GOSHEN
C O L L E G E

Harold and Wilma
Good Library

**Peace
Collection**

Handbook of Forgiveness

HANDBOOK OF FORGIVENESS

Everett L. Worthington, Jr.

Editor

Routledge

New York • Hove

Published in 2005 by
Routledge
Taylor & Francis Group
270 Madison Avenue
New York, NY 10016

Published in Great Britain by
Routledge
Taylor & Francis Group
27 Church Road
Hove, East Sussex BN3 2FA

Printed in the United States of America on acid-free paper
10 9 8 7 6 5 4 3

International Standard Book Number-10: 0-415-94949-1 (Hardcover)
International Standard Book Number-13: 978-0-415-94949-1 (Hardcover)
Library of Congress Card Number 2005003984

Library of Congress Cataloging-in-Publication Data

Handbook of forgiveness / Everett L. Worthington, Jr., editor.
   p. cm.
  Includes bibliographical references and index.
  ISBN 0-415-94949-1 (hardbound)
  1. Forgiveness. 2. Reconciliation. I. Worthington, Everett L., 1946-

BF637.F67H36 2005
155.9'2--dc22   2005003984

Taylor & Francis Group
is the Academic Division of T&F Informa plc.

Visit the Taylor & Francis Web site at
http://www.taylorandfrancis.com

and the Routledge Web site at
http://www.routledge-ny.com

To the funding partners who have generously made a scientific study of forgiveness possible. This includes 14 funding partners for A Campaign for Forgiveness Research *and other foundations, philanthropists, federal funding agencies, and universities.*

Contents

About the Editor

Everett L. Worthington, Jr., Ph.D., is Professor and Chair of Psychology at Virginia Commonwealth University in Richmond. He also serves as Executive Director of *A Campaign for Forgiveness Research*. He has published about 200 articles or chapters and 19 books, many on forgiveness and related topics.

Contributors

Marilyn Peterson Armour, Ph.D., is Assistant Professor at the University of Texas at Austin. She specializes in crime victims, namely, homicide and the use of restorative justice initiatives to treat trauma. She is the author of *At Personal Risk: Boundary Violations in Professional Client Relationships* and numerous articles on the aftermath of homicide. Her current research focuses on the evaluation of victim–offender mediated dialogue in crimes of severe violence, as well as the use of postsentence, in-prison restorative justice programs to reduce recidivism.

Cynthia L. Battle received her Ph.D. in clinical psychology from the University of Massachusetts at Amherst and is now Assistant Professor of Psychiatry and Human Behavior at Brown Medical School in Providence, Rhode Island. Dr. Battle's research and clinical interests focus on family functioning, mood disorders, and women's mental health. She currently has a career development award from the National Institute for Mental Health and is working to develop a family-based treatment for postpartum depression.

Donald H. Baucom, Ph.D., is Professor and Director of Clinical Psychology Training at the University of North Carolina-Chapel Hill. He is the author of over 150 journal articles, book chapters, or books—including his recent books with Norman Epstein, *Enhanced Cognitive-Behavioral Therapy with Couples* and with Patricia Kerig, *Couple Observational Coding Systems*. He has served as Associate Editor of *Behavior Therapy*. His research focuses on developing and evaluating couples-based interventions for a variety of populations, including newly married couples, maritally distressed couples, couples experiencing infidelity, couples and psychopathology, and couples and health concerns.

Steven R. H. Beach, Ph.D., is Professor of Psychology at the University of Georgia in Athens and Director of the Institute for Behavioral Research. He is a Fellow of both the American Psychological Association (APA) and the American Psychological Society (APS). He is the author of two books and over 100 articles on marriage and marital processes. His research focuses on the role of marital and family processes in depression.

Angela L. Boone, M.A., is a doctoral candidate in clinical psychology at George Mason University, Fairfax, Virginia. She is currently studying the emotion of envy, including how individuals cope with the experience of envy, specifically as it relates to occupational settings.

Chris J. Boyatzis, Ph.D., is Associate Professor of Psychology at Bucknell University in Lewisburg, Pennsylvania. He has edited several special journal issues on religious and spiritual development and has published about 40 articles and chapters, including chapters in major handbooks on children's religious development, cultural-cognitive foundations of religious growth, and family socialization processes in religious development. He organized the first preconference on religious and spiritual development at the biennial meetings of the Society for Research in Child Development and conducts many parenting programs at churches.

Ed Cairns, Ph.D., teaches psychology at the University of Ulster and has been a visiting scholar at the Universities of Florida, Cape Town, and Melbourne. Most of his work has investigated the psychological aspects of the conflict in Northern Ireland. He is a Fellow of the British Psychological Society (BPS) and a past president of the Division of Peace Psychology of the APA.

Adam B. Cohen, Ph.D., is a researcher at the Institute of Personality and Social Research at the University of California, Berkeley. He holds a B.A. in psychology and Judaic Studies and a doctorate in psychology. Many of his published articles argue for a contextually grounded approach to the study of religious cultures.

Kathryn L. Cooke, B.S., is enrolled in the Counseling Psychology doctorate program at Virginia Commonwealth University (APA-accredited). She is currently doing research in the area of substance abuse treatment evaluation for incarcerated populations. Her research interests include the process of forgiveness in romantic and family relationships, as well as substance abuse and dependence.

Ronda Dearing earned her Ph.D. in clinical psychology from George Mason University in 2001. She currently is a research scientist at the Research Institute on Addictions, University at Buffalo. She is co-author of the book *Shame and Guilt* (2002) with June Tangney. Dr. Dearing's research interests include help seeking for alcohol problems, treatment engagement and outcome, and issues related to shame and guilt.

Susanne A. Denham, Ph.D., is Professor of Psychology at George Mason University. Her research and publications concern children's social and emotional development. She is especially interested in the role of emotional competence in children's social and academic functioning, as well as the ways in which parents, teachers, and friends help or hinder its development. The development of forgiveness in children is an important facet of such emotional competence. She has served as consultant to several day care and child welfare agencies, assisting with social-emotional programming, as well as writing two books and serving as editor or co-editor on two journals.

Frans B. M. de Waal, Ph.D., is C. H. Candler Professor in the Psychology Department of Emory University in Atlanta and Director of Living Links, which is part of the Yerkes National Primate Research Center. He is world renowned for his studies of conflict resolution, cooperation, and cognition in primates, working with both monkeys and apes. Apart from a stream of scientific publications, he has written six popular books, including *Peacemaking Among Primates* (Harvard, 1989).

Lindon Eaves, Ph.D., D.Sc., is Distinguished Professor of Human Genetics and Psychiatry at Virginia Commonwealth University School of Medicine in Richmond and directs the Virginia Institute for Psychiatric and Behavioral Genetics. His research encompasses statistical genetics and the genetics of human behavior, with a special emphasis on genetic studies of behavioral development and the modeling of biological and cultural inheritance. He is a past president of the Behavior Genetics Association and has received numerous honors and awards for his contributions to behavioral genetics and twin research. He has authored more than 200 papers and a book, *Genes, Culture, and Personality: An Empirical Approach*. He is an Episcopal priest in the Diocese of Virginia and has lectured widely on the relationship between science and theology.

Robert D. Enright, Ph.D., is Professor of Educational Psychology at the University of Wisconsin-Madison, a position he has held since 1978. He is cofounder of the International Forgiveness Institute, a nonprofit organization dedicated to the dissemination of knowledge about forgiveness and community renewal through forgiveness. He is a licensed psychologist. He is the author or editor of four books and over 80 publications centered on social development and the psychology of forgiveness.

Julie Juola Exline, Ph.D., is Assistant Professor of Psychology at Case Western Reserve University in Cleveland, Ohio. Her research focuses on the interface between social and clinical psychology. Many of her empirical projects center on virtues such as forgiveness, repentance, altruistic love, humility, and self-control. She also has a special interest in the study of religious and spiritual struggles.

Tom F. D. Farrow, B.Sc., Ph.D., is a lecturer in psychiatric neuroimaging at the University of Sheffield, United Kingdom and Honorary NHS Clinical Scientist for Sheffield Care Trust. He specializes in structural and functional brain imaging of patients with posttraumatic stress disorder and schizophrenia, particularly in the field of social cognition. He studied neuroscience at the University of Sheffield, United Kingdom before undertaking his Ph.D. in clinical neurology (structural MRI of temporal lobe epilepsy). He was previously a postdoctoral Research Fellow in Psychiatry at Manchester University. In 2002, he was awarded a Royal Society (United Kingdom) Overseas Fellowship and spent a year at the Brain Dynamics Centre, University of Sydney, Australia. He is author of many articles in professional journals and a contributor to several books and research publications.

Frank D. Fincham, Ph.D., is Eminent Scholar and Director, Florida State University Family Institute. He is the recipient of numerous awards for his research and has been listed by the APS as one of the top 25 psychologists in the world in terms of impact. The author of over 200 publications, he is a Fellow of the APA, BPS, National Council for Family Relations, American Society of Applied and Preventive Psychology, and APS.

Eli J. Finkel, Ph.D., is Assistant Professor of Social Psychology at Northwestern University. His research resides at the intersection of self-regulation and interpersonal relationships. He conceptualizes interpersonal processes such as forgiveness and reconciliation as self-regulatory tasks because they require individuals to manage conflicting motivations to arrive at an optimal resolution of their complex circumstances.

Suzanne Freedman, Ph.D., is Associate Professor of Human Development at the University of Northern Iowa, a position she has held since 1994. She was recipient of the APA Dissertation Award in 1993 for her groundbreaking research on forgiveness and incest survivors. She has been studying the topic of forgiveness for 17 years, and her publications focus on the psychology of forgiveness with both adults and adolescents. She has presented her research on forgiveness at numerous national and international conferences, as well as invited workshops.

Kristina Coop Gordon, Ph.D., is Associate Professor in the Clinical Psychology program at the University of Tennessee-Knoxville. She is currently serving as Vice President for Science for the APA's Division 43: Family Psychology and is chair of its task force on empirically validated couples and family therapy. Dr. Gordon has also served as co-president of the AABT Couple Research and Therapy Special Interest Group. She has authored numerous articles and book chapters on forgiveness and couple processes. Dr. Gordon conducts research on forgiveness and family processes, supervises a couples therapy practicum, teaches graduate classes on psychotherapy, and maintains a small private practice.

Leslie Greenberg, Ph.D., is Professor of Psychology at York University in Toronto and Director of the York University Psychotherapy Research Clinic. He has authored the major texts on emotion-focused approaches to treatment. His latest authored book is *Emotion-Focused Therapy: Coaching Clients to Work Through Emotion*. Dr. Greenberg is a founding member of the Society of the Exploration of Psychotherapy Integration and a past president of the Society for Psychotherapy Research (SPR). He recently received the SPR Distinguished Research Career award. He conducts a private practice for individuals and couples, and offers training in emotion-focused approaches.

Julie H. Hall, B.A., is a graduate student in clinical psychology at the University at Buffalo. She received her bachelor's degree from Brown University and is currently pursuing a doctorate in clinical psychology under the advisement of Dr. Frank Fincham. She is the author of several book chapters and journal articles. Her research interests include self-forgiveness, infidelity, and forgiveness within romantic relationships.

Peggy A. Hannon received her Ph.D. in social psychology from the University of North Carolina at Chapel Hill. She is now a research scientist at the University of Washington School of Public Health and Community Medicine. Her research interests focus on romantic relationships and health behavior. Her current research examines how marital partners' forgiveness behaviors affect their own and their partners' health.

Alex H. S. Harris, Ph.D., conducts health psychology and health services research at the Center for Health Care Evaluation, Veterans Affairs Palo Alto Health Care System, and Stanford School of Medicine. He has co-authored several chapters and articles on the relationships between forgiveness and health and has lectured on forgiveness at national conferences. His current interests include forgiveness in the patient–doctor relationship and forgiveness related to substance abuse.

Miles Hewstone, Ph.D., studied psychology at the University of Bristol and obtained his D.Phil. from Oxford University in 1981 and his Habilitation from the University of Tübingen in 1986. He then undertook postdoctoral work with Serge Moscovici in Paris and Wolfgang Stroebe in Tübingen. He has held chairs in social psychology at the University of Bristol, University of Mannheim, and Cardiff University. He is now at Oxford University. He has published widely on the topics of attribution theory, social cognition, stereotyping, and intergroup relations. His current work centers on the reduction of intergroup conflict via intergroup contact, stereotype change, and crossed categorization. He is a former editor of the *British Journal of Social Psychology* and cofounding editor of the *European Review of Social Psychology*. He is a past recipient of the BPS's Spearman Medal and has twice been a Fellow at the Center for Advanced Study in the Behavioral Sciences, Stanford (1987–1988, 1999–2000).

Peter C. Hill, Ph.D., is Professor of Psychology at the Rosemead School of Psychology, Biola University in California and editor of the *Journal of Psychology and Christianity*. In addition to his research on forgiveness, his published research interests include measurement issues, the psychology of religion, and positive psychology. His most recent book, co-authored with Ralph Hood and Paul Williamson, is *The Psychology of Fundamentalism: An Intratextual Approach*, published in 2005 by Guilford Press.

William T. Hoyt, Ph.D., is Associate Professor in the Department of Counseling Psychology at the University of Wisconsin-Madison. His substantive interests focus on social and relational determinants of psychological well-being. He also is interested in research methods and measurement practices and their implications for interpreting research findings.

Beth A. Jerskey, M.A., is a doctoral candidate in the clinical psychology program at Boston University, Massachusetts. She is a student member of the APA, the Massachusetts Psychological Association, the Gerontological Society of America, the International Neuropsychological Society, and the International Society for Traumatic Stress Studies. She is engaged in dissertation research examining three primary issues: the genetic and environmental influences on divorce in Vietnam veterans, the role of combat and posttraumatic stress disorder in marital dysfunction in this sample, and the mediating role of forgiveness on combat as it relates to divorce.

Jeanette Knutson, Ph.D., is the Coordinator of Interventions at the International Forgiveness Institute, writing curricula and supervising teachers and parents as they learn to teach children about forgiveness. She currently is supervising teachers in Belfast, Northern Ireland; Drogheda, the Republic of Ireland; and Madison and Milwaukee, Wisconsin. Her publications center on children from violent and war-torn areas of the world as they learn to forgive.

Michael J. Lyons, Ph.D., is Professor of Psychology, Director of Clinical Training, and Director of the Center for Clinical Biopsychology in the Department of Psychology, Boston University. He is also Chief of Twin Studies at the Harvard Institute of Psychiatric Epidemiology and Genetics. He received his Ph.D. in clinical psychology from the University of Louisville and completed an internship at Yale University and a postdoctoral fellowship at Columbia University. He has published over 100 journal articles and is involved in research on psychopathology, substance abuse, and aging. His current research addresses, among other things, how spirituality may influence aging and psychopathology.

Annette Mahoney, Ph.D., is Full Professor of Psychology at Bowling Green State University and a licensed clinical psychologist. Her primary research interests pertain to the psychology of religion, particularly with regard to family life. Other research interests are links between marriage, parenting, and child behavior problems, and physical aggression in families. She has received research funding from the Ohio Department of Mental Health, the Templeton Foundation, and the Fetzer Institute. She conducts clinical work with children, families, and adults.

Wanda Malcolm, Ph.D., has served as co-investigator with Leslie Greenberg at the York University Psychotherapy Research Clinic, investigating the process of forgiveness and reconciliation in individual and couples therapy. She is Assistant Professor of Psychology at Tyndale University College in Toronto and a registered psychologist, with a private practice in individual and couples emotion-focused therapy.

Alyce Martin is a Ph.D. student in clinical psychology at Case Western Reserve University in Cleveland, Ohio. She is studying self-forgiveness and the role that religiosity plays in accepting forgiveness. Additional research interests include self-compassion, altruism, reconciliation, and humility. She also works as a volunteer therapist at a community mental health facility in Cleveland and seeks to incorporate these ideals in her work.

Michael E. McCullough, Ph.D., is Associate Professor in the Department of Psychology and the Department of Religious Studies at the University of Miami in Coral Gables, Florida. His scholarly work focuses on two topics. First, he studies moral sentiments such as forgiveness, revenge, and gratitude, including their associations with health, well-being, and social behavior. Second, he is interested in the development of religiousness and spirituality and the pathways by which religion and spirituality influence health, well-being, and social behavior.

Julia E. Meyer, B.A., is a graduate student in her first year of the doctoral program in counseling psychology at Iowa State University. She has been involved with forgiveness research from both a social and an applied psychology perspective. This is her first publication.

Ivan W. Miller, Ph.D., received his degree in clinical psychology from the University of Maine. He is currently Professor of Psychiatry and Human Behavior in the Brown Medical School and Director of the Psychosocial Research Program at Butler Hospital. His major research interests are family and cognitive approaches to the assessment and treatment of mood disorders. He has been the recipient of numerous research grants from the National Institutes of Health and private foundations, and he is the author of over 150 articles, chapters, and books.

Etienne Mullet, Ph.D., is a director of research at the Institute for Advanced Studies (EPHE) in Paris. He is the head of the Ethics and Work laboratory of this institute. He is the author of over 100 articles.

Jeffrie G. Murphy is Regents' Professor of Law, Philosophy, and Religious Studies at Arizona State University. He is the author of numerous books and articles on legal and moral philosophy, with a particular emphasis on theories of punishment, mercy, forgiveness, and the moral emotions. His most recent book is *Getting Even: Forgiveness and Its Limits* (Oxford University Press, 2003).

Karen Neal, M.S., is a doctoral candidate in applied developmental psychology at George Mason University. She is a lecturer at the University of North Carolina, Charlotte. Her past professional life has focused on the areas of child and family counseling, child care administration and assessment, and teaching.

Félix Neto, Ph.D., is Professor of Psychology at the University of Oporto, Porto, Portugal. He is the head of the Cognition and Affectivity laboratory of this university. He is the author of numerous books and articles in the area of social psychology.

Ulrike Niens, Ph.D., is a graduate in psychology from the Free University of Berlin. She then completed her Ph.D. in social psychology at the University of Ulster. Since 2002, she has been a Research Fellow with the UNESCO Centre, School of Education at the University of Ulster, where she leads a research program on citizenship education and democracy. Her research interests focus on reconciliation, social identity, and citizenship education.

Tal Nir, M.A., is a doctoral candidate in the clinical psychology program at Boston University, Massachusetts. She is currently involved in clinical training at McLean Hospital, an affiliate of the Harvard Medical School Department of Psychiatry. She is a member of the APA (Division 12) and the Gerontological Society of America. She is engaged in dissertation research that is examining forgiveness and related constructs associated with the Israeli–Palestinian conflict, working with both Israelis and Palestinians. The goal of the research is to identify mechanisms that could contribute to a peaceful resolution of this complex and intractable problem.

Jennie G. Noll, Ph.D., is Associate Professor of Pediatrics at the University of Cincinnati, Children's Hospital Medical Center (CCHMC) in Cincinnati, Ohio. She is a developmental psychologist and holds a joint appointment in the Division of Psychology and the Mayerson Center for Safe and Healthy Children at CCHMC. Her research has been supported by numerous federal and foundation grants, and is primarily concerned with the long-term bio-psych-social effects of childhood abuse on female development.

Kenneth I. Pargament, Ph.D., is Professor of Clinical Psychology at Bowling Green State University and adjunct Professor of Psychology in the Counseling Psychology and Religion Ph.D. program at Boston University. He has published extensively on the vital role of religion in coping with stress and trauma. He is author of *The Psychology of*

Religion and Coping: Theory, Research, Practice and co-editor of *Forgiveness: Theory, Research, Practice.* He is also a licensed clinical psychologist.

Stephanie Pickering, B.S., TLMLP, is a doctoral student in clinical psychology at Seattle Pacific University. She graduated summa cum laude from the University of Washington with a bachelor's degree in psychology in 1996. She has spent the past 2 years researching the link between social competence and forgiveness in first-grade children. Currently she is completing her clinical internship at the Wichita Collaborative Psychology Internship Program in Wichita, Kansas.

Jennifer J. Pokorny, B.A., is a doctoral candidate in the Neuroscience and Animal Behavior Program of the Psychology Department at Emory University in Atlanta. She studies primate cognition and face processing.

Sheila Rivière, Ph.D., is a member of the Ethics and Work laboratory of the Institute for Advanced Studies (EPHE) in Paris. She is the author of several articles.

Lindsey M. Root, B.S., is a doctoral candidate in the Department of Psychology at the University of Miami, Coral Gables, Florida. Her interests involve the effects of positive emotion and virtuous behavior on individuals' psychophysiology. She is currently investigating the effects of forgiving (or not forgiving) on the cardiovascular system.

Caryl E. Rusbult, Ph.D., is Professor and Chair of the Department of Social Psychology at the Free University, Amsterdam. She has published over 90 journal articles or chapters, along with two books. She is best known for her theory and research regarding commitment processes and relationship maintenance behaviors (e.g., forgiveness, accommodation, derogation of alternatives). Much of her recent work is with the "Michelangelo phenomenon," which concerns the ways in which close partners shape one another's dispositions, values, and behavioral tendencies, thereby moving each person closer to (vs. further from) his or her ideal self.

Mark S. Rye, Ph.D., is Associate Professor of Psychology at the University of Dayton and a licensed clinical psychologist. He has co-authored several book chapters and journal articles on forgiveness. Specifically, he has developed measures of forgiveness, designed and evaluated forgiveness interventions for individuals wronged in romantic relationships, and examined the role of religion and spirituality in the forgiveness process.

Steven J. Sandage, Ph.D., LP, is Associate Professor of Marriage and Family Studies at Bethel University, St. Paul, Minnesota. He is also a licensed psychologist in clinical practice with Arden Woods Psychological Services, P.A., in Arden Hills, Minnesota. He is the co-author of two books and several articles on interpersonal forgiveness and directs a research project on forgiveness and culture in collaboration with Hmong-Americans in St. Paul.

Robert M. Sapolsky, Ph.D., is John A. and Cynthia Fry Gunn Professor of Biological Sciences, Neurology, and Neurological Sciences at Stanford University, as well as a research associate at the National Museums of Kenya. He studies stress and stress-related disease, both at the organismal level (in studies of wild baboons) and at the molecular level (examining stress-induced damage to neurons).

Michael Scherer, B.S., is enrolled in the master's program in the Department of Rehabilitation Counseling at Virginia Commonwealth University's Medical College of Virginia. He currently serves as Executive Assistant for *A Campaign for Forgiveness Research*. His research interests involve exploring the interactions between substance abusers and their family members and the impact of forgiveness (or unforgiveness) within these relationships.

Douglas K. Snyder, Ph.D., is Professor and Director of Clinical Psychology Training at Texas A&M University in College Station, Texas. He is a Fellow of the APA in the Divisions of Clinical Psychology, Family Psychology, Psychotherapy, and Evaluation and Measurement. He has served as Associate Editor of the *Journal of Consulting and Clinical Psychology* and *Journal of Family Psychology*. Dr. Snyder is the author of over 100 journal articles, book chapters, or books, as well as co-editor of *Treating Difficult Couples: Helping Clients with Coexisting Mental and Relationship Disorders*.

Ervin Staub, Ph.D., is Professor of Psychology at the University of Massachusetts, Amherst, and Director of the Ph.D. concentration on the psychology of peace and the prevention of violence. He has studied helping behavior and altruism, including their development in children (with lectures and workshops for parents and teachers on how to raise caring and nonaggressive children), the passivity of bystanders, as well as the origins of genocide and mass killing, healing after mass violence, and reconciliation. His books include *The Roots of Evil: The Origins of Genocide and Other Group Violence*, (1989) and the *Psychology of Good and Evil: Why Children, Adults, and Groups Help and Harm Others* (2003). Since 1998, he has been conducting various projects in Rwanda on healing, reconciliation, and the prevention of new violence.

Shevaun L. Stocker, M.A., is a doctoral student in the social psychology program at the University of North Carolina at Chapel Hill. She is currently doing research in the areas of social cognition and romantic relationships. Her research interests include examining the role of accessibility experiences in affecting the judgments people make about their romantic relationships.

Tania Tam is a Ph.D. student at the University of Oxford, studying the effects of contact on intergroup relations in Northern Ireland and ageism in the United Kingdom.

June Price Tangney, Ph.D., is Professor of Psychology at George Mason University, Fairfax, Virginia. She is a Fellow of the APA in the Division of Personality and Social Psychology, co-editor of *Self-Conscious Emotions: Shame, Guilt, Embarrassment, and Pride* (1995) and *The Handbook of Self and Identity* (2004), and has served as Associate Editor of *Self and Identity*. Her primary interest is in the moral emotions of shame and guilt. Her research on the development and implications of moral emotions across the life span is summarized in *Shame and Guilt* (2002), co-authored by Ronda Dearing. She is currently examining the implications of moral emotions and moral cognitions in a longitudinal study of incarcerated offenders, drawing on principles of restorative justice and criminology to learn more about how to better facilitate desistence and rehabilitation.

Lydia R. Temoshok, Ph.D., an internationally respected leader in biopsychosocial oncology, theory in behavioral medicine, psychoneuroimmunology, and HIV prevention research, directs the Behavioral Medicine program in the Institute of Human Virology (IHV) and is Professor of Medicine and Psychiatry, University of Maryland School of Medicine at Baltimore. Before coming to the IHV in 1998, she served as Senior Scientist with the Division of Mental Health in the World Health Organization and the United Nations Programme on AIDS in Geneva, as Scientific Director of HIV behavior research for the U.S. military, and on the faculty at the University of California School of Medicine in San Francisco. She has authored or edited 10 books or monographs, including her well-known 1992 book, *The Type C Connection: The Behavioral Links to Cancer and Your Health* (Random House), in addition to over 40 book chapters and over 100 journal publications. The recipient of numerous academic awards, she has been elected Fellow of the APA, the Academy of Behavioral Medicine Research, and the Society of Behavioral Medicine.

Carl E. Thoresen, Ph.D., is Professor Emeritus of Education and, by courtesy, Psychology and Psychiatry & Behavioral Sciences at Stanford University. He is also Senior Fellow in the Spirituality and Health Institute at Santa Clara University. He served as Principal Investigator of the Stanford Forgiveness Project, a large randomized trial of forgiveness training program. He has published extensively on science and psychology of forgiveness, spirituality, and health.

Loren Toussaint, Ph.D., is Assistant Professor in the Department of Psychology at Luther College, where he teaches courses on forgiveness, stress and coping, and general psychology. He is a former Research Fellow in the Institute for Social Research at the University of Michigan, where he participated in the Psychosocial Factors in Mental and Physical Health and Illness training program sponsored by the National Institute for Mental Health. His research interests are in forgiveness, stress, and health.

Ming T. Tsuang is University Professor, University of California, and Distinguished Professor of Psychiatry and Director of the Institute of Behavioral Genomics in the Department of Psychiatry, University of California, San Diego. He directs the Harvard Institute of Psychiatric Epidemiology & Genetics. He received his M.D. from National Taiwan University and his Ph.D. and D.Sc. from the University of London. Along with his interests in schizophrenia, manic-depressive illness, and substance abuse, he has conducted research on the role of spirituality in promoting mental health. His awards include the American Psychopathological Association's Hoch Award, the Lifetime Achievement Award from the International Society of Psychiatric Genetics, the Gold Medal Award from the American Society of Biological Psychiatry, and the American Psychiatric Association's Award for Research in psychiatry. He is a member of the Institute of Medicine, U.S. National Academy of Sciences, and Academician, Academia

Sinica of Taiwan, the highest academic institution in Taiwan. He has authored over 450 publications and is editor for *Neuropsychiatric Genetics*, a section of the *American Journal of Medical Genetics*.

Mark S. Umbreit, Ph.D., is Professor and founding Director of the Center for Restorative Justice & Peacemaking at the University of Minnesota, School of Social Work. He serves as a Fellow of the International Centre for Healing and the Law in Kalamazoo, Michigan. He is an internationally recognized practitioner and scholar, with more than 33 years of experience as a mediator, trainer, researcher, and author of six books and more than 130 articles, book chapters, and monographs in the fields of restorative justice, mediation, and peacemaking. His most recent book, *Facing Violence: The Path of Restorative Justice & Dialogue*, reports on the first multisite study of victim–offender mediation and dialogue in crimes of severe violence, primarily homicide. He has conducted training seminars and lectures throughout the world. As a practitioner, he specializes in facilitating dialogue between family survivors/victims of severe violence, primarily homicide, and offenders.

Nathaniel G. Wade, Ph.D., is Assistant Professor of Psychology at Iowa State University, where he conducts research on the psychology of forgiveness and religion. He is also a practicing psychologist in Iowa, specializing in group therapy, existential issues, and spirituality. Joining his interests in forgiveness, religion, and psychotherapy, his research expertise is in intervention research, specifically focused on the process and outcome of forgiveness and spiritual interventions.

Rebecca L. Wald, Ph.D., is the Behavioral Medicine Research Coordinator in the Institute of Human Virology, University of Maryland Biotechnology Institute, Baltimore. Her primary research interests are focused on the psychoneuroimmunology of HIV and cancer. In addition to her work on forgiveness in persons living with HIV/AIDS, she also studies adherence to HIV medications and the prevention of transmission risk behaviors.

Serine Warwar, Ph.D., C.Psych. (supervised practice), is a psychologist in supervised practice, working with suicidal patients with borderline personality disorder in the Suicide Studies Unit, University of Toronto, St. Michael's Hospital. Most recently, she was the Research and Treatment Coordinator at the York University Psychotherapy Research Clinic, working on two psychotherapy research studies examining forgiveness in individuals and couples. In addition, she has a private practice in emotion-focused therapy with individuals and couples.

Jon R. Webb, Ph.D., a licensed clinical psychologist, is a Clinical Assistant Professor and the Director of Addiction Psychology and Research in the Clinical Chemical Dependency Fellowship program of the Department of Psychiatry and Behavioral Sciences at the University of Oklahoma Health Sciences Center. His primary professional interest involves the integration of psychology and religion and its application to health. Recent projects have investigated the relationship between forgiveness and health following 9/11, spinal cord injury, and entering substance abuse treatment.

Ian Williamson, Ph.D., is Assistant Professor at New Mexico Highlands University. He just completed his degree in social psychology at the University of Minnesota, where he completed a dissertation on forgiveness anxiety. He is currently working with Steve Sandage on examining the role of forgiveness in people's spiritual lives, and he is hoping to establish a program of research in forgiveness and positive psychology at his new host institution.

Beverly J. Wilson, Ph.D., is Associate Professor of Psychology at Seattle Pacific University. Her research and publications concern children's social and emotional development. She is especially interested in the role of emotion regulation in children's social competence and factors that influence children's emotion regulation skills, such as the ability to manage attentional processes and physiological functioning. She serves as a consultant to several school districts, helping schools identify and develop interventions for children with social and conduct problems.

Charlotte vanOyen Witvliet, Ph.D., is Associate Professor of Psychology at Hope College in Holland, Michigan. She is trained as a scientist-practitioner clinical psychologist. She publishes in the field of emotion and psychophysiology research. Her specialized focus is in unforgiveness, forgiveness, and justice. With the support of the John Templeton Foundation and a four-year Hope College Towsley Research Scholar Award, she has conducted programmatic empirical studies of forgiveness, published journal articles and book chapters, and given presentations in local, national, and international venues.

Peter W. R. Woodruff, M.B., B.S., Ph.D., M.R.C.P., MRCPsych, is Professor and Head of Academic Clinical Psychiatry and Director of the Sheffield Cognition and Neuroimaging Laboratory at the University of Sheffield, United Kingdom and Honorary Consultant Psychiatrist for Sheffield Care Health Trust. He specializes in the application of structural and functional neuroimaging techniques to investigate etiological processes and brain mechanisms underlying psychopathology and its response to treatment in schizophrenia and the major mental illnesses. He trained in medicine at Newcastle upon Tyne Medical School, United Kingdom. He was Medical Lecturer at Kings College London and Visiting Lecturer at Juba University, Sudan. As Assistant Professor at the University of Maryland, seconded to the U.S. Medical Research Unit in Cairo, Egypt, he worked on viral infections of the brain. He trained in clinical psychiatry at the Maudsley Hospital, London and commenced a research career at the Institute of Psychiatry, London, performing neuroimaging studies in schizophrenia and other psychiatric conditions. He studied neuroimaging in Baltimore at Johns Hopkins Hospital and as a Fulbright Fellow at Massachusetts General Hospital, Boston. He was previously a Senior Lecturer at the Institute of Psychiatry, London and Honorary Consultant in Psychiatric Intensive Care at Maudsley Hospital; he was also Senior Lecturer in Psychiatry at Manchester University and Honorary Consultant for Salford Health Trust.

Chapter One

Initial Questions About the Art and Science of Forgiving

Everett L. Worthington, Jr.

Forgiveness is both an art and a science. As an art, it deals with the fundamental questions of our age. It describes how we deal with transgressions and offenses personally and socially. It touches our mental health and well-being. It reaches into our relationships. It colors transactions within society and affects intergroup relations. The art of forgiving revolves around personal experience. Case studies as well as examples from our own and other people's lives teach us about forgiving.

Forgiveness also is now a science. Does that sound strange? A century ago, medicine was more art than science. Visionary philanthropist John D. Rockefeller, on the advice of his financial advisor, Frederick T. Gates, asked whether the healing arts could be studied scientifically and whether Rockefeller could make the most impact philanthropically by funding the art of healing or the scientific study of healing. Fortunately for all of us, Rockefeller invested in medical science. A century later, science has armed practitioners of the art of physical healing with research-revealed tools beyond the wildest dreams of the physician in 1900.

In 1970, virtually no one had studied forgiveness scientifically. Forgiveness was seen as within the domain of religion, and (despite William James and early flirtation between psychology and religion) science was uneasy with religion. Only a few intrepid social scientists conducted isolated studies related to forgiving.

Scientific study of forgiveness began in earnest only in the mid-1980s and has accelerated since that time. It started in the therapeutic community after the publication of a trade book, *Forgive and Forget: Healing the Hurts We Don't Deserve,* by Lewis Smedes (1984). Ironically, Smedes was neither clinician nor scientist. He was a theologian. Yet he started a movement within therapy and science that revolved around the idea that forgiveness can benefit a person's mental health and well-being. That message resonated with therapists, who began to write about how to promote forgiveness in healing for problems in anger, lack of hope, depression, and trauma. In addition, couples counseling and family therapy were natural laboratories for observing the harm of unforgiveness and the healing benefits of forgiveness.

It wasn't long before clinical scientists began to create (and study) interventions to promote forgiveness. Developmental psychologists such as forgiveness studies pioneer Robert Enright began to research how children's reasoning about forgiveness developed. Personality psychologists began to study who did or didn't forgive. Social psychologists examined how forgiveness showed up or didn't in daily social interactions. Health psychologists began to study whether and how forgiveness might affect physical health. In another irony, the study of the relationship between forgiveness and religion lagged the study of forgiveness in nonreligious contexts.

In the mid-1980s, when most people thought about forgiveness, they associated it with religion. Even if people were not religious, common culture had imported the term *forgiveness* from religious usage. So forgiveness had a religious overtone to it, even though both religious and nonreligious people used the word. As society became more postmodern and multicultural, though, forgiveness broke free of the confines of religious communities and even religious connotation. Forgiveness has broadly penetrated popular culture. Tim McGraw, country music superstar, in singing about how he would live if he knew he were dying, said, "I loved deeper and I spoke sweeter. And I gave forgiveness I'd been denying" (McGraw, 2004) Forgiveness has received a lot of public attention.

As more attention has been paid to the study of forgiveness—both in popular culture and in science—more questions have arisen about what it is, how it develops, whether it is always beneficial, whether it can be iatrogenic, and how we might help people forgive if they wish to forgive. As some questions have been answered, new questions have arisen. The depth of our lack of understanding of what forgiveness is and what its limits are has become more obvious.

THE ART OF FORGIVENESS

In 1983 in Texas, Karla Fay Tucker participated in the brutal pickaxe murder of Deborah Thornton and Jerry Lynn Dean. Tucker was apprehended, tried, convicted of capital murder, and sentenced to die by lethal injection, which she did on February 3, 1998. Her case received national attention, however, because of subsequent developments. Then-Governor George W. Bush was a contender for the White House, heightening public interests. Also, Tucker underwent a profound conversion to Christianity while she was incarcerated. To add to the mix, the brother of Deborah Thornton, Ron Carlson, contacted Tucker in prison and asked to meet with her to convey to her that he had forgiven her for the murder. Their meeting resulted in Tucker's expression of remorse, Carlson's granting of forgiveness, and an unlikely friendship. At the execution, Tucker asked Carlson to witness from the side reserved for her supporters. That created a conflict within the Carlson family. On which side would Carlson sit—Tucker's side or his sister's?

The case of Karla Fay Tucker raises many issues of the practicalities of forgiving and not forgiving. For example, when Tucker converted to Christianity, most of the people who knew her testified that she almost certainly was no longer a danger to society. This raised several questions.

1. Should Governor Bush commute her death sentence to life in prison?
2. Does a personal change of heart absolve people from criminal conviction?
3. Was the brutal pickaxe murder simply too heinous to be forgiven by society?
4. Was it too heinous to be forgiven by individuals?

Ron Carlson and Deborah's brother, Tony, disagreed about whether to forgive Tucker. Did Tucker's request for support from Ron Carlson inflict yet another wound to the family she had already harmed? Is there a difference between (a) societal forgiveness or justice, (b) dyadic interaction, and (c) personal forgiveness?

Crimes are presumably against society, not merely against individual members of society. Thus, even if the victims had unanimously agreed to forgive Karla Fay Tucker and to intercede on her behalf with Governor George W. Bush, we can see that the art of forgiving is a messy business.

Possibilities of forgiveness, justice, and their intersection raise numerous questions about ethics and morals. The implications extend through individual lives to their family relationships, work productivity, communities, states, and nations. The practice of forgiveness is an art. Art is creative yet messy—like an artist in a painter's oil-smeared smock. We often see science as pristine in a white lab coat. But is the science of forgiveness any more clear than the art of forgiveness?

THE SCIENCE OF FORGIVENESS

Many questions have been raised and remain unanswered by scientific efforts to study forgiveness. I organize these into eight major questions. In this *Handbook of Forgiveness,* I invited scholars to summarize their areas of expertise. As you read these accounts, I hope you'll discover answers to the eight major questions. Even more, I hope that these scientific reviews reveal additional questions that need to be answered as the science of forgiveness develops. These eight questions might provide your road map for navigating the *Handbook.*

Question 1: What Is Forgiveness?

Definitions are the fountainhead of knowledge. Definitions set the pathway through the processes of forgiveness. Definitions provide a framework for explaining why and how a phenomenon happens. Definitions guide interventionists to develop protocols to help people forgive. Definitions aid therapists in developing healing methods and attitudes. It is not surprising that the major issue characterizing this new science of forgiveness has been how forgiveness ought to be defined.

Enright has written extensively in the early years of the science of forgiveness. The crux of forgiveness for Enright is its complexity as an integration of behavior, cognition, and affect (see Enright & Fitzgibbons, 2000). He advocates replacing negative thinking, action, and feelings with more positive thinking, action, and feelings. He understands forgiveness as a process. Whereas Enright has proposed a process model of forgiveness, that is an intervention model. No scientific evidence suggests that people always move through the 20 steps in his process model (see chapter 24 by Freedman and colleagues) in naturally occurring settings. Nevertheless, his model forms a heuristic hypothesis about the natural occurrence of forgiveness.

McCullough and various collaborators have suggested that forgiveness is a redirection of motivations. They have defined forgiveness as a redirection in negative motivations, which is also accompanied by more conciliatory motivations toward the transgressor. McCullough and his colleagues have shown how such motivations can change (McCullough, Fincham, & Tsang, 2003) and be measured (see chapter 7 by McCullough and Root) over time. Fincham, who has co-authored with McCullough, also champions a motivational view. Working with couples, Fincham and his colleagues (see chapter 13) emphasize a two-component nature of forgiving—reducing negative motivations and increasing positive ones.

Worthington and his colleagues worked closely with McCullough, especially in the early to mid-1990s. McCullough's group and Worthington's group still share an emphasis on the importance of the emotion-motivation connection. Worthington (2003) has described forgiveness as being of two types (see Exline, Worthington, Hill, & McCullough, 2003; Worthington & Scherer, 2004). Decisional forgiveness involves a change in a person's behavioral intentions (hence a change in motivation) toward a transgressor. Emotional forgiveness (Worthington, 2003; Worthington & Wade, 1999; Wade & Worthington, 2003) is a replacement of negative, unforgiving emotions with positive, other-oriented emotions. At first, the positive emotions neutralize some negative emotions, resulting in a decrease in negative emotions. However, once the negative emotion is substantially eliminated, positive emotions can be built. Malcolm, Warwar, and Greenberg (see chapter 23), drawing on attachment theory and emotion-focused therapy, also emphasize emotional transformation that occurs when people forgive.

DiBlasio (1998) has defined forgiveness as a change in willpower to release the person from malevolent behavior toward an offender. DiBlasio calls forgiveness "decision-based forgiveness" (1998, p. 77). DiBlasio wrote with Worthington (see Worthington & DiBlasio, 1990) in the early years of forgiveness studies. Their collaboration undoubtedly affected Worthington's concept of decisional forgiveness.

Cognitive definitions of forgiveness have been well represented. Thompson and her colleagues (2005), Flanigan (1994), Gordon et al. (see chapter 25), and Luskin (2002) advocate cognitive views of forgiveness.

Forgiveness occurs in an interpersonal context. Some theoreticians (Augsburger, 1996), clinicians (Hargrave & Sells, 1997), and basic scientists (Baumeister, Exline, & Sommer, 1998; Exline & Baumeister, 2000; Finkel, Rusbult, Kumashiro, & Hannon, 2002) have emphasized the interpersonal aspects of forgiving. Whereas no one questions the importance of the interpersonal context in which forgiveness might occur, definitional squabbles concern whether the communication of forgiveness or talk and behavior about transgressions should be included within the definition or treated as a separate interpersonal process.

Researchers have often investigated a single aspect of forgiveness at one time, even if they believe forgiveness to be multifaceted. They isolate aspects to study them. However, most interventionists include cognitive, behavioral, affective, and often interpersonal change in their interventions, regardless of which element they believe to be most likely to cause changes. They seek to maximize client change by opening many possible avenues of change.

McCullough, Pargament, and Thoresen (2000) discerned from the chapters in their edited book that investigators had a common core of beliefs about forgiveness. Forgiveness involved prosocial change in people's experiences after a transgression. Their common-core approach was analogous to a shotgun. The next step in scientific progress will be to move beyond the shotgun to the rifle. Investigators must discern a more nuanced understanding of under which circumstances which types of definitions are most accurate and perhaps most useful. Read as a detective for definitions.

Question 2: How Should Forgiveness Best Be Measured?

When forgiveness began to be studied in the late 1980s and early 1990s, few instruments were available to measure it. Typically, nonstandardized questionnaires were used. Early instruments that adduced data to support reliability and validity were rare. Hargrave and Sells (1997) developed a family-oriented measure of forgiveness. Subkoviak et al.'s (1995) measure of forgiveness evolved into the Enright Forgiveness Inventory (see also Al-Mabuk, Enright, & Cardis, 1995). Wade (1989) developed a 90-item measure for her dissertation. Her instrument was refined into two shortened subscales and occasionally a third subscale by McCullough and his colleagues (1998) to become the Transgression-Related Interpersonal Motivations (TRIM) inventory. In later years, Wade's instrument was published in its entirety with some psychometric support in the *Journal of Psychology and Christianity* (Brown, Gorsuch, Rosik, & Ridley, 2001). After 1998, numerous other instruments have been developed to measure forgiveness of transgressions, dispositional forgiveness, and forgiveness of self. Keep an eye out for the variety of measures described by investigators—including a few novel approaches presented for the first time in print within the following pages.

Read as a concerned critic of measures. Are measurements assumed to be valid? Have investigators attempted to triangulate the participants' experiences subsequent to transgressions by measuring other nonforgiveness variables? Have investigators drawn conclusions with circumspection appropriate to the soundness of their methods of assessment?

Question 3: How and for Whom Is Interpersonal Forgiveness Related to Religion?

Merely because scientific methods have been brought to bear in the study of interpersonal forgiveness does not mean that forgiveness is dissociated from all religion. For centuries, forgiveness has been associated with the major religions (Rye et al., 2000) and most centrally with Christianity (Marty, 1998). Christianity has formed much of the backdrop of contemporary U.S. culture, even though most commentators now consider the United States to be a pluralistically religious culture. Thus, forgiveness cannot be considered as completely devoid of religious associations—at least not without detaching it from the experience of most clients and research participants. Because culture has changed, though, religion is not the center of forgiveness, and vice versa, for all (or perhaps most). Social scientists then must investigate how religion and forgiveness do and don't intersect, for whom, and under what conditions.

As you read the subsequent chapters, you might ask yourself whether the writers' conceptualizations will fit well with a religiously diverse society, clientele, or research population. Read with social savvy. Has forgiveness been gutted of religion? How are the highly religious, moderately religious, nominally religious, nonreligious, and irreligious likely to respond to a writer's conceptualization of forgiveness?

Question 4: How Does Forgiveness Affect the Participants in the Forgiveness Process?

Forgiveness involves a transgressor, a victim, sometimes either an involved or an impartial observer, and sometimes wider elements in society. Each is affected differently and experiences different intrapsychic and interpersonal events.

The transgressor may experience guilt, shame, or self-condemnation at having transgressed. Usually, the transgressor must respond to an accusation. He or she might apologize or offer restitution, might be repentant, or might merely express remorse and contrition but continue to inflict transgressions. Some transgressors may be truly guilty as accused; others may be falsely accused or accused of being more unfeeling or harsh than they intended. Some may be narcissistic. Others may be antisocial or manipulative. Still others may be more empathic. Some may be given to self-forgiveness—some to honest self-forgiveness after accepting responsibility and trying to make amends but others simply dodging guilt by letting themselves off scot-free. Still others might stew in their guilt, unable to forgive themselves. Once the victim has forgiven, the transgressor must consider a response—both intrapsychically and interpersonally. Can forgiveness be accepted? The transgressor's experiences, thus, are complex and are intertwined with the experiences and responses of the victim.

The victim, on the other hand, experiences the damage from the transgression and he or she suffers. How the victim perceives the transgression, though, is affected by his or her self-involvement. Victims, for instance, tend to overlook transgressors' attempts to make amends or to discount the costs of apologizing. Victims respond in anger, fear, and resentment. Victims and transgressors talk about the transgressions. Based on interpersonal interactions, victims might approach the offender or might not. Personality attributes of the victims are related to how they deal with forgiveness. They may be vengeful, repressive, fearful, or communicative. Many victims ruminate about wounds they have experienced. The content and intrusiveness of the rumination affects how victims respond.

Offenders and victims (and observers) may be dispositionally oriented toward different ways of acting. They might have a strong justice motive (Lerner, 1980). If justice is not quickly forthcoming, victims might respond by being dispositionally unforgiving, which could manifest as resentful grudge holding or as vengeance. People can deal indirectly with injustice by deflecting it through accepting, excusing, justifying, or even exonerating the offender and offense. With effort, some victims can deal with injustice through forbearance, suppression of feelings, or deciding to forgive. Some might also experience transformative forgiveness. Some people may have more of a forgiving or vengeful personality disposition. A number of personal characteristics are related to such dispositions.

Similarly, offenders are likely influenced by their personalities. They may be guilt prone or shame prone; narcissistic; empathic; preoccupied with saving face; prideful; and characterized by low self-esteem, fragile high self-esteem, or stable high self-esteem.

Forgiveness can also involve others (Helmick & Peterson, 2001). Relatives and neighbors of victims or perpetrators are often touched by transgressions. Crimes affect society and result in laws and rules that govern social interactions. Tribes or other subgroups can be affected. Religious or ethnic conflict can involve the entire social fabric of a country or can extend across national boundaries.

Clearly, forgiveness is highly complex (a) intrapersonally, (b) interpersonally within a dyad, and (c) interpersonally within the societal and political context. Each investigator can tackle only a limited piece of the complex process. You must thus read as a sensitive synthesizer of the forgiveness process.

Question 5: What Are the Benefits of Forgiveness?

The potential benefits of forgiveness are putatively localized in four areas: physical, mental, relational, and spiritual health. Forgiveness might affect people's physical health. Unforgiveness is stressful and makes people feel hostile toward transgressors (Witvliet, Ludwig, & Vander Laan, 2001). A frequently unforgiving person might experience disorders of the cardiovascular or immune system. If we extend the findings from related literatures—such as studies of stress and Type A hostility—we might assume that unforgiveness has a negative impact on physical health. Toussaint, Williams, Musick, and Everson (2001) published results from a national survey suggesting that in elderly people, forgiveness was associated with fewer negative health symptoms. The anticipation is that physical health will be negatively affected if people are chronically unforgiving and positively affected if they practice regular forgiveness.

However, disturbing questions remain. How much (if any) is the impact of unforgive-ness (and forgiveness) on physical health? How much unforgiveness is necessary to create a measurable impact? Is forgiveness important at all?

Forgiveness and unforgiveness might also affect mental health and well-being. At a minimum, it seems obvious that people who are unforgiving experience more anger and depression. Much of the research on forgiveness and mental health outcomes has been done in interventions studies, which do not necessarily reveal whether un-forgiveness or forgiveness might be related to mental health in naturally occurring situations. However, as with physical health, questions remain. How much effect is actually due to forgiving? Could the same benefits accrue if a person obtained revenge or observed civil or criminal justice? Are benefits transitory or lasting? What mecha-nisms link forgiveness to mental health outcomes and to enhanced well-being? Are there negative effects?

On the surface, forgiveness seems logically to be related to relational health. Be-neath the surface, however, the picture is fuzzy. Mere unforgiveness or forgiveness, as experienced internally, might not be related to whether partners in a dyad reconcile with each other. Baumeister et al. (1998) described hollow forgiveness, a forgiveness granted verbally but not experienced psychologically; and silent forgiveness, a for-giveness experienced but never communicated. There can be a disconnect between experience and expression of forgiveness. Yet even if experience and expression are congruent in the victim, that does not guarantee relational harmony. Members of a dyad might perceive events differently, make different attributions of causality, desire different actions, and generally pursue different agendas. The partners interact. Their communication, as well as their pretransgression relationship, ought to be expected to affect whether forgiveness and reconciliation occur. Forgiveness or unforgiveness might be related to better or worse relational health. The fact is that many relationship variables intrude in that relationship.

Forgiveness might be associated with improved spiritual health. As mentioned in Question 3, forgiveness has long been associated with religious experiences. It has particularly been associated with divine forgiveness within a Christian framework and with return to God's path or to *teshuvah* in a Jewish worldview. However, grant-ing, experiencing, and expressing forgiveness might (or might not) produce more peaceful, harmonious points of view, even for those who are not religious. Thus, a boost to nonreligious spirituality may be one benefit of forgiveness.

Optimistic claims of potential benefits of forgiving, without the contamination of much data, have characterized the early years of forgiveness research. However, what do the data say? It is now time to read this literature as a serious skeptic of the puta-tive benefits. The results of that reading could affect the entire field. If benefits can be unambiguously established, there will likely be future governmental funding by some of the Institutes in the National Institutes of Health.

Question 6: What Are the Costs, Limits, and Iatrogenic Effects of Forgiveness?

Much of the research has been done by researchers who assumed that forgiveness, for the most part, is mostly beneficial. However, almost all scientific accounts—in contrast to many mass-market and media accounts—admit that forgiveness can clearly be costly for individuals to undertake. People who forgive often think they are giving up rights to retaliate, even the score, or seek legitimate justice. Thus, significant costs can be incurred by people who express forgiveness.

In addition, there may be limits to what people can forgive. Some people argue that almost any act can be forgiven. Others suggest that forgiveness is limited by the attitude of the transgressor. When transgressors won't take responsibility for their actions or when they continue to perpetrate harmful acts, many people would argue that forgiveness should not be granted.

There might be cases where forgiveness harms individuals. If a person assumes that forgiveness is called for and that person forgives, then as a consequence places himself or herself in danger, some argue that forgiveness has thus had an iatrogenic effect. Others argue that this is a misunderstanding of forgiveness. They say that the person has confused reconciliation and forgiving. Might there be cases in which forgiveness itself is harmful? Might it erode the strength of the justice motive or weaken the resolve to hold a perpetrator accountable? Might forgiving weaken a person's power base or self-esteem? Might it encourage a perpetrator to take advantage?

Have scientists explored the iatrogenic effects of forgiveness? Have studies been undertaken to see whether such harm is actually caused? Instead of reading as a forgiveness advocate, read as a dedicated detractor. Paradoxically, a strong sense of the science of forgiveness can occur only if we define the boundaries sharply.

Question 7: Are There Effective Interventions to Promote Forgiveness Among Families and Larger Social or Societal Units?

In the early history of forgiveness studies, interventionists led the way. Enright was at the forefront of developing such interventions (see chapter 24 by Freedman et al.). He has targeted elderly people (Hebl & Enright, 1993), victims of incest (Freedman & Enright, 1996), and men whose partners had abortions (Coyle & Enright, 1997). On the other hand, Worthington and his group developed psychoeducational interventions to promote forgiveness in groups not aimed at forgiving specific types of transgressions. People were admitted to groups if they experienced *any* transgression they wished to forgive. Both targeted and untargeted interventions to promote forgiveness are useful for different purposes.

Since the early programs, interventionists have developed more interventions to promote forgiveness (see chapter 26 by Wade, Worthington, and Meyer for a meta-analysis).

Are group interventions effective? If so, why? What are the active ingredients of the interventions? Are any particularly effective? If so, with whom and under what conditions?

Few if any interventions have examined forgiveness within the context of a relationship. In troubled couples, families, workplaces, and communities, forgiveness must be contextualized within relationships and within communities. As you read the chapters, try to discern which interventions can be tailored and applied to contexts from couples to communities.

Of great interest also are interventions to promote forgiveness and reconciliation at the societal level. Few researchers have studied societal interventions empirically (see Chapman & Spong, 2003; chapter 28 by Cairns et al.; chapter 27 by Staub; and even chapter 2 by de Waal & Pokorny with primate societies).

Many questions remain about interventions. Are they efficacious? Have controlled studies established evidence-based interventions? On another level, are the interventions effective if applied, not in the carefully controlled clinical trial (called an *efficacy study*), but rather in homes, counseling agencies, community programs, churches, and societies (called *effectiveness studies*)? As you read the following chapters, read as a critical consumer of claims about interventions and their usefulness.

Question 8: Is There a Future for Forgiveness Studies?

There is a fragile future for the scientific study of forgiveness. If new researchers are not drawn into studying forgiveness, there is no future. New investigators depend on mentoring by senior scholars and identification with other areas of psychology. First, mentors must train and attract younger scholars. Perhaps the grant funding achieved by some senior scientists was the prime motivator in attracting some laboratories to the study of forgiveness. When money runs out, those investigators might lose their interest. On the other hand, if young researchers have been attracted to study forgiveness because of the mentoring of the senior investigators, that bodes well for the future of forgiveness studies.

Second, can forgiveness studies be considered part of the larger movement, such as positive psychology? To the extent that forgiveness is commonly accepted as a part of positive psychology, researchers who study positive psychology might include additional variables aimed at forgiveness and its effects. However, if forgiveness studies are isolated within a small subarea, such studies might continue but probably won't expand.

Will funding be forthcoming from philanthropists, foundations, and federal funding sources to support the study of forgiveness? The answer to this question depends on (a) the critical mass of researchers who study forgiveness, (b) whether forgiveness can make a positive impact on physical health, mental health, or relationships that is in line with governmental funding priorities, and (c) whether we can identify weaknesses scientifically and then deal with them. Federal funding depends on mature research programs. Pilot studies are typically required, which (in federal-funding terms) require a quarter or half million dollars to complete. At the present time, are there enough good research track records explicitly involving forgiveness to break into the federal funding arena? Will an Institute pick up forgiveness as an important priority? As you read the following chapters, look for areas that are beginning to approach a critical mass of literature in potentially fundable areas. Read as a future funding recipient.

YOUR PERSPECTIVE AS YOU READ THE FOLLOWING REVIEW CHAPTERS

I have asked experts in their respective areas to write chapters befitting a handbook. As much as possible, we tried to hold to a common structure. Authors begin by defining forgiveness as they understand it.

I asked each author to review the extant research and theory within his or her domain of expertise. As you read, look for areas that are maturing and those still in their infancy. Look for what has been done, what has been found, and what has not yet been studied.

I also asked each author to suggest a research agenda for his, her, or their area, based on the just-completed review. You will encounter hundreds of research topics suggested by these experts. I have suggested eight mindsets you might adopt as you read the following chapters. You can read

as a detective for definitions
as a concerned critic of measures
with social savvy about religious roots
as a sensitive synthesizer of the forgiveness process
as a serious skeptic about putative benefits
as a critical consumer of claims about interventions
as a dedicated detractor who looks for limits of forgiveness
as a future funding recipient.

You might be coming to the book as a clinician looking for practical tips, a scientist just beginning a research career, a seasoned scientist with credentials in some other field, or an experienced forgiveness researcher. The field is wide open for new investigators studying new topics. It is open to practitioners applying scientific insights in new ways. You can contribute to the growth of the science of forgiveness studies and its application.

REFERENCES

Al-Mabuk, R. H., Enright, R. D., & Cardis, P. A. (1995). Forgiving education with parentally love-deprived late adolescents. *Journal of Moral Education, 24,* 427–444.

Augsburger, D. W. (1996). *Helping people forgive.* Westminster, UK: Westminster John Knox Press.

Baumeister, R. F., Exline, J. J., & Sommer, K. L. (1998). The victim role, grudge theory, and two dimensions of forgiveness. In E. L. Worthington, Jr. (Ed.), *Dimensions of forgiveness: Psychological research and theological perspectives* (pp. 79–104). Philadelphia: Templeton Foundation Press.

Brown, S. W., Gorsuch, R., Rosik, C. H., & Ridley, C. R. (2001). The development of a scale to measure forgiveness. *Journal of Psychology and Christianity, 20,* 40–52.

Chapman, A. R., & Spong B. (Eds.). (2003). *Religion and reconciliation in South Africa.* Philadelphia: Templeton Foundation Press.

Coyle, C. T., & Enright, R. D. (1997). Forgiveness intervention with post-abortion men. *Journal of Consulting and Clinical Psychology, 65,* 1042–1045.

DiBlasio, F. A. (1998). The use of decision-based forgiveness intervention within intergenerational family therapy. *Journal of Family Therapy, 20,* 77–94.

Enright, R. D., & Fitzgibbons, R. P. (2000). *Helping clients forgive: An empirical guide for resolving anger and restoring hope.* Washington, DC: American Psychological Association.

Exline, J. J., & Baumeister, R. F. (2000). Expressing forgiveness and repentance: Benefits and barriers. In M. E. McCullough, K. I. Pargament, & C. E. Thoresen (Eds.), *Forgiveness: Theory, research, and practice* (pp. 133–155). New York: Guilford Press.

Exline, J. J., Worthington, E. L., Jr., Hill, P. C., & McCullough, M. E. (2003). Forgiveness and justice: A research agenda for social and personality psychology. *Personality and Social Psychology Review 7,* 337–348.

Finkel, E. J., Rusbult, C. E., Kumashiro, M., & Hannon, P. A. (2002). Dealing with betrayal in close relationships: Does commitment promote forgiveness? *Journal of Personality and Social Psychology, 82,* 956–974.

Flanigan, B. J. (1994). *Forgiving the unforgivable: Overcoming the bitter legacy of intimate wounds.* Foster City, CA: IDG Books Worldwide.

Freedman, S. R., & Enright, R. D. (1996). Forgiveness as an intervention goal with incest survivors. *Journal of Consulting and Clinical Psychology, 64,* 983–992.

Hargrave, T. D., & Sells, J. N. (1997). The development of a forgiveness scale. *Journal of Marital and Family Therapy, 23,* 41–62.

Hebl, J., & Enright, R. D. (1993). Forgiveness as a psychotherapeutic goal with elderly females. *Psychotherapy, 30,* 658–667.

Helmick, R. G., & Peterson, R. L. (2001). *Forgiveness and reconciliation: Religion, public policy, and conflict transformation* (pp. 81–95). Philadelphia: Templeton Foundation Press.

Lerner, M. J. (1980). *The belief in a just world.* New York: Plenum.

Luskin, F. (2002). *Forgive for good: A proven prescription for health and happiness.* San Francisco: HarperCollins.

Marty, M. E. (1998). The ethos of Christian forgiveness. In E. L. Worthington, Jr. (Ed.), *Dimensions of forgiveness: Psychological research and theological perspectives* (pp. 9–28). Philadelphia: Templeton Foundation Press.

McCullough, M. E., Fincham, F. D., & Tsang, J-A. (2003). Forgiveness, forbearance, and time: The temporal unfolding of transgression-related interpersonal motivations. *Journal of Personality and Social Psychology, 84,* 540–557.

McCullough, M. E., Pargament, K. I., & Thoresen, C. E. (2000). The psychology of forgiveness: History, conceptual issues, and overview. In M. E. McCullough, K. I. Pargament, & C. E.

Thoresen (Eds.), *Forgiveness: Theory, research, and practice* (pp. 1–16). New York: Guilford Press.

McCullough, M. E., Rachal, K. C., Sandage, S. J., Worthington, E. L. Jr., Brown, S. W., & Hight, T. L. (1998). Interpersonal forgiving in close relationships II: Theoretical elaboration and measurement. *Journal of Personality and Social Psychology, 73,* 321–336.

McGraw, Tim (2004). Live Like You Were Dying. On *Live Like You Were Dying* [CD]. Nashville: Curb Records.

Rye, M.S., Pargament, K. I., Ali, M. A., Beck, G. L., Dorff, E. N., Hallisey, C., et al. (2000). Religious perspectives on forgiveness. In M. E. McCullough, K. I. Pargament, & C. E. Thoresen (Eds.), *Forgiveness: Theory, research, and practice* (pp. 17–40). New York: Guilford Press.

Smedes, L. (1984). *Forgive and forget: Healing the hurts we don't deserve.* New York: HarperCollins.

Subkoviak, M. J., Enright, R. D., Wu, C. R., Gassin, E. A., Freedman, S., Olson, L. M., et al. (1995). Measuring interpersonal forgiveness in late adolescence and middle adulthood. *Journal of Adolescence, 18,* 641–655.

Thompson, L. Y., Snyder, C. R., Hoffman, L., Michael, S. T., Rasmussen, H. N., Billings, L. S., et al. (2005). Dispositional forgiveness of self, others, and situations. *Journal of Personality, 73,* 313–360.

Toussaint, L. L., Williams, D. R., Musick, M. A., & Everson, S. A. (2001). Forgiveness and health: Age differences in a U.S. probability sample. *Journal of Adult Development, 8,* 249–257.

Wade, N. G., & Worthington, E. L., Jr. (2003). Overcoming interpersonal offenses: Is forgiveness the only way to deal with unforgiveness? *Journal of Counseling and Development, 81,* 343–353.

Wade, S. H. (1989). The development of a scale to measure forgiveness. *Dissertation Abstracts International B, 50,* 5338.

Witvliet, C. v. O., Ludwig, T. E., & Vander Laan, K. L. (2001). Granting forgiveness or harboring grudges: Implications for emotion, physiology, and health. *Psychological Science, 121,* 117–123.

Worthington, E. L., Jr. (2003). *Forgiving and reconciling: Bridges to wholeness and hope.* Downers Grove, IL: InterVarsity Press.

Worthington, E. L., Jr., & DiBlasio, F. A. (1990). Promoting mutual forgiveness within the fractured relationship. *Psychotherapy, 27,* 219–223.

Worthington, E. L., Jr., & Scherer, M. (2004). Forgiveness is an emotion-focused coping strategy that can reduce health risks and promote health resilience: Theory, review, and hypotheses. *Psychology and Health, 19,* 385–405.

Worthington, E. L., Jr., & Wade, N. G. (1999). The social psychology of unforgiveness and forgiveness and implications for clinical practice. *Journal of Social and Clinical Psychology, 18,* 385–418.

Part One

NATURE, PHILOSOPHY, RELIGION, AND FORGIVENESS

Chapter Two

Primate Conflict and Its Relation to Human Forgiveness

Frans B. M. de Waal
Jennifer J. Pokorny

Research on nonhuman primates has produced compelling evidence for so-called reconciliation and consolation, that is, postconflict contacts that serve to repair social relationships and comfort distressed individuals, such as victims of aggression. Although it is difficult and perhaps impossible to demonstrate forgiveness explicitly among nonhuman primates, inferences can be drawn from the behavior these animals use to repair social damage. Their behavior can be seen as an evolutionary precursor to conflict resolution and forgiveness in human societies.

ASSUMPTIONS ABOUT FORGIVENESS AND RECONCILIATION

The best known behavioral mechanism that allows primates to repair social damage caused by hostilities is *reconciliation*. Reconciliation is defined as a friendly reunion between former opponents: The reunion supposedly serves to return the relationship to normal levels of tolerance and cooperation. An early anecdote of this behavior is Köhler's (1925) description of the need for "forgiveness" in a juvenile chimpanzee.

> The little creature, which I had punished for the first time, shrank back, uttered one or two heartbroken wails, as she stared at me horror-struck, while her lips were pouted more than ever. The next moment she had flung her arms round my neck, quite beside herself, and was only comforted by degrees, when I stroked her. (p. 261)

Apes seem to perceive a conflict with those close to them as a threat to the relationship and try to control the damage with affectionate behavior. Although the environment of hand-reared apes is obviously unnatural, human influence does not appear to explain the phenomenon. As we will see below, nonhuman primates have many forms of contact behavior that seems to serve to repair disturbed relationships.

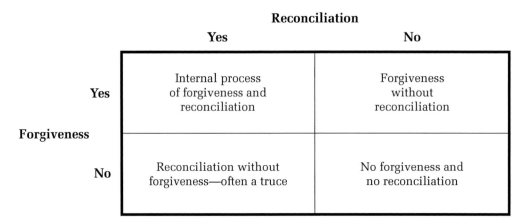

FIGURE 2.1. Possible combinations of reconciliation (a social process between two parties) and forgiveness (an internal process with an offender in mind). After Park and Enright (2000).

When discussing forgiveness, it must be remembered that reconciliation is not forgiveness. It is possible to reconcile with an opponent without actually forgiving the individual. Likewise, it is possible to forgive another without ever formally reconciling (see Figure 2.1). The process of forgiveness occurs when individual A has been wronged in some way by individual B, resulting in A having negative emotions toward B. A then attempts to cope with the situation and overcomes these negative feelings, which usually requires changing one's perception of the other individual. Forgiveness implies acceptance of the situation and the other individual.

Because forgiveness is an internal process to which we have no access in nonhuman primates, if it exists at all, and reconciliation is an externally visible social process, the comparison is difficult to make. Suffice it to say that what the two have in common is some emotional switch, which when turned moves the attitude toward another individual from aggressive and/or fearful to friendly, perhaps even affectionate. This switch is truly remarkable and not something anyone expected to find in animals (Rowell, 2000). It is unlikely that this switching mechanism evolved independently in several species, especially closely related ones. We must assume that if we share it with our close relatives, it derives from the same source: the first group-living mammals perhaps, which arose many millions of years before we appeared on the planet.

REVIEW OF THE LITERATURE

The Need to Preserve Relationships

From an evolutionary perspective, benefits of cooperation are most evident in relationships with a reproductive function, such as male–female and mother–offspring relationships.

Relationships also produce benefits not immediately related to reproduction, however, such as when two individuals protect one another against attack, tolerate one another around resources, provide vigilance against predators, or cooperate during intra- or intergroup competition. It is of course assumed here that cooperative tendencies evolved because they paid off in the long run in terms of survival and reproduction.

Kummer (1978) defined the benefits that individual A provides to B as A's value to B. Any individual will try to improve this value: B will select the best available A, predict A's behavior, and modify A's behavior to its own advantage. In other words, B will invest in the relationship with A. Although most of B's investments may not lead to quick profits, such as immediately useful actions by A, they may help cultivate a relationship that is beneficial to both A and B over the long haul. A good example of such investment is social grooming. One primate may groom another for over an hour without any immediate return favor. After the session, the two will simply part company, each going its own way. There are indications that grooming is altruistic in that it entails costs for the groomer, such as reduced time available for other activities and reduced attention to potential danger, whereas it provides benefits to the groomee in terms of hygiene and a calming effect. Why would one individual provide services to another—grooming is one of the most common activities in primate groups—if not to foster future beneficial exchanges?

The most pervasive and effective cooperation within primate groups is the formation of alliances: Two or more individuals band together against a third. For example, a male attacks a juvenile, and the mother rushes to the juvenile's aid at considerable risk to herself. Or two males together overthrow the reigning alpha male, after which one of the victorious males becomes the new alpha. These kinds of cooperation are critically important to primates: Social rank and sometimes life depend on it. Consequently, they need to get along with others, even with their competitors. Maintenance of valuable relationships despite occasional conflicts of interest is a critical requirement of group life.

Reconciliation Behavior

Initially, reconciliation research contrasted and compared expectations concerning the effect of aggressive behavior on social relations. Two hypotheses existed, the first one being traditional in the extensive aggression literature of the 1960s and 1970s and the second one formulated on the discovery that chimpanzees often reunite following aggression.

Dispersal Hypothesis.   Losers of aggressive incidents are expected to avoid winners. The notion of aggression as a spacing mechanism was based on experience with territorial species and the observation that many animals use aggression to maintain what Hediger (1941) termed *species-typical individual distances.* This hypothesis would predict reduced contact following aggression.

Reconciliation Hypothesis. Individuals are expected to "undo" the damage that aggression inflicts on valuable social relationships. Such a tendency would be expressed in increased contact following aggression and special reassuring and appeasing gestures during these contacts.

In support of the second hypothesis, de Waal and van Roosmalen (1979) were the first to demonstrate that aggression leads to increased contact. Former opponents in the chimpanzee colony of Arnhem Zoo (the Netherlands) were found more often within 2 meters of one another after than before a conflict. Moreover, the chimpanzees engaged in intensive body contacts following conflict, such as kissing and embracing (see Figure 2.2) and preferred such contact with former opponents rather than with individuals who had not been involved in the previous conflict. Interopponent contacts constituted 30% of all postconflict contacts, compared with a random expectation of 5.6%. These results demonstrated a pronounced conciliatory tendency in the chimpanzee, later confirmed by reports from the wild.

Following these findings, de Waal and Yoshihara (1983) developed a controlled methodology to look at reconciliation in a relatively intolerant primate, the rhesus macaque. This new method compared the postconflict observation (PC) with a matched control observation (MC). The MC was usually taken the following day, during the same time of day to control for any diurnal or seasonal behavioral differences. If affiliative contact occurs only in the PC and not in the MC, these individuals are said to be attracted. If contact occurs during the MC and not during the PC, these individuals are said to be dispersed. Therefore, there is a direct comparison between rates of contact following aggression and matched baseline periods (see Figure 2.3). Rather surprisingly, it was found that rhesus macaques also follow peacemaking strategies, although not to the same degree as chimpanzees.

Since then, the PC-MC method has become a staple of research on postconflict behavior across species. Some changes have been made, such as controlling for distance

FIGURE 2.2. Kiss on the mouth by a female to a male chimpanzee. This is a behavior often used between former opponents as a conciliatory gesture. Photograph by Frans de Waal.

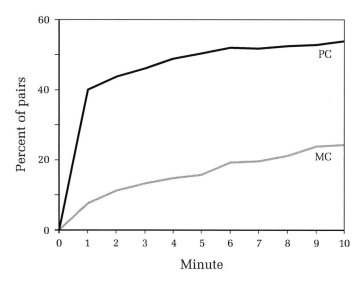

FIGURE 2.3. Primates show a dramatic increase in body contact between former opponents during postconflict (PC), as compared with matched-control (MC) observations. The graph provides the cumulative percentage of opponent pairs establishing friendly contact during a 10-min time window following spontaneous aggressive incidents in a zoo group of stump-tailed macaques.

between former opponents by starting the MC observation only when that distance is similar to the distance at the start of the PC. Others have imposed a time limit on the observation following a conflict, because reconciliation often occurs within the first few minutes. This may be conservative in that some contacts outside this time may function as reconciliation. However, long observations by nature lead to higher chances of contact. These methods also allow one to determine how likely it is for reconciliation to occur with the group (kin vs. nonkin) or species as a whole. Veenema and colleagues (Veenema, Das, & Aureli, 1994) introduced a method to use these observations to measure reconciliation frequencies between different individuals and determine their conciliatory tendency. This is calculated by subtracting the number of dispersed pairs from the number of attracted pairs and dividing by the total number of PC-MC pairs.

Following these methods, similar results have subsequently been reported for a variety of other macaque species, as well as for gorillas, bonobos, golden monkeys, vervets, mangabeys, baboons, and so on. Most of these studies were conducted in captivity, but reconciliation has also been demonstrated in wild primates. In most species studied thus far, affiliative contact between former opponents is more likely during the first few minutes after a conflict, and postconflict attraction is selective. The contact increase does not occur indiscriminately with all possible partners but specifically between recent opponents. For reviews of the literature, see Aureli and de Waal (2000) and de Waal (2000).

According to both the data on captive chimpanzees and descriptions of chimpanzees in the wild, reconciliation in this species involves distinct behavior patterns, such as embracing, gentle touching, and mouth-to-mouth kissing. In fact, chimpanzee opponents kiss one another 10 times more often during the first postconflict contact than during subsequent contacts. Not all primates show a similar behavioral distinction between first postconflict and other contacts, but stump-tailed macaques use another conspicuous behavior pattern rarely observed outside the reconciliation context—the "hold-bottom ritual," in which one individual, usually the recipient of aggression, presents the hindquarters, and the other clasps the presenter's haunches (see Figure 2.4). This ritual occurs in more than 30% of first postconflict contacts, a 20-fold increase compared with control contacts.

The kiss of chimpanzees and the hold-bottom ritual of stump-tailed macaques require high levels of intimacy and coordination. They assist the reconciliation process by making both the context and meaning of the contact more explicit. This is in contrast to the implicit reconciliations of some other species, such as the rhesus macaque, which often reestablish relationships through a brief, inconspicuous brushing contact that is quite meaningful, given the risks involved in mere proximity in this short-tempered species.

Reconciliation serves as a heuristic label for these contacts: It generates ideas about their function, such as that they repair social relationships or reduce social tension. The validity of this label has been confirmed experimentally. Cords (1992), for example, carried out experiments indicating that reconciliation restores tolerance between former opponents. Following an aggressive incident between macaques, the monkeys were presented with two drinking nipples, side by side, from which they could obtain a sweet drink. The monkeys drank together more readily if reconciliation had taken place than without reconciliation. Observational studies of both macaques

FIGURE 2.4. Hold-bottom by a dominant male (right) to a subordinate, which is a specific conciliatory gesture among stump-tailed macaques. Photograph by Frans de Waal.

and chimpanzees confirm that reconciliation reduces the chances of further aggression: The frequency of renewed attack is reduced following reconciliation. These results support the hypothesis that reconciliation restores the relationship between former opponents.

Both macaques and chimpanzees follow what seems a general rule among primates, that is, reconciliation aims to restore the most valuable relationships. In macaques, in which matrilineal kin relationships are particularly valuable, related individuals reconcile conflicts more often than do unrelated individuals. In the chimpanzee, males form stronger bonds than females, and male conflicts are more often reconciled than female conflicts. This general rule, the Valuable Relationship Hypothesis, is reviewed by van Schaik and Aureli (2000) and de Waal (2000), and can be summarized by predicting that reconciliation will be most common between partners that stand most to lose, were conflict to continue.

An experimental investigation of this hypothesis was carried out by Cords and Thurnheer (1993), who trained pairs of macaques to cooperate during feeding, thus enhancing their interdependence. Reconciliation following conflict increased dramatically once a partner had become useful for obtaining food, thus confirming the idea that reconciliation occurs in proportion to the value of the relationship.

Interspecific variability in aggressiveness and peacemaking tendency makes it possible to expose members of a given species to a social environment with dramatically different rates of these behaviors. This can be done by housing them with another species. If reconciliation is a learned social skill, one expects such a manipulation to affect postconflict behavior. This prediction was examined by de Waal and Johanowicz (1993), who exposed rhesus monkeys—a species with low levels of reconciliation—to a highly conciliatory species, the stump-tailed macaque. Both species belong to the genus *Macaca*.

Juveniles were housed in mixed-species groups of seven monkeys each for a period of 5 months. Following this period, they were observed for 6 weeks in groups of conspecifics only. Control rhesus monkeys, matched in age and sex to the experimental subjects, went through the same procedure without contact with another species (i.e., in all-rhesus groups). Initially, individuals of different species lived somewhat separate lives, sleeping and huddling in separate subgroups, but by the end of the 5-month period, they were fully integrated and highly tolerant of each other.

Compared with the control experiment, the main result of the manipulation was a three- to fourfold increase in the proportion of fights followed by reconciliation. Rhesus monkeys who had lived with the kinder, gentler species apparently had learned peacemaking skills. This difference emerged gradually during the co-housing phase but was sustained following removal of the "tutor" species (see Figure 2.5). The experimental setup did not include a control group of stump-tailed monkeys and hence did not allow investigation of whether the tutors had learned to be more aggressive and less conciliatory and after the co-housing stage.

This result, which shows that reconciliation can be modified through environmental manipulation, has important implications. It shows that primate peacemaking is not

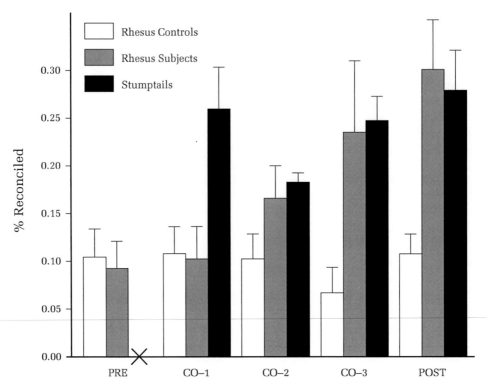

FIGURE 2.5. Mean (+ SEM) proportion per individual of aggressive conflicts followed within 3 min by a reconciliation initiated by the individual. During the pre- and postphase, subjects were housed with conspecifics only; no prephase data are available on stump-tailed monkeys. The 5-month co-housing phase has been divided into three equal parts (CO-1, CO-2, CO-3). The graph shows that rhesus experimental subjects, which lived during co-housing with stump-tails, increased their reconciliation rate and maintained this high rate in the postphase, when they lived with other rhesus monkeys only. Adapted from de Waal & Johanowicz (1993).

some inflexible, "instinctive" pattern but is subject to learning. An instructive confirmation of this learning ability can be found in a study of a wild baboon troop that maintained exceptional peacefulness for over a decade as a result of a past incident (Sapolsky & Share, 2004). This flexibility is even more prominent in our own species.

Complexity and Cognition

Like all macaques, pig-tailed macaques form matrilineal societies in which female kin associate with and support one another. Apart from direct reconciliations between former combatants, Judge (1991) found that relatives of the victim tend to seek contact with the aggressor. For example, a mother may approach and groom the attacker of her daughter in what appears to be a reconciliation "on her offspring's behalf" (p. 234). If such triadic reconciliation protects the victim's matriline against further hostilities, all of its members benefit, including the individual who went to contact the aggressor.

If monkeys sometimes reconcile "for" their matriline, the same mechanism could operate between groups. Intergroup relations tend to be hostile, but on a number of occasions, adult females of different free-ranging groups have been observed to come together for grooming. Several such contacts took place shortly after intergroup fights and involved the alpha females of both groups (Judge & de Waal, 1994). These contacts may serve to reestablish peace between groups.

The complexity of peacemaking interactions is even greater in chimpanzees. In this species, individuals act as though they know the meaning of reconciliation not only for themselves but also for others. The following are typical examples of the cognitive complexity of peacemaking in the Arnhem chimpanzee colony.

Third-Party Mediation. If, after a fight between them, two male rivals stayed in prolonged proximity without engaging in an actual physical reunion (an apparent deadlock situation), an adult female might initiate a grooming contact with one of the two. After several minutes of grooming, she would slowly walk to the other male, often followed by her grooming partner. If he failed to follow, she might return to tug at his arm. After the three individuals had been together for a while with the female in the middle, she would then get up and stroll away, leaving the males alone.

Deception. On six occasions, a dominant female who had been unable to catch a fleeing opponent was observed to approach this individual some time afterward with a friendly appearance, holding out her hand, only to change her behavior when the other came within reach. Reasons to regard the subsequent attack as the female's real intention are its timing (very sudden, without warning signals), the fact that all instances concerned victims capable of outrunning the aggressor, and the intensity of the punishment.

Strategic Reconciliation. Reconciliation may occur in a hurried fashion if continuation of the fight would harm the interests of both individuals. For example, in the years that the Arnhem colony was ruled by a coalition of Nikkie and Yeroen, the alpha male, Nikkie, could get in serious trouble during prolonged conflicts with his partner. A third male would begin an intimidation display, initially terrorizing the females and juveniles but later displaying closer and closer to the two quarreling males themselves. Nikkie was never observed to control the third male on his own. He would first approach his opponent, Yeroen, with a large grin, seeking an embrace. Only after reestablishment of contact with his partner would Nikkie go over to the third male to subdue him.

Control Role. In many primates, high-ranking males break up fights. This so-called control role is perhaps best developed in chimpanzees. Males who adopt this role move from the usual support of winners in fights to loser support and dissociate their intervention tendencies from individual preferences. That is, they are the only group members to intervene in fights impartially. They may move with all hair on end between two combatants until they stop screaming, scatter them with a charging display, or literally pry locked fighters apart with both hands. In all of this, their main objective seems to be to put an end to the hostilities rather than to support one party or the other. The following description illustrates how Luit, within weeks of attaining alpha status in the Arnhem colony, adopted the role.

> On one occasion, a quarrel between Mama and Spin got out of hand and ended in biting and fighting. Numerous apes rushed up to the two warring females and joined in the fray. A huge knot of fighting, screaming apes rolled around in the sand, until Luit leapt in and literally beat them apart. He did not choose sides in the conflict, like the others; instead anyone who continued to fight received a blow from him. I had never seen him act so impressively before. (de Waal, 1982, p. 124)

Distress Alleviation and Empathy

Postconflict contact between former opponents should be distinguished from postconflict contact by one of the participants in a fight with a bystander (i.e., an individual who had not been involved in the fight). Such contacts, especially when initiated by the bystanders themselves, cannot serve the same function as reconciliation (which is to repair a disturbed relationship). The most likely function of contact with bystanders is distress alleviation.

Sensitivity to the emotions of others emerges early in humans, such as when a nursery room with infants bursts out crying in response to the cries of one among them. This process, known as *empathic distress* or *emotional contagion*, provides the ontogenetic basis for cognitively more advanced responses to distress in which the actor understands the other's situation, distinguishes the other's distress from his or her own feelings, and acts out of genuine concern about the other's well-being. Hence, dependent on the precise mechanism involved, empathy, or the capacity to be emotionally affected by someone else's feelings, can be cognitively simple or complex.

An early study of chimpanzees found that affiliative contact between participants in a fight and bystanders occurred more often in the first minute following a conflict than in subsequent minutes (de Waal & van Roosmalen, 1979). Moreover, first-minute contacts included more embracing and gentle touching than did contacts during subsequent minutes. Contacts with bystanders were labeled *consolation*. Recent research confirmed these findings, demonstrating that it is particularly with victims of serious aggression that contact is made (de Waal & Aureli, 1996; see Figure 2.6). These are, of course, also the individuals expected to be most in need of comfort.

In macaques, in contrast, none of the studies addressing this behavior have thus far produced evidence for consolation. Despite various measures and statistical methods, the finding has been the same in four different species: Affiliative contact between recipients of aggression and bystanders does not occur more often following

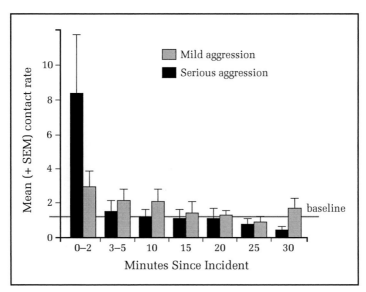

FIGURE 2.6.   The rate with which third parties contact victims of aggression in chimpanzees, comparing recipients of serious and mild aggression. Especially in the first few minutes after the incident, recipients of serious aggression receive more contacts than baseline. Adapted from de Waal & Aureli (1996).

conflict than during control periods. Despite this lack of evidence, qualitative observations suggest that macaques do engage in consolation behavior, at least when very young. We have regularly seen infant rhesus monkeys being attracted to the screams of one among them (e.g., after punishment by an adult or after a fall), approach the vocalizer, and establish contact. Occasionally, this resulted in a pile of infants clambering over each other. Given this strong empathic distress response, why is there so little of it left at later ages?

One possible explanation is that association with the recipient of aggression is fraught with risk. In macaques, recipients of aggression continue to attract aggression in the period immediately following the aggressive incident. If this elevated chance of further aggression extends to bystanders who approach recipients of aggression, this is a risk with which bystanders need to reckon. Perhaps these risks are less important in a chimpanzee society with its looser and more tolerant hierarchy.

The alternative explanation is that chimpanzees achieve a higher level of cognition that allows a sharper distinction between self and other. It is generally recognized that the development of empathy in human children relates to this distinction, hence to the level of self-awareness of the child. Given that chimpanzees can recognize themselves in mirrors, whereas macaques cannot, it is possible that chimpanzees achieve a level of empathy that is simply not present in most other primates (Gallup, 1982).

Physiological Correlates

One finding from clinical observations is that forgiveness negatively correlates with anxiety. Those who have forgiven an opponent show a significant decrease in level of anxiety (Fitzgibbons, 1986). Anxiety studies have also been conducted on nonhuman primates, making use of a behavioral index. It was proposed by Schino and colleagues (Schino, Scucchi, Maestripieri, & Turillazzi, 1988) that anxiety can reliably be measured in nonhuman primates through certain self-directed behaviors, such as self-scratching. In fact, Aureli and van Schaik (1991) found that among long-tailed macaques, the levels of self-scratching increased among recipients of aggression soon after having been attacked. Aureli also showed that among Barbary macaques, not only the recipients of aggression but also the aggressors increased self-scratching immediately following a conflict (Aureli, Das, & Veenema, 1997). This anxiety may reflect generalized arousal following conflict or it may in fact be a result of the temporary uncertainty within the relationship between two individuals. Support of the later explanation came from the observation that scratching occurred more often after conflict between strongly affiliated individuals. Most importantly, the studies by Aureli indicate that reconciliation is very effective in reducing or eliminating arousal, as measured by self-directed behavior.

Heart rate studies support some of these conclusions. Heart rate was measured in captive rhesus macaques engaged in aggressive conflicts (Smucny, Price, & Byrne, 1997). The heart rate of both the aggressor and victim rose following an aggressive interaction, taking longer to drop back to baseline in the victim than the aggressor. If reconciliation occurred between two opponents, there was a significant reduction in the elevated heart rate, returning to baseline levels. Aureli and colleagues also looked at changes in heart rate associated with different interactions between individual rhesus macaques living in a group situation (Aureli, Preston, & de Waal, 1999). Subjects showed a significantly increased heart rate if approached by a dominant individual but no change if approached by kin or a subordinate. It was further found that heart rates dropped in individuals engaged in social grooming.

Another study looking at physiological aspects of emotional response in the chimpanzee was conducted by Parr (2001). In this experiment, chimpanzees were shown videos and images that were believed to cause an emotional reaction while recording changes in skin temperature. In humans, it has been shown that decreases in skin temperature are associated with negative emotional arousal. The stimuli presented contained images of a hypodermic needle or dart gun, scenes of unknown conspecifics being injected, and veterinarians threatening chimpanzees with the dart gun. The largest decreases in temperature were recorded when individuals were shown the needle or dart gun, as well as when observing conspecifics being injected. It is not possible from this study to determine whether these changes were due to the subject's own fear of those stimuli or whether they indeed were responding with empathy toward the individual in the images.

How Is Aggression Avoided?

One function of dominance hierarchies, as found in many animals, is to regulate access to resources so that individuals do not need to contest priority every time there is a potential for competition. Mostly, the subordinate withdraws, and the dominant obtains the resource. This way, aggression is avoided, and the relationship is not undermined. Loss of the resource by the subordinate may appear costly, but had this individual attempted to prevent the other from claiming the resource, it most likely would not have gained much more than injuries and a damaged relationship. Conformity to the dominance hierarchy through avoidance of dominants is an effective way of resolving routine disputes.

Apart from avoidance, the approach of a dominant individual can also elicit special gestures or facial expressions in the subordinate. Primates have evolved ritualized status signals. Well-known examples are the bared-teeth display of rhesus macaques and the pant-grunt of chimpanzees. These submissive displays are completely unidirectional (i.e., only one individual in a given pair shows these signals toward the other). The most likely function is appeasement in order to avoid harmful confrontation.

Social conflict can also occur under circumstances and for reasons that do not involve direct competition. As Mason (1993) points out, the most common source of conflict occurs when one individual expects some form of "satisfaction" from another but fails to achieve it. For example, one individual seeks to have sex with or groom another and is rebuffed. This type of conflict rarely leads to aggression but is resolved by a process of negotiation in which the participants exchange signals to increase the predictability of the other's future behavior and to facilitate the achievement of a common goal.

This process is more evident when individuals encounter one another for the very first time, as arranged in some introduction experiments. At the beginning, the encounter is characterized by mistrust and/or hostility, after which various signals help reduce the level of uncertainty and establish a relationship. This process of negotiation leads to the reduction of ambivalence and the achievement of common objectives or a compromise between the objectives of the two parties involved.

Sometimes negotiation is not successful, and one participant may attack the other. One of the most striking examples of overt aggression is when males compete over access to a mate. Among baboons, one male, alone or together with an ally, may attack another male who is in consort with an estrous female. However, nonaggressive tactics are also available to solve these competitive situations. Greeting rituals, in which one male gently touches or mounts another, are common during tensions among male baboons over sexual access to a female. When the number of estrous females is low, compared with the number of males, the chance of mating for an individual male is reduced. Interestingly, under these circumstances, the rate of male aggression stays the same but greeting rituals occur more often. This suggests that greetings decrease tension between males and lower the risk of intermale aggression through increased tolerance (Colmenares, 1991).

In captivity, primates have even more reasons to stop or prevent aggression than in the wild. This situation, with its reduced interindividual distances, offers an excellent opportunity to study conflict management capacities. A traditional view predicts that aggression increases under crowded conditions. Recent research on nonhuman primates has suggested an alternative view. Primates, and perhaps other animals as well, cope with high population density by conflict-avoidance strategies (de Waal, 1989). The way space restrictions affect social behavior varies per species and per situation, but the expected aggression increase under high-density conditions is often minimal and sometimes even reversed. In chimpanzees, it was found that during short-term crowding, the rate of agonistic behaviors was lower than during normal conditions (Aureli & de Waal, 1997). Under short-term crowding in rhesus monkeys, there was no significant increase in intense aggressive behaviors (Judge & de Waal, 1993). In fact, submissive behaviors such as avoidance actually increased under these conditions. Likewise, during long-term crowding, male rhesus monkeys increased grooming and huddling, but there was no increase in the rates of aggression (Judge & de Waal, 1997). This affiliation strategy probably functions to increase social tolerance and limit the potentially damaging effects of aggression.

NEW RESEARCH DIRECTIONS

Advances in technology may provide us with more direct insight into the underlying cognitive and possible emotional processes that are involved during conflicts and reconciliation. Brain regions have been identified in humans that appear to correspond to empathy and forgiveness processes. Through the use of functional magnetic resonance imaging (fMRI), it may be possible to present tasks to nonhuman primates, which may elicit similar responses, while monitoring the brain activity. If these regions are similar, more definite conclusions can be drawn as to the cognitive and emotional similarities and differences across species.

Another area for further research is the inclusion of data from wild populations. This process is currently well underway, with at least a dozen projects on wild primates either being published (e.g., Kutsukake & Castles, 2004; Wittig & Boesch, 2003) or ongoing. The rates of reconciliation are sometimes lower in the wild, but it is obvious that the principles of conflict resolution are essentially the same, meaning that we can gain a fuller understanding of the mechanisms and their evolution by combining controlled studies in captivity with detailed data from the field.

CONCLUSION

Nonhuman primates live in socially complex groups in which they rely for survival on other individuals. It is crucial to maintain cooperative relationships. Although there are competitive situations in which aggression may be inevitable, it is also essential to repair the damage to ensure future cooperation. We have provided evidence showing that reconciliation and other forms of conflict resolution among nonhuman primates are widespread. Given the problem of determining the psychological underpinnings of these behaviors, we are unable to conclude that nonhuman primates do in fact forgive former opponents. However, studies have clearly shown that behavioral correlates of anxiety are significantly reduced following reconciliation between former opponents. In some species, such as the chimpanzee, the importance placed on maintaining relationships may be seen in the repertoire of behavior used specifically for reconciliation. However, the tendency to reconcile is not necessarily hard-wired and can be modified by the surrounding environment, as seen when species with differing conciliatory tendencies are brought together. Conflict resolution is a highly flexible process and, therefore, a social skill that takes into account the value of social relationships and the level of cooperation required for successful group life.

REFERENCES

Aureli, F., Das, M., & Veenema, H. C. (1997). Differential kinship effect on reconciliation in three species of macaques (*Macaca fascicularis, M. fuscata,* and *M. sylvanus*). *Journal of Comparative Psychology, 111,* 91–99.

Aureli, F., & de Waal, F. B. M. (1997). Inhibition of social behavior in chimpanzees under high-density conditions. *American Journal of Primatology, 41,* 213–228.

Aureli, F., & de Waal, F. B. M. (2000). *Natural conflict resolution.* Berkeley, CA: University of California Press.

Aureli, F., Preston, S. D., & de Waal, F. B. M. (1999). Heart rate responses to social interactions in free-moving rhesus macaques (*Macaca mulatta*): A pilot study. *Journal of Comparative Psychology, 113,* 59–65.

Aureli, F., & van Schaik, C. P. (1991). Post-conflict behaviour in long-tailed macaques (*Macaca fascicularis*): II. Coping with the uncertainty. *Ethology, 89,* 101–114.

Colmenares, F. (1991). Greeting, aggression, and coalitions between male baboons: Demographic correlates. *Primates, 32,* 453–463.

Cords, M. (1992). Post-conflict reunions and reconciliation in long-tailed macaques. *Animal Behaviour, 44,* 57–61.

Cords, M., & Thurnheer, S. (1993). Reconciling with valuable partners by long-tailed macaques. *Ethology, 93,* 315–325.

de Waal, F. B. M. (1982). *Chimpanzee politics: Power and sex among apes.* London: Jonathan Cape.

de Waal, F. B. M. (1989). The myth of a simple relation between space and aggression in captive primates. *Zoo Biology Supplement, 1,* 141–148.

de Waal, F. B. M. (2000). Primates: A natural heritage of conflict resolution. *Science, 289,* 586–590.

de Waal, F. B. M., & Aureli, F. (1996). Consolation, reconciliation, and a possible cognitive difference between macaques and chimpanzees. In A. E. Russon, K. A. Bard, & S. T. Parker (Eds.), *Reaching into thought: The minds of the great apes* (pp. 80–110). Cambridge: Cambridge University Press.

de Waal, F. B. M., & Johanowicz, D. L. (1993). Modification of reconciliation behavior through social experience: An experiment with two macaque species. *Child Development, 64,* 897–908.

de Waal, F. B. M., & van Roosmalen, A. (1979). Reconciliation and consolation among chimpanzees. *Behavioral Ecology and Sociobiology, 5,* 55–66.

de Waal, F. B. M., & Yoshihara, D. (1983). Reconciliation and redirected affection in rhesus monkeys. *Behaviour, 85,* 224–241.

Fitzgibbons, R. P. (1986). The cognitive and emotive uses of forgiveness in the treatment of anger. *Psychotherapy, 23,* 629–633.

Gallup, G. G., Jr. (1982). Self-awareness and the emergence of mind in primates. *American Journal of Primatology, 2,* 237–248.

Hediger, H. (1941). Biologische gesetzmäbigkeiten im verhalten von wirbeltieren. *Mitteilungen Naturforschungs Gesellschaft Bern 1940, 37*–55.

Judge, P. G. (1991). Dyadic and triadic reconciliation in pigtail macaques (*Macaca nemestrina*). *American Journal of Primatology, 23,* 225–237.

Judge, P. G., & de Waal, F. B. M. (1993). Conflict avoidance among rhesus monkeys: Coping with short-term crowding. *Animal Behaviour, 46,* 221–232.

Judge, P. G., & de Waal, F. B. M. (1994). Intergroup grooming relations between alpha females in a population of free-ranging rhesus macaques. *Folia Primatologica, 63,* 63–70.

Judge, P. G., & de Waal, F. B. M. (1997). Rhesus monkey behaviour under diverse population densities: Coping with long-term crowding. *Animal Behaviour, 54,* 643–662.

Köhler, W. (1925). *The mentality of apes.* New York: Vintage.

Kummer, H. (1978). On the value of social relationships to nonhuman primates: A heuristic scheme. *Social Science Information, 17,* 687–705.

Kutsukake, N., & Castles, D. L. (2004). Reconciliation and post-conflict third-party affiliation among wild chimpanzees in the Mahale Mountains, Tanzania. *Primates, 45,* 157–165.

Mason, W. A. (1993). The nature of social conflict: A psycho-ethological perspective. In W. A. Mason & S. P. Mendoza (Eds.), *Primate social conflict* (pp. 13–47). Albany, NY: SUNY Press.

Park, S. R., & Enright, R. D. (2000). Forgiveness across cultures. In F. Aureli & F. B. M. de Waal (Eds.), *Natural conflict resolution* (pp. 359–361). Berkeley, CA: University of California Press.

Parr, L. A. (2001). Cognitive and physiological markers of emotional awareness in chimpanzees (*Pan troglodytes*). *Animal Cognition, 4,* 223–229.

Rowell, T. E. (2000). The ethological approach precluded recognition of reconciliation. In F. Aureli & F. B. M. de Waal (Eds.), *Natural conflict resolution* (pp. 227–228). Berkeley, CA: University of California Press.

Sapolsky, R. M., & Share, L. J. (2004). A pacific culture among wild baboons: Its emergence and transmission. *PLoS Biology, 2,* 534–541.

Schino, G., Scucchi, S., Maestripieri, D., & Turillazzi, P. G. (1988). Allogrooming as a tension-reduction mechanism: A behavioral approach. *American Journal of Primatology, 16,* 43–50.

Smucny, D. A., Price, C. S., & Byrne, E. A. (1997). Post-conflict affiliation and stress reduction in captive rhesus macaques. *Advances in Ethology, 32,* 157.

van Schaik, C. P., & Aureli, F. (2000). The natural history of valuable relationships in primates. In F. Aureli & F. B. M. de Waal (Eds.), *Natural conflict resolution* (pp. 307–333). Berkeley, CA: University of California Press.

Veenema, H. C., Das, M., & Aureli, F. (1994). Methodological improvements for the study of reconciliation. *Behavioural Processes, 31,* 29–38.

Wittig, R. M., & Boesch, C. (2003) "Decision-making" in conflicts of wild chimpanzees (*Pan troglodytes*): An extension of the relational model. *Behavioral Ecology and Sociobiology, 54,* 491–504.

Chapter Three

Forgiveness, Self-Respect, and the Value of Resentment

Jeffrie G. Murphy

A s a moral philosopher rather than a psychologist, I will not be able to follow the format typical for this volume. I have no experiments or studies to report, no recommendations for further research, and no clinical recommendations. My interest is in ethical questions, and my discipline is not empirical but is essentially conceptual and normative—seeking to clarify the concepts that we use in moral evaluation and to suggest ways in which such evaluation might profitably be structured. One goal—one that goes back at least as far in time as Socrates—is to raise skeptical doubts when certain moral views have uncritically become a part of the conventional wisdom of the day.

PERSONAL ASSUMPTIONS ABOUT FORGIVENESS

It has for some time seemed to me that such skepticism should be directed to much contemporary thinking on forgiveness. There is, I think, a powerful contemporary "forgiveness movement" that often suggests that forgiveness is an unambiguously good thing—promising psychological, moral, and even physical benefit to those who practice it. If one looks at the self-help and recovery sections of most bookstores, for example, one will see an enormous number of books with forgiveness in the title, and many of these books represent little more than uncritical, sentimental boosterism. In fairness, however, it should be noted that this kind of boosterism is most commonly found in works of popular psychology. Works of scientific psychology are typically (though not always) more nuanced and critical.

Although by no means an enemy of forgiveness, I seek to throw a bit of a wet blanket on this trendy movement by highlighting the dangers of hasty forgiveness. Hasty forgiveness can in my view undermine self-respect, respect for the moral order, respect for the wrongdoer, and even respect for forgiveness itself. This final consequence occurs when the genuine and valuable article is reduced to a set of posturing clichés and becomes what is sometimes called "cheap grace." I am not the only one who urges such caution, of course; indeed, psychologist Sharon Lamb (Lamb & Murphy, 2002) and I have recently edited a book in which a variety of authors, both philosophers and psychologists, express a variety of cautions. My own views on the positive value of resentment and its link to self-respect have been greatly influenced by Joseph Butler (1718/1896), Jean Améry (1986), Aurel Kolnai (1978), Thomas Hill, Jr. (1991), and Peter Strawson (1974).

Before I proceed to make this case, however, let me emphasize my view that philosophy on such matters should not pretend to lay out any final truths. Its job is rather to raise interesting (often skeptical) questions and to develop a framework for discussion that will (it is hoped) advance the conversation. This framework will necessarily be somewhat personal to its author and thus can represent no more than one perspective on the issues in question. My own perspective has been deeply formed by my own philosophical and religious (specifically Christian) studies, but other perspectives could emerge from different studies of equal depth.

WHAT IS FORGIVENESS?

My own thinking on forgiveness has been most influenced by the writings of the great 18th-century moral philosopher and theologian (and Anglican Bishop), Joseph Butler (1718/1896). Most of Butler's philosophy was developed in his published sermons, and two are of particular relevance to the present topic: "Upon Resentment" and "Upon Forgiveness of Injuries."

In the second of these sermons, Butler (1718/1896)—rightly, in my judgment—characterizes forgiveness as primarily an internal matter, a change of heart. It often does, of course, have external behavioral consequences, but its essence is internal.

What is this inner state or change of heart that is the essence of forgiveness? It is not itself an emotion or passion but is rather, according to Butler, the overcoming or limiting of certain passions, namely, the vindictive passions that are naturally aroused when we are wronged by others. These vindictive passions—anger, the desire to strike back, the desire to see the wrongdoer punished, sometimes even hatred—are called by Peter Strawson (1974) "reactive attitudes" (p. 6), and he with Butler sees them as natural responses to being wronged. Butler uses the term *resentment* to refer to these vindictive passions.

It is easy to see why forgiveness, as a way of overcoming or transcending resentment, is often a good thing. Forgiveness may allow us to reconcile with others and restore relations of value, free us from the inner turmoil that may come from harboring grudges, and free us from an overly narcissistic involvement with our own injuries—a tendency to sometimes (but not always) see ourselves as more victimized than we really are. Forgiveness may also have social value—blunting vindictive responses that might result in a kind of revenge taking that would undermine civil order.

None of the above, however, shows that forgiveness—particularly hasty forgiveness—is *always* a good thing. Neither does it show that the resentment that is overcome is always a bad thing. So it is time to say, with Butler, something on behalf of resentment.

THE CASE FOR RESENTMENT

Bishop Butler, in his powerful sermon "Upon Resentment," seeks to make a case for the legitimacy of resentment and other vindictive passions, arguing that a just and loving God would not have universally implanted these passions within his creatures unless the passions served some valuable purpose. (A similar point—without any reference to God—might be made by an evolutionary biologist.) The danger of resentment, he argued, lies not in having it but rather in being dominated by it to such a degree that one can never overcome it and thus acts irresponsibly on the basis of it. As the initial response to being wronged, however, the passion stands in defense of important values—values that might be compromised by immediate and uncritical forgiveness of wrongs.

What are the values defended by resentment and threatened by hasty and uncritical forgiveness? In my own writings (Murphy, 2003; Murphy & Hampton, 1988), I have argued that three of the most important are self-respect, self-defense, and respect for the moral order. A person who never resented any injuries done to him or her might be a saint. It is equally likely, however, that such lack of resentment reveals a servile personality—a personality lacking in respect for himself or herself and respect for the rights and status that attach to a free and equal moral being. (This is the point behind S. J. Perelman's famous quip, "To err is human, to forgive supine.") Just as indignation over the mistreatment of others stands as emotional testimony that we care about them and their rights, so does resentment stand as emotional testimony that we care about ourselves and our rights.

This is a very important point to emphasize: Moral commitment is not merely a matter of intellectual commitment; it requires emotional allegiance as well, for a moral person is not simply a person who holds the abstract belief that certain things are wrong. The moral person is also driven to do something about the wrong; and what drives us is found mainly in our emotions or passions. It is not enough for me simply to say, "I respect myself." If this is indeed true, I will also convey emotionally, typically by resentment, that my being wronged truly matters to me and that the wrongdoer should expect a strong negative response.

Related to this is an instrumental point: Those who have vindictive dispositions toward those who wrong them give potential wrongdoers an incentive *not* to wrong them. If I were going to set out to oppress other people, I would surely prefer to select for my victims persons whose first response is forgiveness rather than persons whose first response is revenge. Those temperamentally given to hasty forgiveness or nudged toward it by an overly enthusiastic forgiveness therapist may also be given to hasty reconciliation—letting abusive people back into their lives—and thus putting themselves at continuing risk. Although these people no doubt deserve our sympathy, Kant

(1797/1996) was not totally off base when he noted that "one who makes himself into a worm cannot complain afterwards if people step on him" (p. 559). It is important to stress, however, that resentment does not stand merely as emotional testimony of self-respect. This passion and the reluctance to transcend it in hasty forgiveness also stands as testimony to our allegiance to the moral order itself. We have a duty to support—both intellectually and emotionally—the moral order, an order represented by clear understandings of what constitutes unacceptable treatment of one human being by another. If we do not show resentment or indignation to those who, in victimizing others, flout those understandings, then we run the risk—as Aurel Kolnai (1978) has warned—of being complicitous in evil. We also run the risk of failing to show moral respect for wrongdoers themselves who, if regarding themselves as free and responsible moral agents, *should* expect to find their wrongdoing met with resentment. Any other response would flirt with treating them as nonresponsible and would be patronizing. I certainly want my own wrongdoing to be met with resentment and would feel insulted and degraded if others viewed me merely as pitiful, sick, and myself as much a victim as those whom I have wronged. Do I not thus owe other wrongdoers at least the initial presumption that they, too, are legitimate objects of blame, resentment, and punishment?

It should be noted that the link I am suggesting between resentment and such values as self-respect may help to explain why *repentance* on the part of the wrongdoer often opens the door to legitimate forgiveness. For example, if a man offends me and is unrepentant, standing behind the wrong he has done to me, then I run the risk that in forgiving him I am endorsing the symbolic message that he conveyed in wronging me—the message that he matters more than I do and can use me like an object for his purposes. If the wrongdoer is truly repentant, however, he seeks to break the symbolic and emotional connection between his present self and his previous wrongful self—now joining me in condemning that previous self. Thus, I can relate positively to what he now is with less risk of complicity in evil.

Repentance is generally viewed as a necessary condition for forgiveness in the Jewish tradition, but there are deep disagreements about this within Christianity. Many Christians advocate universal and unconditional forgiveness, whereas others retain the idea that repentance should first be required. These Christians are, not surprisingly, fond of quoting Jesus' remark at Luke 17:3:

> If thy brother trespass against thee, rebuke him; and if he repents, forgive him.

If the vindictive passion of righteous and punitive anger is regarded as totally unchristian, and if Christians seek to follow in the imitation of Christ tradition, then what are they to make of the story (John 2:14) where Jesus, moved it would appear by righteous anger, inflicts punitive violence (whipping) on the money changers in the temple?

If what I have said thus far—with the aid of Butler—is correct, then there is much of positive value to be found in resentment, in the vindictive passions. Why then do these passions enjoy such bad press? Why do so many people think that, like cruelty or malice, they are unambiguously irrational (sick or evil) and that one may transcend them with no loss of value at all? Why has opposition to these passions taken such a firm root in ordinary language that even to call a person "vindictive" is normally taken to express severe criticism of that person?

It is possible, of course, that what people say—and think they are supposed to say—about such matters is not always an accurate index of how they actually believe and feel. Indeed, the great popularity of revenge entertainment in books and films suggests that many people take vicarious delight in seeing wronged people get even through acts of revenge. To the degree that people really do believe that the vindictive passions are sick or evil, however, it is at least possible they have been seduced by some arguments that—though plausible on their face—may not survive close rational scrutiny. I will explore a few of the most prominent of these.

One typically argues for the irrationality (sickness or evil) of an emotion by attempting to show that it is not fitting to its object, is harmful to the person who experiences it, is inherently self-defeating, necessarily leads to pathological excess, or is pointless—lacking in any useful purpose.

I do not think that vindictiveness can easily be shown to be irrational on any of these tests. It certainly seems fitting that one strikes back when one has been injured—indeed, such a response seems encoded in us by our evolutionary history—and thus the vindictive person does not seem like the neurotic who does indeed have an emotion that is not fitting to its object—for example, a person who is phobic, who has an irrational fear of something that is not in fact dangerous.

Neither does the emotion seem pointless. Vindictive people want to get even, and no doubt will often, having asserted their own equal worth and rights, feel much better when such revenge is realized. That is just its point. To say it is pointless only because it does not have a point of which the critic of vindictiveness would approve is simply to beg the question at issue.

Many people love to say, of course, that forgiveness provides (I hate the word) "closure," but getting even can sometimes provide closure as well. And forgiveness does not always provide this anyway. My first philosophy professor told a story (perhaps apocryphal) of Lord Bacon visiting a seacoast church and asking the priest the meaning of a large painting on a wall. "It represents," said the priest, "all those who were saved from drowning through prayer." Bacon replied: "And where do you hang the picture of those who were not saved?" Sometimes the boosters for forgiveness remind me of this priest—keeping the successes vividly in sight while remaining blind to the failures.

It is commonly argued that the resentful, grudge-holding person tends to harm himself or herself, like a scorpion stinging itself to death with its own tail. It is, of course, irrational to regard as legitimate emotions that are self-poisoning, and this looks like a good case for the irrationality of the vindictive passions. But such a conclusion would, I think, be hasty for two reasons.

First, it is possible that vindictiveness will poison only if *repressed.* If so, this is as much an argument in favor of expressing our vindictiveness in acts of revenge as it is an argument for the elimination of vindictiveness. In short, there are at least two ways to avoid nursing a grudge: forgive or get even. (There are, of course, varieties of other options as well.)

Second, we need to distinguish between the rationality of the emotion itself and the rationality of the *role* that this emotion plays in the overall psychological economy of the person. Recall Spinoza (1677/1985) on the fear of death. He did not argue that the fear of death is, like a phobia, itself irrational. He did not, for example, counsel against looking both ways before crossing a street. Rather he argued that it is irrational to be *led* by the fear of death—that is, to let the fear play such a dominant role in one's life that it sours all the good things that life has to offer. Thus, unless it can be shown that vindictiveness must always be the dominant passion and thus lead the vindictive person in some self-destructive or other-destructive way, we do not yet have a case for the undesirability of the passion itself.

Of course, some writers have argued this very thing—that vindictiveness will in fact always so dominate a person's life as to prevent that person's human flourishing. Here as one example is what the psychoanalyst Karen Horney (1948) says about vindictiveness:

> There is no more holding back a person driven toward revenge than an alcoholic determined to go on a binge. Logic no longer prevails. Whether or not the situation is appropriate does not matter. It overrides prudence. Consequences for himself and others are brushed aside. He is as inaccessible as anybody who is in the grip of a blind passion. (p. 5)

This is a serious claim, because, if true, it would reveal the vindictive person as having both an irrational and destructively immoral self—a self likely to harm others and to undermine the social order.

But is Horney's (1948) claim true? I think that it is not. Speaking (as almost any Irishman can) from personal experience as a somewhat vindictive person, I believe that I have often gotten even with people in ways that, in addition to being satisfying to me, were moderate and proportional. My chosen strategy of revenge sometimes involved nothing more than a few well-selected (and hurtful, I hoped) words or by actions no more extreme than no longer extending lunch invitations or rides to work to them.

Rarely have I been dominated by my vindictive feelings. I often let them float harmlessly in the back of my mind until an appropriate occasion for their expression occurs. I am not suggesting that this makes me particularly admirable—and I might even accept the charge that it reveals in me a streak of pettiness—but I do not think that it qualifies me as dangerously crazy or evil.

Where then do Horney (1948) and others get this idea that vindictive people are all potentially dangerous lunatics just waiting to inflict unjust harm and destroy the social fabric? Therapists, I imagine, often get it from their clients, because people of proportional and moderate emotions tend to be rare in their practices. Others may get it from art—particularly film and literature—where revenge is often mistakenly identified with illegal and socially disruptive vigilante activity that at least borders on insanity. This theme goes back at least as far as the ancient story of Medea and is to be found in classic Western movies and in the most recent best-seller thrillers.

Of course, these works portray vindictiveness in extreme ways because moderate and proportional revenge taking is *boring*. However, just because the extreme cases are more interesting and gripping, it does not follow that there are not many more cases where revenge is taken in moderate and proportional ways. But who would want to read a revenge novel or view a revenge film where the central character ultimately gets back at his victimizer by no longer extending lunch invitations to him?

To summarize: None of the arguments I have surveyed establishes either the irrationality or the immorality of vindictiveness or even of moderate acts of revenge.

Because the arguments against vindictiveness are weak and because something (recall Butler) has been found to say in its favor, I think that it is justified to conclude—at least provisionally—that vindictive passions can legitimately be attributed to sane and virtuous people. Virtuous people can, I think, sometimes even enjoy without guilt the knowledge that those who have wronged them—particularly if unrepentant—are "getting theirs" through such mechanisms as criminal punishment.

CONCLUSION

Because others in this volume (and I in many of my other writings) have much to say on behalf of forgiveness, I have in this entry set myself a very limited objective: to introduce some cautions with respect to its hasty and uncritical bestowal. The vindictive passions have some positive value—they are not, like cruelty or malice, simply sick and evil—and thus seeking to overcome them always carries with it the danger that something of value is being improperly sacrificed. This sacrifice may be of proper self-respect, sacrifice of respect for the moral order, or—if hasty forgiveness leads to hasty reconciliation—sacrifice of reasonable self-protection. Even as we rightly preach the virtues of forgiveness, we should recognize that victims deserve to have their vindictive passions to some degree validated. Even if these passions should generally not be the last word, they have a legitimate claim to be the first word. Even when they should not control, they should be listened to with respect instead of met with pious sermons and sentimental, dismissive clichés. In short: Even if one subscribes to a brand of Christianity that must ultimately reject the legitimacy of Elie Wiesel's (1995) prayer at Auschwitz or is committed to forgiveness for purely psychological reasons, one must surely still have *some* sympathy with that prayer and not see it merely as a symptom of irrational illness or evil:

> God of forgiveness, do not forgive those who created this place. God of mercy, have no mercy on those who killed here Jewish children. (p. 1)

REFERENCES

Améry, J. (1986). Resentments. *At the mind's limits.* New York: Schocken.

Butler, J. (1718/1896). Sermons upon resentment and upon forgiveness of injuries preached at Rolls Chapel, London, in 1718. In W. E. Gladstone (Ed.), *Works of Joseph Butler, Vol. 2,* (pp. 136–167). Oxford: Clarendon Press.

Hill, T. E., Jr. (1991). Servility and self-respect. *Autonomy and self-respect* (pp. 4–18). Cambridge: Cambridge University Press.

Horney, K. (1948). The value of vindictiveness. *American Journal of Psychoanalysis, 8,* 3–12.

Kant, I. (1797/1996). *The metaphysics of morals. Practical philosophy.* [Mary Gregor, translator], Cambridge: Cambridge University Press.

Kolnai, A. (1978). Forgiveness. *Ethics, value, and reality—selected papers of Aurel Kolnai.* Indianapolis: Hackett.

Lamb, S., & Murphy, J.G. (Eds.). (2002). *Before forgiving: Cautionary views on forgiveness and psychotherapy.* New York: Oxford University Press.

Murphy, J. G. (2003). *Getting even: Forgiveness and its limits.* New York: Oxford University Press.

Murphy, J. G., & Hampton, J. (1988). *Forgiveness and mercy.* Cambridge: Cambridge University Press.

Spinoza, B. (1677/1985). Ethics demonstrated in a geometrical manner. *Collected works of Spinoza, Vol. 1.* [Edited and translated by E. Curley]. Princeton, NJ: Princeton University Press.

Strawson, P. (1974). *Freedom and resentment and other essays.* London: Methuen.

Wiesel, E. (1995). Prayer given at an unofficial ceremony commemorating the liberation of Auschwitz. *CNN Transcript 720-1,* January 26, 1995.

Chapter Four

Forgiveness in Cultural Context

Steven J. Sandage
Ian Williamson

orgiveness is a construct that can be traced and studied in connection with diverse streams of literature from cultures around the globe. As psychologists, we are most familiar with the body of psychological literature on forgiveness that has developed over the past two decades (for reviews, see Enright & Fitzgibbons, 2000; Fincham, 2000; McCullough & Witvliet, 2002). Numerous psychological definitions, measures, and models of forgiveness are currently available for researchers and practitioners. Forgiveness represents a scholarly landscape that is much stronger in variety than orderly coherence. Wuthnow's (2000) sociological study of a nationally representative sample of adult Americans suggested that respondents' understandings of forgiveness had "fuzzy edges" (p. 126), reflecting considerable diversity about the definitions, boundaries, and moral contingencies of forgiveness. Based on his interviews, Wuthnow concluded:

> Forgiveness is a culturally available category that people associate with a loosely defined set of attitudes and behavior that often includes making sense of or giving a new interpretation to a past action, overcoming anger or guilt, gaining a feeling of cleansing or wholeness, and being able to think about or interact with an offending or aggrieved person in a new way. (p. 127)

Despite how culturally available and embedded forgiveness is as a construct, surprisingly little empirical research has focused on investigating cultural and contextual variables in relationship to forgiveness (Lamb, 2002; Sandage, Hill, & Vang, 2003). Is forgiveness valued and practiced in similar ways across cultures? How do particular cultural and contextual factors influence individual and group processes of forgiveness and unforgiveness? These kinds of questions remain largely unaddressed in contemporary social science, but a few studies and theoretical papers do offer starting points for charting next steps for researchers and practitioners interested in forgiveness and culture. Our primary goals in this chapter are to (a) review the limited available social science literature that pertains directly to relationships between forgiveness and culture, (b) suggest some promising directions for future research on forgiveness and culture, and (c) highlight some cultural implications for applied work in the area of forgiveness. However, attempting to understand the ways in which culture influences processes of forgiveness requires defining both *culture* and *forgiveness*. In the following section, we will outline our present understandings of culture and forgiveness.

PERSONAL ASSUMPTIONS ABOUT FORGIVENESS AND CULTURE

Defining Culture

The American Psychological Association (APA, 2003) multicultural guidelines define *culture* as "the belief systems and value orientations that influence customs, norms, practices, and social institutions, including psychological processes (language, care-taking practices, media, educational systems) and organizations" (p. 380). These APA guidelines further describe culture as "the embodiment of a worldview" and say that "all individuals are cultural beings and have a cultural, ethnic, and racial heritage" (p. 380). APA encourages psychologists to be "culture-centered" by using a "cultural lens" and recognizing that "all individuals, including themselves, are influenced by different contexts, including the historical, ecological, sociopolitical, and disciplinary" (p. 380). This inclusive APA definition of culture suggests that every definition, model, or theory of forgiveness is influenced by cultural and contextual dimensions in numerous ways. The recent emergence of cultural psychology as a discipline represents an effort to understand the reciprocal influences and mutual constitution of culture and mind (Cole, 1996; Fiske, Kitayama, Markus, & Nisbett, 1998). In this view, cultural practices and meanings inform psychological processes, which recursively "generate and transform these cultural practices and meanings" (Fiske et al., 1998, p. 916).

Cole (1996) draws on Russian cultural-historical psychologists, such as Vygotsky and various anthropologists, in offering an intriguing definition of culture as a "system of artifacts" (p. 142) that serve to coordinate individuals with their environmental contexts. Artifacts, in Cole's view, are simultaneously material and ideal (or cognitive) and include culturally shaped tools that mediate human action. The various levels of artifacts include physical objects (e.g., a peace pipe, storycloth weaving, communion chalice), the symbolic tools of words and written materials (e.g., a sacred text, a self-help book, a journal entry), and cognitive scripts or schemas that culturally shape moral and religious values and interpretations of behavior (e.g., only apologize to those with higher power and status, "don't let the sun go down on your anger," forgiveness requires giving a gift). Cultural artifacts mediate the action processes through which subjects transform objects in relationship to contexts or ecologies at multiple levels (e.g., dyads, families, clans, communities, etc.). This view of culture challenges researchers and practitioners to consider the complex interactions between these differing dimensions of culture.

Cole's definition and model of culture does not negate the value of experimental and quantitative research on forgiveness, although his view does expose the limitations of viewing culture as simply a categorical independent variable based on demographic sheets. Forgiveness definitions, models, and interventions developed by psychologists and other cultural workers (e.g., spiritual leaders) can be understood as culture-laden tools or practices (i.e., artifacts) used to describe certain ways of coping with interpersonal conflict. In fact, we are intrigued with the sociological thesis that the growing psychological and therapeutic literature on forgiveness in North America may be a response to new historical challenges of coping with interpersonal conflict and resentment in an individualistic societal context with declining social capital. At other points in history, religious and family influences may have offered stronger social networks that helped mediate interpersonal conflict through communal forgiveness-like artifacts (e.g., religious teachings and practices, intergenerational family mediation). As many individuals have become less connected to the social capital and moral authority of tightly knit communities, new psychological construals of forgiveness might be offering cultural tools for those trying to adapt to an individualistic ecology by freeing the self from negative attachments to others. This thesis could be loosely supported by the fact that most of the contemporary psychological literature has focused on forgiving others or on self-forgiveness with comparably less focus on seeking forgiveness or reconciliation (Sandage & Wiens, 2001).

Defining Forgiveness

Among the many psychological definitions of individual forgiveness toward others, we have been most influenced by McCullough's (McCullough & Witvliet, 2002) social psychological model of intrapersonal forgiveness of an offender as a process of prosocial transformation in interpersonal motivations toward that offender where motivations become less vengeful and avoidant, and more benevolent. This definition suggests there are both active (vengeful) and passive (avoidant or exclusionary) motivational alternatives to forgiveness.

Theoretical Assumptions

We will briefly outline some of the contours of our present theoretical assumptions about forgiveness and culture as a way of admitting our expectations and potential biases.

1. Forgiveness emerges at multiple levels of human development as ways relational subsystems attempt to adapt to their *ecological* or *systemic contexts*. These subsystems could be individuals, dyads, families, communities, nations, or other groupings. The subsystem unit of focus in forgiveness research and practice (e.g.,

individual, dyad, community) is itself a culture-laden decision (McCullough & Witvliet, 2002). For example, traditional, highly collectivistic Hmong tend to view forgiveness as a communal process of restoring face and harmony between clans rather than an individual decision or dyadic process. Ecological or multisystemic perspectives also suggest forgiveness could be one form of systemic equilibrium or ecological balancing between subsystems (Maddock & Larson, 1995; Trzyna, 1997). These perspectives serve to widen the frame of reference for determining whether a particular form of forgiveness meets optimal standards for social justice and ecological health. For example, forms of forgiveness that threaten the integrity or survival of a particular subsystem could be considered unjust, unhealthy, and potentially ecologically damaging, such as when abuse victims remain in abusive relationships with perpetrators (Lamb, 2002).

2. More specifically, forgiveness represents one way in which subsystems attempt to balance *power* and *control* in their ecosystemic contexts. The dynamics of power and control are largely neglected in the psychological literature on forgiveness (Fincham, 2000; Lamb, 2002; Shults & Sandage, 2003). Maddock and Larson (1995) use dictionary definitions of *power* ("the capacity to influence") and *control* ("the capacity to restrain or regulate influence") to develop a single dialectical construct (power/control) reflecting the interactive nature of these constructs in human systems (p. 55). They assert that power and control are both necessary components of social interaction and, if unbalanced, become distorted and oppressive. For example, the distorted dynamics of power/control can be replicated by the very social systems charged to intervene in abusive relationships. Authority figures who use coercion to demand forgiveness from someone may unintentionally perpetuate a cycle of overpowering and victimization. Conversely, healthy forgiveness might be an empowering way of negotiating boundaries. Forgiveness can be described as resulting from the intersubjective and self-differentiating capacity to recognize both self and other as subjects and agents rather than objects for domination or rigid control (Sandage, in press).

3. The cultural worldview contours of *individualism* and *collectivism* represent a promising set of dimensions for understanding cultural differences in models of forgiveness (Sandage et al., 2003; Sandage & Wiens, 2001). In Table 4.1, we provide an outline for contrasting individualistic and collectivistic worldviews as they might influence models of forgiveness. Our contrast is offered as a general heuristic and is based largely on theory rather than empirical data at this point, although we will review some empirical support in this chapter.

Individualistic worldviews tend to construe selfhood as independent and self-reflexive, emphasizing personal boundaries and self-definition. Individualistic worldviews are likely to construe forgiveness as a personal choice to fit with exchange or contractual views of relationships. The primary individualistic face-concern would be saving self-face, so forgiveness might be practiced if it heals a loss of self-esteem. Forgiveness and reconciliation would be considered sharply distinct in order to preserve

TABLE 4.1. Comparison of Individualistic and Collectivistic Worldviews in Relation to Forgiveness

Factor viewed	Individualistic worldview	Collectivistic worldview
View of self	Independent, self-reflexive	Interdependent, socially embedded
View of relationships	Exchange/contractual	Communal/covenantal
Primary face concern	Self-face	Other-face and self-face
Forgiveness and reconciliation	Sharply distinct	Closely related
Value of self-forgiveness	High	Low
Central goal of forgiveness	Personal well-being	Social well-being
Primary tools for forgiveness	Professional psychotherapy, self-help resources, and individual coping skills	Communal mediators/healers, narratives, rituals, and symbols

Note: Adapted from Sandage & Wiens (2001), this table is intended to provide a general heuristic for outlining and comparing models of forgiveness based on individualistic and collectivistic worldviews. Admittedly, there are many versions of individualism and collectivism, and some bicultural individuals can even employ both. The hypothesized differences are based mostly on theory rather than empirical data.

individual boundaries. Self-forgiveness fits an individualistic emphasis on self-reflexivity and freedom from communal authority. The goal of individualistic forgiveness would be personal well-being for the one who forgives. It would utilize tools such as professional psychotherapy, self-help resources, and individual coping skills.

Collectivistic cultures construe selfhood as interdependent and socially embedded, emphasizing social connections and group norms. The collectivistic view of relationships as communal or covenantal suggests forgiveness would be less a personal choice and more a proscribed duty in certain culturally defined situations. For a highly collectivistic group, an offense or loss of face may not happen to just one person but to several people. Collectivistic concerns for saving both other- and self-face require community involvements in forgiveness. Therefore, when forgiveness occurs, it is not extended by just one person but by a family, group, or clan. Forgiveness and reconciliation are likely to be closely related or synonymous in collectivistic cultures. Self-forgiveness is likely to be implausible from a collectivistic worldview because the self is socially defined and socially sustained. The collectivistic goal of forgiveness will prioritize restoring social harmony and well-being above personal benefits. Members of collectivistic societies are also likely to utilize third-party mediators (e.g., family or clan leaders) and cultural healers (e.g., priests, clergy, shamans) to negotiate conflict and forgiveness through communal rituals and ceremonies. Collectivistic cultural traditions often include narratives and symbols that can provide shared understandings of the cultural tools for forgiveness.

REVIEW OF EMPIRICAL AND THEORETICAL LITERATURE

As we suggested earlier, there is not a well-developed coherent body of research on forgiveness and culture. In this section, we will review the loose collection of studies we found most pertinent to understanding connections between forgiveness and culture. There are so few published studies on forgiveness and culture that a relatively comprehensive review is possible, yet drawing broad conclusions is dangerous. For this reason, the reader should be aware that our review is tentative, with a strong possibility that initial trends might be disconfirmed. We will first describe and illustrate the main empirical and theoretical approaches researchers have utilized in studying forgiveness and culture. Then we will review the empirical evidence for both general trends in forgiveness across cultures and culturally unique trends in forgiveness.

Empirical and Theoretical Approaches to Studying Forgiveness and Culture

Social science researchers approaching forgiveness and culture empirically have largely relied on three main approaches. One quantitative strategy involves cross-cultural psychological research *within* a particular cultural domain outside of the United States in an effort to test the validity of a forgiveness model previously developed in the United States. For example, Huang and Enright (2000) tested Enright's developmental model of forgiveness in South Korea. Similarly, Park and Enright (1997) used a Taiwanese sample to determine whether older adolescents (ages 20–23) would be more intrinsically forgiving than their younger counterparts (ages 12–14), who were hypothesized to be more extrinsically motivated. In both cases, the researchers were looking to other cultures to *generalize*, providing evidence of the potential universality of a certain forgiveness process. The main advantage of this approach is that it can show how certain aspects of forgiveness may be universal or similar for people across many or all cultures. The main limitation of this approach is that models and measures from one cultural context might be used in a different cultural context without adequate attention to subtle variants in cultural meaning.

Another quantitative approach that researchers have implemented involves cross-cultural psychological research comparing samples from two or more different cultural, ethnic, or racial groups on forgiveness measures. For example, Kadiangandu, Mullet, and Vinsonneau (2001) compare Congolese and French samples, and Takaku, Weiner, and Ohbuchi (2001) compare Japanese and American samples. It should be noted that this type of cross-cultural research includes not only comparisons between cultures across the national divide but sometimes between cultures within the same nation. Azar and Mullet's (2001) comparison of forgiveness schemas between Christian and Muslim religious samples within Lebanon provide one illustration. A major benefit to this type of approach, in addition to supplying direct evidence for similarities and differences across cultures, is that comparisons can still be made *within* cultures. For instance, Kadiangandu and his colleagues (2001) not only compare the French and the Congolese but also look for gender differences within each culture.

The third empirical approach includes the general category of qualitative methods that anthropologists, psychologists, and sociologists have used to try to understand the cultural and social functions and meanings of forgiveness in particular contexts (e.g., Gobodo-Madikizela, 2002). The chief advantage of many qualitative approaches is that researchers can be placed in close proximity to the cultural communities and lived experiences of those being studied. These approaches can provide access to narratives and other cultural artifacts involved in social processes of forgiveness, demonstrating the meaning and functions that forgiveness serves for people of various cultural traditions.

Kratz's (1991, 1994) ethnographic study is a good example in describing how the Okiek of Kenya use a communal ritual of confession and forgiveness as a culturally proscribed rite of passage for the initiation of adolescent girls into adulthood. Kratz's fieldwork with the Okiek spanned 14 years and involved detailed ethnographic analyses of ritual events. For example, 14-year-old Okiek girls confess all of their "social debts" in the form of personal narratives (or *pesenweek*) during a late-night community ceremony in front of a fire. During their confessions, the girls are questioned by a male announcer who challenges them to admit all hidden sins. As the girls confess, they are publicly harangued and jeered by laughter from adult community members, who then come forward in a line and demonstrate absolution and forgiveness by taking turns anointing the girls' faces with a mixture of fat and saliva. This ceremony is followed by the girls' excision (a form of genital mutilation) and culminates in their status transformation as part of the adult community.

One function of this ritual of confession and forgiveness is to alleviate any lingering anger or resentment toward the girls by adults who might be involved in the excision cutting. Kratz (1991) contrasts this ceremony with Catholic confession in which the ritual of confession and forgiveness is played out repeatedly and privately in confessional over the course of an individuals' adult life rather than as a single developmental rite of passage. In a later volume, Kratz (1994) employs semiotics (the study of signs and cultural symbols) to construct her interpretation of the ritual efficacy of Okiek initiation ceremonies in transforming cultural identities. A strength of this type of ethnographic research is the rich, in-depth descriptive data of a cultural practice that would be impossible (and unethical) to study in a lab setting.

Nqweni's (2002) phenomenological interview study with South African families that were victimized by apartheid-related political violence and publicly shared their stories with the Truth and Reconciliation Commission (TRC) represents a different kind of qualitative approach (for a related case study, see Gobodo-Madikizela, 2002). The interview data offers a thick narrative description of how these families had suffered and the systemic complications involved in forgiving alleged perpetrators. For example, some participants found the public testimony of alleged perpetrators to be unconvincing, and this particularly hindered forgiveness when the location of personal remains was at issue. In some cases, disunity within victimized families seemed to be exacerbated by the TRC process. Some participants objected to cases where perpetrator amnesty was granted before reparations were clarified. Despite these and other systemic barriers, some of the participants articulated forgiveness toward perpetrators. Community support was described as a primary healing resource for families. Unfortunately, Nqweni did not report the frequencies or location of these themes within the sample, which compromises the adequacy of the description of the data and limits phenomenological validity.

Empirical Findings Supporting General Trends in Forgiveness Across Cultures

Initial empirical research on forgiveness and culture supports the notion that some dimensions of forgiveness may occur in similar ways across cultures. Azar and colleagues (Azar & Mullet, 2001; Azar, Mullet, & Vinsonneau, 1999) demonstrate, in both of their vignette studies, that a general "forgiveness schema" is shared independent of participants' religious or cultural community. In the first study (Azar et al., 1999), Christian (Catholic, Maronite, and Orthodox sects) participants from Beirut ($N = 48$) read stories of a harmful act committed against a child in the Lebanese civil war and indicated their levels of forgiveness. The stories were manipulated on four dimensions: whether the transgressor had in-group or out-group membership (Muslim or Christian), the degree of intent, the severity of the offense consequences, and apologies for the offense. The second study (Azar & Mullet, 2001) used an identical procedure but exposed a larger sample ($N = 96$) with a balance of Christians and Muslims (Druze , Shiite, and Sunni sects).

Whether participants were Muslim or Christian, Druze or Maronite, they all stated they would be more forgiving when a hypothetical shooting was not intentional, did not carry long-term consequences, and was followed by a perpetrator's apology. These studies confirm and extend prior research on intentionality, apology, and offense consequences as strong predictors of forgiveness (Girard & Mullet, 1997; McCullough & Witvliet, 2002). This pair of cultural studies (Azar & Mullet, 2001; Azar et al., 1999) also goes beyond previous work by providing evidence that the in-group/out-group distinction may reduce in importance when making forgiveness determinations. Christians were just as likely to forgive Muslims as to forgive fellow Christians for gun violence in a hypothetical scenario, and the same was true of Muslims forgiving Christians. Nevertheless, an avenue for future research is whether this finding would hold up in real scenarios of in-group versus out-group offenses.

Cognitive moral reasoning about forgiveness is another area of possible cross-cultural generalizability. Enright and his colleagues (Huang & Enright, 2000; Park & Enright, 1997) have found evidence that certain cross-sectional trends in the development of forgiveness occur in Eastern cultures in ways that parallel trends in U.S. culture. In Enright's initial research on adolescents, an age-graded typology of forgiveness was developed (see Enright & Fitzgibbons, 2000). It was based loosely on Kohlberg's stages of moral reasoning. Level 1 and 2 forgivers, who tended to be younger, desired forgiveness only after some level of revenge or compensation has taken place. Level 3 and 4 forgivers, who tended to be older, were largely responding out of a felt obligation to others or society. Level 5 and 6 forgivers, who tended to be the oldest, forgave intrinsically, out of a genuine sense of compassion and love.

Park and Enright (1997) confirmed part of this model on a Korean sample of adolescents who had experienced a personal injury from a friend in the previous 6 months. The researchers used an understanding–forgiveness interview to assess participants' responses to moral dilemmas regarding forgiveness and level of development of reasoning about forgiveness. Younger Koreans (ages 12–14) showed lower levels of forgiveness understanding than did older Koreans (ages 20–22). Huang and Enright's (2000) study of adults in Taiwan further extended the developmental model by gathering behavioral and physiological data. A screening measure similar to the understanding–forgiveness interview was used to select only Level 4 (Lawful) forgivers and Level 6 (Loving) forgivers. Level 4 forgivers were more prone to cast down their eyes, use masked smiles, and show higher blood pressure during the telling of the offending incident than were Level 6 forgivers. This initial evidence seems to suggest a cross-cultural developmental trend in forgiveness that is motivated initially by egocentrism, then social conformity, and finally an intrinsic expression of love. It is important to note that Huang and Enright's (2000) study used a sample that consists exclusively of adults. Therefore, a substantial amount of variation in people's level of forgiveness remained in later life, even within the same developmental cohort. However, these studies were cross-sectional rather than longitudinal and did not include research strategies that could have provided data about cultural differences in forgiveness.

Empirical Findings Supporting Culturally Unique Trends in Forgiveness

There is some empirical evidence and theoretical work that points toward culturally unique trends in the practice of forgiveness. Scobie, Scobie, and Kakavoulis (2002) conducted a comparative factor analysis of undergraduate student samples in Britain ($n = 315$), Greece ($n = 130$), and Cyprus ($n = 119$) using the Scobie Forgiveness Scale, which attempts to measure seven different linguistic components of forgiveness. The groups did not differ on overall willingness to forgive or be forgiven; however, there were some cross-cultural differences on the components of forgiveness as well as item loadings on those components. For example, the British group endorsed guilt-release language more and relationship-repairing language less in connection with forgiveness than did the Greek or Cypriot groups. The authors offered little interpretation of the cultural differences in their results.

The most common explanatory framework for cultural differences contrasts individualistic, legalistic societies with collectivistic, communal societies (Fiske et al., 1998). Takaku et al. (2001) conducted an experimental study in which Japanese and American participants were placed in a condition where they visualized a time they were wrongdoers (hypocrisy-inducing condition) or in a condition where they visualized a time they had been victims. Results showed that although both Japanese and Americans forgave more after being exposed to a hypocrisy-inducing manipulation, the psychological process by which the hypocrisy induction works is different across cultures. Whereas Americans were more attuned to the perceived controllability of the offense (i.e., did the offender have a choice), Japanese were more attentive to the stability of an offense (i.e., the recidivism) and their relationship to the offender. Furthermore, Americans framed the offense more in terms of a violation of justice, whereas Japanese were more apt to frame offenses as violations of norms and roles. A less assimilable finding is that while the Japanese tendency to forgive was mediated entirely by negative emotions toward the offender, the American tendency to forgive was directly affected by several variables: (a) negative emotions, (b) positive emotions, (c) perceived controllability of offense, and (d) the hypocrisy induction (Takaku et al., 2001).

Individualism and collectivism also emerged as potential explanatory constructs for differences between the French and Congolese in the tendency to forgive (Kadiangandu et al., 2001). In a questionnaire study, Kadiangandu and his colleagues found that Congolese claimed to be more forgiving, less vengeful, and more responsive to personal and social circumstances that suggest forgiveness. Older adults in the Congolese sample were more sensitive to circumstances when forgiving, whereas within-group age differences were not found in the French sample.

Beyond cultural differences in individualism and collectivism, Congo and France have very different systems of justice (Kadiangandu et al., 2001). The French system of justice, similar to most Western systems, traditionally involves sanction and control by third party authorities (e.g., police, judges, and juries). By contrast, the Congolese system relies more heavily on relational exclusion and subsequent forgiveness and reintegration in a system based more on restorative justice. Furthermore, because the community is more deeply integrated and interdependent, forgiveness, at times, becomes a necessity for sustaining societal functioning.

Collectivistic societies may also differ simply in how offenses are construed and how many people are involved throughout the forgiveness process. Temoshok and Chandra (2000) found that when Indian women contracted AIDS, 80% blamed their family of origin for their woeful circumstances, whereas only 40% blamed their husbands, who actually gave them the disease. In this study, women in a collectivistic society with family-arranged marriages viewed an offense not strictly as a failure of a husband to exercise responsibility for his sexual behavior but as a failure of their families to marry them to the correct person. Forgiveness, therefore, implies more than just forgiving their husbands but also forgiving their families.

In summary, though forgiveness may have some cross-cultural dimensions, it also appears that forgiveness is understood and practiced in ways that are culturally shaped. Preliminary work suggests that victims from collectivistic societies are more inclined to pay attention to the likelihood the offender will reoffend, whereas victims from individualistic societies focus attention on the offenders' control over the initial offenses. Furthermore, collectivists may be more inclined to relational motivations for forgiveness, whereas individualists are more motivated by justice considerations. One study (Kadiangandu et al., 2001) showed that a more behaviorally interdependent and relational tribal culture was more forgiving than a comparatively individualistic and legalistic culture; however, no other studies have shown differences in people's overall level of forgiveness across cultures.

NEW DIRECTIONS NEEDED IN FORGIVENESS AND CULTURE RESEARCH

Optimal progress in understanding the relationships between forgiveness and culture in various contexts will require multimethod interdisciplinary approaches to research. In recommending multiple methods, we are suggesting there are scientific strengths to both qualitative and quantitative methods. Qualitative research strategies could start with ethnographic fieldwork studies with various cultural groups, using interview and observational methods to gain thick descriptions of forgiveness-related conflicts, rituals, practices, and other cultural artifacts. These research strategies could employ the paradigms of cultural psychology and indigenous psychology, which value local knowledge and bottom-up model building (Kim, Park, & Park, 2000). Qualitative studies could investigate indigenous definitions of forgiveness and the specific rituals or cultural tools used to generate forgiveness. Collaborative action-research approaches should be utilized, particularly with underserved populations, in order to dialog with participant stakeholders about the benefits of a given study for that group.

It could be particularly helpful to have qualitative data related to the community and contextual dimensions of culture that seem to promote or impede experiences of forgiveness. For example, what types of cultural or systemic factors maintain un-forgiveness? And what cultural or systemic factors promote in-group and out-group forms of forgiveness? Longitudinal designs with immigrant or refugee populations could examine the potential health benefits of forgiveness in groups experiencing rapid cultural change.

Quantitative research on forgiveness and culture should prioritize measurement development, an area where there has been virtually no cross-cultural validation of forgiveness measures. This means there is almost no solid data on the degree to which forgiveness is valued or understood universally. As measurement limitations are overcome, structural equations modeling could be used to examine cross-cultural between-group differences on individual forgiveness items beyond analyses of overall scale scores or factor structures. Culture-laden developmental and personality variables that have been previously related to forgiveness, such as empathy or shame, should be studied with cross-cultural samples. A host of cultural variables could be tested for mediator or moderator effects on various forgiveness measures, including individualism and collectivism, acculturation conflicts, family coping styles, and spiritual and religious variables, among others. The interactions between cultural dynamics and understandings of desecration (i.e., assaults on sacred space) could be a particularly important area of study in order to reduce politically and religiously volatile forms of unforgiveness. Culturally accommodative psychoeducational, counseling, parent education, and substance abuse interventions with forgiveness modules also need to be developed and empirically tested.

RELEVANCE FOR CLINICAL AND APPLIED INTERVENTIONS

Surprisingly few published psychological forgiveness interventions include explicit consideration of culturally appropriate target populations or recommended ways of adapting interventions for cultural diversity. As an example of the relevance of these issues, forgiveness interventions that promote forgiving someone else as an individual choice or decision that can be legitimately motivated by personal benefits may represent an individualistic cultural tool but may not fit the worldviews of highly collectivistic groups. Counselors and therapists should be sensitive to cultural influences on definitions and practices of forgiveness and develop the needed skills for intercultural dialog in this area.

It is also important to consider forgiveness and related issues within various cultural and systemic contexts. Most people live within numerous interpenetrating cultural or relational systems, which can be a source of the very conflicts that raise forgiveness issues. For example, intergenerational acculturation differences are a source of conflict in many families and cultural groups. Awareness of cultural dynamics of power and control in various systems can help prevent the use of forgiveness interventions that are ineffective or even harmful.

Cultural diversity also means that differing groups of people will approach and transform cultural tools for forgiveness in differing ways. For example, writing exercises are common in forgiveness studies and interventions. Yet many recent refugee and immigrant populations are comprised of many individuals with limited English writing skills, making English-based forgiveness writing exercises ineffective as a culturally sensitive tool. One Hmong-American therapist in our area described helping many of his Hmong clients cope with anger and practice forgiveness using the nonverbal cultural tools of weaving storycloth and hammering nails (Sandage et al., 2003). Recent refugee or immigrant populations are among those populations that are often less inclined to visit a mental health professional, so psychoeducational groups might be a primary forgiveness intervention for this group.

PERSONAL THEORETICAL PERSPECTIVES ON THE FIELD

The growing field of positive psychology is helping advance scientific and applied contributions related to a variety of developmental strengths and virtues, including forgiveness. We are encouraged that positive psychologists are joining those in other disciplines who have been studying the human strengths that contribute to personal and communal well-being. Peterson and Seligman (2004) have classified what they take to be universal, cross-cultural virtues supported by evolution. Sandage et al. (2003) argued for the development of a multicultural positive psychology that embraces scientific rigor and cross-cultural research but also explores cultural influences in the diverse expressions of virtues such as forgiveness.

Our current research related to forgiveness and culture involves a partnership with several leaders in the Hmong-American community in the twin cities. The Hmong are a Southeastern Asian ethnic group that fought with the U.S. in Laos against the North Vietnamese. Starting in the 1970s, the U.S. eventually helped many Hmong families relocate to the U.S. from refugee camps in Thailand. Sandage et al. (2003) describe some initial fieldwork consultation with Hmong cultural informants about Hmong understandings of forgiveness. A case study of forgiveness described by a Hmong-American therapist is also used to provide descriptive data of cultural meanings of forgiveness. The fieldwork and case study reveal several dimensions of highly collectivistic Hmong culture that shape the dynamics of forgiveness in ways that differ markedly from many of the dominant models in Western psychology. For example, traditional Hmong spirituality is a mix of animism and ancestor worship, which tends to promote a concern for securing forgiveness from ancestral spirits through correct funeral practices and other ritual sacrifices. The etiology of many physical and emotional problems is interpreted by traditional Hmong as resulting from an unforgiving spirit.

Traditional Hmong also practice forgiveness in a highly collectivistic way where conflicts are expected to utilize family and clan mediation. Interpersonal offenses are often viewed as losses of face for an entire family or clan. Forgiveness ceremonies are held between clans and can include very specific rituals, gifts, and even face washing as symbolic gestures of restoring the face that was lost or shamed during conflict. We are currently working with Hmong therapists in conducting semistructured interviews with Hmong-Americans who are willing to describe their experiences of forgiveness. One research participant clearly referred to one cultural artifact or script that informed his attempt to seek forgiveness:

> Because I broke the [axe] handle, I was somewhat afraid. Therefore, I went and bought some good-tasting liquor because we knew that person well. . . . I went to the person and in the Hmong way, I asked him for forgiveness. (Sandage, Xiong, & Chang, 2005)

To our knowledge, published psychological approaches to forgiveness and reconciliation in the West have not included the suggestion of giving "good-tasting liquor" or other gifts. But "the Hmong way" and many other cultural "ways" of forgiveness represent fascinating streams that researchers have not previously explored.

REFERENCES

American Psychological Association. (2003). Guidelines for multicultural education, training, research, practice, and organizational change for psychologists. *American Psychologist, 58,* 377–402.

Azar, F., & Mullet, E. (2001). Interpersonal forgiveness among Lebanese: A six-community study. *International Journal of Group Tensions, 30,* 161–181.

Azar, F., Mullet, E., & Vinsonneau, G. (1999). The propensity to forgive: Findings from Lebanon. *Journal of Peace Research, 36,* 169–181.

Cole, M. (1996). *Cultural psychology: A once and future discipline.* Cambridge, MA: Harvard University Press.

Enright, R. D., & Fitzgibbons, R. P. (2000). *Helping clients forgive: An empirical guide for resolving anger and restoring hope.* Washington, DC: American Psychological Association.

Fincham, F. D. (2000). The kiss of the porcupines: From attributing responsibility to forgiving. *Personal Relationships, 7,* 1–23.

Fiske, A. P., Kitayama, S., Markus, H. R., & Nisbett, R. E. (1998). The cultural matrix of social psychology. In D. T. Gilbert, S. T. Fiske, & G. Lindzey (Eds.), *Handbook of social psychology* (4th ed., pp. 915–981). Boston: McGraw-Hill.

Girard, M., & Mullet, E. (1997). Propensity to forgive in adolescents, young adults, older adults, and elderly people. *Journal of Adult Development, 4,* 209–220.

Gobodo-Madikizela, P. (2002). Remorse, forgiveness, and rehumanization: Stories from South Africa. *Journal of Humanistic Psychology, 42,* 7–32.

Huang, S. T., & Enright, R. D. (2000). Forgiveness and anger-related emotions in Taiwan: Implications for therapy. *Psychotherapy, 37,* 71–79.

Kadiangandu, J. K., Mullet, E., & Vinsonneau, G. (2001). Forgiveness: A Congo-France comparison. *Journal of Cross-Cultural Psychology, 32,* 504–511.

Kim, U., Park, Y. S., & Park, D. (2000). The challenge of cross-cultural psychology: The role of the indigenous psychologies. *Journal of Cross-Cultural Psychology, 31,* 63–75.

Kratz, C. A. (1991). Amusement and absolution: Transforming narratives during confession of social debt. *American Anthropologist, 93,* 826–851.

Kratz, C. A. (1994). *Affecting performance: Meaning, movement, and experience in Okiek women's initiation.* Washington, DC: Smithsonian Institution Press.

Lamb, S. (2002). Introduction: Reasons to be cautious about the use of forgiveness in psychotherapy. In S. Lamb & J. G. Murphy (Eds.), *Before forgiving: Cautionary views of forgiveness in psychotherapy* (pp. 3–14). New York: Oxford University Press.

Maddock, J. W., & Larson, N. R. (1995). *Incestuous families: An ecological approach to understanding and treatment.* New York: W. W. Norton.

McCullough, M. E., & Witvliet, C. V. O. (2002). The psychology of forgiveness. In C. R. Snyder & S. Lopez (Eds.), *Handbook of positive psychology* (pp. 446–458). New York: Oxford University Press.

Nqweni, Z. (2002). A phenomenological approach to victimization of families subjected to political violence. *Journal of Psychology in Africa, 12,* 180–195.

Park, Y. O, & Enright, R. D. (1997). The development of forgiveness in the context of adolescent friendship conflict in Korea. *Journal of Adolescence, 20,* 393–402.

Peterson, C., & Seligman, M. E. P. (2004). *Character strengths and virtues: A handbook and classification.* Washington, DC: American Psychological Association.

Sandage, S. J. (in press). Intersubjectivity and the many faces of forgiveness: A reply to Wangh. *Psychoanalytic Dialogues.*

Sandage, S. J., Hill, P. C., & Vang, H. C. (2003). Toward a multicultural positive psychology: Indigenous forgiveness and Hmong culture. *Counseling Psychologist, 31,* 564–592.

Sandage, S. J., & Wiens, T. W. (2001). Contextualizing models of humility and forgiveness: A reply to Gassin. *Journal of Psychology and Theology, 29,* 201–211.

Sandage, S. J., Xiong, L., & Chang, Z. (2005). *Forgiveness narratives of Hmong clients: A qualitative study.* Unpublished manuscript, Bethel Seminary, St. Paul, MN.

Scobie, G. E., Scobie, E. D., & Kakavoulis, A. K. (2002). A cross-cultural study of the construct of forgiveness: Britain, Greece, and Cyprus. *Psychology: Journal of the Hellenic Psychological Society, 9,* 22–36.

Shults, F. L., & Sandage, S. J. (2003). *The faces of forgiveness: Searching for wholeness and salvation.* Grand Rapids, MI: Baker.

Takaku, S., Weiner, B., & Ohbuchi, K. (2001). A cross-cultural examination of the effects of apology and perspective taking on forgiveness. *Journal of Language and Social Psychology, 20,* 144–166.

Temoshok, L. R., & Chandra, P. S. (2000). The meaning of forgiveness in a specific situational and cultural context: Persons living with HIV/AIDS in India. In M. E. McCullough, K. I. Pargament, & C. E. Thoresen (Eds.), *Forgiveness: Theory, research, and practice* (pp. 41–64). New York: Guilford Press.

Trzyna, T. (1997). The social construction of forgiveness. *Christian Scholars Review, 27,* 226–241.

Wuthnow, R. (2000). How religious groups promote forgiving: A national study. *Journal for the Scientific Study of Religion, 39,* 125–139.

Chapter Five

When the Sacred Is Violated: Desecration as a Unique Challenge to Forgiveness

Annette Mahoney
Mark S. Rye
Kenneth I. Pargament

In this chapter, we address unique challenges that arise when people interpret interpersonal violations from a religious frame of reference. Although the construct of forgiveness has long been embedded within religious systems of meaning in many cultures (Rye et al., 2000), contemporary psychological theory and research on forgiveness have largely avoided explicit discussion of the spiritual dimension of forgiveness. However, most people in the United States and in many other parts of the world adhere to religious frameworks of meaning. For example, most Americans believe in God or a higher power and commonly engage in religious practices, such as prayer (Gallup & Jones, 2000). Thus, it would seem important for social scientists to integrate religiously based beliefs and behaviors into models of how people interpret and come to terms with interpersonal violations. For example, the terrorist attacks on September 11, 2001, reflected more than a terrible loss of life and property in the eyes of many Americans; these public tragedies also represented a violation of fundamental spiritual symbols and values, including the sacredness of the nation, the sanctity of life, and the sublime virtues of justice and compassion. Private traumas can likewise affect people spiritually, as we hear in the pain and anger voiced by a 48-year-old woman after she discovered that her partner was in a three-year-long affair with a mutual friend: "I could not comprehend the level of ongoing purposeful deceit on the part of my significant other. [It was] unimaginable that an 'upstanding, prominent, religious, moral, preaching' person could be so utterly deceitful in so many ways for such an extended period of time" (Pargament, Magyar, Benore, & Mahoney, in press).

In this chapter, we offer a set of researchable propositions about how religion could shape the way that people interpret interpersonal violations and render forgiveness. In particular, we focus on how perceiving interpersonal violations as having a spiritual dimension (i.e., desecrations) may affect how people come to terms with a wrongdoing. *Desecration*, a newly emerging construct in the psychology of religion, is defined as the violation of a sanctified aspect of life (Pargament et al., in press). Specifically, we elaborate on three major propositions about desecration. First, desecration adds to the psychological trauma experienced when a violation occurs. Second, desecration incorporates an additional component—the sacred—into the interpersonal dynamics between a victim and perpetrator when a violation occurs. Third, depending on a variety of contextual factors, perceiving an event as a desecration could increase or decrease peoples' motivation to forgive.

At the onset, it should be recognized that this chapter is conceptually oriented and speculative in nature because little empirical research has been conducted thus far on desecration. Further, because the psychology of religion emphasizes individual religiousness, few studies speak to the interplay of religion and interpersonal processes such as forgiveness. To foster integration of religion and interpersonal psychology, we focus here on a victim's responses to a perpetrator who commits a desecration. We do not address a perpetrator's perceptions of, or responses to, committing a desecration toward the self or others. Neither do we address victims' responses to communal desecrations. Also, although desecration is a construct that presumably transcends specific religions, our propositions about desecration and forgiveness may be especially pertinent to believers of monotheistic religions in which God is identified as a separate entity with whom people have a relationship. Our hope is that this chapter will expand the psychology of religion's attention to the interpersonal realm, particularly with regard to forgiveness in a dyadic social context.

PERSONAL ASSUMPTIONS ABOUT DESECRATION AND FORGIVENESS

Desecration

Sanctification as a Conceptual Prerequisite. A prerequisite to understanding desecration is the concept of *sanctification* (Mahoney et al., 1999; Pargament & Mahoney, in press), which refers to perceiving an aspect of life as having divine character and significance. Two such processes have been highlighted in previous studies. *Theistic sanctification* refers to experiencing an aspect of life as being a manifestation of one's images, beliefs, or experience of God. *Nontheistic sanctification* occurs without reference to a specific deity and takes place when an aspect of life is imbued with divine qualities, such as timelessness, ultimate value, and transcendence. Thus, marriage can become a sacred covenant between both spouses and God, a job can become a God-given vocation, a piece of land can become blessed ground, a nurse can become a saint, and a day of the week can become the Sabbath. The process of sanctification extends the realm of the sacred beyond concepts of God, the Divine, and transcendence to include most, if not all, aspects of life.

Empirical research suggests that people imbue many life experiences with sacred meaning. For example, Mahoney et al. (in press) asked adults to rate the degree to which each of their top 10 strivings in life was sanctified. Although some types of strivings were more sacred than others, the participants perceived a wide array of strivings as connected to God or imbued with sacred qualities, including the family, self-development, work and money, physical health, and existential concerns. Studies also suggest that sanctification has important implications for individual and interpersonal functioning. Namely, people appear to invest more of themselves in things they hold sacred. In this vein, Mahoney et al. (in press) found that adults devoted more time and energy on their most highly sanctified strivings, compared with their least sanctified strivings. Second, people are more likely to preserve and protect the sacred aspects of their lives. For example, working with a community sample, Mahoney et al. (1999) found that husbands and wives who sanctified their marriages to a greater degree were more protective of their relationships; they responded to conflict with better problem-solving strategies, such as more collaboration, less verbal aggression, and less stalemating. Third, people are likely to derive greater satisfaction and well-being from aspects of life that are experienced as divine. For instance, greater sanctification of the marriage has been tied to greater marital satisfaction and more personal benefits from marriage (Mahoney et al., 1999). In sum, people view many aspects of life as possessing a deeper, more ultimate level of reality. As a result, they are approached differently. Jones (2002) puts it this way: "The sacred is not, necessarily, a unique and special object or domain split off from the rest of life, but is rather the world of ordinary objects experienced in a particular way" (p. 61).

Definition of Desecration.   Sanctification provides the backdrop for our understanding of desecration, which we define as the violation of a sanctified aspect of life (Pargament et al., in press). A desecration is tantamount to destroying a perceived point of connection between the human and the Divine. In religious language, the perpetrator commits a sacrilege by failing to treat a sacred aspect of life with obligatory awe and reverence. In psychological language, the violation threatens the divine status of an aspect of life by breaking presumed or explicit standards of conduct (i.e., behavior, cognitions, or emotion) with respect to the sanctified object.

To our knowledge, three empirical studies have been conducted on desecration (Magyar, Pargament, & Mahoney, 2000; Mahoney et al., 2002; Pargament et al., in press). In these studies, participants answered items about the degree to which they perceived an event as a desecration. Two interlocking beliefs are necessary to endorse the items. An individual must perceive that the aspect of life under question had previously been sanctified and that the event violated this aspect of life. In theistically oriented items on the desecration measure, God is overtly mentioned. Examples include: A part of my life that God made sacred was attacked; something from God was torn out of my life; the Divine in my life was intentionally harmed through this event; something symbolic of God was purposely damaged; something sacred that came from God was dishonored; this event ruined a blessing from God; and this event was both an offense against me and against God. Other items on the scale refer to the sanctified aspect of life without reference to a specific higher power. Examples of these items include: A violation of something spiritual to me occurred; something evil ruined a blessing in my life; a sacred part of my life was violated; the event was a sinful act involving something meaningful in my life; something that was sacred to me was destroyed; this event was an immoral act against something I value; this event was a transgression of something sacred. In studies thus far, the items with and without reference to God correlate highly and do not load onto separate factors.

Impact of Desecration.   The theory of sanctification sets the stage for why negative life events that are interpreted to be desecrations are likely to have special power and significance. Namely, three interrelated issues could heighten the psychological trauma of a desecration. First, assumptions that people make about sanctified aspects of life represent critical ingredients of the individual's worldview (Pargament & Mahoney, in press). For example, sacred objects, such as family bonds, may often be presumed to be everlasting and deserving of reverence by believers and nonbelievers alike. Others may assume that sanctified objects hold a special power that protects the objects and their owners from violation (e.g., God will protect this aspect of life from harm). Even if these assumptions are held implicitly, they can be psychologically powerful. The death of a loved one, the end of a marriage, or the experience of victimization may be terribly traumatic because they damage not only a person's sense of benevolence, justice, and self-worth, but also his or her core spiritual worldview. Qualitative research suggests that unforgivable injuries tend to fracture assumptions about personal control, justice, self-worth, or the goodness of others (Flanigan, 1992). In a similar manner, desecrations may be especially painful because such violations may raise serious doubts about the sacred nature of the violated object as well as undermine the individual's larger spiritual system of meaning. Furthermore, these types of offenses entail the destruction of a connection to the divine realm.

Second, the sacred may be central to the stories and themes by which people live. Narrative theorists have described how people lend meaning to their lives by structuring their experiences into "macronarratives," encompassing life stories, and "micronarratives," smaller stories (Neimeyer & Levitt, 2001, p. 48). Narratives that are interwoven with a sacred dimension may be particularly compelling. Relevant here is the work by Emmons (1999) who examined the role of spirituality in personal strivings. Strivings describe "what a person is typically trying to do" (p. 26). They add unity and coherence to daily behavior and to the individual's life story. Emmons, Cheung, and Tehrani (1998) found that overtly spiritual strivings may be particularly valuable in this regard. They asked a sample of 78 adults to report their strivings. Twenty-five percent of these goals were coded as either theistic (e.g., live a godly life) or spiritual (e.g., teach my children spiritual truths). People with a higher proportion of theistic and spiritual strivings reported significantly greater purpose in life, greater subjective well-being, and greater coherence and integration among their goals. Spiritual strivings, Emmons concluded, can help to unify and integrate personality.

Similarly, Mahoney et al. (in press) found that the more people sanctified major life strivings, the more they reported a sense of joy, meaning, and purpose in life. However, there is a potential downside to the sanctification of an individual's strivings and larger life narrative. Events that violate sanctified aspects of life are likely to disrupt the narrative flow of an individual's life. The old story the individual had planned to live by may no longer be viable, and a new tale must be constructed. Ultimately, the individual may see this unfolding story as facilitating personal growth, but the process is likely to be painful.

Third, as cited earlier, empirical research on sanctification indicates that people make greater investments in and derive greater benefits from sanctified objects. In turn, the destruction of a connection to the sacred realm may be especially frightening to a victim, who presumably would want to protect and defend vigorously the sacred realm from further threat.

Together, these three arguments provide the basis for asserting that perceiving an offense as a desecration is likely to evoke more intense intrapersonal reactions to the offense. These responses could include greater fear because something of divine value has unexpectedly been harmed and may not be repairable; greater anger because fundamental expectations of how sacred objects should be treated have been broken; and greater sadness because a sacred object has been lost, and basic assumptions about the world have been compromised (Mahoney et al., 2002; Pargament et al., in press). The added stress from a desecration may also be manifested by poorer health by the victim (Magyar et al., 2000). In light of this greater suffering, a victim of a desecration may also experience a deeper need to repair or protect the sacred object as well as find it necessary to reevaluate and modify core beliefs. Desecrations may also evoke stronger interpersonal reactions by victims toward perpetrators (Mahoney et al., 2002). This includes a greater desire for punishment of the offender because of the damage done to the sacred; greater confidence in judging the violator because the victim has the sacred on his or her side; and a stronger sense of self-righteousness and moral superiority relative to the perpetrator.

Empirically, three studies lend initial support to our suppositions about the effects of desecration. First, Magyar et al. (2000) examined the intrapersonal implications of desecration in a sample of 359 college students, predominantly women, who had been recently hurt in a romantic relationship. Consistent with hypotheses, the more that students perceived the interpersonal hurt or betrayal as a desecration of a sacred relationship, the more they reported negative emotions and mental and physical health symptoms. In addition, higher levels of desecration were linked with greater posttraumatic psychological growth and spiritual change in the process of coming to terms with the offense. Both sets of links remained significant even after controlling for the negativity of the event. Thus, the interpretation of a relationship violation as a desecration had significant ties to the psychological adjustment, physical health, and identity development of college students beyond the mere severity of the incident.

In another study that dealt with the implications of a desecration for personal well-being, Pargament et al. (in press) asked 117 adults randomly selected from the community to rate the degree to which they perceived the most negative event in their lives in the past 2 years as a desecration. Higher ratings were related to greater anger, depression, and anxiety, as well as more intrusive thoughts about the event. But after controlling for global religiousness and two event-related variables (i.e., whether the individual identified a perpetrator; the number of objects the participant reported lost or violated in the event), greater desecration was related only to higher levels of anger and avoidance strategies (e.g., tried not to think or talk about the event, immersion in school or work) and to lower levels of posttraumatic psychological growth (e.g., less reevaluation of values and relationship commitments). Thus, mature adults who have experienced a desecration may be energized by anger and the sense of deep spiritual violation, which then strongly motivates a shift in focus from the trauma itself to doing things to reestablish control over one's life. Although this coping approach may deflect some of the distress tied to the violation, it may not lead to more positive change for adults who have well-established identities.

A third study on desecration assessed not only the intrapsychic functioning of the victims but also the victims' reactions toward perpetrators (i.e., interpersonal variables). Specifically, Mahoney et al. (2002) surveyed college students living in the Midwest and in New York City about the 9/11 terrorists attacks in the United States. Consistent with earlier research, the more that the students perceived the attacks as a desecration, the more likely they were to report depression, anxiety, and a sense of threat. Higher levels of desecration were also tied to greater likelihood of altering life priorities, reaching out more to others for support, and deepening one's spirituality (e.g., prayer, feeling closer to God and religious community). In addition, higher levels of desecration were robustly related to endorsement of extreme retaliatory responses toward terrorists (e.g., use of nuclear bombs and biological weapons), as well as a higher level of solidarity with U.S. citizens and government. Thus, Mahoney et al. (2002) suggests that interpretations of violence as spiritual violations can heighten fear, mobilize people to reevaluate priorities and join together, invoke a sense of self-protectiveness, and solidify people's desire to strike back against perpetrators.

Forgiveness

In our view, forgiveness is best defined as a victim releasing or foregoing bitterness and vengeance toward the perpetrator of an offense while acknowledging the seriousness of the wrong. Thus, we agree with most psychologists that forgiveness does not imply forgetting (Smedes, 1996), condoning (Veenstra, 1992), reconciliation (Freedman, 1998), or release from legal accountability (Enright & Fitzgibbons, 2000). Further, we assume that the absence of negative feelings toward the offender is sufficient for forgiveness. This definition allows maximum applicability across religious worldviews, which vary as to whether acknowledgment of wrongdoing and restitution by the offender are prerequisites of forgiveness and whether positive feelings or actions by the victim are a necessary part of forgiveness (Rye et al., 2000).

FORGIVENESS AND DESECRATION

Desecration Expands the Relationship Context of Forgiveness

In applying forgiveness to a desecration, it is critical to recognize that the interpersonal context expands from a dyadic interaction between the victim and perpetrator to a broader, systemic context involving spiritual entities. A desecration is not merely an offense between the victim and perpetrator. From the victim's point of view, the violation also involves a third "party," namely the sacred aspect of life with whom the victim has a psychological relationship, accompanied by responsibilities to this sacred object. For example, a sanctified marriage would have a life of its own that supercedes each spouse and calls forth certain obligations. Further, believers from monotheistic religions may feel a responsibility to God for the safeguarding of sanctified objects that are perceived to be a manifestation of divinity. Thus, a desecration is a violation not only against the self but also an attack against a sacred aspect of life and possibly God. In turn, the victim is faced with choices to balance what is best for all parties. As will be elaborated, the psychological experience of being caught in a triangle between the perpetrator-sacred object, self-sacred object, and self-perpetrator can create complexities for the victim in how to respond to a desecration.

Of course, a victim could bypass the complications that a desecration creates for forgiveness in two ways. First, even though it may seem obvious that the victim had previously sanctified the violated object, the victim may repudiate this spiritual dimension after the offense occurs. For example, the Catholic church teaches that some behaviors by spouses are grounds for the annulment of a marriage, which essentially means that the relationship never met criteria for sanctification (Zwack, 1983). Second, the victim could transform his or her core spiritual worldview, deciding that the damaged aspect of life had erroneously been elevated to sacred status. For example, after being maligned and terminated for exposing workplace fraud to authorities, an individual may decide that he or she had mistakenly perceived a particular career track as a sacred pathway. In these circumstances, an offense would still be perceived as a wrongdoing, but the added challenges for forgiveness would be neutralized because the offense is no longer perceived as a desecration.

Factors That May Influence Motivation to Forgive a Desecration

As discussed earlier, a desecration appears to heighten the severity of the intrapsychic and interpersonal effects of a violation. In turn, a desecration should generally be more difficult to forgive than an offense that involves a nonsacred aspect of life. Nevertheless, in some cases, the desire to restore the sacred status of the desecrated object and/or maintain a connection to God may facilitate forgiveness. We propose that the following factors could tip the balance for or against the forgiveness of a desecration.

Intentionality of Offender.   The victim's perception of the perpetrator's intentionality in committing a desecration is likely to influence the victim's motivation to forgive. A victim may be more likely to forgive a perpetrator who is seen as ignorant of the sacred status of what was violated. In contrast, a victim may have more difficulty forgiving if he or she believes that the perpetrator understood the victim's beliefs about the sacredness of the relationship or object. Indeed, forgiveness is likely to be the most difficult when the offender has previously promised to invest in and protect the sanctified object. For example, because clergy sexual abuse represents a desecration committed by a person presumed to be a guardian of a sacred aspect of life, it takes on even greater power to shatter the victim's fundamental assumptions about the self, the perpetrator, and the sacred world (e.g., McLaughlin, 1994). Indeed, victims may feel especially conflicted about forgiving offenders who seem intentionally to violate the parameters surrounding sacred objects, such as a spouse who deliberately pursues an affair. Previous research has shown that participants consider intentionality of the offender's action when deciding whether to forgive, and forgiveness is inversely related to perceived intentionality (Boon & Sulsky, 1997). To forgive a perpetrator who commits a desecration with clear premeditation may seem like an abdication of God's principles of morality and a condonation of the sacred object's fall from grace into the profane world.

Apology and Restitution by the Offender.   The victim's perception of the perpetrator's willingness to apologize and provide restitution for a desecration to the victim and/or God is also likely to influence the victim's willingness to forgive. Research has found that apologies decrease negative thoughts, feelings, and behaviors toward a perpetrator in both adults (Ohbuchi, Kameda, & Agarie, 1989) and children (Darby & Schlenker, 1982). Although prior research has not focused on offenses that victims perceived as desecrations, this pattern seems likely for desecrations. Further, victims may worry that forgiving a desecration without contrition by the offender may place the sacred object at risk for ongoing damage as well as represent an act of disrespect to the object and/or God. In this vein, a recent experiment suggested that when people imagine a loved one suffering an interpersonal offense, they expect to feel principled anger on behalf of the loved one, particularly if they feel protective toward him or her (Exline, 2002). In a similar manner, a victim may believe that forgiving desecrations without an apology by the perpetrator would be disloyal to God.

Many religious traditions, in fact, have special purification rituals designed precisely for the offender to acknowledge his or her transgressions and make amends. In the Roman Catholic tradition, parishioners can participate in the Sacrament of Reconciliation in which they confess their sins and engage in acts of penance as a prelude to forgiveness. Within Judaism, individuals may go through a process called *teshuvah*, a ritual whereby an offender publicly acknowledges a wrongdoing, expresses remorse for his or her actions, offers compensation to the victim, and promises not to commit the offense in the future (Dorff, 1998). A Jewish victim is encouraged to forgive only if the offender has gone through this process (Rye et al., 2000). Victims from other religious traditions who believe that an offender is genuinely contrite and has made peace with God for an offense may likewise feel reassured that it is permissible in God's eyes for the victim to forgive the offense.

Nature of the Relationship Between the Offender and the Sanctified Aspect of Life. A victim's motivation to forgive a desecration may also depend on the degree to which the offender is connected to the sanctified aspect of life. At one end of the continuum, victims may be most likely to forgive offenders who play an integral role in the aspect of life that was violated for two reasons. First, from a cost-benefit analysis, a victim may decide that putting aside negative feelings toward the perpetrator is better than losing access to this sacred conduit. For example, a husband may forgive his wife's infidelity to rebuild their sacred marriage. A parent may forgive a teenager for getting pregnant outside of marriage and work to sustain this relationship to protect the spiritual well-being of the entire family system. A businessman may forgive a partner for violating their contract and continue to work together because their business is perceived to be a holy mission dependent on both of their talents. Second, a victim may experience cognitive dissonance when an offender is embedded within the desecrated aspect of life. Cognitive dissonance occurs when an individual experiences discomfort due to two inconsistent thoughts (Festinger, 1957). Particularly if an offender has played a central role within the sacred aspect of life, a victim is likely to experience both positive and negative thoughts about the offender. According to cognitive dissonance theory, such conflicting thoughts lead to emotional discomfort that, in turn, motivates individuals to modify their thoughts. One way for a victim of a desecration to reduce cognitive dissonance is to let go of negative thoughts about the offender through forgiveness.

On the other end of the continuum, a victim may perceive an offender to be disconnected from the sacred aspect of life, as in the case of a stranger who commits a criminal act that desecrates the victim's body. In other cases, an offender's violation may trigger a shift in the victim's perceptions of the offender from being an "insider" to an "outsider" of the sacred sphere under question. One example would be a respected clergy member who is found to be a sexual perpetrator and is subsequently cut off from all contact with the victim's family. Victims may be less motivated to forgive offenders who are disconnected from a sacred object for two reasons. First, maintaining a cordial relationship with the offender is unnecessary to restore the sacred status of the violated object. Second, the victim may view the offender as a spiritual enemy who does not merit forgiveness either from the victim or from God. For instance, the more that college students viewed the 9/11 attacks as a desecration, the more they believed that the terrorists embodied demonic characteristics (e.g., evil, satanic; Mahoney et al., 2002). Such beliefs may represent an especially potent form of the fundamental attribution error. This error is defined as the tendency to overestimate the role of internal traits and underestimate situational variables when explaining the behavior of another person (Jones & Harris, 1967). McCullough (1996) has suggested that this kind of attributional bias may contribute to difficulties in forgiving an offender. Specifically, a victim may be more likely to attribute the offender's behavior to deficiencies of the person's character while ignoring possible situational contributors to the behavior. This may make it more difficult to experience empathy, which is an integral part of the forgiveness process (McCullough, Worthington, & Rachal, 1997). Victims may have an especially hard time feeling empathy for people seen as evil outsiders who have defiled a sacred aspect of life.

Nature of the Relationship Between the Victim and the Divine.   Some individuals may be motivated to forgive the perpetrator to protect their relationship with God or some divine higher power, which may be seen as the most sanctified aspect of their life. That is, a victim's beliefs about what is necessary to sustain a direct bond with the Divine may promote forgiveness when a less central, albeit sanctified, aspect of life is violated. The victim may feel that the anger felt toward the perpetrator for ruining a gift from God becomes an obstacle to experiencing God's compassion and understanding. Indeed, one of the most important theological rationales for forgiveness in monotheistic religions is that because God forgives humans, we should forgive each other (Rye et al., 2000). Failure to emulate God's forgiving nature may, in the minds of some, lead to difficulties in one's relationship with the Divine. Thus, the solution is to let go of negative feelings toward the perpetrator about the desecration and even extend acts of love, compassion, and kindness toward the perpetrator. Here the relationship between the victim and God takes precedence over the victim's relationship with other aspects of life through which God has been experienced.

Victims' Orientation Toward Justice.   Social scientists have recently begun to explore justice as a complementary process of forgiveness. Two types of justice have been examined. First, retributive or punitive justice involves the punishment of the offender for the wrongdoing and is typically the focus of the legal system (Exline, Worthington, Hill, & McCullough, 2003). Second, restorative justice involves compensation for damages along with conciliatory behaviors, such as the offender's expression of remorse. This form of justice is gaining attention as a means to address victims' needs to air grievances and obtain direct apologies and restitution from the offender (Exline et al., 2003). Although seeking justice and rendering forgiveness are not mutually exclusive, a gap between the desired and actual level of justice has been hypothesized to decrease the likelihood of forgiveness (Worthington, 2003).

With regard to a desecration, the victim's view of his or her responsibility for bringing about justice is likely to affect his or her ability to forgive an offender. On one hand, the victim may believe redressing the desecration is the responsibility of God, not the victim. This would presumably free the victim to concentrate on forgiveness. An underlying factor that may facilitate this attitude is a strong sense of humility. Humility refers to an ability to take a realistic view of one's limitations, to see oneself as part of a larger world beyond the self, and to recognize one's own potential for wrongdoing (Exline, Bushman, Faber, & Phillips, 2000). Empirical research suggests that people who feel a stronger sense of humility are more able to forgive transgressions

(Exline et al., 2000). Rather than taking a spiritually "one-up" orientation, victims of desecrations who believe they should take a humble stance toward the offender and God may be more able to forgive and relinquish justice into the hands of God.

Conversely, the victim may feel a strong responsibility to carry out retributive justice to rectify damage done to a sacred aspect of life. To avoid such action may seem like betrayal of divine mandates, standards, and intentions for human conduct. In this situation, the victim would perceive God as aligned with himself or herself against the perpetrator. Here the victim would hold a spiritually one-up position relative to the perpetrator in order to reestablish the sanctified object's status and protect it from future harm. The victim would take action to ensure that punishment is delivered to the perpetrator to force him or her into a submissive position vis-à-vis the sacred realm. Here the perpetrator would not necessarily be required to be repentant, rather the victim would concentrate on retaliatory actions to deter the perpetrator from acting out against the sacred in the future.

NEW RESEARCH DIRECTIONS NEEDED IN THE AREA

To date, empirical research has not examined the forgiveness of offenses that are perceived by a victim to be a desecration. As we elaborate above, however, several promising hypotheses merit attention. First, desecrations would be expected to be more difficult to forgive than are other types of offenses because desecrations have higher intrapsychic and interpersonal costs. Second, several factors that call on a victim's beliefs about the sacred realm are likely to raise or lower a victim's ability to forgive a desecration. To briefly reiterate, forgiveness would presumably be easiest when: (a) the victim views the offender as naive, rather than fully informed, about the sacred nature of the violated object; (b) the offender confesses and makes amends to the victim with the goal of restoring the object to its rightful sacred status, rather than deny the desecration; (c) the offender plays an integral role in restoring the sacred aspect of life, rather than being an "outsider"; (d) the victim believes forgiveness is required to protect his or her bond with God; and (e) the victim believes that justice can be brought about only by supernatural actions, not his or her own retributive actions. Evidence for such hypotheses would highlight the power of the spiritual dimension of interpersonal offenses.

RELEVANCE FOR CLINICAL AND APPLIED INTERVENTIONS

Although research on the forgiveness of desecrations specifically has yet to be done, other research shows that religious beliefs and practices are often involved in the interpretation and recovery from offenses. As cited earlier, people commonly interpret negative life events as desecrations (Pargament et al., in press). In addition, when coming to terms with offenses, religious individuals place a more positive value on forgiveness (e.g., Gorsuch & Hao, 1993). Also, many individuals rely on religious strategies when trying to forgive (Rye & Pargament, 2002). This research highlights the need for clinicians to assess carefully clients' spiritual lives when interpersonal offenses occur. In particular, clinicians should be sensitive to the spiritual dimension of traumatic life events; when a violation is defined in spiritual terms, solutions to the transgression may also be drawn from this realm. One powerful set of religious coping methods to promote forgiveness are individually based (Pargament, 1997). These include a victim (a) seeking spiritual support from God or higher power, (b) seeking support from a religious community, (c) making benevolent religious reappraisals of violation, and (d) engaging in religious rituals (Pargament, 1997). For instance, the individual may pray to God to develop a sense of empathy toward the perpetrator and gain perspective on situational factors underlying an offense. Fellow believers may also encourage forgiveness by reminding a victim of his or her need for forgiveness. A second class of religious coping methods available to facilitate forgiveness includes adaptive interpersonal processes promoted by some religious traditions (Mahoney & Tarakeshwar, in press). For example, the concept of "theistic mediation" refers to both parties of a dyad viewing God as an objective but compassionate third person in the relationship who would encourage both the victim and offender to do whatever is necessary to recover from the damage to the sacred object without inflicting further harm. Clinicians could help their clients to identify and access these religious resources in coping with desecrations.

Of course, clinicians should also process with clients the risks of forgiving a desecration. For example, a victim may need to redefine the parameters surrounding sacred objects, such that a prior absolute standard of conduct with regard to the sacred object becomes forgivable. For example, a husband may decide that, although his wife's infidelity violated a sacred marital vow, such events can take place in holy marriages. But a victim may sometimes feel that shifting the criteria of a sanctified aspect of life denigrates both the sacred and one's own sense of spiritual integrity. As an illustration, a woman may believe that her body is a holy temple and if she forgives her partner for mistreating her physically or sexually, she may fail to require sufficiently high standards of conduct for herself as a sacred being. Recent studies indicate that victims have stronger feelings of regret about forgiveness when this action leads to feelings of stupidity, weakness, being cheated, or negativity about self (Exline, Ciarocco, & Baumeister, 2001). Such feelings of a betrayal of the self may be especially strong if a victim alters his or her core spiritual beliefs to forgive the perpetrator. Particularly if the desecration occurs again, a victim may experience added regret for not making a different decision that would have better protected the sacred. Finally, the victim may experience a deeper sense of anger at God for not preventing the reinjury. Such feelings may be unique risks of the forgiveness of desecrations.

CONCLUSIONS

For many years, psychologists have been intensely interested in the impact of life traumas on the psychological, social, and physical functioning of people. Yet life events also affect people spiritually. Moreover, the most painful of life events can take on even greater power when interpreted within a spiritual context. In short, a desecration is more than a stressful life event. It is a violation of the deepest, most precious aspects of a person's life. Desecrations are, in the words of Elkins (1998), a violation of one's soul. In this chapter, we have taken some initial steps to clarify the nature of desecration and its implications for forgiveness. We have suggested that the violation of a sacred aspect of life poses unique challenges for forgiveness in part because the process of forgiveness shifts from dyadic (self-perpetrator) to triadic (self-perpetrator-sacred) in nature. To put it another way, analyzing the relationship between the victim and perpetrator is not sufficient in coming to terms with a desecration. The victim must also explore the nature of his or her relationship with the sacred. This is a difficult balancing act that deserves attention from clinicians and researchers alike. Clinicians should be cognizant of the dilemmas raised for forgiveness evoked when their clients struggle with interpersonal violations they perceive as desecrations. Researchers should also extend their studies of trauma and forgiveness to examine the spiritual character of life's most painful events and most powerful resources for resolution.

REFERENCES

Boon, S. D., & Sulsky, L. M. (1997). Attributions of blame and forgiveness in romantic relationships: A policy capturing study. *Journal of Social Behavior and Personality, 12,* 19–44.

Darby, B. W., & Schlenker, B. R. (1982). Children's reactions to apologies. *Journal of Personality and Social Psychology, 43,* 742–753.

Dorff, E. N. (1998). The elements of forgiveness: A Jewish approach. In E. L. Worthington, Jr. (Ed.), *Dimensions of forgiveness: Psychological research and theological perspectives* (pp. 29–55). Philadelphia: Templeton Foundation Press.

Elkins, D. N. (1998). *Beyond religion: A personal program for building a spiritual life outside the walls of traditional religion.* Wheaton, IL: Theosophical.

Emmons, R. E. (1999). *The psychology of ultimate concerns.* New York: Guilford Press.

Emmons, R. A., Cheung, C., & Tehrani, K. (1998). Assessing spirituality through personal goals: Implications for research on religion and subjective well-being. *Social Indicators Research, 45,* 391–422.

Enright, R. D., & Fitzgibbons, R. P. (2000). *Helping clients forgive: An empirical guide for resolving anger and restoring hope.* Washington, DC: American Psychological Association.

Exline, J. J. (2002, February). *When loved ones suffer harm: Protectiveness, loyalty, and other's forgiveness as predictors of one's own anger.* Poster presented at a meeting of the Society for Personality and Social Psychology, Savannah, GA.

Exline, J. J., Bushman, B., Faber, J., & Phillips, C. (2000, February). Pride gets in the way: Self-protection works against forgiveness. In J. J. Exline (Chair), *Ouch! Who said forgiveness was easy?* Symposium at a meeting of the Society for Personality and Social Psychology, Nashville, TN.

Exline, J. J., Ciarocco, N., & Baumeister, R. F. (2001, February). *Forgive and regret? Misgivings in the wake of forgiveness and apology.* Poster presented at a meeting of the Society for Personality and Social Psychology, San Antonio, TX.

Exline, J. J., Worthington, E. L., Jr., Hill, P. C., & McCullough, M. E. (2003). Forgiveness and justice: A research agenda for social and personality psychology. *Personality and Social Psychology Review, 7,* 337–348.

Flanigan, B. (1992). *Forgiving the unforgivable.* New York: Macmillan.

Festinger, L. (1957). *A theory of cognitive dissonance.* Evanston, IL: Row Peterson.

Freedman, S. (1998). Forgiveness and reconciliation: The importance of understanding how they differ. *Counseling and Values, 42,* 200–216.

Gallup, G., & Jones, T. (2000). *The next American spirituality: Finding God in the twenty-first century.* Colorado Springs, CO: Cook Communications.

Gorsuch, R. L., & Hao, J. Y. (1993). Forgiveness: An exploratory factor analysis and its relationships to religious variables. *Review of Religious Research, 34,* 333–347.

Jones, E. E., & Harris, V. A. (1967). The attribution of attitudes. *Journal of Experimental Social Psychology 3,* 1–24.

Jones, J. W. (2002). *Terror and transformation: The ambiguity of religion in psychoanalytic perspective.* New York: Brunner-Routledge.

Magyar, G. M., Pargament, K. I., & Mahoney, A. (2000, August). *Violating the sacred: A study of desecration among college students.* Paper presented at the annual meeting of the American Psychological Association, Washington, DC.

Mahoney, A. M., Pargament, K. I., Ano, G., Lynn, Q., Magyar, G., McCarthy, S., et al. (2002, August). *The devil made them do it? Demonization and the 9/11 attacks.* Paper presented at the annual meeting of the American Psychological Association, Chicago.

Mahoney, A., Pargament, K. I., Cole, B., Jewell, T., Magyar, G. M., Tarakeshwar, N., et al. (in press). A higher purpose: The sanctification of strivings. *The International Journal for the Psychology of Religion.*

Mahoney, A., Pargament, K. I., Jewell, T., Swank, A. B., Scott, E., Emery, E., et al. (1999). Marriage and the spiritual realm: The role of proximal and distal religious constructs in marital functioning. *Journal of Family Psychology, 13,* 321–338.

Mahoney, A., & Tarakeshwar, N. (in press). Religion's role in marital and family relationships. In R. Paloutzian & C. Park (Eds.), *Handbook of the psychology of religion and spirituality.* New York: Guilford Press.

McLaughlin, B. R. (1994). Devastated spirituality: The impact of clergy sexual abuse on the survivor's relationship with God and the church. *Sexual Addiction and Compulsivity, 1,* 145–158.

McCullough, M. E. (1996, April). *Promoting forgiveness with clients who can't: An empathy-based model for psychoeducation.* Paper presented at the National Conference on Forgiveness in Clinical Practice, Baltimore.

McCullough, M. E., Worthington, E. L., Jr., & Rachal, K. C. (1997). Interpersonal forgiving in close relationships. *Journal of Personality and Social Psychology, 73,* 321–336.

Neimeyer, R. A., & Levitt, H. (2001). Coping and coherence: A narrative perspective on resilience. In C. R. Snyder (Ed.), *Coping with stress: Effective people and processes* (pp. 46–67). New York: Oxford University Press.

Ohbuchi, K., Kameda, M., & Agarie, N. (1989). Apology as aggression control: Its role in mediating appraisal of and response to harm. *Journal of Personality and Social Psychology, 56,* 219–227.

Pargament, K. I. (1997). *The psychology of religion and coping: Theory, research, practice.* New York: Guilford Press.

Pargament, K. I., Magyar, G. M., Benore, E., & Mahoney, A. (in press). Sacrilege: A study of sacred loss and desecration and their implications for health and well-being in a community sample. *Journal of Personality and Social Psychology.*

Pargament, K. I., & Mahoney, A. (in press). Sacred matters: Sanctification as vital topic for the psychology of religion. *The International Journal for the Psychology of Religion.*

Rye, M. S., Pargament, K. I., Ali, M. A., Beck, G. L., Dorff, E. N., Hallisey, C., et al. (2000). Religious perspectives on forgiveness. In M. E. McCullough, K. I. Pargament, & C. E. Thoresen (Eds.), *Forgiveness: Theory, research, and practice* (pp. 17–40). New York: Guilford Press.

Rye, M. S., & Pargament, K. I. (2002). Forgiveness and romantic relationships in college: Can it heal the wounded heart? *Journal of Clinical Psychology, 58,* 419–441.

Smedes, L. B. (1996). *The art of forgiving.* Nashville, TN: Moorings.

Veenstra, G. (1992). Psychological concepts of forgiveness. *Journal of Psychology and Christianity, 11,* 160–169.

Worthington, E. L., Jr. (2003). *Forgiving and reconciling: Bridges to wholeness and hope.* Downers Grove, IL: InterVarsity Press.

Zwack, J. P. (1983). *Annulment: Your chance to remarry within the Catholic church.* Cambridge: Harper & Row.

Chapter Six

Anger Toward God: A New Frontier in Forgiveness Research

Julie Juola Exline
Alyce Martin

The experience of anger is not limited to the interpersonal domain. When suffering occurs that seems uncontrollable and unfair, individuals sometimes blame God and become intensely angry toward God. However, people often believe that it is morally inappropriate to feel angry toward God, which implies that they may be reluctant to admit such feelings or even to discuss the possibility (Novotni & Petersen, 2001). But taboo or not, anger toward God appears to be common. In the 1988 General Social Survey, a broad-based survey of American households, 63% of respondents reported that they sometimes felt anger toward God. Frequent or unresolved anger toward God has been linked with emotional distress (e.g., Exline, Yali, & Lobel, 1999; Pargament, Zinnbauer, et al., 1998), suggesting that the topic has clinical relevance. Because research on anger toward God is in its infancy, our goal here is to describe the handful of studies that exist while highlighting many questions that still need to be addressed.

PERSONAL ASSUMPTIONS ABOUT ANGER TOWARD GOD

Suffering can prompt a variety of negative emotions regarding God, including confusion (Exline, 2002a), mistrust (Murray-Swank, 2003), and a sense of being punished (Pargament, Zinnbauer, et al., 1998). Positive feelings toward God can also occur in the wake of negative events. For example, undergraduates in one study typically reported moderate levels of love, trust, and closeness toward God after a crisis (Exline, 2002a). Because our goal for this chapter is to suggest comparisons with interpersonal anger and forgiveness, we will focus on anger toward God.

People can conceivably feel anger toward God even if they view God as an impersonal source of energy or power, as in many Eastern faiths. However, our discussion will apply most directly to belief systems that emphasize personal relationships between humans and God.

Although we suggest parallels between anger toward God and interpersonal anger, we have chosen not to use the terms *forgiving God* or *forgiveness of God*. Most forgiveness definitions emphasize the moral culpability of offenders. Many people do not believe that God is capable of moral wrongdoing, rendering the term *forgiveness* inappropriate (see Moon, 1999). To avoid confusion, we will speak of resolving anger toward God, rather than forgiving God.

The topic of anger toward God is not entirely new in psychology. Ideas relevant to anger toward God appear in research on God images (e.g., Benson & Spilka, 1973), spiritual development (e.g., Hall & Edwards, 2002), "amazing apostates" (Altemeyer & Hunsberger, 1997), religious conflict (e.g., Nielsen & Fultz, 1995), negative religious coping and spiritual struggles (e.g., Pargament, Koenig, Tarakeshwar, & Hahn, 2001; Pargament, Murray-Swank, Magyar, & Ano, 2004; Pargament, Smith, Koenig, & Perez, 1998; Pargament, Zinnbauer, et al., 1998), spiritual risk (e.g., Fitchett, 1999a, 1999b; Fitchett, Rybarczyk, & DeMarco, 1999), and spiritual injury (Lawson, Drebing, Berg, Vincellette, & Penk, 1998). Although all of these literatures are relevant to our topic, space constraints dictate that we emphasize ideas and findings that focus specifically on anger toward God. Readers seeking an overview of religious and spiritual struggles more generally are referred to other recent overviews (e.g., Exline, 2002b; Exline & Rose, in press; Fitchett, 1999a, 1999b; Pargament, 1997, 2002; Pargament et al., 2004).

REVIEW OF THEORETICAL AND EMPIRICAL LITERATURE

We have organized this section as follows. First, we suggest some predictors of anger toward God. Second, we briefly discuss potential consequences of anger toward God. Finally, we outline some means that people may use to resolve anger toward God.

Predictors of Anger Toward God

Although empirical research remains sparse, studies have identified some situational and individual difference factors that predict anger toward God. Many of these factors parallel predictors of interpersonal anger and unforgiveness, as reviewed below. We also suggest some potential predictors that have not yet been empirically tested.

Undeserved Suffering as a Dominant Theme.   Most discussions of anger toward God center on a common theme: God's willingness to cause or permit undeserved suffering (Kushner, 1981; McCloskey, 1987; Novotni & Petersen, 2001; Smedes, 1984; Yancey, 1998). In some situations, people attribute blame to God because there is no evident human cause. For instance, people often blame God for untimely deaths, illnesses, accidents, and natural disasters. Yet even when it is easy to identify human causes of suffering, people may hold God responsible for failing to prevent the harm. Examples include atrocities such as the Holocaust (Brenner, 1980), the private pain of sexual abuse (Murray-Swank, 2003), and common offenses, such as infidelity and divorce (Exline, 2002a).

Regardless of the specific form of suffering, the notion of injustice emerges as a core theme in cases of anger toward God. Anger toward God parallels interpersonal anger in this respect. Worthington uses the term *injustice gap* to describe this discrepancy between how things are and how they would be if things were fair (Worthington, 2003). The larger the injustice gap, the more anger a person is likely to feel, and the more difficult it will be to resolve the anger.

Severity of Harm and Beliefs About Underlying Motives. Severe offenses create larger injustice gaps than do mild offenses (Worthington, 2003). Forgiveness research suggests that the more severe and intentional an offense, the more difficult it is to forgive (e.g., Boon & Sulsky, 1997; Zechmeister & Romero, 2002). Parallel findings are starting to emerge from studies of anger toward God. In one recent study (Exline & Bushman, 2004), undergraduates were asked to recall a negative event in which they believed that God may have played a role. Negative feelings were greater to the extent that God was viewed as responsible for the suffering—particularly when God's actions were viewed as malevolent, punitive, disappointing, illogical, or shaming. Here we see a direct parallel between interpersonal anger and anger toward God. People become angry toward others—and toward God—if they believe that they have been hurt deeply and intentionally.

Inflated Sense of Entitlement. Anger toward God may be especially characteristic of a specific group of individuals: those with an inflated, narcissistic sense of entitlement. High-entitlement persons believe that they merit special treatment, and they are highly invested in collecting on the debts they believe others owe them (e.g., Campbell, Bonacci, Shelton, Exline, & Bushman, 2004; Emmons, 1987). Because of its link with narcissism, entitlement also implies a desire to "save face" and a reluctance to compromise personal pride. As such, it seems likely that highly entitled persons should readily perceive injustices toward themselves, and they should hold on to anger about these events. Consistent with this reasoning, studies have shown that entitlement predicts both readiness to take offense (McCullough, Emmons, Kilpatrick, & Mooney, 2003) and reluctance to forgive (Exline, Baumeister, Bushman, Campbell, & Finkel, 2004).

In a recent study focused on anger toward God, entitlement predicted greater negative emotion toward God and more negative attributions about God's intentions; it decreased belief in God when negative emotions did occur (Exline & Bushman, 2004). High-entitlement individuals were especially sensitive to the issue of being repaid. If they believed that God had repaid them (even partially) for their suffering, they tended to report a positive impact of the event on their bond with God. If they did not feel repaid, they tended to report a negative impact. Being repaid was less crucial for those scoring lower on entitlement.

Emphasis on Justice Versus Mercy.   According to recent research (Worthington, 2003; Worthington, Berry, & Parrott, 2001), people differ in their relative favoring of conscientiousness-based virtues (e.g., duty, responsibility) versus warmth-based virtues (e.g., love, mercy). One might speculate that those favoring conscientiousness would hold onto anger toward God until a sense of justice was restored. On the other hand, those favoring mercy might have difficulty accepting the harsh side of divine justice—for example, biblical references to God-ordained capital punishment, war, eye-for-an-eye retribution, and the prospect of hell. These hypotheses await empirical testing.

Religiosity/Spirituality and Perceived Closeness to God.   The forgiveness literature suggests various reasons why feeling close to God should protect against developing grudges toward God. First, forgiveness is more likely when two parties share a close, committed relationship before the offense (e.g., Fincham, Paleari, & Regalia, 2002; Finkel, Rusbult, Kumashiro, & Hannon, 2002). Second, religiosity predicts more positive attitudes about forgiveness in general (e.g., Tsang, McCullough, & Hoyt, in press). Both of these factors would suggest that people will not want to stay angry toward God if they feel close to God and want to maintain this close relationship.

Consistent with the above predictions, our survey research with undergraduates suggests lower levels of anger toward God among students who report high current religiosity and retrospectively report greater perceived closeness to God prior to the event (Exline & Bushman, 2004). However, higher religiosity was also strongly linked with belief that anger toward God was morally unacceptable. This association raised the question of whether devout followers reported less anger toward God simply because they were afraid to admit their anger. This did not appear to be the case. The negative correlation between religiosity and anger toward God remained significant when we controlled for beliefs about the acceptability of such feelings. Nonetheless, the finding that religiously committed individuals often see anger toward God as morally wrong suggests a need for careful, sensitive assessment within religiously committed samples.

Although the above findings emphasize religiosity, distinctions between organized religion and personal spirituality may be important in understanding anger toward God. For example, some people might turn away from organized religion in reaction to teachings that present harsh images of God. These spiritual (but not religious) individuals might have attributions and images of God that would differ from those of religious affiliates. Such issues await empirical testing.

Also, it seems probable that people's images of God would moderate the associations between religious or spiritual commitment and anger toward God. Those who view God as angry and punitive might find themselves in a difficult bind, fearful of admitting anger toward God but also reluctant to trust God or draw close to God. On the other hand, those whose images of God emphasize love and mercy face a different challenge. Assuming that they hold God responsible for suffering, they need to reconcile God's role in suffering with their benevolent views of God.

Parental Relationships and Attachment.   Prior research and theory suggest that images of God often mirror images of human fathers (e.g., Beit-Hallahmi & Argyle, 1975; Hall, 2004; Rizzuto, 1979). Would a strained relationship with one's father predict problems in one's perceived relationship with God as well? Consistent with this logic, studies suggest that women who suffer sexual abuse from their fathers often have negative God images and difficulty trusting God (see Murray-Swank, 2003, for a review). Complementary results emerged from an interview study of homeless men (Smith & Exline, 2002). In that study, reports of a poor current relationship with one's father were associated with (a) more problems in one's perceived relationship with God, (b) a more frequent sense that God was punishing the self, and (c) somewhat greater belief that it was morally appropriate to hold on to negative feelings toward God. The men's earlier histories with their fathers were also important, particularly in terms of the simple presence versus absence of their fathers in the home: Participants were much less likely to recall problems in their early relationships with God if their fathers had lived with them during childhood.

The data on homeless men also raised the possibility that maternal relationships may be important in predicting one's perceived relationship with God. Such a finding would be consistent with prior research and theorizing, showing links between God images and maternal relationships (Vergote & Tamayo, 1981). Only 4 of the 52 homeless men in our sample reported that their mothers had been absent during their childhood years, which renders our findings tentative. However, despite the relative rarity of a mother's absence, a statistically significant effect emerged: The absence of one's mother during childhood predicted a higher level of recollected problems in the men's early relationships with God (Smith & Exline, 2002). Also, a sense of having been treated well by one's mother was associated with fewer perceived problems in one's relationship with God—and with greater odds of resolving such problems when they did occur. Although preliminary and awaiting replication, these data suggest that both maternal and paternal relationships may be important predictors of people's perceived relationships with God.

Because parental relationships are so central to attachment bonds, it seems sensible to predict that attachment styles would be linked with a person's propensity to experience negative feelings toward God (see Kirkpatrick, 1999). Secure attachment is associated with a greater propensity to forgive others (e.g., Davidson, 2001; Luebbert, 2000). Also, some evidence demonstrates that people can turn to God as a substitute attachment figure (e.g., Hall, 2004; Kirkpatrick, 1998). Data from two studies offer some support for a link between attachment style and anger toward God. Among college students, insecure attachment predicted more negative feelings toward God after life crises (Exline, 2002a). Among homeless men, insecure attachment (in particular, avoidant attachment) was associated with greater recollection of problems in one's early relationship with God (Smith & Exline, 2002). Though preliminary, these results suggest that secure attachment bonds predict fewer problems in people's perceived relationships with God.

Summary. These preliminary data suggest that predictors of anger toward God often parallel predictors of interpersonal anger and unforgiveness. People become angry toward God when they view God as responsible for severe offenses. Perceived closeness to God might buffer against anger, whereas insecure attachment and a sense of entitlement seem to contribute to angry feelings.

Possible Consequences of Anger Toward God: Physical, Psychological, and Spiritual

Data on the consequences of anger toward God are still sparse. However, a number of findings suggest that anger toward God may have consequences for physical, psychological, and spiritual well-being.

Physical Effects. One study of 96 medical rehabilitation inpatients showed a link between anger toward God at admission and poorer recovery (as assessed via performance on activities of daily living) at 4 months postadmission (Fitchett et al., 1999). Negative religious coping, more generally, has also been linked with negative outcomes in terms of health and well-being (for reviews, see Pargament, 2002; Pargament et al., 2004). For example, in a longitudinal cohort study of 596 medical patients aged 55 and older, religious struggle at baseline predicted greater mortality risk over a 2-year period, even when controlling for demographic factors, physical health status, and mental health indices (Pargament et al., 2001). Notably, two of the religious struggle items that predicted mortality risk were relevant to anger toward God: They assessed feelings of abandonment by God and of questioning God's love for the self.

Psychological Correlates. Frequent or prolonged anger toward God has been linked with global indices of distress and poor adjustment, although the causal relationships remain unclear. In a study of 92 caregivers of terminally ill patients, seeing one's situation as unjust, as unfair punishment from God, or as desertion by God was associated with greater reports of depression and anxiety (Mickley, Pargament, Brant, & Hipp, 1998). Studies of college students suggest that frequent or unresolved anger toward God correlates with low self-esteem (Pargament, Zinnbauer et al., 1998), depression (Exline et al., 1999), anxiety (Pargament, Zinnbauer et al., 1998), trait anger (Exline et al., 1999), poor problem-solving skills (Pargament, Zinnbauer et al., 1998), and insecure attachment (Exline, 2002a; Hall & Edwards, 2002). Unfortunately, because studies to date have used cross-sectional, correlational designs, we cannot determine the direction of causality.

Spiritual Effects: Angry Withdrawal and Unbelief.   It seems likely that anger toward God would often appear as part of a constellation of spiritual distress. Consistent with this logic, correlational studies have revealed that frequent anger toward God tends to co-occur with other spiritual struggles, including guilt and interpersonal conflict surrounding religious issues (e.g., Nielsen & Fultz, 1995; Pargament, Smith, et al., 1998; Pargament, Zinnbauer, et al., 1998).

We are particularly interested in the issue of whether anger toward God might lead to decreased belief in God's existence. Our interest was piqued by an early study of anger toward God among undergraduates (Exline et al., 1999), which revealed a counterintuitive finding: Those who reported no belief in God reported more grudges toward God than believers. At first glance, this finding seemed to reflect an error. How could people be angry with God if they did not believe in God? Reanalyses of a second dataset (Exline, Fisher, Rose, & Kampani, 2004; Kampani & Exline, 2002) revealed similar patterns: Those who endorsed their religious beliefs as "atheist/agnostic" or "none/unsure" reported more anger toward God than those who reported a religious affiliation. Further analyses identified a group of *conflicted believers* (or *slipping believers*), all of whom had previously believed that God exists (or might exist) but no longer believed at the time of the study. When compared with believers, these individuals reported more anger toward God. These findings raised the question of whether anger might actually affect belief in God's existence, an idea in line with Novotni and Petersen's (2001) clinical descriptions of *emotional atheism.*

Studies of traumatic events suggest a possible link between suffering, anger toward God, and doubts about God's existence. According to Cook and Wimberly (1983), 33% of parents who suffered the death of a child reported doubts about God in the first year of bereavement. In another study, 90% of mothers who had given birth to a profoundly retarded child voiced doubts about the existence of God (Childs, 1985). Our survey research with undergraduates has focused directly on the association between anger at God and self-reported drops in belief (Exline et al., 2004). In the wake of a negative life event, anger toward God predicted decreased belief in God's existence. Furthermore, when we looked only at those who showed some drop in belief, belief was least likely to recover for those who reported that they were angry toward God and had chosen to turn away from God. In addition, an open-ended question revealed that 9% of those who had resolved negative feelings stated that they had done so by deciding not to believe in God (Exline, 2002a). Because these data were based on retrospective reports rather than longitudinal analysis, they should be interpreted with caution. Yet they raise the possibility that anger toward God—and subsequent decisions to withdraw—may lead to reduced belief in God's existence.

Summary.   Clearly, longitudinal and experimental studies are needed to make firm conclusions about the consequences of anger toward God. However, studies to date suggest that anger toward God could impair health and might also decrease belief in God's existence. Data on mental health consequences are correlational, creating a chicken-and-egg problem: Anger toward God could lead to distress or vice versa, or a third variable might account for the link. Future studies might also compare the consequences of interpersonal grudges with the consequences of grudges toward God—a topic that, to the best of our knowledge, remains completely unexplored.

Resolving Negative Feelings Toward God

Once people become angry toward God, how do they resolve the anger? Of course, this question assumes a desire to reduce the anger—a desire that not everyone has. Nonetheless, our study of undergraduates showed that 80% of those who reported negative feelings toward God indicated that the feelings decreased over time (Exline, 2002a). What prompts this decreased anger? Research has not been sufficiently sophisticated to offer systematic, process-oriented models. However, preliminary data do exist. We describe these findings briefly below.

Parallels with Interpersonal Forgiveness.   Some of the findings about resolution of anger toward God suggest clear parallels with interpersonal forgiveness. For example, people are more likely to forgive others if they receive apologies (e.g., Darby & Schlenker, 1982; McCullough et al., 1998; Ohbuchi, Kameda, & Agarie, 1989) or other restitution (e.g., Witvliet, Worthington, Wade, & Berry, 2002; Worthington, 2003). Odds are that God will not appear to a person with a confession of wrongdoing or an apology. Nonetheless, people may believe that God has repaid them in some positive way for their suffering. In one recent study (Exline & Bushman, 2004), undergraduates reported more benevolent attributions about God's intentions when they believed that God had repaid them in some way for their distress. When participants rated the overall impact of the event, feeling repaid also predicted more positive evaluations of their relationship with God.

Repayment is not the only way to reduce the injustice gap. People might also see injustices as smaller if they see benefit from the suffering or if they see a perpetrator's motives as benevolent. They might decide that the party in question was not responsible for the offense, which would also reduce the sense of injustice. Among students in our sample (Exline, 2002a), 25% cited benign reappraisal of God's intentions as a reason for reduced anger, whereas 14% cited benefits from the situation. A substantial minority (27%) reported that their anger subsided because they had obtained a meaningful explanation or insight into why the event occurred. In addition, 12% became less angry because they saw the event as God's will, whereas 11% decided that God was not at fault.

The same study (Exline, 2002a) suggests another parallel with interpersonal forgiveness. Research on interpersonal offenses suggests that anger may fade with the passage of time (e.g., McCullough, Fincham, & Tsang, 2003). Consistent with this finding, 27% of those in our undergraduate sample cited the simple passage of time as a reason for decreased anger toward God.

Some Likely Differences. Despite clear parallels between anger toward God and anger toward others, fundamental differences between humans and God imply important distinctions. For example, the major monotheistic traditions (Christianity, Judaism, and Islam) all center on a God infinite in knowledge and power. People are extremely limited in comparative terms. God has full access to people's thoughts, whereas people cannot fully know the thoughts of God (except as given through divine revelation). God is also viewed as holy and perfect, whereas people commit sins and errors. People can also see and talk to other humans, whereas contact with God is less tangible. Although many try to communicate with God through prayer, not everyone prays. Attempts to hear from God are likely to be even more rare, and these perceived messages (by healthy, nonpsychotic individuals) may arrive in ways that seem fuzzy and prone to distortion—through images, visions, thoughts, prophetic words, decontextualized scripture verses, or presumably God-ordained events.

Although we are not aware of empirical data on these issues, it seems likely that the aforementioned ways in which monotheists view God should affect their means of resolving anger toward God. For example, seeing God's power as unlimited may make people angry toward God for not preventing disasters; however, it may also make them wary about expressing negative feelings toward God out of fear of retribution—particularly if they are convinced of God's power but are not convinced of God's benevolence toward them. Seeing God as holy implies that believers must convince themselves that God did not actually commit a wrongdoing. This condition differs markedly from those of interpersonal forgiveness, in which people typically hold offenders accountable for wrongdoing. Not being able to talk with God face to face is likely to raise barriers to understanding, barriers that offended parties may need to surmount through their own efforts (e.g., prayer, study of scripture, reflection, or seeking clues in the external world).

When people strive to be close to God, they may need to engage in considerable mental effort to find explanations and attributions that help to resolve their anger. If they are not willing to turn away from God, they must find other solutions that satisfy them. The popular literature suggests some ways of reframing. For example, some people frame suffering as a tool for refining character (e.g., Arthur, 1997; Wilkinson, 2001). Others blame Satan, evil forces, or the fallen nature of humankind for suffering, rather than blaming God. Some propose that God actually suffers along with people or on their behalf (e.g., Moon, 1999), with perhaps the most dramatic case being the atoning death of Christ on the cross in Christianity. Others argue that the need for free will opens the door to suffering and evil, and God may not choose or be able to prevent suffering for this reason (e.g., Kushner, 1981; McCloskey, 1987). Some might find comfort in believing that justice will be restored in the afterlife (McCloskey, 1987). Others contend that because human perspectives are so limited in comparison with God's, there are many mysterious aspects of God's character and plans that humans cannot comprehend; therefore, we must accept a certain degree of mystery while trusting in God's infinite wisdom, love, and power (Jeffress, 2000; Moon, 1999;

Yancey, 1988). In our current research, we are trying to assess some of these forms of appraisal using empirical tools.

Cognitive gymnastics may not be the most effective way to resolve anger toward God. Experiential tools might also prove helpful. For example, some authors have argued for the importance of first acknowledging—and perhaps communicating—one's negative feelings toward God (e.g., Novotni & Petersen, 2001, Smith, 1997; Zornow, 2001). This might be accomplished through techniques such as prayer, journaling, writing letters to God (Murray-Swank, 2003), or empty-chair techniques in which people imagine themselves talking with God (e.g., Smith, 1997). Individuals from Judeo-Christian traditions might also meditate on holy texts written by fellow sufferers, such as the Hebrew Psalmists, as a way of facilitating the process of "crying out" to God (see Zornow, 2001, for an intervention based on this technique).

Tools to rebuild a sense of trust and closeness to God might include use of contemplative prayer, worship, imagery, or meditation on sacred texts that emphasize God's love and power. Some preliminary data support the notion that eliciting imagery of unconditional love, caring, and acceptance from God can help to reduce anger toward God (Exline, 2004; see also Murray-Swank, 2003). In Charismatic Christian circles, some believers might also turn to supernaturally based techniques involving inner healing or deliverance from evil forces (see Exline & Rose, in press, for a discussion). Other techniques might be more interpersonal, as in the form of healing therapeutic relationships. Finally, to the extent that God images indeed reflect parental images (Rizzuto, 1979), working to forgive one's parents might be a helpful starting point for resolving anger toward God (Bliss, 2003). Each of these techniques merits empirical attention, and there are doubtless many other useful techniques available that are not mentioned here.

NEW RESEARCH DIRECTIONS NEEDED IN THIS AREA

We see the empirical study of anger toward God as a rich and largely unexplored frontier. The field is currently wide open, with a great need for studies on virtually every aspect of the topic. Future studies should tap more diverse forms of stressors (e.g., natural disasters, accidents, wartime atrocities, crime, problems in fertility and pregnancy, serious illness, and injury). It is also crucial to study samples that are diverse in terms of age, culture, and religion. There should be an advancement in methodology that includes longitudinal and experimental designs. For example, one might follow participants over a period of years to determine (a) how their perceived relationships with God (including anger) shift over time, (b) predictors of such shifts, and (c) consequences of such shifts for mental, physical, and spiritual well-being. From an applied perspective, it is very important to begin to evaluate empirically the effectiveness of various techniques for managing anger toward God. For example, laboratory-based research could examine the physiological effects of expressing versus suppressing anger toward God, whereas a controlled clinical trial could be used to evaluate an intervention.

RELEVANCE FOR CLINICAL AND APPLIED INTERVENTIONS

The topic of anger toward God would seem to be an extraordinarily ripe area for the development of interventions. This seems especially true given the recent attention to spiritually oriented treatments and the recent burst of interpersonal forgiveness interventions. We are aware of some recent interventions that address anger toward God (see, e.g., Murray-Swank, 2003; Novotni & Petersen, 2001; Zornow, 2001), and there are doubtless others of which we are unaware. There seems to be considerable room for development and empirical evaluation in this area. Interpersonal forgiveness interventions might incorporate themes related to anger toward God, and stand-alone interventions might also be created to focus specifically on this issue. Interventions that focus on anger toward God should probably also include some emphasis on receiving forgiveness from God, because the two issues are likely to be intertwined for many people.

Development of interventions should provide a natural opportunity to collaborate with religious professionals, such as pastoral counselors, theologians, chaplains, and members of the clergy. Relative to the typical psychologist, religious professionals are likely to have greater experience in dealing with issues involving anger toward God. Although our need to focus on empirical work in this chapter prevented us from delving into theological and religious works on suffering and anger toward God, such writings do exist and should not be overlooked. An interdisciplinary perspective seems highly appropriate for research and intervention on the theme of anger toward God, especially given the inherently theological and pastoral nature of the topic.

As a cautionary note, it seems that intervening when a person is angry with God requires sensitivity and a keen sense of ethics. If a person's faith is slipping, as we found in some cases, who should provide counsel? Should a religious leader or counselor try to bolster a flagging faith? Should an atheist hasten the slippage and help a person feel comfortable with losing faith? Should one attempt neutrality, which might be impossible to attain? These ethical and moral issues are contextualized by the personal experience of the struggler, and the counselor must accurately read what is in the client's best interests. These are difficult issues—not for the glib or the faint-hearted. Yet there are desperate needs in this area to help struggling people, and interventionists need to identify and address the issues thoughtfully.

PERSONAL THEORETICAL PERSPECTIVES ON THE FIELD

We see anger toward God as an exciting and largely untapped area in which to conduct research. In the past decade, much of the research on forgiveness has emphasized its secular and interpersonal sides. Research to date has revealed many of the basic processes behind transgression and forgiveness. However, given the importance of anger toward God in many people's lives, it seems like an appropriate time to devote attention to this important (but often taboo) topic.

One of the authors (J. E.) became involved in this work through two different avenues: one line of research in interpersonal forgiveness and another emphasizing religious and spiritual struggles. After she and her colleagues published a small correlational study on anger toward God (Exline et al., 1999), their work received an unusually high amount of media attention for what they viewed as a modest scientific contribution. There seems to be a good deal of public interest in the topic. In conversations with others, we find that the religiously devout are often intrigued (and sometimes shocked) by this line of research. Because of the taboo nature of anger toward God, many people with strong faith commitments rarely have opportunities to discuss it. Some welcome the opportunity. Atheists and agnostics have also expressed considerable interest in the topic, with many using it as a launching pad to discuss their own religious and spiritual struggles.

The other author (A. M.) became involved in this work by first looking at the opposite side of the coin: receiving forgiveness from God and its relationship to one's ability to forgive the self. Recent correlational data have demonstrated a link between self-forgiveness and feeling forgiven by God for an incident where participants felt they might have offended God (Cafaro & Exline, 2002). Believing that one has been forgiven by God and accepting God's forgiveness were both positively correlated with self-forgiveness. Current research (Martin, 2004) is investigating the effects of religiously oriented mini-interventions—such as letter writing to God and imagery—on one's ability to accept God's forgiveness. We imagine that accepting God's forgiveness may help people to realize their innate worth as humans and may encourage them to view themselves in a more loving, compassionate, and forgiving way. Because anger toward God often co-occurs with a belief that God is angry toward one, we propose that future research and interventions on anger toward God should include elements that focus on receiving forgiveness from God.

Given the amount of public interest in anger toward God and the potential for unique contributions to both basic science and intervention, we are enthusiastic about continuing to pursue research in this area. We encourage others to do so as well, and we are particularly eager to encourage collaborations between empiricists, clinicians, and religious professionals.

Also, for those who are interested in directly participating in studies on this topic (or know others who might be interested), please note that we are currently developing online studies on anger toward God and spiritual struggles to run from our Web site. At the time of this writing, the Web site address is as follows: http://www.cwru.edu/artsci/pscl/faculty/exline/exline3.htm.

CONCLUSIONS

Individuals can experience anger not only toward one another but also toward God. Although empirical research on this topic is in its infancy, existing data suggest parallels between anger toward God and interpersonal anger. For example, people become angry (toward other people or God) when they experience or witness serious injustices, especially when they do not feel repaid, when they feel entitled to repayment, and when there is no preexisting close relationship to serve as a buffer. The consequences of anger toward God are not yet well understood, but there is some evidence suggesting the potential for spiritual, psychological, and physical health effects. Once people become angry toward God, it appears that a majority of them resolve the anger. However, the processes behind this resolution are not yet understood.

The prospect of anger toward God raises thorny theological and psychological issues, and the topic is one that many people consider taboo. Given the prevalence of anger toward God, the level of public interest in the findings, and the prospect for creative interdisciplinary and clinical work, we see the topic of anger toward God as a fruitful and exciting area for future research.

REFERENCES

Altemeyer, B., & Hunsberger, B. (1997). *Amazing conversions: Why some turn to faith and others abandon religion.* Amherst, NY: Prometheus.

Arthur, K. (1997). *As silver refined: Learning to embrace life's disappointments.* Colorado Springs, CO: WaterBrook.

Beit-Hallahmi, B., & Argyle, M. (1975). God as a father projection: The theory and the evidence. *British Journal of Medical Psychology, 48,* 71–75.

Benson, P. L., & Spilka, B. (1973). God image as a function of self-esteem and locus of control. *Journal for the Scientific Study of Religion, 13,* 297–310.

Bliss, P. (2003). *Debt-canceling: Forum on forgiveness.* Unpublished workshop materials, The City Mission, Cleveland, OH.

Boon, S. D., & Sulsky, L. M. (1997). Attributions of blame and forgiveness in romantic relationships: A policy-capturing study. *Journal of Social Behavior and Personality, 12,* 19–44.

Brenner, R. R., (1980). *The faith and doubt of holocaust survivors.* New York: The Free Press.

Cafaro, A., & Exline, J. (2002, March). *Correlates of self-forgiveness after offending God.* Poster session presented at the Midwinter Conference on Spirituality, Baltimore.

Campbell, W. K., Bonacci, A. M., Shelton, J., Exline, J. J., & Bushman, B. J. (2004). Psychological entitlement: Interpersonal consequences and validation of a new self-report measure. *Journal of Personality Assessment, 83,* 29–45.

Childs, R. E. (1985). Maternal psychological conflicts associated with the birth of a retarded child. *Maternal-Child Nursing Journal, 14,* 175–182.

Cook, J. A., & Wimberley, D. W. (1983). If I should die before I wake: Religious commitment and adjustment to the death of a child. *Journal for the Scientific Study of Religion, 22,* 222–238.

Darby, B. W., & Schlenker, B. R. (1982). Children's reactions to apologies. *Journal of Personality and Social Psychology, 43,* 742–753.

Davidson, L. L. (2001). Forgiveness and attachment in college students. *Dissertation Abstracts International: Section B: The Sciences and Engineering, 61*(11-B), 6129.

Emmons, R. A. (1987). Narcissism: Theory and measurement. *Journal of Personality and Social Psychology, 52,* 11–17.

Exline, J. J. (2002a, August). *Rifts and reconciliation between humans and God: An overview.* Presentation at an annual meeting of the American Psychological Association, Chicago.

Exline, J. J. (2002b). Stumbling blocks on the religious road: Fractured relationships, nagging vices, and the inner struggle to believe. *Psychological Inquiry, 13,* 182–189.

Exline, J. J. (2004, March). Anger toward God: A brief overview. In E. L. Worthington, Jr. (Chair), *Current basic and applied research on forgiveness.* Symposium presented at the annual meeting of the Christian Association for Psychological Studies, St. Petersburg, FL.

Exline, J. J., Baumeister, R. F., Bushman, B. J., Campbell, W. K., & Finkel, E. J. (2004). Too proud to let go: Narcissistic entitlement as a barrier to forgiveness. *Journal of Personality and Social Psychology, 87,* 894–912.

Exline, J. J., & Bushman, B. J. (2004). *Anger toward others versus God: A comparison of predictors, consequences, and means of resolution.* Unpublished manuscript, Case Western Reserve University.

Exline, J. J., Fisher, M., Rose, E., & Kampani, S. (2004). *The emotional side of unbelief: Links between anger toward God and decreased belief in God.* Unpublished manuscript, Case Western Reserve University.

Exline, J. J., & Rose, E. (in press). Religious and spiritual struggles. In R. F. Paloutzian & C. Park (Eds.), *Handbook of the psychology of religion and spirituality.* New York: Guilford Press.

Exline, J. J., Yali, A. M., & Lobel, M. (1999). When God disappoints: Difficulty forgiving God and its role in negative emotion. *Journal of Health Psychology, 4,* 365–379.

Fincham, F. D., Paleari, F. G., & Regalia, C. (2002). Forgiveness in marriage: The role of relationship quality, attributions, and empathy. *Personal Relationships, 9,* 27–37.

Finkel, E. J., Rusbult, C. E., Kumashiro, M., & Hannon, P. (2002). Dealing with betrayal in close relationships: Does commitment promote forgiveness? *Journal of Personality and Social Psychology, 82,* 956–974.

Fitchett, G. (1999a). Screening for spiritual risk. *Chaplaincy Today, 15*(1), 2–12.

Fitchett, G. (1999b). Selected resources for screening for spiritual risk. *Chaplaincy Today, 15*(1), 13–26.

Fitchett, G., Rybarczyk, B. D., & DeMarco, G. A. (1999). The role of religion medical rehabilitation outcomes: A longitudinal study. *Rehabilitation Psychology, 44,* 333–353.

Hall, T. W. (2004). *Relational spirituality: Implications of the convergence of attachment theory, interpersonal neurobiology, and emotional information processing.* Unpublished manuscript, Biola University, Los Angeles.

Hall, T. W., & Edwards, K. J. (2002). The Spiritual Assessment Inventory: A theistic model and measure for assessing spiritual development. *Journal for the Scientific Study of Religion, 41,* 341–357.

Jeffress, R. (2000). *When forgiving doesn't make sense.* Colorado Springs, CO: WaterBrook.

Kampani, S., & Exline, J. J. (2002, August). *Can unbelievers be angry at God?* Presentation at the annual meeting of the American Psychological Association, Chicago, IL.

Kirkpatrick, L. A. (1998). God as a substitute attachment figure: A longitudinal study of adult attachment style and religious change in college students. *Personality and Social Psychology Bulletin, 24,* 961–973.

Kirkpatrick, L. A. (1999). Attachment and religious representations and behavior. In J. Cassidy, & P. R. Shaver (Eds.), *Handbook of attachment: Theory, research, and clinical applications* (pp. 803–822). New York: Guilford Press.

Kushner, H. S. (1981). *When bad things happen to good people.* New York: Avon Books.

Lawson, R., Drebing, C., Berg, G., Vincellette, A., & Penk, W. (1998). The long-term impact of child abuse on religious behavior and spirituality in men. *Child Abuse and Neglect, 22,* 369–380.

Luebbert, M. C. (2000). Attachment, psychosocial development, shame, guilt, and forgiveness. *Dissertation Abstracts International: Section B: The Sciences and Engineering, 60*(8-B), 4234.

Martin, A. (2004). *Facilitating self-forgiveness through religiously oriented interventions.* Unpublished manuscript. Cleveland, OH: Case Western Reserve University.

McCloskey, P. (1987). *When you are angry with God.* New York: Paulist Press.

McCullough, M. E., Emmons, R. A., Kilpatrick, S. D., & Mooney, C. N. (2003). Narcissists as "victims": The role of narcissism in the perception of transgressions. *Personality and Social Psychology Bulletin, 29,* 885–893.

McCullough, M. E., Fincham, F. D., & Tsang, J. (2003). Forgiveness, forbearance, and time: The temporal unfolding of transgression-related interpersonal motivations. *Journal of Personality and Social Psychology, 84,* 540–557.

McCullough, M. E., Rachal, K. C., Sandage, S. J., Worthington, E. L., Jr., Brown, S. W., & Hight, T. L. (1998). Interpersonal forgiving in close relationships II: Theoretical elaboration and measurement. *Journal of Personality and Social Psychology, 75,* 1586–1603.

Mickley, J. R., Pargament, K. I., Brant, C. R., & Hipp, K. M. (1998). God and the search for meaning among hospice caregivers. *Hospice Journal, 13*(4), 1–17.

Moon, G. W. (1999). "Forgiving" God: A matter of heart over head. *Marriage and Family: A Christian Journal, 2,* 177–185.

Murray-Swank, N. A. (2003). *Solace for the soul: An evaluation of a psycho-spiritual intervention for female survivors of sexual abuse.* Unpublished doctoral dissertation, Bowling Green State University.

Nielsen, M. E., & Fultz, J. (1995). Further examination of the relationships of religious orientation to religious conflict. *Review of Religious Research, 36,* 369–381.

Novotni, M., & Petersen, R. (2001). *Angry with God.* Colorado Springs, CO: Piñon.

Ohbuchi, K., Kameda, M., & Agarie, N. (1989). Apology as aggression control: Its role in mediating appraisal of and response to harm. *Journal of Personality and Social Psychology, 56,* 219–227.

Pargament, K. I. (1997). *The psychology of religion and coping.* New York: Guilford Press.

Pargament, K. I. (2002). The bitter and the sweet: An evaluation of the costs and benefits of religiousness. *Psychological Inquiry, 13,* 168–181.

Pargament, K. I., Koenig, H. G., Tarakeshwar, N., & Hahn, J. (2001). Religious struggle as a predictor of mortality among medically ill elderly patients: A two-year longitudinal study. *Archives of Internal Medicine, 161,* 1881–1885.

Pargament, K. I., Murray-Swank, N., Magyar, G. M., & Ano, G. G. (2004). Spiritual struggle: A phenomenon of interest to psychology and religion. In W. R. Miller & H. Delaney (Eds.),

Judeo-Christian perspectives on psychology: Human nature, motivation, and change (pp. 245–268). Washington, DC: American Psychological Association.

Pargament, K. I., Smith, B. W., Koenig, H. G., & Perez, L. (1998). Patterns of positive and negative religious coping with major life stressors. *Journal for the Scientific Study of Religion, 37,* 710–724.

Pargament, K. I., Zinnbauer, B. J., Scott, A. B., Butter, E. M., Zerowin, J., & Stanik, P. (1998). Red flags and religious coping: Identifying some religious warning signs among people in crisis. *Journal of Clinical Psychology, 54,* 77–89.

Rizzuto, A. M. (1979). *The birth of the living God: A psychoanalytic study.* Chicago: University of Chicago Press.

Smedes, L. B. (1984). *Forgive and forget: Healing the hurts we don't deserve.* New York: Simon & Schuster.

Smith, C., & Exline, J. J. (2002, August). *Effects of homelessness on a person's perceived relationship with God.* Presentation at the annual meeting of the American Psychological Association, Chicago, IL.

Smith, R. F., Jr. (1997). *Sit down, God. . . . I'm angry.* Valley Forge, PA: Judson Press.

Tsang, J-A., McCullough, M. E., & Hoyt, W. T. (in press). Psychometric and rationalization accounts for the religion-forgiveness discrepancy. *Journal of Social Issues.*

Vergote, A., & Tamayo, A. (Eds.). (1981). *The parental figures and the representation of God: A psychological and cross-cultural study.* The Hague: Mouton.

Wilkinson, B. (2001). *Secrets of the vine.* Sisters, OR: Multnomah Press.

Witvliet, C. V. O., Worthington, E. L., Jr., Wade, N. G., & Berry, J. W. (2002, April). *Physiological reactivity to apology and restitution.* Paper presented at a meeting of the Society of Behavioral Medicine, Washington, DC.

Worthington, E. L., Jr. (2003). *Forgiving and reconciling: Bridges to wholeness and hope.* Downers Grove, IL: InterVarsity Press.

Worthington, E. L., Jr., Berry, J. W., & Parrott, L. III. (2001). Unforgiveness, forgiveness, religion, and health. In T. G. Plante & A. Sherman (Eds.), *Faith and health* (pp. 107–138). New York: Guilford Press.

Yancey, P. (1988). *Disappointment with God: Three questions no one asks aloud.* New York: HarperCollins.

Zechmeister, J. S., & Romero, C. (2002). Victim and offender accounts of interpersonal conflict: Autobiographical narratives of forgiveness and unforgiveness. *Journal of Personality and Social Psychology, 82,* 675–686.

Zornow, G. B. (2001). *Crying out to God: Prayer in the midst of suffering.* Unpublished manuscript, Evangelical Lutheran Church in America, Chicago, IL.

Part Two

METHODS OF STUDYING FORGIVENESS

Chapter Seven

Forgiveness as Change

Michael E. McCullough
Lindsey M. Root

Imagine for a moment that instead of being interested in forgiveness, you are interested in the athletic performance of mountain climbers. One morning, five climbers are dropped by helicopter at random points between 1,000 and 5,000 feet above sea level. They climb for the next 12 hours. Your climbers are carrying altimeters that record their altitude at the beginning and at the end of the 12-hour period. At the end of the observation period, you want to figure out how much each of your climbers progressed. What would you do with the available data to get an answer?

People are quite accustomed to this sort of problem so most probably would not consider the assumptions involved in solving it. First, one usually assumes that we know each climber's altitude when the 12-hour period begins and ends, which is only possible if the stopwatch and the altimeter readings are somehow coordinated. One usually assumes that the altimeters measure with perfect reliability, but if these altitude measurements were accurate only to ± 500 feet, one would have to doubt an apparent 500-foot gain in altitude. Fortunately, measurement error in altimeters is small, relative to the gains that our hikers are likely to be making, so we are probably safe to assume that measurement error is only trivially different from zero.

We must also remember that our five climbers start out at different altitudes on the mountain; therefore, we cannot use their final altitudes as a proxy for progress up the mountain. Therefore, we must subtract their starting altitudes from their final altitudes. In fact, when we plot a straight line between each climber's starting and ending altitudes, as in Figure 7.1, we can easily see why this is important. Three climbers appeared to make some progress; the climber who began at the highest altitude seemed to make no progress whatsoever during the 12-hour period; and the climber with the lowest altitude at the end of the 12-hour period actually appeared to be climbing in the wrong direction!

So imagine that we decide to ignore their differing starting points and instead use their final altitudes as proxies for progress. This would give us a greatly distorted impression of each hiker's progress. We might begin correlating traits such as their body weights, physical fitness, prior food intake, or other characteristics with their final altitudes, but these correlations would tell us nothing about the traits associated with

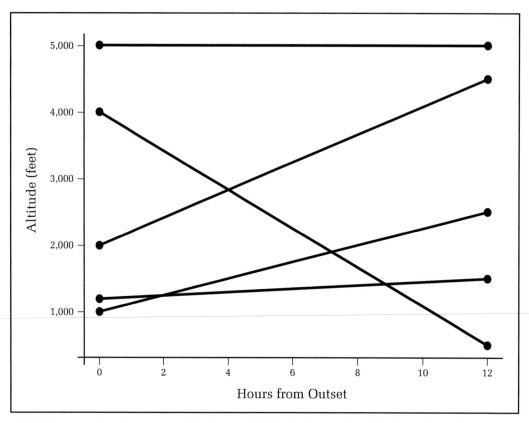

FIGURE 7.1. Altitudes of five climbers at the beginning and end of a 12-hour observation period.

our climbers' progress. To study change in altitude or correlates of change in altitude, we need to know where each individual started on the mountain.

Researchers who study forgiveness and helping professionals are in similar positions to those of the researchers or professionals who wish to study or improve the five climbers' performance. Just as performance researchers and professionals cannot determine how much altitude our climbers gained by simply consulting the altimeter readings at the end of the 12-hour period, researchers and professionals interested in forgiveness cannot learn how much an individual has forgiven a transgressor by simply measuring how the individual feels toward a transgressor at any given time. Yet much of forgiveness research to date has interpreted cross-sectional differences in the forgiveness equivalent of "altitude" as "changes in altitude."

This chapter was written to introduce readers to modern methods for studying change with longitudinal data collected on multiple individuals (sometimes called *panel data*) that permit explicit models of forgiveness as change.

PERSONAL ASSUMPTIONS ABOUT FORGIVENESS

Researchers have defined forgiveness in different ways. For example, Enright, Gassin, and Wu (1992) defined *forgiveness* as "the overcoming of negative affect and judgment toward the offender, not by denying ourselves the right to such affect and judgment, but by endeavoring to view the offender with compassion, benevolence, and love" (p. 101). Exline and Baumeister (2000) defined *forgiveness* as the "cancellation of a debt" by "the person who has been hurt or wronged" (p. 133). Finally, McCullough, Worthington, and Rachal (1997) defined *forgiveness* as "the set of motivational changes whereby one becomes (a) decreasingly motivated to retaliate against an offending relationship partner; (b) decreasingly motivated to maintain estrangement from the offender; and (c) increasingly motivated by conciliation and goodwill for the offender, despite the offender's hurtful actions" (pp. 321–322).

Despite the obvious differences among such definitions, they are all based on the assumption that forgiveness involves prosocial change regarding a transgressor on the part of the transgression recipient. Most theorists concur that when people forgive, their responses (i.e., thoughts, feelings, behavioral inclinations, or actual behaviors) toward a transgressor become more positive and/or less negative. This point of consensus led McCullough, Pargament, and Thoresen (2000) to propose that *intraindividual prosocial change toward a transgressor* is a foundational and uncontroversial feature of forgiveness. We assume this to be true as well.

REVIEW OF THE THEORETICAL AND EMPIRICAL LITERATURE

Several models for studying forgiveness as change are available. Change is a long-standing problem in social sciences research, and tremendous progress has been made in the methods used to study change in human systems. We will review some of what we have learned from some of these approaches and describe some of their strengths and weaknesses. We will also address some common practical questions about using these methods. We close by introducing two models for studying change that may be useful for future work on forgiveness.

Cross-Sectional Approach to Studying Change

Research on forgiveness of specific transgressors received a big push forward with the development of several self-report questionnaires (e.g., McCullough et al., 1998; Subkoviak, Enright, Wu, & Gassin, 1995; Wade, 1990). Such measures prompt respondents to think of a single transgressor who has hurt them in the past, then to answer questions that assess their current thoughts and feelings about the transgressor (e.g., "I want to get even with him/her" vs. "I have overcome my resentment toward him/her"). Researchers often aggregate participants' responses to these items and interpret the scores as measures of how much the individuals have forgiven their various transgressors. These individual differences can then be correlated with characteristics that might influence forgiveness or outcomes that forgiveness might influence.

This approach is problematic. Using a single measurement to assess forgiveness is analogous to using our climbers' altitudes at the end of the 12 hours to determine their progress. This is because some individuals are more deeply wounded and, thus, have more to forgive. Like our climbers, people who have been harmed begin the climb at different places. A few years ago, our group began looking for research approaches that could better depict forgiveness as change.

Two-Wave Panel Model

The simplest model that permits one to observe change is a two-wave panel design in which people complete measures of their thoughts, feelings, emotions, or behaviors regarding a transgressor (i.e., measures traditionally conceptualized as "forgiveness" scales) on two different occasions. Each individual's Time 1 score can be subtracted from or covaried out of his or her Time 2 score to create a value representing the individual's net change between the two time points. This method statistically equates individuals by removing between-persons differences at Time 1. This is the approach one would likely use to ascertain the progress of our five climbers. Our climbers did not begin at the same altitude, but by subtracting or statistically controlling for initial differences, we can pretend that they did. McCullough and colleagues (McCullough, Bellah, Kilpatrick, & Johnson, 2001) used a two-wave panel model to examine vengefulness and rumination as correlates of forgiving. By computing change scores for individuals who completed measures of forgiveness on two occasions, the researchers found that people with high scores on a self-report measure of their vengeful behaviors and their attitudes regarding revenge experienced less reduction in their revenge motivation in the months after an interpersonal transgression than did people with lower scores. They also found that people who experienced reduced avoidance and revenge motivations regarding a transgressor also tended to experience reduced ruminative cognition and reduced effort to suppress those cognitions.

Researchers often use two-wave panel designs to evaluate forgiveness interventions to improve statistical power, but apparently not because they believe it is a better representation of forgiveness. Two-wave panel designs are certainly better than using cross-sectional individual differences to measure forgiveness, but they still have drawbacks. First, researchers using a two-wave design would typically measure people who had been hurt at some point in the past twice (possibly with random assignment to an experimental condition between the two measurements) and compute change scores. In such a design, the only values of time attached to the two scores are values representing their placement in the research design, not values that have psychological meaning (i.e., the amount of time that had passed since the transgression occurred).

Second, by using pre- and post-differences to approximate forgiveness, one necessarily assumes that any given individual changes at a constant rate: Like cannon balls fired into the sky at different angles on a planet with no gravity, the two-wave design assumes that an individual's rate of change stays the same forever and, therefore, can be estimated with fidelity from any two given points in his trajectory. One might not want to assume this, but it is impossible to do otherwise because the most rational trajectory between two points is a straight line.

A third problem with the two-wave design is that true change cannot be separated from measurement error. With our five climbers, this probably is not a problem because our altimeters have low measurement error; however, when using self-reports, one is not so fortunate.

Multilevel Linear Growth Models

The limitations of the two-wave panel model can be addressed with methods called *multilevel linear growth models* (also called *hierarchical linear models, mixed models*, or *random coefficient models*). These models are called *multilevel, hierarchical*, or *mixed* because they accommodate a nested data structure—for example, the data structure that arises when multiple measurements are obtained from each of several individuals. These models can be tested with various software packages, including SPSS, SAS, HLM, MLWin, and R, as well as various programs for structural equation modeling, but our focus is on the models themselves and what they can teach us about forgiveness. For a fuller examination of mixed models for analyzing longitudinal data, see Bryk and Raudenbush (2002) and Nezlek (2001).

We can use these models if we change our plan for data collection in two ways: We need to measure participants on three occasions or more; and with each measurement, we must record how much time has passed since each person's transgression occurred. Suppose we have three measures of how vengeful an individual feels toward a transgressor (e.g., the values 3.5, 2.0, and 2.1) from three different occasions (e.g., 2, 10, and 15 days after a transgression). We can write:

$$Revenge_{ij} = \beta_{0j} + \beta_{1j}(Time_{ij}) + r_{ij} \tag{1}$$

In Equation (1), the revenge score of person j (let's call him Jim) at time i is modeled as a function of an intercept β_{0j}, which represents Jim's expected revenge motivation when $Time = 0$ (i.e., just after the transgression) and a rate of change β_{1j}, which represents the rate at which Jim's revenge scores change as a linear function of time. The residual r_{ij} is the deviation of Jim's revenge score at time i from what would be expected, based on his initial revenge status (that is, the revenge score that would be expected when time since the transgression = 0, or β_{0j}) and the rate of linear change in his revenge scores (or β_{1j}). For forgiveness research, this equation does three important things. First, Jim's change in revenge motivation (called *trend forgiveness* for reasons we will describe shortly) is separated from his initial level of revenge motivation. We have separated progress up the mountain from initial altitude. Second, by attaching the amounts of time that elapsed between the transgression and each individual measurement to the revenge scores, time is expressed in a psychologically meaningful metric—the amount of time since Jim was harmed. Third, true change is separated from measurement error. Equation (1) is identified with three data points, and we can estimate the two β parameters (i.e., initial status and rate of change).

If we measure Jim's revenge motivation on a fourth occasion, we can identify a linear model that allows for more complex forms of change:

$$Revenge_{ij} = \beta_{0j} + \beta_{1j}(Time_{ij}) + \beta_{2j}(Time^2_{ij}) + r_{ij} \tag{2}$$

In Equation (2), Jim's revenge score on occasion i results from three parameters: (a) his expected revenge score immediately after the transgression (β_{0j}), (b) the rate of linear change in his revenge scores over the measured interval (β_{1j}), and (c) the rate of quadratic change (also called *curvature*) in his revenge scores over the measured interval (β_{2j}). As in Equation (1), r_{ij} is the deviation of Jim's revenge score at time i from what would be expected, based on his initial revenge status and his rates of linear and quadratic change in revenge scores over the measured interval. By including the coefficient for quadratic change, β_{2j}, Jim's trajectory can possess curvature. If, from this regression, we find that Jim's value for β_{0j} is 3.10, for example, we can conclude that when *Time* = 0 (that is, immediately after the transgression) Jim's revenge motivation score was 3.10. If we find that β_{1j} is, for example, −0.04, we can conclude that Jim's revenge motivation went down, on average, 0.04 scale score units per day. If Jim's value for β_{2j} is positive—say, +0.002—then we conclude that Jim's trajectory was "concave upward," and that the declines in Jim's revenge motivation slowed down, on average, 0.002 scale score units per day. In other words, the rate at which Jim was shedding his revenge motivations decreased over time.

Fixed Effects, Random Effects, and Interindividual Differences in Forgiveness

Equations such as (1) and (2) are called *Level 1* or *within-person* equations because they parameterize the observations at the first level in a multilevel design (i.e., in this example, they explain where the variation among the repeated measures of revenge motivation comes from). Recall that these research designs are called *multilevel designs* because several observations are obtained for each of several individuals. Now suppose that we have five people who have been harmed in the last few days by a transgressor. For each of these individuals, we might estimate Level 1 linear equations of the form of Equation (2), which would yield different estimates for their initial status, linear change, and quadratic change parameters. How should we conceptualize the interindividual variation in these parameter estimates? The simplest way is to model the parameters as the result of expected parameter estimates for the entire sample and person-specific deviations from the expected values. In the language of multilevel models, the expected values of the parameters for the sample are called *fixed effects*, and the person-specific deviations from the expected values are called *random effects*. Person-specific variations in linear change in revenge, for example, can be decomposed according to the following between-persons, or Level 2 model:

$$\beta_{1j} = \gamma_{10} + u_{1j} \qquad (3)$$

In Equation (3), we have expressed Jim's rate of linear change in revenge motivation (β_{1j}) as a function of a fixed effect and a random effect. The fixed effect γ_{10} (often called the *grand mean*) is the expected linear change for the sample, and the random effect u_{1j} is the deviation of Jim's parameter estimate for linear change β_{1j} from the fixed effect γ_{10}. Note that the γ coefficient has two subscripts, the first of which corresponds to the numerical subscript on the β from the Level 1 equation in which it was used. The fixed effect answers the question, "What is the typical degree of linear change that an individual from our sample can be expected to experience?" To answer the question, "To what extent does Jim's degree of forgiveness differ from the 'average' person in the sample?" we simply interpret Jim's random effect u_{1j}. When we consider our sample of individuals as a whole, the variation in random effects is a variance component that can be predicted based on other variables. If we want to know whether a personality trait or some characteristic of the transgression itself is associated with linear reductions in revenge, for example, we can evaluate whether a personality trait or transgression characteristic explains some of the variation among the person-specific estimates for the β_1 parameters. This is equivalent to correlating the trait or transgression characteristic with the random effects because the fixed effect is a constant that does not contribute to between-persons variance. We can write:

$$\beta_{1j} = \gamma_{10} + \gamma_{11}Neuroticism_j + u_{1j} \qquad (4)$$

This decomposes Jim's parameter estimate for linear change into (a) the fixed effect γ_{10}, (b) Jim's score on a self-report measure of *Neuroticism* (which we have centered around the sample mean) multiplied by a parameter γ_{11} that relates *Neuroticism* scores to individual differences in linear change, and (c) a random effect u_{1j}, which now represents variation that cannot be explained by the fixed effect and between-persons differences in *Neuroticism*. If γ_{11} is statistically significant, we can conclude that *Neuroticism* is a significant predictor of individual differences in linear change. If we wish to examine whether a forgiveness intervention is effective, we can create a dummy variable *ForgInt*, for which we assign zero to participants in a control group and 1 to participants in a forgiveness intervention. Then we can write:

$$\beta_{1j} = \gamma_{10} + \gamma_{11}ForgInt_j + u_{1j} \qquad (5)$$

where $ForgInt_j$ = Jim's score on the dummy variable. To examine whether the intervention is particularly efficacious for people low in *Neuroticism*, we can create a product variable *Neur*Int* representing the interaction of *Neuroticism* and the treatment effect, and write:

$$\beta_{1j} = \gamma_{10} + \gamma_{11}ForgInt_j + \gamma_{12}Neuroticism_j + \gamma_{13}Neur*Int_j + u_{1j} \qquad (6)$$

If γ_{13} is statistically significant, we can conclude that the effects of the forgiveness intervention are moderated by *Neuroticism*. As the random effects variance becomes smaller with successive models, we are doing a better job of accounting for interindividual differences in forgiveness.

Our research group has written several papers that used multilevel linear growth models to study forgiveness (Bono & McCullough, 2004; McCullough & Bono, 2004; McCullough, Fincham, & Tsang, 2003). The studies described in those papers involved longitudinal data from undergraduates who had suffered transgressions in the recent past and whom we measured repeatedly for several months. We obtained up to five measurements per person.

The first question we asked was whether the typical person tended to forgive in the months following their transgressions. By examining the fixed effects obtained from running multilevel models as in Equation (1) on repeated measures of people's avoidance, revenge, and benevolence motivations toward their transgressors, we found that the expected rate of reduction in participants' avoidance and revenge motivations was statistically significant. The typical person became less avoidant and vengeful toward his or her transgressor. However, this was not true of benevolence motivations: The fixed effect for linear change in benevolence was not significantly different from zero. This indicates that we can expect undergraduates to become less avoidant and vengeful toward their transgressors as time passes after a transgression but that we cannot expect them to become more benevolent. This difference suggests that it might be worthwhile to maintain a conceptual distinction between the decay of negative motivations and the restoration of positive ones as components of forgiveness (McCullough et al., 2003), because some of these changes can be expected of the typical individual, whereas others cannot.

In the same paper, we examined the extent to which appraisals of transgression severity, empathy for a transgressor, and responsibility attributions influenced interindividual differences in the linear change of avoidance, revenge, and benevolence motivations (McCullough et al., 2003). We were somewhat surprised to find that initial appraisals of how severe transgressions were and participants' feelings of empathy toward their transgressors were not correlated with individual differences in the rates at which avoidance, revenge, and benevolence motivations changed. However, we did find evidence that people who initially made stronger attributions of responsibility experienced steeper increases in benevolence motivations over time. This latter finding implies that attributing responsibility to one's transgressor may set psychological or social processes in motion that facilitate the return of benevolent motivations.

In a more recent paper (McCullough & Bono, 2004), we were more successful in accounting for individual differences in forgiveness using multilevel linear growth models. By adapting a method for modeling longitudinal change in two variables concurrently (Raudenbush, Brennan, & Barnett, 1995), we examined a question that we had addressed earlier using a two-wave panel design (McCullough et al., 2001): To what extent are reductions in avoidance and revenge motivations associated with reductions in rumination about the transgression? In a first study, we found that the correlations of linear changes in avoidance motivation and revenge motivation with longitudinal changes in rumination were rs = .65 and .19, respectively. The revenge-rumination correlation was likely attenuated by a lack of random effects variance for linear change in revenge motivation (i.e., people did not vary much in how much linear change they experienced in revenge motivation). However, we performed the same analyses on a second data set in which there was significant random effects variance for linear changes in revenge, and the correlations of linear change in avoidance motivation and revenge motivation with linear change in rumination were surprisingly strong, rs = .87 and .87, respectively (McCullough & Bono, 2004).

To this point in the chapter, we have described how multilevel linear growth models offer a way to model forgiveness as a process of continuous change that is produced by one or more latent growth parameters (e.g., linear and curvilinear change). Because the trajectories produced by this formulation are continuous trends that operate across the entire measured interval on which they are based, we have called this type of forgiveness *trend forgiveness*. However, the multilevel linear growth model can shed light on another aspect of forgiveness that we have called *temporary forgiveness* (McCullough et al., 2003).

Temporary Forgiveness.   Notice that the Level 1 (or within-persons) equations (Eqs. 1 and 2) that we specified for our multilevel models include a residual term r_{ij}. Jim's residual r at time i is the degree to which his instantaneous TRIM value deviates from what we would expect for Jim at that point in time following the transgression, *given what we know about Jim's initial level of revenge motivation and the way in which his revenge motivation changed continuously* (due to a constant growth rate and a degree of acceleration or deceleration imposed on that growth rate) across the measured interval. These deviations r_{ij} from the expected values, based on Jim's Level 1 parameters, are inevitable because of measurement error and occasion-specific error. However, some of the residual variance in Jim's revenge motivations might reflect meaningful, substantive variations in his motivations regarding his transgressor. That is, Jim might feel more vengeful on one day than on another (even after taking his growth trajectory into account) because he is in a particularly good (or bad) mood that day, has had a particularly good (or bad) interaction with his transgressor, or experiences some other transient change. Such transient changes would likely exert real, though fleeting, effects on Jim's revenge motivations. On days when Jim's measured revenge motivations fall below his regression line, we might say that Jim became *temporarily* less vengeful toward his transgressor, or alternatively, temporarily more forgiving.

In contrast, on days when Jim has more revenge motivation than would be expected based on his parameters for initial status and change, we might say that he has become *temporarily* less forgiving. Thus, the fluctuations of Jim's revenge motivation scores around his trajectory might be thought to reflect, in part, a sort of *temporary forgiveness*—a transient and reversible change in his thoughts, feelings, motivations, or behaviors regarding his transgressor that might also tell us something important about the factors that promote or deter forgiveness.

If we add to our data set a measure of Jim's state negative affect (or NA) for each occasion when we also measured his revenge motivations, we can center each of the NA measures around Jim's mean NA value and write:

$$Revenge_{ij} = \beta_{0j} + \beta_{1j}(Time_{ij}) + \beta_{2j}(Time^2_{ij}) + \beta_{3j}(NA_{ij}) + r_{ij} \tag{7}$$

In (7), the coefficient β_{3j} expresses the strength of the relationship of (a) fluctuations in Jim's *NA* scores around the values that would be expected based on his initial status, rate of linear change, and curvature with (b) fluctuations in Jim's *Revenge* scores around the values that would be expected on the basis of his initial status, rate of linear change, and curvature. We now have a total of four parameters in our Level 1 model. To identify this model, we must measure Jim on at least five occasions (to identify a Level 1 model, the number of observations per person must exceed the number of Level 1 parameters). Also, note that *temporary forgiveness* is entirely independent of *trend forgiveness*. Trend forgiveness is an attribute of persons in transgression situations (that is, some people demonstrate trend forgiveness vis-à-vis a given transgression, whereas others do not, making it a *between-persons* phenomenon) but temporary forgiveness is an attribute of individuals on certain occasions but not on others (i.e., a within-persons phenomenon). There is no parameter for temporary forgiveness—it is an unobservable entity that we detect by accounting for fluctuations of people's scores around their growth trajectories.

Our research group has used this method for modeling temporary forgiveness to investigate several substantive questions. First, we used repeated measures of the degree to which individuals experienced ruminative thoughts about a transgression they had recently incurred to examine whether within-persons variation in rumination was associated with within-persons variation in avoidance and revenge motivations. This was the case, which is consistent with the hypothesis that rumination deters temporary forgiveness (McCullough & Bono, 2004). Moreover, through multilevel mediational analyses (Krull & MacKinnon, 2001), we found that rumination deters temporary forgiveness by making people angrier toward (but not more fearful of) their transgressors. We have used similar methods to shed light on the relationship between temporary forgiveness and psychological well-being (Bono & McCullough, 2004).

The multilevel linear growth model provides several different perspectives from which to ask questions about forgiveness as a process of change. In the following few paragraphs, we address some frequently asked practical questions about using these models to study forgiveness.

How Do Multilevel Models Handle Missing and Unbalanced Data? A virtue of the multilevel approach to conceptualizing forgiveness is that the analytic tools that are available for conceptualizing forgiveness this way are themselves quite forgiving of imperfect data. In traditional repeated measures analysis of variance, if a participant is missing any single datum that is named in the model, the participant's data are deleted listwise. In studies with even modest attrition between any two waves of data collection, listwise deletion can lead to a substantial loss of data. Most multilevel programs use estimation procedures that allow missing data on the outcome variables, compensating for this missingness by relying more heavily on the fixed effects to estimate a given individual's parameters. However, few if any of these software programs can accommodate missing data at the highest level (in this case, Level 2, or the between-persons level). If an individual is missing a score on *Neuroticism* per Equation (4) above, his or her data are still deleted listwise.

Another virtue of multilevel models from a design perspective is that the data need not be balanced (i.e., individuals' observations need not be obtained according to a fixed measurement schedule). If Jim's measurements were taken 2, 10, and 15 days after a transgression, and Julie's were obtained 3, 12, and 20 days following a transgression, most multilevel programs can take these differences into account.

How Many Measurements per Participant Do I Need? This is an important consideration for multilevel models. One should measure participants on at least three occasions. Otherwise, it is not possible to estimate the two growth parameters (initial status and linear change), which seem to us to be the minimum for conceptualizing forgiveness as change. Once this "three-minimum" criterion has been met, our quick answer to the question is "as often as possible for as long as possible," but there are two caveats to add to this quick answer. The first caveat is that oversampling participants may cause fatigue that leads them to stop taking the questions seriously. In our published work, we have endeavored to sample once every 2 weeks, but surely one could sample more frequently than that. We are currently analyzing data from a study in which we measured participants each day for 21 days following a transgression, and we expect to learn some important lessons about sampling rates from that study.

The second caveat is that at some point, people's feelings, thoughts, and motivations toward their transgressors must surely stop changing. Theoretically, one could sample an individual for the rest of his or her life, but at some point, presumably that individual's feelings toward his or her transgressor would stabilize around an asymptote. However, how long this takes is currently unknown. We return to this point below in our discussion of nonlinear models.

How Many Participants Do I Need? Judgments of sample size should be based on considerations of statistical power. The power of these models has been studied extensively (Snijders & Bosker, 1993), and software is available for estimating power (Bosker, Snijders, & Guldemond, 2003). Unfortunately for many research areas, including the forgiveness area, the statistical power for multilevel models is hard to estimate because some of the necessary parameters (including the means, variances, and covariances of the random effects) are unknown, and it would be hard to arrive at a reasonable guess. Precise power calculations notwithstanding, to some extent the lack of power that comes from small N can be offset by collecting a large number of observations for each individual and vice versa, but adding Level 1 observations boosts power only insofar as it assists researchers in developing more precise estimates of each individual's growth parameters. At some point, precision cannot be increased substantially by adding more Level 1 units, and adding participants is the best way to boost power.

When Should I Try to Get Participants Into My Study?   As quickly as possible after the transgression. We have had good success at locating undergraduates within a few days of incurring significant interpersonal transgressions by repeatedly visiting their classes. This is, no doubt, considerably more difficult when working with samples of individuals who have been harmed in extraordinary ways. Nevertheless, taking time seriously is an important, even indispensable, prerequisite for using multilevel analyses to model forgiveness, so researchers should begin measuring participants as soon after their transgressions as possible. When it is not possible to begin data collection relatively quickly after the transgressions occur, researchers should try to obtain highly accurate information about when people's transgressions occurred.

NEW RESEARCH DIRECTIONS NEEDED IN THE AREA

There are two other multilevel methods for modeling longitudinal data that might be useful complements to multilevel linear growth models that we have discussed here. These methods are called *growth mixture models* and *multilevel nonlinear growth models*.

Growth Mixture Models

The multilevel linear growth model rests on the assumption that there is only one type of trajectory for describing every person's pattern of longitudinal change (Muthén, 2001), although there is variation among people's values on the growth parameters. In other words, even if people's forgiveness trajectories do not conform to the same general shape, the (single-class) multilevel linear growth model assumes that they do. Thus, interindividual differences can be discussed only as parametric differences, not qualitative ones.

One can appreciate the tenuousness of this assumption by considering differences in the TRIM trajectories of three hypothetical individuals, all of whom were harmed on Day 0 (see Figure 7.2). Following the transgression, Person A experiences a very high level of revenge motivation regarding the transgressor and maintains this level for the next month. Person B experiences a very low level of revenge motivation

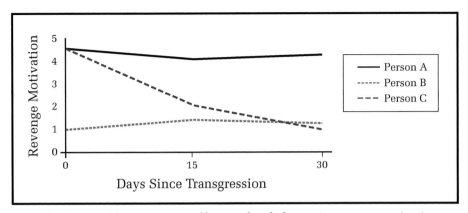

FIGURE 7.2.   Three patterns of longitudinal change in revenge motivation.

and maintains this low level for the next month. Person C, however, begins with a very high level of revenge motivation—as high as that of person A—but over the next month, this level decreases until it is as low as that of Person B.

If we fit linear equations to data points of Persons A, B, and C, we would find that Person A's initial revenge parameter estimate was relatively high, but the parameter estimate for his rate of change over time was negligible (i.e., he changed at the rate of approximately zero units per week). For Person B, we would find a very low initial revenge value, but like person A, those values changed at a rate of approximately zero units per week. One can see that the meaning of lack of decay in one's revenge motivations means something very different if one was not very vengeful at the outset (like Person B) from what it means if one was extremely vengeful at the outset (like Person A). Moreover, only Person C demonstrated initially high levels of revenge motivation that decayed over time; therefore, only the Person C could be said to have forgiven.

This example shows that the reduction in Person C's revenge motivations is meaningful only in light of the fact that he was highly vengeful at the outset. In other words, the significance of Person C's longitudinal trajectory comes from treating his initial status and rate of change in tandem, not by considering them individually. This interpretation is not possible in multilevel linear models that do not examine the overall *shape* of a trajectory, instead using decontextualized estimates of linear change without considering initial values.

In (single-class) multilevel linear models for studying forgiveness, estimates of initial status and linear change are almost always negatively correlated—in many cases considerably so. This is because people with very little revenge or avoidance motivation directly following a transgression have very little negative motivation to dissipate, whereas people with the highest initial levels of revenge and avoidance motivations are precisely the people who have the most to forgive and, therefore, are the ones who can experience steep linear reductions in those motivations over time. This dependence between initial status and linear change makes the predictors and consequences of forgiveness difficult to isolate because variables that are associated positively with forgiveness tend to be correlated negatively with initial status. In other words, decomposing people's TRIMs into initial status and slope estimates that are interpreted independently of each other makes it difficult to know whether a predictor or outcome of change in people's TRIMs is caused by its relationship with initial status, forgiveness, or both.

It would be more informative to conceptualize longitudinal change in terms of a set of qualitatively discrete classes of trajectories (Muthén, 2001). We can imagine one trajectory class that is characterized by initially high levels of revenge motivation and no change over time (we might call this trajectory *chronic unforgiveness*, depicted by Person A in Figure 7.2); a second class that is characterized by low levels of revenge initially with no change over time (we might call this trajectory *chronic forbearance*, depicted by Person B in Figure 7.2); and a third class characterized by high levels of revenge that decrease at a steady rate over time (we might call this trajectory *forgiveness*, as depicted by Person C in Figure 7.2).

Using growth mixture modeling (Muthén, 2001, 2003; Muthén et al., 2002), we can develop an efficient taxonomy of such trajectory classes, then use class memberships as a set of variables to be predicted on the basis of background variables or used as predictors of other (e.g., psychological, physiological, or behavioral) outcomes. Growth mixture models have been used to study several problems related to interindividual differences in intraindividual change, including the developmental pathways in cigarette smoking and alcohol use from adolescence to early adulthood (Tucker, Orlando, & Ellickson, 2003), the development of aggression among at-risk adolescents (Muthén et al., 2002), and even the developmental pathways of religious development from the postcollege years to late adulthood (McCullough, Enders, Brion, & Jain, in press). With these models, it is the entire shape of a trajectory—expressed as a discrete, categorical variable—rather than the growth components of a single trajectory that become variables to be predicted on the basis of background variables and to be used as predictors of distal outcomes. Thus, these models lead to novel interpretations of how forgiveness relates to other variables.

We know of only two statistical programs that can be used for growth mixture models—Mplus (Muthén & Muthén, 1998–2004) and the "Traj" procedure developed for SAS (Jones, Nagin, & Roeder, 2001). In our experience, growth mixture models are more difficult to specify and are more sensitive to start values than are (single-class) multilevel linear growth models, but we think they hold considerable promise for forgiveness research, nonetheless.

Multilevel Nonlinear Growth Models

Linear growth models are "linear" not because they force growth to be modeled as a straight-line function of time but because they express the outcome variable as a linear function of the parameters. In reality, however, many things change in a nonlinear way. Washing out of a drug from the blood stream and radioactive decay both involve nonlinear change, even though a linear equation might provide a good fit to observed data over a bounded interval. In such instances, the linear approximations are approximations nonetheless, and it is difficult to give their parameters meaningful interpretations (e.g., knowing that something decays in a linear fashion over a bounded interval does not explain the mechanism that produces the change).

For this reason, it might be useful in the future for researchers to explore equations for forgiveness in which the outcome variable is expressed as a nonlinear function of time. Multilevel nonlinear growth models such as these can be tested with Proc NLMixed in the SAS system or with nlme in S, S-PLUS, and R (Pinheiro & Bates, 1998). In our limited experience, nlme is more flexible and is less picky about start values than is Proc NLMixed, although SAS is considerably more user-friendly and probably more familiar to most forgiveness researchers.

RELEVANCE FOR CLINICAL AND APPLIED INTERVENTIONS

For the practicing clinician, the take-home message is that forgiveness is a change process and that one should not confuse initial status with change when evaluating where clients are. People who come to professionals with help in forgiving by definition are starting with fairly low levels of forgiveness, so even small amounts of progress should be seen as genuine progress.

PERSONAL THEORETICAL PERSPECTIVES ON THE FIELD AND CONCLUSIONS

Scientific progress often is characterized by a transition from static to dynamic views of phenomena (Boker & Nesselroade, 2002), perhaps because thinking about how systems change allows scientists to develop models that predict larger proportions of a system's possible states. Many scientists are expanding the theoretical reach of the social sciences by explicitly considering how we can model change in human systems, just as physical scientists have broadened the reach of the natural sciences by focusing on changes such as motion, growth, decline, and transitions between discrete states. We think that forgiveness is a concept that is ripe for the kind of theorizing that takes seriously the proposition that forgiveness is a dynamic psychological process that unfolds over time rather than a static property of individuals. Modern methods for the analysis of change that allow scientists to take time seriously in how forgiveness is modeled and measured will aid them in advancing theory and, ultimately, providing the world with tools that people can use to experience forgiveness in their own lives.

REFERENCES

Boker, S. M., & Nesselroade, J. R. (2002). A method for modeling the intrinsic dynamics of intra-individual variability: Recovering the parameters of simulated oscillators in multi-wave panel data. *Multivariate Behavioral Research, 37*, 127–160.

Bono, G., & McCullough, M. E. (2004). *Forgiveness and well-being.* Unpublished manuscript, Coral Gables, FL, University of Miami.

Bosker, R. J., Snijders, T. A. B., & Guldemond, H. (2003). *PINT (Power IN Two-level designs): Estimating standard errors of regression coefficients in hierarchical linear models for power calculations. User's Manual Version 2.1.* The Netherlands: University of Groningen.

Bryk, A. S., & Raudenbush, S. W. (2002). *Hierarchical linear models: Applications and data analysis methods* (2nd ed.). Thousand Oaks, CA: Sage.

Enright, R. D., Gassin, E. A., & Wu, C. (1992). Forgiveness: A developmental view. *Journal of Moral Development, 21*, 99–114.

Exline, J. J., & Baumeister, R. F. (2000). Expressing forgiveness and repentance: Benefits and barriers. In M. E. McCullough, K. I. Pargament, & C. E. Thoresen (Eds.), *Forgiveness: Theory, research, and practice* (pp. 133–155). New York: Guilford Press.

Jones, B. L., Nagin, D. S., & Roeder, K. (2001). A SAS procedure based on mixture models for estimating developmental trajectories. *Sociological Methods and Research, 29*, 374–393.

Krull, J. L., & MacKinnon, D. P. (2001). Multilevel modeling of individual and group level mediated effects. *Multivariate Behavioral Research, 36*, 249–277.

McCullough, M. E., Bellah, C. G., Kilpatrick, S. D., & Johnson, J. L. (2001). Vengefulness: Relationships with forgiveness, rumination, well-being, and the Big Five. *Personality and Social Psychology Bulletin, 27*, 601–610.

McCullough, M. E., & Bono, G. (2004). *How rumination deters forgiveness: Two longitudinal studies.* Unpublished manuscript, Coral Gables, FL, University of Miami.

McCullough, M. E., Enders, C. K., Brion, S. L., & Jain, A. R. (in press). The varieties of religious development in adulthood: A longitudinal investigation of religion and rational choice. *Journal of Personality and Social Psychology,*

McCullough, M. E., Fincham, F. D., & Tsang, J. (2003). Forgiveness, forbearance, and time: The temporal unfolding of transgression-related interpersonal motivations. *Journal of Personality and Social Psychology, 84*, 540–557.

McCullough, M. E., Pargament, K. I., & Thoresen, C. E. (2000). The psychology of forgiveness: History, conceptual issues, and overview. In M. E. McCullough, K. I. Pargament, & C. E. Thoresen (Eds.), *Forgiveness: Theory, research, and practice* (pp. 1–14). New York: Guilford Press.

McCullough, M. E., Rachal, K. C., Sandage, S. J., Worthington, E. L., Jr., Brown, S. W., & Hight, T. L. (1998). Interpersonal forgiving in close relationships. II: Theoretical elaboration and measurement. *Journal of Personality and Social Psychology, 75*, 1586–1603.

McCullough, M. E., Worthington, E. L., Jr., & Rachal, K. C. (1997). Interpersonal forgiving in close relationships. *Journal of Personality and Social Psychology, 73*, 321–336.

Muthén, B. O. (2001). Second-generation structural equation modeling with a combination of categorical and continuous latent variables: New opportunities for latent class/latent growth modeling. In L. M. Collins & A. G. Sayer (Eds.), *New methods for the analysis of change* (pp. 291–322). Washington, DC: American Psychological Association.

Muthén, B. O. (2003). Statistical and substantive checking in growth mixture modeling: Comment on Bauer and Curran. *Psychological Methods, 8*, 369–377.

Muthén, B., Brown, C. H., Masyn, K., Jo, B., Khoo, S. T., Yang, C. C., et al. (2002). General growth mixture modeling for randomized preventive interventions. *Biostatistics, 3*, 459–475.

Muthén, B. O., & Muthén, L. K. (1998–2004). *Mplus user's guide* (3rd ed.). Los Angeles: Muthén & Muthén.

Nezlek, J. B. (2001). Multilevel random coefficient analyses of event- and interval-contingent data in social and personality psychology research. *Personality and Social Psychology Bulletin, 27*, 771–785.

Pinheiro, J. C., & Bates, D. M. (1998). *lme and nlme: Mixed effects methods and classes for S and S-Plus.* Bell Labs, Lucent Technologies, and University of Wisconsin-Madison.

Raudenbush, S. W., Brennan, R. T., & Barnett, R. C. (1995). A multivariate hierarchical model for studying psychological change within couples. *Journal of Family Psychology, 9*, 161–174.

Snijders, T. A. B., & Bosker, R. J. (1993). Standard errors and sample sizes for two-level research. *Journal of Educational Statistics, 18*, 237–259.

Subkoviak, M. J., Enright, R. D., Wu, C., & Gassin, E. A. (1995). Measuring interpersonal forgiveness in late adolescence and middle adulthood. *Journal of Adolescence, 18*, 641–655.

Tucker, J. S., Orlando, M., & Ellickson, P. L. (2003). Patterns and correlates of binge drinking trajectories from early adolescence to young adulthood. *Health Psychology, 22*, 79–87.

Wade, S. H. (1990). The development of a scale to measure forgiveness. *Dissertation Abstracts International, 50*(11-B), 5338.

Chapter Eight

Issues in the Multimodal Measurement of Forgiveness

William T. Hoyt
Michael E. McCullough

Although the recommendation to include multiple indicators of a construct of interest is commonplace in research design texts (e.g., Cook & Campbell, 1979), investigators conducting basic and applied research on forgiveness have typically relied on a single measure of this construct. There are many reasons why forgiveness researchers may fail to use multimodal measurement. Certainly, inclusion of additional questionnaires or other measurement procedures poses a burden to participants as well as researchers. Perhaps investigators simply do not believe that a concomitant benefit to research validity will compensate for this additional burden. In this relatively new research area, selecting multiple indicators that overlap sufficiently to constitute measures of the same underlying construct, but not so much that they are essentially redundant, may pose a challenge. Finally, researchers may avoid including more than one measure of forgiveness because this augmentation to the research design creates challenges at the data analysis phase. Our goal in this chapter is to address each of these challenges. In the sections that follow, we review the rationale for preferring multimodal measurement, provide a conceptual framework to assist researchers and research consumers in evaluating forgiveness measures, and describe common models for data analysis using multiple measures, with illustration of their relevance to the forgiveness domain.

PERSONAL ASSUMPTIONS ABOUT FORGIVENESS

The authors come to forgiveness research from the perspective of counseling psychology, with its emphasis on positive development and enhancing human strengths. Forgiveness is of interest as a human virtue from the perspective of numerous religious and spiritual traditions (McCullough & Snyder, 2000). As scientists, counseling psychologists have typically been sensitive to the importance of environmental and contextual determinants of human behavior, and to the importance of social relationships

109

as an indicator of quality of life (Heppner, Casas, Carter, & Stone, 2000). Because of its relationship-enhancing potential, the capacity for forgiveness may well be an important indicator of both relational and individual health. In this chapter, we consider forgiveness as first and foremost an interpersonal process, with little attention to other aspects of forgiving (e.g., forgiveness of self; forgiveness of God or of inanimate objects or events). We conceptualize interpersonal forgiveness as a transactional process between two individuals. As such, it has multiple determinants, which include characteristics of the forgiver, the transgressor, the relationship, and the offense. As discussed below, this concept has implications for interpretation of scores on forgiveness measures and may provide a rationale in many research contexts for multimodal measurement procedures.

REVIEW OF LITERATURE: CONSTRUCT VALIDITY AND MULTIMODAL MEASUREMENT

The process of construct validation addresses the fundamental question, posed by Cronbach and Meehl (1955): What constructs account for variance in test performance? (p. 282). The use of the plural *constructs* embodies the fundamental insight that scores on any psychological test (or questionnaire, or behavioral rating scale) contain *surplus meaning*—that is, they inevitably reflect systematic variance in one or more characteristics of the respondents, in addition to standing on the construct they are intended to measure. This is easy to see in the case of domain-specific achievement tests. Reliable differences on such tests must reflect reading ability and perhaps differences in proficiency with the item formats, as well as familiarity with the content domain under investigation. These unwanted components of systematic variance, which we refer to as *bias* variance, make interpretation of scores on a test problematic.

Sources of Bias in Forgiveness Measures

In this and the following section, we develop a conceptual framework for exploring bias in forgiveness measures. In the absence of such a framework, investigators are unlikely to be motivated to make use of multiple measures and may fail to make best use of the data from multiple indicators when they do take the trouble to include them in their research designs.

Forgiveness measures (in common with most personality ratings) contain a form of bias not present in ability tests, namely, distortions in ratings due to idiosyncratic characteristics or motives of the rater. These *rater biases* are different for self- and other-ratings. Because most forgiveness measures consist of self-ratings (McCullough, Hoyt, & Rachal, 2000), we focus on self-reports here. Readers interested in biases in ratings of others are referred to previous work in this area (Hoyt, 2000; Hoyt & Kerns, 1999).

Bias in self-ratings has been studied under the rubric of *response sets*—styles of responding that contribute systematic but construct-irrelevant variance to ratings.

Well-known response sets include acquiescence and social desirability. *Acquiescence* variance is characterized by differences in the extent to which people tend to agree that descriptors (regardless of content) apply to themselves. To minimize confounding with acquiescence, many forgiveness measures include at least some reverse-scored items.

Social desirability variance is attributable to differences in the degree to which respondents modify their self-reports so as to make a good (or socially desirable) impression. Social desirability bias contributes more strongly to score variance for attributes that are culturally valued (e.g., intelligence) than for those that are value-neutral (e.g., perfectionism).

Although scholars debate about the validity of measures that purport to control for these biases (McCrae & Costa, 1983; Ones, Viswesvaran, & Reiss, 1996), the important (and uncontroversial) point is that self-reports are contaminated to an unknown degree with construct-irrelevant variance, referred to by Campbell and Fiske (1959) as *method variance*. A corollary is that high correlations between two sets of scores "might be explained as due either to basic trait similarity or to shared method variance" (p. 85), that is, to the tendency to evoke similar biases on the part of respondents. Thus, Campbell and Fiske emphasized the importance of convergent validity across methods (and discriminant validity with measures of different traits by similar methods) as criteria for construct validation.

Multiple Measures Versus Multimodal Measurement

At this point, we can define *multimodal measurement* as inclusion of two or more measures of a construct by methods (or *modes*) of measurement that are different enough to provide unique perspectives on the construct of interest. What constitutes "different enough" methods depends on the research question and will be the subject of detailed consideration in connection with the examples presented below.

As we will see, most of the studies in the forgiveness literature that have employed multiple measures have not been true multimodal studies, because the two (or more) measures (usually self-reports) share bias variance as well as construct-relevant variance. Such multiple-measure, mono-method studies are an improvement over single-measure research designs, in that they may include different facets of the complex forgiveness construct. For example, studies of transgression-related interpersonal motivations (e.g., McCullough & Hoyt, 2002) typically examine increases in benevolence motives and decreases in avoidance and revenge motives. Similarly, Enright's Forgiveness Inventory (EFI; Subkoviak, Enright, Wu, & Gassin, 1995) attempts to measure forgiveness as increases in positive affect, cognition, and behavior regarding a transgression, as well as reductions in negative affect, cognition, and behavior through a set of self-report items. However, measures such as those developed by McCullough and Hoyt (2002), and Enright (Subkoviak et al., 1995) do not do much to eliminate the confounding bias variance, because this variance is probably common to each of the subscales on these measures.

REVIEW OF LITERATURE: WHAT ARE "METHODS" OF MEASUREMENT?

Campbell and Fiske (1959) were intentionally vague in defining *method*, preferring to construe this term broadly to encompass a wide range of measurement procedures (Fiske & Campbell, 1992). Investigators seeking to study method variance have examined both fine and coarse differences in these procedures as sources of variance in personality scores. Many published studies using techniques developed by Campbell and Fiske examine method differences (e.g., different question formats in two self-report measures) that are probably too trivial to constitute different *modes* of measurement, in the sense discussed here.

Our field is at an early stage in its appreciation of the effects of method, and it is not yet possible to give comprehensive guidelines for determining when two methods are different enough to comprise a multimodal assessment of a construct such as forgiveness. The critical consideration is that the variance shared among the two measures should be valid variance, not bias variance. That is, the two measures should share construct-relevant (or *common factor*) variance but contain different sources of method (or *specific factor*) variance. In this section, we suggest two broad categories of measurement differences that could be considered by investigators seeking to use multimodal measurement: the source of the measured data and the level of measurement.

Source Differences

A method factor that is likely to contribute substantially to variance in ratings is the source of the information about forgiveness. Personality psychologists have long been exhorted to collect data from multiple sources (Cattell, 1957). Cattell's enthusiasm for a diversity of data sources has been commemorated with the LOTS acronym, reminding researchers of four broad classes of personality information on: life events data (L data); observational data (O data); test data (T data); and self-reports (S data; John & Benet-Martinez, 2000).

Life events data have the advantage that they are obtained objectively from life records. Although not used, to date, by forgiveness researchers, L data can provide one perspective on forgiveness in some populations. For example, in a study of divorced couples, compliance with alimony payment schedule may be related to level of forgiveness (among other things).

Observational data may be collected in a variety of settings and from a variety of sources. Forgiveness researchers have occasionally used O data—usually from acquaintance ratings of participants' forgivingness. For example, Brown (2003) validated a dispositional measure of forgiveness by documenting convergence with romantic partner ratings. Acquaintances have the advantage of depth of knowledge of the participants, but their ratings can be relatively unreliable because (a) acquaintances may have idiosyncratic interpretations of scale items, which usually cannot be mitigated by rater training; (b) acquaintances are unique to each participant, which increases bias variance; and (c) it is difficult to aggregate ratings across many observers because acquaintances are difficult to recruit (Hoyt, 2000). To our knowledge, no one has made use of O data derived from trained observers, laboratory settings, and/or standardized interaction partners (confederates) to measure forgiveness, although Ripley and Worthington (2002) did use observational ratings of couple interactions to assess the ratio of positive to negative communication behaviors following a forgiveness intervention. These procedures enhance reliability of measurement, at some cost to generalizability of ratings to naturalistic interactions.

Test data are based on laboratory situations that yield objective scores on the variable of interest. T data on forgiveness could be derived from several existing laboratory tests, such as defections in the Prisoner's Dilemma game (Kassinove, Roth, Owens, & Fuller, 2002) or laboratory analogs of aggressive responding in response to a simulated provocation (e.g., Anderson & Bushman, 1997; Bushman & Baumeister, 1998).

Finally, *self-report data* are data from questionnaires (or interviews) in which participants describe their own attitudes or behavior. As already noted, self-reports are by far the most common source of data in forgiveness research. S data are also a common source for other variables that researchers believe are correlated with forgiveness. Correlations between two variables are difficult to interpret when both are measured by self-report because they reflect trait correlations but also (and to an unknown degree) method covariance. To avoid "mono-operation bias" (Cook & Campbell, 1979, p. 65), it behooves forgiveness researchers to consider augmenting their measurement of forgiveness with data from L, O, and T sources.

Levels of Analysis of Forgiveness: Offense, Relationship, and Individual

Although method variance is often described disparagingly as "nuisance" variance or statistical "noise" (e.g., Lubinski & Dawis, 1992), Campbell and Fiske (1959) left open the possibility that methods may be worthy of study in their own right (see also Cronbach, 1995). In the domain of forgiveness research, causal determinants at multiple *levels of analysis* are important for our theoretical understanding of forgiveness yet contribute to variance in forgiveness scores that in some research contexts is irrelevant to the construct of interest.

Forgiveness processes are studied at multiple levels. As a behavior, forgiveness is inherently linked to a particular event or *offense*. A person hurts or offends me in some way, and I react with changes in my feelings, attitudes, and motivations toward him or her. My (eventual) willingness to forgive this transgression is based in part on numerous situation-level details, including the severity of the offense, its intentionality, and the transgressor's willingness to apologize and make amends. Each of these factors contributes to variance in scores on transgression-based measures of forgiveness (McCullough et al., 2000).

Forgiveness may also be studied as a *relational* or *dyadic* process. Some relationships are more forgiving than others, and people's willingness to forgive a particular relationship partner is likely to be at least somewhat consistent across unique offenses that occur within that relationship.

Finally, forgiveness at the *individual* level refers to individual differences in the disposition to forgive that are at least somewhat consistent across relationships and offenses within relationships. The premise underlying the many studies of individual-level correlates of forgiveness (e.g., correlations with measures of personality, psychopathology, or well-being) is that some people are more forgiving (across a variety of relationships and specific transgressions) than are others and that this forgiving disposition is rooted in stable personality traits and has consequences for their mental health.

Considering the appropriate level of analysis is crucial to evaluating the construct validity of forgiveness measures. The *level of measurement* of the variables must correspond to the *level of analysis* of the constructs in the research hypothesis. Scores derived from a different measurement level inevitably contain substantial construct-irrelevant variance. For example, if an investigator hypothesizes that more forgiving couples are likely to be more satisfied and committed, the hypothesis is at the relationship level of analysis. What happens if he or she tests this hypothesis with variables measured at the situational level (i.e., with an offense-specific measure of forgiveness)? Forgiveness scores based on a single transgression would then serve to operationalize relational (or dyadic) forgiveness. But these scores differ from the *typical* forgiveness in the relationship to the extent that, for some or all couples, the specified offense differs from the typical offense for that couple. Any transgression-specific variance in scores, which would be valid variance for research at the level of specific offense, is nuisance variance in the context of the present research hypothesis and reduces the validity of measurement (by reducing the proportion of variance in scores that is attributable to general tendencies to forgive the relationship partner).

To enhance validity in this example, we could aggregate forgiveness scores based on two or more specific offenses. Using these two or more sets of offense-specific forgiveness scores as indicators of relationship-level forgiveness constitutes *multimodal* measurement in the sense described above: These measures share construct-relevant variance (i.e., variance in consistent tendencies to be forgiving or unforgiving toward the partner) but not method variance (i.e., deviations from these stable tendencies attributable to temporal or offense-specific factors). Although the correlation between forgiveness scores over any arbitrarily selected pair of offenses within a relationship is likely to be modest, by aggregating a number of such modestly correlated measures, we may obtain a highly reliable (and valid) composite index of relational forgiveness (Lubinski & Dawis, 1992; see also McCullough & Hoyt, 2002).

Summary of Recommendations

In this section, we have suggested that investigators wishing to use multimodal measurement could think about two different conceptual schemes that represent diverse measurement modes for forgiveness research. One scheme (LOTS) identifies four distinct sources of data on forgiveness; including data from more than one source constitutes multimodal measurement. The other scheme identifies three levels of analysis (individual, relationship, and offense-specific) that are relevant to the study of forgiveness; an alternative strategy is to collect data of multiple types at a lower level of analysis (e.g., relationship-level data with friends, parents, and romantic partner) as a multimodal approach to assessment of forgiveness at a higher level of analysis (e.g., dispositional forgiveness, which should be consistent across these different relationship types). Below, we consider how to work with multimodal data to address questions of interest to forgiveness researchers.

MAKING BEST USE OF MULTIPLE MEASURES: ANALYTICAL STRATEGIES AND EXAMPLE STUDIES

We have already discussed one strategy for using data from multiple measures of forgiveness: aggregation to create a composite variable. This is advantageous because the composite will have a higher proportion of valid variance (and lower proportion of error variance) than its component variables. When component variables are measured by different methods (i.e., in the case of multimodal measurement), the proportion of method variance is also lower in the composite than in its components. A related approach with similar benefits is to treat forgiveness as a latent variable in a structural equation model with two or more measures as multiple indicators. In this section, we present alternatives to conventional aggregation approaches. These may be useful when different aspects of forgiveness are theorized to load on the two (or more) measures or when the measures use different methods, and the role of method variance is of substantive interest. When two or more measures embody different aspects of forgiveness, it can be instructive to analyze them separately, comparing patterns of correlations with criterion variables. When method variance is of substantive interest (Cronbach, 1995), a number of statistical models can be used to explore the role of method in determining ratings of forgiveness. We describe three such models: the multitrait multimethod matrix (MTMM), generalizability theory (GT), and the social relations model (SRM). When possible, we illustrate with an example drawn from the literature on forgiveness.

Extrinsic Convergent Validation: Exploring Patterns of Correlations with Criterion Variables

Fiske (1971) noted that a strong correlation between two measures is necessary but not sufficient evidence of their conceptual equivalence. Fiske recommended that, in addition to reporting convergent validity correlations between two measures thought to assess the same construct, investigators should examine their patterns of *extrinsic convergent validity* (ECV)—that is, their patterns of correlation with criterion variables. When these patterns are highly similar for both measures, a strong argument can be made for empirical equivalence. (See Lubinski, 2004, p. 99, for an example of an argument via ECV analysis for the equivalence of three measures of verbal intelligence.) When two similar measures have different patterns of correlation, this can be important for elaborating the theory of the construct being assessed.

ECV analysis has the virtue that it is methodologically simple (involving straightforward comparison of correlation coefficients) but conceptually powerful. An example of the use of ECV to study forgiveness is the research program by McCullough and colleagues investigating a motivational model of forgiveness.

McCullough et al. (1998) equated forgiveness with decreases in motivation to avoid the perpetrator and to obtain revenge on him or her. McCullough et al. reported avoidance-revenge correlations between .4 and .5 in two samples, and comparable (negative) correlations with a single-item measure of forgiveness. However, subsequent studies revealed different patterns of correlation with relationship satisfaction and commitment in heterosexual couples. Most notably, male partners' revenge (but not avoidance) motives (negatively) predicted their female partners' relationship satisfaction (McCullough et al., 1998). Avoidance and revenge motives were also differentially related to transgression-relevant variables, with avoidance motives more strongly ameliorated by offender apology and victim empathy for the offender than are revenge motives (McCullough et al., 1998). When examined at the individual level of analysis, these motives were linked differentially to broad personality styles, with dispositional avoidance consistently uniquely predicted by neuroticism and dispositional revenge uniquely (negatively) predicted by agreeableness (McCullough & Hoyt, 2002). These findings confirm that, although they share considerable common variance (up to 25%), the avoidance and revenge scales measure distinct dimensions of forgiveness that have different correlates and different implications for relationship partners.

Multitrait Multimethod Matrix

The multitrait multimethod matrix (MTMM; Campbell & Fiske, 1959) has proven to be far and away the most popular tool for examining method variance in psychological measures. However, we do not recommend this method without reservation. Campbell and Fiske's guidelines for analysis are impressionistic rather than quantitative, and alternative procedures for conducting MTMM analyses using confirmatory factor analysis are temperamental, with models often failing to converge (Kenny & Kashy, 1992). Below, we discuss two generalizability-based approaches that we believe have more potential to address methodological and substantive issues for researchers using multimodal measurement.

Generalizability Theory: Decomposing Score Variance

Cronbach's inquiries into the meaning of test scores in the 1940s and 1950s eventually led to the development of another analytic framework for understanding the role of method variance in psychological measures. Although originally conceived as a liberalization of the assumptions of classical reliability theory (Cronbach, Rajaratnam, & Gleser, 1963), generalizability theory (GT) eventually emerged as a broad analytic framework for investigating the generalizability of scores across different measurement conditions, or *facets* (Cronbach, Gleser, Nanda, & Rajaratnam, 1972). As such, GT straddles the conventional boundary between classic reliability and validity theory, and provides a flexible tool for investigating sources of variance that contribute to scores derived from a variety of measurement procedures.

Probably partly as a consequence of its flexibility, GT is underutilized in contemporary psychological research. GT does not lend itself to cookbook "default" applications that are the norm in statistical software packages. Researchers wishing to use these techniques must learn to use a specialized computer application (GENOVA; Crick & Brennan, 1983; free download at http://www.uiowa.edu/~itp/pages/SWGENOVA .SHTML). Although helpful primers are available for using GT to estimate reliability of measurement (e.g., Hoyt & Melby, 1999; Shavelson & Webb, 1991), few attempts have been made to extend GT principles to examine score validity. We here present some initial thoughts on applicability of GT techniques to addressing questions of interest to forgiveness researchers.

In our discussion of levels of analysis for studying forgiveness, we noted that forgiveness occurs in response to discrete offenses but that responses to multiple offenses within a given dyad are likely to show some consistency, such that forgiveness can also be considered as a characteristic of the dyad or relationship. Further, it is likely that a person who is relatively forgiving in one relationship will also be forgiving in others, so that study of forgiveness at the individual (dispositional) level will also be fruitful. McCullough et al. (2000, table 4.1) showed how this three-tiered hierarchy (offenses embedded in streams of dyadic interactions embedded in individuals' responding in a variety of interpersonal contexts) could be modeled as a GT design. For each participant in the proposed study, six offenses are studied. The offenses encompass three of that person's relationships, with two of the offenses having been perpetrated by each of the three relationship partners. The data for the study are the participant's feelings of forgiveness in response to each of the six offenses.

Note that although each of the six measures is a self-report of willingness to forgive, measurement procedures in this research design are multimodal in the sense described above. Scores on each of the six forgiveness measures contain variance attributable to dispositional forgiveness, and the six measures include different subsets of method variance due to relationship partners and situations. McCullough and Hoyt (2002) carried out a version of this research design in two studies, operationalizing relationship as *relationship type* (in Study 1, for example, each participant reported forgiveness of same-sex friend, opposite-sex friend, and romantic partner) and offense as a function of the *severity* of the transgression (so that each participant reported on one severe and one mild offense in each relationship type).

Meaning of Variance Components.   The purpose of the generalizability analysis (in McCullough & Hoyt, 2002) was to *partition variance* in forgiveness ratings into variance attributable to four main factors of interest. The relative size of each variance component reflects the importance of the corresponding determinant of forgiveness. To give a sense of the types of questions that can be addressed in a GT analysis, we first describe the meaning of each variance component for this study design, then present a brief summary of our findings.

Person variance (P) reflects the extent to which forgiveness in response to a given offense is predictable from the victim's general disposition to forgive others (across offense severity and relationship type). If P variance is large, this indicates that people are relatively consistent in their forgivingness across relationships and offenses. If P variance is small, then willingness to forgive is strongly conditioned on relational or situational factors, and we look to the remaining variance components to gauge the relative importance of these factors.

Variance attributable to the *Person × Relationship Type interaction* (PR) reflects the extent to which persons' rank (on forgivingness) differs as a function of relationship type. If PR variance is large, then persons who are most forgiving in one relationship may not be so forgiving in another. (Knowing that someone is very forgiving of her romantic partner, for example, would not help you to predict her forgivingness of a same-sex friend.)

Variance attributable to the *Person × Severity interaction* (PS) reflects the extent to which persons' rank (on forgivingness) differs in response to moderate or severe offenses. If PS variance is large, then people who are the most forgiving of a minor offense may not be the most forgiving of a more severe hurt.

Finally, variance attributable to the three-way interaction (*Person × Relationship × Severity)* is notated *PRS,e* to reflect the limitation that the highest order interaction is confounded with error in any generalizability study. This is because there is only one data point per combination of these three factors, so we cannot separate stable (reliable) variance from random error. Thus, variance attributable to the highest order interaction in any generalizability study is referred to as *residual* variance and reflects variance due to random error, the three-way (in this case) interaction, and interactions with other facets (measurement conditions) not explicitly measured in this research design.

GT analyses also produce variance estimates for the main effects of relationship type and severity (i.e., R and S) and for the interaction of these facets (i.e., RS). These are of theoretical interest as well. The S main effect, for example, will be large if (as expected) people are generally less forgiving of severe offenses than of mild ones. We focus on variance components involving persons (P, PR, PS, and residual) because of their importance for understanding the consistency (or lack thereof) in people's willingness to forgive—that is, the importance of dispositional forgiveness in determining responses to specific offenses.

Summary of Findings. Using the motivational framework described above to measure forgiveness, McCullough and Hoyt (2002) found that persons accounted for 25% and 44% of variance in avoidance and revenge motivation, respectively, in Study 1. Thus, people showed much more consistency in their vengeful motivations than in their avoidant impulses. Relationship type was one factor in this inconsistency (*PR* accounted for 13% of variance in both avoidance and revenge): People who were most forgiving of same-sex friends, for example, were not necessarily most forgiving of romantic partners. *PS* accounted for little variance in either measure (i.e., persons who were relatively forgiving of severe transgressions were also relatively forgiving of mild transgressions) but residual variance was large (37% and 36% for avoidance and revenge, respectively), undoubtedly reflecting, at least in part, other sources of variance in response to single offenses (e.g., apology, intentionality) that were not investigated here.

These findings are important in that they suggest that revenge motivation is more strongly influenced by dispositions (i.e., more consistent across offenses and relationships) than is avoidance motivation. Additional analyses provided guidance for future users of scenario measures, presenting G coefficients (analogous to reliability coefficients) for composites derived from aggregating forgiveness scores across scenarios, and examining congruence between forgiveness scores derived from historical offenses (discussed above) with those from fictional offenses (not described here). By conducting variance partitioning analyses, we learn about the relative importance of various determinants of forgiveness.

Social Relations Model: A Special Case of GT for Round-Robin Designs

A final model useful for analyzing multimodal measures of forgiveness is the social relations model (SRM; Kenny, 1994). Like GT, SRM is a variance partitioning model, with the advantage that it incorporates ratings from both members of a dyad. SRM data must be collected in round-robin format (each person in a group rates each other person), so it is most useful for studying naturally occurring groups, such as friendship groups, roommates, or families. Like GT, SRM requires specialized software (SOREMO; Kenny, 1987; download for a fee at http://users.rcn.com/dakenny/srmp.htm), which may be one reason why it is underused in social and personality research.

To highlight the potential of SRM for studying forgiveness, we present selected findings from a study by Hoyt, Fincham, McCullough, Maio, and Davila (in press; Study 1) who conducted SRM analyses on data from 94 families (father, mother, and daughter in 8th grade), each of whom reported her or his general level of forgiveness to the other two family members.

SRM analyses partition variance in dyadic ratings into actor, partner, relationship, and error variance. *Actor variance*, which accounted for more than 50% of variance in most dyads, reflects consistency in forgiving across relationships (i.e., *forgivingness*). *Partner variance* reflects individual-level differences in *forgivability*—a construct that has been little researched. Partner variance was significant for mothers and children but not for fathers. Thus, whereas there was no evidence of individual differences in forgivability among fathers, some mothers (and some children) were perceived as more forgivable than others in the eyes of other family members. *Relationship variance* indicates unique forgiveness (or unforgiveness) toward a relationship partner, controlling for the victim's general forgivingness and the offender's general forgivability. Relationship variance was high only for mothers' ratings of fathers (accounting for 75% of variance in mothers' ratings of fathers), indicating unique adjustments in wives' forgivingness toward their husbands based on relational factors.

The SRM framework allows for examination of many phenomena of interest in dyadic relationships. *Reciprocity* addresses whether people who are forgiving also tend to be forgiven. SRM examines reciprocity at both the individual level (where we found evidence of reciprocity for both mothers and children) and the dyadic level (where we found no evidence of reciprocity, as expected based on the paucity of relationship variance). In addition to collecting data on forgiveness in multiple relationships, we also examined both victim and offender perspectives on forgiveness, which allows for checks on congruence among scores from different data sources (i.e., self-reports and other-reports). Congruence correlations indicated moderate to strong levels of self-other agreement at both individual and dyadic levels of analysis.

RELEVANCE FOR CLINICAL AND APPLIED INTERVENTION

The importance of multimodal assessment will not be surprising to practitioners. Every couples counselor is aware that relationship partners have differing perspectives on both positive and negative relationship events, and that both perspectives are important. Questions about generalizability of measurement also bear formal similarity to questions about generalizability of treatments. For example, if I assist an adult victim of child sexual abuse to forgive the abuser, I may believe that this process has value in itself and that it serves as a model for how current relationships can be repaired when trust is damaged. Yet I recognize that generalizability is inherently limited and that forgiveness is a function of particularities of a given relationship as well as of the skill, perceptiveness, and willingness of the forgiver.

For practitioners relying on research-supported theories or measures of forgiveness, the limitations of studies using unimodal measurement are useful to keep in mind. Thus, when self-reported forgiveness is found to be correlated with other self-report measures (e.g., depression, well-being), readers should be aware that these correlations reflect correlated method variance as well as trait variance, so that the true strength of association between traits is obscured. On the other hand, when forgiving for a single offense (e.g., a relationship conflict) is correlated with indicators of well-being, there is a mismatch in level of measurement between predictor and criterion variables. Because forgiveness scores contain substantial situational and dyadic variance, they will not correlate as highly with well-being as would a trait-level forgiveness measure. Thus, the source and level of measurement are important to keep in mind when interpreting both theoretical and applied research findings.

CONCLUSION

In this chapter, we reviewed the literature on construct validity, focusing on the problem of surplus meaning (or method variance), to provide a rationale for the use of multimodal measurement by forgiveness researchers. We presented two category systems (source of data and level of measurement) that may assist researchers in selecting multiple measures that contain common trait variance but distinct sources of method variance. We described the benefits of aggregation across measurement methods and presented several specialized analytic techniques to examine variations in research findings across different measures and measurement methods. We hope that this conceptual framework will be useful to both researchers and consumers of research as they consider how to design studies and interpret study findings. We hope the analytical toolkit presented here will provide a stimulus to forgiveness researchers to move beyond mono-operation bias in creative ways to advance both our psychometric and substantive knowledge about forgiveness processes.

REFERENCES

Anderson, C. A., & Bushman, B. J. (1997). External validity of "trivial" experiments: The case of laboratory aggression. *Review of General Psychology, 1*, 19–41.

Brown, R. P. (2003). Measuring individual differences in the tendency to forgive: Construct validity and links with depression. *Personality and Social Psychology Bulletin, 29*, 759–771.

Bushman, B. J., & Baumeister, R. F. (1998). Threatened egotism, narcissism, self-esteem, and direct and displaced aggression: Does self-love or self-hate lead to violence? *Journal of Personality and Social Psychology, 75*, 219–229.

Campbell, D. T., & Fiske, D. W. (1959). Convergent and discriminant validation by the multi-trait-multimethod matrix. *Psychological Bulletin, 56*, 81–105.

Cattell, R. B. (1957). *Personality and motivation structure and measurement.* Oxford, England: World Book.

Cook, T. D., & Campbell, D. T. (1979). *Quasi-experimentation: Design and analysis issues for field settings.* Boston: Houghton Mifflin.

Crick, J. E., & Brennan, R. L. (1983). *GENOVA: A generalized analysis of variance system.* Iowa City, IA: American College Testing.

Cronbach, L. J. (1995). Giving method variance its due. In P. E. Shrout & S. T. Fiske (Eds.), *Personality research, methods, and theory: A festschrift honoring Donald W. Fiske* (pp. 145–157). Hillsdale, NJ: Lawrence Erlbaum.

Cronbach, L. J., Gleser, G. C., Nanda, H., & Rajaratnam, N. (1972). *The dependability of behavioral measurements: Theory of generalizability for scores and profiles.* New York: Wiley.

Cronbach, L. J., & Meehl, P. E. (1955). Construct validity in psychological tests. *Psychological Bulletin, 52,* 281–302.

Cronbach, L. J., Rajaratnam, N., & Gleser, G. C. (1963). Theory of generalizability: A liberalization of reliability theory. *British Journal of Statistical Psychology, 16,* 137–163.

Fiske, D. W. (1971). *Measuring concepts of personality.* Chicago: Aldine-Atherton.

Fiske, D. W., & Campbell, D. T. (1992). Citations do not solve problems. *Psychological Bulletin, 112,* 393–395.

Heppner, P. P., Casas, J. M., Carter, J., & Stone, G. L. (2000). The maturation of counseling psychology: Multifaceted perspectives, 1978–1998. In S. D. Brown, & R. W. Lent (Eds.), *Handbook of counseling psychology* (3rd ed., pp. 3–49). New York: Wiley.

Hoyt, W. T. (2000). Rater bias in psychological research: When is it a problem and what can we do about it? *Psychological Methods, 5,* 64–86.

Hoyt, W. T., Fincham, F., McCullough, M. E., Maio, G., & Davila, J. (in press). Responses to interpersonal transgressions in families: Forgivingness, forgivability, and relationship-specific effects. *Journal of Personality and Social Psychology.*

Hoyt, W. T., & Kerns, M. D. (1999). Magnitude and moderators of bias in observer ratings: A meta-analysis. *Psychological Methods, 4,* 403–424.

Hoyt, W. T., & Melby, J. N. (1999). Dependability of measurement in counseling psychology: An introduction to generalizability theory. *Counseling Psychologist, 27,* 325–352.

John, O. P., & Benet-Martinez, V. (2000). Measurement: Reliability, construct validation, and scale construction. In H. T. Reis, & C. M. Judd (Eds.), *Handbook of research methods in social and personality psychology* (pp. 339–369). New York: Cambridge University Press.

Kassinove, H., Roth, D., Owens, S. G., & Fuller, J. R. (2002). Effects of trait anger and anger expression style on competitive attack responses in a wartime prisoner's dilemma game. *Aggressive Behavior, 28,* 117–125.

Kenny, D. A. (1987). *SOREMO: A FORTRAN program for round robin data structures* [computer program]. Storrs: University of Connecticut.

Kenny, D. A. (1994). *Interpersonal perception: A social relations analysis.* New York: Guilford Press.

Kenny, D. A., & Kashy, D. A. (1992). Analysis of the multitrait multimethod matrix by confirmatory factor analysis. *Psychological Bulletin, 112,* 165–172.

Lubinski, D. (2004). Introduction to the special section on cognitive abilities: 100 Years after Spearman's (1904) "'General intelligence,' objectively determined and measured." *Journal of Personality and Social Psychology, 86,* 96–111.

Lubinski, D., & Dawis, R. V. (1992). Aptitudes, skills and proficiencies. In M. D. Dunnette, & L. M. Hough (Eds.), *Handbook of industrial and organizational psychology* (Vol. 3, 2nd ed., pp. 1–59). Palo Alto, CA: Consulting Psychologists Press.

McCrae, R. R., & Costa, P. T. (1983). Social desirability scales: More substance than style. *Journal of Consulting and Clinical Psychology, 51,* 882–888.

McCullough, M. E., & Hoyt, W. T. (2002). Transgression-related motivational dispositions: Personality substrates of forgiveness and their links to the Big Five. *Personality and Social Psychology Bulletin, 28,* 1556–1573.

McCullough, M. E., Hoyt, W. T., & Rachal, K. C. (2000). What we know (and need to know) about assessing forgiveness constructs. In M. E. McCullough, & K. I. Pargament (Eds.), *Forgiveness: Theory, research, and practice* (pp. 65–88). New York: Guilford Press.

McCullough, M. E., Rachal, K. C., Sandage, S. J., Worthington, E. L. Jr., Brown, S. W., & Hight, T. L. (1998). Interpersonal forgiving in close relationships: II. Theoretical elaboration and measurement. *Journal of Personality and Social Psychology, 75*, 1586–1603.

McCullough, M. E., & Snyder, C. R. (2000). Classical source of human strength: Revisiting an old home and building a new one. *Journal of Social and Clinical Psychology, 19*, 1–10.

Messick, S. (1989). Validity. In R. L. Linn (Ed.), *Educational measurement* (3rd ed., pp. 13–103). Washington, DC: American Council on Education.

Ones, D. S., Viswesvaran, C., & Reiss, A. D. (1996). Role of social desirability in personality testing for personnel selection: The red herring. *Journal of Applied Psychology, 81*, 660–679.

Ripley, J. S., & Worthington Jr., E. L. (2002). Hope-focused and forgiveness-based group interventions to promote marital enrichment. *Journal of Counseling and Development, 80*, 452–463.

Shavelson, R. J., & Webb, N. M. (1991). *Generalizability theory: A primer.* Thousand Oaks, CA: Sage.

Subkoviak, M. J., Enright, R. D., Wu, C., & Gassin, E. A. (1995). Measuring interpersonal forgiveness in late adolescence and middle adulthood. *Journal of Adolescence, 18*, 641–655.

Part Three

THE PSYCHOLOGY OF FORGIVENESS

Chapter Nine

Emotional Development and Forgiveness in Children: Emerging Evidence

Susanne A. Denham
Karen Neal
Beverly J. Wilson
Stephanie Pickering
Chris J. Boyatzis

Phillip's birthday is coming, and he's hoping for a new scooter, silver with red handles and a brake; it folds down so that he can carry it over his shoulder with a strap. He keeps telling his mom, "I want this scooter." He even showed a picture of it to his best friend since first grade, Juan. On his birthday, his mother surprised him with the scooter. She warned, "Just don't ride your scooter down the big hill." Phillip took the new scooter to show Juan. Juan thought the scooter was really cool, too. But then he said, "I want to go faster. I'm going down the big hill." Phillip said, "No, my mom said not to." But Juan did it anyway; the scooter got out of control. He jumped off, so he was all right, but the scooter went flying and smashed into a tree, ruined.

Jameil loves roller coasters. The faster, the higher, the wilder, the better; he is never afraid. There's a new roller coaster at the park, called the Looney Loop; it has three loops and no floor. You go upside down three times, with your feet dangling, and you see everything below you. Jameil begged his dad to ride the Looney Loop together, and Dad promised. But when he got home the night before Opening Day, Dad said, "I've got some bad news. We can't go tomorrow. I'm going to have to work all day and Sunday, too, and I need the car, so mom can't take you. We can go to the park in a couple of weeks." (Neal & Caswell, 2002)

What will happen next in these scenarios? Will Phillip blame Juan and end up not being best friends after all their time together? Will Jameil hold a grudge against his dad all summer long? Because people so frequently hurt each other, it is plausible that events requiring forgiveness occur in all types of relationships, even between childhood best friends or children and parents. One person unjustly offends the other,

128   Handbook of Forgiveness

and the other person suffers. The victim then must choose how to respond, in terms of internal thoughts, feelings, and motivations, as well as external behaviors—to acknowledge the transgression but forgive the offender, or to refuse to forgive.

With these issues in mind, we have several goals in this chapter: (a) to outline the importance of forgiveness and offer a working definition for this phenomenon that can be used with children and their families; (b) to discuss ways in which forgiveness could be an important component of children's socioemotional competence; (c) to generate interest in the study of forgiveness and emotional development in children and youth by reporting on some very new research; and (d) to generate research questions that future scholars might address.

PERSONAL ASSUMPTIONS ABOUT FORGIVENESS

Why, though, might forgiveness be important? As Phillip and Jameil probably found out, it isn't easy to forgive someone who treats your treasured possession irresponsibly or breaks promises. In fact, other people might even consider the forgiver a "pushover." So why bother?

Several reasons for going through what can be a difficult cognitive, affective, motivational, and often behavioral process include: (a) maintenance of close relationships, (b) lessening of violence, and (c) promotion of well-being. Forgiveness poses an option for repairing and maintaining relationships, which serve to nurture and protect people. Childhood peer relationships are especially important; they promote cooperation, conflict management, and self-esteem (Hartup, 1996). Furthermore, youth violence is an increasing concern in our society. An important element in these tragic situations seems to be inability to resolve conflict, which might deescalate if forgiveness were involved; many adolescents involved in violence say they were motivated by anger and revenge (Pfefferbaum & Wood, 1994). Forgiveness research may assist in developing interventions to improve peer relationships and deter negative long-term outcomes.

At the same time, psychology needs to understand not only psychopathology but also the capacity for positive, prosocial interactions. "Psychology is not just the study of weakness and damage, it is also the study of strength and virtue" (Seligman, 1998, p. 1). Accordingly, it is important to note that forgiveness is psychologically beneficial for victim *and* offender, influencing physical, mental, and social health (Worthington, Berry, & Parrott, 2001). It allows anger and resentment to dissipate (Worthington & Wade, 1999). Forgivers are more adjusted, securely attached, other-oriented, and unselfish; they also better understand the transgressor's perspective than do unforgivers (McCullough et al., 1998; Tangney, Boone, Fee, & Reinsmith, 1999). Studying forgiveness may allow us to understand not only factors associated with the developmental course of aggression and distress but also pathways toward health.

But what do these issues mean for children? Children—like adults—often get their feelings hurt when involved in conflicts with siblings, parents, or peers. Thus, forgiveness should be as important for children as it is for adults. Once we are convinced that forgiveness is important, however, we are faced with a second thorny task—defining it.

WORKING TOWARD A DEFINITION FOR FORGIVENESS

Forgiveness is a construct in search of a comprehensive definition (Tangney et al., 1999). Until the crispest possible definition of forgiveness is depicted, both conceptual and methodological problems will proliferate. We have considered many definitions of forgiveness and found points of disagreement (Enright, Freedman, & Rique, 1998; McCullough, 2001; North, 1987; Worthington & Wade, 1999). Some explicitly cite behavior—or at least the motivation toward prosocial behavior—as part of forgiveness. Others emphasize the emotional transformations and/or the important motivational changes wrought by forgiveness. Still others focus on the cognitive reasoning involved in forgiveness decisions.

Judgments about emotional, cognitive, motivational, and behavioral elements of forgiveness—which are inherent in and correlates of forgiveness—are crucial. We use the following working definition of forgiveness:

> Forgiveness is a transformation of one's affect, cognitive judgments, and motivations toward an offender. The victim makes an assessment of the harm done and acknowledges the perpetrator's responsibility but voluntarily chooses to cancel the debt, giving up the need for revenge, punishments, or restitution. Importantly, one removes oneself from the negative emotions directly related to the transgression. Over time, there is a motivational transformation, including a reduction in negative motivations and an increase in constructive motivations toward the perpetrator. The forgiver may be motivated toward positive social behaviors toward the offender.

We consider the affective transformation of forgiveness to be of primary importance. Phillip could be really mad at Juan but realize, "Wow, he's really going to be in trouble. I hate to think of my best friend getting that much heat from his parents, my parents, *and me!*" Empathy, along with the allied ability of perspective taking, are related to forgiveness and lack of blame (Sandage, Worthington, Hight, & Berry, 2000; Tangney et al. 1999; Worthington et al., 2000).

Shame, anger, and guilt have radically different forgiveness-related consequences. Anger and shame are often associated with unforgiveness in victims, whereas guilt may be seen as a precursor to some events of forgiveness. When transgressed against, anger- and shame-prone people often resort to defensive tactics, such as ruminating or seeking revenge, to escape the intolerable experience of shame and the force of their anger (Tangney, 1991). For guilt-prone individuals, guilt for one's part in the transaction, or one's own fallibility, may accompany forgiving; the tension and regret associated with such guilt can motivate constructive changes.

Although realistic reasoning about the offender and about oneself as victim are important parts of forgiveness, solely cognitive forgiveness may be what Enright et al.

(1998) called *pseudoforgiveness* or what McCullough and Worthington (1994) referred to as *role-expected, expedient, detached*, or *limited forgiveness*. In contrast, the "true" forgiver's cognitive, affective, and motivational changes toward the wrongdoer are essential. Furthermore, behaviors such as reconciliation, pardoning, excusing, and altruism should be seen as *consequences of*, not *part of*, forgiveness. Similarly, revenge and restitution seeking can be *consequences of* but not *part of*, unforgiveness (McCullough & Worthington, 1994). Nonvindictive *behavior* toward the perpetrator could occur without cancellation of the emotional debt and arise from numerous personal and contextual attributes other than motivational change (e.g., inhibition, incomplete understanding).

However, we do need to examine behaviors linked to the cognitive, affective, and motivational changes wrought during forgiveness, because positive behaviors toward the transgressor and relationship repair are key advantages of forgiveness. Decisions concerning forgiveness are often followed by accommodation behaviors. The victim can choose to respond in a relationship-enhancing way instead of a relationship-destructive way (Rusbult, Verette, Whitney, Slovik, & Lipkus, 1991). Because much of children's inner lives are played out in "outer" behavior, relations between their forgiveness and social behavior merit close scrutiny.

REVIEW OF THEORETICAL AND EMPIRICAL LITERATURE ON CHILDREN AND FORGIVENESS

The inception and developmental course of forgiveness and its behavioral aftermaths need to be discerned. Forgiveness is likely a vital component of children's social competence, but where do we start to study forgiveness "from the beginning?"

Developmental Perspective on Forgiveness and Children's Emotional and Social Competence

Clearly, any investigation of the inception and developmental course of forgiveness must include emotional, cognitive, motivational, and behavioral elements, which allow us to examine forgiveness within a developmental perspective. Any given age has unique emotional, cognitive, and social tasks that determine a child's success in development. By zeroing in on these special tasks, we can pinpoint the nature of forgiveness during childhood and how it may change.

Young Children's Social-Emotional Developmental Tasks. Children moving into elementary school are becoming proficient with peers. Their interactions center on reducing negative affect and maintaining positive affect during play while resolving conflicts. They begin to understand moral rules and conventions, appreciate how intention, motives, and apology may mitigate a transgressor's actions, and experience complex emotions, such as guilt, shame, and empathy. The essentials for forgiveness are in place. However, even though young children may learn that it is morally and socially important to forgive, they may not understand forgiveness conceptually or do it easily or well. They often fail in integrating social information sources, appreciating implications of social interactions, and canceling the emotional debt (Darby & Schlenker, 1982).

Older Children's Social-Emotional Developmental Tasks.   During middle childhood, new developments multiply and determine the need for and emergence of forgiveness. The peer world is central to children of this age; the subtlety of social interaction grows exponentially (Denham, von Salisch, Olfhof, Kochanoff, & Caverly, 2002). Regulation of emotion in the service of smoother peer interaction matures, as does understanding of others' unique emotional viewpoints. Such complex peer interactions are complemented by increased social cognitive ability to identify, evaluate, and enact solutions for social problems (Crick & Dodge, 1994) and more sophisticated forgiveness reasoning (Enright, 1994). However, many children still act in ways that lead to the worst possible fate: social rejection. Reactive and relational aggression also emerge—some children react to provocations very unpleasantly; others use aggression to manipulate and hurt others (Crick & Grotpeter, 1995; Dodge & Coie, 1987). So older children are equipped to forgive but also may more often require forgiveness and need to forgive others.

Along with the centrality of the larger peer group, dyadic friendships become key contexts in which lifelong social and emotional abilities may be fostered. Friendship has been described as a close, dyadic relationship of two people with shared history (Rose & Asher, 1999). It differs from larger peer-group relationships in that it is reciprocal, voluntary, interdependent, and acknowledged by both partners. Unlike roles in relationships with adults, childhood friends must negotiate, compromise, and share while remaining assertive (Rubin, Bukowski, & Parker, 1998). Older children's friendships also become more intimate, providing self-validation and support. The development and maintenance of mature friendships underscore older children's forgiveness potential. Friends are more likely than distant peers to resolve conflicts positively (Rubin et al., 1998), and forgiveness can be part of such relationship-enhancing conflict resolution (Laursen, Hartup, & Koplas, 1996). Forgiveness-related social cognitive abilities, such as determining offenders' motives or intentionality and selecting prosocial goals and strategies, also are related to peer acceptance and friendship quality (Rose & Asher, 1999).

Thus, forgiveness is crucial to satisfactory social relationships. Adult research has shown that forgiveness more often occurs when apologies take place, victims empathize with the offender, and relationships are close and stable (McCullough et al., 1998; Worthington & Drinkard, 2000). These forgiveness mechanisms have been postulated but not explored empirically within childhood friendships. We must examine these children's conflict-resolution techniques, as well as their social cognitive goals and strategies, within a forgiveness framework.

Research Focusing Directly on Children's Forgiveness:
Justice-Related Reasoning

So far, the sparse body of research has focused on forgiveness in children or adolescents from a cognitive developmental perspective (e.g., Enright, Santos, & Al-Mabuk, 1989; Park & Enright, 1997; Subkoviak et al., 1995). Enright and colleagues suggest that forgiveness occurs within the context of justice (i.e., when the victim believes justice has been served) and that forgiveness reasoning parallels that for justice. They have proposed a stage model of forgiveness development. The initial stage depicts forgiveness as contingent on a level of revenge equal to the hurt caused by the offender. In the second, reciprocal forgiveness stage, one will forgive if the offender makes restitution for the offense or if forgiving will relieve guilt. The third stage of forgiveness emphasizes the expectations of others. In the fourth stage of forgiveness, society's expectations and religion are paramount influences. Individuals at the fifth stage reason in ways that maintain social unity. In the final stage, forgiveness is an unconditional gift given in love by the victim. The victim sees the transgressor as worthy of forgiveness merely because he or she is a person and not because of regret or restitution for the offense.

After testing fourth, seventh, and tenth graders, college students, and adults with moral dilemmas, Enright et al. (1989) concluded that the understanding of forgiveness is related to age. Only a very few adults demonstrated the highest level of reasoning. Most adult descriptions of forgiveness centered on religious or lawful expectations. Adolescent forgiveness was strongly influenced by peers. For most children, forgiveness depended on reversing negative consequences. Enright et al.'s (1989) work warrants some criticism. First, the dilemmas involve adults in adult situations, which children may not comprehend. Second, the theory does not allow for the influence of modeled behaviors. Third, advancement through the stages requires logical, abstract thought.

Children no doubt make cognitive decisions whenever they need to forgive or be forgiven; such decisions may, however, require more practical reasoning and intuition than formal reasoning. Moreover, Enright's model does not allow for differentiating among transgressions. We would expect that children's attributions about varying dimensions of transgressions would impact their perceptions about the likelihood of forgiveness. For example, Darby and Schlenker (1982) found that older children accept increasingly elaborate apologies. They also found that children considered intention, motive, and apology in determining the fate of the offender. In fact, even preschoolers can make mature moral judgments concerning the severity of transgressions. Smetana, Schlagman, and Adams (1993) found that 3- and 4-year-olds rated moral transgressions as more offensive than social ones. If even young children have a better understanding of intentionally and the severity of moral errors than previously recognized, they are also likely to have a better understanding of forgiveness than previous research has indicated.

Research Emanating From Our Working Definition

In programs of research on children's forgiveness at George Mason and Seattle Pacific Universities, we are examining such cognitive attributions that may contribute to children's decisions to forgive. Equally or more important are the links between children's forgiveness and empathy and prosocial motivations and behaviors (Scobie & Scobie, 2000; Worthington, in press); so we are focusing on emotions—children's empathy in response to characters' distress in children's movies; anger-, guilt-, and shame-proneness; and expectations of the victim's negative affect following offenses. We wish to see whether empathy, along with anger-, guilt-, and shame-proneness, play the same roles in children's forgiveness as in adults'.

To meet these goals, we needed a measure of children's forgiveness. Our goal was to create parallel scenario-based measures for children and parents, following our working definition of forgiveness and including cognitive, motivational, and emotional aspects (Denham, Neal, Hamada, & Keyser, 2002). We first examined the Multidimensional Forgiveness Inventory (MFI) as a model for the tools we wished to create (Tangney et al., 1999).

Prior to measure construction, we interviewed parents, teachers, and children about situations calling for forgiveness in families and children's peer groups. Armed with this information, we created parallel scenarios appropriate for child-peer interactions and adult-adult interactions. The scenario-based questionnaire format allows us to assess forgiveness with fidelity via (a) developmentally appropriate and phenomenological scenarios, (b) specific aspects of the process, and (c) minimization of social desirability and error variance. The final dimensions in the Children's and Parents' Forgiveness Inventories (CFI and PFI) include cognitive dimensions (act severity, receiving punishment) and motivational/behavioral dimensions (e.g., the likelihood of forgiveness under certain circumstances—when the act was purposeful or an accident, when the transgressor felt bad, apologized, made an excuse, or said nothing—and the length of time before forgiveness takes place). The CFI also includes affective dimensions of how hurt, angry, and sad the victim would be (parents' reports on affect came from Tangney's MFI).

Each questionnaire consists of four scenarios naming the child as victim from whom another should seek forgiveness and four scenarios naming a perpetrator, who must seek forgiveness from the child (see Figure 9.1). Analyses of responses from 7- to 12-year-olds and their parents prove the measures highly reliable for children, mothers, and fathers (Mincic, Kalb, Bassett, & Denham, 2004). Pickering and Wilson (2003) have uncovered methodological and theoretical issues in using CFI with first graders. Children this young did not clearly understand the term *forgive* but did understand forgiveness in behavioral terms of accidents and apologies.

Early findings with the CFI show that overall propensity to forgive does not vary across age categories (Neal, Bassett, & Denham, 2004). Age may be related to increasingly abstract reasoning about forgiveness and conflict resolution, but it is not a strong

FIGURE 9.1. CFI Item: Your best friend stole your project idea and got an "A" on it.

predictor of forgiveness *motivation* (see also Park & Enright, 1997). Means for the propensity to forgive or to expect forgiveness did differ across contexts (with items for self and other as transgressors aggregated). Specifically, forgiveness decisions differed according to offender behavior, perceived intent, and posttransgression affect. Children considered forgiveness most likely when the offense was accidental or when the offender apologized or felt really bad. Saying nothing, offending on purpose, or making excuses demonstrates lack of repentance or sincerity; children predicted forgiveness would be less likely in such contexts (Neal, Bassett, & Denham, 2004).

When a transgressor feels really bad, a child's beliefs about an offender's feelings may be the result of empathy, fueled by guilt after one's own transgressions. The child expects transgressors to have similar discomfort or for victims to empathize with the transgressor's situation. Though replication is needed, results so far support those with adults: first graders' empathy and forgiveness are related (Wilson, 2004). Analyses of children's empathic responses to and knowledge of movie characters' emotions are ongoing. Although both relate to peer evaluations of *prosocial behavior*, we await more finely grained analyses including forgiveness.

Considering "made an excuse" and "did it on purpose" responses together, children are less forgiving when offenses are committed with a lack of concern or with cruel intentions. Children were particularly judgmental about the "made an excuse" response. Excuses may be seen as insincere statements that get the offender "off the hook," as opposed to more empathy-evoking reasons. Again, children's evaluations point to moral reasoning based on intentionality and motivation.

The frequency of these less forgiving responses when an offense occurred "on purpose" was related to the children's emotions, again consistent with adult research. For example, shame- and anger-prone children reported a lower likelihood of forgiveness in this context (Denham, Neal, & Bassett, 2004; Neal, Bassett, & Denham, 2004). If the perpetrator made an excuse, children high on anger intensity also reported less likely forgiveness. Highly shame- and anger-prone children reported that it would take them longer to forgive than it would other children. In contrast, guilt-proneness was related to children's likelihood of forgiveness when the action was accidental.

We have begun to examine how forgiveness relates to children's social competence. CFI reports of forgiving accidents and apologetic transgressors are predictive of first graders' social competence (Pickering & Wilson, 2003). Forgiveness, peer status, and prosocial behavior are positively related, and forgiveness is negatively related to aggression and grudge holding (Pickering & Wilson, 2004). Denham and colleagues also are collecting reports of social competence, friendship quality, and conversations about transgressions between friends.

Pickering and Wilson (2003) considered the motivational side of forgiveness important to explore, because social motivations have been successfully measured in adults as a measure of forgiveness (McCullough et al., 1998) and in children in terms of revenge/aggression and prosocial social goals (Erdley & Asher, 1996). Such goals are correlated with children's social behavior, as well as number and quality of friendships (Erdley & Asher, 1996; Rose & Asher, 1999). Wilson and Pickering modified the CFI, asking children whether their goals after each scenario would be to enact revenge/aggression, avoid the matter, or talk things over and make things better. They also asked children to describe how they dealt with a friend disappointing or angering them, over time. Children endorsing revenge/aggressive goals or avoidance were less well liked by peers and seen as more aggressive (Pickering & Wilson, 2004). Children who had prosocial goals regarding a friend's transgressions were less likely to be seen as aggressive. Those who held grudges over time were the most aggressive; most children showed forbearing or forgiving stances. Assessing children's detailed motivations is a useful window on forgiveness.

Finally, children can be classified according to patterns of forgiveness in a person- rather than a variable-centered manner. For example, Bassett (2004) found groups that could be termed *forgivers, nonforgivers*, and *discerning forgivers* (i.e., less forgiving when the transgression was on purpose or the perpetrator said nothing but not different from other groups on forgiving when the act was an accident or the perpetrator felt bad or apologized). She found the discerning forgivers to be more fearful than either other group but less impulsive than nonforgivers. Finally, this study showed anger more via talking badly about others than did the forgiving group. It will be interesting to continue these person-centered analyses with larger samples.

Socialization and Children's Forgiveness

Thus, although data collection and analyses continue, researchers are beginning to isolate important aspects of children's forgiveness and their correlates in social behavior and emotion. If children *are* learning to forgive, *where* are they learning this vital quality? Parental socialization is a best bet, laying the foundation for a substrate of empathy, lessened anger and shame, appropriate guilt, needs-oriented forgiveness reasoning, and motivational and behavioral aspects of forgiveness. Parents in our study provide information on their forgiveness, proneness to anger, shame, and guilt, and empathy/perspective taking, along with ratings of conflict with spouses, religiosity, and parenting styles and practices. Children give opinions of parents' childrearing practices and conflict. In mothers but not fathers, forgiveness is correlated with children's forgiveness (Denham et al., 2004). Parent-child conversations about times when each offended the other also are being collected; these conversations are awaiting coding but appear to be rich sources of parents' and children's possibly bidirectional effect on each other's forgiveness.

Mothers' self-reported anger, especially self-aggression and fractious intentions when angry, were negatively associated with aspects of children's forgiveness (i.e., when the transgressor transgressed on purpose, gave an excuse, or felt bad); empathy in a fantasy situation was related to children's forgiveness (Denham et al., 2004). In contrast, fathers' *lack* of empathy (in either realistic or fantasy situations) and seething anger or outer-directed aggression when angry were *positively* associated with dimensions of their children's forgiveness. These counterintuitive findings with fathers make one wonder whether children are *reacting to* fathers' angry, nonempathic stances as they are *modeling* their mothers' forgiveness. Parental guilt- and shame-proneness so far make few contributions to children's CFI ratings.

Interparental conflict and its resolution may be important fodder for the development of forgiveness (Getman, 2004; Grych & Fincham, 1993). Generally, positive resolution to conflict is seen as important for child outcomes (Cummings, Simpson, & Wilson, 1993; Denham & Grout, 1992; see also Ohbuchi & Sato, 1994, on the value of apologies to children). In our work, however, children were more likely to forgive on a number of dimensions if they also reported feeling that they were triangulated within their parents' conflicts. Perhaps self-involvement may lead children to be more forgiving because they learn more resolution strategies within parents' conflicts. Alternatively, children may feel so bad in triangulated situations that they learn to avoid conflict by forgiving, even when others make excuses. Furthermore, children tended to forgive when the transgression was an accident or an apology was made and when parent-reported conflict was *more* frequent; perhaps these children were exposed to more resolutions accompanied by forgiveness strategies. In contrast, less constructive modes of conflict, such as physical aggression reported by mothers or fathers and avoidance or stonewalling by fathers, were related to children's lower forgiveness ratings. Finally, relations among parents' reports of conflict and PFI scores suggested an indirect effect—mothers who reported more cooperative conflict strategies had higher

PFI scores, whereas fathers' more frequent resolutions were positively associated and their avoidance strategies negatively associated with PFI scores.

Parents' childrearing practices and their children's evaluations of these same practices may contribute directly and in interaction to children's notions of forgiveness. Mincic et al. (2004) found that mothers who reported more negative parenting practices had children with lower propensities to forgive. In contrast, both mothers' and children's perceptions of positive childrearing practices were positively related to children's forgiveness. Over and above the direct contributions of mothers' and children's perceptions of childrearing practices, children who perceived their mothers' parenting practices less positively were particularly unforgiving overall when their mothers reported their own parenting practices as less positive, and children were most likely to forgive a perpetrator who felt bad when they perceived their mothers to use more positive parenting practices *and* mothers perceived their own parenting practices as less negative. Children's and mothers' perceptual agreements may facilitate a positive emotional environment, which could promote forgiveness in children. These results, although they bear replication, offer an interesting glimpse into parents' and children's behaviors, perceptions, and beliefs that may interact in the inception of forgiveness.

Parents' religion also should at least indirectly relate to children's forgiveness, given that forgiveness is given varying emphases in many major religions. Wyatt, Bassett, and Denham (2004) have found that existential aspects of religious experience are positively and extrinsic aspects negatively related to children's forgiveness. We hope to expand this inquiry greatly.

Our last suggestive area involving parents' promotion of forgiveness involves attachment. Paleari, Regalia, and Fincham (2003) found that adolescents' willingness to forgive parents was directly predicted by their benign responsibility attributions about their parents, their negative affective reactions, and their emotional empathy, and was indirectly predicted, via these constructs, by children's positive relationships with their parents. It is easy to imagine that feeling that one can find distress relief from an attachment figure and enjoy being near him or her—the essence of attachment—should at least indirectly support the development of forgiveness. In Denham's as-yet-unpublished research, we are assessing children's attachment via their family drawings; coding is ongoing.

New Research Directions Needed in the Area

The investigation of forgiveness as it relates to children's emotions, cognitions, motivations, behaviors, social relationships, and personal well-being is at an exciting point of embarkation. We have numerous questions to ask about the inception of developmental progression of children's forgiveness and its socialization, and we are eager to begin this effort.

- Is there individual continuity in forgiveness?
- Can we assume that socialization mechanisms are similar to those for other social behaviors (i.e., modeling, induction/reactions, open discussion of forgiveness)? What are the frequencies of these mechanisms? Do they differ with age? Might second grader Jameil (see initial vignettes) have different discussions about forgiveness with his parents than sixth grader Phillip?
- Can we assess the "forgiveness climate" in families rather than in individuals? For example, do Phillip and Jameil's families differ on such a dimension?
- To what degree do parents use forgiveness discussions during conflict resolution within different relationships (e.g., parent–child, spouse–spouse)? What if Jameil's parents got into a big fight about going to the amusement park? What would Jameil learn about forgiveness?
- How do children display forgiveness behaviors toward peers, toward parents, and toward self? How did Jameil end up feeling and acting toward his father?
- What is the role of extended family? Did Phillip get some sage advice from his grandmother?
- What forgiveness do siblings display toward each other in their relationships and conflicts? Maybe Jameil's sister helped him understand how exhausted Dad was and how he meant well.
- What about peers? Did another friend help Phillip process his righteous anger at Juan?
- How are religion, denomination, and church involvement related to children's forgiveness?
- Do teachers ever discuss forgiveness with children beyond stating, "Say you're sorry"?
- How often is forgiveness modeled in the media (e.g., TV shows, movies, kids' shows)?
- Do children learn more about forgiveness when the ecosystems in which they live are consistent in promoting it (e.g., both family and church promoting forgiveness similarly)?
- What are cultural differences in children's forgiveness?
- What do *children* believe forgiveness is? Young children may define forgiveness via reconciliatory behaviors; their notions, although not fully mature, deserve examination (Neal & Caswell, 2002; cf. Pickering & Wilson, 2004). Scobie and Scobie (2003) have found no difference in school children's and adults' understanding of forgiveness; either it is present earlier than predicted or, as a relational mechanism, it is common to children and adults. Denham's as-yet-unpublished data also suggest no differences between children and parents on any CFI/PFI dimensions except that parents feel less hurt and angry after transgressions. Maybe Phillip's father is less angry, but both he and Phillip may consider Juan's attitude as unworthy of forgiveness.

Relevance for Clinical and Applied Interventions

The theoretical stance and burgeoning research outlined here have the potential to spawn many useful applications. For example, parents and parent educators could benefit from evidence on childhood forgiveness to tailor parenting practices and programs that would maximize children's interpersonal and intrapersonal health. Child clinicians could make use of forgiveness research in developing individual and group prevention and intervention programs that could help children improve their peer relationships and deter negative long-term outcomes. Finally, public policy experts could use evidence of the positive outcomes of forgiveness in recommendations for curricula and other child-related regulations.

PERSONAL THEORETICAL PERSPECTIVES

Given our theoretical stance and reviewing promising research on childhood forgiveness, we agree with Worthington's (in press) theoretical assumptions about its development. We must come to understand the roots of children's *decisional* and *emotional* forgiveness (i.e., deciding to not seek revenge or avoid the transgressor vs. emotional replacement of negative, unforgiving emotions)—how these aspects of forgiveness emerge in development, what factors promote them, and how parents and teachers facilitate them. We need to explore not only cognitive underpinnings of forgiveness but also those related to temperament, attachment, emotion regulation and coping, parental emotion coaching, and the religious/spiritual environment of the home. Our theory of forgiveness can only become richer through these efforts.

CONCLUSION

We hope that other investigators will join us in studying cognitive, affective, and motivational elements of forgiveness and behavioral sequelae in children. Given the importance of peer and parent–child relationships, it would seem that knowing the answers to some of the questions noted above could be pivotal in interventions to lessen peer difficulties and in family therapy. Much work needs to be done before we can reach evidence-based applications of forgiveness for children, but we must start now.

ACKNOWLEDGMENTS

The authors wish to thank the families who have assisted them in beginning the journey toward understanding the development of forgiveness in children. As well, we thank Hideko Bassett, Miranda Getman, Sara Kalb, Melissa Mincic, Samantha Shapiro, and Todd Wyatt for their assistance in conceptualizing studies and collecting data.

The authors wish to thank the John Templeton Foundation, *A Campaign for Forgiveness Research*, the Council of Christian Colleges and Universities, as well as George Mason and Seattle Pacific Universities for their support of the research reported on herein.

REFERENCES

Crick, N. R., & Dodge, K. A. (1994). A review and reform of social information-processing mechanisms in children's social adjustment. *Psychological Bulletin, 115,* 76–101.

Crick, N. R., & Grotpeter, J. K. (1995). Relational aggression, gender, and social-psychological adjustment. *Child Development, 66,* 710–722.

Cummings, E. M., Simpson, K. S., & Wilson, A. (1993). Children's responses to interadult anger as a function of information about resolution. *Developmental Psychology, 29,* 978–985.

Darby, B. W., & Schlenker, B. R. (1982). Children's reactions to apologies. *Journal of Personality and Social Psychology, 43,* 742–753.

Denham, S. A., & Grout, L. A. (1992). Mothers' emotional expressiveness and coping: Topography and relations with preschoolers' social-emotional competence. *Genetic, Social, and General Psychology Monographs, 118,* 75–101.

Denham, S. A., Neal, K., & Bassett, H. H. (2004). *"You hurt my feelings pretty bad": Parents' and children's emotions as contributors to the development of forgiveness.* Paper presented at the biennial Conference on Human Development, Washington, DC.

Denham, S.A., Neal, K., Hamada, H., & Keyser, M. (2002). *Child/Parent Forgiveness Inventories.* Unpublished measures, George Mason University: Fairfax, VA.

Denham, S. A., von Salisch, M., Olthof, T., Kochanoff, A., & Caverly, S. (2002). Emotions and peer relationships. In C. Hart & P. K. Smith (Eds.), *Handbook of child social development* (pp. 307–328). New York: Blackwell.

Dodge, K. A., & Coie, J. D. (1987). Social-information processing factors in reactive and proactive aggression in children's peer groups. *Journal of Personality and Social Psychology, 53,* 1146–1158.

Enright, R. D. (1994). Piaget on the moral development of forgiveness: Identity or reciprocity? *Human Development, 37,* 63–80.

Enright, R. D., Freedman, S. R., & Rique, J. (1998). The psychology of interpersonal forgiveness. In R. D. Enright & J. North (Eds.). *Exploring forgiveness* (pp. 46–62). Madison, WI: University of Wisconsin Press.

Enright, R. D., Santos, M. J. D., & Al-Mabuk, R. (1989). The adolescent as a forgiver. *Journal of Adolescence, 12,* 95–110.

Erdley, C. A., & Asher, S. R. (1996). Children's social goals and self-efficacy perceptions as influences on their responses to ambiguous provocation. *Child Development, 67,* 1329–1344.

Getman, M. (2004). *Conflict and forgiveness: Relations between parental conflict and child forgiveness.* Unpublished senior thesis, George Mason University, Fairfax, VA.

Grych, J. E., & Fincham, F. D. (1993). Children's appraisal of marital conflict: Initial investigations of the cognitive-contextual framework. *Child Development, 64,* 215–230.

Hartup, W. W. (1996). The company they keep: Friendships and their developmental significance. *Child Development, 67,* 1–13.

Laursen, B., Hartup, W. W., & Koplas, A. L. (1996). Towards understanding peer conflict. *Merrill-Palmer Quarterly, 42,* 6–102.

McCullough, M. E. (2001). Forgiveness: Who does it and how do they do it? *Current Directions in Psychological Science, 10,* 194–197.

McCullough, M. E., Rachal, K. C., Sandage, S. J., Worthington, E. L., Jr., Brown, S.W., & Hight, T. L. (1998). Interpersonal forgiving in close relationships II. Theoretical elaboration and measurement. *Journal of Personality and Social Psychology, 75,* 1586–1603.

McCullough, M. E., & Worthington, E. L., Jr. (1994). Models of interpersonal forgiveness and their applications to counseling: Review and critique. *Counseling and Values, 39,* 2–14.

Mincic, M., Kalb, S. Bassett, H., & Denham, S. A. (2004, April). *Reliabilities of the cognitive understanding forgiveness inventory for children and the cognitive understanding forgiveness inventory for parents.* Poster presented at the biennial Conference on Human Development, Washington, DC.

Mincic, M. S., Wyatt, T., Kalb, S., Shapiro, S., Bassett, H., & Denham, S. A. (2004, August). *Perceptions of parent styles' effects on children's forgiveness.* Poster presented at the annual meeting of the American Psychological Association, Honolulu, HI.

Neal, K., Bassett, H. H., & Denham, S. A. (2004, April). *Affective processes and children's propensity to forgive.* Paper presented in the symposium, S. Denham, Chair, *Children's Forgiveness,* at the biennial meeting of the Conference on Human Development, Washington, DC.

Neal, K., & Caswell, C. (2002, April). *How do children perceive forgiveness?* Poster session presented at the biennial Conference on Human Development, Charlotte, NC.

Neal, K., & Denham, S. (2003, April). *The development of forgiveness in children.* Paper presented at the Society for Research in Child Development Religious and Spiritual Development Preconference, Tampa, FL.

North, J. (1987). Wrongdoing and forgiveness. *Philosophy, 62,* 499–508.

Ohbuchi, K-I., & Sato, K. (1994). Children's reactions to mitigating accounts: Apologies, excuses, and intentionality of harm. *Journal of Social Psychology, 131,* 791–805.

Paleari, F. G., Regalia, C., & Fincham, F. D. (2003). Adolescents' willingness to forgive their parents: An empirical model. *Parenting: Science and Practice, 3,* 155–174.

Park, Y. O., & Enright, R. D. (1997). The development of forgiveness in the context of adolescent friendship conflict in Korea. *Journal of Adolescence, 20,* 393–402.

Pfefferbaum, B., & Wood, P. B. (1994). Self-report study of impulsive and delinquent behavior in college students. *Journal of Adolescent Health, 15,* 295–302.

Pickering, S. R., & Wilson, B. J. (2003, October). *Forgiveness in first grade children: Relations with social competence.* Paper presented at the meeting Scientific Findings about Forgiveness, Atlanta, GA.

Pickering, S. R., & Wilson, B. J. (2004, April). *Forgiveness in first grade children: Links with social preference, aggression, social problems, and reciprocal friendships.* Paper presented at the biennial Conference on Human Development, Washington, DC.

Rose, A. J., & Asher, S. R. (1999). Children's goals and strategies in response to conflicts within a friendship. *Developmental Psychology, 35,* 69–79.

Rubin, K. H., Bukowski, W., & Parker, J. G. (1998). Peer interactions, relationships, and groups. In W. Damon (Series Ed.) & N. Eisenberg (Vol. Ed.), *Handbook of child psychology: Vol. 3. Social, emotional, and development* (5th ed.; pp. 619–700). New York: Wiley.

Rusbult, C.E., Verette, J., Whitney, G. A., Slovik, L. F., & Lipkus, I. (1991). Accommodation processes in close relationships: Theory and preliminary empirical evidence. *Journal of Personality and Social Psychology, 60,* 53–78.

Sandage, S. J., Worthington, E. L., Jr., Hight, T. L., & Berry, J. W. (2000). Seeking forgiveness: Theoretical context and an initial empirical study. *Journal of Psychology and Theology, 28,* 21–35.

Scobie, G. E. W., & Scobie, E. D. (2000). A comparison of forgiveness and pro-social development. *Early Child Development and Care, 160,* 33–45.

Scobie, G. E. W., & Scobie, E. D. (2003). Measuring children's understanding of the construct of forgiveness. In P. H. Roelofsma, J. M. T. Coreleyn, & J. W. van Saane (Eds.), *One hundred years of psychology and religion (*pp. 105–121). Amsterdam: VU University Press.

Seligman, M. E. P. (1998). Building human strength: Psychology's forgotten mission. *APA Monitor, 29*(1), 1.

Smetana, J. G., Schlagman, N., & Adams, P. W. (1993). Preschool children's judgments about hypothetical and actual transgressions. *Child Development, 64,* 202–214.

Subkoviak, M. J., Enright, R. D., Wu, C., Gassin, E. A., Freedman, S., Olson, L. M., et al. (1995). Measuring interpersonal forgiveness in late adolescence middle adulthood. *Journal of Adolescence, 18,* 641–655.

Tangney, J. P. (1991) Moral affect: The good, the bad, and the ugly. *Journal of Personality and Social Psychology, 61,* 598–607.

Tangney, J., Boone, A. L., Fee, R., & Reinsmith, C. (1999). *Individual differences in the propensity forgive: Measurement and implications for psychological and social adjustment.* Unpublished manuscript, George Mason University, Fairfax, VA.

Wilson, B. J. (2004, April). *Forgiveness in children: Relations to empathy and individual differences.* Paper presented at the Biennial Conference on Human Development, Washington, DC.

Worthington, E. L., Jr. (in press). The development of forgiveness. In E. M., Dowling, & W. G. Scarlett (Eds.), *Encyclopedia of spiritual and religious development in childhood and adolescence.* Thousand Oaks, CA: Sage.

Worthington, E. L., Jr., Berry, J. W., & Parrott, L. III (2001). Unforgiveness, forgiveness, religion, and health. In T. G. Plante & A. C. Sherman (Eds.), *Faith and health: Psychological perspectives* (pp. 107–138). New York: Guilford Press.

Worthington, E. L., Jr., & Drinkard, D. T. (2000). Promoting reconciliation through psychoeducational and therapeutic interventions. *Journal of Marital and Family Therapy, 26,* 93–101.

Worthington, E. L., Jr., Kurusu, T. A., Collins, W., Berry, J. W., Ripley, J. S., & Baier, S. N. (2000). Forgiving usually takes time: A lesson learned by studying interventions to promote forgiveness. *Journal of Psychology and Theology, 28,* 3–20.

Worthington, E. L., Jr., & Wade, N. G. (1999). The psychology of unforgiveness and forgiveness and implications for clinical practice. *Journal of Social and Clinical Psychology, 18,* 385–418.

Wyatt, T., Bassett, H. H., & Denham, S. A. (2004, April). *Parental religiosity and its influence on the emergence of forgiveness in childhood.* Paper presented at the Biennial Conference on Human Development, Washington, DC.

Chapter Ten

Forgiving the Self: Conceptual Issues and Empirical Findings

June Price Tangney
Angela L. Boone
Ronda Dearing

Most theory and research on forgiveness focuses on people's capacity or willingness to forgive others. Forgiveness, however, is a complex process that involves both interpersonal and intrapersonal dimensions. Based on extensive clinical experience, Enright and the Human Development Study Group (1996) proposed a "forgiveness triad" to capture the multiple layers of forgiveness in human experience. In addition to the capacity to forgive others, Enright et al. (1996) also called attention to the importance of receiving forgiveness and forgiving the self.

CONCEPTUALIZING SELF-FORGIVENESS

Much of our previous research has focused on shame and guilt, so it is perhaps not surprising that we would take a special interest in the concept of self-forgiveness. Shame and guilt are two painful "self-conscious" emotions that people experience when they have failed or transgressed—that is, when they are in the perpetrator, not the victim role. The human capacity for these "moral emotions" is both a blessing and a curse. Feelings of shame and guilt serve as a moral barometer, alerting us when we have violated important personal, societal, and moral standards. These feelings and the *anticipation* of these feelings often inhibit us from yielding to temptation. They can also motivate us in constructive directions that are healthy for both the self and others.

However, there are costs. Clinicians and clergy see the worst of it—people wrestling with debilitating, chronic feelings of shame and guilt that interfere with the quality of life and important relationships. For example, in mental health settings, clinicians often encounter clients who appear debilitated by unresolved feelings of shame, guilt, and remorse—distressing feelings that are very often out of proportion to the severity of transgression. It has been suggested that in such cases, successful treatment involves helping the client process his or her deep feelings of guilt and remorse, then to resolve those feelings constructively by, for example, reparation and self-forgiveness. Thus, there may be an intimate link between self-forgiveness and the resolution of feelings of shame and guilt.

To date, theory and research on moral emotions and self-forgiveness have proceeded largely independent from one another. Most psychologists have discussed the nature of self-forgiveness within the context of interpersonal forgiveness theory, drawing clear parallels between forgiveness of the self and forgiveness of others. Enright (1996) defined *self-forgiveness* as "a willingness to abandon self-resentment in the face of one's own acknowledged objective wrong, while fostering compassion, generosity, and love toward oneself" (p. 115). Hall and Fincham (in press) defined *self-forgiveness* as "a set of motivational changes whereby one becomes decreasingly motivated to avoid stimuli associated with the offense, decreasingly motivated to retaliate against the self (e.g., punish the self, engage in self-destructive behaviors etc.), and increasingly motivated to act benevolently towards the self" (p. 4). DeShea and Wahkinney (2003) defined *self-forgiveness* as "a process of releasing resentment toward oneself for a perceived transgression or wrongdoing."

In a recent integrative review, Hall and Fincham (in press) further delineated the parallels between forgiveness of the self and forgiveness of others. Both are processes that unfold over time. Both involve an objective wrong. In both cases, forgiveness is freely given (i.e., self-forgiveness is not a requirement or entitlement). Both self-forgiveness and forgiveness of others are distinct from condoning, excusing, or forgetting a transgression.

Nonetheless, the two types of forgiveness differ in some important respects (Hall & Fincham, in press). First, Hall and Fincham observe that whereas forgiveness of others is by definition unconditional (true interpersonal forgiveness does not hinge on the perpetrator's future behavior), self-forgiveness may be granted *on the condition that* one makes reparation or *on the condition that* one changes one's behavior in the future. Second, interpersonal forgiveness does not require reconciliation with the perpetrator. Forgiveness is an intrapersonal process that may or may not be accompanied by reconciliation at the interpersonal level. In contrast, reconciliation with the self is a necessary component of self-forgiveness. Third, Hall and Fincham speculate that the consequences of not forgiving the self may be more severe than the consequences of not forgiving another. One can avoid an unforgiven perpetrator, but one cannot escape an unforgiven self.

Finally, in discussing the nature of self-forgiveness, psychologists emphasize the importance of distinguishing between "true" self-forgiveness and "pseudo," or false self-forgiveness (Baumeister, Exline, & Sommer, 1998; Hall & Fincham, in press). A requirement for true self-forgiveness is that the offender acknowledge the wrongdoing and accept responsibility. In pseudo-self-forgiveness, the offender essentially lets himself or herself off the hook—the offense and its consequences are brushed off, minimized, excused, and/or blamed on others. Hall and Fincham (in press) further add the explicit requirement that significant angst be experienced as a result of the acceptance of responsibility. "The realization of wrongdoing and acceptance of responsibility generally initiate feelings of guilt and regret, which must be fully experienced before one can move towards self-forgiveness. Attempts to forgive oneself without cognitively and emotionally processing the transgression and its consequences are likely to lead to denial, suppression, or pseudo-forgiveness. . . . True self-forgiveness is often a long and arduous process that requires much self-examination and may be very uncomfortable" (p. 10). In short, nontrivial pangs of conscience (some combination of shame, guilt, regret, and perhaps embarrassment) are necessary for true self-forgiveness to occur. Pseudo self-forgiveness may appear to result in a similar end state (being at peace with oneself), but it is essentially gained by a moral, cognitive, and affective shortcut—bypassing acceptance of responsibility, acknowledgement of harmful consequences, and negative self-conscious emotions. What is not clear in this nascent literature is how much self-conscious anguish needs to be experienced in order to have adequately processed and achieved self-forgiveness, the real thing.

Owing to the nature of their work, clinicians see the most extreme cases of problems with self-forgiveness. However, ordinary people in the course of daily life routinely stumble and fail. Almost everyone (with perhaps the exception of psychopathic individuals) at times faces the dilemma of an estranged, denounced self and the need to move toward self-forgiveness. In our research, we have been interested in the psychological and social implications of self-forgiveness in the normal range—that is, for people in general, not in a clinical population. A key question addressed by our research concerns the links between self-forgiveness and the capacity for moral emotions. A second, more general question is whether the capacity to forgive the self is a psychological strength, much as the capacity to forgive others is a psychological strength and virtue. Is self-forgiveness an element one might want to include in character education curricula? Is it a capacity parents might want to encourage in their children?

ASSESSING SELF-FORGIVENESS

Very little research has examined the psychological and social correlates of self-forgiveness, in part because of the heavy emphasis in the literature on forgiveness of *others* and in part because there simply aren't many measures available to assess this construct. Mauger et al. (1992) blazed the trail with the development of their dispositional Forgiveness of Self scale. Mauger et al.'s measure, however, includes items that clearly fall outside the construct of self-forgiveness (e.g., "I often get into trouble for not being careful to follow the rules"). More recently, Wahkinney (2001; see also DeShea & Wahkinney, 2003) developed a situation-specific measure of self-forgiveness, much along the lines of Enright's Forgiveness Inventory. Here the focus of assessment is not on people's general capacity to forgive the self across time and situations but rather on a person's level of self-forgiveness with respect to a particular offense, whether or not they are more generally inclined or able to forgive the self.

Our interest is in trait self-forgiveness—people's general propensity to forgive (or not forgive) the self for failures and transgressions that cause harm to others, to the self (see Hall & Fincham, in press), or both. To assess individual differences in the propensity to forgive the self across situations, we developed the Multidimensional Forgiveness Inventory (MFI; Tangney, Boone, Fee, & Reinsmith, 1999), which assesses (a) a propensity to forgive others (FO), (b) a propensity to ask for forgiveness *from* others (AF), and (c) a propensity for self-forgiveness (FS). The structure of the MFI is similar to our scenario-based Test of Self Conscious Affect (TOSCA; Tangney, Wagner, & Gramzow, 1989) assessing proneness to shame and guilt, and our Anger Response Inventories (ARIs; Tangney, Wagner, Marschall, & Gramzow, 1991) assessing characteristic ways of responding to and managing anger. Respondents are presented with a series of common, everyday situations involving transgressions (some with the respondent as victim and others with the respondent as perpetrator). Each victim situation is followed by questions assessing likelihood of forgiving the perpetrator (FO) and an estimate of how long it would take to forgive. We also include items assessing how hurt and angry the respondent-victim would be. These are intended to engage respondents while providing an index of the likely impact of each event on the respondent. Each perpetrator situation is followed by questions assessing the respondent's likelihood of seeking or asking for forgiveness (AF), his or her propensity to forgive the self (FS), as well as the likelihood of externalizing blame and blaming the self.

Results from two studies, one with multiple respondents (index participants plus parents and friends of index participants), indicate that the MFI reliably assesses three distinct dimensions of forgiveness. Both internal consistency estimates and test-retest correlations over a 1- to 3-week period provide strong support for the MFI. For example, internal consistency of the MFI self-forgiveness scale across five samples ranged from .76 to .86. Test-retest reliability over a 1- to 3-week period was .70. Moreover, the scenario-based format of the MFI appears to have circumvented social desirability biases. The average correlation of measures of social desirability with Forgiveness of Others and Self-Forgiveness scales were .15 and −.17, respectively (Tangney & Boone, 2004).

SELF-FORGIVENESS: EMPIRICAL FINDINGS

We examined the psychological and social correlates of self-forgiveness in two independent studies using the MFI. Participants in Study 1 were 285 undergraduate students attending a large state university. Participants in Study 2 were 268 undergraduate students (index participants), 264 friends of the participants (also largely undergraduates), and 85 mothers and 68 fathers of the index participants.

Self-Forgiveness and the Moral Emotions

Of particular interest is the relationship of self-forgiveness to individual differences in proneness to shame and proneness to guilt. The terms *shame* and *guilt* are often used interchangeably, but a large body of research now indicates that these are distinct emotions with very different implications for subsequent moral and interpersonal behavior (Lewis, 1971; Lindsay-Hartz, de Rivera, & Mascolo, 1995; Tangney, 1990b, 1992, Tangney & Dearing, 2002).

To summarize briefly, feelings of shame involve a painful focus on the self—the humiliating sense that "*I* am a bad person." Such shameful humiliation is typically accompanied by a sense of shrinking, of being small, and feelings of worthlessness and powerlessness. Ironically, research has shown that such painful and debilitating feelings of shame do not motivate constructive changes in behavior. Instead, people in the midst of a shame experience often resort to defensive tactics, seeking to hide or escape the shameful feeling, denying responsibility, and even shifting the blame outside, holding others responsible for their dilemma. In contrast, guilt involves a focus on a specific behavior—the sense that "I did a bad thing" rather than "I am a bad person." Feelings of guilt involve a sense of tension, remorse, and regret over the bad thing done, which typically motivates reparative action (confessing, apologizing, or somehow repairing the damage done).

Enright and colleagues (1996) suggested that "true self-forgiveness . . . originates from a position of guilt, remorse, and shame" (p. 117). Recent research, making a distinction between shame and guilt, however, suggests that these moral emotions should have very different implications for self-forgiveness. People who are prone to feelings of guilt (about a specific behavior) may indeed be well placed to seek and receive forgiveness from others and to forgive themselves—in part because a bad behavior is much easier to change than a bad self. However, people prone to feelings of shame (about the entire self) are very likely to have difficulties in these areas. In shame, the task of self-forgiveness is much more daunting. It is the self at issue. On the other hand, it has been observed that shamed individuals are no less likely to repeat their transgressions and often are more so, and they are no more likely to attempt reparation and often are less so (Tangney & Dearing, 2002). Rather, because shame is so intolerable, the shamed individual is inclined to respond defensively—even aggressively (Tangney, 1990a; Tangney & Dearing, 2002; Tangney, Wagner, Barlow, Marschall, & Gramzow, 1996; Tangney, Wagner & Gramzow, 1992). Shame has been associated with a tendency to deny responsibility and externalize blame, holding others responsible for failures and transgressions. Not infrequently, shamed individuals become irrationally angry with others. They sometimes resort to overtly aggressive and destructive actions. Thus, the propensity to experience shame may be associated with difficulties in forgiving the self. However one also can imagine an inclination toward something akin to pseudo-forgiveness, given shame-prone individuals' propensity to defensively deny, rationalize, and externalize blame.

Results from two independent studies, one with multiple respondent groups, indicate that people who readily forgive themselves are somewhat less prone to both shame and guilt, relative to their peers. The findings did not consistently replicate across the various subsamples of respondents in Study 2. In some cases, the correlations were substantial, negative, and statistically significant; in other cases, the relationship was negligble. But in no case was there a significant positive correlation between self-forgiveness and the propensity to experience the moral emotions of shame *or* guilt.

Empathy is also relevant in situations where one harms others (as opposed to being the harmed victim). On one hand, empathic resonance with the distress of a harmed victim might intensify feelings of shame and guilt, making such feelings more difficult to resolve. On the other hand, it has been suggested that the capacity for other-oriented empathy might enhance the capacity for self-forgiveness because a shamed or guilty offender may be able to direct some of that empathy and understanding to the self, thereby facilitating self-forgiveness.

As it turns out, in both studies, other-oriented perspective taking was negligibly related to the propensity to forgive the self. Self-forgiveness, however, was inversely correlated with both empathic concern *and* personal distress scales from Davis's (1983) Interpersonal Reactivity Index. Individuals who are inclined to forgive themselves seem relatively immune to the distress of others.

Taken together, the profile of moral emotional dispositions associated with the MFI self-forgiveness scale raise the possibility that this measure taps pseudo-self-forgiveness, not necessarily the true self-forgiveness that involves a complex sequence of cognitive and affective events—acknowledgement of wrongdoing, acceptance of responsibility, recognition of negative consequences, attendant experiences of other-oriented empathic concern, consequent experiences of guilt and/or shame, and an ultimate reconciliation with and forgiveness of a truly regretful self.

Other Characteristics of the Self-Forgiving Individual

Characteristics of the Self.   Self-forgiveness necessarily involves forgiving misdeeds, failures, or transgressions—in a word, shortcomings in oneself or one's behavior. Thus, our readiness to forgive may hinge on the degree to which we hold ourselves to unrealistically high standards of perfection. One can imagine the difficulties with self-forgiveness faced by a relatively perfectionistic person. Similarly, "socially oriented" perfectionism (the perception that important others expect perfection, as described by Hewitt & Flett, 1993), fear of shame and/or negative evaluation, global self-esteem, and other self-evaluative personality dimensions should be relevant to one's propensity to forgive the self.

Our results indicate that people who are inclined to forgive themselves are less troubled by the self-evaluative concerns that color most people's lives. Self-forgiveness was negatively correlated with fear of negative evaluation, fear of shame, and socially prescribed perfectionism. In addition, both level and stability of self-esteem were positively related to self-forgiveness in Study 1. Narcissism had even more substantial implications for forgiveness of self. Self-forgiveness was positively associated with narcissism across both studies. Narcissistic individuals may be slow to forgive others, but when they themselves transgress, they quickly forgive themselves and move on.

When the Shoe Is on the Other Foot.   We also examined the feelings, attitudes, and behaviors of self-forgiving individuals when the shoe is on the other foot—when they are the victims of someone else's transgression. In response to the MFI victim scenarios, the propensity to forgive others was positively correlated with self-forgiveness. However, a different pattern of results was observed when considering the ARI, which assesses people's characteristic responses when angered by others. Results indicate that people who easily forgive the self tend to be harsher in response to others' transgressions. For example, self-forgiveness was positively correlated (statistically significant in at least one study, with an analogous trend in the other) with direct physical and verbal aggression, indirect harm, and displaced physical aggression. Self-forgiveness was negatively correlated with self-aggression, the two adaptive anger management scales (rational discussion and corrective action), and most consistently with cognitive reappraisals of both the self and target roles. In short, people who forgive themselves easily when they harm others are the very same people who are least open-minded when they are the victims of others' misdeeds. Self-forgiveness in perpetrator scenarios was negatively correlated with the propensity to rethink one's own role or a partner's role in anger scenarios (where the respondent is presumably the victim).

Quality of Relationships.   The propensity to forgive the self was relatively independent of a variety of relationship-relevant dimensions, including attachment style and loneliness. There was some indication that people prone to jealousy are less inclined to self-forgive, compared with their less jealous peers. Considering respondents' reports of their actual romantic relationships, no significant correlations were observed beyond what one would expect by chance. Thus, it remains to be seen whether our observed positive link between number of sex partners and self-forgiveness replicates in future studies.

Big Five.   We also examined the relationship of self-forgiveness to the Big Five personality characteristics (openness, extraversion, conscientiousness, agreeableness, and neuroticism) and to a measure of self-control. The propensity to forgive the self was largely independent of personality factors, apart from a negative correlation with agreeableness (see chapter 11 by Mullet, Neto, and Rivière for a review of research on personality factors and forgiveness of self). In addition, self-forgiveness was negatively correlated with the Brief Self-Control Scale (Tangney, Baumeister, & Boone, 2004).

Psychological Adjustment.   What are the implications of self-forgiveness for our psychological adjustment and well-being? Here, an intriguing pattern of results was observed. Across two independent studies, self-forgiveness was positively related to an antisocial personality pattern. Further, in at least one of the two samples, self-forgiveness was associated with drug and alcohol dependence; manic bipolar symptoms; and histrionic, narcissistic, and aggressive personality patterns. It is worth noting that people who readily forgive themselves are not generally more vulnerable to psychological symptoms. In fact, self-forgiveness was associated with a general sense of psychological well-being and an absence of psychological symptoms in such key areas as depression and thought problems.[1]

Religion and Gender.   To what degree does religion play a role in people's willingness to forgive the self? In our studies, we focused on Buddhist, Muslim, Protestant, and Catholic groups—groups that were sufficiently represented in the samples. We conducted analyses of variance across five subsamples—participants in Study 1 and the index participants, friends, mothers, and fathers in Study 2. In general, forgiveness dimensions varied surprisingly little as a function of religious affiliation. In Study 1, people's propensity to forgive the self varied significantly across religious groups. Post-hoc Newman-Keuls tests indicated that, on average, Protestants reported being more self-forgiving than Muslim and Buddhist respondents. However, no significant differences were observed among the multiple groups of informants in Study 2.

If self-forgiveness does not vary substantially as a function of religious doctrine, does the *quality* of one's religious involvement relate to forgiveness? Our results indicate that self-forgiveness is unrelated to respondents' degree of religious involvement and their religious orientation (i.e., intrinsic vs. extrinsic reasons for being religiously involved).

Similarly, there were few gender differences in self-forgiveness across the subsamples. In Study 2, male index participants reported a higher propensity to forgive the self than did female index participants, but this gender difference did not replicate in the other Study 2 subsamples or in Study 1.

Psychological Portrait of the Self-Forgiving Individual

People with a dispositional tendency to forgive themselves appear to be rather self-centered, insensitive, narcissistic individuals, who come up short in the moral emotional domain, showing lower levels of shame, guilt, and empathic responsiveness. Relatively "shameless," they feel little remorse for their transgressions, little empathy for their victims, and little concern about what others think of them. Although quick to forgive themselves, when angered, they're harsh in response to others' transgressions. For example, when provoked to anger, they are inclined to become aggressive, have difficulty seeing things from the other person's point of view, and disinclined to take constructive action.

These characteristics of self-forgiving individuals may cause distress to those around them, but self-forgivers are themselves unfazed. Regarding individual adjustment, the propensity to forgive the self was positively correlated with self-reports of psychological well-being and negatively correlated with internal psychological distress. The only clinical problems associated with self-forgiveness were those related to a lack of self-control (e.g., drug and alcohol abuse, chronic antisocial behavior). In short, self-forgivers may act bad, but they don't feel bad.

RECONCEPTUALIZING SELF-FORGIVENESS AND ITS MEASUREMENT

Given these results, it is clear that the MFI self-forgiveness scale does not necessarily capture a person's propensity to experience genuine feelings of remorse *and then* to resolve those feelings constructively. Rather, it appears that the self-forgiveness scale reflects a propensity to let oneself easily off the hook. Self-forgivers may easily forgive the self precisely because they fail to feel a sense of responsibility, remorse, and regret for their transgressions at the outset. In examining the intercorrelations of the MFI subscales, we found a strong negative correlation between forgiving the self and blaming the self. Thus, self-forgivers were inclined not to take responsibility for harming others in the first place.

The available research on the few alternative measures of self-forgiveness suggests that the MFI is not alone in capturing a substantial proportion of variance attributable to pseudo-forgiveness (for a review, see chapter 11 by Mullet, Neto, and Rivière). For example, using Mauger's measure, researchers have found a negative relationship between self-forgiveness and measures of neuroticism, anxiety, and depression (Leach & Lark, 2003; Maltby, Macaskill, & Day, 2001; Mauger et al., 1992; Seybold, Hill, Neuman, & Chi, 2001). Correlations between self-forgiveness and emotional empathy were nonsignificant but in a negative direction (Macaskill, Maltby, & Day, 2002). Similarly, Walker and Gorsuch (2002) replicated the inverse relationship between self-forgiveness and both neuroticism and anxiety using an alternative measure of self-forgiveness.

Similar results have been found when examining self-forgiveness with respect to specific events. For example, Zechmeister and Romero (2002) found that people who reported having forgiven the self for a specific event expressed high levels of regret and self-blame, but they also tended to blame their victims. Relative to those who did not forgive the self, self-forgivers were inclined to justify their actions and were rated by coders as "self-focused and portrayed victims as deserving what they got" (p. 683). Paralleling our findings regarding trait self-forgiveness and self-esteem, DeShea and Wahkinney (2003) found that people who reported having forgiven the self for a specific event expressed substantially higher levels of unconditional self-regard, relative to those who had not forgiven a significant transgression. In addition, self-forgivers scored low on neuroticism and high on agreeableness, replicating other researchers' findings at the trait level.

In short, each of these studies employed measurement strategies that appear to tap a heavy component of pseudo-self-forgiveness. Part of the problem is that all existing measures of self-forgiveness essentially measure an outcome—an endpoint—without assessing crucial elements of the process that lead up to that outcome. To distinguish between true self-forgiveness and pseudo-self-forgiveness, it is necessary to capture critical aspects of the *process* that leads to the outcome of a self at peace with the self. Most likely, in solely assessing that endpoint, the MFI (and its sister measures) captures *both* individuals prone to pseudo-self-forgiveness and those who have the propensity to experience the sequence of events that theorists have in mind when they describe true self-forgiveness—a sequence that requires an acceptance of responsibility and the experience of some level of moral discomfort that must be resolved.

NEW RESEARCH DIRECTIONS

One advantage of scenario-based measures such as the MFI (see also the Transgression Narrative Test of Forgiveness [Berry, Worthington, Parrott, O'Connor, & Wade, 2001]; the TOSCA measures of shame and guilt [Tangney & Dearing, 2002]; and the ARIs [Tangney et al., 1996]) is that they can be readily modified to test hypotheses about *processes*, not just outcomes (e.g., by incorporating the assessment of theoretically defined criteria and of hypothesized moderators and mediators *at the situational level*). Future research could modify the MFI to include scales assessing sense of responsibility and level of moral discomfort. In this way, guided by recent impressive theoretical advances (e.g., DeShea & Wahkinney, 2003; Hall & Fincham, in press), future studies could capitalize on the power of scenario-based methods by incorporating qualifying criteria and other process variables of interest.

A scientific understanding of the correlates and consequences of the propensity for true self-forgiveness (that complex process) awaits future empirical work. Ideally, such work would employ a combination of appropriately modified scenario-based measures, studies of the process of self-forgiveness in the context of specific offenses (with or without a consideration of individual differences), and the systematic observations by clinicians in the field.

MORE GENERAL THOUGHTS ON THE MFI

The pace of research on forgiveness since 1999 has been astounding. Owing to Sir John Templeton's generous philanthropic contribution to this field, there has been an unprecedented development in our knowledge and understanding of forgiveness and the "virtues" more generally. So, too, has there been a tremendous growth in the assessment of these scientifically measurable constructs. Researchers interested in forgiveness of *others* are fortunate to have a range of measures from which to choose. Thus, the question is always, Which one?

Based on our findings from two large validation studies (Tangney & Boone, 2004) in conjunction with a review of the recent literature, we would recommend one of the shorter, global self-report measures over the MFI if one is interested in simply assessing the propensity to forgive others (trait forgiveness). We are especially impressed with Brown's recent (2003) Tendency to Forgive scale (TTF) and the Trait Unforgiveness-Forgiveness scale (TUF; Berry & Worthington, 2001; see Berry, Worthington, O'Connor, Parrott, & Wade, 2005). A key aim in electing to use a scenario-based approach for the MFI was to circumvent the problem of social desirability bias often seen in measures that rely on ratings of global attributes, especially when considering self-reports of moral emotions, strengths, and virtues (e.g., Harder & Lewis, 1987; Kugler & Jones, 1992; Mosher, 1966; for a discussion, see Tangney, 1996; Tangney & Dearing, 2002). Results from the current studies indicate that the MFI largely succeeded in circumventing possible confounds with social desirability (average correlation of forgiveness of others with social desirability was .15). However, the TUF performed reasonably well in this domain as well (average correlation with measures of social desirability in our Study 2 was −.29). Moreover, Brown's recent (2003) TTF scale was only modestly correlated with social desirability ($r = .25$). Notably, the TTF is composed of a mere four items that can be completed in a fraction of the time required by the MFI, and multiple studies attest to its reliability and validity.

When might the MFI be useful? Scenario-based measures such as the MFI may be especially useful when conducting research with subpopulations in which concerns about social desirability come to the fore (e.g., parents engaged in custody disputes). Respondents are often more willing to endorse a specific socially undesirable action in the context of a specific situation, compared with reporting on more generalized traits or tendencies. In addition, scenario-based assessments can be useful when working with young children who may not have the abstract thinking skills required to evaluate self-traits. Young children are cognitively equipped to report that they would forgive in situations a, b, and c, but they may not yet be able to view themselves as "a person who easily forgives." Denham and colleagues (see chapter 9) have developed a modified version of the MFI for use with parents and children, with promising results.

In the future, scenario-based assessments such as the MFI may be most useful when the focus of research is on theoretically relevant processes. With the addition of relevant response items, researchers can incorporate an empirical assessment of hypothesized mediators and moderators, as well as key construct criteria, for example, to distinguish between true and pseudo-self-forgiveness.

Scenario-based measures are lengthy. The payoff can be substantial, depending on the context, construct, and research question. If a researcher is interested in simply a quick dispositional assessment of interpersonal forgiveness, the MFI is probably not the measure of choice.

RELEVANCE FOR CLINICAL AND APPLIED INTERVENTIONS

Clinical Implications: Forget the Self

Clearly, based on the range of undesirable traits shown to be associated with the propensity to experience pseudo-self-forgiveness, it is not a characteristic we want to foster and encourage. True self-forgiveness—the process and the capacity to engage in the process—is what clinicians aim to facilitate when faced with clients who struggle with self-forgiveness. Yet we do wonder whether the focus on the endpoint—*self*-forgiveness—can be just as misleading for the practicing clinician or member of the clergy as it is for the researcher. Self-forgiveness is an awfully self-focused construct that seriously misses the point. One can waste away precious hours, months, or even years delving into what is essentially a self-focused analysis of selfish concerns when the real issue is a harmed other—be it a specific person, a group, the community, or (as Hall & Fincham [in press] argue) the self.

As Holmgren (2002) so aptly stated, "To dwell on one's own past record of moral performance, either with a sense of self-hatred and self-contempt or with a sense of superiority, is an activity that is overly self-involved and devoid of any real moral value. The client will exercise his moral agency much more responsibly if he removes his focus from the fact that he did wrong and concentrate instead on the contribution he can make to others and on the growth he can experience in the moral and nonmoral realms" (p. 133).

Application to Restorative Justice

This is at the heart of the restorative justice movement—an innovative, promising approach to work with criminal offenders (see chapters 29 and 30). Restorative justice is a philosophical framework that requires active participation by the victim, the offender, and the community with the aim of repairing the fabric of the community (Braithwaite, 1989, 2000; Cragg, 1992; Morrell, 1993). For example, the "Impact of Crime" workshop implemented in Fairfax County, VA's Adult Detention Center emphasizes principles of community, personal responsibility, and reparation. Utilizing cognitive restructuring techniques, case workers and group facilitators challenge common distorted ways of thinking about crime, victims, and locus of responsibility. As clients grapple with issues of responsibility, the question of blame inevitably arises, as do emotions of self-blame. In the process of reexamining the causes of their legal difficulties and revisiting the circumstances surrounding their offense and its consequences, many clients experience new feelings of shame, guilt, or both.

Although not explicitly stated, another important feature of the restorative justice philosophy is the "guilt-inducing, shame reducing" nature of this approach. In early stages of treatment, offenders may feel a predominance of shame, focusing on themselves rather than the plight of the victims. Although not optimal, feelings of shame can serve as a therapist's "hook"—yielding intense feelings that can be processed, transformed, and harnessed as more adaptive feelings of guilt. In the long term, restorative justice approaches (e.g., Maruna, 2001) encourage offenders to take responsibility for their behavior, acknowledge negative consequences, feel guilt for having *done* the wrong thing, empathize with their victims, and act to make amends. But offenders are ultimately discouraged from feeling shame about *themselves.* In short, from a restorative justice perspective, the emphasis is not on moral angst but on moral change and moral action.

CONCLUSION

Elsewhere (Tangney & Mashek, 2004), we have argued that one need not feel bad (really bad) to be a good person. In fact, we reviewed a range of psychological theories and empirical findings that, taken together, seriously challenge the notion that suffering is a useful barometer of moral worth.

Neither is self-focus a useful barometer of moral worth. Quite the reverse. For example, true humility—in the sense of recognition of one's place in the world, not self-abasement—goes hand-in-hand with a relative lack of self-focus or self-preoccupation (Halling, Kunz, & Rowe, 1994; Tangney, 2000, 2002; Templeton, 1997). Having become "unselved" (Templeton, 1997), the person who has gained a sense of humility is no longer phenomenologically at the center of his or her world. The focus is on the larger community of which he or she is one part.

In addressing clients' difficulties with self-forgiveness, it may be that clinicians will be better served by focusing on the process rather than its endpoint.

NOTES

1. In this nonclinical sample of traditional and nontraditional college students, as is typical in community samples, there was sufficient variability in clinical symptoms, with distressed individuals scoring in the mild-to-moderate rather than severe range.

ACKNOWLEDGMENTS

This research was supported by a grant from the John Templeton Foundation. Portions of this paper were presented at the November 2003 conference sponsored by *A Campaign for Forgiveness Research*, Scientific Findings About Forgiveness, Atlanta. We are grateful for wisdom and assistance from Everett Worthington, Julie Exline, David Manning, Deb Mashek, and Jeff Stuewig.

REFERENCES

Baumeister, R. F., Exline, J. J., & Sommer, K. L. (1998). The victim role, grudge theory, and two dimensions of forgiveness. In E.L. Worthington, Jr. (Ed.), *Dimensions of forgiveness: Psychological research and theological perspectives* (pp. 79–104). Philadelphia: Templeton Foundation Press.

Berry, J. W., & Worthington, E. L., Jr. (2001). Forgivingness, relationship quality, stress while imagining relationship events, and physical and mental health. *Journal of Counseling Psychology, 48,* 447–455.

Berry J. W., Worthington, E. L., Jr., O'Connor, L. E., Parrott, L., III, & Wade, N. G. (2005). Forgiveness, vengeful rumination, and affective traits. *Journal of Personality, 73,* 1–43.

Berry, J. W., Worthington, E. L., Jr., Parrott, L. III, O'Connor, L. E., & Wade, N. G. (2001). Dispositional forgivingness: Development and construct validity of the Transgression Narrative Test of Forgivingness (TNTF). *Personality and Social Psychology Bulletin, 27,* 1277–1290.

Braithwaite, J. (1989). *Crime shame and reintegration.* Melbourne: Cambridge University Press.

Braithwaite, J. (2000). Shame and criminal justice. *Canadian Journal of Criminology, 42,* 281–298.

Brown, R. P. (2003). Measuring individual differences in the tendency to forgive: Construct validity and links with depression. *Personality and Social Psychology Bulletin, 29,* 759–771.

Cragg, W. (1992). *The practice of punishment: Towards a theory of restorative justice.* London: Routledge.

Davis, M. H. (1983). Measuring individual differences in empathy: Evidence for a multidimensional approach. *Journal of Personality and Social Psychology, 44,* 113–126.

DeShea, L., & Wahkinney, R. L. (2003, November). *Looking within: Self-forgiveness as a new research direction.* Paper presented at the conference Scientific Findings about Forgiveness, Atlanta.

Enright, R. D., & the Human Development Study Group (1996). Counseling within the forgiveness triad: On forgiving, receiving forgiveness, and self-forgiveness. *Counseling and Values, 40,* 107–126.

Hall, J. H., & Fincham, F. D. (in press). Self-forgiveness: The stepchild of forgiveness research. *Journal of Social and Clinical Psychology.*

Halling, S., Kunz, G., & Rowe, J. O. (1994). The contributions of dialogal psychology to phenomenological research. *Journal of Humanistic Psychology, 34,* 109–131.

Harder, D. W., & Lewis, S. J. (1987). The assessment of shame and guilt. In J. N. Butcher & C. D. Spielberger (Eds.), *Advances in personality assessment* (Vol. 6, pp. 89–114). Hillsdale NJ: Lawrence Erlbaum Associates.

Hewitt, P. L., & Flett, G. L. (1993). Dimensions of perfectionism, daily stress, and depression: A test of specific vulnerability hypothesis. *Journal of Abnormal Psychology, 102,* 58–65.

Holmgren, M. R. (2002). Forgiveness and self-forgiveness in psychotherapy. In S. Lamb & J. G. Murphy (Eds.), *Before forgiving: Cautionary views of forgiveness in psychotherapy* (pp. 112–135). New York: Oxford University Press.

Kugler, K., & Jones, W. H. (1992). On conceptualizing and assessing guilt. *Journal of Personality and Social Psychology, 62,* 318–327.

Leach, M. M., & Lark, R. (2003). Does spirituality add to personality in the study of trait forgiveness? *Personality and Individual Differences, 30,* 881–885.

Lewis, H. B. (1971). *Shame and guilt in neurosis.* New York: International Universities Press.

Lindsay-Hartz, J., de Rivera, J., & Mascolo, M. (1995). Differentiating shame and guilt and their effects on motivation. In J. P. Tangney & K. W. Fischer (Eds.), *Self-conscious emotions: Shame, guilt, embarrassment, and pride* (pp. 274–300). New York: Guilford Press.

Macaskill, A., Maltby, J., & Day, L. (2002). Forgiveness of self and others and emotional empathy. *Journal of Social Psychology, 142,* 663–665.

Maltby, J., Macaskill, A., & Day, L. (2001). Failure to forgive self and others: A replication and extension of the relationship between forgiveness, personality, social desirability, and general health. *Personality and Individual Differences, 30,* 881–885.

Maruna, S. (2001). *Making good: How ex-convicts reform and rebuild their lives.* Washington, DC: American Psychological Association.

Mauger, P. A., Perry, J. E., Freeman, T., Grove, D. C., McBride, A. G., & McKinney, K. E. (1992). The measurement of forgiveness: Preliminary research. *Journal of Psychology and Christianity, 11,* 170–180.

Morrell, V. (1993). Restorative justice: An overview. *Criminal Justice Quarterly, 5,* 3–7.

Mosher, D. L. (1966). The development and multitrait-multimethod matrix analysis of three measures of three aspects of guilt. *Journal of Consulting and Clinical Psychology, 30,* 25–29.

Seybold, K. S., Hill, P. C., Neuman, J. K., & Chi, D. S. (2001). Physiological and psychological correlates of forgiveness. *Journal of Psychology and Christianity, 20,* 250–259.

Tangney, J. P. (1990a). Assessing individual differences in proneness to shame and guilt: Development of the self-conscious affect and attribution inventory. *Journal of Personality and Social Psychology, 59,* 102–111.

Tangney, J.P. (1990b). Sharing shame and guilt: Another social-clinical interface. *Contemporary Social Psychology, 14,* 83–88.

Tangney, J. P. (1992). Situational determinants of shame and guilt in young adulthood. *Personality and Social Psychology Bulletin, 18,* 199–206.

Tangney, J. P. (1996). Conceptual and methodological issues in the assessment of shame and guilt. *Behaviour Research and Therapy, 34,* 741–754.

Tangney, J.P. (2000). Humility: Theoretical perspectives, empirical findings and directions for future research. *Journal of Social and Clinical Psychology, 19,* 70–82.

Tangney, J. P. (2002). Humility. In C. R. Snyder & S. J. Lopez (Eds.), *The handbook of positive psychology* (pp. 411–419). New York: Oxford University Press.

Tangney, J. P., Barlow, D. H., Wagner, P. E., Marschall, D., Borenstein, J. K., Sanftner, J., et al. (1996). Assessing individual differences in constructive vs. destructive responses to anger across the lifespan. *Journal of Personality and Social Psychology, 70,* 780–796.

Tangney, J. P., Baumeister, R. F., & Boone, A. (2004). High self-control predicts good adjustment, less pathology, better grades, and interpersonal success. *Journal of Personality, 72,* 271–324.

Tangney, J. P., & Boone, A. L. (2004). Assessing individual differences in the propensity to ask for forgiveness, to forgive the self, and to forgive others: Development of the Multidimensional Forgiveness Inventory (MFI). Unpublished manuscript, George Mason University, Fairfax, VA.

Tangney, J. P., Boone, A. L., Fee, R., & Reinsmith, C. (1999). *Multidimensional Forgiveness Scale.* George Mason University, Fairfax VA.

Tangney, J. P., & Dearing, R. (2002). *Shame and guilt.* New York: Guilford Press.

Tangney, J. P., & Mashek, D. J. (2004). In search of the moral person: Do you have to feel really bad to be good? In J. Greenberg, S. L. Koole, & T. Pyszczynski (Eds.), *Handbook of experimental existential psychology* (pp. 156–166). New York: Guilford Press.

Tangney, J. P., Wagner, P. E., Barlow, D. H., Marschall, D. E., & Gramzow, R. (1996). The relation of shame and guilt to constructive vs. destructive responses to anger across the lifespan. *Journal of Personality and Social Psychology, 70*, 797–809.

Tangney, J. P., Wagner, P., & Gramzow, R. (1989). *The Test of Self-Conscious Affect (TOSCA).* George Mason University, Fairfax, VA.

Tangney, J. P., Wagner, P. E., & Gramzow, R. (1992). Proneness to shame, proneness to guilt, and psychopathology. *Journal of Abnormal Psychology, 103*, 469–478.

Tangney, J. P., Wagner, P. E., Marschall, D., & Gramzow, R. (1991). *The Anger Response Inventory (ARI).* George Mason University, Fairfax VA.

Templeton, J. M. (1997). *Worldwide laws of life*. Philadelphia: Templeton Foundation Press.

Wahkinney, R. L. (2001). *Self-forgiveness scale: A validation study.* Unpublished doctoral dissertation, University of Oklahoma, Norman.

Walker, D. F., & Gorsuch, R. L. (2002). Forgiveness within the Big Five personality model. *Personality and Individual Differences, 32*, 1127–1137.

Zechmeister, J., & Romero, C. (2002). Victim and offender accounts of interpersonal conflict: Autobiographical narratives of forgiveness and unforgiveness. *Journal of Personality and Social Psychology, 82*, 675–686.

Chapter Eleven

Personality and Its Effects on Resentment, Revenge, Forgiveness, and Self-Forgiveness

Etienne Mullet
Félix Neto
Sheila Rivière

Previous research shows that the decision to forgive depends on numerous factors, such as: (a) situational factors (intention of harm, repetition of offense, severity of the consequences, cancellation or not of the consequences, presence of apologies, and/or compensation from the offender [e.g., Mullet & Girard, 2000]), (b) relational factors (offender's identity and his or her proximity with the victim, his or her hierarchical status, his or her attitude after the offense, and environmental pressures [e.g., Aquino, Tripp, & Bies, 2001]), and (c) personality factors (McCullough & Worthington, 1999). This chapter will focus on the latter group of factors. What are the personality traits that could predict the duration and intensity of the post-offense resentment, the choice of forgiveness (self-forgiveness or forgiveness of others), or the choice of revenge?

Examining the impact of personality factors on forgiveness and revenge is important for reasons that are both theoretical and practical. On the theoretical level, it is essential, for instance, to understand how the personality influences attitudes and decisions at crucial moments of our lives, such as in the face of opposition, arguments, and conflicts of interest; and in reaction to adversity or offense. It is often in these particular moments that important—often irreversible—decisions are made. Such decisions can impact a person's entire life. It is, therefore, essential to investigate the role of personality factors to identify those that are the most important in these critical life situations.

On the practical level for psychologists and other practitioners, when dealing with therapies aimed at healing and forgiveness, it is essential to know how and to what extent to take into the account the personality of the patient (Enright & Fitzgibbons, 2000). Indeed, the method used by the practitioner needs to be adapted to the personality of the patient. It wouldn't be conceivable to apply the same method with a highly neurotic patient as with a stable one. Knowledge of the patient's personality would thus inform the practitioner as to the nature of the resentment (intensity and duration), the willingness to forgive, or the tendency to seek revenge.

PERSONAL ASSUMPTIONS ABOUT FORGIVENESS, REVENGE, AND RESENTMENT

We define *forgiveness* as the overcoming of resentment toward an offender, not by denying the right to such feelings but by endeavoring to view the offender with compassion. *Revenge* is defined as the infliction of harm to an offender in return for perceived wrong. *Resentment* is defined as a cold, emotional complex consisting of bitterness, hostility, residual fear, and residual anger in response to perceived harm from an offender.

Different instruments have been devised for measuring forgiveness in particular circumstances and dispositional forgiveness (also called *forgivingness*; Roberts, 1995). A careful study of these different instruments reveals that not all exclusively measure the intended dimension. For instance, the scale Forgiveness-Nonretaliation (Ashton, Paunonen, Helmes, & Jackson, 1998) includes four categories of items. Some refer to forgiveness (e.g., "My attitude toward people who have tried to harm me is 'forgive and forget'"). Others focus on revenge (e.g., "When someone treats me really unfairly, I want to 'get even' with them, even if it is inconvenient to do so"). Others focus on lasting resentment (e.g., "I tend to 'hold a grudge' against people who have wronged me"). Others refer more to neuroticism than forgiveness (e.g., "I usually start out by suspecting other people and only trusting them after getting to know them well").

In the same vein, the Forgiveness of Others scale (Mauger et al., 1992) contains items referring to reconciliation (e.g., "I am able to make up pretty easily with friends who have hurt me in some way"), revenge (e.g., "People who criticize me better be ready to take some of their own medicine"), or lasting resentment (e.g., "I have grudges which I have held on to for months or years"). Other items measure attitudes toward forgiveness or revenge (e.g., "I feel that other people have done more good than bad for me"). Others have little to do with forgiveness (e.g., "I often use sarcasm when people deserve it"). Even if factorial analysis may allow us to classify these different elements under the same name, this does not signify that the underlying construct is unitary and nonambiguous.

As illustrated by Wade and Worthington (2003; see also Brown, 2003; Thompson et al., 2005), revenge is not the contrary of forgiveness, and resentment does not necessarily mean absence of forgiveness in the future. When one is the victim of an intentional offense, a feeling of resentment seems logical, the duration of which would usually depend on the circumstances of the offense, the attitude of the offender, and, of course, the personality of the victim. Mullet, Houdbine, Laumonnier, and Girard (1998) and Mullet, Barros, Frongia, Usai, and Neto (2003) have shown that individual differences concerning the intensity of resentment are sufficiently notable to help identify a separate factor: lasting resentment (see also McCullough & Hoyt, 2002;

McCullough et al., 1998; Rye et al., 2001). Lasting resentment clearly coincides with the concept of unforgiveness proposed by Worthington and Wade (1999).

The end of the resentment (or unforgiveness) state could take many forms, which are probably directly in relation with the victim and offender's personalities and the environment. Mullet et al. (1998, 2003) have shown that the individual differences in relation with sensitivity to circumstances are sufficiently important to help identify another separate factor: sensitivity to personal and social circumstances. Different forms of resentment naturally end with either forgiveness, revenge, or other types of closure (such as formal complaint or oblivion). Thus, the absence of revenge does not necessarily mean forgiveness. A victim can be still in the resentment mode yet have made a formal complaint or be trying to forget. It is also important to note that the presence of resentment is not synonymous with revenge. Forgiveness can follow the state of resentment, even a long-lasting one. Thus, the presence of (moderate to strong) statistical correlations among reduced forgiveness, revenge, and resentment do not constitute an argument for mixing these three concepts into one scale. These statistical correlations are in fact directly related to the nature of the process that goes from offense to resentment, which would end by either forgiveness or revenge.

Mullet et al. (2003) have argued that it is essential to differentiate these concepts and measure the impact of different personality measures on each component. We described six constructs: enduring resentment toward others, revenge, sensitivity to circumstances, forgiveness of others, forgiveness of self, and forgiveness of situations. We excluded from this classification the measures of forgiveness toward and from God and forgiveness seeking. It should be also noted that categories were not always clear-cut. Some subscales contain items that belong to two or more categories. For instance, the Forgiveness of Others scale (Mauger et al., 1992) was considered, despite its title, as a revenge scale because a majority of this scale's items are more in relation with revenge than with forgiveness. For the more recent scales, the choice of the categories has been more straightforward. The three subscales of state measure Transgression-Related Interpersonal Motivations Inventory (TRIM; McCullough, Bellah, Kilpatrick, & Johnson, 2001), for instance, were without much ambiguity, classified in enduring resentment (avoidance subscale), forgiveness of others (benevolence subscale), and revenge (revenge subscale). Considering that the measures in relation with self-forgiveness are still not numerous, only one category was considered for this construct (despite the fact that the items were not all homogenous).

MEASURING PERSONALITY: A COMMON FRAMEWORK

To organize the existing data and explore the possible correlations with personality factors, a common framework was needed. The Big Five model of personality was chosen: agreeableness, neuroticism, extraversion, conscientiousness, and openness. We examined those factors and forgiveness-relevant dispositions related to them.

Another factor that has been studied often is religion or spirituality. According to some authors (MacDonald, 2000; Piedmont, 1999), this factor is largely orthogonal to the Big Five. Spirituality is mainly related to the vision that the individual may have of his or her place in time and space and in relation to the world and the universe. Piedmont (1999) has proposed the following facets for this factor: sense of universality, prayer fulfillment, and sense of connectedness. In contrast, religion may be conceived as the strength of one's beliefs in a doctrine and the frequency of participation in activities linked with this doctrine (e.g., regular attendance in church). On *a priori* grounds, it is conceivable that a highly religious or spiritual individual would be much less inclined to lasting resentment and that to the contrary, such an individual would choose more rapidly and more frequently the path to forgiveness as opposed to resentment and revenge (see Rye et al., 2000). With regard to self-forgiveness—although it is more difficult to formulate any hypothesis—it is conceivable that a highly spiritual individual would be more inclined to recognize his or her faults and ask for forgiveness, which in turn could only help the self-forgiveness process.

REVIEW OF THE THEORETICAL AND EMPIRICAL LITERATURE

A total of 27 studies have been identified on the basis of three criteria: (1) they present a good enough description of the used items; (2) they contain at least one measure among the ones classified into the six categories previously defined; and (3) they contain at least one personality measure. These studies have been marked with an asterisk in the references. We will examine the results for the four measures for which a sufficient number of studies have been identified: resentment, revenge, forgiving others, and forgiving self. For sensitivity to situations and forgiveness of situations, too few studies were identified to tabulate.

In Table 11.1, we present the correlations between personality dimensions and lasting resentment toward others. Correlations between enduring resentment and agreeableness ranged from −.10 to −.43. The strongest negative correlation was observed for altruism. The correlation between enduring resentment and neuroticism were mostly positive, ranging from .24 to .39. Depression presented the highest positive correlation with lasting resentment (.51), followed by anger, anxiety, and rumination. Extraversion, conscientiousness, and openness were only infrequently related to enduring resentment (see Table 11.1). Measures of religiousness were correlated strongly and negatively with enduring resentment, ranging from −.12 to −.46. The strongest negative correlation was observed for spirituality and enduring resentment (−.46).

In Table 11.2, we present the correlations between personality dimensions and revenge. Correlations between revenge and agreeableness were all strongly negative, ranging from −.29 to −.51. The correlation between revenge and neuroticism was positive, although weaker than what was observed for agreeableness, ranging from .01 to .36, with the exception of the Maltby, Macaskill, and Day (2001) study. Hostility presented the highest positive correlation, followed by anger, anxiety, depression, and rumination.[1] Correlations between revenge and extraversion were negative, ranging from .00 to −.36. They were especially notable among men. Correlations between revenge and conscientiousness were also negative, ranging from −.02 to −.46. Responsibility presented the highest negative correlation (−.46). Correlations between revenge and openness were the weakest observed. Correlations between revenge and religiousness were all negative and among the highest observed, ranging from −14 to −.39.

TABLE 11.1. **Personality and Enduring Resentment**

Personality variable	Personality scale	Resentment scale	r	Study
Agreeableness				
Agreeableness	Big Five Inventory	TTF	−.43	Brown (2003)
	Big Five Inventory	TRIM*-A	−.23, −.10	McCullough et al. (2001)
Altruism	Batson Empathy Scale	TRIM*-A	−.52	Wade et al. (2003)
Emotional empathy	IRI (Empathic concern)	TTF	−.01	Brown (2003)
Perspective taking	IRI (Perspective taking)	TTF	−.29	Brown (2003)
Attitude toward forgiveness	ATF	TTF	−.37	Brown (2003)
Extraversion				
Extraversion	Big Five Inventory	TTF	−.08	Brown (2003)
	Big Five Inventory	TRIM*-A	.02, .04	Brown (2003)
Shyness	Shyness	FS-R	−06^m, .02^f	Neto & Mullet (2004)
	Embarrassability	FS-R	−09^m, −.09^f	Neto & Mullet (2004)
Independence	Independence	FS-R	.21^m, .29^f	Neto & Mullet (2004)
	Interdependence	FS-R	.02^m, −.16^f	Neto & Mullet (2004)
Loneliness	Loneliness	FS-R	.16^m, .10^f	Neto & Mullet (2004)
Neuroticism				
Neuroticism	Big Five Inventory	TTF	.39	Brown (2003)
	Big Five Inventory	TRIM*-A	.22, .32	McCullough & Hoyt (2002)
	Big Five Inventory	TRIM*-A	.36, .24	McCullough & Hoyt (2002)
Positive affectivity	PANAS	TRIM*-A	−.12	McCullough et al. (1998)
Negative affectivity	PANAS	TRIM*-A	.13	McCullough et al. (1998)
	PANAS	TRIM*-A	.28	McCullough et al. (2001)
Anger	State Anger Scale	RFS*-AN	.41	Rye, Loiacono, Folck, Olszewski et al. (2001)
	State Anger Scale	RFS*-AN	.38	Rye, Folck, Heim, Olszewski et al. (in press)

TABLE 11.1.   Personality and Enduring Resentment *(continued)*

Personality variable	Personality scale	Resentment scale	*r*	Study
Anger	State Anger Scale	EFI*	.26	Gisi & d'Amato (2000)
	Trait Anger Scale	RFS*-AN	.34	Rye et al. (2001)
	Trait Anger Scale	RFS*-AN	.32	Rye et al. (in press)
	Trait Anger Scale	TTF	.44	Brown (2003)
Paranoid style	Paranoid Personality Scale	FS-R	.30[f], .38[m]	Muñoz Sastre, Vinsonneau, Chabrol, & Mullet (2004)
Anxiety	Anxiety Scale (S+T)	EFI*	.15	Subkoviak, Enright, & Wu (1992)
	State Anxiety Scale	EFI*	.43	Subkoviak et al. (1995)
Depression	CES-D	RFS*-AN	.51	Rye et al. (in press)
	CES-D	TTF	.34	Brown (2003)
Rumination	IES-Rumination	TRIM*-A	.39	McCullough et al. (2001)
	IES-Suppression	TRIM*-A	.37	McCullough et al. (2001)
	IES-Rumination	TRIM*-A	−.08	McCullough et al. (1998)
Self-esteem	RSES	TTF	−.31	Brown (2003)
	RSES	FS-R	−.08[m], −.07[f]	Neto & Mullet (2004)
Conscientiousness				
Conscientiousness	Big Five Inventory	TTF	−.04	Brown (2003)
	Big Five Inventory	TRIM*-A	.08, −.07	McCullough et al. (2001)
Openness				
Openness	Big Five Inventory	TTF	−.07	Brown (2003)
	Big Five Inventory	TRIM*-A	−.13, .07	McCullough et al. (2001)
Self-deception	Self-Deception	TRIM*-A	.12	McCullough et al. (1998)
Religiousness				
Religiousness	Religiosity Scale	EFI*	−.37	Subkoviak et al. (1995)
	RWBS	RFS*-AN	−.20	Rye et al. (2001)
	RWBS	RFS*-AN	−.30	Rye et al. (2001)
	RWBS	RFS*-AN	−.22	Rye et al. (in press)
Spirituality	EWBS	RFS*-AN	−.40	Rye et al. (2001)
	EWBS	RFS*-AN	−.46	Rye et al. (in press)
	Religious Faith	HFS-O	−.30	Edwards et al. (2002)
Hope	HS-Avoid. Hope Threats	RFS*-AN	−.35	Rye et al. (2001)
	Hope Scale	RFS*-AN	−.12	Rye et al. (in press)

TABLE 11.1. Personality and Enduring Resentment *(continued)*

Note: ATF = Attitude Towards Forgiveness Scale, CES-D = Center for Epidemiological Studies Depression Scale, EFI* = Enright Forgiveness Inventory, EWBS = Existential Well-Being Scale, FS-R = Forgivingness Scale-Resentment, HFS-O = Heartland Forgiveness Scale-Others, HS = Hope Scale, IES = Impact of Event Scale, IRI = Interpersonal Reactivity Inventory, PANAS = Positive and Negative Attitude Scale, RRFS-AN = Rye Forgiveness Scale-Absence of Negative, RSES = Rosenberg Self-Esteem Scale, RWBS = Religious Well-Being Scale, TRIM*-A = Transgression Related Interpersonal Motivations-Avoidance, TTF = Tendency to Forgive Scale. The references to the precise measures of personality used may be found in the reference in the right column.
*State forgiveness scales; ᵐ = Male; ᶠ= Female

TABLE 11.2. Personality and Revenge

Personality variable	Personality scale	Revenge scale	*r*	Study
Agreeableness				
Agreeableness	Big Five Mini-Markers	AFNRS	−.29	Ashton et al. (1998)
	HA-HESC	AFNRS	−.50	Ashton et al. (1998)
	BARS	FOOS	−.51	Leach & Lark (2003)
	Big Five Inventory	FOOS	−.49	McCullough et al. (2001)
	Big Five Inventory	TRIM*-R	−.36, −.50	McCullough et al. (2001)
Altruism	AMAS	AFNRS	−.26	Ashton et al. (1998)
Empathy	Empathy Scale	VS	−.38	Stuckless & Goranson (1992)
Neuroticism				
Neuroticism	BARS	FOOS	.31	Leach & Lark (2003)
	REPQ	FOOS	.09ᵐ, −.07ᶠ	Maltby et al. (2001)
	Big Five Inventory	FOOS	.36	McCullough et al. (2001)
	Big Five Inventory	TRIM*-R	.06, .01	McCullough et al. (2001)
Emotional stability	Big Five Mini-Markers (-)	AFNRS	.21	Ashton et al. (1998)
Positive affectivity	PANAS (-)	TRIM*-R	.10	McCullough et al. (1998)
Negative affectivity	PANAS	TRIM*-R	.17	McCullough et al. (2001)
	PANAS	TRIM*-R	.32	McCullough et al. (1998)
Anger	SAEI	FOOS	.50	Seybold, Hill, Neuman, & Chi (2001)
	TAEI	FOOS	.62	Seybold et al. (2001)
	Trait Anger Scale	VS	.58	Stuckless & Goranson (1992)
Hostility	CISS-Cynical Hostility	FOOS	.63	Seybold et al. (2001)

TABLE 11.2. **Personality and Revenge** *(continued)*

Personality variable	Personality scale	Revenge scale	r	Study
Hostility	CISS-Hostile Attribution	FOOS	.65	Seybold et al. (2001)
	CISS-Hostile Affect	FOOS	.64	Seybold et al. (2001)
Anxiety	State Anxiety Scale	FOOS	.54	Seybold et al. (2001)
	Trait Anxiety Scale	FOOS	.55	Seybold et al. (2001)
	GHQ-Anxiety	FOOS	.11[m], .16[f]	Maltby et al. (2001)
Paranoid style	PPSS	FS-V	.39[f], .50[m]	Muñoz Sastre et al. (2005)
Depression	Depression Inventory	FOOS	.49	Seybold et al. (2001)
	MMPI-Depression	FOOS	.16	Mauger et al. (1992)
	GHQ-Depression	FOOS	.37[m], .23[f]	Maltby et al. (2001)
	CES-D	VI	.02	Brown (2003)
Rumination	IES-Rumination	TRIM*-R	.40	McCullough et al. (2001)
	IES-Suppression	TRIM*-R	.19	McCullough et al. (2001)
	IES-Rumination	TRIM*-R	.27	McCullough et al. (1998)
Psychoticism	MMPI-Defective Inhibition	FOOS	.46	Mauger et al. (1992)
	MMPI-Poignancy	FOOS	.32	Mauger et al. (1992)
	MMPI-Persecutory Ideas	FOOS	.49	Mauger et al. (1992)
	MMPI-Need for Affection	FOOS	.53	Mauger et al. (1992)
	MMPI-Naiveté	FOOS	.45	Mauger et al. (1992)
	MMPI-Self-Alienation	FOOS	.45	Mauger et al. (1992)
	MMPI-Social Alienation	FOOS	.54	Mauger et al. (1992)
	MMPI-Hypochondriasis	FOOS	.12	Mauger et al. (1992)
	MMPI-Hysteria	FOOS	−.09	Mauger et al. (1992)
	MMPI-Psychopathy	FOOS	.21	Mauger et al. (1992)
	MMPI-Paranoia	FOOS	.24	Mauger et al. (1992)
	MMPI-Psychastenia	FOOS	.26	Mauger et al. (1992)
	MMPI-Schizophrenia	FOOS	.36	Mauger et al. (1992)
	MMPI-Hypomania	FOOS	.28	Mauger et al. (1992)
	REPQ	FOOS	.03[m], .17[f]	Maltby et al. (2001)
Extraversion				
Extraversion	BARS	FOOS	−.23	Leach & Lark (2003)
	MMPI-Social Introversion (-)	FOOS	−.28	Mauger et al. (1992)

TABLE 11.2.   **Personality and Revenge** *(continued)*

Personality variable	Personality scale	Revenge scale	*r*	Study
Extraversion	REPQ	FOOS	$-.25^m, -.11^f$	Maltby et al. (2001)
	Big Five Mini-Markers	FNRS	$-.02$	Ashton et al. (1998)
	Big Five Inventory	FOOS	$.00$	McCullough et al. (2001)
	Big Five Inventory	TRIM*-R	$-.36, .10$	McCullough et al. (2001)
Conscientiousness				
Conscientiousness	BARS	FOOS	$-.25$	Leach & Lark (2003)
	Big Five Mini-Markers	AFNRS	$-.09$	Ashton et al. (1998)
	Big Five Inventory	FOOS	$-.24$	McCullough et al. (2001)
	Big Five Inventory	TRIM*-R	$-.36, -.02$	McCullough et al. (2001)
Responsibility	JPI-Responsibility	AFNRS	$-.46$	Ashton et al. (1998)
Self-deception	Self-Deception (-)	TRIM*-R	$-.30$	McCullough et al. (1998)
Openness				
Openness	BARS	FOOS	$-.13$	Leach & Lark (2003)
	Big Five Mini-Markers	AFNRS	$-.17$	Ashton et al. (1998)
	Big Five Inventory	FOOS	$-.07$	McCullough et al. (2001)
	Big Five Inventory	TRIM*-R	$-.08, .07$	McCullough et al. (2001)
Religiousness				
Religiousness	RWBS	FOOS	$-.39$	Leach & Lark (2003)
Spirituality	SCRS	FOOS	$-.38$	Mauger et al. (1996)
	EWBS	FOOS	$-.39$	Leach & Lark (2003)
	STS-Universality	FOOS	$-.14$	Leach & Lark (2003)
	STS-Prayer	FOOS	$-.19$	Leach & Lark (2003)
	STS-Connectedness	FOOS	$-.15$	Leach & Lark (2003)

Note: AFNRS = Ashton Forgiveness Non Retaliation Scale, AMAS = Altruistic Money Allocation Scale, BARS = Bipolar Adjective Rating Scale, CES-D = Center for Epidemiological Studies Depression Scale, CISS = Coping Inventory for Stressful Situations, EWBS = Existential Well-Being Scale, FOOS = Forgiveness of Others Scale, GHQ = General Health Questionnaire, HA-HESC = High Agreeableness-High Emotional Stability Scale, IES = Impact of Event Scale, JPI = Jackson Personality Inventory, MMPI = Minnesota Multiphasic Personality Inventory, PANAS = Positive and Negative Attitude Scale, PPSS = Paranoid Personality Style Subscale, REPQ = Revised Eysenk Personality Questionnaire, RWBS = Religious Well-Being Scale, SAEI = State Anger Expression Inventory, SCRS = Spiritual Coping Scale, STS = Spiritual Transcendence Scale, TAEI = Trait Anger Expression Inventory, TRIM*-R = Transgression Related Interpersonal Motivations-Revenge, VS = Vengeance Scale. The references to the precise measures of personality used may be found in the reference in the right column.
*State forgiveness scales; ^{m} = Male; ^{f} = Female

In Table 11.3, we present the correlations between personality dimensions and forgiveness of others. Correlations between forgiveness of others and agreeableness were all positive, ranging from .25 to .33, with the exception of Walker and Gorsuch's study (2002), which systematically reported lower numbers. Emotional empathy presented the strongest positive correlation, followed by attitude toward forgiveness and perspective taking. Correlations between forgiveness of others and neuroticism were all negative, ranging from −.27 to −.32, with the exception of the Brown (2003) study, which was made on a small sample. Anger presented the strongest negative correlation, followed by rumination and narcissism. Regarding self-esteem, all correlations were weak, but they did change dramatically with gender. Correlations between forgiveness of others and extraversion were mostly positive, although weaker than for agreeableness and neuroticism, ranging from −.02 to .20. Interdependence presented the highest correlations with forgiveness (with values higher for women than for men). Correlations between forgiveness of others and conscientiousness were all positive and in the same range as those observed for extraversion (.04 to .24). Dutifulness presented the highest positive correlation. Correlations between forgiveness of others and openness were weak. Correlations between forgiveness of others and religiousness were positive and notable, ranging from .12 to .29, with the exception of the Enright, Santos, and Al-Mabuk (1989) study, in which different instruments were used. Between hope and forgiveness; however, the correlation was weak and negative.

TABLE 11.3. **Personality and Forgiveness of Others**

Personality variable	Personality scale	Forgiveness scale	r	Study
Agreeableness				
Agreeableness	Big Five Inventory	TNTF	.25, .33, .28	Berry et al. (2001)
	Big Five Inventory	TNTF	.27	Brown (2003)
	IPIP	WFS-O	.07	Walker & Gorsuch (2002)
Warmth	16PF-A	WFS-O	.06	Walker & Gorsuch (2002)
Sensitivity	16PF-I	WFS-O	.05	Walker & Gorsuch (2002)
Emotional empathy	Batson Empathy Scale	SIFS	.52	Wade & Worthington (2003)
	Batson Empathy Scale	TNTF	.24	Wade & Worthington (2003)
	IRI (Empathic concern)	TNTF	.16	Brown (2003)
	Emotional Empathy Scale	FI	.43[m], 61[m], .36[f], .49[f]	Coleman & Byrd (2003)
Perspective taking	IRI	TNTF	.40	Brown (2003)
Gratitude	Gratitude Questionnaire	DTFS	.36	McCullough, Emmons, & Tsang (2002)
	Gratitude Adjectives	DTFS	.30	McCullough et al. (2002)

TABLE 11.3.   **Personality and Forgiveness of Others** *(continued)*

Personality variable	Personality scale	Forgiveness scale	r	Study
Attitude toward forgiveness	ATF	TNTF	.51	Brown (2003)
Extraversion				
Extraversion	Big Five Inventory	TNTF	−.02, .19, −.02	Berry et al. (2001)
	Big Five Inventory	TNTF	.20	Brown (2003)
	IPIP	WFS-O	.02	Walker & Gorsuch (2002)
Introversion	16PF-Q2 (-)	WFS-O	.16	Walker & Gorsuch (2002)
Friendliness	16PF-H	WFS-O	.00	Walker & Gorsuch (2002)
Reserve	16PF-N	WFS-O	−.06	Walker & Gorsuch (2002)
Gregariousness	16PF-F	WFS-O	−.01	Walker & Gorsuch (2002)
Assertiveness	16PF-E	WFS-O	−.02	Walker & Gorsuch (2002)
Independence	Interdependence	FS-F	.11[m], .36[f]	Neto & Mullet (2004)
	Independence (-)	FS-F	.13[m], .17[f]	Neto & Mullet (2004)
Loneliness	Loneliness	FS-F	−.18[m], .13[f]	Neto & Mullet (2004)
Shyness	Shyness (-)	FS-F	.07[m], .19[f]	Neto & Mullet (2004)
	Embarrassability (-)	FS-F	−.06[m], .12[f]	Neto & Mullet (2004)
Neuroticism				
Neuroticism	Big Five Inventory	TNTF	−.29, −.27, −.32	Berry et al. (2001)
	Big Five Inventory	TNTF	−.10	Brown (2003)
	IPIP	WFS-O	−.27	Walker & Gorsuch (2002)
Emotional stability	16PF-C (-)	WFS-O	−.17	Walker & Gorsuch (2002)
	16PF-Q4	WFS-O	−.34	Walker & Gorsuch (2002)
Distrust	16PF-L	WFS-O	−.21	Walker & Gorsuch (2002)
Paranoid style	PPSS	FS-F	−.22[f], −.40[m]	Muñoz Sastre et al. (2005)
Anxiety	16PF-O	WFS-O	−.15	Walker & Gorsuch (2002)
Anger	AQ-Anger	TNTF	−.33, −.35, −.45	Berry et al. (2001)
	State Anger Scale	RFS*-PP	−.11	Rye et al. (in press)
	Trait Anger Scale	TNTF	−.43, −.38, −.43	Berry et al. (2001)
	Trait Anger Scale	TNTF	−.43	Berry & Worthington (2001)

TABLE 11.3.   **Personality and Forgiveness of Others** *(continued)*

Personality variable	Personality scale	Forgiveness scale	r	Study
	Trait Anger Scale	TUFS	−.66	Berry & Worthington (2001)
	Trait Anger Scale	RFS*-PP	−.21	Rye et al. (2001)
	Trait Anger Scale	RFS*-PP	−.09	Rye et al. (in press)
	Trait Anger Scale	FLS	−.31	Rye et al. (2001)
Hostility	AQ-Hostility	TNTF	−.21, −.37, −.32	Berry et al. (2001)
Depression	CES-D	RFS*-PP	−.14	Rye et al. (in press)
Rumination	DRS	TNTF	−.49	Berry et al. (2001)
Self-esteem	Self-Esteem Scale	FS-F	.14[m], −.23[f]	Neto & Mullet (2004)
Narcissism	NPI	DLFS	−.43	Sandage, Worthington, Hight, & Berry (2000)
Conscientiousness				
Conscientiousness	Big Five Inventory	TNTF	.15, .24, .16	Berry et al. (2001)
	Big Five Inventory	TNTF	.04	Brown (2003)
	IPIP	WFS-O	.13	Walker & Gorsuch (2002)
Dutifulness	16PF-G	WFS-O	.21	Walker & Gorsuch (2002)
Orderliness	16PF-Q3	WFS-O	.13	Walker & Gorsuch (2002)
Openness				
Openness	Big Five Inventory	TNTF	.14, .14, .02	Berry et al. (2001)
	Big Five Inventory	TNTF	.11	Brown (2003)
	IPIP	WFS-O	−.02	Walker & Gorsuch (2002)
Intellect	16PF-B	WFS-O	−.01	Walker & Gorsuch (2002)
Imagination	16PF-M	WFS-O	−.18	Walker & Gorsuch (2002)
Complexity	16PF-Q1	WFS-O	.12	Walker & Gorsuch (2002)
Religiousness				
Religiousness	Religious Belief Scale	Dilemmas	.33, .54	Enright et al. (1989)
	Religiousness Scale	RFS*-PP	.29	Rye et al. (2001)
	Religiousness Scale	FLS	.22	Rye et al. (2001)
	RWBS	RFS*-PP	.23	Rye et al. (2001)
	RWBS	RFS*-PP	.12	Rye et al. (in press)

TABLE 11.3.   Personality and Forgiveness of Others (continued)

Personality variable	Personality scale	Forgiveness scale	r	Study
Religiousness	Religiosity Scale	DTFS	.27	Sandage et al. (2000)
Spirituality	EWBS	RFS*-PP	.21	Rye et al. (2001)
	EWBS	RFS*-PP	.21	Rye et al. (in press)
Hope	Hope Scale	RFS*-PP	−.05	Rye et al. (in press)

Note: 16PF = 16 Primary Factors, AQ = Aggression Questionnaire, ATF = Attitude Towards Forgiveness Scale, CES-D = Center for Epidemiological Studies Depression Scale, DRS = Dissipation Rumination Scale, DTFS = Disposition to Forgive Scale, FS-F = Forgivingness Scale-Forgiveness, IPIP = International Personality Item Pool, IRI = Interpersonal Reactivity Inventory, NPI = Narcissism Personality Inventory, PPSS = Paranoid Personality Style Subscale, RFS*-PP = Rye Forgiveness Scale-Presence of Positive, TNTF = Transgression Narrative Test of Forgivingness, TUFS = Trait Unforgiveness Forgiveness Scale, WFS-O = Walker Forgiveness Scale-Others. The references to the precise measures of personality used may be found in the reference in the right column.
*State forgiveness scales; [m] = Male; [f] = Female

In Table 11.4, we present the correlations between personality dimensions and self-forgiveness. Correlations between self-forgiveness and neuroticism were all quite strong and negative. The facets that presented the highest correlations were anxiety, hostility, depression, and anger.[2] Correlations between self-forgiveness and extraversion were weak but positive. Assertiveness presented the highest positive correlation. As regards agreeableness, openness, conscientiousness, and religiousness, the observed correlations were heterogeneous; therefore, it is premature to draw any conclusions.

To demonstrate that the four constructs are related but similar, an individual study might employ a variety of methods, such as using confirmatory factor analyses and showing that different patterns of predictors connect variables. We have examined patterns of connections for four forgiveness-related variables and personality. We conclude that the patterns are similar in general but are differentiated enough to justify conceptualizing the variables as different from each other. The starkest differences are between forgiveness of self and revenge. The most similar patterns are between resentment and revenge.

We do not want to overemphasize the magnitude, significance, or importance of the correlations. We recognize the perils in comparing across studies. However, we are trying to establish that regardless of different types of samples, sample sizes, and measures, some consistency is apparent. In addition, we acknowledge as a further limitation of our approach that several studies are overrepresented in Tables 11.1 through 11.4 by virtue of their multiple correlations (e.g., Mauger et al., 1992).

TABLE 11.4.   Personality and Forgiveness of Self

Personality variable	Personality scale	Forgiveness scale	r	Study
Agreeableness				
Agreeableness	BARS	FOSS	.22	Leach & Lark (2003)
	IPIP	WFS-S	.02	Walker & Gorsuch (2002)
Warmth	16PF-A	WFS-S	.02	Walker & Gorsuch (2002)
Sensitivity	16PF-I	WFS-S	.01	Walker & Gorsuch (2002)
Emotional empathy	EES	FOSS	−.11[m], .07[f]	Macaskill et al. (2002)
Extraversion				
Extraversion	Big Five Inventory	FOSS	.11	Berry et al. (2001)
	IPIP	WFS-S	.14	Walker & Gorsuch (2002)
Introversion	16PF-Q2 (-)	WFS-S	.10	Walker & Gorsuch (2002)
Friendliness	16PF-H	WFS-S	.20	Walker & Gorsuch (2002)
Reserve	16PF-N (-)	WFS-S	.14	Walker & Gorsuch (2002)
Gregariousness	16PF-F	WFS-S	.13	Walker & Gorsuch (2002)
Assertiveness	16PF-E	WFS-S	.23	Walker & Gorsuch (2002)
	REPQ	FOSS	−.19[m], −.05[f]	Maltby et al. (2001)
Neuroticism				
Neuroticism	BARS	FOSS	−.54	Leach & Lark (2003)
	IPIP	WFS-S	−.12	Walker & Gorsuch (2002)
Emotional stability	16PF-C (-)	WFS-S	−.52	Walker & Gorsuch (2002)
	16PF-Q4	WFS-S	−.52	Walker & Gorsuch (2002)
Distrust	16PF-L	WFS-S	−.13	Walker & Gorsuch (2002)
Anxiety	16PF-O	WFS-S	−.44	Walker & Gorsuch (2002)
	REPQ	FOSS	−.53[m], −.41[f]	Maltby et al. (2001)
	State Anxiety Scale	FOSS	−.64	Seybold et al. (2001)
	Trait Anxiety Scale	FOSS	−.76	Seybold et al. (2001)
	GHQ-Anxiety	FOSS	−.22[m], −.22[f]	Maltby et al. (2001)
Anger	SAEI	FOSS	−.36	Seybold et al. (2001)
	TAEI	FOSS	−.58	Seybold et al. (2001)
Hostility	CISS-Cynical Hostility	FOSS	−.62	Seybold et al. (2001)
	CISS-Hostile Attribution	FOSS	−.62	Seybold et al. (2001)
	CISS-Hostile Affect	FOSS	−.52	Seybold et al. (2001)
Depression	Depression Inventory	FOSS	−.50	Seybold et al. (2001)
	MMPI-Depression	FOSS	−.46	Mauger et al. (1992)

TABLE 11.4. Personality and Forgiveness of Self *(continued)*

Personality variable	Personality scale	Forgiveness scale	r	Study
	GHQ-Depression	FOSS	−.32[m], −.27[f]	Maltby et al. (2001)
Psychoticism	REPQ	FOSS	.05[m], −.08[f]	Maltby et al. (2001)
	MMPI-Defective Inhibition	FOSS	−.47	Mauger et al. (1992)
	MMPI-Poignancy	FOSS	−.44	Mauger et al. (1992)
	MMPI-Need for Affection	FOSS	.44	Mauger et al. (1992)
	MMPI-Naiveté	FOSS	.27	Mauger et al. (1992)
	MMPI-Persecutory Ideas	FOSS	−.49	Mauger et al. (1992)
	MMPI-Social Introversion	FOSS	−.47	Mauger et al. (1992)
	MMPI-Self Alienation	FOSS	−.69	Mauger et al. (1992)
	MMPI-Social Alienation	FOSS	−.62	Mauger et al. (1992)
	MMPI-Hypochondriasis	FOSS	−.23	Mauger et al. (1992)
	MMPI-Hysteria	FOSS	−.14	Mauger et al. (1992)
	MMPI-Psychopathy	FOSS	−.40	Mauger et al. (1992)
	MMPI-Paranoia	FOSS	−.41	Mauger et al. (1992)
	MMPI-Psychastenia	FOSS	−.56	Mauger et al. (1992)
	MMPI-Schizophrenia	FOSS	−.49	Mauger et al. (1992)
	MMPI-Hypomania	FOSS	−.16	Mauger et al. (1992)

Conscientiousness

Conscientiousness	BARS	FOSS	.30	Leach & Lark (2003)
	IPIP	WFS-S	−.11	Walker & Gorsuch (2002)
Dutifulness	16PF-G	WFS-S	−.11	Walker & Gorsuch (2002)
Orderliness	16PF-Q3	WFS-S	−.06	Walker & Gorsuch (2002)

Openness

Openness	BARS	FOSS	.16	Leach & Lark (2003)
	IPIP	WFS-S	.12	Walker & Gorsuch (2002)
Intellect	16PF-B	WFS-S	.22	Walker & Gorsuch (2002)
Imagination	16PF-M	WFS-S	−.10	Walker & Gorsuch (2002)
Complexity	16PF-Q1	WFS-S	.12	Walker & Gorsuch (2002)

Religiousness

Religiousness	RWBS	FOSS	−.02	Leach & Lark (2003)
Spirituality	Religious Faith	HFS-S	.13	Edwards et al. (2002)

TABLE 11.4.   **Personality and Forgiveness of Self** *(continued)*

Personality variable	Personality scale	Forgiveness scale	r	Study
Spirituality	EWBS	FOSS	.31	Leach & Lark (2003)
	STS-Universality	FOSS	−.01	Leach & Lark (2003)
	STS-Prayer	FOSS	−.13	Leach & Lark (2003)
	STS-Connectedness	FOSS	.01	Leach & Lark (2003)

Note: 16PF = 16 Primary Factors, AFNRS = Ashton Forgiveness Non Retaliation Scale, BARS = Bipolar Adjective rating Scale, CISS = Coping Inventory for Stressful Situations, EES = Emotional Empathy Scale, EWBS = Existential Well-Being Scale, FOSS = Forgiveness of Self Scale, GHQ = General Health Questionnaire, HFS-S = Heartland Forgiveness Scale-Self, IPIP = International Personality Item Pool, MMPI = Minnesota Multiphasic Personality Inventory, REPQ = Revised Eysenk Personality Questionnaire, RWBS = Religious Well-Being Scale, SAEI = State Anger Expression Inventory, STS = Spiritual Transcendence Scale, TAEI = Trait Anger Expression Inventory, WFS-S = Walker Forgiveness Scale-Self. The references to the precise measures of personality used may be found in the reference in the right column; [m] = Male; [f] = Female

IMPORTANCE OF PERSONALITY FACTORS AS COMPARED WITH RELATIONAL AND SITUATIONAL FACTORS

McCullough and Hoyt (2002) examined the respective impact of situational, relational, and personal variables in the prediction of resentment, revenge, and forgiveness of others. In a first study, they used fictional and freely evoked (real) situations in which the transgressor was a romantic partner, a same-sex friend, or an opposite-sex friend. The transgressions ranged from less severe to severe. The authors also assessed the personality scores for each participant. Personality accounted for 18% (resentment), 18% (revenge), and 15% (forgiveness) of the variance of the responses (correlations of .42, .42, and .39, respectively). In a second situation, they used the same device but this time the transgressor was the mother, the father, a same-sex friend, or an opposite-sex friend. The transgressions still ranged from less severe to severe. Personality scores for each participant were also assessed using peer ratings. Personality accounted for 30% (resentment), 33% (revenge), and 40% (forgiveness) of the variance of the responses when assessed via self-ratings and 19%, 24%, and 30% of the variance when assessed via peer ratings.

In summary, personality factors explained 20% to 35% of the variance in variables that we examined in this chapter (resentment, revenge, forgiveness of others, and forgiveness of self).

NEW RESEARCH DIRECTIONS NEEDED IN THE AREA

Despite the existence of an important body of research in this area, it would be essential to continue the research in numerous new directions. A first direction, which is the direct continuation of the studies presented in this chapter, would be to research more systematically the relations between forgiveness (or revenge) and personality by examining different facets of each personality factor. This is an important new direction as the analysis we have proposed in the previous section suggests, and existing research demonstrates that not all facets are equal with regard to their correlations with forgiveness (or revenge). For instance, as shown by Berry, Worthington, Parrott, O'Connor, and Wade (2001) and Walker and Gorsuch (2002), the correlation between extraversion and self-forgiveness is rather low (about .10). However, regarding one of the facets of this factor, assertiveness, this correlation becomes much more notable. It is indeed expected that a more assertive individual would experience less difficulty in coming to self-forgiveness, compared with a less assertive individual. It would therefore be interesting to explore the correlations between self-forgiveness and other facets of extraversion, such as poise or leadership.

Another direction already explored by some researchers would be to study more systematically the influence of gender in the correlations between forgiveness (or revenge) and personality. As shown by Neto and Mullet (2004), some correlations are reversed with gender (see Table 11.3). We could cite here the case of forgiveness and self-esteem. Neto and Mullet (2004) found a negative correlation for women and a positive one for men: Women who scored high on self-esteem were less likely to forgive; whereas for men, this same score correlated positively with forgiveness, although to a lesser extent (see also Maltby et al., 2001).

Another possible approach would be to study the correlations between personality and forgiveness (or revenge) from a developmental standpoint. As shown by Mauger, Saxon, Hamill, and Pannel (1996), the correlations between agreeableness and revenge are notably different in adolescents (−.72) and adults (−.34). Further studies of these differences may contribute to a better understanding of forgiveness and what motivates it at different ages. One hypothesis would be that forgiveness of others is mainly correlated with agreeableness in childhood and adolescence but that with age it becomes increasingly less correlated with agreeableness and more correlated with neuroticism. It is also possible that this pattern of correlations changes again for the elderly (see also Mullet & Girard, 2000).

A fourth approach would be to study the correlations between personality and forgiveness cross-culturally (for a review, see chapter 4 by Sandage & Williamson). Fu, Watkins, and Hui (2003) found that the correlations between anxiety and forgiveness were quite low in a Chinese sample. This correlation was shown to be one of the strongest in most Western studies (see Seybold et al., 2001). More intercultural studies are needed to help understand how the impact of personality on forgiveness and revenge vary (and as a result, what they mean) from one cultural context to another. The existing intercultural studies seem to indicate important cultural variations on the willingness to forgive (Fu, Watkins, & Hui, 2003; Kadima Kadiangandu, Mullet, & Vinsonneau, 2001), and these differences merit further analysis (see also Azar & Mullet, 2002).

Another possible approach would be to study more systematically the interactions between personality and situational factors (McCullough & Hoyt, 2002). For instance, how does the correlation between forgiveness and neuroticism vary according to the type (psychological, physical, or material) or the intensity (not severe, moderately severe, severe) of the offense? It could be hypothesized that the correlation between forgiveness and neuroticism is stronger in the case of a psychological offense as compared with a material loss (see Gauché & Mullet, in press) and in the case of a mild offense as compared with a severe one (McCullough & Hoyt, 2002). In the same vein, we recommend more systematic study of the interactions between personality and forgiveness as a function of the proximity of the offender (McCullough & Hoyt, 2002). For instance, how does the correlation between agreeableness and revenge vary according to the proximity of the offender? Is this correlation the same for an unknown, a casual relation (e.g., a colleague at work), a distant relative, and a close family member? It could be hypothesized that this correlation is stronger in the first and second cases, compared with the last two.

We suggest extending the study of forgiveness and personality to variables other than the willingness to forgive or revenge. It would be interesting to investigate the extent to which the conceptualizations of forgiveness are related to personality. For instance, what is the relation between agreeableness and the concept that forgiveness implies a change of heart (the replacement of negative emotions toward the offender with more positive emotions)? In other words, do the conceptualizations of forgiveness change as an individual scores higher on agreeableness? Or what is the relation between conscientiousness and the concept that forgiveness is "good and moral?" More generally, is the impact of personality on forgiveness a direct one, or is it more or less "filtered" by each person's conceptualizations of forgiveness (Mullet, Girard, & Bakhshi, 2004)?

Finally, it would be essential to study the relations between forgiveness and personality using instruments other than those presented in this chapter. Emmons (2000) recommended the use of more diversified instruments. Based on McAdams (1996), he suggested that in addition to the personality measures of Level I "relatively noncon-ditional, decontextualized, and comparative dimensions of personality called traits" (p. 157), researchers use Level II measures: "contextualized strategies, plans and con-cerns that enable a person to solve various life tasks and achieve personally important life goals" (p. 158). Also, Emmons suggested that researchers use Level III measures or life narratives: "While constructs at Levels I and II can lead to a healthy understand-ing of forgiveness, it may be only through incorporation of constructs at Level III that a complete account of forgiveness within personality can be constructed" (p. 171).

This is because "forgiveness is the integrated state of a person who is in right relationship with God, with others, and within himself or herself" (p. 171).

RELEVANCE FOR CLINICAL AND APPLIED INTERVENTIONS

These results have implications for the practice of forgiveness-oriented counseling. As an example, individuals experiencing more lasting resentment toward others were shown to be the ones who present low scores on agreeableness in general (especially low on altruism and perspective taking and high in cynicism) and religiousness (especially low on spirituality), and high on neuroticism (especially high scores on anger, anxiety, depression, and rumination). As a result, patients facing lasting resentment problems may be systematically invited to express their anger in order to take control of it and to take the perspective of others. Clinicians might also help them overcome depressive tendencies. As another example, vengefulness appeared to be strongly related to neuroticism in general and to a paranoid personality style in particular. An area of concern here is the difficulty of diagnosing paranoid personality disorders or strong paranoid tendencies: Individuals with paranoid personalities may conceal their paranoid tendencies quite well, and the diagnosis can be easily missed. In some cases, strong vengefulness must systematically lead one to consider the possibility of paranoid tendencies or personality disorders and to take them into account in the psychotherapeutic process.

PERSONAL THEORETICAL PERSPECTIVES ON THE FIELD

We are currently conducting research in two different directions. First, we examine in a systematic way the relationships between resentment, revenge, forgiveness of others, and the many facets that are subsumed under the neuroticism factor (stability, happiness, calmness, moderation, toughness, impulse control, imperturbability, cool-headedness, and tranquility), as well as the many facets that are subsumed under the agreeableness factor (understanding, warmth, morality, pleasantness, empathy, cooperation, sympathy, tenderness, and nurturance). One of our hypotheses, based on the double nature of forgiveness (intrapersonal and interpersonal), is that the main relationships between forgivingness and personality concern the interpersonal facets of personality (e.g., cooperation, toughness) much more than the intrapersonal, strictly self-referential facets of personality (e.g., happiness, morality). Second, we examine the relationships between conceptualization of forgiveness and personality at the level of the factors as well as at the level of the facets. One of our hypotheses is that the effect of personality on forgiveness is largely mediated by the conceptualizations one has about forgiveness (e.g., implying the replacement of negative emotions toward the offender with more positive emotions).

CONCLUSION

Forgiveness is a complex "state" for which there is more than one path. It is conceivable that one accesses the state of forgiveness only after integrating multiple data and trying numerous paths, not all straightforward. Indeed, forgiveness is the outer translation of a long and often difficult inner process, a process that is a reflection of the victim's personality.

NOTES

1. From a psychopathological standpoint, persecutory ideas, schizophrenia, self-alienation, social alienation, and defective inhibition are aspects of neuroticism that highly correlated with revenge.
2. From a psychopathological standpoint, practically all indices obtained with MMPI highly correlate with self-forgiveness.

ACKNOWLEDGMENTS

This work was supported by POCTI/PSI/46245/2002, the Laboratoire Cognition et Décision of the Ecole Pratique des Hautes Etudes, and the UMR Travail et Cognition of the Mirail University.

REFERENCES

Note: Studies that contain at least one personality measure are marked with an asterisk.

Aquino, K., Tripp, T. M., & Bies, R. J. (2001). How employees respond to personal offense: The effect of blame attribution, victim status, and offender status on revenge and reconciliation in the workplace. *Journal of Applied Psychology, 86,* 52–59.

*Ashton, M. C., Paunonen, S. V., Helmes, E., & Jackson, D. N. (1998). Kin altruism, reciprocal altruism, and the Big Five personality factors. *Evolution and Human Behavior, 19,* 243–255.

Azar, F., & Mullet, E. (2002). "Forgiveness": Overall level and factor structure in a sample of Muslim and Christian-Lebanese. *Peace and Conflict: A Peace Psychology Journal, 8,* 17–30.

*Berry, J. W., & Worthington, E. L., Jr. (2001). Forgivingness, relationship quality, stress while imagining relationship events, and physical and mental health. *Journal of Counseling Psychology, 48,* 447–455.

*Berry, J. W., Worthington, E. L., Jr., Parrott, L., III, O'Connor, L. E., & Wade, N. G. (2001). Dispositional forgivingness: Development and construct validity of the Transgression Narrative Test of Forgivingness (TNTF). *Personality and Social Psychology Bulletin, 27,* 1277–1290.

*Brown, R. P. (2003). Measuring individual differences in the tendency to forgive: Validity and links with depression. *Personality and Social Psychology Bulletin, 29,* 759–771.

*Coleman, P. K., & Byrd, C. P. (2003). Interpersonal correlates of peer victimization among young adolescents. *Journal of Youth and Adolescence, 32,* 301–314.

*Edwards, L. M, Lapp-Rinker, R. H., Magyar-Moe, J. L., Rehfeldt, J. D., Ryder, J. A., Brown, J. C., et al. (2002). A positive relationship between religious faith and forgiveness: Faith in the absence of data. *Pastoral Psychology, 50,* 147–152.

Emmons, R. A. (2000). Personality and forgiveness. In M. E. McCullough, K. I. Pargament, & C. E. Thorensen (Eds.), *Forgiveness: Theory, research and practice* (pp. 156–178). New York: Guilford Press.

Enright, R. D., & Fitzgibbons, R. P. (2000). *Helping clients forgive: An empirical guide for resolving anger and restoring hope.* Washington, DC: American Psychological Association.

*Enright, R. D., Santos, M. J. D., & Al-Mabuk, R. (1989). The adolescent as forgiver. *Journal of Adolescence, 12,* 95–110.

Fu, H., Watkins, D., & Hui, E. K. F. (2003). *Personality correlates of the disposition towards interpersonal forgiveness: A Chinese perspective.* Unpublished manuscript, University of Hong Kong, Hong Kong, China.

Gauché, M., & Mullet, E. (in press). Do we forgive physical aggression in the same way that we forgive psychological aggression? *Aggressive Behavior.*

Gisi, T. M., & d'Amato, R. C. (2000). What factors should be considered in rehabilitation: Are anger, social desirability, and forgiveness related in adults with traumatic brain injuries? *International Journal of Neurosciences, 105,* 121–133.

Kadima Kadiangandu, J., Mullet, E., & Vinsonneau, G. (2001). Forgivingness: A Congo-France comparison. *Journal of Cross-Cultural Psychology, 32,* 504–511.

*Leach, M. M., & Lark, R. (2003). Does spirituality add to personality in the study of trait forgiveness? *Personality and Individual Differences, 30,* 881–885

*Macaskill, A., Maltby, J., & Day, L. (2002). Forgiveness of self and others and emotional empathy. *Journal of Social Psychology, 142,* 663–665.

MacDonald, D. A. (2000). Spirituality: Description, measurement, and relation to the five factor model of personality. *Journal of Personality, 68,* 153–197.

*Maltby, J., Macaskill, A., & Day, L. (2001). Failure to forgive self and others: A replication and extension of the relationship between forgiveness, personality, social desirability, and general health. *Personality and Individual Differences, 30,* 881–885.

*Mauger, P. A., Perry, J. E., Freeman, T., Grove, D. C., McBride, A. G., & McKinney, K. E. (1992). The measurement of forgiveness: Preliminary research. *Journal of Psychology and Christianity, 11,* 170–180.

*Mauger, P. A., Saxon, A., Hamill, C., & Pannel, M. (1996, October). *The relationship of forgiveness to interpersonal behavior.* Paper presented at the annual convention of the Southeastern Psychological Association, Norfolk, VA.

McAdams, D. P. (1996). Personality, modernity and the storied self: A contemporary framework for studying the self. *Psychological Inquiry, 7,* 295–321.

*McCullough, M. E., Bellah, C. G., Kilpatrick, S. D., & Johnson, J. L. (2001). Vengefulness: Relationships with forgiveness, rumination, well-being, and the Big Five. *Personality and Social Psychology Bulletin, 27,* 601–610.

*McCullough, M. E., Emmons, R. A., & Tsang, J-A. (2002). The grateful disposition: A conceptual and empirical topography. *Journal of Personality and Social Psychology, 82,* 112–127.

*McCullough, M. E., & Hoyt, W. T. (2002). Transgression-related motivational dispositions: Personality substrates of forgiveness and their links to the Big Five. *Personality and Social Psychology Bulletin, 28,* 1556–1573.

*McCullough, M. E., Rachal, K. C., Sandage, S. J., Worthington, E. L., Jr., Brown, S. W., & Hight, T. L. (1998). Interpersonal forgiving in close relationships: II. Theoretical elaboration and measurement. *Journal of Personality and Social Psychology, 75,* 1586–1603.

McCullough, M. E., & Worthington, E. L. (1999). Religion and the forgiving personality. *Journal of Personality, 67,* 1141–1164.

Mullet, E., Barros, J., Frongia, L., Usai, V., & Neto F. (2003). Religious involvement and the forgiving personality. *Journal of Personality, 71,* 1–19.

Mullet, E., Girard, M., & Bakshi, P. (2004). Conceptualizations of forgiveness. *European Psychologist, 9,* 78–86.

Mullet, E., Houdbine, A., Laumonnier, S., & Girard, M. (1998). Forgivingness: Factorial structure in a sample of young, middle-aged, and elderly adults. *European Psychologist, 3,* 289–297.

Mullet, E., & Girard, M. (2000). Developmental and cognitive points of view on forgiveness. In M. E. McCullough, K. I. Pargament, & C. E. Thoresen (Eds.), *Forgiveness: Theory, research and practice* (pp. 111–132). New York: Guilford Press.

*Muñoz Sastre, M. T., Vinsonneau, G., Chabrol, H., & Mullet, E. (2005). Forgivingness and the paranoid personality style. *Personality and Individual Differences, 38,* 765–772.

*Neto, F., & Mullet, E. (2004). Personality, self-esteem, and self-construal as correlates of forgivingness. *European Journal of Personality, 18,* 15–30.

Piedmont, R. L. (1999). Does spirituality represent the sixth factor of personality? Spiritual transcendence and the five-factor model. *Journal of Personality, 67,* 985–1013.

Roberts, R. C. (1995). Forgivingness. *American Philosophical Quarterly, 32,* 289–306.

*Rye, M. S., Folck, C. D., Heim, T. A., Olszewski, B. T., & Traina, E. (in press). Forgiveness of an ex-spouse: How does it relate to mental health following a divorce? *Journal of Divorce and Remarriage.*

*Rye, M. S., Loiacono, D. M., Folck, C. D., Olszewski, B. T., Heim, T. A., & Madia, B. P. (2001). Evaluation of the psychometric properties of two forgiveness scales. *Current Psychology, 20,* 260–277.

Rye, M. S., Pargament, K. I., Ali, M. A., Beck, G. L., Dorff, E. N., Hallisey, C., et al. (2000). Religious perspectives on forgiveness. In M. E. McCullough, K. I. Pargament, and C. E. Thoresen (Eds.), *Forgiveness: Theory, research, and practice* (pp. 17–40). New York: Guilford Press.

*Sandage, S. J., Worthington, E. L., Jr., Hight, T. L., & Berry, J. W. (2000). Seeking forgiveness: Theoretical context and an initial empirical study. *Journal of Psychology and Theology, 28,* 21–35.

*Seybold, K. S., Hill, P. C., Neuman, J. K., & Chi, D. S. (2001). Physiological and psychological correlates of forgiveness. *Journal of Psychology and Christianity, 20,* 250–259.

*Subkoviak, M. J., Enright, R. D., & Wu, C.-R. (1992, October). *Current developments related to measuring forgiveness.* Paper presented at the annual meeting of the Mid-Western Educational Research Association, Chicago.

*Subkoviak, M. J., Enright, R. D., Wu, C-R., Gassin, E. A., Freedman, S., Olson, L. M., et al. (1995). Measuring interpersonal forgiveness in late adolescence and middle adulthood. *Journal of Adolescence, 18,* 641–655.

*Stuckless, N., & Goranson, R. (1992). The Vengeance Scale: Development of a measure of attitudes toward revenge. *Journal of Social Behavior and Personality, 7,* 25–42.

Thompson, L. Y., Snyder, C. R., Hoffman, L., Michael, S. T., Rasmussen, H. N., Billings, L. S., et al. (2005). Dispositional forgiveness of self, other, and situations. *Journal of Personality, 73,* 316–360.

*Wade, N. G., & Worthington, E. L., Jr. (2003). Overcoming interpersonal offenses: Is forgiveness the only way to deal with unforgiveness? *Journal of Counseling and Development, 81,* 343–353.

*Walker, D. F., & Gorsuch, R. L. (2002). Forgiveness within the Big Five personality model. *Personality and Individual Differences, 32,* 1127–1137.

Worthington, E. L., Jr., & Wade, N. G. (1999). The social psychology of unforgiveness and forgiveness and implications for clinical practice. *Journal of Social and Clinical Psychology, 18,* 385–418.

Part Four

CLOSE RELATIONSHIPS AND FORGIVENESS

Chapter Twelve

Forgiveness and Relational Repair

Caryl E. Rusbult
Peggy A. Hannon
Shevaun L. Stocker
Eli J. Finkel

Many social scientists conceptualize forgiveness as an *intra*personal phenomenon, adopting victim-focused explanations of its causes and consequences. For example, some empirical work has examined the precise cognitive and affective processes by which victims come to forgive those who have perpetrated acts of violence against them; other work has examined the circumstances under which it is beneficial for a victim to forgive such offenses (for a review, see McCullough, 2001). This is well and good—a victim-focused approach may be entirely suitable in settings wherein victim and perpetrator have neither a past nor a future with one another, because in temporally bounded, fundamentally ahistoric settings, the forgiveness process essentially rests on the victim's capacity to "heal the self" and move on.

However, in settings wherein victim and perpetrator have a past and (potentially) a future with one another—that is, in ongoing relationships—there is much to be gained by adopting an *inter*personal conceptualization of forgiveness. To begin with, we note the obvious: We live our lives in relationships. In comparison to time spent with strangers, we spend more time with people with whom we have some sort of relationship, whether as spouse, parent, friend, or co-worker. In comparison to interactions with strangers, interactions with relational partners are more important to us, are more central to our identities and values, and have a greater impact on our physical and psychological well-being (Reis, Collins, & Berscheid, 2000). Also, many transgressions come about within ongoing relationships, and those transgressions are consequential—we have a stake in addressing and resolving them. Moreover, in ongoing relationships, the forgiveness process itself is inherently interpersonal—it is a process to which both victim *and* perpetrator contribute. In this broad context, it is self-evident that understanding forgiveness rests on questions larger than how victims forgive and whether this is a good thing; we must also understand when, how, and why forgiveness is good for relationships.

The goal of this chapter is to provide a conceptual framework for understanding forgiveness and relational repair. We begin by introducing key tenets of interdependence theory (Kelley et al., 2003; Kelley & Thibaut, 1978; Thibaut & Kelley, 1959), discussing concepts and principles that are central to analyzing transgression, forgiveness, and reconciliation. Then we use this framework to (a) analyze victim and perpetrator reactions to transgressions, (b) describe forgiveness as a temporally extended phenomenon that rests on the character of victim–perpetrator interaction, and (c) discuss personal and relational processes that are relevant to understanding reconciliation and relational repair. We also consider the relevance of this theoretical framework for clinical and applied interventions, and conclude with suggestions regarding future theoretical and empirical work regarding forgiveness and relational repair.

THEORETICAL ASSUMPTIONS REGARDING FORGIVENESS

Transgressions and Norms.   From an interdependence perspective, a *transgression* is an incident in which a perpetrator is perceived (by the victim and perhaps by the perpetrator as well) to have knowingly departed from the norms that govern their relationship, thereby harming the victim. *Norms* are rule-based inclinations to respond in a specified manner to specified types of interpersonal situation (Rusbult & Van Lange, 2003)—that is, partners implicitly or explicitly agree that under certain circumstances, some courses of action are mandated (e.g., always "being on one another's side"), whereas other courses of action are forbidden (e.g., extra-relationship romantic involvement). Although norms may initially be established as a simple matter of convenience—for example, as rules by which partners may coordinate specific types of interaction—over time, such rules often "take on the characteristics of a moral obligation" (Thibaut & Kelley, 1959, p. 128).

In light of the fact that transgressions cause victims harm and violate moral obligations, it is not surprising that such incidents instigate a rather potent constellation of victim and perpetrator cognition, affect, and behavior. This signature constellation is characterized by victim vengeance and perpetrator guilt—a pattern of response that can be seen as functionally adaptive (at least in the short run), in that such inclinations provide some measure of reassurance that a transgression will not recur. Indeed, it has been argued that among social animals—for whom mutual cooperation and rule adherence have tremendous functional value—there may be an underlying, evolutionary basis for tendencies toward vengeance and guilt (Ridley, 1996).

Forgiveness and the Transformation Process.   Moving beyond this potent constellation of victim and perpetrator negativity rests on victim forgiveness, which entails "granting pardon," or "canceling a debt." Consistent with other interpersonal conceptualizations (Baumeister, Exline, & Sommer, 1998; McCullough, Worthington, & Rachal, 1997), we define *forgiveness* as the victim's willingness to resume pretransgression interaction tendencies—the willingness to forego grudge and vengeance, instead coming to behave toward the perpetrator in a positive and constructive manner

(Rusbult, Kumashiro, Finkel, & Wildschut, 2002). We propose that forgiveness rests on a psychological transformation of the transgression situation. Given that victims experience powerful, gut-level impulses toward vengeance, to make way for forgiveness, these destructive impulses must be tempered. *Transformation* describes the process by which a victim takes broader considerations into account than the transgression per se, including not only concern for the perpetrator and relationship but also broader norms or values. The individual's immediate, gut-level impulses are termed *given preferences*; the psychologically transformed preferences that directly guide behavior are termed *effective preferences* (Kelley & Thibaut, 1978).

How is victim motivation transformed from righteous indignation and craving for vengeance to willingness to entertain the possibility of forgiveness? Prosocial transformation comes about via changes in the victim's cognitive and emotional experiences: The victim essentially thinks through the causes and implications of the transgression, developing a more benevolent, less blameful understanding of the event (e.g., identifying extenuating circumstances, acknowledging personal culpability). More or less concurrent with such cognitive activity, the victim undergoes a critical affective shift, moving (sometimes slowly) from fury and antagonism to compassion and caring for the perpetrator.[1]

The process by which benevolence replaces blame and compassion replaces antagonism is not necessarily (or typically) an immediate, unilateral response on the part of victims. To begin with, the transformation process itself typically takes some time. It is important to note that perpetrators, too, play a role in promoting (vs. impeding) the victim's prosocial transformation. If perpetrators behave badly—for example, by reacting in a defensive manner, minimizing the severity of a transgression, denying responsibility for it, or offering insincere apology—the transformation process and forgiveness become very effortful and psychologically threatening for victims. Defensive maneuvers on the part of perpetrators to some degree are understandable in that victims and perpetrators often have differing perspectives on transgressions, and perpetrators feel the need to justify their behavior not only to victims but also to themselves. In contrast, when perpetrators exhibit genuine remorse, it becomes easier for victims to undergo the sorts of cognitive and affective tempering upon which prosocial transformation rests.

Relational Repair. Of course, perpetrator apology and victim forgiveness do not automatically yield *reconciliation*, defined as the resumption of pretransgression relationship status. From an interdependence perspective, the two most important considerations in understanding reconciliation center on restoring *commitment*, defined as the extent to which each partner intends to persist in the relationship, feels psychologically attached to it, and exhibits long-term orientation toward it; and *trust*, defined as the strength of each partner's conviction that the other can be counted on to behave in a benevolent manner. Commitment reliably motivates prosocial acts, such as accommodation and sacrifice; trust is based on each person's perception that the other is willing to engage in such prosocial acts (Rusbult, Olsen, Davis, & Hannon, 2001). Thus, trust represents conviction regarding the strength of a partner's commitment.

Reconciling following a significant transgression entails mutual investment, whereby both partners exert significant, coordinated effort to achieve a desired end state—restored couple functioning (Kelley et al., 2003). To progress toward reconciliation, each partner must enact prosocial behaviors during interaction, and each must sustain the energy and motivation to do so over an extended period of time. For example, the victim must exhibit considerable good will, setting aside blame and demonstrating willingness to begin afresh with a clean slate; the perpetrator must exhibit mature acceptance of responsibility and enact repeated acts of amends to "repay his or her debt." The partners may also need to *renegotiate the norms* that govern their relationship, resolving conflicting views on what constitutes a transgression, clarifying the terms of amends and forgiveness, or specifying the consequences of future transgressions.[2] Such behaviors are not always easy, especially in the wake of an emotionally charged transgression. Accordingly, many couples experience a rough road to reconciliation, in that the investments required of each person tend to be costly or effortful. For example, the perpetrator may be tempted to justify his or her actions by blaming the victim for the transgression; the victim may be tempted to reject the perpetrator's apology and insist on retribution. Such lapses represent serious setbacks, making it more challenging for each partner to opt for prosocial, reconciliation-facilitating behaviors in subsequent interactions.

Following relationship-shattering transgressions, does complete reconciliation ever really come about, or does a powerful transgression forever leave its stamp on a relationship? Can perpetrators offer sufficient amends to assuage their feelings of guilt, or does the sense of indebtedness persistently color perpetrator-victim interactions? Do victims readily recover faith in their partners' reliability and good will, or is it simply too difficult to abandon transgression-relevant anxiety? We suggest that forgiveness and reconciliation are not all-or-nothing propositions and that in many instances—particularly among resilient and resourceful partners, and in relationships with strong pretransgression circumstances—reconciliation can come about even in the wake of relationship-shattering transgressions.

REVIEW OF EMPIRICAL LITERATURE

As noted earlier, we believe that interdependence theory is a very useful means of conceptualizing forgiveness as an inherently interpersonal phenomenon. Accordingly, in the following pages we make use of this theoretical framework in reviewing the empirical literature regarding (a) reactions to transgressions, (b) the forgiveness process, and (c) relational repair. Throughout this review, we refer readers to information presented in Table 12.1, which includes summary information regarding participants, methods, and findings for studies that examine transgressions, forgiveness, or reconciliation in a relational context (i.e., transgressions in ongoing relationships). At the same time, in reviewing the empirical literature, we also cite findings from nonrelational studies that are relevant to a given issue (these nonrelational studies are not listed in Table 12.1).[3]

TABLE 12.1. Empirical Research Regarding Reactions to Transgressions, the Forgiveness Process, and Relational Repair

Reference	Method	Participants	Transgressors	Results
		Reactions to transgressions		
Baumeister, Stillwell, & Heatherton (1995)	St 1 Narratives St 2 Narratives	Undergraduates Undergraduates	Not specified (reports as perpetrator)	Transgressions against close partners ↔ greater perpetrator guilt. Perpetrator interpersonal neglect, unfulfilled obligations, selfish actions ↔ greater perpetrator guilt. Guilt ↔ greater perpetrator confession, apology, changes in behavior.
Baumeister, Stillwell, & Wotman (1990)	St 1 Narratives	Undergraduates	Not specified (reports as both victim, perpetrator)	Compared with perpetrators, victims regard transgressions as more arbitrary, incomprehensible, gratuitous. Victims perceive more continuing harm, lasting damage, long-term consequences. Perpetrators regard victims' reactions as excessive.
Feldman, Cauffman, Jensen, & Arnett (2000)	St 1 Scenario study	Undergraduates	Relational partners (50% DP, 50% FP)	Low tolerance of deviation, high self-restraint ↔ transgressions judged more harshly, as less acceptable.
Finkel, Rusbult, Kumashiro, & Hannon (2002)	St 2 Survey	Undergraduates	Dating partners	Commitment ↔ more positive immediate and delayed victim cognition and behavior, more negative immediate victim emotion but more positive delayed emotion.
Kowalski, Walker, Wilkinson, Queen, & Sharpe (2003)	St 1 Narratives	Undergraduates	Relational partners (23% RP, 37% FP)	Compared with perpetrators, victims describe transgressions as more aversive, perceive more negative consequences, rate self less blameful and partner more blameful. Perpetrators report more guilt.
Leary, Springer, Negel, Amsell, & Evans (1998)	St 1 Narratives	Undergraduates	Relational partners (32% DP, 39% FP)	Transgressions ↔ victim hurt, anxiety, anger, hostility. Relational devaluation, responsibility attributions ↔ greater victim distress. Compared with perpetrators, victims report greater perpetrator responsibility, relational harm, erosion of trust.
Smolen & Spiegel (1987)	St 1 Survey	Community sample	Marital partners	Provocative perpetrator behavior ↔ lower couple adjustment. Provocation-adjustment association stronger among men with low internal locus of control.

TABLE 12.1. Empirical Research Regarding Reactions to Transgressions, the Forgiveness Process, and Relational Repair *(cont.)*

Reference	Method	Participants	Transgressors	Results
Zechmeister & Romero (2002)	St 1 Narratives	Community sample	Relational partners (19% RP, 34% FP)	Compared with perpetrators, victims perceive transgression as continuing to exert negative effects. Victim empathy ↔ benign victim interpretations of transgressions, greater forgiveness. Perpetrator empathy ↔ less perpetrator self-forgiveness.
			Forgiveness process	
Brown (2003)	St 2 Survey	Undergraduates	Dating partners	Victim perspective taking, agreeableness, positive attitude toward forgiveness ↔ greater victim forgiveness. Victim depression, neuroticism, vengeance motivation, number of transgressions recalled ↔ lesser victim forgiveness.
	St 2 Survey	Undergraduates	Relational partners	
	St 4 Survey	Undergraduates	Not specified	
Fincham & Beach (2002)	St 1 Survey	Community sample	Marital partners	Wife psychological aggression ↔ lesser husband forgiveness (St 1). Husband psychological aggression ↔ greater wife retaliation (St 1). Partner psychological aggression ↔ greater retaliation (St 2). Partner constructive communication ↔ greater forgiveness.
	St 2 Survey	Community sample	Marital partners	
Finkel, Rusbult, Kumashiro, & Hannon (2002)	St 1 Experiment	Undergraduates	Dating partners	Commitment prime → greater victim forgiveness (absence of destructive reactions).
	St 2 Survey	Undergraduates	Dating partners	Commitment ↔ more positive immediate and delayed victim cognition and behavior, more negative immediate victim emotion but more positive delayed emotion.
	St 3 Interaction records	Undergraduates	Dating partners	Commitment ↔ greater victim forgiveness (positive cognition, emotion, behavior).
Hannon (2001)	St 1 Survey	Undergraduates	Dating partners	Pretransgression trust, commitment ↔ greater victim forgiveness, perpetrator amends.
Hannon, Rusbult, Finkel, & Kumashiro (2004)	St 1 Survey	Undergraduates	Dating partners	Perpetrator amends ↔ greater victim forgiveness.
	St 2 Interaction records	Undergraduates	Dating partners	Both amends and forgiveness account for unique variance in resolving transgression incidents.
	St 3 Observational	Community sample	Marital partners	Effective resolution is associated with enhanced couple well-being.

Study		Method	Sample	Participants	Findings
Hargrave & Sells (1997)	St 1	Scale development	Community sample	Relational partners (type not specified)	Opportunity for perpetrator compensation, victim insight, victim understanding ↔ greater victim forgiveness.
McCullough, Bellah, Kilpatrick, & Johnson (2001)	St 1	Longitudinal	Undergraduates	Relational partners (type not specified)	Victim vengefulness ↔ lesser victim forgiveness, greater rumination, greater negative affectivity, lower life satisfaction, lower agreeableness, greater neuroticism.
	St 2	Survey	Undergraduates	Not specified	
McCullough, Fincham, & Tsang (2003)	St 1	Longitudinal	Undergraduates	Relational partners (43% DP, 39% FP)	Transgressions ↔ victim avoidance, revenge motivation. Lesser transgression severity, greater victim empathy ↔ greater victim trend forgiveness. Lesser victim responsibility attributions, greater empathy ↔ greater victim temporary forgiveness.
	St 2	Longitudinal	Undergraduates	Relational partners (42% DP, 39% FP)	
McCullough & Hoyt (2002)	St 1	Survey	Undergraduates	Relational partners (33% RP, 67% FP)	Transgression severity, victim neuroticism ↔ lesser victim forgiveness (benevolence, avoidance, revenge). Victim agreeableness ↔ greater victim forgiveness.
	St 2	Survey	Undergraduates	Relational partners (50% FP)	
McCullough, Rachal, Sandage, Worthington, Brown, & Hight (1998)	St 3	Survey	Undergraduates	Dating partners	Couple adjustment/commitment, victim empathy, perpetrator apology ↔ greater victim forgiveness (benevolence, avoidance, revenge). Victim rumination ↔ lesser victim forgiveness.
	St 4	Survey	Undergraduates	Relational partners (49% DP, 21% FP)	
McCullough, Worthington, & Rachal (1997)	St 2	Intervention	Undergraduates	Relational partners (32% DP, 21% FP)	Victim empathy intervention → greater victim empathy, forgiveness (compared with forgiveness-only intervention and wait-list control group).
Rusbult, Davis, Finkel, Hannon, & Olsen (2004)	Sts 1–2	Experiments	Undergraduates, Community sample	Dating partners (1), Marital partners (2)	Compared with later victim reactions, immediate reactions to transgressions are more angry, blameful, vengeful, destructive. Compared with later victim reactions, immediate reactions are less forgiving. Forgiveness rests on a transformation process.
	Sts 3–4	Surveys	Undergraduates, Community sample	Dating partners (3), Marital partners (4)	

TABLE 12.1. Empirical Research Regarding Reactions to Transgressions, the Forgiveness Process, and Relational Repair *(cont.)*

Reference	Method		Participants	Transgressors	Results
				Relational repair	
Fincham, Paleari, & Regalia (2002)	St 1	Survey	Community sample	Marital partners	Benign victim attributions ↔ greater victim forgiveness ↔ greater marital quality. Attributions–forgiveness association stronger among women. Empathy–forgiveness association stronger among men.
Fincham, Beach, & Davila (2004)	St 1	Survey	Community sample	Marital partners	Male retaliation ↔ lesser resolution (report by women). Female benevolence ↔ greater resolution (report by men). Male avoidance ↔ lesser resolution (report by women).
	St 2	Survey	Community sample	Marital partners	
Gordon & Baucom (2003)	St 1	Survey	Community sample	Marital partners	Victim forgiveness ↔ greater marital adjustment, more positive beliefs about marriage.
Holeman (2003)	St 1	Qualitative study	Clinical sample	Marital partners	Relationship with God ↔ greater couple resolution, reconciliation.
Karremans & Van Lange (2004)	St 1	Experiment	Undergraduates	Not specified	Victim forgiveness → greater victim willingness to accommodate, willingness to sacrifice, cooperative behavior. Effects evident independent of commitment to relationship. Forgiveness restores (rather than enhances) pro-relationship motivation.
	St 2	Survey	Undergraduates	Relational partners (type not specified)	
	St 3	Experiment	Undergraduates	Not specified	
Karremans, Van Lange, Ouwerkerk, & Kluwer (2003)	St 4	Survey	Community sample	Marital partners	Victim forgiveness ↔ greater victim life satisfaction, primarily in high-commitment relationships.

Note: For Method column, Survey = cross-sectional survey study, Longitudinal = longitudinal study. For Transgressors column, for Relational partners only, we indicate the proportion of transgressions that were committed by DP = dating partners, FP = friends, MP = marital partners, and RP = romantic partners. For Results column, → = causal impact demonstrated, ↔ = association demonstrated.

Reactions to Transgressions

In introducing our theoretical assumptions, we noted that transgressions entail victim harm and represent norm violations, and therefore instigate a rather potent constellation of victim and perpetrator cognition, affect, and behavior. Indeed, the empirical literature reveals that following transgressions, victims experience diverse negative emotions, including anxiety, hurt, sadness, anger, and hostility (Leary, Springer, Negel, Amsell, & Evans, 1998; Ohbuchi, Kameda, & Agarie, 1989; Rusbult, Davis, Finkel, Hannon, & Olsen, 2004; see reactions to transgressions in Table 12.1). Victims also develop negative patterns of cognition, including confusion regarding the event and its implications, tendencies to review transgression-relevant events obsessively, and inclinations toward blameful attributions (Baumeister, Stillwell, & Wotman, 1990; Rusbult et al., 2004). Finally, victims adopt negative behavioral tendencies, including avoidance of the perpetrator, holding of a grudge or vengeance seeking, and demands for atonement or retribution (Kremer & Stephens, 1983; McCullough, Fincham, & Tsang, 2003; Rusbult et al., 2004).

Victim reactions have been shown to be moderated by personal dispositions, properties of transgressions, and characteristics of the victim-perpetrator relationship. Reactions tend to be harsher, more hostile, and more vengeful among victims with low empathy, low tolerance of deviation, high self-restraint, and external locus of control (Feldman, Cauffman, Jensen, & Arnett, 2000; McCullough et al., 2003; Smolen & Spiegel, 1987). Reactions also vary as a function of the nature of transgressions: Victims experience greater anxiety, avoidance, hostility, and desire for vengeance in response to more severe transgressions, transgressions that imply relational devaluation, and transgressions that are perceived to be deliberate and controllable. Also, reactions tend to be stronger immediately following a transgression than at a later time (Finkel, Rusbult, Kumashiro, & Hannon, 2002; McCullough et al., 2003). Finally, victim reactions vary as a function of the nature of the victim-perpetrator relationship—cognitive and behavioral reactions tend to be less negative in highly committed relationships (although committed victims' immediate emotional reactions tend to be *more* negative than their later emotional reactions; Finkel et al., 2002).

The empirical literature also reveals findings that are consistent with our assumptions regarding perpetrator behavior. Perpetrators experience guilt and remorse when they commit transgressions by behaving selfishly, neglecting their partners, or otherwise violating relational obligations (Baumeister, Stillwell, & Heatherton, 1995; Tangney, Wagner, Hill-Barlow, Marschall, & Gramzow, 1996). Typically, feelings of guilt induce patterns of perpetrator affect, cognition, and behavior that are conducive to promoting victim forgiveness. For example, perpetrator guilt is associated with displays of sadness and remorse, thoughts centering on concern for the victim, and inclinations toward confession, apology, and amends.

However, victims and perpetrators do not always construe transgressions similarly. Research using narrative techniques has revealed that in comparison with perpetrators, victims experience greater distress; regard perpetrator behavior as more arbitrary, incomprehensible, and gratuitous; attribute responsibility more to the perpetrator than to the self; describe the transgression as more severe; and report that the transgression exerted more damaging and enduring effects on the relationship (Baumeister et al., 1990; Gonzales, Manning, & Haugen, 1992; Kowalski, Walker, Wilkinson, Queen, & Sharpe, 2003; Leary et al., 1998; Zechmeister & Romero, 2002). Perpetrators experience greater guilt than victims but also tend to regard victims' reactions as somewhat excessive and out of line with the magnitude of the transgression (Baumeister et al., 1990; Kowalski et al., 2003). Such findings suggest that when post-transgression interaction reveals victim hostility, blame, and vengeance seeking that implies culpability beyond what the perpetrator perceives is appropriate (e.g., when victims fail to account for extenuating circumstances), perpetrators exhibit defensive maneuvers. Under such circumstances, perpetrators deflect blame, cognitively justify transgressions (to others and to themselves), and become reluctant to offer amends commensurate with what victims believe is owed. Thus, and consistent with our theoretical framework, transgressions are problematic interdependence dilemmas. On the basis of victims' and perpetrators' initial reactions, the road to forgiveness would appear to be a difficult one.

The Forgiveness Process

Forgiveness Rests on Prosocial Motives.   Our interdependence-based analysis suggests that forgiveness should be conceptualized as a psychological transformation of the transgression, such that the victim's powerful impulse toward vengeance is tempered, thereby clearing the way for forgiveness. We describe this process as a prosocial transformation whereby the victim takes broader considerations into account than the transgression per se (e.g., concern for the partner, prosocial norms or values). Consistent with this claim, a variety of prosocial dispositions have been shown to be associated with forgiveness. For example, victims are more forgiving to the extent that they attempt to "walk in their partners' shoes," exhibiting greater empathy and more pronounced tendencies toward perspective taking (Brown, 2003; Fincham, Paleari, & Regalia, 2002; McCullough et al., 2003; McCullough et al., 1997; see Forgiveness process in Table 12.1). Greater forgiveness is also evident among victims who score higher in agreeableness, are more tolerant of deviation, and exhibit greater insight and understanding (Brown, 2003; Feldman et al., 2000; Hargrave & Sells, 1997; McCullough, Bellah, Kilpatrick, & Johnson, 2001; McCullough & Hoyt, 2002). In addition, victims tend to be *less* forgiving when they possess dispositions or values that *interfere* with compassionate orientation toward others—for example, to the extent that they score higher in depression, neuroticism, negative affectivity, and vengeance motivation (Brown, 2003; McCullough et al., 2001, 2003; McCullough & Hoyt, 2002). Thus, it would appear that prosocial transformation and forgiveness are promoted to the extent that victims (a) possess the ability and inclination to see the world through others' eyes (empathy, perspective taking), (b) possess dispositions or values that allow them to "make themselves open" to alternative points of view (agreeableness, tolerance, understanding), and (c) do *not* dedicate undue energy to their personal interests and concerns (do *not* exhibit undue entitlement, narcissism, neuroticism, negative affectivity, vengeance motivation).

Forgiveness Rests on Prosocial Cognition and Affect. Our interdependence-based analysis also outlines the means by which prosocial transformation takes place via changes in the victim's cognitive and emotional state. Specifically, we suggest that the victim thinks through the causes and implications of the transgression, develops a more benevolent and less blameful understanding of the event, and (concurrently) develops increased compassion and caring for the perpetrator. Consistent with this point of view, victim mental processes appear to play a central role in promoting (vs. impeding) forgiveness. Victims are less likely to forgive to the extent that they exhibit greater rumination and recall a greater number of prior transgressions, and are more likely to forgive to the extent that they develop more benign attributions regarding the causes of the perpetrator's actions (Brown, 2003; Fincham et al., 2002; McCullough et al., 2001, 2003). In addition, it appears that in highly committed relationships, victims experience stronger prosocial motivation, which yields more benign attributions and benevolent affect, and in turn promotes positive behavior and enhanced forgiveness (Finkel et al., 2002). Moreover—and not surprising—victims find it easier to develop benign interpretations and experience benevolent affect in response to transgressions that are less severe and that do not imply relational devaluation (Leary et al., 1998; McCullough et al., 2003; McCullough & Hoyt, 2002).

Forgiveness Takes Time. Our interdependence-based framework also suggests that the forgiveness process is not necessarily (or usually) immediate. Interestingly, whereas most (or all) theoretical analyses imply that forgiveness is a *process* that involves prosocial *change* in victim orientation, most empirical investigations of this process examine forgiveness at a single point in time (see chapter 7 by McCullough & Root). In a landmark paper, McCullough, Fincham, and Tsang (2003) presented a thought experiment to demonstrate why such single-assessment methods are inadequate to capture the forgiveness process. We are asked to imagine Alan and Bill, each of whose partners committed a transgression on Day 0. On a vengeance-seeking scale, Alan scores 4.0 in vengeance seeking on Day 0 and scores 3.1 on Day 35, whereas Bill scores 3.1 in vengeance seeking on Day 0 and scores 3.1 on Day 35. Who is more forgiving? Three conclusions are plausible: (a) Bill is more forgiving, because on Day 0 he is less vengeful than Alan (3.1 vs. 4.0), (b) the two are equally forgiving, because on Day 35 they exhibit equal vengeance seeking (3.1 vs. 3.1), or (c) Alan is more forgiving, because he exhibits a greater decline over time in vengeance seeking (4.0 to 3.1) than does Bill (3.1 to 3.1). McCullough and his colleagues (2003) propose that the third conclusion is correct and suggest that forgiveness should be measured in terms of change over time in prosocial motivation. Based on this analysis, forgiveness is argued to include two components: forbearance, which describes the degree to which a victim *initially* exhibits forgiveness; and trend forgiveness, which describes the degree to which a victim becomes increasingly forgiving over time.[4] These authors also present empirical evidence demonstrating that both components account for unique variance in forgiveness and that the two components may sometimes be shaped by differing causes.

Despite the strengths of this analysis—and despite our rather wholehearted endorsement of this general approach—we propose that the McCullough et al. (2003) forbearance construct conflates two distinct processes that we term *restraint* and *forbearance*. From an interdependence perspective, restraint (one aspect of psychological transformation) transpires in the seconds immediately following a transgression and entails overriding gut-level impulses toward vengeance; whereas forbearance (a second aspect of transformation) transpires in the minutes and hours following a transgression, rests on relatively conscious and active meaning analysis (including both cognitive and affective events), and entails developing increased prosocial orientation (the latter roughly parallels the analysis of McCullough et al., 2003). The third process in our three-stage model is *extended forgiveness*, which roughly parallels trend forgiveness, except that this stage spans a period from several hours following a transgression to several days or months following a transgression.[5]

Why is it important to distinguish between restraint and forbearance? Our analysis suggests that victims' gut-level impulses tend to be hostile and vengeful. Thus, to understand fully how far a victim has progressed toward forgiveness, it is important to assess victims' immediate impulses (i.e., given preferences)—their cognition, affect, and behavioral impulses *immediately following* a transgression (i.e., within minutes or seconds; McCullough et al. [2003] assessed forgiveness several days or weeks following a transgression). From a theoretical point of view, gut-level, given impulses are the logical starting point for analysis, in that these behavioral preferences are a close approximation of the character of the interpersonal situation in which victim and perpetrator find themselves. Moreover, human mental processes can be very fast—close to instantaneous. Thus, some portion of the psychological tempering that transpires following a transgression will take place in the seconds and minutes following the victim's initial perception of a transgression. This is particularly true in ongoing relationships, in that partners with a history (and perhaps a future) with one another have adapted to one another over the course of prior interactions; they have developed assumptions and beliefs about one another; and they have shaped one another's dispositions, values, and behavioral tendencies. In short, they have developed habitual patterns of response (Rusbult & Van Lange, 2003). Thus, to ascertain how far a victim has progressed toward forgiveness (i.e., to track the transformation process), we must tap into gut-level impulses; to tap into gut-level impulses, it is necessary to assess truly immediate reactions to transgressions.

Rusbult et al. (2004) presented two sets of studies to support their three-stage model of forgiveness. First, they conducted two studies (of dating and marital relations) to demonstrate that the forgiveness process begins within seconds (not days) following a transgression. Participants listened to a tape recording that presented hypothetical (yet common) transgressions (e.g., "your partner lies to you about something

important"). For each transgression, they confronted a forced choice between a constructive (forgiving) reaction and a destructive (vengeful) reaction. Participants were
given either 7 or 14 s to read and respond to the forced-choice options. In comparison
with participants in the plentiful reaction time condition (14 s), those in the limited
reaction time condition (7 s) were 50% more likely to select vengeful, retaliatory reactions. These findings support the claim that the forgiveness process (restraint, in
particular) begins within seconds of experiencing a transgression.

In a second set of studies (of dating and marital relations), participants were
asked to recall a prior transgression committed by their partners, to vividly bring
that incident to mind, and to provide descriptions of their reactions at three points in
time—the responses they considered enacting immediately following the transgression, the reactions they actually enacted immediately following the transgression,
and the reactions they enacted at a later time. Consistent with our interdependence-
based analysis, participants exhibit significant increases over time in forgiveness. It is
important to note that different variables predict responses across the three stages:

1. Restraint is predicted by the severity of a transgression but not by empathy or
   commitment (in support of the claim that preferences at this stage are essentially
   "given" by the transgression situation).
2. Forbearance is predicted by restraint tendencies but not by severity or empathy
   (among married individuals, habit, as embodied in commitment level, is also a
   significant predictor).
3. Extended forgiveness is predicted by commitment level but not by severity or forbearance (among dating individuals, meaning analysis, as embodied in empathy,
   is also a significant predictor).

The slight differences in findings for dating versus marital relationships are attributable to strength of habit. Married individuals have stronger histories, or stronger
commitment-driven tendencies; dating individuals lack such habit, so forgiveness is a
more extended process that rests on empathy as well as commitment.

Forgiveness is Interpersonal.   As noted earlier, much of the existing work regarding forgiveness has been victim-centered, emphasizing the *intra*personal processes
by which victims come to forgive perpetrators (Freedman, 1998; Kremer & Stephens,
1983). We suggest that whereas this approach may be entirely suitable in settings
wherein victim and offender have neither a past nor a future with one another, it is a
less suitable orientation for understanding forgiveness in ongoing relationships. We
suggest that perpetrators, too, may play a role in promoting (or impeding) prosocial
transformation and forgiveness. In this regard, we define *amends* as the perpetrator's
inclination to accept responsibility for a transgression, offering sincere apology and
genuine atonement.

Why should perpetrator amends promote forgiveness? First, amends may exert
beneficial effects on victim cognition and emotion, thereby enhancing the probability

of prosocial victim transformation. For example, by discussing the incident in a concerned and apologetic manner, the perpetrator may help the victim develop feelings
of empathy, thereby promoting a more positive emotional state, or may identify extenuating circumstances, thereby promoting less malevolent attributions regarding
the perpetrator's motives (Fincham et al., 2002; McCullough et al., 1998). Second,
amends may yield superior immediate outcomes for the victim, providing partial debt
repayment and thereby "cooling" the interaction: When a perpetrator responds to the
victim's righteous indignation with heartfelt apology rather than anger and defensiveness, the victim experiences superior immediate outcomes, which should inhibit
the victim's tendency toward vengeance and hostility. Third, by admitting guilt and
accepting personal responsibility, the perpetrator improves future interaction opportunities (i.e., helps to create "a better future") in that heartfelt amends acknowledges
the existence of a debt that the perpetrator wishes to repay (making it easier for the
victim to move toward renewed trust) and provides reassurance that the transgression will not recur (Baumeister et al., 1995). Thus, in the wake of perpetrator amends,
the victim should find it less psychologically costly—less risky or humiliating—to
offer the healing hand of forgiveness.

Unfortunately, few empirical studies have examined how perpetrator behavior
affects the forgiveness process. Narrative studies of guilt experiences suggest that
guilt-inducing incidents are more likely to involve close partners than strangers or
acquaintances and that the experience of guilt frequently motivates acts of amends
(apology, confession, behavior change; Baumeister et al., 1995). Experimental research
suggests that perpetrator apology promotes victim forgiveness, at least in the context
of stranger interactions (Gonzales et al., 1992; Weiner, Graham, Peter, & Zmuidinas,
1991). Finally, studies of ongoing relationships—relationships in which partners have
a past and a future with one another—have revealed the following:

1. Perpetrators are more likely to offer amends in relationships characterized by
   strong pretransgression trust and commitment (Hannon, 2001).
2. When victims perceive that perpetrators seek to "cancel" the negative consequences of their actions and communicate in a positive manner, forgiveness is
   more probable (Fincham & Beach, 2002; McCullough et al., 1998).
3. During conversations regarding transgression incidents, perpetrator amends promote increases over time in levels of victim forgiveness (Hannon, Rusbult, Finkel,
   & Kumashiro, 2004).

Relational Repair

There is no guarantee that perpetrator amends and victim forgiveness will necessarily yield reconciliation. Even in the event of complete forgiveness, one or both partners may find that they continue to monitor one another's actions carefully, interact
in an unnatural manner, or find it difficult to recover pretransgression levels of trust.

Thus, to understand the aftermath of transgressions fully, it is important to examine not only forgiveness but also reconciliation, or the successful resumption of pretransgression relationship status. Earlier, we suggested that two key issues in reconciliation are commitment and trust (on the part of both partners): Were commitment and trust of sufficient strength prior to the transgression to provide a solid basis for reconciliation? and, Can commitment and trust be recovered following a transgression? We also proposed that reconciliation entails mutual investment whereby both partners exert significant, coordinated effort to achieve restored couple functioning (e.g., setting aside blame, offering repeated acts of amends, renegotiating couple norms). Reconciliation does not necessarily mean that a relationship does not change or that conditions revert fully to "the way it was before." Depending on the nature and severity of a transgression, a relationship may return to its pretransgression state or may move forward with new norms and expectations.

Relatively little research has been oriented toward studying the reconciliation process. The few studies that have examined posttransgression relational circumstances have revealed that later couple well-being (e.g., marital quality, dyadic adjustment) is promoted by the sorts of victim and perpetrator behaviors discussed earlier. On the victim's part, couple well-being is promoted by empathy, benign attributions regarding the transgression, "letting go" of hurt feelings, and forgiveness; on the perpetrator's part, couple well-being is promoted by apology, amends, and promises not to repeat the transgression (Fincham et al., 2002; Gordon & Baucom, 2003; see Relational repair in Table 12.1). Research regarding relational repair has also demonstrated that male partners' retaliation is negatively associated with conflict resolution and that female partners' benevolence is positively associated with conflict resolution; that is, wives' forgiveness promotes conflict resolution, whereas their husbands' unforgiveness impairs conflict resolution (Fincham, Beach, & Davila, 2004). Finally, it appears that forgiveness indeed helps couples move toward reconciliation, in that following forgiveness, victims recover their inclinations to engage in a wide range of prosocial relationship-maintenance behaviors, including accommodation, willingness to sacrifice, and other cooperative, prosocial acts (this work did not examine perpetrators' postforgiveness behavior; Karremans & Van Lange, 2004). Collectively, these findings suggest that in the wake of transgression, both partners' actions have important implications for future couple well-being.

Although transgressions tend to be very upsetting and potentially quite harmful, it is important to recognize that such incidents can also be highly diagnostic (Holmes & Rempel, 1989). In the aftermath of transgression, the manner in which partners comport themselves provides meaningful information that would not be evident during periods of "smooth sailing"—information about each person's dispositions, values, and motives, as well as their probable future behavior. For example, if perpetrators promise that the transgression will not recur, apologize for causing pain, and work to "repay their debt," victims have reason to believe that perpetrators value the relationship and are committed to relational norms. Similarly, if victims listen to the "other side of the story" and accept perpetrator apology, perpetrators gain important information about how the victim responds to conflict. Conciliatory behavior of this sort may do much to reduce uncertainty, assuage anxiety, and increase intimacy; such behavior may also enhance the couple's ability to deal with stressful situations and may reduce the likelihood of further transgressions. Therefore, in the wake of serious transgressions, it is not surprising that in comparison with couples who have not yet achieved forgiveness, those who report forgiveness also report higher levels of marital adjustment (Gordon & Baucom, 2003). Moreover, it appears that reconciliation-relevant behaviors (e.g., victim forgiveness) are associated with later life satisfaction, particularly in the context of highly committed relationships (Karremans, Van Lange, Ouwerkerk, & Kluwer, 2003). Thus—and consistent with our interdependence theoretic analysis—it would appear that "reconciliation is worth it," particularly to the extent that "a relationship is worth it."

RELEVANCE FOR CLINICAL INTERVENTIONS

What are the implications of an interdependence-based analysis for clinical interventions? We are gratified that the implications of our analysis align well with existing interventions of demonstrated utility. To begin with, it should be clear that for transgressions committed in the context of ongoing relationships, interventions must be conjoint—interventions that are oriented toward just one partner are unlikely to be maximally effective. At present, the most prominent conjoint techniques are those involving both behavioral and cognitive interventions—for example, integrative behavior therapy, emotion-focused couple therapy, and insight-oriented couple therapy (Baucom & Epstein, 1990). Behavioral interventions should include skills training and exercises designed to increase rates of constructive interpersonal acts centering on victim restraint (e.g., controlling the impulse to lash out when hurt, reducing the frequency of hostile accusations), perpetrator amends (e.g., offering genuine apology, engaging in heartfelt amends), and couple reconciliation (e.g., sustained, coordinated investments toward the goal of restoring mutual trust). Such interventions might be augmented by constructive renegotiation of the norms that govern a relationship—how does each partner interpret "the rules," what constitutes reasonable "debt repayment" on the part of a perpetrator, and what are the consequences of future transgressions? For example, although one transgression of a specified type might eventually be forgivable, a second such transgression would not be.

Cognitive interventions should be oriented toward promoting the sorts of benevolent, partner-oriented mental events (cognitive and affective) upon which prosocial transformation rests. To begin with, interventions should address problematic beliefs or expectations. For example, the victim may believe that a transgression is indicative of a complete lack of respect on the part of the perpetrator, or the perpetrator may believe that a victim's impulse toward vengeance reflects excessive sensitivity or irrationality. Moreover, interventions should address the attributions partners form about one another's actions—for example, guiding victims away from stable, global, internal attributions regarding the causes of transgressions and toward attributions that recognize extenuating factors and possible personal culpability. Indeed, interventions oriented toward enhancing empathy and perspective taking presumably are beneficial because they inhibit distress-maintaining attributions and promote relatively benevolent cognition and affect, thereby paving the way for prosocial transformation and forgiveness (McCullough et al., 1997). Finally, cognitive interventions should address the core, prosocial motives upon which forgiveness, amends, and reconciliation rest. For example, couples could be encouraged to recognize and acknowledge the extent of their reliance on one another, thereby priming underlying commitment; couples could be encouraged to recall and acknowledge one another's prior acts of benevolence, thereby priming underlying trust.

THEORETICAL PERSPECTIVES ON THE FIELD

Our interdependence-based analysis has numerous implications for the manner in which social scientists conceptualize and empirically examine forgiveness. We limit our comments to two implications that we believe are particularly important. First, we believe it is critical to conceptualize forgiveness as a process that rests on a fundamental, psychological transformation of the transgression situation. As such, we can learn much about forgiveness by attending to the micro-level mental events that transpire following transgressions. For example, precisely how do victims manage to restrain their gut-level impulses toward vengeance, what sorts of dispositional and situational factors influence the exercise of restraint, and precisely how does the exercise of restraint affect perpetrators? What cognitive, affective, and behavioral tendencies—on the part of both victim and perpetrator—most effectively and reliably promote forgiveness, and do key tendencies operate similarly in promoting both short-term and long-term benevolence (i.e., do parallel factors promote both forbearance and extended forgiveness)? At present, very few theoretical, methodological, or statistical models incorporate such features.

Second, and importantly, we return to the assertion advanced at the beginning of this chapter. We believe that although the traditional, victim-focused approach may be informative as a means of characterizing forgiveness in fundamentally ahistoric settings (following transgressions committed by strangers, e.g., hit-and-run drivers), such an approach is quite limited as a means of understanding forgiveness in ongoing relationships. Given that many consequential transgressions are committed by those who are closest to us, we have argued that scientists should adopt an inherently interpersonal approach to understanding forgiveness—an approach that examines the critical roles played by both victim *and* perpetrator. Thus, we call for further theoretical and empirical work regarding the relatively understudied, inherently interpersonal aspects of forgiveness, particularly the roles of perpetrator behavior in promoting forgiveness and of both victim and perpetrator in bringing about reconciliation and relational repair.

CONCLUSIONS

Our goals in this chapter were twofold. First, we sought to underscore the impediments to forgiveness—thereby illuminating the psychological challenges of this process—by highlighting the fundamental human tendency of victims to react to norm violations with righteous indignation and vengeful impulses (as well as the fundamental human tendency of perpetrators to defend and justify their actions). We argued that the concept of psychological transformation provides a good means of characterizing the process by which individuals find their way to genuine forgiveness (as well as to heartfelt amends). We also suggested that a more carefully articulated model of this process may be warranted. We proposed a three-stage model of forgiveness, including restraint, forbearance, and extended forgiveness. Second—and hand in hand with our first goal—we sought to promote an essentially interpersonal characterization of forgiveness in the context of ongoing relationships, emphasizing the critical roles played by both victim and perpetrator in promoting (vs. impeding) forgiveness and relational repair. We believe that interdependence theory provides a very useful set of concepts and principles for understanding these phenomena—a set of concepts that not only illuminate our scientific understanding of these phenomena but also suggest why certain types of clinical interventions are most likely to be effective.

NOTES

1. Of course, the transformation process may also become relatively automatic. Over the course of extended involvement, partners may develop habitual tendencies toward specific types of transformation, such that psychological transformation comes about with little or no mediation by mental events (e.g., strong commitment or high trust may automatically instigate prosocial transformation).
2. Importantly, renegotiation may help reintroduce the sense of predictability and controllability that was shattered by the transgression, promoting restored commitment and trust.
3. In light of the fact that the forgiveness literature is growing dramatically, this review should be regarded as selective rather than comprehensive.
4. These authors also describe a third component, termed *temporary forgiveness*. We will not discuss this component because it is irrelevant to the concerns of this chapter.
5. Moreover, in discussing both forbearance and extended forgiveness, we highlight the fact that critical interpersonal events may transpire during the latter two stages—interpersonal events that may play a crucial role in shaping the forgiveness process, including perpetrator confession, apology, or amends. We return to this point later.

REFERENCES

Baucom, D. H., & Epstein, N. (1990). *Cognitive-behavioral marital therapy.* New York: Bruner-Mazel.

Baumeister, R. F., Exline, J. J., & Sommer, K. L. (1998). The victim role, grudge theory, and two dimensions of forgiveness. In E. L. Worthington, Jr. (Ed.), *Dimensions of forgiveness: Psy-*

chological research and theological perspectives (pp. 79–104). Philadelphia: Templeton Foundation Press.

Baumeister, R. F., Stillwell, A. M., & Heatherton, T. F. (1995). Personal narratives about guilt: Role in action control and interpersonal relationships. *Basic and Applied Social Psychology, 17*, 173–198.

Baumeister, R. F., Stillwell, A., & Wotman, S. R. (1990). Victim and perpetrator accounts of interpersonal conflict: Autobiographical narratives about anger. *Journal of Personality and Social Psychology, 59*, 994–1005.

Brown, R. P. (2003). Measuring individual differences in the tendency to forgive: Construct validity and links with depression. *Personality and Social Psychology Bulletin, 29*, 759–771.

Feldman, S. S., Cauffman, E., Jensen, L. A., & Arnett, J. J. (2000). The (un)acceptability of betrayal: A study of college students' evaluations of sexual betrayal by a romantic partner and betrayal of a friend's confidence. *Journal of Youth and Adolescence, 29*, 499–523.

Fincham, F. D., & Beach, S. R. H. (2002). Forgiveness in marriage: Implications for psychological aggression and constructive communication. *Personal Relationships, 9*, 239–251.

Fincham, F. D., Beach, S. R. H., & Davila, J. (2004). Forgiveness and conflict resolution in marriage. *Journal of Family Psychology, 18*, 72–81.

Fincham, F. D., Paleari, F. G., & Regalia, C. (2002). Forgiveness in marriage: The role of relationship quality, attributions, and empathy. *Personal Relationships, 9*, 27–37.

Finkel, E. J., Rusbult, C. E., Kumashiro, M., & Hannon, P. A. (2002). Dealing with betrayal in close relationships: Does commitment promote forgiveness? *Journal of Personality and Social Psychology, 82*, 956–974.

Freedman, S. (1998). Forgiveness and reconciliation: The importance of understanding how they differ. *Counseling and Values, 42*, 200–216.

Gonzales, M. H., Manning, D. J., & Haugen, J. A. (1992). Explaining our sins: Factors influencing offender accounts and anticipated victim responses. *Journal of Personality and Social Psychology, 62*, 958–971.

Gordon, K. C., & Baucom, D. H. (2003). Forgiveness and marriage: Preliminary support based on a model of recovery from a marital betrayal. *American Journal of Family Therapy, 31*, 179–199.

Hannon, P. A. (2001). *Perpetrator behavior and forgiveness in close relationships.* Unpublished doctoral dissertation, University of North Carolina at Chapel Hill.

Hannon, P. A., Rusbult, C. E., Finkel, E. J., & Kumashiro, M. (2004). *Forgiveness as an interaction-based phenomenon: Perpetrator amends, victim forgiveness, and the resolution of betrayal incidents.* Unpublished manuscript, University of Washington, Seattle.

Hargrave, T. D., & Sells, J. N. (1997). The development of a forgiveness scale. *Journal of Marital and Family Therapy, 23*, 41–63.

Holmes, J. G., & Rempel, J. K. (1989). Trust in close relationships. In C. Hendrick (Ed.), *Review of personality and social psychology* (Vol. 10, pp. 187–220). London: Sage.

Holeman, V. T. (2003). *Reconciling differences.* Downers Grove, IL: InterVarsity Press.

Karremans, J. C., & Van Lange, P. A. M. (2004). Back to caring after being hurt: The role of forgiveness. *European Journal of Social Psychology, 34*, 207–227.

Karremans, J. C., Van Lange, P. A. M., Ouwerkerk, J. W., & Kluwer, E. S. (2003). When forgiving enhances psychological well-being: The role of interpersonal commitment. *Journal of Personality and Social Psychology, 84*, 1011–1026.

Kelley H. H., Holmes, J. G., Kerr, N. L., Reis, H. T., Rusbult, C. E., & Van Lange, P. A. M. (2003). *An atlas of interpersonal situations.* New York: Cambridge University Press.

Kelley, H. H., & Thibaut, J. W. (1978). *Interpersonal relations.* New York: Wiley.

Kowalski, R. M., Walker, S., Wilkinson, R., Queen, A., & Sharpe, B. (2003). Lying, cheating, complaining, and other aversive interpersonal behaviors: A narrative examination of the darker side of relationships. *Journal of Social and Personal Relationships, 20*, 471–490.

Kremer, J. F., & Stephens, L. (1983). Attributions and arousal as mediators of mitigation's effect on retaliation. *Journal of Personality and Social Psychology, 45*, 335–343.

Leary, M. R., Springer, C., Negel, L., Ansell, E., & Evans, K. (1998). The causes, phenomenology, and consequences of hurt feelings. *Journal of Personality and Social Psychology, 74*, 1225–1237.

McCullough, M. E. (2001). Forgiveness: Who does it and how do they do it? *Current Directions in Psychological Science, 10*, 194–197.

McCullough, M. E., Bellah, C. G., Kilpatrick, S. D., & Johnson, J. L. (2001). Vengefulness: Relationships with forgiveness, rumination, well-being, and the Big Five. *Personality and Social Psychology Bulletin, 27*, 601–610.

McCullough, M. E., Fincham, F. D., & Tsang, J. (2003). Forgiveness, forbearance, and time: The temporal unfolding of Transgression-related interpersonal motivations. *Journal of Personality and Social Psychology, 84*, 540–557.

McCullough, M. E., & Hoyt, W. T. (2002). Transgression-related motivational dispositions: Personality substrates of forgiveness and their links with the Big Five. *Personality and Social Psychology Bulletin, 28*, 1556–1573.

McCullough, M. E., Rachal, K. C., Sandage, S. J., Worthington, E. L., Brown, S. W., & Hight, T. L. (1998). Interpersonal forgiving in close relationships: II. Theoretical elaboration and measurement. *Journal of Personality and Social Psychology, 75*, 1586–1603.

McCullough, M. E., Worthington, E. L., & Rachal, K. C. (1997). Interpersonal forgiving in close relationships. *Journal of Personality and Social Psychology, 73*, 321–336.

Ohbuchi, K., Kameda, M., & Agarie, N. (1989). Apology as aggression control: Its role in mediating appraisal of and response to harm. *Journal of Personality and Social Psychology, 56*, 219–227.

Reis, H. T., Collins, W. A., & Berscheid, E. (2000). The relationship context of human behavior and development. *Psychological Bulletin, 126*, 844–872.

Ridley, M. (1996). *The origins of virtue: Human instincts and the evolution of cooperation.* New York: Penguin.

Rusbult, C. E., Davis, J. L., Finkel, E. J., Hannon, P., & Olsen, N. (2004). *Forgiveness of transgressions in close relationships: Moving from self-interested impulses to relationship-oriented actions.* Unpublished manuscript, Free University at Amsterdam, Amsterdam, The Netherlands.

Rusbult, C. E., Kumashiro, M., Finkel, E. J., & Wildschut, T. (2002). The war of the Roses: An interdependence analysis of betrayal and forgiveness. In P. Noller & J. A. Feeney (Eds.), *The intricacies of marital interaction* (pp. 251–281). New York: Cambridge University Press.

Rusbult, C. E., Olsen, N., Davis, J. L., & Hannon, P. (2001). Commitment and relationship maintenance mechanisms. In J. H. Harvey & A. Wenzel (Eds.), *Close romantic relationships: Maintenance and enhancement* (pp. 87–113). Mahwah, NJ: Lawrence Erlbaum.

Rusbult, C. R., & Van Lange, P. A. M. (2003). Interdependence, interaction, and relationships. *Annual Review of Psychology, 54*, 351–375.

Smolen, R. C., & Spiegel, D. A. (1987). Marital locus of control as a modifier of the relationship between the frequency of provocation by spouse and marital satisfaction. *Journal of Research in Personality, 21*, 70–80.

Tangney, J. P., Wagner, P. E., Hill-Barlow, D., Marschall, D. E., & Gramzow, R. (1996). Relation of shame and guilt to constructive versus destructive responses to anger across the lifespan. *Journal of Personality and Social Psychology, 70,* 797–809.

Thibaut, J. W., & Kelley, H. H. (1959). *The social psychology of groups.* New York: Wiley.

Weiner, B., Graham, S., Peter, O., & Zmuidinas, M. (1991). Public confession and forgiveness. *Journal of Personality, 59,* 281–312.

Zechmeister, J. S., & Romero, C. (2002). Victim and offender accounts of interpersonal conflict: Autobiographical narratives of forgiveness and unforgiveness. *Journal of Personality and Social Psychology, 82,* 675–686.

Chapter Thirteen

"'Til Lack of Forgiveness Doth Us Part": Forgiveness and Marriage

Frank D. Fincham
Julie H. Hall
Steven R. H. Beach

Because those we love are paradoxically the ones we are most likely to hurt, it is critical to understand forgiveness in close relationships. Indeed, spouses report that the capacity to seek and grant forgiveness is one of the most important factors contributing to marital longevity and marital satisfaction (Fenell, 1993), and marital therapists note that forgiveness is a challenging but necessary part of the healing process for major relationship transgressions such as infidelity (Gordon & Baucom, 1999). Likewise, forgiveness of everyday hurts may contribute to relationship strength in numerous ways (Fincham, Beach, & Davila, 2004). This chapter explores forgiveness as it operates within the context of marriage, considering the existing research that has been done in this area as well as identifying promising directions for future research. We also address how forgiveness can be applied in interventions with individual couples and groups of couples within the community. Finally, we discuss our theoretical perspectives on the forgiveness field as a whole. Before embarking on this exploration, we first make explicit our theoretical assumptions about the construct of forgiveness.

ASSUMPTIONS ABOUT FORGIVENESS

Notwithstanding the lack of a consensual definition of forgiveness, common to most definitions is the idea of a freely chosen motivational transformation in which the desire to seek revenge and to avoid contact with the transgressor is lessened, a process sometimes described as an altruistic gift (e.g., Enright, Freedman, & Rique, 1998; Worthington, 2001). However, recent studies of marital forgiveness have challenged this assumption of a unidimensional motivational change, questioning the notion that forgiveness is limited to a decrease in negative motivation (Fincham, 2000; Fincham & Beach, 2002; Fincham et al., 2004). There is emerging evidence that forgiveness also entails a positive motivational state that forms the foundation for approach, or conciliatory, behavior. It is therefore important to consider both positive and negative dimensions of forgiveness, because the presence of positive motivation cannot be inferred from the absence of negative motivation. We also distinguish our definition of forgiveness from constructs such as denial (unwillingness to perceive the injury), condoning (removes the offense and hence need for forgiveness), pardon (granted only by a representative of society, such as a judge), forgetting (removes awareness of offense from consciousness; to forgive is more than not thinking about the offense), and reconciliation (restores a relationship and is therefore a dyadic process). In sum, we assume forgiveness constitutes a transformation in motivation toward a transgressor that comprises both positive and negative dimensions (for details see Fincham & Beach, 2001).

What Do We Know About Forgiveness in Marriage?

Despite a burgeoning literature on forgiveness, relatively little is known about how forgiveness operates in marriage. It is evident that general theoretical accounts of forgiveness may not apply to forgiveness in marriage, because the forgiveness process may have different antecedents, correlates, or consequences in marital relationships than in other relationships. This has led some researchers to cite the lack of integration of forgiveness theory and marriage theory as one of the most significant problems in the current forgiveness literature (Gordon, Baucom, & Snyder, 2000). In Table 13.1, we summarize existing research on forgiveness in marriage. It can be seen that forgiveness has a number of correlates in marriage, including relationship and life satisfaction, intimacy, attributions, and affect, and that it predicts psychological aggression, marital conflict, and behavior toward the spouse after a transgression.

Critique.   Although important first steps have recently been taken in the exploration of marital forgiveness, several limitations of this research are evident. One major shortcoming is the tendency, also found in forgiveness research more generally, to obtain data on forgiveness and its correlates from a single source. Even when obtained from both spouses, data tend to be analyzed separately by spouse. Both of these circumstances fail to take into account interdependence between spouses. It is undoubtedly important to explore how a husband's forgiveness relates to his reports of marital quality, communication, and so on. However, it is equally important to assess how husbands' forgiveness is related to wives' perceptions of these same relationship variables. It is therefore important to include both spouses in the same analysis and to examine cross-spousal effects. This approach is illustrated in a recent study in which wives' benevolent motivation predicted husbands' reports of better conflict resolution, and husbands' retaliation and avoidance predicted wives' reports of poorer

TABLE 13.1. Studies That Have Investigated Forgiveness in Married Couples

Study and source	Sample type and description	Findings
Alvaro (2001) Dissertation	Community; 46 married couples in a forgiveness intervention or a control group	Positive associations with marital satisfaction, communication, emotional intimacy, and intellectual intimacy. A forgiveness-based intervention was shown to enhance each of these four variables.
Burchard et al. (2003) Journal	Community; 20 newlywed couples assigned to 1 of 2 marital enrichment programs or a control group	Trait forgiveness positively associated with quality of life, and couples in the forgiveness-based condition showed a marginally significant increase in quality of life.
Fincham (2000) Journal	Community; 71 British couples in third year of marriage	Negative associations with conflict-promoting responsibility attributions and positive associations with communication behavior and marital quality. Forgiveness fully mediated the relationship between responsibility attributions and communication behavior when controlling for marital quality. Forgiveness also predicted retaliatory and conciliatory responses to partner injury when controlling for marital quality, hurt, and time.
Fincham & Beach (2002) Journal	Community Study 1: 44 British couples in the first year of marriage	Negative dimension of forgiveness positively associated with aggression and negatively associated with marital satisfaction. Positive dimension of forgiveness positively associated with marital satisfaction for Hs. Hs' positive forgiveness was negatively related to Ws' aggression and positively related to Ws' satisfaction. Hs' willingness to forgive predicted Ws' psychological aggression, controlling for marital satisfaction. Ws' retaliation predicted Hs' psychological aggression after controlling for satisfaction.
	Study 2: 66 British couples	A two-factor model of forgiveness was supported, and the negative and positive dimensions of forgiveness showed similar associations with marital variables as in Study 1. Negative forgiveness was inversely associated with communication, whereas positive forgiveness was positively related to communication. Spousal negative forgiveness was positively related to the partner's psychological aggression and negative forgiveness, and negatively related to the partner's satisfaction, communication, and positive forgiveness.

(continues)

TABLE 13.1. Studies That Have Investigated Forgiveness in Married Couples (continued)

Study and source	Sample type and description	Findings
Fincham, Beach, & Davila (2004) Journal	Community Study 1: 52 British couples in their third year of marriage	Spousal positive forgiveness was positively related to the partner's satisfaction, communication, and positive forgiveness. Spousal positive forgiveness was negatively related to the other partner's aggression. The two forgiveness dimensions accounted for significant variance in satisfaction. However, positive dimension accounted for unique variance in Ws' satisfaction, whereas the negative dimension accounted for unique variance in Hs' satisfaction.
		A two-factor model of forgiveness was supported, in which the positive and negative dimensions were moderately and inversely related. For Hs only, the negative dimension was positively associated with ineffective conflict resolution and negatively associated with own marital satisfaction and Ws' satisfaction.
		For both spouses, the positive dimension of forgiveness was negatively related to ineffective conflict resolution and positively associated with own marital satisfaction. Hs' retaliatory impulses predicted Ws' reports of ineffective conflict resolution after controlling for marital satisfaction. Ws' benevolence negatively predicted Hs' reported ineffective conflict resolution.
	Study 2: 96 American couples from long-term marriages	A three-factor model (i.e., benevolence, retaliation, avoidance) of forgiveness was supported. A pattern of correlations similar to those in Study 1 was found.
		Hs' avoidance predicted Ws' reported ineffective conflict resolution, even after controlling for marital satisfaction. Ws' benevolence negatively predicted Hs' reported ineffective conflict resolution.
Fincham, Paleari, & Regalia (2002) Journal	Community Italian Hs ($n = 79$) and Ws ($n = 92$) from long-term marriages	Positive associations with marital quality, benign attributions, and emotional empathy, and inverse association with negative affective reactions. Responsibility attributions, negative affective reactions, and emotional empathy directly predicted forgiveness. Responsibility attributions were more predictive of forgiveness for Ws, whereas emotional empathy was a better predictor of forgiveness in Hs. Marital quality facilitated forgiveness indirectly through attributions but did not account for unique variance in forgiveness.

Citation	Sample	Findings
Gordon & Baucom (2003) Journal	Community; 107 married couples	Spouses were grouped into three stages of forgiveness. Groups differed in global ratings of forgiveness; spouses in Stage 1 report the least forgiveness, least positive marital assumptions, and lowest marital satisfaction, whereas spouses in Stage 3 report the highest levels of these variables. In terms of psychological closeness, spouses in Stage 1 scored lowest, and those in Stage 3 scored highest. This pattern was reversed for perceptions of partners' power in the marriage.
Hoyt, Fincham, McCullough, Maio, & Davila (in press) Journal	Community Study 1: 96 American couples in long-term marriages	Spouses concurred on how likely they were to forgive their child. Hs and Ws showed variability in their unique willingness to forgive and perceptions of being forgiven by their spouse, beyond the variance accounted for by actor or partner effects. Reactions to spouse transgressions were determined largely by relationship-specific factors, rather than individual tendencies toward forgiveness or forgivability. Same pattern was found for perceived forgiveness by one's spouse for one's own transgressions. Ineffective arguing accounted for significant variance in these relationship effects, for both forgiveness and perceived forgiveness.
	Study 2: 79 British couples in long-term marriages	Parents did not concur on how likely they were to forgive their child. As in Study 1, Hs and Ws showed variability in their unique willingness to forgive and perceptions of being forgiven by their spouse, beyond the variance accounted for actor/partner effects. Again, reactions to spouse transgressions determined largely by relationship-specific factors, rather than individual tendencies toward forgiveness or forgivability. The same pattern was found for perceived forgiveness by one's spouse for one's own transgressions. After controlling for transgression severity and closeness, trust accounted for significant variance in these relationship effects for forgiveness, but only for Ws' forgiveness of Hs. In terms of perceived forgiveness, trust and closeness predicted significant variance in Ws' ratings of being forgiven by their Hs.
Kachadourian, Fincham, & Davila (2004) Journal	College and community Study 1: 184 undergraduates in dating relationships	Positive associations with model of self, model of other, and relationship satisfaction. Models of self and other predicted the tendency to forgive, and there was a significant interaction between these two predictors. For individuals with more negative models of self, there was no relationship between model of other and the *(continues)*

TABLE 13.1.   Studies That Have Investigated Forgiveness in Married Couples *(continued)*

Study and source	Sample type and description	Findings
		tendency to forgive. However, model of other predicted a greater tendency to forgive among those with more positive models of self. Tendency to forgive also predicted relationship satisfaction and partially mediated the association between model of other and relationship satisfaction.
	Study 2: 96 couples in long-term marriages	Tendency to forgive and actual forgiveness were positively associated with one another and to model of self, model of other, and relationship satisfaction. Hs' marital satisfaction was positively associated with Ws' tendency to forgive, and Ws' models of self and other were positively related to Hs' forgiveness. Models of self and other predicted the tendency to forgive, but there was a significant interaction between these two predictors for Ws only. For Ws with more negative models of self, there was no relationship between model of other and the tendency to forgive. However, model of other predicted a greater tendency to forgive among those with more positive models of self. Tendency to forgive also predicted marital satisfaction. Tendency to forgive partially mediated the association between model of other and marital satisfaction for Hs, and partially mediated the association between model of self and marital satisfaction for both spouses. The tendency to forgive predicted actual forgiveness of a transgression. However, for Hs there was an interaction such that the tendency to forgive predicted actual forgiveness only for high-severity events.
Kachadourian, Fincham, & Davila (2005) Journal	Community; 87 couples in long-term marriages	Forgiveness positively associated with marital satisfaction and negatively related to rumination and ambivalence. There was a significant interaction between ambivalence and rumination, even after controlling for marital quality and event severity. For spouses who ruminated frequently, increased ambivalence was associated with lower forgiveness. There was no relationship between ambivalence and forgiveness for individuals who did not ruminate.
Karremans, Van Lange, Ouwerkerk, & Kluwer (2003) Journal	Community; 119 married couples	Partner-specific forgiveness was positively associated with life satisfaction, and this association was stronger than the association between general forgiveness and life satisfaction. Partner-specific and general forgiveness were positively related, as were spouses' reports of partner-specific forgiveness.

Study	Sample	Findings
Paleari, Regalia, & Fincham (2005) Journal	Community; 198 married couples in Italy assessed at two points separated by a 6-month interval	Rumination and empathy independently predicted concurrent unforgiveness and benevolence. Unforgiveness and benevolence concurrently affected marital quality. The rumination → unforgiveness → marital quality path was stronger for Ws than for Hs, whereas the empathy → benevolence path was stronger for Hs than for Ws. Marital quality at Time 1 influenced unforgiveness and benevolence 6 months later via Time 2 rumination. Unforgiveness and benevolence at Time 1 influenced marital quality 6 months later through the mediation of Time 1 marital quality, Time 2 unforgiveness, benevolence, and rumination.
Rackley (1993) Dissertation	Community; 170 married individuals	Forgiveness significantly predicted marital adjustment.
Ripley & Worthington (2002) Journal	Community; 43 married couples assigned to one of two marital enrichment programs or a control group	Forgiveness was positively associated with marital satisfaction and communication. Couples in the forgiveness-based group showed a greater improvement in communication at follow-up than couples in the control group but did not differ from couples in the hope-focused group. The three treatment groups did not differ in terms of marital quality or forgiveness at post-test and follow-up.
Sells, Giordano, & King (2002) Journal	Clinical; 5 married couples seeking therapy	At posttreatment, forgiveness skills had increased, with gains for subscales of insight, trust, and overt forgiveness. However, at follow-up, gains were maintained only for trust.
Vaughan (2001) Dissertation	Community; 20 newly married couples assigned to a control group or 1 of 2 marital enrichment programs*	Trait forgiveness was positively associated with religious commitment and Time 2 marital satisfaction. Religious commitment and trait forgiveness predicted marital satisfaction at posttreatment. Forgiveness accounted for most of the variance. However, marital satisfaction declined slightly in the forgiveness treatment group.
Woodman (1992) Dissertation	Community; 84 married individuals	Positive association with marital adjustment.

Note: H = husband, W = wife
* The same sample used by Burchard et al. (2003).

conflict resolution (Fincham et al., 2004). However, this study did not investigate interactional behavior between husbands and wives, and thus does not tell us how these associations between forgiveness dimensions and conflict resolution were overtly manifested in couples' exchanges.

A second methodological challenge involves differentiating forgiveness from potentially overlapping constructs, such as marital quality. The marital literature is brimming with constructs and measures that unknowingly tap into the same domain (see Fincham & Bradbury, 1987). As a result, the field is strewn with an unknown number of tautological findings owing to content overlap in the operations used to assess purportedly different constructs. In light of this observation, it is encouraging that some recent studies have found associations between forgiveness and other relationship constructs when controlling for marital quality, suggesting that forgiveness is a unique and informative process (Fincham & Beach, 2002; Fincham et al., 2004).

Third, despite emerging evidence of the bidimensional nature of forgiveness, few studies have considered both positive and negative aspects of forgiveness. This will be crucial to enhancing our understanding of marital forgiveness, because these dimensions have different correlates and perform differently for husbands and wives (Fincham & Beach, 2002; Fincham et al., 2004). Having identified three important methodological limitations of the current marital forgiveness literature, we are now in a position to offer specific recommendations about how to address these challenges. Although these recommendations are framed in the context of marriage, they can easily be extended to forgiveness in other dyads or to forgiveness research in general.

METHODOLOGICAL RECOMMENDATIONS

Given that forgiveness within marriage represents a process involving both spouses, one of the first steps to improving research is to obtain data from each partner and to examine how both self-reported and partner-reported forgiveness relate to other marital processes. As has been highlighted thus far, the determinants, correlates, and consequences of forgiveness appear to be different among husbands and wives. Further, obtaining data from both partners will allow consideration of how one spouses' forgiveness affects the other spouse and how it affects relationship-level variables. Implicit in this recommendation is the need to examine spousal interactions to assess the behaviors that might facilitate one spouse's forgiveness of the other. Such assessment may include self-report in which both partners maintain a diary and complete daily measures for several weeks following a transgression within the marriage. However, there is also a great need to move beyond self-reports and to supplement these measures with other sources of information, such as observational data. For example, partners might be asked to reenact a recent conflict centered around an unforgiven transgression, as well as one pertaining to a forgiven offense, in order to contrast the behavioral patterns that characterize these interactions. Regardless of the approach taken, we must broaden the scope of our research to consider both partners' perspectives, as well as cross-spousal effects.

In response to the potential conceptual overlap between relationship constructs, we must be vigilant in constructing forgiveness measures to ensure that we do not include items that tap related constructs, such as communication, because this overlap would overestimate associations between forgiveness and other interpersonal processes within marriage. As noted, this problem has plagued the assessment of marital quality (e.g., Fincham & Bradbury, 1987), leading some researchers in this field to suggest that global measures of marital satisfaction are the most appropriate way to capture an individual's overall sentiment toward the marriage (see Bradbury, Fincham, & Beach, 2000; Fincham & Beach, in press). Perhaps we can avoid similar item/construct overlap by heeding this advice and focusing on global ratings of the extent to which one has forgiven one's partner. However, global measures are appropriate only when a researcher is seeking to measure forgiveness as an overall judgment and are less useful when information is sought about specific dimensions of forgiveness. Whether assessing marital forgiveness at a global or specific level, the most important guideline is that we maintain the conceptual clarity that will distinguish forgiveness from other marital processes.

Our third methodological recommendation pertains to the assessment of forgiveness as a bidimensional process. The positive (i.e., approach) and negative (i.e., avoidance) dimensions of forgiveness represent distinct motivational systems (Gray, 1987) and must be measured separately. Work by McCullough, Fincham, and Tsang (2003) suggests that the temporal unfolding of avoidant, retaliatory, and benevolent motivation can take several forms, underscoring the need to assess all three forms at various levels. Within the context of marriage, positive and negative dimensions of forgiveness appear to operate differently for husbands and wives, indicating that the determinants and consequences of forgiveness may differ across spouses. In addition, the negative and positive dimensions of forgiveness may themselves have different determinants, correlates, and consequences. Finally, this simple two-dimensional scheme also allows us to distinguish among four types of forgiveness, as shown in Table 13.2 (see also Fincham & Beach, 2001). In short, bidimensional assessment is necessary to furthering our understanding of marital forgiveness.

Our final recommendation does not concern forgiveness per se but instead stems from an important observation about relationship research. Weiss (1980) coined the term *sentiment override* to describe the hypothesis that spouses respond noncontingently

TABLE 13.2. Forgiveness Typology Resulting from Bidimensional Concept of Forgiveness

Dimension		Positive	
		High	Low
Negative	High	Ambivalent forgiveness	Nonforgiveness
	Low	Complete forgiveness	Detached forgiveness

to partner behavior or questions about the marriage. In other words, partners simply respond to each other or research questions in terms of their dominant feelings or sentiments about the relationship, and this is reflected "in as many tests as one chooses to administer" (Weiss & Heyman, 1990, p. 92). As a result, measures of constructs such as forgiveness *in the context of a relationship* can serve as proxy indices of relationship satisfaction and thereby give rise to tautological findings. This has prompted at least one marital researcher to assert that attempts to explain variance in relationship satisfaction using self-reports are "invalid from a scientific standpoint" (Gottman, 1990, p. 79).

We do not agree with this conclusion but instead suggest a solution to this problem. Simply stated, we propose that a test of "surplus conceptual value" be passed whenever a construct is assessed via self-report in relationships. This test can be provided by controlling statistically the relationship satisfaction of both partners whenever two relationship variables are investigated, lest any association between them simply reflect their status as proxies of relationship satisfaction. A conceptually similar test can easily be applied to experimental research on relationship variables. With this test applied, forgiveness has been found to be related to marital processes (see Fincham et al., 2004).

NEW RESEARCH DIRECTIONS

We now turn to identify needed areas of basic research, including the need to study (a) different levels of forgiveness (i.e., for a specific transgression vs. repeated transgressions and for major transgressions vs. less serious transgressions), (b) the temporal unfolding of forgiveness in marriage and the way in which it relates to level of forgiveness called for, (c) the communication of forgiveness among intimates, (d) the causal relations among forgiveness and its correlates in marriage, and (e) self-forgiveness for the perpetration of transgressions against the partner. After exploring each of these areas, we consider implications for clinical and applied interventions.

Basic Research

Different Levels of Forgiveness. Although most marital forgiveness research has studied specific offenses, transgressions in marriage can also be considered at the dyadic level. Dyadic forgiveness represents a person's general tendency to forgive offenses within a particular relationship (McCullough, Hoyt, & Rachal, 2000). This level of forgiveness is likely characterized by different predictors and correlates than is offense-specific forgiveness, making it important to assess the association between dyadic forgiveness and offense-specific forgiveness. Similarly, when exploring different levels of forgiveness, it is necessary to compare specific and repeated transgressions. For example, a husband trying to forgive his wife for her one-time infidelity likely experiences a different forgiveness process than a partner faced with his wife's fourth affair. How does the trangressional history of a relationship influence the forgiveness of subsequent offenses within that relationship? Do past transgressions influence the forgiveness of subsequent offenses only when the wrongdoing is similar in nature, severity, or proximity to a past offense?

Chronic transgressions must also be considered, such as long-standing patterns of emotional neglect. How do spouses forgive one another for hurts that are endured day after day? Such questions cannot be answered by examining forgiveness at the offense-specific level; we must move beyond single transgressions to consider the various patterns of wrongdoing in marriage. This entails considering not only major transgressions but also fairly minor offenses. When looking at forgiveness in nondistressed, long-term marriages, researchers are more likely to encounter minor transgressions than major offenses, such as infidelity and physical abuse. It will be important to explore how the marital forgiveness process differs, depending on both the pattern and the severity of the transgressions.

Temporal Unfolding of Forgiveness.   There is the temptation to identify forgiving with a specific statement of forgiveness or an overt act of forgiveness (e.g., Baumeister, Exline, & Sommer, 1998). However, the verb form *to forgive* is not performative but instead signals that a decision to forgive has occurred. It therefore sets in motion a process with a presumed endpoint that may be sudden or may be slowly achieved (for a more complete analysis, see Fincham, 2000).

This creates particular challenges in ongoing relationships. Consider the spouse who offers a verbal statement of forgiveness. As indicated, such a statement does not constitute forgiveness per se and more likely indicates the decision to try to forgive the partner. Even when worded as such (though in the normal course of events one expects "I forgive you" to occur more commonly than "I want to try and forgive you"), the partner is likely to experience the statement as performative and be puzzled, annoyed, or angry when incompletely resolved feelings of resentment about the transgression intrude on subsequent discourse or behavior in the relationship. Thus, the words *I forgive you* can signal the beginning of a process for the spouse but be seen as the end of the matter by the partner, who may be only too willing to put the transgression in the past and act as though it never happened. The timing of such a verbalization and where the spouse stands with regard to our typology of forgiveness are likely to be particularly important. For example, the verbalization may have a different impact, depending on whether the spouse offering it is seen to be ambivalent versus detached.

Communication of Forgiveness.   Kelley (1998) was among the first to recognize the importance of exploring how forgiveness is expressed between individuals in daily interactions and found that victims used three strategies to communicate forgiveness to an offender. Direct strategies involved overtly granting forgiveness, whereas indirect strategies included more subtle expressions of forgiveness. In the third group of strategies, forgiveness was conditional and was granted only with certain stipulations. These three types of strategies also characterized the offenders' attempts to seek forgiveness. Although these communication techniques capture the general expression of forgiveness, research has yet to explore forgiveness transactions specifically within the context of marriage. It will be informative to compare partners' communication strategies and their perceptions of being forgiven by the other spouse. Similarly, certain ways of expressing forgiveness may be more adaptive and may be associated with or predictive of healthy relationships.

Such research is important because communication of forgiveness can easily be bungled or abused. First, genuinely motivated attempts to tell the partner that he or she is forgiven can easily be seen as a put-down or a form of retaliation if unskillfully executed. Thus, they can lead to conflict and might themselves end up being a source of hurt. Second, the transgressor is likely motivated to see forgiven behavior as condoned behavior if the spouse does not explicitly and clearly communicate that the transgression and the hurt it has caused are unacceptable. Because victims experience greater loss than transgressors feel they gain from the transgression, this communication requires some skill to avoid being seen as an overreaction and, hence, a possible source of conflict. Third, statements of forgiveness may be abused. They can be used strategically to convey contempt, engage in one-upmanship, and so on.

Causal Relations.   The paucity of longitudinal or experimental research on marital forgiveness renders it difficult to draw any conclusions about the causal relationships between forgiveness and its correlates in marriage. For example, although there is a robust association between forgiveness and marital satisfaction in cross-sectional studies, forgiveness may enhance marital satisfaction, marital satisfaction may promote forgiveness, or these constructs may be reciprocally related. This ambiguity also characterizes the associations that have been found between forgiveness and marital communication, conflict resolution, intimacy, and psychological aggression. Future research is needed to identify causal relations between specific forgiveness dimensions and other relationship variables.

Self-Forgiveness.   The topic of self-forgiveness has been largely neglected by marital research, as well as by the general forgiveness literature. Self-forgiveness is necessary when one has behaved in a way that he or she acknowledges as wrong and accepts responsibility for such behavior (Dillon, 2001; Holmgren, 1998). We conceptualize self-forgiveness as a set of motivational changes whereby one becomes decreasingly motivated to avoid stimuli associated with the offense, decreasingly motivated to retaliate against the self (e.g., punish the self, engage in self-destructive behaviors etc.), and increasingly motivated to act benevolently toward the self. Self-forgiveness plays an interesting role in marriage. Spouses must frequently deal with having behaved hurtfully to their partners. The victimized spouse's behavior may play an important part in facilitating the perpetrator's self-forgiveness; it has been hypothesized that being granted forgiveness by the victim may promote self-forgiveness (Hall & Fincham, in press). In this respect, the interplay between interpersonal forgiveness and self-forgiveness in marriage has yet to be explored. Further, although attributions and conciliatory behavior have been proposed as variables that may promote self-forgiveness, there may also be unique relationship-level processes in marriage that facilitate self-forgiveness.

Implications for Clinical and Applied Interventions

In recent years, forgiveness-based psychoeducation and intervention programs have become more prominent in the marital literature (e.g., Burchard et al., 2003; Gordon et al., 2000; Ripley & Worthington, 2002). However, most interventions have focused on facilitating forgiveness by increasing empathy for the offender. Increased empathy may have a direct effect on retaliatory impulses by making the transgressor more understandable. However, we are not aware of any forgiveness interventions that have focused specifically on increasing benevolence motivations. Given the likely divergence of influences on the positive and negative dimensions of forgiveness, this oversight seems striking. At best, it appears that forgiveness interventions may not be capitalizing on all possible means of enhancing forgiveness. At worst, it may be that a dimension has been overlooked that could be critical for long-term outcomes in marriage.

Much of what is known from psychological research on marital interaction can be fruitfully conceptualized in terms of relationship goals, particularly the "emergent" goals that characterize couples locked in destructive interactions (Fincham & Beach, 1999). In such interactions, couples commonly switch from the goals they profess on a day-to-day basis—that is, goals that are largely cooperative—to emergent goals that are adversarial in nature. For example, rather than focus on generating a solution to the problem at hand, couples locked in the destructive pattern of escalation may find themselves focused on beating their partners—or at least on not losing the argument to their partners. This sets the stage for couples to engage in negative behaviors, even when they "know better" and want to behave differently (in the heat of the moment, they simply fail to employ requisite skills; Worthington, 2003). In the context of past partner offenses, such emergent goals may lead to previously forgiven transgressions being used as ammunition in the escalating battle. Because of the power of emergent goals to disrupt marital interaction, communication skills and empathy for the partner may not be enough to ensure translation of partner forgiveness into a dyadic process that is helpful to the couple. In particular, if partners have been successful in reducing retaliatory goals, this need not protect them from the reemergence of retaliatory goals during conflict. It may be that benevolence motives are a better, or perhaps just an additional, protection against the reemergence of retaliatory motives during conflict. Likewise, it may be that benevolence motives are necessary for optimal conflict resolution in a dyadic context.

This framework suggests that current programs for facilitating forgiveness may not provide a complete answer to marital breakdown or relationship reconciliation, even if they are relatively effective in promoting a reduction in retaliatory motives in the relatively calm, nonconflictual setting of the forgiveness group. As Fincham and Beach (1999) noted, the marital area has long been in need of an intervention that can modify problematic emergent goals. Similarly, it may be that a critical missing element in current forgiveness programs is something that will protect couples against the emergent retaliatory goals that may arise during the common, everyday conflict situations that characterize marriage. If so, current forgiveness interventions may prove to be of short-lived value with regard to relationship outcomes and may never fulfill their promise in the marital context. The key to enhanced longer term outcomes, therefore, is to find an intervention that will help partners recognize and respond effectively to their own emergent retaliatory goals. To be maximally effective, such an intervention should readily occur to the couple, require minimal reasoning, and have a calming effect on both parties. At the same time, if the intervention were able to prime partner forgiveness, this would be an especially important additional strength.

One possibility is to combine empathy for the partner with an intervention to enhance benevolence for the partner. Such a program might build on current forgiveness programs by adding a series of elements designed to promote benevolence. The first element of the benevolence intervention might focus on making the intellectual case for benevolence (e.g., the benefits that accrue from one's partner doing well). The intellectual case could set the stage for an emotional argument for benevolence (it provides opportunities for positive basking; it supports one's positive self-view; it provides an opportunity for personal spiritual growth). In turn, the emotional argument might set the stage for exploring with the partner the possible benefits of regular activities to express benevolence or cognitively to rehearse benevolent intentions toward the partner. Overall, the proposal to add benevolence training to current forgiveness interventions can be seen as combining forgiveness interventions with motivational interviewing. Motivational interviewing helps clients overcome the ambivalence that prevents them from making positive changes in their lives (Miller & Rollnick, 2002), suggesting that it is well suited to the promotion of benevolence in the context of forgiveness interventions, because clients must overcome a negative motivational state toward the offender and replace it with positive motivation.

PERSONAL THEORETICAL PERSPECTIVES ON THE FIELD

In this section, we introduce three new theoretical viewpoints that have important implications for research on forgiveness.

The Phenomenology of Forgiveness: Concepts of Forgiveness Among Spouses

A fundamental distinction in family research is that between insider (family member) and outsider (scientific observer) perspectives. This distinction can be usefully applied to thinking about the very definition of forgiveness. Most research on forgiveness reflects the outsider perspective because, even though it obtains subjective judgments of forgiveness, the questions asked about forgiveness are chosen a priori by the researcher. Even the few empirical attempts to develop empirically based definitions of forgiveness have been limited to "expert" judgments and, therefore, still reflect an outside perspective.

It is also important to understand the insider perspective and examine spouses' concepts of forgiveness and their understanding of what it means to forgive. Why? For a start, it is likely that how a spouse conceptualizes forgiveness will matter when attempting to understand the likelihood of forgiveness in specific circumstances. For instance, if a spouse believes that in order to forgive, he or she must literally forget the transgression and thereby place himself or herself at risk of future harm, he or she may be reluctant to forgive.

Understanding the phenomenology of forgiveness also has important implications for its measurement. Even psychometrically sophisticated measures of forgiveness (e.g., Berry, Worthington, Parrott, O'Connor, & Wade et al., 2001), as well as many studies (e.g., Boon & Sulsky, 1997), rely on some form of the question, "Have you forgiven?" If we do not understand what people mean when they say they forgive or do not forgive, it is difficult to understand what these measures mean. Furthermore, an assumption in most measures of forgiveness is that what the investigator is measuring corresponds with the idea of forgiveness in the mind of the participant. An important step in forgiveness research is to describe what spouses mean when they say they forgive or do not forgive and to compare these meanings to expert definitions of forgiveness.

Finally, understanding the phenomenology of forgiveness has the potential to advance forgiveness as a psychotherapeutic process. Understanding how people outside of the research community conceptualize and experience forgiveness may help researchers to develop improved psychoeducational and therapeutic techniques. For example, a wife may be unwilling to forgive her husband because of the fear of being viewed as weak or the fear of putting herself at an increased risk for future betrayals. Therefore, it is important to know how people think about forgiveness so that we can address any negative notions that they may have about it.

Implicit Versus Explicit Forgiveness: A Polygraph for Forgiveness?

A common distinction in social cognition research is between explicit and implicit cognitive processes (e.g., memory, judgments, attitudes). Paralleling Shiffrin and Schneider's (1977) discussion of controlled (initiated deliberately and is effortful, slow, often verbalizable, and controllable) and automatic (fast, effortless, involuntary, ballistic, and involves no awareness) processing, explicit processes are something one can talk about or declare (e.g., "declarative memory"), whereas implicit processes entail little or no ability to describe or become conscious of what one knows or thinks. What has this to do with forgiveness in marriage?

As any marital therapist can testify, marital interactions are often overlearned, unfold at an astonishing speed, and appear to proceed without much thought. This does not deny the importance of forgiveness for marital interactions; it simply suggests that the kind of deliberate and effortful judgments of forgiveness that we have studied thus far will provide an incomplete picture of its role. For example, it is not uncommon to come across a spouse who says and believes that he or she has forgiven the partner, only to discover that resentment or a desire for revenge is instigated by the slightest cue during interaction with the partner. If we are to understand how forgiveness in marriage influences marital interaction, we will also need to study forgiveness at this implicit level. Unlike explicit forgiveness that can be adopted quickly, implicit forgiveness, like any automatic process, requires extensive practice to develop.

There are numerous ways to assess implicit judgments but space precludes their discussion here (for an example in marital research, see Fincham, Garnier, Gano-Phillips, & Osborne et al., 1995). Can assessment of forgiveness at the implicit level provide a polygraph test? Hardly. The subtitle of this section is an attention-focusing device more than anything else because it is quite common to find discrepancies between explicit and implicit measures. We expect this to be no different in the case of forgiveness. Indeed, one might expect the discrepancy to be particularly pronounced in this field because the explicit decision to forgive, as noted, sets in motion a process that may take a long time to complete.

There is, however, one sense in which we might take the polygraph notion seriously. That is, when a spouse shows forgiveness on both explicit and implicit measures, we might safely conclude that he or she has truly forgiven the partner. Conversely, discrepancy between the two measures is not diagnostic in that it cannot distinguish among cases that reflect the need for more work to be done to achieve complete forgiveness, socially desirable responses on the explicit measure, and outright deception of the researcher or the self.

Forgiveness and Ambivalence

Implicit in the last section is the possibility that a spouse may experience ambivalence toward forgiving the partner or toward the partner more generally. Again, this can be assessed by asking the spouse explicitly about feelings of ambivalence, or it can be assessed implicitly. A recent study illustrates the relevance of ambivalence for understanding forgiveness in marriage. Kachadourian et al. (2005) used an open-ended listing of partner characteristics to assess ambivalence toward the partner and argue that in marriage, the occurrence of a negative event such as a transgression is likely to prime the negative component of a spouse's ambivalence toward the partner. Moreover, ruminating about the transgression is likely to chronically prime this negative component of ambivalence, leading to the hypothesis that there should be an interaction between ambivalence and rumination on forgiveness. They found support for this hypothesis: Greater ambivalence was associated with less forgiveness when the spouse ruminated about the transgression. However, for husbands and wives who did not think about the transgression frequently, the association between attitudinal ambivalence and forgiveness was not significant.

CONCLUSION

Forgiveness or a lack thereof appears to be essential in understanding satisfaction and relationship dynamics in marriage. Although much remains to be done in exploring its correlates, especially in exploring the causal connections between forgiveness and marital outcomes, it is clear that there are many connections and that these connections are consequential for many things, ranging from marital satisfaction to destructive arguments. Likewise, recent evidence indicates that the connections between forgiveness and marital outcomes do not depend on single source reports, overlap with global marital satisfaction, or item-overlap between measures. A remaining challenge for intervention research is to capitalize fully on the underlying structure of forgiveness. To the extent that forgiveness is comprised of two or more functionally distinct elements, current programs may not be capitalizing on the full potential of forgiveness interventions. Likewise, it will be important to continue to integrate research on forgiveness with basic research on other interpersonal processes, including the distinction between insider and outsider perspectives, implicit and explicit attitudes, and the sources and consequences of attitude ambivalence. By doing so, we will place our understanding of forgiveness on a firmer scientific footing and provide the foundation for continuing progress in forgiveness interventions.

REFERENCES

Alvaro, J. A. (2001). An interpersonal forgiveness and reconciliation intervention: The effect on marital intimacy. *Dissertation Abstracts International, 62*(3). (UMI 3011552).

Baumeister, R. F., Exline, J. J., & Sommer, K. L. (1998). The victim role, grudge theory, and two dimensions of forgiveness. In E. L. Worthington, Jr. (Ed.), *Dimensions of forgiveness: Psychological research and theological perspectives* (pp. 79–106). Philadelphia: Templeton Foundation Press.

Berry, J. W., Worthington, E. L., Parrott, L., O'Connor, L. E, & Wade, N. G. (2001). Dispositional forgivingness: Development and construct validity of the Transgression Narrative Test of Forgivingness (TNTF). *Personality and Social Psychology Bulletin, 27,* 1277–1290.

Bradbury, T.N., Fincham, F.D., & Beach, S.R.H. (2000). Research on the nature and determinants of marital satisfaction: A decade in review. *Journal of Marriage and the Family, 62,* 964–980.

Boon, S. D., & Sulsky, L. M. (1997). Attributions of blame and forgiveness in romantic relationships: A policy-capturing study. *Journal of Social Behavior and Personality, 12,* 19–44.

Burchard, G. A., Yarhouse, M. A., Kilian, M. K., Worthington, E. L., Berry, J. W., & Canter, D. E. (2003). A study of two marital enrichment programs and couples' quality of life. *Journal of Psychology and Theology, 31,* 240–252.

Dillon, R. S. (2001). Self-forgiveness and self-respect. *Ethics, 112,* 53–83.

Enright, R. D., Freedman, S., & Rique, J. (1998). The psychology of interpersonal forgiveness. In R. D. Enright & J. North (Eds.), *Exploring forgiveness* (pp. 46–62). Madison, WI: University of Wisconsin Press.

Fenell, D. (1993). Characteristics of long-term first marriages. *Journal of Mental Health Counseling, 15,* 446–460.

Fincham, F. D. (2000). The kiss of the porcupines: From attributing responsibility to forgiving. *Personal Relationships, 7,* 1–23.

Fincham, F. D., & Beach, S. R. (in press). Relationship satisfaction. In D. Perlman & A. Vangelisti (Eds.), *The Cambridge handbook of personal relationships.* Cambridge, England: Cambridge University Press.

Fincham, F. D., & Beach, S. R. (1999). Marital conflict: Implications for working with couples. *Annual Review of Psychology, 50,* 47–77.

Fincham, F. D., & Beach, S. R. (2001). Forgiving in close relationships. *Advances in Psychology Research, 7,* 163–198.

Fincham, F. D., & Beach, S. R. (2002). Forgiveness in marriage: Implications for psychological aggression and constructive communication. *Personal Relationships, 9,* 239–251.

Fincham, F. D., Beach, S. R., & Davila, J. (2004). Forgiveness and conflict resolution in marriage. *Journal of Family Psychology, 18,* 72–81.

Fincham, F. D., & Bradbury, T. N. (1987). The assessment of marital quality: A reevaluation. *Journal of Marriage and the Family, 49,* 797–809.

Fincham, F. D., Garnier, P. C., Gano-Phillips, S., & Osborne, L. N. (1995). Pre-interaction expectations, marital satisfaction, and accessibility: A new look at sentiment override. *Journal of Family Psychology, 9,* 3–14.

Fincham, F. D., Paleari, G., & Regalia, C. (2002). Forgiveness in marriage: The role of relationship quality, attributions, and empathy. *Personal Relationships, 9,* 27–37.

Gordon, K. C., & Baucom, D. H. (1999). A multitheoretical intervention for promoting recovery from extramarital affairs. *Clinical Psychology: Science and Practice, 6,* 382–399.

Gordon, K. C., & Baucom, D. H. (2003). Forgiveness and marriage: Preliminary support for a measure based on a model of recovery from a marital betrayal. *American Journal of Family Therapy, 31,* 179–199.

Gordon, K. C., Baucom, D. H., & Snyder, D. K. (2000). The use of forgiveness in marital therapy. In M. E. McCullough, K. I. Pargament, & C. E. Thoresen (Eds.), *Forgiveness: Theory, research, and practice* (pp. 203–227). New York: Guilford Press.

Gottman, J. M. (1990). How marriages change. In G. R. Patterson (Ed.), *Depression and aggression in family interaction* (pp. 75–102). Hillsdale, NJ: Erlbaum.

Gray, J. A. (1987). *The psychology of fear and stress.* Cambridge, England: Cambridge University Press.

Hall, J. H., & Fincham, F. D. (in press). Self-forgiveness: The stepchild of forgiveness research. *Journal of Social and Clinical Psychology.*

Holmgren, M. R. (1998). Self-forgiveness and responsible moral agency. *Journal of Value Inquiry, 32,* 75–91.

Hoyt, W. T., Fincham, F. D., McCullough, M. E., Maio, G., & Davila, J. (in press). Responses to interpersonal transgressions in families: Forgivingness, forgivability, and relationship-specific effects. *Journal of Personality and Social Psychology.*

Kachadourian, L. K., Fincham, F. D., & Davila, J. (2004). The tendency to forgive in dating and married couples: The role of attachment and relationship satisfaction. *Personal Relationships, 11,* 373–393.

Kachadourian, L. K., Fincham, F. D., & Davila, J. (2005). Attitudinal ambivalence, rumination and forgiveness of partner transgressions in marriage. *Personality and Social Psychology Bulletin, 31,* 334–342.

Karremans, J. C., Van Lange, P. A., Ouwerkerk, J. W., & Kluwer, E. S. (2003). When forgiving enhances psychological well-being: The role of interpersonal commitment. *Journal of Personality and Social Psychology, 84,* 1011–1026.

Kelley, D. (1998). The communication of forgiveness. *Communication Studies, 49,* 1–17.

McCullough, M. E., Fincham, F. D., & Tsang, J. (2003). Forgiveness, forbearance, and time: The temporal unfolding of transgression-related interpersonal motivations. *Journal of Personality and Social Psychology, 84,* 540–557.

McCullough, M. E., Hoyt, W. T., & Rachal, K. C. (2000). What we know (and need to know) about assessing forgiveness constructs. In M. E. McCullough, K. I. Pargament, & C. E. Thoresen (Eds.), *Forgiveness: Theory, research, and practice* (pp. 65–90). New York: Guilford Press.

Miller, W. R., & Rollnick, S. (2002). *Motivational interviewing.* New York: Guilford Press.

Paleari, F. G., Regalia, C., & Fincham, F. D. (2005). Marital quality, empathy, and rumination: A longitudinal analysis. *Personality and Social Psychology Bulletin, 31,* 368–378.

Rackley, J. V. (1993). The relationships of marital satisfaction, forgiveness, and religiosity. *Dissertation Abstracts International, 54*(4). (UMI 9319792).

Ripley, J. S., & Worthington, E. L. (2002). Hope-focused and forgiveness-based group interventions to promote marital enrichment. *Journal of Counseling and Development, 80,* 452–463.

Sells, J. N., Giordano, F. G., & King, L. (2002). A pilot study in marital group therapy: Process and outcome. *The Family Journal: Counseling and Therapy for Couples and Families, 10,* 156–166.

Shiffrin, R. M., & Schneider, W. (1977). Controlled and automatic human information processing. II. Perceptual learning, automatic attending, and a general theory. *Psychological Review, 84,* 127–190.

Vaughan, L. (2001). The relationship between marital satisfaction levels associated with participation in the FREE (Forgiveness and Reconciliation through Experiencing Empathy) and hope-focused marital enrichment program. *Dissertation Abstracts International, 62*(2). (UMI 3004950).

Weiss, R. L. (1980). Strategic behavioral marital therapy: Toward a model for assessment and intervention. In J. P. Vincent (Ed.), *Advances in family intervention, assessment and theory* (Vol. 1, pp. 229–271). Greenwich, CT: JAI Press.

Weiss, R. L., & Heyman, R. E. (1990). Observation of marital interaction. In F. D. Fincham & T. N. Bradbury (Eds.), *The psychology of marriage* (pp. 87–117). New York: Guilford Press.

Woodman, T. (1992). The role of forgiveness in marital adjustment. *Dissertation Abstracts International, 53*(4). (UMI 9225999).

Worthington, E. L., Jr. (2001) Unforgiveness, forgiveness, and reconciliation and their implications for societal interventions. In R. G. Helmick & R. L Petersen (Eds.), *Forgiveness and reconciliation: Religion, public policy, and conflict transformation* (pp. 161–182). Philadelphia: Templeton Foundation Press.

Worthington, E. L., Jr. (2003). Hope focused marriage: Recommendations for researchers, clinicians, and church workers. *Journal of Psychology and Theology, 3,* 231–239.

Chapter Fourteen

Families and Forgiveness

Cynthia L. Battle
Ivan W. Miller

My mom gave us up—we had to go live in a home. Didn't care if we were little, or what. That's what hurt. It took me a long time, but I forgave.... I tried to put myself in her position. What would I do?... My father used to beat her up. We could hear it. He used to get us out of bed.... "You see this?! You see her?!" My mother there with a black eye.... She had to get out of that situation.... I didn't see her for 12–13 years. I went to talk to her when I was 35. She explained everything...said she was sorry, crying and everything, apologizing.... She knew how much it hurt me. [When she was dying], I'd pray to God that my brother would come and say, "Ma, I love you" before she died. And he wouldn't. I won't ever forgive him for that. (participant in Forgiveness and Families Study)

Despite the great increase in attention to the construct of forgiveness in the psychological and broader social science literature over the past 15–20 years (e.g., Enright & North, 1998; Worthington, 1998a), a number of significant gaps exist in our understanding of the ways in which forgiveness is important for families and family functioning. For example, what types of events or interpersonal transgressions arise in families that most often call for one person to forgive another? Without intervention, how do families typically negotiate the process of forgiveness? How does this process vary for different types of families? Finally, and perhaps most important, how does forgiveness—or lack of forgiveness—following relational injuries relate to the overall functioning and well-being of a family? Although these are critical clinical and research questions to address, the answers remain unclear. In this chapter, we review the emerging theoretical and empirical literature relevant to the process of forgiveness within the family context. In addition, we describe our group's research in this area, which includes interview-based assessments of 102 community families. Finally, we discuss clinical implications based on existing data and present recommendations for future research.

PERSONAL ASSUMPTIONS ABOUT FORGIVENESS

We would like to identify aspects of our background and professional training that have likely shaped our personal assumptions about forgiveness. First, as family researchers, our perspective is influenced by systems theory, an approach that emphasizes the interrelatedness of individuals within a family group, and the importance of understanding how one individual's behavior has an effect on the entire system. More broadly, our assumptions about forgiveness are influenced by our training as clinical psychologists, both valuing empiricism and recognizing the importance of individual differences. Finally, our perspectives are influenced by our backgrounds as European-Americans raised within and influenced by Judeo-Christian culture.

Because the terms *forgiveness* and *family* can mean different things to different people, we would like to be explicit about how we use these terms. As several writers have noted (Butler, Dahlin, & Fife, 2002; McCullough & Worthington, 1995), the concept of forgiveness is often not clearly distinguished from other similar constructs. In our view, forgiveness is an intentional process that is both intrapersonal and interpersonal in nature and, as described by Enright and the Human Development Study Group (1991), consists of multiple cognitive, affective, and behavioral elements. The description of forgiveness offered by McCullough, Pargament, and Thoresen (2000) is consistent with our view: forgiveness is an "intra-individual, pro-social change toward a perceived transgressor that is situated in an interpersonal context" (p.12). We see forgiveness as related to but clearly distinct from reconciliation, exoneration, and acceptance-based conflict resolution strategies.

Just as there are many ways to define forgiveness, there are many ways to define what constitutes a family. We use a relatively simple and broad definition. By *family*, we are referring to people who are related to one another, including an individual's family of origin (parents, siblings, any other relatives in the household), as well as one's current family system (partner, children, other relatives in the household). Thus, our perspective includes traditional couples and marital research/therapy within a more overarching framework of family research/therapy. We use a family systems perspective because it is inclusive of different types of family structures (e.g., wife, husband, and their children; a mother-daughter dyad; a same-sex couple). This perspective allows research and treatment to be generalized to many types of families and couples, an important consideration, given the increasingly diverse demographics of the United States. Finally, family treatment can help address difficulties between family members other than two adult partners (e.g., problems between parents and a teenager; problems with in-laws).

REVIEW OF THEORETICAL AND EMPIRICAL LITERATURE

Very little published literature, either theoretical or empirical in nature, has directly addressed forgiveness in the family context. The literature that does exist primarily targets forgiveness within marital (as opposed to other family) relationships and often is focused on the development of interventions. Because another chapter in this book is devoted exclusively to the topic of forgiveness within married couples (see chapter 13 by Fincham, Hall, & Beach), we will provide only a brief review of the couples literature here. In the following sections, we will first discuss how the concept of forgiveness is addressed in theoretical writings on normal family processes and in theories of family/marital psychotherapy. Next, we will review the relevant empirical literature on forgiveness in families. Finally, we will describe our current ongoing study of forgiveness in families and present some preliminary findings.

FAMILY THEORY RELEVANT TO FORGIVENESS

Forgiveness as a Construct in Traditional Family Theory

We begin by examining how the concept of forgiveness fits into the "classic" theories of family process and family therapy. Surprisingly, there has been little attention to the construct of forgiveness in major family theories, despite the fact that most approaches consider resolving family conflict and coping with negative family events to be important to the health and longevity of families. In our review of some of the dominant family theories, including Bowen family systems theory (Bowen, 1978), the Beavers family systems model (Beavers et al., 1965), the McMaster model of family functioning (Epstein, Bishop, & Levin, 1978), and the Circumplex model (Olson, Russell, & Sprenkle, 1989), few references are made to the concept of forgiveness. Forgiveness is also virtually absent from major theories of family therapy, including Ericksonian family therapy (Lankton, Lankton, & Matthews, 1991), strategic family therapy (Haley, 1963), structural family therapy (Minuchin, 1974), and behavioral marital therapy (Jacobson & Margolin, 1979). However, these theories and therapeutic approaches all promote strategies for healthy family adaptation, conflict management, and relationship repair. For example, family theorists have emphasized that healthy families must be flexible and adaptable to changes over time (Olson & Gorall, 2003); they must be able to tolerate imperfections of family members and foster a climate in which it is comfortable to admit to mistakes (Beavers & Hampson, 2003); they must be able to resolve even emotionally laden problems (Epstein, Bishop, & Levin, 1978); and they must maintain a hopeful outlook for the future, even in the presence of a painful, uncertain reality (Beavers & Hampson, 2003). Thus, although not directly stated, many theories are consistent with the notions that the ability to forgive is integral to the overall functioning of the family and that forgiveness is an important mechanism by which healthy family relationships are maintained.

Several writers have offered reasons for the lack of attention to forgiveness within traditional family systems literature. Coleman (1998) posited that forgiveness may be viewed as somewhat at odds with the family systems approach in that most systemic theories emphasize the transactional nature of relationships and ways in which family members' behaviors are inextricably linked. Coleman suggests that in some systems therapists deemphasize individuals' behaviors and instead look at relational patterns that have evolved in the family, even in instances when one person's behavior was hurtful to another. Thus, if individuals' behaviors are not viewed as wrong or unjust, the concept of forgiveness becomes less relevant. However, Coleman goes on to suggest that forgiveness should in fact be viewed as consistent with a family systems perspective, because evaluating and changing relational patterns promotes forgiveness, which in turn promotes greater ability to change. It is also possible that forgiveness has not been addressed in family therapy because of the neutral stance that is typically advocated in traditional systems and other therapeutic approaches. Forgiveness is commonly conceptualized as having moral undertones relating to justice, injustice, and fairness—concepts difficult to embrace if one has a neutral stance. Moreover, several writers note that forgiveness may be avoided in the psychological literature because of its association with religion (e.g., Walrond-Skinner, 1998).

Although the majority of traditional family theories make no direct reference to forgiveness, one family therapy approach that does address issues highly related to the construct of forgiveness is contextual family therapy (Boszormenyi-Nagy, 1987; Boszormenyi-Nagy, Grunebaum, & Ulrich, 1991). In the contextual model, there is an emphasis on understanding the balance of fairness, or *equitability,* within the family system, as well as assessing the dynamics of family loyalties, interpersonal trust, and reciprocity. As a cornerstone of contextual family therapy, Boszormenyi-Nagy (1987) introduced the concept of *relational ethics,* or balance of fairness between family members, which he described as a "fundamental force in holding family and societal relationships together through reliability and trustworthiness" (p. 204). During treatment based on the contextual approach, therapists identify relational injuries that have occurred in the family and help family members in the process of exoneration.

Related to contextual family theory is the work of Boss (2001) and Walsh (2003) on family resilience, stress management, and hardiness. These strength (rather than deficit)-based theories of family functioning identify positive qualities and behaviors that promote healthy functioning over time, such as making meaning from adversity, maintaining connectedness, and holding a positive outlook in the face of change and uncertainty. Thus, the skills recognized by these models are consistent with promoting forgiveness in the family system.

Theoretical Models of Forgiveness in Families

We turn our attention now to some contemporary theoretical models that have explicitly addressed forgiveness in family and marital relationships. Not surprisingly, several contemporary family and marital researchers with interests in forgiveness have drawn on the contextual approach to family therapy. For example, Hargrave (1994) and colleagues (Hargrave, Jennings, & Anderson, 1991; Hargrave & Sell, 1997) developed a theoretical model of forgiveness in families particularly well integrated within Boszormenyi-Nagy's contextual family therapy approach. Hargrave suggests that to recover from interpersonal transgressions, families must go through a process of forgiveness consisting of two overarching dimensions: exoneration and forgiveness. In this model, exoneration includes the two "stations" of *insight* (recognizing patterns that perpetuate unjust reenactments) and *understanding* (recognizing the limits of the offender without removing his or her responsibility). Similarly, forgiveness includes the stations of *giving the opportunity for compensation* (providing a chance for the victimizer to restore the relationship) and the *overt act of forgiveness* (victim and offender openly discuss the hurtful behavior). Based on their model, they have developed and validated scales to measure relational ethics (Hargrave et al., 1991) and the forgiveness process (Interpersonal Relationship Resolution Scale; Hargrave & Sells, 1997).

Other contemporary researchers have also developed models for forgiveness in families. Gordon and Baucom (1998; 1999; 2003) developed an approach to forgiveness of extramarital affairs by integrating contextual therapy with cognitive-behavioral and insight-oriented marital therapies. DiBlasio detailed a model for "decision-based forgiveness" with intergenerational families (1998) and couples coping with infidelity (2000). Finally, Worthington (1998b) and colleagues (Worthington & Wade, 1999) have described a model for forgiving (*empathy-humility-commitment* model) with special attention to forgiveness within close family dyads.

In sum, although traditional family theories describing family processes and family psychotherapies have been essentially silent on the topic of forgiveness, contemporary forgiveness theorists (particularly those developing interventions) have had little difficulty incorporating forgiveness within a family framework, particularly the contextual approach. Forgiveness has been conceptualized in various ways, but generally is described as a complex process with multiple stepwise phases (e.g., Enright, 2001) that can promote healing from interpersonal transgressions on both the individual and relational level. Forgiveness is promoted not only as a process that helps individuals achieve greater emotional well-being but also as a critical process for families that need to restore trust following serious transgressions.

Empirical Research on Families and Forgiveness

The past decade has seen steady growth in the empirical study of forgiveness. The majority of studies pertaining to forgiveness in families have been with married couples (for review, see chapter 13 by Fincham et al. and chapter 25 by Gordon, Baucom, & Snyder). This includes a series of basic research studies by Fincham (2000) and colleagues (e.g., Fincham, Beach, & Davila, 2004; Fincham, Paleari, & Regalia, 2002) on spouses' responsibility attributions, empathy, and conflict-resolution skills, as well as several intervention studies targeting forgiveness in couples (e.g., Gordon & Baucom's 2003). Research addressing family forms other than couples is primarily focused on the development of forgiveness interventions. Group, individual, and family interventions have been developed for incest survivors (Freedman & Enright, 1996), college students deprived of parental affection (Al-Mabuk, Enright, & Cardis, 1995), parents whose children committed suicide (Al-Mabuk & Downs, 1996), men whose partners had abortions (Coyle & Enright, 1997), intergenerational families with unresolved issues (DiBlasio, 1998), and adults sharing parenting duties (Kiefer, et al., 2004).

Interestingly, most research that pertains to forgiveness within couples and families is based on individual data. That is, rather than draw upon information from more than one member of a family, investigators typically have relied on the report of a single individual. In addition, much research has examined "dispositional" forgiveness rather than reactions to actual interpersonal events or patterns in families (for an exception, see Fincham, 2000). These findings generally suggest that individuals with higher levels of dispositional forgiveness—that is, those who have a greater tendency to forgive those close to them after transgressions—are more likely to experience higher quality relationships, both in their families and in other realms of their lives.

The importance of using methodology that includes input from more than one family member can be seen by emerging data suggesting that men and women may view forgiveness differently. For example, in Fincham and colleagues' (Fincham et al., 2002) study with 92 married Italian couples, responsibility attributions were the best predictor of forgiveness for women; however, empathy was a stronger predictor of forgiveness for men. In addition, Fincham et al.'s (2004) two-site study of forgiveness and conflict resolution behaviors suggested that three identified components of forgiveness had different roles for wives and husbands in predicting future conflict resolution. Specifically, wives' positive forgiveness behaviors (i.e., benevolence) were most important in predicting the couple's conflict resolution, whereas husbands' negative forgiveness behaviors (i.e., retaliation, avoidance) mattered most.

The growing body of research on forgiveness provides support for the general premise that forgiveness plays an important role in family relationships. To our knowledge, however, no basic research has examined forgiveness among multiple members of a family system aside from those addressing marital forgiveness.

THE BROWN FORGIVENESS AND FAMILIES STUDY

To begin the process of elucidating how forgiveness works within family systems, our research group is currently examining forgiveness in a diverse sample of families from the community. The Brown Forgiveness and Families Study has three primary aims. First, we hope to identify the events that take place within families that create the greatest need for forgiveness. As Enright and Coyle (1998) have noted, the need for forgiveness arises from some type of event that causes injury. The topology of these events remains unclear, particularly within a family context. Although much of the literature on forgiveness within families has focused on infidelity (e.g., DiBlasio, 2000; Gordon & Baucom, 2003) and to a lesser extent on domestic abuse and incest (e.g., Freedman & Enright, 1996), no studies have documented a more complete range of situations that necessitate forgiveness.

The second goal of the study is to delineate the processes by which individuals after an interpersonal transgression do (or do not) arrive at a state of forgiveness with their family members. Although several interventions have been developed to help promote forgiveness in families, the effectiveness of these strategies remains largely unknown, as does the extent to which these strategies resemble the process of forgiving in the "real life" development of families. In addition to gathering open-ended responses regarding key elements in the forgiveness process, we are inquiring about the role of several specific elements (e.g., presence or absence of apology, offender's behaviors following the transgression).

The third goal of the study is to explore the associations among forgiveness, family functioning, and individual coping and adaptation. As noted earlier, prior research has suggested that individuals and families who are able to forgive important transgressions are more likely to experience healthy family relationships and better emotional and physical well-being. This has been less examined in the context of family systems other than marital relationships.

In our ongoing study, we are examining these questions by asking family members to participate in an in-depth, semistructured interview and provide self-report data regarding a number of individual and family characteristics (e.g., empathy, forgiveness, family functioning). The Forgiveness in Families Interview was modeled after the Life Events and Difficulties Schedule (Brown & Harris, 1989). It identifies key interpersonal transgressions in the family and examines factors leading to forgiveness or lack of forgiveness following the transgression.

Our preliminary findings suggest that a wide range of events necessitate forgiveness in families. In addition to infidelity and abuse, many other types of transgressions are reported as important experiences calling for forgiveness. These include (a) unequal treatment of siblings by one or both parents, (b) failure of a parent to protect a child from harm, (c) hurt feelings from divorce and/or remarriage, (d) lack of parental acceptance of a spouse or romantic partner (particularly in interracial or same-sex relationships), (e) irresponsible or dishonest financial decisions made by a family member, (f) problems associated with a family member's addiction or mental illness, (g) inequitable distribution of household tasks, (h) repeated instances of broken family commitments or prolonged absences, (i) disagreements regarding care of an ill or elderly relative, and (j) disputes regarding funerals and estate settlement.

In addition, our initial examination of the data reveals that there is considerable variation in how the process of forgiveness occurs in different families. For example, some families in our sample achieved forgiveness via overt discussion of the transgression and explicit granting of forgiveness; however, others reported success with much less direct ways of communicating about events. Consistent with findings regarding the role of forgiveness in marital relationships, preliminary analyses suggest that when individuals in families report a history of forgiving recent transgressions in the family (forgiveness averaged over several events), they tend to report better individual mental health, as well as higher levels of family functioning (Miller, Battle, Rossi, & Sasaki, 2003).

NEW RESEARCH DIRECTIONS NEEDED IN THE AREA

Research on forgiveness in families is still in its infancy. In the broadest sense, we believe that much more basic research is needed to clarify the nature and importance of forgiveness in families. Findings from these studies will play a key role in shaping and evaluating forgiveness-based interventions currently being developed for couples and families.

Before outlining what we believe are the most important questions facing the field, we would like to highlight some fundamental ways that forgiveness (and lack of forgiveness) in families may be distinguished from forgiveness in other relationships, as well as some ways in which the process of forgiveness research is different with families.

Perhaps most important, family relationships involve longer term and more intimate affiliations than do the majority of other social relationships. Because of the frequent nature of interactions and the high level of emotional involvement and interdependence that typically exists between family members, transgressions are likely to occur more often than in other relationships, and the stakes are higher when such hurts remain unresolved. In addition, because of the everyday nature of family relations and interactions, family members often face the challenge of coping with minor, yet repeated transgressions more so than in other relationships.

Another important aspect of forgiveness in families pertains to the complex nature of family relationships and the affective connections and loyalties that exist among family members: When transgressions occur, *multiple* family members are usually affected, and effects on individual family members may vary depending on the person's developmental status, family role, and affiliation with other family members. Thus, a single event may spur a complex series of reactions and effects across the family, necessitating forgiveness among multiple individuals. Major transgressions in families (e.g. violence, infidelity, abandonment) can result in particularly deep and wide-reaching effects, affecting not only those directly involved but also others in the household, extended family, and in some cases, even future generations.

A third unique aspect of forgiveness in families is that family systems will often adhere to or develop their own philosophies, values, and rules for behavior. A family's value system and behavioral rules may directly stem from a shared religious orientation or from the family's ethnic or cultural background; however, it may also be unrelated to these factors. Some families may therefore explicitly adopt and nurture a "culture" of forgiveness within their family system—teaching, modeling, and encouraging forgiveness among its members—and others may not. This family-level variable and its relation to individual behavior will be interesting to measure as more research is conducted within family systems.

Finally, we would like to acknowledge that research with families can be quite challenging, both conceptually and methodologically, and often more so than research with individuals or couples. For example, defining and measuring the primary variables of interest may not be straightforward, especially when multiple family members' perspectives are taken into consideration. On a practical level, enrolling and maintaining the research involvement of multiple, key family members can be difficult, given family members' work and school schedules and caretaking responsibilities for young children or elderly relatives. However, despite these challenges, we believe the additional effort involved in research with families is well worth it, and indeed essential, depending on the research questions of interest. Although research with individuals can help tap into some family-level processes, most questions regarding families can be adequately addressed only by including multiple family members in the research process.

In terms of specific areas of study, we propose the following progression of research:

1. It will be important to describe the phenomenology of forgiveness in family settings in terms of explicating both the types of events that necessitate forgiveness and the process by which forgiveness happens or is unable to happen. How is forgiveness in families similar to or different from forgiveness in other settings? As noted earlier, because individuals in families are affiliated for long periods of time, it will be particularly important to understand the impact of chronic or repeated transgressions within families, as well as the effectiveness of different strategies for coping with such patterns of hurtful behavior. Are acute, severe transgressions in the family more or less damaging than more minor, yet ongoing transgressions?

2. How important is forgiveness (or lack of forgiveness) between family members to the overall functioning of a family system? What types of positive effects on health and functioning might forgiveness have for the family as a whole and the individuals within it—and what are the negative effects when forgiveness does not take place?

3. What other aspects of family functioning are most closely related to forgiveness in terms of facilitating the forgiveness process? For example, is the best predictor of forgiveness in the family the overall level of cohesion or connectedness in the family system, or is forgiveness more associated with other aspects of functioning, such as communication or problem-solving ability? Are family qualities that predict greater tendency to forgive changeable?

4. What are the specific processes by which forgiveness occurs and by which forgiveness can lead to better family functioning? Initial research indicates that the ability to forgive is associated with better family/marital adjustment; however process mechanisms remain unclear and are important to address. For example, does forgiveness lead to better family functioning by strengthening the degree of trust, cohesion, or closeness among family members? Does forgiveness promote

healthy functioning by decreasing the likelihood or severity of family conflict? Regardless of whether overt conflict takes place, does the experience of multiple, unforgiven transgressions over time lead to an erosion of positive feelings or "good will" among family members and increase feelings of hostility and resentment?

5. Because family systems can develop their own values and rules for behavior, it would be important to understand to what extent families explicitly nurture a culture of forgiveness. If present, how might this value influence behavior of individuals following hurtful events, both with family members and with others? Would it lead to a greater tendency to forgive others even when the individual is living in a different environment? For families who explicitly value forgiveness, how is the practice of forgiveness taught to family members, particularly children (i.e., via social modeling or via family "rules" about apologizing and granting forgiveness)?

6. Depending on their age and level of cognitive/social/emotional development, children who experience hurtful events from parents, siblings, or other family members are likely to have different levels of understanding regarding the context and precipitating factors leading to a hurtful event. They will also differ in their ability to view events from another's perspective and develop empathy for the offender. Because the skill of perspective taking and the capacity for empathy develop over time, it will be important to examine how the developmental status of family members relates to forgiveness. Participants in our study frequently noted that they were unable to forgive some of their earliest and most significant hurts (e.g., an absent, alcoholic parent; being given up for adoption) because they lacked a full understanding of the situation, explaining that it was only years later that they could forgive, after developing a more nuanced perspective. When children (or adult children) are unable to forgive hurtful events in their families of origin, how does this affect their capacity for healthy intimate relationships as adults?

7. As noted before, research on forgiveness in families should take into account the complexity of family relationships and far-reaching impact that some transgressions may have. In our research, we have seen evidence of how a single event can affect multiple members of the family system. For example, participants described strong feelings of betrayal regarding transgressions not directly experienced by them but by another family member (e.g., a sibling who stole money from an elderly parent). In such cases, the love and loyalty felt for the offended family member can fuel lingering feelings of resentment that may influence the relationship for years. How does the forgiveness process work when multiple family members have taken offense by a transgression? What if one family member forgives and another does not? Research is needed to examine the impact of transgressions across multiple family members and over time.

8. It will be important to explore the ways in which empirical findings regarding the above questions vary across different types of individuals and different types of families. The majority of couples research focuses on married, predominantly White, middle-class, heterosexual couples. Greater diversity is needed in terms of family structure (e.g., single-parent families, same-sex families), as well as based

on race, ethnicity, religion, and socioeconomic status. Cross-cultural studies examining Western and non-Western families will also be important, particularly because aspects of healthy family functioning that are likely related to forgiveness (e.g., level of cohesion, family loyalty) differ across cultures.

In addition to these specific research questions, improvements are needed in the measurement of forgiveness within families. In their review of approaches to assess forgiveness at various levels (i.e., offense-based, dyadic, and dispositional), McCullough, Hoyt, and Rachal (2000) discuss several ways in which forgiveness measurement warrants improvement. With regard to dyadic and relationship-based measures, for example, no validated interview measures have been described in the literature. Moreover, measures are needed to assess forgiveness not only from an individual perspective but also from multiple informants in the family and perhaps using multiple methods (interview, self-report, observed interaction). McCullough and colleagues (2000) note that there are no validated partner-report forgiveness measures. Finally, although forgiveness is typically conceptualized as a process that unfolds over time, measurement usually approaches forgiveness as a state or dispositional construct with just one individual at one time point assessed. An exception is the measure of recovery from marital betrayal by Gordon and Baucom (2003), but most measures do not take this perspective.

In addition to basic research, another important area is the development and more rigorous evaluation of forgiveness interventions for a wider range of families and family dyads, using randomized controlled trial methodology. As many writers have noted, forgiveness is not unidimensional but a complex construct that has multiple components (e.g., Enright & the Human Development Study Group, 1991). Thus, in addition to using more rigorous designs, intervention studies would be strengthened by greater attention to mediators of treatment effect and proposed mechanisms of action (e.g., increased empathy for the offender) to help clarify key behavioral, affective, and/or cognitive components of forgiveness among family members.

RELEVANCE FOR CLINICAL AND APPLIED INTERVENTIONS

Forgiveness research is highly relevant for family and marital therapy, especially the growing number of interventions for families and couples that focus specifically on forgiveness. Although basic research is limited, the research that does exist suggests that forgiveness may be associated with better marital and family adjustment, as well as more effective conflict resolution behaviors between relationship partners. Moreover, long-term couples have reported using forgiveness as an important strategy to maintain the health of the relationship (Fennel, 1993). Based on these findings, it follows that clinical interventions (both preventive and treatment-oriented psychotherapies) that focus on building forgiving attitudes and behaviors in families may be useful in promoting healthy family functioning. When unresolved relational transgressions from the past have a negative impact on an individual's functioning, it may be useful to add an adjunctive family component to individual treatment, focused specifically on forgiveness of a hurtful event (such as the "forgiveness session/s" for families described by DiBlasio & Proctor, 1993). As Worthington and Drinkard (2000) note, however, in many cases, individuals in close relationships will need to be taught how to communicate about hurtful past events and forgiveness in order to make such meetings useful. In general, more basic research is needed to draw conclusions regarding the value of forgiveness for families, the mechanisms by which forgiveness can occur, and how to facilitate this process in psychotherapy.

PERSONAL THEORETICAL PERSPECTIVES ON THE FIELD

We are encouraged to see the growing number of studies addressing forgiveness in various contexts, including increased attention to understanding how forgiveness works in family relationships. Because so few basic research studies have been conducted regarding the role of forgiveness in family relationships, we see many exciting opportunities for research in the area. We hope that the coming years will include more refined techniques for measuring forgiveness processes, including methods to capture perspectives of multiple family members. We believe that greater integration between the new and growing body of empirical research on forgiveness and other existing lines of research on close relationships, family processes, and marital/family therapy can lead to key developments in our understanding of what helps families function well, stay connected, and promote optimal functioning of individual members.

CONCLUSIONS

Even though family relationships are arguably one of the most critical contexts for forgiveness, strikingly little research has examined how family members forgive one another. Problems in close relationships often serve as the impetus for seeking psychotherapy (Veroff, Kulka, & Douvan, 1981), and family turmoil, marital dissatisfaction, and divorce are common (Martin & Bumpass, 1989). Family dysfunction and marital discord are consistently associated with depression and other forms of psychiatric distress (Keitner & Miller, 1990). The importance of family stability on individual mental health and on social, behavioral, and emotional child outcomes has also been observed (Amato & Keith, 1991). If forgiveness can promote such stability within families, this research may have critical clinical and public health implications. Greater empirical attention to the meaning and impact of forgiveness within families will help inform theory and intervention research, as well as a wider scale of public health programs that may be useful in promoting long-term family resilience and longevity.

ACKNOWLEDGMENTS

We wish to thank Rita Rossi, Ryan G. Sasaki, Linda Bigden, and Jackie Albro for their assistance with data collection and data management. This research was supported by a grant from *A Campaign for Forgiveness Research.*

REFERENCES

Al-Mabuk, R. H., Enright, R. D., & Cardis, P. (1995). Forgiveness education with parentally love-deprived college students. *Journal of Moral Education, 24,* 427–444.

Al-Mabuk, R. H., & Downs, W. R. (1996). Forgiveness therapy with parents of adolescent suicide victims. *Journal of Family Psychotherapy, 7,* 21–39.

Amato, P. R., & Keith, B. (1991). Consequences of parental divorce for the well-being of children: A meta-analysis. *Psychological Bulletin, 110,* 26–46.

Beavers, W. R., Blumberg, S., Timken, K. R., & Weiner, M. D. (1965). Communication patterns of mothers of schizophrenics. *Family Process, 4,* 94–104.

Beavers, W. R., & Hampson, R. B. (2003). Measuring family competence: The Beavers systems model. In F. Walsh (Ed.), *Normal family processes: Growing diversity and complexity* (3rd ed.; pp. 549–580). New York: Guilford Press.

Boss, P. (2001). *Family stress management: A contextual approach.* Newbury Park, CA: Sage.

Bowen, M. (1978). *Family therapy in clinical practice.* New York: Jason Aronson.

Boszormenyi-Nagy, I. (1987). *Foundations of contextual family therapy: Collected papers of Boszormeny-Nagy, M.D.* Philadelphia: Brunner/Mazel.

Boszormenyi-Nagy, I., Grunebaum, J., & Ulrich, D. (1991). Contextual therapy. In A. S. Gurman & D. P. Kniskern (Eds.), *Handbook of family therapy* (Vol. II, pp. 200–238). New York: Brunner/Mazel.

Brown, G. W., & Harris, T. O. (1989). Depression. In G. W. Brown & T. O. Harris (Eds.), *Life events and illness* (pp. 49–93). New York: Guilford Press.

Butler, M. H., Dahlin, S. K., & Fife, S. T. (2002). Languaging factors affecting clients acceptance of forgiveness intervention in marital therapy. *Journal of Marital and Family Therapy, 28,* 285–298.

Coleman, P. W. (1998). The process of forgiveness in marriage and the family. In R. D. Enright & J. North (Eds.), *Exploring forgiveness* (pp. 75–94). Madison, WI: University of Wisconsin Press.

Coyle, C. T., & Enright, R. D. (1997). Forgiveness intervention with postabortion men. *Journal of Consulting and Clinical Psychology, 65,* 1042–1046.

DiBlasio, F. A. (1998). The use of a decision-based forgiveness intervention within intergenerational family therapy. *Journal of Family Therapy, 20,* 77–94.

DiBlasio, F. A. (2000). Decision-based forgiveness treatment in cases of marital infidelity. *Psychotherapy, 37,* 149–158.

DiBlasio, F. A., & Proctor, J. H. (1993). Therapists and clinical use of forgiveness. *American Journal of Family Therapy, 21,* 175–184.

Enright, R. D. (2001). *Forgiveness is a choice: A step-by-step process for resolving anger and restoring hope.* Washington, DC: American Psychological Association.

Enright, R. D., & Coyle, C. T. (1998). Researching the process model of forgiveness within psychological interventions. In E. L. Worthington, Jr. (Ed.), *Dimensions of forgiveness: Psychological research and theological perspectives* (pp. 139–161). Philadelphia: Templeton Foundation Press.

Enright, R. D., & the Human Development Study Group (1991). The moral development of forgiveness. In W. Kurtines & J. Gerwirtz (Eds.), *Handbook of moral behavior and development* (Vol. 1, pp. 123–152). Hillsdale, NJ: Lawrence Erlbaum.

Enright, R. D., & North, J. (Eds.). (1998). *Exploring forgiveness.* Madison, WI: University of Wisconsin Press.

Epstein, N. B., Bishop, D. S., & Levin, S. (1978). The McMaster model of family functioning. *Journal of Marriage and Family Counseling, 4*, 19–31.

Fennel, D. L. (1993). Characteristics of first-time marriages. *Journal of Mental Health Counseling, 15*, 446–460.

Fincham, F. D. (2000). The kiss of the porcupines: From attributing responsibility to forgiving. *Personal Relationships, 7*, 1–23.

Fincham, F. D., Beach, S. R. H., & Davila, J. (2004). Forgiveness and conflict resolution in marriage. *Journal of Family Psychology, 18*, 72–81.

Fincham, F. D., Paleari, G., & Regalia, C. (2002). Forgiveness in marriage: The role of relationship quality, attributions, and empathy. *Personal Relationships, 9*, 27–37.

Freedman, S. R., & Enright, R. D. (1996). Forgiveness as an intervention with incest survivors. *Journal of Consulting and Clinical Psychology, 64*, 938–992.

Gordon, K. C., & Baucom, D. H. (1998). Understanding betrayals in marriage: A synthesized model of forgiveness. *Family Process, 37*, 425–449.

Gordon, K. C., & Baucom, D. H. (1999). A multitheoretical intervention for promoting recovery from extramarital affairs. *Clinical Psychology: Science and Practice, 6*, 382–399.

Gordon, K. C., & Baucom, D. H. (2003). Forgiveness and marriage: Preliminary support for a measure based on a model of recovery from marital betrayal. *American Journal of Family Therapy, 31*, 179–199.

Haley, J. (1963). *Strategies of psychotherapy.* New York: Grune & Stratton.

Hargrave, T. D. (1994). *Families and forgiveness: Healing wounds in the intergenerational family.* New York: Brunner/Mazel.

Hargrave, T. D., Jennings, G., & Anderson, W. T. (1991). The development of a relational ethics scale. *Journal of Marital and Family Therapy, 17*, 311–320.

Hargrave, T. D., & Sells, J. N. (1997). The development of a forgiveness scale. *Journal of Marital and Family Therapy, 23*, 41–62.

Jacobson, N. S., & Margolin, G. (1979). *Marital therapy: Strategies based on social learning and behavior exchange principles.* New York: Brunner/Mazel.

Keitner, G. I., & Miller, I. W. (1990). Family functioning and major depression: An overview. *American Journal of Psychiatry, 147*, 1128–1137.

Kiefer, R. P., Worthington, E. L., Jr., Myers, B. J., Kliewer, W. L., Kilgour, J. M., Jr., et al. (2004). *Training parents in forgiving and reconciling.* Unpublished manuscript currently under editorial review, Virginia Commonwealth University, Richmond.

Lankton, S. R., Lankton, C. H., & Matthews, W. J. (1991). Ericksonian family therapy. In A. S. Gurman & D. P. Kniskern (Eds), *Handbook of family therapy* (Vol. II; pp. 239–283). New York: Brunner/Mazel.

Martin, T., & Bumpass, L. (1989). Recent trends in marital disruption. *Demography, 26*, 37–52.

McCullough, M. E., Hoyt, W. T., & Rachal, K. C. (2000). What we know (and need to know) about assessing forgiveness constructs. In M. E. McCullough, K. I. Pargament, & C. E. Thoresen, (Eds.), *Forgiveness: Theory, research, and practice* (pp. 65–90). New York: Guilford Press.

McCullough, M. E., Pargament, K. I., & Thoresen, C. E. (Eds.). (2000). *Forgiveness: Theory, research, practice*. New York: Guilford Press.

McCullough, M. E., & Worthington, E. L., Jr. (1995). Promoting forgiveness: A comparison of two brief psychoeducational group interventions with a waiting list control. *Counseling and Values, 40*, 55–68.

Miller, I. W., Battle, C. L., Rossi, R., & Sasaki, R. G. (2003, October). *Forgiveness in families.* Paper presented at Scientific Findings About Forgiveness. Atlanta, GA.

Minuchin, S. (1974). *Families and family therapy.* Cambridge, MA: Harvard University Press.

Olson, D. H., & Gorall, D. M. (2003). Circumplex model of marital and family systems. In F. Walsh (Ed.), *Normal family processes: Growing diversity and complexity* (3rd ed., pp. 514–548). New York: Guilford Press.

Olson, D. H., Russell, C. S., & Sprenkle, D. H. (1989). *Circumplex model: Systematic assessment and treatment of families.* New York: Haworth Press.

Veroff, J., Kulka, R. A., & Douvan, E. (1981). *Mental health in America: Patterns of help-seeking from 1957–1976.* New York: Basic Books.

Walrond-Skinner, S. (1998). The function and role of forgiveness in working with couples and families: Clearing the ground. *Journal of Family Therapy, 20*, 3–19.

Walsh, F. (2003). Family resilience: Strengths forged through adversity. In F. Walsh (Ed.). *Normal family processes: Growing diversity and complexity* (3rd ed.; pp. 399–423). New York: Guilford Press.

Worthington, E. L., Jr. (1998a). The pyramid model of forgiveness: Some interdisciplinary speculations about unforgiveness and the promotion of forgiveness. In E. L. Worthington, Jr. (Ed.), *Dimensions of forgiveness: Psychological research and theological perspectives* (pp. 107–137). Philadelphia: Templeton Foundation Press.

Worthington, E. L., Jr. (1998b). An empathy-humility-commitment model of forgiveness applied within family dyads. *Journal of Family Therapy, 20*, 59–76.

Worthington, E. L., Jr., & Drinkard, D. T. (2000). Promoting reconciliation through psycho-educational and therapeutic interventions. *Journal of Marital and Family Therapy, 26*, 93–101.

Worthington, E. L., Jr., & Wade, N. G., (1999). The psychology of unforgiveness and forgiveness and implications for clinical practice. *Journal of Social and Clinical Psychology, 18*, 385–418.

Part Five

THE BODY AND FORGIVENESS

Chapter Fifteen

Genetic Influences on Forgiving

Ming T. Tsuang
Lindon Eaves
Tal Nir
Beth A. Jerskey
Michael J. Lyons

The significant genetic influences that have been demonstrated for a wide range of human behaviors provide a strong a priori basis for expecting that individual differences in forgiving, just as in many other behaviors, are influenced by genetic factors. Behavioral geneticists regularly investigate genetic factors that may make an individual more or less likely to carry out a behavior (e.g., to forgive). We are interested in identifying genetic factors that influence the probability that an individual will forgive.

Despite the vast literature attempting to resolve the contributions of genetic and environmental factors to individual differences in human behavior, the role of biological and social factors in making people more or less forgiving has hardly been explored empirically. Insofar as forgiveness is a temperamental trait, we might expect it to show similar genetic and nongenetic influences, as do other temperamental and personality traits that have been studied more extensively. However, insofar as the act of forgiving is contingent on exposure to hurt, we expect the role of social factors and perhaps the interaction of genetic and environmental influences to be substantially greater.

BEHAVIORAL GENETICS METHODOLOGY

Family studies are typically the first step in addressing the question of whether a given characteristic is influenced by genetic factors. If a characteristic is genetic, it should run in families. However, if a characteristic runs in families, there are two plausible explanations—sharing the same genes can produce similarities among individuals and sharing the same environment can produce similarities. Two approaches utilized to disentangle genetic from family environmental influences are adoption studies and twin studies. In adoption studies, one set of parents provides the individual with his or her genes (the biological parents), and another set provides his or her family environment (the adoptive parents). By contrasting the degree to which the individual resembles the biological versus the adoptive parents, we can draw inferences about the relative influence of genes and the family environment. For a number of reasons (e.g., improved contraception, greater acceptance of single parenthood, confidentiality of birth-parent identity, and "open adoption," in which birth parents select and interact with adoptive parents), adoption studies are difficult to conduct in contemporary America.

Twin studies offer another approach to disentangling genes from the environment as the source of family resemblance. Twins offer a naturally occurring experiment in which two individuals share the same environment from conception and either 100% (monozygotic twins; MZ) or 50% of their genes (dizygotic twins; DZ). Resemblance within twin pairs is typically quantified by calculating the correlation between twins within pairs separately for MZ and DZ pairs. To the extent that MZ resemblance exceeds DZ resemblance, genetic influences are implicated. To the extent that DZ resemblance exceeds 50% of the MZ resemblance, influences from the shared family environment are implicated. Biometrical modeling is used to quantify the relative contributions of genetic factors, the shared family environment, and the unique or nonshared environment.

ASSUMPTIONS ABOUT FORGIVENESS

Because we are unaware of any previous research on the relationship between genetics and forgiving, we start by describing our view and assumptions regarding the construct of forgiveness. First, although no consensual definition of forgiveness exists (Worthington, 1998), we agree with McCullough, Pargament, and Thoresen (2000) that all the existing definitions share core features—when people forgive, their responses toward people who have transgressed against them become more positive and less negative. In particular, Worthington and Wade's definition (1999) of forgiveness as the emotional replacement of negative emotions of unforgiveness with positive emotions such as empathy, sympathy, compassion, or love informs our approach to studying forgiveness. After conducting a review of the available literature on the genetic influences on these putatively forgiveness-related emotions, we found that a genetic influence on empathy is the best established. Second, according to Worthington and Scherer (2004), unforgiveness is conceptualized as a stress reaction, and forgiveness is one way people reduce unforgiveness. Thus, forgiveness can be used as a coping strategy to reduce a stressful reaction to a transgression (Worthington & Scherer, 2004). Third, forgiveness may be related to the broader constructs of religion and spirituality (McCullough & Worthington, 1999 for a review). Fourth, forgiveness is related to personality traits such as neuroticism and agreeableness (Symington, Walker, & Gorsuch, 2002).

Described above are assumptions that inform our approach to forgiveness. Because there is little research specifically addressing genetic influences on forgiving, we will examine genetic influences on constructs that we assume are related to forgiving.

REVIEW OF THE THEORETICAL AND EMPIRICAL LITERATURE

Assumption One—Empathy

One current conceptualization of forgiveness is based on Batson's empathy-altruism hypothesis (Batson & Oleson, 1991) that empathy motivates individuals to help others, including strangers, by activating the human aptitude for altruism. Although the interpersonal context in which forgiveness occurs is often more complex than the context in which altruism occurs, McCullough, Worthington, and Rachal (1997) view empathy as vital to the notion of forgiveness as an altruistic behavior. They present evidence from two studies that forgiveness is a prosocial act largely mediated by empathy toward the transgressor. The first study found that the association between forgiveness and apology was mediated in part by increased empathy facilitated by the apology. The second study found that the usefulness of a psychosocial intervention for promoting forgiveness was partly mediated by the efficacy of the intervention in promoting empathy toward the offender. This link between empathy and forgiveness was also found by McCullough and colleagues (1998). According to the empathy-forgiveness link, empathy toward the transgressor seems to be a critical condition for the individual's capacity to forgive after experiencing a transgression. McCullough, Worthington, and Rachal (1997) considered various aspects of empathy and asserted that empathy is primarily an affective phenomenon but also considered perspective taking as an important element of empathy.

Influences on Empathy.   Matthews and colleagues (Matthews, Batson, Horn, & Rosenman, 1981) investigated the heritability of empathy using adult men twin pairs. They found a correlation of .41 for MZ twins and .05 for DZ twins, yielding a heritability of 72%. Rushton, Fulker, Neale, Nias, and Eysenck (1986), using adult twin pairs, found evidence of substantial heritability of empathy. According to their results, 51% of the variance in empathy was due to genetic factors, 49% was due to the nonshared environment, and the shared environment had no detectable influence. Although both Matthews et al. (1981) and Rushton et al. (1986) reported high levels of heritability of empathy, both studies have been criticized for analytic approaches that may overestimate heritability (see Davis, Luce, & Kraus, 1994).

Zahn-Wexler, Robinson, and Emde (1992) studied the development of empathic concern in 14- and 20-month-old twin pairs. They found significant heritability at both 14 and 20 months, with MZ correlations of .29 and .30, respectively, and DZ correlations of .05 and .09. Heritability was of 23% at age 14 months and 28% at 20 months. Because behavior in young children may be different from that of older individuals, caution should be used when comparing aspects of empathy across developmental periods.

Davis et al. (1994) investigated the heritability of three facets of empathy: (a) empathic concern (feeling of sympathy, compassion, and concern for others), (b) personal distress (feelings of discomfort when confronting another's distress), and (c) perspective taking (dispositional tendency to consider the psychological point of view of others). The first two are considered to be within the affective domain, whereas the last one is nonaffective and has not been previously researched. They used data from Loehlin and Nichols's (1976) study of twins. For empathic concern, they observed an MZ correlation of .22 and a DZ correlation of .08, producing a heritability estimate of 28%; for personal distress, the MZ twins correlated .22, and the DZ twins correlated .06, producing a heritability estimate of 32%. In contrast, the difference between MZ and DZ correlations for the perspective-taking aspect of empathy was not significant. These results suggest that dispositional affective empathy is substantially influenced by genetic factors.

Although there are only a few studies of the influence of genetic factors on empathy, all provide evidence for genetic influences. In general, previous research has not detected a significant shared environmental influence on trait empathy. This may be because it is nonshared aspects of the environment—whether within or outside the family—that have the greatest influence on empathy, or it may be due to the relatively lower power of the twin method for demonstrating shared environmental effects.

Assumption Two—Coping

Coping reflects thinking, feeling, or acting so as to preserve a satisfied psychological state when threatened (Snyder, 2001). Therefore, forgiveness as a means of coping can be thought of as a way to preserve a prosocial state between people in an interpersonal relationship. Although coping styles have often been studied with regard to their relationship to specific quality-of-life outcomes (i.e., coping after a diagnosis of a medical disorder), coping is also an important construct for geneticists interested in understanding more about individuals' "sensitivity to the environment" (Kendler & Eaves, 1986). Although forgiveness after being a victim of wrongdoing can generate various responses (e.g., emotional, motivational, cognitive, and/or behavioral; Snyder, 2001), many researchers interested in coping mechanisms divide strategies into two primary categories—those that are emotion-focused and those that are problem-focused. It has been postulated that forgiveness is principally an emotion-focused coping strategy, although it can be problem-focused as well (Worthington & Scherer, 2004).

Kendler and colleagues (Kendler, Kessler, Heath, Neale, & Eaves, 1991) were the first to investigate genetic and environmental influences on coping styles. Using the Ways of Coping checklist (Folkman & Lazarus, 1980), they conducted a factor analysis and found three factors—turning to others, problem solving, and denial. They categorized problem solving as a cognitive and problem-focused style, denial as emotion-focused, and turning to others as both problem-focused and emotion-focused. Their twin data indicated that familial resemblance for turning to others and problem solving was due solely to genetic factors (30% and 31%, respectively) but that shared environmental factors accounted for most of the familial influence on denial (19%). They concluded that genetic factors, presumably related to temperament, influence the more problem-solving coping strategies of turning to others and problem solving. There was no strong evidence of familial environmental influences on the more problem-focused strategies, which is not consistent with a "social learning" model of learned behaviors from parents. In contrast, shared family environmental influences significantly influenced the more emotion-focused denial strategy.

Mellins, Gatz, and Baker (1996) investigated coping methods in children from a behavioral genetic standpoint. They found that genetic influences accounted for a substantial percentage of the reliable variance in problem-focused coping strategies, whereas the shared environment was a significant influence in emotion-focused alternatives. These are similar to Kendler et al. (1991): Problem-focused strategies are significantly influenced by genes, and emotion-focused strategies are influenced by the family environment. One caveat to this study was that the investigators measured the same construct using both open-ended and closed-ended instruments, but these measures yielded conflicting results, making clear-cut conclusions difficult to draw.

Using multivariate path analysis to test the hypothesis that different coping styles share some of the same genetic influences as well having unique or unshared genetic influences, Busjahn and colleagues (Busjahn, Faulhaber, Freier, & Luft, 1999) used a coping questionnaire with 19 different types of reactions (e.g., "play down," avoidance, self-medication/alcohol use). The majority of the response types (14 of 19) showed genetic influences without significant shared environmental effects, 2 of the 19 scales showed effects from the family environment without genetic effects (aggression and distraction from situation), and 3 of 19 scales showed a combination of genetic and shared environmental effects (situational control, avoidance, self-pity). Results from multivariate analyses demonstrated a complex genetic architecture with specific as well as shared genetic influences on coping behaviors.

Forgiveness has primarily been viewed as an emotion-focused coping strategy. Empirical evidence suggests that emotion-focused coping strategies may be primarily influenced by the shared family environment. More research is needed to determine what specific aspects of the family environment may mediate emotion-focused coping strategies specific to forgiveness.

Assumption Three—Spirituality and Religion

Religion Versus Spirituality.   The relationship between religiosity and spirituality was examined by Wink and Dillon (2003), under the assumption that they are related but distinct constructs (Marty, 1993). They used different measurements for spirituality and religiosity and examined their interrelationship and relationship to psychosocial well-being. Religiosity was assessed using items regarding institutionalized beliefs and practice, and spirituality was assessed using items regarding daily personal (noninstitutionalized) beliefs and behaviors. Results indicated that religiosity is more related to communal behaviors, whereas spirituality is more concerned with one's self (i.e., asserting, protecting, and expanding the self). Although there was some overlap between religiosity and spirituality (both constructs correlated substantially with some communal characteristics), Wink and Dillon concluded that the two constructs are distinct. In contrast, Hill et al. (2000) reported that religion and spirituality represent related rather than independent constructs. According to Wuthnow (1998), associating religiosity and spirituality to institutional versus personal domains disregards the fact that all forms of spiritual expression unfold in a social context and that organized faith traditions are concerned with the ordering of personal affairs as well. In addition, empirical evidence indicates that most individuals experience spirituality within the context of an organized religion and do not decontextualize spirituality from religion (Marler & Hadaway, 2002; Zinnbauer et al., 1997).

The relationship between forgiveness and religion was explored by McCullough and Worthington (1999) within the three major monotheistic traditions in the West (Christianity, Islam, and Judaism). They also examined the extent to which forgiveness and religion are connected in human functioning by reviewing the existing body of research on these two constructs. Based on their review, they concluded that forgiveness is a concept that generally has deep religious roots in Western culture.

Kendler and colleagues (2003), using adult twins, conducted a factor analysis to assess religiosity, spirituality and related attitudes. They found seven dimensions of religiosity. One was named *forgiveness* and included items reflecting caring, loving, and a forgiving approach to the world. Another dimension, named *unvengefulness*, was partly extracted from the same measure as the items of forgiveness but reflected an attitude that emphasized avoiding retaliation rather than promoting forgiveness. Other dimensions were general religiosity, social religiosity, involved God, God as judge, and thankfulness. These results indicate the complexity and multidimensionality of the construct of religiosity. Moreover, although some have argued that religiosity and spirituality are different dimensions (i.e., religiousness represents an institutional, formal, inhibiting expression; spirituality represents a personal, subjective, freeing expression; Koenig, McCullough, & Larson, 2001), Kendler et al. (2003) observed no major distinction between the two constructs.

Genetics and Spirituality/Religion. Using adolescent twins, Loehlin and Nichols (1976) reported that the frequency of religious activities was substantially correlated in twin pairs and that there were only moderately higher correlations for MZ than for DZ pairs. Similarly, Rose (1988), using the MMPI, found that twin resemblance for religious orthodoxy was mainly influenced by shared environmental factors. Rose (1988) found that 10% of the variance in religious orthodoxy was due to genetic influence, 61% was due to the shared environment, and 29% was due to the nonshared environment.

Using adult twins reared together and reared apart, Waller and colleagues (Waller, Kojetin, Bouchard, Lykken, & Tellegen, 1990) examined five measures of religiosity and reported substantial heritability for all scales, including an MMPI-based measure of religious fundamentalism. They found that for fundamentalism, 46% of the variance was contributed by genetic factors, and the remaining variance was contributed by the nonshared environment. Truett et al. (1994) used a large twin-family study (29,698 subjects, of which 5,670 were twin pairs) that included data on frequency of church attendance. Applying a gender-dependent model, they found that in males, genes and the family environment each contributed about one quarter of the variance in frequency of church attendance, whereas the nonshared environment accounted for about half. In females, genetic factors, the family environment, and the nonshared environment contributed roughly equally to the variance. Some variance was attributable to the covariance of genes and environment. Kendler, Gardner, and Prescot (1997) studied resemblance for religiosity (i.e., personal devotion, personal conservatism, institutional conservatism) in female twin pairs. They found that personal conservatism could be explained mainly on the basis of twins' nonshared environment (55%), but shared environment contributed to the variance as well (45%). No evidence was found for the influence of any genetic factors on personal conservatism. For institutional conservatism, genetic factors had a minor role (12%); the nonshared environment explained 37% of the variance, but most of the variance could be explained by the shared environment (51%). Interestingly, for personal devotion, family environment and genetic factors made similar contributions to twin resemblance (24% and 29%, respectively), and the balance was due to the nonshared environment (47%).

D'Onofrio and colleagues (1999), using twin pairs and their family members, found that additive genetic effects explained 18% of the variance for females and 19% for males for church attendance. The contribution of nonadditive genetic influences accounted for approximately 30% in females and 23% in males. Using adult male twin pairs from the Vietnam Era Twin Registry, Tsuang, Williams, Simpson, and Lyons (2002) reported that shared environmental factors accounted for 45% of the variance in spiritual involvement, nonshared environmental factors accounted for 32%, and genetic factors accounted for 23%. These results are suggestive only due to the relatively small sample size (100 pairs). It appears as though both shared environmental and genetic factors influence dimensions of religiosity. (For further information on twin correlations and parameter estimates of other religious constructs, see D'Onofrio, Eaves, Murrelle, Maes, & Spilka, 1999.)

Assumption Four—Personality

It has been suggested that a variety of factors influence forgiving a transgression and that at times, individual differences such as personality are significant contributors to forgiveness, whereas at other times, social and relational factors are more important (for a review, see chapter 11 by Mullet, Neto, & Riviére; Snyder, 2001). Symington and colleagues (2002) found that neuroticism and agreeableness were personality traits that played a significant role in a variety of forgiveness dimensions; researchers have also found these traits to have an opposite effect on forgiveness. Agreeableness is positively correlated with forgiveness, and neuroticism is negatively correlated (Brose, Rye, Lutz, & Ross, 2002). McCullough and colleagues (McCullough, Bellah, Kilpatrick,

& Johnson, 2001) found vengefulness to play a major role in forgiveness (i.e., vengeful people are less forgiving). They also found that vengefulness was positively correlated to neuroticism and negatively correlated to agreeableness.

Loehlin (1992) summarized five large twin studies that investigated neuroticism and found that model-fitting analyses across twin and adoption designs produced heritability estimates of 41%. With regard to environmental effects, no more than 10% of the variance in neuroticism was accounted for by shared environment, and the greatest variance was attributed to nonshared environmental influences (and error).

Bergeman and colleagues (1993) published a genetic analysis of twins reared together and apart on other dimensions of personality, including the other primary personality trait related to forgiveness—agreeableness. Using model-fitting techniques, they found that the total genetic influences were approximately 12%, shared environmental effects were 21%, and nonshared environmental effects accounted for 67% of the variance. Jang and colleagues (Jang, Livesley, & Vernon, 1996) reported that 41% of the variance for both neuroticism and agreeableness was genetically determined. The evidence supporting a significant genetic influence on agreeableness is not as well established as that for the genetic influence on neuroticism.

RELEVANCE FOR CLINICAL AND APPLIED INTERVENTIONS

It seems highly unlikely that any knowledge we may gain about the influence of genetic factors on forgiveness, either at the quantitative or molecular level, will have any applied implications in the foreseeable future. The relationship of genes and the proteins for which they code to the behavior of forgiving will undoubtedly prove to be complex, and manipulation of the relevant genes would be morally and ethically problematic, even if it were scientifically possible. If all we are interested in is the technical application of scientific understanding of genetic influences on forgiveness, we will inevitably be disappointed.

However, genetic research into behavior has the potential to address questions about human nature that may be more meaningful: Why are we humans the way we are? Suggesting that a trait or behavior is influenced by genetic factors has various implications. Genetic explanations are antithetical to some ideologies because they are assumed to imply deterministic mechanisms that preclude any possibility of changing or influencing the characteristic. For some people, concluding that a trait or behavior is influenced by genetic factors may lead to therapeutic nihilism; that is, they may conclude that if a factor is genetically influenced, it is immutable or unchangeable. Fortunately, this view is misguided.

The disorder phenylketonuria (PKU) is a convenient example of the shortcomings of this view. If an infant has two defective copies of the gene that codes for the enzyme that metabolizes phenylalanine, the result is a buildup of phenylpyruvic acid, which damages that developing nervous system, leading to mental retardation. However, for individuals who have the genotype for PKU, an environmental manipulation (i.e., excluding phenylaline from the diet) can prevent the clinical syndrome. This demonstrates that "genetically determined" outcomes are not necessarily inevitable. Evidence that may demonstrate significant genetic influences on an individual's probability of forgiving would not be incompatible with efforts to improve understanding of forgiveness and environmental interventions to promote forgiveness.

Although for some people the belief in genetic influences might lead to pessimism about the efficacy of interventions, genetic explanations can also be used to promote a nonjudgmental stance (and perhaps forgiveness itself). Tolerance toward traits such as obesity or homosexuality that have often been stigmatized in our culture may be promoted by evidence supporting the influence of genetic factors. If obesity to a great extent reflects genetic predispositions, it is more difficult to sustain a view of the obese individual as having a character flaw; if sexual orientation is a reflection of genetic influences, it is more difficult to characterize an orientation as "sinful." An appreciation of genetic influences on human behavior may help reduce blame and promote tolerance. Although understanding genetic influences on forgiveness will not translate into a clinical intervention, it can inform how we think about people in a way that will lead to attitudes that are both more realistic and more humane.

NEW RESEARCH DIRECTIONS NEEDED IN THE AREA

To date there has been little work on the genetic and environmental influences on forgiving, so additional exploration in the field could prove to be valuable. Twin studies might be the best starting point for research on genetic influences on forgiving. Twin studies could inform our understanding of genetic influences on the construct of forgiveness but might also provide information about the nature of the relationships of other relevant constructs to forgiveness. Such research could, for example, explicate that nature of the relationship between forgiveness and personality traits such as neuroticism.

Another factor to keep in mind in trying to understand genetic influences on forgiving is the complexity introduced by the potential for environmental factors to influence gene expression. At any given time or context, many genes remain unexpressed. Developmental and environmental factors can alter the expression of genes. It may be that certain developmental or environmental factors affect the expression of genes that influence the probability of forgiving. There may be an interaction between genes and the environment in which certain genetic influences are manifested only under certain environmental conditions.

We are aware of only two ongoing studies of genetic influences on forgiveness—each study is being conducted by an author of this chapter. Tsuang and colleagues (Tsuang, 2005) recently completed data collection on a project entitled, "Is There a Role for Forgiveness and Spirituality in Coping with Combat Trauma?" In this study, we conducted an empirical investigation of the role of forgiveness in coping with trauma associated with military service in Vietnam. The overall objective is to explicate the actual and potential roles of forgiveness for coping with combat and other traumatic life-threatening experiences. This study utilized 170 pairs of identical twins from the Vietnam Era Twin Registry in which one twin served in Vietnam and experienced high levels of combat exposure and the co-twin served in the military but did not serve in Vietnam.

The second study, "The Causes and Effects of Forgiveness: A Twin Family Study" by Eaves (2005), investigates whether religion and forgiveness protect against drug use. The study is investigating whether genetic and psychological factors play a part in using drugs as well as factors that may influence forgiveness. Questionnaires on religiosity, adolescent behavioral outcomes, and social risk and protective factors were mailed to adolescent twins and their parents. Data are also being collected on adult twins, along with their spouses and children, examining similar constructs. Preliminary analyses indicate that the correlation for MZ twins is greater than that for DZ twins and lead to the inference that there is a small genetic influence on forgiveness, such as is found with a number of other temperamental traits.

PERSONAL THEORETICAL PERSPECTIVES ON THE FIELD

The approach we have taken in our twin study of forgiveness in Vietnam veterans provides an example of how we believe that genetic factors can be incorporated into a study examining forgiveness. We are investigating the influence that forgiveness may have on the individual's ability to cope with combat stress. The outcomes we are examining include variables such as physical health, psychiatric disorders (e.g., post-traumatic stress disorder, depression, substance abuse), demoralization (nonspecific distress), and "life success" as indicated by occupational functioning, family functioning, and life satisfaction. In our model, the question of the moderating effect of forgiveness on combat exposure is addressed by determining whether forgiveness influences the relationship between combat and social/psychological outcomes later in life. This question may seem straightforward, but answering the question unambiguously may actually be fairly complicated. One way to think of this design is that each pair of twins represents two copies of a single set of genes and family environmental influences. Conceptually speaking, one copy of the genes and family environment is sent to Vietnam and exposed to combat trauma; the other set is not exposed. The outcome of the unexposed individual is the best predictor of the status of the combat-exposed twin if he had not been exposed to combat. In this way, we are not judging the influence of forgiveness on the psychological and social outcomes per se. Rather, we are judging the influence of forgiveness based on the deviation of the combat-exposed twin's outcomes from the outcomes of his unexposed co-twin. This will allow us to determine whether forgiveness can ameliorate some of the adverse consequences of combat trauma.

Although it is still the "early days" in the behavior-genetic study of forgiveness, the above theoretical perspective has its precedent in other areas of psychiatric genetics. A recent study by Eaves, Silberg, and Erkanli (2003) focused on the relationship between prepubertal anxiety, adverse life events, and later depression in a sample of adolescent female twins. Briefly, they showed how early genetic differences on anxiety (the analogy of a forgiving temperament in our model) created differences in later depression through three distinct pathways. The first pathway is due to the fact that the same genes that affect early anxiety also influence later depression. Such a process is known to geneticists as *pleiotropy* and to developmental pychopathologists as *heterotypic continuity*. The second pathway arises because early genetic effects on anxiety increase exposure to life events that in turn increase risk to depression ("genotype-environment correlation;" rG-E). Finally, the genes that create differences in early anxiety also make young women more sensitive to the depressogenic effects of environmental adversity ("genotype × environment interaction," GxE). This basic threefold mechanism, *mutatis mutandis,* is exactly that envisioned on our model for the relationship between a forgiving temperament, exposure to wrong, and subsequent successful social adaptation.

CONCLUSIONS

Studying genetic (and environmental) influences on forgiving will be difficult because forgiving occurs in the context of an event that provides the opportunity to forgive or not to forgive. That is, if the individual has not been wronged, there is not an opportunity to determine whether he or she would forgive the wrong. Because traditional approaches to studying genetic influences depend on assessing similarity among relatives, this creates a situation in which relatives could be dissimilar in their forgiving for reasons having to do with forgiveness per se, or they could be dissimilar because they did not both experience a transgression or experienced different transgressions. To have a clear-cut assessment of the degree of similarity among relatives for their forgiving behavior, it would be very helpful if both relatives had experienced a similar transgression from which to judge their forgiving. Perhaps on a lifetime basis, it would be possible to identify comparable instances of being wronged for each individual, then to assess how forgiving he or she was in that situation.

Because most human behavior is influenced by genetic factors, it seems very likely that forgiving will be found to be as well. Although there has been dramatic progress in biological and statistical aspects of genetic research, the rate-limiting step in explicating the genetic influences on forgiving is likely to be the complex and multifaceted nature of the construct and the difficulty of measuring and quantifying the phenomenon.

ACKNOWLEDGMENTS

The authors wish to thank the Atlantic Philanthropic Services, *A Campaign for Forgiveness Research*, and the John Templeton Foundation for separate contributions that helped fund the work described in this chapter.

REFERENCES

Batson, C. D., & Oleson, K. C. (1991). Current status of the empathy-altruism hypothesis. In M. S. Clark (Ed.), *Prosocial behavior* (pp. 62–85). Newbury Park, CA: Sage Publications.

Bergeman, C. S., Chipuer, H., Plomin, R., Pedersen, N., McClearn, G. E., Nesselroade, J. R., et al. (1993). Genetic and environmental effects on openness to experience, agreeableness, and conscientiousness: An adoption twin study. *Journal of Personality, 61,* 159–179.

Brose, L. A., Rye, M. S., Lutz, C. J., & Ross, S. R. (2002 August). *Forgiveness and the five-factor model of personality.* Poster presented at the 110th annual convention of the American Psychological Association, Chicago.

Busjahn, A., Faulhaber, H.-D., Freier, K, & Luft, F. C. (1999). Genetic and environmental influences on coping styles: A twin study. *Psychosomatic Medicine, 61,* 469–475.

Davis, M. H., Luce, C., & Kraus, S. J. (1994). The heritability of characteristics associated with dispositional empathy. *Journal of Personality, 62,* 369–391.

D'Onofrio, B. D., Eaves, L. J., Murrelle, L., Maes, H .M., & Spilka, B. (1999). Understanding biological and social influences on Religious affiliation, attitudes, and behaviors: A behavior genetic perspective. *Journal of Personality, 67,* 953–984.

Eaves, L. J. (2005). [The causes and effects of forgiveness: A twin family study]. Unpublished raw data, Virginia Commonwealth University, Richmond.

Eaves, L. J., Silberg, J. L., & Erkanli, A. (2003). Resolving multiple epigenetic pathways to adolescent depression. *Journal of Child Psychology and Psychiatry, 44,* 1006–1014.

Folkman, S., & Lazarus, R.S. (1980). An analysis of coping in a middle-aged community sample. *Journal of Health and Social Behavior, 21,* 219–239.

Hill, P. C., Pargament, K. I., Hood, R. W., Jr., McCullough, M. E., Swyers, J. P., Larson, D. B., et al. (2000). Conceptualizing religion and spirituality: Points of commonality, points of departure. *Journal for the Theory of Social Behaviour, 30,* 51–77.

Jang, K. L., Livesley, W. J., & Vernon, P. A. (1996). Heritability of the Big Five personality dimensions and their facets: A twin study. *Journal of Personality, 64,* 577–591.

Kendler, K. S., & Eaves, L. J. (1986). Models for the joint effect of genotype and environment on liability on psychiatric illness. *American Journal of Psychiatry, 143,* 279–289.

Kendler, K. S., Gardner, C. O., & Prescot, C. A. (1997). Religion, psychopathology, and substance use and abuse: A multimeasure, genetic-epidemiologic study. *American Journal of Psychiatry, 154,* 322–329.

Kendler, K., Kessler, R. C., Heath, A. C., Neale, M. C, & Eaves, L. J. (1991). Coping: A genetic epidemiological investigation. *Psychological Medicine, 21,* 337–346.

Kendler, K. S., Liou, X. Q., Gardner, C. O., McCullough, M. E., Larson, D., & Prescot, C. A. (2003). Dimensions of religiosity and their relationship to lifetime psychiatric and substance use disorders. *American Journal of Psychiatry, 160,* 496–503.

Koenig, H. G., McCullough, M, E., & Larson, D. B. (2001). *Handbook of religion and health.* New York: Oxford University Press.

Loehlin, J. C. (1992). *Genes and environment in personality development.* Newbury Park, CA: Sage.

Loehlin, J. C., & Nichols, R. C. (1976). *Heredity, environment, and personality.* Austin, TX: University of Texas Press.

Marler, P. L., & Hadaway, C. K. (2002). "Being religious" or "being spiritual" in America: A zero-sum proposition? *Journal for the Scientific Study of Religion, 41,* 289–300.

Marty, M. (1993). Where the energies go. *Annals of the American Academy of Political and Social Sciences, 553,* 11–26.

Matthews, K. A., Batson, C. D., Horn, J., & Rosenman, R. H. (1981). "Principles in his nature which interest him in the fortune of others...": The heritability of empathic concern for others. *Journal of Personality, 49,* 237–247.

McCullough, M. E., Bellah, C. G., Kilpatrick, S. D., & Johnson, J. L. (2001). Vengefulness: Relationships with forgiveness, rumination, well-being, and the Big Five. *Personality and Social Psychology Bulletin, 27,* 601–610.

McCullough, M. E., Pargament, K. I., & Thoresen, C. E. (2000). The psychology of forgiveness: History, conceptual issues, and overview. In M. E. McCullough, K. I. Pargament, & C. E. Thoresen (Eds.), *Forgiveness: Theory, research, and practice* (pp. 1–14). New York: Guilford Press.

McCullough, M. E., Rachal, K. C., Sandage, S. J., Worthington, E. L., Jr., Brown, S. W., & Hight, T. L. (1998). Interpersonal forgiving in close relationships II: Theoretical elaboration and measurement. *Journal of Personality and Social Psychology, 75,* 1586–1603.

McCullough, M. E., & Worthington, E. L., Jr. (1999). Religion and the forgiving personality. *Journal of Personality, 67,* 1141–1164.

McCullough, M. E., Worthington, E. L., Jr., & Rachal, K. C. (1997). Interpersonal forgiving in close relationships. *Journal of Personality and Social Psychology, 73,* 321–336.

Mellins, C. A., Gatz, M., & Baker, L. (1996). Children's methods of coping with stress: A twin study of genetic and environmental influences. *Journal of Child Psychology and Psychiatry, 378,* 721–730.

Rose, R. J. (1988). Genetic and environmental variance in content dimensions of the MMPI. *Journal of Personality and Social Psychology, 55,* 302–311.

Rushton, J. P., Fulker, D. W., Neale, M. C., Nias, D. K. B., & Eysenck, H. J. (1986). Altruism and aggression: The heritability of individual differences. *Journal of Personality and Social Psychology, 50,* 1192–1198.

Snyder, C. R. (Ed.). (2001). *Coping with stress: Effective people and processes.* Oxford: Oxford University Press.

Symington, S. H., Walker, D. F., & Gorsuch, R. L. (2002). The relationship between forgiveness and reconciliation to five and sixteen factors of personality. *Journal of Psychology and Christianity, 21,* 141–150.

Truett, K. R., Eaves, L. J., Walters, E. E., Heath, A. C., Hewitt, J. K., Meyer, J. M., et al. (1994). A model system for analysis of family resemblance in extended kinships of twins. *Behavior Genetics, 24,* 35–49.

Tsuang, M. T. (2005). [Is there a role for forgiveness and spirituality in coping with combat trauma?] Unpublished raw data, Harvard Institute for Psychiatric Epidemiology and Genetics, Cambridge, MA.

Tsuang, M. T., Williams, W. M., Simpson, J. C., & Lyons, M. J. (2002). Pilot study of spirituality and mental health in twins. *American Journal of Psychiatry, 159,* 486–488.

Waller, N. G., Kojetin, B. A., Bouchard, T. J., Jr., Lykken, D. T., & Tellegen A. (1990). Genetic and environmental influences on religious interests, attitudes, and values: A study of twins reared apart and together. *Psychological Science, 1,* 138–142.

Wink, P., & Dillon, M. (2003). Religiousness, spirituality, and psychosocial functioning in late adulthood: Finding from a longitudinal study. *Psychology and Aging, 18,* 916–924.

Worthington, E. L., Jr. (Ed). (1998). *Dimensions of forgiveness: Psychological research and theological perspectives.* Philadelphia: Templeton Foundation Press.

Worthington, E. L., Jr., & Scherer, M. (2004). Forgiveness is an emotion-focused coping strategy that can reduce health risks and promote health resilience: Theory, review, and hypotheses. *Psychology and Health, 19,* 385–405.

Worthington, E. L., Jr., & Wade, N. G. (1999). The social psychology of unforgiveness and forgiveness and implication for clinical practice. *Journal of Social and Clinical Psychology, 18,* 385–418.

Wuthnow, R. (1998). *After Heaven: Spirituality in America since the 1950s.* Berkeley: University of California Press.

Zahn-Wexler, C., Robinson, J., & Emde, R. N. (1992). The development of empathy in twins. *Development Psychology, 28,* 1038–1047.

Zinnbauer, B. J., Pargament, K. I., Cole, B. C., Rye, M. S., Butter, E. M., Belvich, T. G., et al. (1997). Religion and spirituality: Unfuzzying the fuzzy. *Journal for the Scientific Study of Religion, 36,* 549–564.

Chapter Sixteen

Neuroimaging of Forgivability

Tom F. D. Farrow
Peter W. R. Woodruff

orgiveness may be defined as compassionate feelings that support a willingness to forgive or as the act of excusing a mistake or offense (WordNet, 1997). One component of forgiveness may be judging the forgivability of others' actions (possibly taking contextual information or extenuating circumstances into account).

Neuroimaging of forgivability is initially both very attractive and potentially quite disturbing. To the layperson, brain scanning equates with scientists examining which part of the brain "lights up" or activates when a particular action, emotion, or thought happens. The attractiveness of this possibility is therefore in the promise to reveal a physical basis to what is generally regarded as an ethereal and psychologically complex concept.

The disturbing aspect though, is the possibility posed by neuroimaging of exposing our innermost thoughts, moral judgments, and emotions to scrutiny and quantitative analysis. In this chapter, we will explore the ways in which neuroimaging can be used to strengthen our understanding of the physiology of forgiveness and can provide the means by which we can explore relevant brain mechanisms. For instance, we report how functional magnetic resonance imaging (fMRI) has been used to explore the brain activations associated with component processes of forgivability judgments and has allowed examination of brain regions involved in actively giving—or withholding—forgiveness.

fMRI is a noninvasive imaging technique that relies on the differing properties of oxyhemoglobin and deoxyhemoglobin (oxygenated and deoxygenated blood) in a magnetic field. This allows mapping of the distribution of oxygenated blood (and by inference, neuronal activity) in response to a particular task. fMRI scans are designed such that subjects perform contrasting tasks, the demands of which are matched as far as possible, so as to differ only by the specific cognitive process of interest. By subtracting the "baseline" task from the "active" task, many of the background and other processes unrelated to cognitive processes of interest (such as perceiving the noise of the scanner) are excluded. Brain activations to complex psychological paradigms (as opposed to, e.g., visual cortex activation to viewing a flashing checkerboard pattern) are rarely significantly strong enough for reliable and meaningful areas to be identified in individual subjects. It is, therefore, more common for activations to be group averaged.

Such techniques also allow examination of brain changes within a group, such as those induced by psychotherapeutic or pharmacological intervention and symptom resolution. Successful imaging of complex psychological brain processes is ultimately completely reliant on the ability of the paradigm to elicit the cognitive task of interest.

PERSONAL ASSUMPTIONS ABOUT FORGIVENESS

In our early scanning studies (Farrow et al., 2001), we neither attempted to nor claim to have imaged subjects in the process of actively forgiving. To achieve such an aim would have required the application of individually tailored scenarios and would have relied on the engagement of a personally sensitive and fairly unconstrained cognitive process at the required time in an unfamiliar environment (an MRI scanner). However, more recently, this more ambitious paradigm has been attempted (Pietrini, 2003).

We were initially interested in imaging subjects making judgments about the forgivability of another's actions. To do so, we identified putative component cognitive processes according to the following rationale:

1. Forgivability judgments are likely to be dependent on our interaction with and perception of the people around us and the cultural and societal norms to which we subscribe. Hence, we sought a social cognition paradigm that probed the cognitive thoughts and processes underlying social perception and social judgments.
2. Forgivability is likely to involve moral judgments. The task therefore had to concern a moral judgment about behavior.
3. Forgivability depends on empathy. The task therefore needed to involve the person in identifying with and understanding another's situation, feelings, and motives.
4. Forgivability depends on the capacity for a theory of mind (ToM). Hence, the task would require the attribution of independent mental states to self and others in order to explain and predict others' behavior. This capacity is often described as seeing the world from someone else's point of view or perspective.

We attempted, therefore, to elucidate the component processes that together are required to make a forgivability judgment. Social cognition, moral judgments, empathy, and ToM have all been examined using neuroimaging, and their study is also of relevance to many neuropsychiatric conditions. Empathy includes the interpretation and expression of emotions and contains a cognitive (understanding a conspecific's behavior and his or her intentions) and an affective (visceral emotional) component. Successful human social interaction (cohesion) requires understanding of other people's intentions, actions, and emotions. Specific to neuropsychiatry, empathic ability is often compromised in psychopathy, borderline personality disorder, and orbitofrontal and ventromedial cortex damage, whereas ToM deficits exist in autism, Asperger's syndrome, and schizophrenia. Posttraumatic stress disorder (PTSD) is known, in contrast with the other neuropsychiatric conditions mentioned, to respond well to a course of cognitive behavioral therapy (CBT; Tarrier et al., 1999). PTSD has been characterized as an impairment of the accurate evaluation and categorization of experiences (Stein, Jang, Taylor, Vernon, & Livesley, 2002), which may lead to a reduced or conditioned "normal" emotional physiological response and subsequently affect information processing (see chapter 22 by Noll for a review). The possibility therefore exists of conducting pre- and posttherapy brain imaging in patients with PTSD, using a paradigm such as empathic or forgivability judgments.

In this chapter, we will consider studies that attempt to image forgivability, then those that have examined the four component processes previously described.

REVIEW OF THE THEORETICAL AND EMPIRICAL LITERATURE

Neuroimaging Studies of Forgivability and Forgiveness

To date, there have been four separate studies of neuroimaging of forgiveness. These involved forgivability judgments in healthy controls (Farrow et al., 2001), forgivability judgments in patients with PTSD pre- and posttherapy (Farrow et al., 2002), forgivability judgments in patients with schizophrenia (Egleston et al., 2004; Green et al., 2003), and "actively forgiving" in healthy controls (Pietrini, 2003; Ricciardi et al., 2004).

Empathic and Forgivability Judgments in Healthy Controls

In Farrow et al. (2001), 10 healthy control subjects (mean age 31 years [range 21–51 years]; 7 men and 3 women) underwent an fMRI scan while making empathic and forgivability judgments. Subjects began by reading a short scenario before making five serial forced-choice decisions from two possible answers (see Table 16.1). Each scenario (empathic or forgivability judgments) was alternated with "baseline" social reasoning judgments to allow activation-of-no-interest subtraction that focused on activations related to the effect of the cognition of interest. Data analysis and results were restricted to brain activations in response to the judgment-making process, as scenario-reading activations were excluded. It was hypothesized that frontotemporal brain regions would be differentially activated by empathic and forgivability judgment tasks.

Areas of activation are reported by two methods—neuroanatomical name (i.e., brain region) and Brodmann's area (BA; a functional and cytoarchitectonic parcellation of brain grey matter, similar but not identical to the brain's gyral folds). Empathy judgments relative to social reasoning were associated with significant activations of left anterior middle temporal (BA 21), left superior frontal (BA 9), left inferior frontal (BA 47), orbitofrontal gyri (BA 11), and precuneus (BA 7; see Figure 16.1a). Judgments of forgivability relative to social reasoning were associated with significant activations

TABLE 16.1.   Examples of Presentation Paradigms

Social reasoning judgments (baseline)

Scenario: Approaching a large traffic jam on the motorway.

Details: It is not rush hour. There have been no road work signs.

Decision: More likely explanation for the delay.

A car crashed ahead	OR	A lorry crashed ahead
A local football match	OR	A local hockey match
A car burst into flames	OR	A car ran out of petrol
A slow lorry ahead	OR	A slow tractor ahead
Flooding on the road	OR	An oil spill on the road

Empathic judgments

Scenario: Your friend's daughter is happy.

Details: She is nine years old, in high spirits, and excited about a forthcoming event.

Decision: More likely explanation for her emotional state.

Her birthday the following day	OR	Her birthday the following week
Favourite football team won a match	OR	Favourite football team won the league
Going to the cinema that afternoon	OR	Going to the ice-rink that afternoon
Buying a new school uniform	OR	Buying a new party dress
Going to her grandmother's house	OR	Going to her friend's house

Forgivability judgments

Scenario: A celebrity appearing in court.

Details: You read in the newspaper that a well-known television presenter has appeared in court, charged with an offense.

Decision: Which of the following crimes you would see as more forgivable?

Income tax evasion	OR	Council tax evasion
Driving while drunk	OR	Driving while disqualified
Speeding on a motorway	OR	Speeding on a country road
Assaulting a journalist	OR	Assaulting an autograph hunter
Shoplifting from a food store	OR	Shoplifting from a clothes store

Note: Examples of paradigms used in scanner. Each functional scan lasting 306 s incorporated six 51-s epochs in a boxcar design of paradigm presentation (3 "active" empathic or forgivability judgments alternated with 3 "baseline" social reasoning judgments). Each 51-s condition consisted of a 16-s visually presented scenario followed by five serially presented pairs of possible answers. Each pair of possible answers was displayed for 7 s, thereby creating a 35-s epoch during which subjects made serial forced-choice judgments about the same index scenario.

(a)

(b)

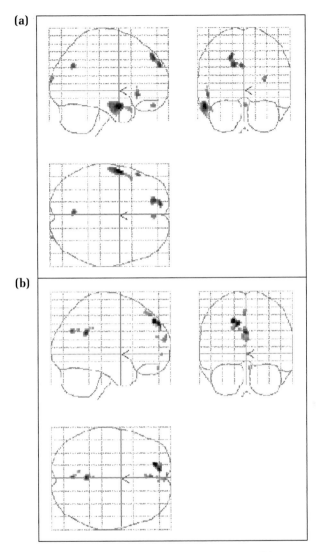

FIGURE 16.1. **(a)** Empathic vs. social reasoning judgments. **(b)** Forgivability vs. social reasoning judgments. SPM activation maps depict "averaged" regional brain activations from 10 subjects performing empathic judgments (Figure 16.1a) and forgivability judgments (Figure 16.1b) relative to social reasoning judgments. Extent of activation is shown in grey voxel clusters ($p < 0.05$, corrected for multiple comparisons) within 3 "transparent" brain projections viewed from the right aspect (sagittal projection; top left of figure), the posterior aspect (coronal projection; top right of figure), and from the superior aspect (axial projection; bottom left of figure). Reproduced with permission of Lippincott, Williams, & Wilkins Publishers. From Farrow, T. F. D., Zheng, Y., Wilkinson, I. D., Spence, S. A., Deakin, J. F. W., Tarrier, N., Griffiths, P. D., & Woodruff, P. W. R. (2001). Investigating the functional anatomy of empathy and forgiveness. *NeuroReport, 12,* 2433–2438.

of [left] superior frontal (BA 8/9/10) and posterior cingulate gyri (BA 31; see Figure 16.1b). Both empathic and forgivability judgments were associated with significant activations of left superior frontal (BA 9); orbitofrontal gyri (BA 11); and precuneus (BA 7). The activation areas common to empathic and forgivability judgments are distinct from the activations seen for each judgment paradigm individually.

Farrow et al. (2001) investigated the functional anatomy of forgiveness by examining one of many (postulated) cognitive components of forgiving—the neural correlates of making empathic and forgivability judgments. In keeping with previous studies of social cognition (as we will see later), making empathic and forgivability judgments clearly implicates frontotemporal brain regions. In particular, there was a discrete activation of left middle temporal gyrus while making empathic judgments, which was not seen during judgments of forgivability. These preliminary results suggest that attempting to understand others (i.e., empathizing) is physiologically distinct from determining the forgivability of their actions. The middle temporal gyrus has been described as "a common neural system of stored knowledge of personal identity" (Gorno-Tempini et al., 1998, p. 2103). The lack of middle temporal gyrus activation in response to the forgivability judgments may have been due to the forgivability scenarios being based on unknown individuals, whereas the empathic scenarios were based on personal acquaintances. The empathic judgments in our study required the imagining of a known person's responses, whereas the forgivability judgments centered on unknown people. This possible confound could have been addressed by adapting the empathy protocol so that it referred to persons unknown to the experimental subjects. However, it could be argued that by nature, empathy is likely to be applied most accurately with reference to another person known to the individual. Left frontal cortex was activated by both empathic and forgivability judgments, a finding that is congruent with reports of impaired empathy following left frontal cortical lesions (Grattan & Eslinger, 1992). In particular, left medial prefrontal cortex exhibits highly circumscribed activation common to both conditions, suggesting that they share a common neurocognitive substrate.

Lack of empathy is of central importance to many psychiatric conditions (e.g., schizophrenia, narcissistic personality disorder, antisocial personality disorder). Our results give a strong indication that activations of very high-level cognitive processes are recordable and that abnormal mental states could be reasonably predicted to show differing patterns of activation. There is an emerging literature on the beneficial effects of forgiveness as a psychotherapeutic intervention for many conditions (e.g., PTSD, postabortion grief, and incest; Coyle & Enright, [1997], Freedman & Enright, [1996]). "Abnormal" brain activations may therefore be amenable to "normalization" through cognitive intervention, possibly containing a forgiveness component.

Empathic and Forgivability Judgments in Posttraumatic Stress Disorder

Farrow et al. (2002) reported preliminary findings from an ongoing study using 13 patients with PTSD (following a road traffic accident or assault). We wished to explore the way in which PTSD symptoms would impact on emotional and social cognition processing (i.e., patients' ability to make empathic and forgivability judgments). We hypothesized that the psychological impact of PTSD would be reflected in attenuation of brain activation in regions previously shown to subserve social cognition (Farrow et al., 2001) and that CBT tailored to include a forgiveness component, would result in "normalization" of brain activation on tasks that probe empathy and forgivability.

Subjects were scanned while making the empathic and forgivability judgments described in Farrow et al. (2001) both before and after CBT that specifically addressed issues of forgiveness of the perpetrator. The CBT comprised up to 10 weekly 1-hour sessions of fixed content, together with intersessional tasks (e.g., writing a trauma impact statement to be regularly read and rewritten during the therapeutic course). The concepts of empathy and forgiveness were discussed in the context of the expression of anger, frustration, and the need for revenge. In subsequent sessions, empathy with the perpetrator was discussed as a positive emotional state competing with potential negative emotional states. Topics included types of empathy, expression of empathy, and techniques for promoting empathy and making statements to the offender promoting empathy. Patients' intersessional tasks at this stage included writing a letter to themselves from the offender's perspective.

Patients then spent three sessions specifically investigating forgiveness in relation to their index incident. The first of these specific sessions, "forgiveness as a meaningful skill," included exposure to hurt, identifying events to focus forgiveness on, identifying personal ways of forgiving, and forgiveness role-play. The intersessional tasks included writing a letter from the offender's perspective and rehearsal of forgiving.

The second of three specific sessions focused on the "promoting of a commitment to forgive" by investigating techniques and personal ways of exploring commitment to forgive, reading the letter written from the offender's perspective, and role playing of empathic understanding. For their intersessional task, patients wrote a "letter of forgiveness."

The final session focused specifically on the ideas of forgiveness and "holding on to forgiveness," together with techniques for holding on to forgiveness—reading their forgiveness letter, discussing attribution errors, and role-playing exercises involving forgiveness.

All patients fulfilled DSM-IV (American Psychological Association [APA], 1994) criteria for PTSD pretherapy but, with significant symptom resolution, did not fulfill them posttherapy. Preliminary results suggested that pretherapy, PTSD patients' empathic and forgivability judgments relative to social reasoning were associated with significantly less activation in relevant areas, as identified from healthy controls (Farrow et al., 2001). For the same patients posttherapy, empathic and forgivability judgments produced activations similar to those seen in healthy control subjects.

The main finding from this study was therefore that patients with PTSD showed enhanced brain activation following symptom resolution in brain areas that were previously shown to be involved in social cognition (Farrow et al., 2001). Symptom resolution was facilitated by therapeutic input that involved a central, structured forgiveness component.

Patients with PTSD were often dealing in therapy with issues of forgiveness (toward someone that they saw as to blame for their incident) and reported reduced empathy (numbing of affect toward family, friends, and colleagues). However, the scanning tasks engaged processes linked with social cognition judgments rather than directly invoking inherent emotions. It is therefore difficult at this stage to state categorically how specific the effect is to forgiveness, as opposed to other, higher order information-processing abnormalities observed in PTSD (Blomhoff, Reinvang, & Malt, 1998; McFarlane, Weber, & Clark , 1993).

This fMRI study in PTSD (Farrow et al., 2002), however, does provide convincing evidence that a psychotherapeutic intervention might lead to changes in brain activity. The issue of forgiveness is pertinent to many cases of PTSD, and this is clearly an area that would benefit from further investigation. These results are encouraging in general for similar neuroimaging studies of psychotherapeutic intervention in serious mental disorders that concern difficulties in social interaction.

Empathic and Forgivability Judgments in Schizophrenia

Difficulty with social interactions is a key clinical feature of schizophrenia, which has been characterized as "a disorder of the representation of [others'] mental states" (Frith, 1992, p. 107). These deficits may impact patients' ability to make judgments about, for example, empathic and forgivability scenarios. A better understanding of the neural basis of social cognition might ultimately help to explain brain mechanisms underlying some of the deficits in social functioning in people with schizophrenia.

One ongoing study (Egleston et al., 2004; Green et al., 2003) has been concerned with repeating the empathic and forgivability judgment paradigms (Farrow et al., 2001) in patients with schizophrenia. Data were also collected from a new set of healthy controls to confirm the reproducibility of "normal" activations. In both the healthy controls and patients with schizophrenia, scanning was conducted twice (approximately 2.5 months apart) to provide a pre- and posttreatment comparison for the patients with schizophrenia and a measure of the reproducibility of activations in healthy controls over time.

Fourteen patients with schizophrenia and fourteen age-, sex-, and IQ-matched healthy controls were scanned on two occasions. At initial scan, healthy controls showed very similar activations to those previously reported. Those data supported the reproducibility of the paradigm. At second scan, healthy control subjects showed reduced activation to both empathic and forgivability judgments, thereby giving a more valid comparator for patients' second scans. Preliminary results suggest an increased activation in schizophrenia patients following treatment, compared with controls (i.e., schizophrenia [Time 2 – Time 1] minus control [Time 2 – Time 1]) in task-relevant regions (Egleston et al., 2004; Green et al., 2003).

These findings support other neuroimaging studies implicating frontotemporal underactivation in patients with schizophrenia during social cognition tasks (e.g., Russell et al., 2000). The findings suggest that treatment-induced increases in brain activation occur in areas implicated in empathic and forgivability judgments.

Active Imaginal Forgiving in Healthy Control Subjects

Pietrini, Ricciardi, and their colleagues at the University of Pisa, Italy (Pietrini, 2003, Ricciardi et al., 2004) state in their abstract that, "While designating regions involved in evaluating forgivability and ethical judgments, these results [Farrow et al., 2001] do not provide any insight about neural responses associated with the process of giving or withholding forgiving" (Ricciardi et al., 2004, p. 1). Having previously successfully used fMRI combined with visual imagery strategies to explore the neural correlates of aggressive behavior (Pietrini, Guazzelli, Basso, Jaffe, & Grafman, 2000), they sought to determine the brain correlates associated with the imaginal evocation of giving or withholding forgiveness. In the fMRI scanner, six healthy volunteers (four female; mean age 26 years) evoked individually specific scenarios that comprised a hurtful event. They were then randomly instructed to imagine giving or withholding forgiveness. Activations to evocation of the hurtful event and engaging in forgiving or unforgiving behavior were all examined. Preliminary results from the evocation of the hurtful condition showed increases in anterior middle frontal and ventral temporal cortices associated with activity reductions in visual, motor, and subcortical regions, compared with the baseline control condition. The enactment of forgiving versus unforgiving behavior was associated with differences in neural activity in the right medial, middle and superior frontal cortices, right amygdala, bilateral striatum, left anterior cingulate, bilateral posterior parietal cortices, and cerebellum. These anterior areas, such as frontal cortex, amygdala, anterior cingulate and striatum; are involved with the regulation of emotional responses, moral judgments (Greene & Haidt, 2002), perception of physical and moral pain, and decision-making processes (Vogt, Finch, & Olson, 1992). Hence, there may be a convergence in our understanding of psychological component processes to forgiving and their neural correlates. Pietrini and colleagues' results are novel in that they may tap the affective (i.e., bodily, autonomic) component of *actively* forgiving and *feeling* emotional experiences (albeit from recalled memories). This may explain why their results contain areas of activation common to previous studies (Egleston et al., 2004; Farrow et al., 2001, 2002; Green et al., 2003) as well as additional regions.

RELEVANT PREVIOUS RESEARCH

Previously reported research on fMRI of empathic and forgivability judgments and giving and withholding forgiving supports the existence of components of such high-level cognitions. These components have been elucidated by neuroimaging in healthy volunteers regarding theory of mind (ToM; Fletcher et al., 1995; Gallagher et al., 2000; Goel, Grafman, Sadato, & Hallett, 1995), moral judgments (Greene, Sommerville, Nystrom, Darley, & Cohen, 2001; Greene & Haidt, 2002; Moll, Eslinger, & de Oliveira-Souza, 2001), moral sensitivity (Moll et al., 2002), general emotional activation (Phan, Wager, Taylor, & Liberzon, 2002), and sympathy (Decety & Chaminade, 2003). ToM paradigms have also been extensively conducted in patients with autism and Asperger's syndrome (e.g., Happé et al., 1997), and patients with schizophrenia (e.g., Mazza, De Risio, Surian, Roncone, & Casacchia, 2001; Russell et al., 2000). Both of these patient groups are considered to have specific ToM deficits.

ToM tasks involve left medial prefrontal cortex, left ventrolateral prefrontal cortex, orbitofrontal cortex, and posterior cingulate gyrus in healthy control subjects. Medial prefrontal cortical (and to a lesser extent, posterior cingulate gyrus) activation during ToM tasks is not observed in patients with Asperger's syndrome. In patients with schizophrenia, ToM tasks fail to activate the ventrolateral prefrontal cortex (and to a lesser extent, medial prefrontal cortex).

Sympathy has been defined as "the affinity, association, or relationship between persons wherein whatever affects one similarly affects the other" (*Merriam-Webster Medical Dictionary*, 2002). A positron emission tomography (PET) neuroimaging study of sympathy (Decety & Chaminade, 2003) used videos of sad and emotionally neutral stories to elicit brain activations. Decety and Chaminade (2003) found that emotional expression of any kind in the videos was associated with activation of left inferior frontal gyrus. Medial prefrontal gyrus activation was associated with incongruity between an actor's emotional expression and the narrative content of a story. The authors proposed that the medial prefrontal gyrus is involved in evaluating social conflict. However, they also noted that the inferior frontal and medial prefrontal activations were modulated by subjects' assessment of the likeability of the story actors. The interaction between objective emotional interpretation and subjective judgment of a person's "likeability" may have relevance for further neuroimaging studies of forgiveness. For instance, one interpretation of this finding may be that we more easily forgive people we like.

A further area of research relevant to forgiveness is neuroimaging moral judgments. Greene et al. (2001) presented subjects with stories about which they made moral judgments. An example of such a story was one in which a runaway train was heading toward a number of people down one fork of the track. By switching the points on the track, it would be possible to divert the train down another railway track, resulting in only one person dying. Subjects were asked to decide whether they would switch the points. This was contrasted with a (ostensibly similar) judgment of whether it would be morally correct to push a stranger in front of a train to save the lives of many people. This study reported that moral personal judgments were associated (in contrast with moral impersonal judgments) with activations including left medial prefrontal cortex and posterior cingulate gyrus. This specifically relates to forgiveness research because moral judgments about others' actions are invariably a factor in whether those actions are forgivable.

NEW RESEARCH DIRECTIONS

An important research direction is likely to be the application of current knowledge of the neuroscience of emotional processing to our understanding of forgiveness. For instance, the functional neuroanatomy of such emotions (Phan et al., 2002) as fear, happiness, sadness, and disgust tells us about how the brain responds to distinct emotions. At some level, these emotions presumably influence our ability to forgive or make forgivability judgments. How they do so could aid our insight into the processes that lead to forgiveness. For instance, emotions are important to forgiveness because a person's decision whether to forgive may be modulated by the giver's emotional evaluation of the subject of their forgiveness. Phan and colleagues concluded that, as a generalization, the medial prefrontal cortex was specifically involved in emotional processing, whereas emotional recall, imagery, and emotional tasks that demanded a heavy cognitive load recruited both the anterior cingulate and the insula. These brain regions form candidate areas identified as significant in the generation of forgiveness. Future studies may enable us to be more specific about brain areas responsible for emotional and other psychological processes that may influence an individual's ability to forgive.

RELEVANCE FOR CLINICAL AND APPLIED INTERVENTIONS

Neuroimaging of forgiveness and forgivability have to date been used only in research settings. There are developmental and psychiatric disorders associated with deficits of ToM (autism) and empathy (psychopathy). Furthermore, adherence to social conventions may in health depend on ventrolateral prefrontal cortex function. Because all these brain regions comprise the substrate for putative component processes that lead to forgiveness, it would be tempting to speculate that lesions in these regions would lead to "deficits" in the ability to forgive. However, there are no medical disorders characterized by an inability to forgive or make forgivability judgments. On the other hand, some evidence does support the idea that the ability to forgive does confer a prognostic advantage on patients who are victims of assault (DiBlasio & Proctor, 1993). If established, it may be that neuroimaging techniques could be used to monitor an individual's psychological response to therapy or even help make predictions of their likely response to treatment. However, though the possibility of utilizing a forgivability neuroimaging paradigm in pre- and postintervention (therapeutic) clinical application is feasible, the power to detect individual changes of potential clinical utility is probably some way off.

PERSONAL THEORETICAL PERSPECTIVES ON THE FIELD

In common with many complex cognitions, forgiveness can be considered as comprising component cognitive processes, which ultimately have a representation in the brain. Rather than being reductionist, this notion merely demonstrates that many of the underlying processes can be elucidated and disentangled from one another. Choosing whether to forgive someone may still be conceptualized as a psychological process beyond the sum of these (postulated) component parts. However, by examining such parts in healthy controls and patients with known social cognition, empathy, and theory of mind deficits, our understanding of forgiveness may be further illuminated.

CONCLUSIONS

This chapter reviewed the attractive and potentially disturbing connotations of imaging forgiveness and forgivability. The early results in neuroimaging of forgiveness would suggest that further research in the area may help determine how the brain enables complex psychological processes to interact and modulate one another that may lead to variation in the capacity to forgive and determine the impact of this variation on psychological "health."

ACKNOWLEDGMENTS

We thank Mr. Camal Gouneea for conducting the "CBT with a forgiveness component" therapy, Dr. Mike D. Hunter for psychiatric patient clinical assessments, Dr. Kwang H. Lee for providing data from his schizophrenia patient study, Dr. Pietro Pietrini for preliminary data from his imaginal forgiveness study, and all patients and healthy subjects who participated in the reported studies. The work resulting in the Farrow et al. (2001) paper and abstract (2002) was funded by the John Templeton Foundation (Grant No. 5184). We thank Janssen-Cilag for kindly helping fund the studies on neuroimaging empathy and forgivability in schizophrenia from which preliminary findings are reported in this chapter.

REFERENCES

American Psychiatric Association. (1994). *Diagnostic and statistical manual of mental disorders* (4th ed; DSM-IV). Washington, DC: Author.

Blomhoff, S., Reinvang, I., & Malt, U. F. (1998). Event related potentials to stimuli with emotional impact in post-traumatic stress patients. *Biological Psychiatry, 44,* 1045–1053.

Coyle, C. T., & Enright, R. D. (1997). Forgiveness intervention with postabortion men. *Journal of Consulting and Clinical Psychology, 65,* 1042–1046.

Decety, J., & Chaminade, T. (2003). Neural correlates of feeling sympathy. *Neuropsychologia, 41,* 127–138.

DiBlasio, F. A., & Proctor J. H. (1993). Therapists and the clinical use of forgiveness. *Journal of Family Therapy, 21,* 175–184.

Egleston, P. N., Lee, K. H., Brown, W. H., Green, R. D. J., Farrow, T. F. D., Hunter, M. D., et al. (2004). Treatment induced brain changes during forgiveness tasks in patients with schizophrenia. *Schizophrenia Research, 67,* 193.

Farrow, T. F. D., Zheng, Y., Wilkinson, I. D., Spence, S. A., Deakin, J. F. W., Tarrier, N., et al. (2001). Investigating the functional anatomy of empathy and forgiveness. *NeuroReport, 12,* 2433–2438.

Farrow, T. F. D., Hunter, M. D., Fawbert, D., Smith, R., Mason, S., Gouneea, C., et al. (2002). Differential fMRI activations to social reasoning paradigms in patients with PTSD pre- and post-therapy. *NeuroImage HBM2002 CD.* 289.

Fletcher, P., Frith, U., Baker, S. C., Dolan, R. J., Frackowiak, R. S. J., & Frith, C. D. (1995). Other minds in the brain: A functional imaging study of "theory of mind" in story comprehension. *Cognition, 57,* 109–128.

Freedman, S. R., & Enright, R. D. (1996). Forgiveness as an intervention goal with incest survivors. *Journal of Consulting and Clinical Psychology, 64,* 983–992.

Frith, C. D. (1992). *The cognitive neuropsychology of schizophrenia.* Hillsdale, NJ: Lawrence Erlbaum.

Gallagher, H. L., Happé, F., Brunswick, N., Fletcher, P. C., Frith, U., & Frith, C. D. (2000). Reading the mind in cartoons and stories: An fMRI study of "theory of mind" in verbal and nonverbal tasks. *Neuropsychologia, 38,* 11–21.

Goel, V., Grafman, J., Sadato, N., & Hallett, M. (1995). Modeling other minds. *NeuroReport, 6,* 1741–1746.

Gorno-Tempini, M. L., Price, C. J., Josephs, O., Vandenberghe, R., Cappa, S. F., Kapur, N., et al. (1998). The neural systems sustaining face and proper-name processing. *Brain, 121,* 2103–2118.

Grattan, L. M., & Eslinger, P. J. (1992). Long-term psychological consequences of childhood frontal lobe lesion in patient DT. *Brain and Cognition, 20,* 185–195.

Green, R. D. J., Lee, K. H., Brown, W. H., Egleston, P. N., Farrow, T. F. D., Hunter, M. D., et al. (2003). Effect of treatment on brain activation during judgements of forgivability in people with schizophrenia. *NeuroImage, 19,* S106.

Greene, J. D., Sommerville, R. B., Nystrom, L. E., Darley, J. M., & Cohen, J. D. (2001). An fMRI investigation of emotional engagement in moral judgement. *Science, 293,* 2105–2108.

Greene, J., & Haidt, J. (2002). How (and where) does moral judgment work? *Trends in Cognitive Sciences, 6,* 517–523.

Happé, F., Ehlers, S., Fletcher, P., Frith, U., Johansson, M., Gillberg, C., et al. (1997). "Theory of mind" in the brain: Evidence from a PET scan study of Asperger syndrome. *NeuroReport, 8,* 197–201.

Mazza, M., De Risio, A., Surian, L., Roncone, R., & Casacchia M. (2001). Selective impairments of theory of mind in people with schizophrenia. *Schizophrenia Research, 47,* 299–308.

McFarlane, A. C., Weber, D. L., & Clark C. R. (1993). Abnormal stimulus processing in posttraumatic stress disorder. *Biological Psychiatry, 34,* 311–320.

Merriam-Webster's Medical Desk Dictionary. (2001). Springfield, MA: Merriam-Webster.

Moll, J., Eslinger, P. J., & de Oliveira-Souza, R. (2001). Frontopolar and anterior temporal cortex activation in a moral judgment task. *Arquivos de neuro-psiquiatria. 59,* 657–664.

Moll, J., de Oliveira-Souza, R., Eslinger, P. J., Bramati, I. E., Mourao-Miranda, J., Andreiuolo, P.A., et al. (2002). The neural correlates of moral sensitivity: A functional magnetic resonance imaging investigation of basic and moral emotions. *Journal of Neuroscience, 22*, 2730–2736.

Phan, K. L., Wager, T., Taylor, S. F., & Liberzon, I. (2002). Functional neuroanatomy of emotion: A meta-analysis of emotion activation studies in PET and fMRI. *NeuroImage, 16*, 331–348.

Pietrini, P., Guazzelli, M., Basso, G., Jaffe, K., & Grafman, J. (2000). Neural correlates of imaginal aggressive behavior assessed by positron emission tomography in healthy subjects. *American Journal of Psychiatry, 157*, 1772–1781.

Pietrini, P. (2003, October). *Neural correlates of imaginal forgiveness and unforgiveness: A functional magnetic resonance imaging study in healthy human subjects.* Paper presented at Scientific Findings About Forgiveness, Atlanta, GA.

Ricciardi, E., Gentili, C., Rizzo, M., Vanello, N., Sani, L., Landini, L., et al. (2004). *Brain activity associated with forgiving and unforgiving behavior in humans as assessed by fMRI.* Poster presented at 10th annual meeting of the Organization for Human Brain Mapping (HBM2004), Budapest, Hungary.

Russell, T. A., Rubia, K., Bullmore, E. T., Soni, W., Suckling, J., Brammer, M.J., et al. (2000). Exploring the social brain in schizophrenia: Left prefrontal underactivation during mental state attribution. *American Journal of Psychiatry, 157*, 2040–2042.

Stein, M. B, Jang, K. L., Taylor, S., Vernon, P. A., & Livesley, W. J. (2002). Genetic and environmental influences on trauma exposure and posttraumatic stress disorder symptoms. *American Journal of Psychiatry, 159*, 1675–1681.

Tarrier, N., Pilgrim, H., Sommerfield, C., Faragher, B., Reynolds, M., Graham, E., et al. (1999). A randomised trial of cognitive therapy and imaginal exposure in the treatment of chronic post-traumatic stress disorder. *Journal of Consulting and Clinical Psychology, 67*, 13–18.

Vogt B. A., Finch D. M., & Olson C. R. (1992). Functional heterogeneity in cingulate cortex: The anterior executive and posterior evaluative regions. *Cerebral Cortex, 2*, 435–443.

WordNet 1.6, (1997). WordNet. Retrieved May 20, 2004 from www.cogsci.princeton.edu/~wn/.

Chapter Seventeen

The Physiology and Pathophysiology of Unhappiness

Robert M. Sapolsky

PROLOGUE, 2004

Stress physiology, as applied to the average vertebrate, is the study of the defenses mobilized by the body in response to physical challenges—being chased by a predator when injured or sprinting after a meal when starving. In contrast, humans have the cognitive sophistication to activate the identical stress response habitually for purely psychological or social reasons—worries about mortgages, relationships, and the thinning ozone layer. Although activation of the stress response is critical for surviving pursuit by a lion, it is pathogenic when mobilized chronically, and many Westernized diseases are caused or worsened by overactive stress responses. How do psychological and social factors—such as unhappiness—activate the stress response? Broadly, for the same physical stressor, an organism is more likely to have a stress response if it lacks outlets for frustration, social support, control, or predictability. Social status also modulates the stress response. Many studies of social primates suggest that low-ranking individuals have chronically activated stress responses and are more prone toward stress-related diseases. This likely reflects their being subject to higher rates of both physical and psychological stressors than are dominant individuals. However, in primates, social subordination is not always associated with such maladaptive physiology; it is not just rank that influences physiology but also the sort of society in which the rank occurs, as well as that individual's experience of rank and society.

These same principles can be applied to interpreting social status and patterns of diseases in humans. Particular emphasis is placed on the extensive literature showing the health risks of low socioeconomic status (SES), interpreting them in the context of the psychological stressors particular to low SES. Personality and temperament also modulate the stress response; for example, there are overactivated stress responses in primates with a "hot reactor" temperament and in humans with major depression, anxiety disorders, Type A personality, or repressive personality. Finally, social status and personality can interact in a critical manner—specifically, an inner locus of control is highly adaptive in one position in society, whereas in another, it is highly predictive of cardiovascular disease.

When humans experience transgressions, their physiology is affected. Injustices, threats, and physical or psychological harms can lead to unforgiveness. Such unforgiveness entails rumination. Physically, unforgiveness and rumination may well create similar stress responses as are experienced in all animals in response to more classic, physical stressors. Some humans become chronically unforgiving. Chronic physiological arousal with frequent unforgiveness has the potential to create a pathophysiological pattern, which can lead to illness or can exacerbate preexisting illness.

In this chapter, which is reprinted from an earlier review chapter,[1] I describe the physiology and pathology of unhappiness—of which unforgiveness may be a subcategory. Evidence is accumulating to suggest a link (for two recent reviews, see chapter 19 by Harris & Thoresen; Worthington & Scherer, 2004), but the jury is still out as to the degree of similarity and its physical impact.

INTRODUCTION: THE HUMAN STRESS RESPONSE

Imagine that an earnest young wildebeest in the early stages of its PhD program in psychobiology has finally selected a thesis project. The ambitious ungulate plans to study the physiological correlates of social behavior of the primate *Homo sapiens*. Thanks to anesthetic dartings of groups of tourists that frequent the savanna, a study population is outfitted with telemetry devices, remote blood-collection systems, and ambulatory EKG monitors. All is going well, and a degree seems conceivable for this scholarly wildebeest when an inexplicable set of data appear. On certain occasions, specifically afternoons, when the humans lounge in the shade of their camp, pairs of them perform a strange behavior. Two males, for example, might begin these odd ritualized interactions, and along with that, blood pressure quickly soars; heart rate increases dramatically; muscle tension rises, as does caloric expenditure; and androgenic steroid hormones pour into the circulation. The wildebeest knows precisely what the physiology implies, namely an intense male-male dispute. The physiological profile is identical to when two male wildebeest contest females in heat as they lunge at each other. Yet the two humans do nothing more than sit in close proximity, decrease their rates of vocalization and eye contact, and occasionally do nothing more physically taxing than move a small piece of wood.

A startling aspect of human psychobiology: People who care about such things get physiologically aroused during chess matches and get aroused in ways that are indistinguishable from animals having territorial disputes (Leedy & DuBeck, 1971). The poor wildebeest has just discovered a startling fact about humans, one that makes no sense to virtually any other animal (particularly those comprising its dissertation committee): Humans mobilize the same physiology as any other animal but for reasons unrelated to physical demands.

This chapter concerns another circumstance in which humans mobilize a common set of physiological responses but for novel reasons. For most species, this system signals either a physical insult or the imminent threat of one. For humans, in contrast, it far more frequently signals a state of unhappiness, of psychological or social unease.

The *stress response* is a set of hormonal and neural events that are fairly stereotyped among vertebrates. This phylogenetic conservation implies a vital role in physiology, namely, saving your neck during a crisis. For most species, the stress response mediates adaptation to threats to *homeostasis.*[2] This term, coined by the physiologist Walter Cannon early in the century and a cornerstone of our ninth-grade biology education, refers to a sense of physiologic equilibrium where body temperature, acidity, blood glucose level state, and so on are all in balance and ideal. A *stressor* can be something in the environment that disrupts homeostatic balance, and the stress response represents the adaptations that help reestablish homeostasis. For most species, such disruptions can be anything but subtle—starvation, injury, an attack by a predator, combat with a conspecific—nature bloody in tooth and claw. In that context, the stress response represents the adaptations that help save your life.

In some cases, a stressor can also be the *anticipation* that one is just about to be thrown out of balance. Thus, a wildebeest seeing a lion charging toward it may immediately mobilize the stress response—increasing its heart rate and blood pressure, diverting energy to its muscles—even though it has not yet been torn asunder. In the same way, a lion may mobilize its stress response in anticipation of a threat to allostasis, such as having to sprint after a meal. Stress responses in anticipation of the immediacy of a physical stressor are obviously adaptive, insofar as they give the organism a head start in physiologically coping.

Among humans, however, the stress response is mobilized in ways unimaginable in the rest of the animal kingdom. When scanning the cloudless skies and the parched soil during a drought, a subsistence farmer in the developing world might mobilize the stress response in the knowledge that months from now, his children will be starving, even though their current nutritional state is perfectly adequate. When scanning a calendar, an overextended American might mobilize a stress response with the realization that April 15th is just around the corner; this may come despite this individual being unmenaced by carnivores. And virtually all humans at some sleepless point at night will mobilize the stress response in recognizing that their time on this earth is horribly finite.

Humans can activate the typical vertebrate stress response in anticipation of physical stressors that are extremely displaced in time. This is made possible by a vast extension of the cognitive skills that allow a wildebeest to react in alarm at the sight of a rapidly approaching lion, allowing us instead to fret over challenges long in the future. Moreover, humans can readily activate the identical stress response for purely psychological or social reasons when there are *no* conceivable physical challenges. This requires features of thought and emotion that are shared with only a handful of other species and that are possessed by them to a far lesser extent. Experiments will be discussed in which stress responses in rats can be triggered by purely psychological manipulations or where a primate's endocrine profile reflects its cognitive assessment of its role in its society. Nonetheless, no rat or primate is ever going to understand why these humans get stressed by blind dates, promotions, public speaking, or traffic jams.

The centerpiece of stress physiology in humans is that we can mobilize the system for psychological or social reasons. The centerpiece of stress *patho*physiology is that *chronic* mobilization of the stress response increases the likelihood of disease, and this is mostly a human province. Stressors for most animals are typically short term and physical, because either the crisis or the animal is soon over with. Wildebeests do not have 30-year sprints from lions, but we can be stressed with 30-year mortgages, and it is the chronicity of the stress response that increases the risk of disease (for reasons to be explained below).

This chapter reviews the physiology and pathophysiology of the stress response, focusing on features that are most central to understanding humans and their psychological stressors. Why bother? Perhaps monitoring the stress response is a particularly accurate way of detecting the emotive state of an individual. This is precisely what is being done in studies with nonhuman primates. Animal care laws commendably mandate that attention be paid to the "psychological well-being" of laboratory primates, generating the nontrivial task of determining when that state has been achieved. In the absence of the extensive observation that would be required of each animal, a reasonable solution is to decide that animals that have elevated circulating levels of stress responsive hormones probably do not have a psychological sense of well-being. However, this approach is not particularly needed for humans. In general, you do not need to monitor a dozen different hormones in someone's bloodstream to know that he or she is unhappy (nor, as will be discussed below, is that likely to actually tell you much).

The important reason for studying stress physiology is because of its relevance to disease. Few of us will die of bubonic plaque, malnutrition, or dengue fever—infectious disease and diseases of poor nutrition or hygiene have mostly been vanquished in Western societies. Instead, we die of diseases of slow accumulation of damage—the gradual blockade of blood vessels that can cause heart or cerebrovascular disease, the slow derangement of metabolism of adult-onset diabetes, the repeated challenge and ultimate defeat of immune defenses that is cancer. Lifestyle, emotional temperament, and psychological factors have virtually nothing to do with how a body manages exposure to a massive and rapidly acting insult such as cholera, but they have much to do with the progression of some of our most common Western diseases. Insofar as chronic unhappiness, anxiety, and depression can cause sustained overactivation of the stress response, they increase the risk of some of these diseases. Humans are unique in the extent to which they can mobilize the stress response for sustained, psychological reasons, and Westernized humans are unique in living well enough and long enough to pay the price for this.

In the first part of this chapter, I review the physiology of the stress response and how stress-related disease occurs. I recognize that readers are neither physiologists nor wish to become one; to make this section more user-friendly, a summary occurs at its end, which can be skipped to immediately by the faint-hearted. Moreover, I give only broad references to reviews of the subject. Following that, I review how psychological, social, and personality factors can modulate or cause the stress response.

THE PHYSIOLOGY OF THE STRESS RESPONSE AND THE EMERGENCE OF STRESS-RELATED DISEASE

As noted, varied stressors trigger a fairly stereotyped set of endocrine and neural responses known as the stress response. At the heart of this is the activation of the sympathetic nervous system (a division of the autonomic, or involuntary, nervous system). This leads to the secretion of the hormones adrenaline and noradrenaline (also known as *epinephrine* and *norepinephrine*) into the bloodstream, which mediate the classic "fight or flight" syndrome. Of equal importance is the secretion during stress of other hormones called *glucocorticoids*. These steroids come from the adrenal gland, with the human version being cortisol (also known as *hydrocortisone*). Stress also stimulates the secretion of additional hormones, such as beta-endorphin, glucagon, prolactin, and vasopressin (reviewed in chapter 2 of Sapolsky, 1994).

The stress response inhibits other endocrine and neural systems. There is decreased secretion of insulin, hormones related to sexual behavior, and reproduction and growth and tissue repair, and inhibition of the parasympathetic nervous system. Whereas the sympathetic activation mediates arousal, parasympathetic activation works in opposition, having a calming, vegetative effect (see chapter 2, Sapolsky, 1994).

Remarkably, the actions of this daunting array of hormones make sense when one considers the physiological needs of a prey species desperately trying to evade a predator or a predator desperately trying to obtain a meal. For both animals, this crisis requires the immediate mobilization of energy into the bloodstream and its subsequent diversion to exercising muscle; this would be a singularly inauspicious time to be depositing energy into fat cells for a project for next spring. As such, during stress, energy storage is blocked, and energy that is already stored is liberated into the bloodstream and diverted to muscle. These steps are accomplished by the inhibition of insulin secretion and of parasympathetic tone and by the activation of the sympathetic nervous system, glucocorticoids, and glucagon, which were named for their ability to mobilize energy; to increase circulating levels of glucose (reviewed in Munck, Guyre, & Holbrook, 1984). It is also adaptive to deliver those nutrients to muscle as rapidly as possible, and sympathetic hormones plus glucocorticoids increase heart rate and blood pressure.

During a crisis, it is also useful to inhibit any physiological processes that are unessential, wasteful drains on resources. As such, the stress response also involves triaging a variety of functions. Digestion is inhibited (including the inhibition of salivary secretion, accounting for our dry mouths when we are nervous); for the hungry predator, digestion is irrelevant, whereas for the prey, the energy being mobilized comes from glycogen stored in the liver (rather than from glucose in the gut), and this is no time for the slow and costly process of digestion. Growth, inflammation, and tissue repair are also deferred for later. In addition, reproductive physiology is inhibited; a desperate sprint across the savanna is no time to ovulate. As another feature of the stress response, immune function is inhibited because of the danger of overactivation of immunity (to the point of autoimmune disease) during stressors (an idea first hypothesized by Munck et al., 1984 and heavily supported by both experimental and clinical data). Finally, during certain types of stressors, pain perception is blunted—the phenomenon of stress-induced analgesia, where someone in the middle of combat might be unaware of being injured (reviewed by Terman, Shavit, Lewis, Cannon, & Liebeskind, 1984).

Collectively, these steps are vital for surviving a physical stressor, as demonstrated by a handful of rare diseases in which components of the stress response fail. For example, in Addison's disease, sufferers are depleted of glucocorticoids, and in Shy-Drager syndrome, it is the sympathetic nervous system that is impaired. In both cases, individuals are extremely fragile if untreated, and a major variety of physical stressors can prove fatal.

Yet sustained overactivation of this same stress response (most typically, for psychological reasons) can be pathogenic. To be more precise, it is not that stress makes you sick but that it increases the likelihood of contracting a disease that makes you sick.

When the pathogenic potential of stress was first recognized in the 1930s (Selye, 1936), an explanation emerged that is now considered wrong. In the face of a short-term stressor, as just described, the stress response is mobilized, and a state of adaptation, a re-establishment of allostatic balance, can be achieved. As conceptualized back then, prolonged stress causes a state of exhaustion—literally, the body is depleted of hormones such as glucocorticoids, epinephrine, or norepinephrine, and disease occurs because the external stressor now pummels the body unopposed (see Selye, 1971). In this scenario, stress-related disease arises because the defending army of the stress response runs out of ammunition.

As a first demonstration that this cannot be the explanation for stress pathophysiology, purely psychological stressors (in which there is no external insult to pummel the body, should defenses fail) are pathogenic when prolonged. Moreover, it is exceedingly rare that chronic stress of any sort leads to the hypothesized exhaustion stage, where stores of stress hormones are depleted. The facets of the stress response just outlined are generally costly and inefficient but are essential for surviving an acute crisis. When those same facets are chronically activated, they exact a price; in effect, stress-related disease does not arise because the army runs out of ammunition but because the rest of the economy is bankrupted by the size of the defense budget.

This principle applies to numerous organismal systems. As outlined, when running at full speed during a physical stressor, it is adaptive to divert energy to muscle. Yet if one mobilizes the same metabolic stress response chronically when worrying about the ozone layer, there is atrophy of storage tissues and fatigue, and increased risk of adult-onset diabetes or worsening of preexisting cases (see Surwit, Ross, & Feingloss, 1991). Moreover, although increasing blood pressure in order to sprint away from a predator is adaptive, doing the same repeatedly in the face of daily traffic jams places significant wear and tear on blood vessels.

The triaging of nonessential tasks also becomes damaging when prolonged. Repeated inhibition of blood flow to the stomach (part of the inhibition of digestion) increases the risk of certain types of ulcers, which are probably unrelated to the recently discovered ulcerogenic bacteria (see Yabana & Yachi, 1988). Prolonged stress also wreaks havoc with reproduction. In females, cycles become irregular or cease altogether, implantation of fertilized eggs become less likely due to thinning of the uterine lining, and there is increased risk of miscarriage. In males, prolonged stress decreases testosterone concentrations and, of even more functional significance, causes impotence or premature ejaculation (reviewed in Sapolsky, 1991).

Continuing this theme, one cannot constantly defer long-term building and repair in the body without paying a price. In young organisms, chronic stress disrupts growth. At an extreme, growth can cease entirely, despite adequate food intake. Such cases have been given a number of labels, including failure to thrive, stress dwarfism, or psychogenic or psychosocial dwarfism (see Green, Campbell, & David, 1984). Remarkably, removal of the child from the stressful environment typically reinstates growth.

Finally, insofar as stress is immunosuppressive, tremendous attention has focused on the possibility that chronic stress will increase the vulnerability to infectious disease and cancer. This forms a cornerstone of the nascent discipline of psychoneuroimmunology (Ader, Felten, & Cohen, 1991). It appears as though stress will indeed increase the risk of some relatively minor infectious diseases (for example, the common cold). Far more attention has focused on possible links between chronic stress and cancer; a careful reading of the literature indicates any such links to be quite weak and inflated in many circles (reviewed in chapter 8 of Sapolsky, 1994). Finally, there are some immensely complicated relations between chronic stress and autoimmune disease that are beyond the scope of this chapter.

In summary, various physical and psychological stressors trigger the fairly stereotyped stress response, which includes secretion of the adrenal steroid hormones called *glucocorticoids*, activation of the "flight-or-fight" sympathetic nervous system (leading to the secretion of epinephrine and norepinephrine), and inhibition of secretion of hormones related to growth and sex. Collectively, these responses are adaptive during an acute physical crisis, such as a sprint across the savanna: Energy is mobilized from storage sites and delivered to exercising muscle, cardiovascular tone is enhanced to accelerate such nutrient delivery, and anything unessential to surviving the immediate crisis—digestion, reproduction, growth, tissue repair, immunity—is deferred until a more auspicious time. However, if these same responses are prolonged, there is increased risk of disease or worsening of preexisting disease, mainly because these responses are sufficiently costly to eventually become damaging themselves. Thus, with prolonged stress, there is often worsening of metabolic diseases such as adult-onset diabetes (due to chronic mobilization of energy stores), hypertension (due to the cardiovascular effects of the stress response), certain types of ulcers (due to the inhibition of digestion), amenorrhea and impotence (due to the inhibition of reproduction), and stress dwarfism (due to the inhibition of growth), and there is sufficient suppression of immunity to increase the risk of some infectious diseases.

Although it is highly maladaptive if an organism cannot mobilize the stress response during an acute physical challenge, it can be just as deleterious if the system is activated for too long, as is often the case for the psychological stressors of humans. From a physiological standpoint, the most commonly accepted indices of such overactivation involve elevated resting levels of glucocorticoids or of the hormones of the sympathetic nervous system (epinephrine and norepinephrine).

PSYCHOLOGICAL MODULATORS OF THE STRESS RESPONSE

The two central concepts of this chapter are that (a) although most animals activate the stress response because of an acute physical challenge to physiological equilibrium or the impending threat of such a challenge, humans tend to activate the stress response for purely psychological or social reasons and that (b) chronic activation of the stress response (as humans often do for those nonphysical reasons) can increase the risk of certain diseases or can worsen certain preexisting diseases. The preceding section detailed how the adaptive features of the short-term stress response turn into maladaptive pathophysiology when chronic. In this next section, I focus on what is perhaps the most important question in this chapter: What features make psychological stressors stressful? One might initially assume that answering this question involves rather imprecise, nonquantitative psychological approaches.[3] However, some rigorous and clear-cut paradigms have emerged (reviewed in Levine, Coe, & Wiener, 1989; Weiss, 1968). It is worth reviewing them here, and I present them, at times, in a somewhat simplified, schematic form.

In one scenario, two rats would be in adjacent cages and would receive, for example, mild electric shocks through an electrified floor grid. Critically, both animals would receive the same shocks of equal intensity at precisely the same times; by all of the rules of the now-classic stress physiology, their bodies would be challenged to identical extents. The sole difference would be some psychological variable manipulated in one of the rats. The endpoint would then be a measure of the stress response (e.g., blood pressure, heart rate, glucocorticoid or epinephrine levels in the bloodstream) or a measure of a stress-related disease (e.g., the incidence of stress ulcers). This approach has provided extremely clear demonstrations of the psychological variables that modulate the stress response.

The first critical variable is whether an organism has *outlets* for the frustration caused by a physical stressor. Expose two rats to the identical shocks, and there will be less of a stress response and less risk of a stress-related disease in the one with access to a running wheel or a bar of wood to gnaw. This has been generalized to other paradigms and species, producing the general observation that a physical stressor is more pathogenic when an individual lacks outlets or sources of displacement. These studies form the scientific rationale for the stress management emphasis on outlets such as hobbies or exercise.

These studies gave some insight into another, less adaptive coping response in many humans—a rat being shocked is buffered from the stress response if it is allowed to be polydipsic or polyphagic—stress can trigger overeating or drinking. Finally, these studies showed another, even more disquieting coping response—a rat exposed to shocks has less of a stress response if it can attack another rat. The tendency of organisms to reduce stress by displacing aggression onto other individuals is at the heart of the stress-management caveat that you shouldn't avoid getting ulcers by giving them to others. It might give us some insight into the links between socioeconomic stress and increased rates of spousal or child abuse (discussed in Lenington, 1981).

The classic yoked-rat paradigm revealed a second psychological variable. Expose two rats to a pattern of electric shocks; in one cage, however, there is a warning light which, 10 s before each shock, signals that impending stressor. The rat receiving *predictive information* has less chance of a stress response or a stress-related disease. This finding, too, has generalized across paradigms and species (including humans exposed to loud noises with or without a prior warning [e.g. Brier et al., 1987]) and shows that under circumstances of certain inevitable stressors, it is protective to know how bad and long that stressor will be and when it will start. When asking a dentist whether some painful drilling is almost finished, all of us take more comfort from the answer, "I just need to drill X more times and we're done" than from hearing, "Hmm, hard to say with these things, could be a few more seconds, could be hours, I remember a patient once. . ."

Predictability protects for two reasons. First, by telling when the stressor is coming and how bad it will be, it helps shape the type of coping response mobilized. This can be detected with physiological measures, demonstrating that predictive information decreases the size of the stress response *during* the stressor. For example, an individual undergoes a surgical procedure and is given some predictive information—the first postsurgical day will involve a fair amount of pain and the second day, only some minor discomfort. Most would find that helpful in planning their coping outlets: plan to watch the four distracting action movies on video during the first day while waiting until the second day to peruse that collection of delicate haikus.

Predictive information helps in a second, perhaps even more important way. By signaling when a stressor is impending, the absence of that signal indicates when an organism can relax (termed the *safety-signal hypothesis* by Seligman, 1975). For the rat without the warning light, one might always be a half-second away from a shock. This can be detected with physiological measures, demonstrating that predictive information makes for a faster recovery of the stress response *after* the abatement of the stressor—the organism knows that it is over with until the next warning.

The relevance of predictability in explaining patterns of human stressors is obvious. The simplest demonstration is that our students hate pop quizzes. The more important arenas are considerably more complicated. As will be discussed below, predictability works only in certain circumstances.

Another psychological variable is critical. Expose two rats, once again, to the same shocks. One rat has been trained in an active avoidance task. Specifically, that rat has learned to repeatedly press a lever to decrease the likelihood of receiving shocks. Make that lever available to the rat and, irrespective of the fact that the lever is disconnected and the rat receives the same number of shocks as does its yoked neighbor, it has less of a stress response. The same physical stressor can be less pathogenic when the individual has a sense of *control*. Identical studies have been done with humans exposed to aversive noise, with or without access to a (placebo) lever. The relevance of this variable to real-life circumstances is obvious as well and underlies stress management counseling to find footholds of control in stressful circumstances. A striking example of this is seen with the person working as a secretary for a temporary agency who, when asked if it isn't stressful to be constantly thrown into a new setting and often having to deal with difficult, demanding individuals, replies, "Not at all—if it's too much of a drag, I'm out of there"—and you know that this person rarely actually walks off a job.

It should be clear that control and predictability are closely related concepts (and as will also be discussed below, an increased sense of control does not always protect against stress, either). Some investigators have conceptualized them as falling under the umbrella of *novelty*: lack of control or predictability augments the stress response, insofar as events turn out to be discrepant from expectations, increasing the demands for vigilance on an organism's part as it tries to discern and master whatever new rules are in effect (Levine et al., 1989).

The power of novelty as a stressor is shown with an extremely informative study (Goldman, Coover, & Levine, 1973). A rat is maintained on an interval-reinforcement schedule where it must lever-press to receive pellets of food. Over the course of any 10-min period, an average of 20 lever presses are needed per food pellet, with the requirement fluctuating randomly between 15 and 25 lever presses. The animal has settled into this reinforcement schedule when a change is made. Specifically, the average of 20 lever presses per food pellet is maintained, but the variability is increased, now ranging from 10 to 30 lever presses. Note that the animal is fed the exact same amount as before, but it simply has less predictability or control over outcome, and this triggers a physiological stress response. The key in this study is that this occurs in the context of food reward, rather than of aversive shocks. The prior studies showed that psychological factors could modulate the response to physical stressors. This study demonstrates that psychological factors can trigger the stress response in the absence of any physical stressor, even in a rat. One can even see evidence of an increased stress response where there was more novelty but *less* actual physical challenge. During the London blitz, there was more of an increase in ulcer rates in the suburbs, which was bombed only intermittently, than in the city center, which was bombed like clockwork each night (Stewart & Winser, 1942).

Another important psychological variable concerns whether one *perceives events as improving or worsening*. A version of this can be shown with two rats. On one day, one rat receives 50 shocks, the other 10. The next day, both receive 25. Once again, by the rules of classic stress physiology, their bodies are now being exposed to identical physical challenges and should mobilize identical stress responses. However, the individual who has been shifted from 10 to 25 is far more reactive—its life is getting worse, in contrast with its yoked conspecific. A similar finding emerged from some of my own work with male baboons in East Africa (Sapolsky, 1992). Such animals live in linear dominance hierarchies that are often quite stable and unchanging (where Number 5 in the hierarchy, for example, consistently dominates Number 6 and is consistently subordinated to Number 4). Periods of instability (where 5 still dominates 6 but barely, winning perhaps 51% of the interactions, rather than 95% of them) should be stressful because of their unpredictability. However, I observed very different glucocorticoid concentrations in baboons, depending on whether instability occurred with animals below or above them in the hierarchy. This is logical: Unstable interactions with subordinates signal that you are about to drop in the hierarchy and were associated with elevated glucocorticoid levels. In contrast, equivalent rates of unstable interactions with dominant individuals does not signal a stressor but instead a promotion—and was not associated with elevated glucocorticoid levels. Thus, it is not just the external stressor that regulates the stress response but its interpretation. One can see the same principle in humans. Imagine some corporation where the mailroom clerk, because of superb work, is given a raise from minimum wage to $50,000 a year, whereas the senior vice-president, because of lackluster work, is punished with the equivalent salary. Both have equal ability to buy items that will buffer them from allostatic challenge, yet you know who will be making angry calls about a new job from the cellular phone in the BMW.

A final psychological variable also modulates the stress response and is most readily demonstrated with primates. Place a monkey into a new, empty cage, and it will have a stress response. Place it in there and fill the room with strange monkeys, and the stress response worsens. Place it in there with a group of familiar friends, and the stress response is blunted (Levine et al., 1989). Allowing the animals to sit in contact or to groom prevents the stress response even further. This finding generalizes across paradigms and species as well. It is protective to have someone to lean on.

Why *sociality* should protect in a nonhuman primate is complex and appears to incorporate some of the variables raised previously. There is a component of modulating the novelty of the situation—the novelty of a new cage setting is decreased when it is filled with known individuals. Sociality also provides outlets for frustration, such as grooming someone. It also signals that life is improving in that, even in this novel new cage, there is at least a friend who can be relied on to groom you.

These issues contribute to one of the most important observations in behavioral medicine. When considering the mortality and morbidity rates across a wide variety of diseases, an enormous risk factor in a human is social isolation (House, Landis, & Umberson, 1988). As another example of this, following the loss of an adult child, it is socially isolated parents (i.e., those who are divorced or widowed) who are significantly at risk of death in the following year (Levav, Friedlander, Kark, & Peritz, 1988). Are these relationships simply due to some confounds? For example, a socially isolated individual won't be reminded to take daily medicine or is more likely to eat a half-cooked, nonnutritive meal out of a can. Careful work has shown these relationships to hold even after controlling for those factors (Berkman, 1983; House et al., 1988). For social primates, such as we are, isolation appears to be an aching and potent stressor.

Collectively, these studies demonstrate that for the same physical stressor, stress response and stress-related disease become more likely if the individual lacks outlets for frustration, lacks a sense of control or predictability, perceives events as worsening, and lacks social affiliation. Moreover, these psychological factors can generate a stress response even in the absence of a physical stressor. As noted, many of stress management techniques involve manipulating some of these psychological variables. The next section briefly reviews the considerable complexity in such an approach.

SOME CAVEATS IN UNDERSTANDING PSYCHOLOGICAL MODIFIERS OF THE STRESS RESPONSE

One might come away from the preceding section concluding that an optimal strategy for reducing psychological stress is to maximize a sense of predictability, control, outlets, and so on. The relationship is more subtle than that, and if these variables are manipulated incorrectly, they can actually worsen the stress response.

A first example will make sense to denizens of singles bars—social support and affiliation are helpful only insofar as they are real. A particularly powerful example of this comes from psychoimmunology: Although marriage constitutes one version of protective affiliation, a *bad* marriage is associated with immune suppression (Kiecolt-Glaser et al., 1987).

These issues are more subtle concerning the variable of predictability. Consider a circumstance in which a stressor is inevitable. When is it protective to be informed that it will occur? One important parameter is time course (see Natelson, Dubois, & Sodetz, 1977; Weiss, 1972). Giving a rat a warning signal 10 s before a shock is protective. In contrast, a warning that comes a quarter of a second before is not—there is no opportunity for the preparation prior to the stressor or the relaxation with the implied signaling of no impending stressor. Even more importantly, giving the signal half an hour before the stressor worsens the stress response. This makes considerable sense; would one find it to be stress reducing, for example, to be informed that a dozen years hence, a limb would be lost in a horrible accident?

Predictive information helps only with intermediate time lags between the signal and stressor. It is also helpful only when it signals the onset of moderately common stressors. Predictability about a rare (and remember, inevitable) stressor is of little help, in that one was not worrying about it anyway—few of us would derive comfort from being told exactly when a meteor will crash into our garage. Conversely, information about extremely common stressors is also of little help, in that one already is taking their occurrence for granted.

The previous section emphasized that predictive information helps in part because it aids the individual in planning coping strategies. As such, information will not be helpful when individuals are in no position to cope. For example, most health professionals would probably agree that it is not wise to inform an accident victim that no other members of the family survived when that individual is still barely holding on to life in intensive care. This taps into subtle ideas in stress management concerning the uses of denial, to be considered below (also see Lazarus, 1983).

The studies in the preceding section demonstrated that in some cases, a sense of control is protective, independent of whether the individual actually has any control in that circumstance. This is not always the case, however. Some of the most compassionate things we do involve minimizing someone's sense of control when true disaster has struck—no one could have stopped the car in time, the way she darted out; it wouldn't have mattered even if you had gotten him to the doctor 2 months ago. And some of the most brutal things we do is to artificially elevate a sense of control in victims to make them responsible for their victimization—what does she expect, if she's going to dress that way; of course they're going to be persecuted if they refuse to assimilate. In general, a sense of control aids in coping in the face of minor or moderate stressors, in that it biases the individual to focus on how much worse things would have been if they hadn't been in charge. In contrast, a sense of control worsens outcome when the stressor is major, because the individual is biased to focus on how much better things could have been, and how it is their fault that that is not the case; you do not want someone to feel as though they could have controlled the uncontrollable.

Thus, predictability and control help only within certain narrow parameters and can even worsen outcomes when outside those bounds. As will be seen in the coming sections, this idea is extremely applicable when considering stress response and stress-related diseases in the context of social status and personality.

INDIVIDUAL DIFFERENCES IN THE STRESS RESPONSE AND SOCIAL STATUS

What does an individual's position in society have to do with the stress response and proclivity toward stress-related disease? There is ample evidence that social status is relevant to understanding individual differences in both physical and psychological components of the stress system.

Most work in this area has been done with animals. Since the discernment of pecking orders in chickens, scientists have recognized the role of dominance hierarchies in many species. The most common and simplistic picture of such systems is of there being a fairly linear hierarchy, with high rank initially being attained through aggression and maintained thereafter through the threat of it. In this scenario, dominance carries with it numerous perks, including preferential access to contested resources and sources of social support, and the ability to displace aggression onto subordinates when frustrated. As will be seen, this is but one version of dominance systems but one that monopolized early thinking on the subject, because it is what is seen among rats and among the males of some of the more frequently-studied Old World primates.

When considering dominance systems like these, it is easy to generate some predictions as to who will have the most active stress responses and stress-related disease—subordinates. Under the most ideal ecological circumstances, these are the animals who spend the most time and effort to obtain their calories, and during times of famine, these are the first to be hungry. In many social systems, it is subordinates who are most subject to predation or to attack due to displacement aggression from higher ranking individuals in their group.

Subordination also carries considerable psychological stress. Low-ranking animals often cannot predict or control access to resources, generating psychological stress in addition to the physical costs of such limits. In addition to the physical injury that may result from random displaced aggression, there is the psychological stress of the lack of predictability. Finally, subordinates are often limited in their access to social support (for example, being groomed) or to outlets for frustration (such as displacement aggression).

A fairly consistent literature demonstrates that in stable versions of such dominance hierarchies (as seen in rats, macaque monkeys, baboons, and a large number of other species), the predictions above are borne out (reviewed in Sapolsky, 1993a, 1997). When compared to dominant individuals, subordinates (a) secrete elevated levels of glucocorticoids and overactivate the sympathetic nervous system under basal, nonstressed circumstances; (b) are more prone toward cardiovascular disease; (c) if female, have significantly higher rates of anovulatory cycles and lower estradiol levels; if male, have testicular systems that are more readily suppressed during stress; and (d) are immunosuppressed and may be more prone toward infectious diseases.

These findings, derived from studies of animals in cages, in seminatural outdoor enclosures, as well as in the wild, seem quite logical and suggest that social rank is an important determinant of the stress response and vulnerability to stress-related disease. However, there are numerous complications that must be considered before considering stress physiology and human social status.

A first important qualifier is that it is not just one's rank that is important but the sort of society in which it occurs. An example was alluded to above, with the indication that not all species have dominance systems in which high rank is achieved through aggressive success, after which dominant individuals rule a stable and linear hierarchy through bluff and intimidation and garner the perks of office. One exception to this occurs in those same species (for example, male baboons or rhesus monkeys) when the hierarchy is unstable. In the wild, this is rare, occurring after the death or transfer of some key individual; in captive populations, instability is the norm during the first months when animals are formed into a group and must establish their dyadic dominance relations. Whether in the wild or captivity, periods of instability are marked by high rates of aggression, frequent reversals of dyadic relations that change the direction of dominance, rapid formation and collapse of coalitions, and reduced rates of sociality—in other words, a time when high-ranking animals, who are at the center of the most intense competition within the shifting hierarchy, undergo particularly high rates of physical stressors over which they have little control or predictability and with fewer outlets or sources of support. At such times, it is now dominant animals, rather than the usual subordinates, who have the highest basal levels of glucocorticoids (Sapolsky, 1993b). Therefore, social dominance is associated with an optimal stress response only when dominance is associated with the psychological advantages of stability.

The theme that it is not just rank that is important but also the sort of society in which it occurs is shown in considering a very different type of dominance system. Numerous New World monkeys (such as marmosets and tamarins) and mongooses are "cooperative breeders" where social units are extended and cooperative families. Among macaques, subordination is brought about through aggression and harassment. In contrast, a subordinate marmoset female is typically a younger relative waiting her turn and helping older relatives with child care in the interim; in these species, subordination is not associated with high rates of being the target of displaced aggression. Importantly, among these animals, subordination is not associated with elevated glucocorticoid levels (Abbott et al., 2003). The rank/physiology relationship is also sensitive to what it is like to be a dominant or subordinate individual in this particular (macaque, baboon, marmoset, mongoose, etc.) group. Among rhesus monkeys and baboons, for example, the usual pattern of elevated glucocorticoid levels in subordinates is less pronounced if they happen to live in a troop with atypically high rates of reconciliative behaviors or low rates of displacement aggression by dominant males (Gust, Gordon, Hambright, & Wilson, 1993; Sapolsky, 1986). This latter case was based on my studies of male baboons in the Serengeti. Among these animals, subordinates are subject to the highest rates of displacement aggression and have the highest basal glucocorticoid concentrations. During the 1984 East African drought, these baboons, although not starving, devoted all of their day to foraging. Rates of displacement aggression declined markedly, as did the hypercortisolism of the subordinates. Thus, ironically for those low-ranking animals, an ecological stressor protected them from a greater social stressor.

As a second caveat to emerge from the more subtle animal studies, stress-related physiology is not influenced by just rank and by the society in which that rank occurs but by the personal experience of both. One example of this was discussed—times of social instability among baboon males are not particularly stressful for those rising in the hierarchy during the tumult, independent of the number of unpredictable, dominance interactions in which they participate.

As another example, among female macaques, the severity of basal hypercortisolism varies as a function of how often animals are subject to dominance or aggressive interactions and how often they are given affiliative support (Gust et al., 1993). A similar relationship was observed among female baboons between the rate of being subject to aggression and the extent of suppression of circulating white blood cell counts (Alberts, Sapolsky, & Altmann, 1992). Moreover, among young macaques placed in peer groups after separation from their mothers, the smallest decline in antibody levels occurred in animals with the highest rates of social contact (Laudenslager, Held, Boccia, Reite, & Cohen, 1990). As another example of the importance of personal experience, in groups of wolves and macaques, the highest glucocorticoid concentrations occurred in animals whose ranks were most unstable (the beta male among the wolves and recent transfer animals among the macaques; McLeod, Moger, Ryon, Gadbois, & Fentress, 1997; van Schaik, van Noordwijk, van Bragt, & Blankenstein, 1991). Another example comes from orangutans, among whom dominant males are big, muscular beasts with conspicuous secondary sexual characteristics (such as dramatic cheek flanges). In contrast, subordinate males are either slender individuals (lacking the secondary sexual characteristics) or in a transitional state between this gracile form and the more robust one. Both types of subordinate males are reproductively active, with the gracile individuals doing their mating covertly and the transitional animals more overtly challenging dominant males for access to females. Not surprising, it is the latter type of subordinate individual who has the chronically elevated stress hormone levels (Maggioncalda, 1995).

These studies show that there is not a monolithic relationship between social rank and the pathogenicity of the stress response. Instead, absolutely opposite physiological correlates of rank can occur, depending on the societal and personal context of that rank.

One can readily predict that these subtleties should apply with a vengeance to human "rank" and the stress response. Some investigators have been inspired by the fact that rank differences among animals of some species often emerge from aggressive interactions and have examined physiological differences between winners and losers of athletic events (e.g., Elias, 1981). I find these to be of limited use. Aggression is only one of many factors playing a role in establishing and maintaining dominance in animals. I suspect that we learn even less in humans by studying aggressive interactions that are rare and highly symbolic (for example, it is not common for weekend tennis matches to determine one's access to adequate calories).

Other studies have focused on more permeating systems of status in humans, such as different ranks in the military or different positions in hierarchical work places. Some investigators have considered the most salient feature of differential rank in animals to be differential access to contested resources and have drawn parallels between that and differential income in humans as a function of occupational status. Again, I question the value of this, because differences in one's place in the corporate hierarchy may influence the readiness with which one can afford to get a large-screen television but not the ability to get sufficient calories.

Others have emphasized the idea that among animals, different psychological implications are the most important thing about different ranks. These investigators have attributed some of the high rates of stress-related disease in certain occupations (e.g., air traffic controllers, middle-level management, bus drivers [e.g., Rose & Fogg,

1993]) to the psychological milieu in which there are high degrees of demand and responsibility with little autonomy. This seems quite valid to me, so long as one factors in the ability of humans to belong to multiple hierarchies simultaneously, with some being more psychologically meaningful than others; thus, a "low-ranking" individual in some workplace may be deriving most of his sense of hierarchical status from the fact that he is, nonetheless, an elder of his church. Furthermore, the human capacity for rationalization, internalization of standards, and so on, greatly confounds the impact of any ranking system.

In many ways, it seems to be that the most meaningful way that a Westernized human can be "low-ranking" is by being of low SES. One would assume this to be one of the surest ways of being chronically stressed. Low SES involves increased exposure to a variety of physical stressors, ranging from greater demands for physical labor and greater risk of injury in the workplace to, at the more depressing extremes of our unequal society, decreased access to appropriate nutrition. Moreover, low SES involves vastly increased exposure to psychological stressors—low levels of control or predictability about employment, housing, and so on; limited time and funds for protective outlets (e.g., hobbies, vacations); and decreased access to many sources of social support (reflecting the time demands of second jobs).

This predicts that low-SES individuals should have chronically elevated stress responses. To my knowledge, this has not been examined in any systematic way. However, there is literature concerning another consequence of low SES—the extraordinarily powerful link between low SES and adverse health—which could be interpreted in part as reflecting physical and psychological stressors.

A large number of studies from an array of Western nations have demonstrated that SES (as measured by income, occupation, housing, or most reliably, educational level) powerfully predicts risk of various diseases, prognoses, likelihood of successful aging, and life expectancy (e.g., Kitagawa & Huaser, 1973; Marmot, Kogevinas, & Elston, 1987). This arguably constitutes the single most consistent finding in health psychology. Not surprisingly, droves of investigators have sought to understand its bases.

The most immediate explanation is a factor quite unique from discussions of stress, physiology, and social status in animals, namely, differential access to medical care. Obviously, individuals who cannot afford regular checkups, preventive measures, or the best of care when sick will have illnesses that will be detected later and treated less effectively. However, differential access cannot be the sole, or even a major explanation for the SES gradient in health (and is, in fact, a relatively minor factor). First, there are strong SES gradients for diseases whose incidences could not be decreased by improved medical access (e.g., diabetes; Pincus & Callahan, 1995). Even more striking, the SES gradient still occurs in countries with universal health coverage and equal access to medical care (Diderichsen, 1990; Kunst & Mackenbach, 1994).

Other investigators have emphasized another relatively unique human feature— that low SES is associated with higher rates of risk factors for disease, such as smoking, alcohol abuse, or increased fat and cholesterol intake. Multivariate analyses, however, have demonstrated the persistence of robust health gradients even after controlling for these factors (Adler, Boyce, Chesney, Folkman, & Syme, 1993; Feldman, Makuc, Kleinman, & Cornoni-Huntley, 1989).

Other investigators have explored the impact of variables more related to the animal studies, namely, differential exposure to physical stressors revolving around nutrition and adequate shelter. Remarkably, SES gradients exist (albeit often to a considerably lesser extent) even after controlling for those factors. In one notable example, the health and life expectancy of elderly nuns was significantly predicted by SES differences at adolescence, despite an intervening half-century of all subjects sharing diet, health care, and living conditions (Snowdon, Ostwald, & Kane, l989).

Because of these findings, some researchers believe that a significant proportion of the SES gradient is attributable to many of the psychological factors related to stress (Adler et al., 1993; Antonovsky, 1968; Pincus & Callahan, 1995). This is reinforced by the finding that diseases that are not particularly stress-related (such as cancer, as discussed earlier) show the shallowest SES gradients, whereas those that are most stress-related (such as psychiatric disorders) show the most dramatic (Pincus, Callahan, & Burkhauser, 1987).

This section allows for one conclusion that strikes me as rather ironic. Early observations concerning dominance hierarchies in animals suggested that social subordination should be associated with overactivated stress responses and increased risk of certain stress-related diseases. Subsequent studies showed some support for this but with far more qualifiers than originally anticipated (particularly with primates), reflecting the importance of the type of society and the personal experience of both the society and rank. This stands as a testimonial to the social and psychological complexities of nonhuman primates. Similarly, the nature of SES in Western societies suggests that low SES should be associated with increased risk of certain stress-related diseases as well. This has been borne out dramatically and, most important, is consistent *despite* variations in the type of society and the personal experience of both the society and low SES. It strikes me that this is either a testimonial to humans being less complex than related species or that with the invention of societal stratification, humans have come up with a form of subordination whose impact is unprecedented in the primate world.

INDIVIDUAL DIFFERENCES IN THE STRESS RESPONSE AND PERSONALITY

An understanding of rank, the society in which it occurs, and the personal experience of both gives considerable information as to the physical and psychological stressors to which an individual is exposed. Just as important is whether an individual accurately *perceives* the stressors and sources of coping. In this regard, individual differences in temperament and personality are critical to understanding differences in the stress response in both humans and primates.

One temperamental style among primates is associated with elevated basal glucocorticoid secretion and increased risk of stress-related disease (e.g., atherosclerosis).

Among macaques, this temperamental style is seen in animals who are most behaviorally and physiologically reactive to novelty (Suomi, 1987). Among baboon males and after controlling for rank, these are individuals who are least adept at distinguishing between threatening and merely neutral interactions with rivals—for them, everything constitutes a provocation (Ray & Sapolsky, 1992; Sapolsky & Ray, 1989). This style of animal has been called a "hot reactor," a term akin to many used in the Type A literature (discussed later in this section). I think this temperamental type can also be understood in the context of predictability. These animals are particularly poor at discerning the predictive information that should discriminate stressful from non-stressful circumstances and thus must be atypically vigilant and aroused.

A second cluster of temperamental traits also predicts elevated glucocorticoid levels among these baboons after controlling for rank. These are animals who are the least adept at inserting a degree of control during stressors (for example, when overtly threatened by a rival, they are least likely to be the ones to start the inevitable fight), and are least capable of behaviorally distinguishing between good and bad outcomes of fights (Ray & Sapolsky, 1992; Sapolsky & Ray, 1989). Again, this can be framed psychologically—these animals either do not attempt coping responses that would give them control, cannot recognize their efficacy when it happens, or cannot determine whether a situation is improving or worsening.

Finally, elevated glucocorticoid levels occur in male baboons with the lowest levels of affiliative behaviors such as grooming, sitting in contact with others, or playing with infants (Ray & Sapolsky, 1992). Again, this is after controlling for social rank.

Similar themes emerge from studies linking certain human personality types with overly active stress responses. One example involves individuals with anxiety disorders, who can be viewed as attempting defensive coping responses that are overactivated. The world is perceived as filled with endless challenges that demand searches for safety. In contrast, major depressive disorder has been conceptualized as reflecting "learned helplessness," where the individual perceives the world to be full of stressful challenges but feels incapable of managing coping responses (Seligman, 1975). Both disorders can be viewed as cases of stress responses that are discrepant with the stressor. It is important that both also involve chronic overactivation of the stress response; anxiety is most closely aligned with moderately elevated sympathetic tone and depression with elevated basal levels of glucocorticoids (APA Taskforce, 1987; Gulley & Nemeroff, 1993; Lundberg & Frankenhaeuser, 1980; Sapolsky & Plotsky, 1990).

One of the more carefully studied links between personality and stress-related disease concerns Type A personality and cardiovascular disease. As originally conceptualized, Type A individuals were competitive, overachieving, time-pressured, impatient, and hostile. At present, there remains considerable debate as to whether it is the hostility or the time-pressured features of this disorder that are most critical to the cardiovascular disease risk (Matthews & Haynes, 1986; Williams, 1991). These are individuals who respond to minor social provocations as though far from minor, and frustrations are typically interpreted as being personally motivated. This is the epitome of hot reacting, and laboratory studies indicate that for the same small frustration,

Type A individuals have the largest and most prolonged sympathetic arousal. When played out over a lifetime of mobilizing stress responses during situations that others view as no big deals, a price is paid in terms of heart disease risk.

Some recent work has revealed an additional and surprising personality type associated with elevated glucocorticoid levels, namely, repressive personalities (Brown et al., 1996). By definition, these people are neither depressed nor anxious. Instead, they have an emotionally controlled style, are people who dot their *i*'s and cross their *t*'s; who strive for structured, predictable lives without surprises; and who are relatively emotionally inexpressive. Personality tests show repressive individuals to have a strong need for social conformity, a discomfort with ambiguity (for example, on questionnaires, they disproportionately endorse statements with words such as "never" or "always"), and a tendency to repress negative emotions. Studies have shown that forcing healthy volunteers to repress the expression of emotional responses to stressful stimuli exaggerates the physiological responses (Gross & Levenson, 1997), suggesting that this is what occurs chronically in repressive individuals. A lesson of depressives, anxious individuals, and Type A individuals seems to be the danger of stress responses that do not match the magnitude of the stressor. In the face of contentment and high level of functioning, repressives appear to teach the lesson that sometimes, it can be quite stressful to construct a world in which there are no stressors.

A final point is quite important for the purposes of this chapter. There is considerable individual variation in these links between personality and physiology. For example, not all anxious individuals have elevated sympathetic tone, and not all Type As are hypertensive. As the most carefully documented example, elevated glucocorticoid levels are seen in only half of depressives, and its manifestations are often quite subtle. Thus, although there are many ways to be unhappy (for example, by being hypervigilant and anxious or by having a sense of helpless depression), they do not always manifest in a reliable physiological marker. Again, one does not study these links between unhappiness and physiology in order to develop a more scientific way of proving that someone is unhappy; that is not only unnecessary but probably unlikely to work. Instead, one studies these links in order to gain insights into the mechanisms by which emotional states (including unhappiness) might have pathologic consequences.

THE INTERACTIONS BETWEEN SOCIAL STATUS AND PERSONALITY, AND SOME CONCLUDING WARNINGS

In the section on modulators of the stress response, I emphasized the importance of basic psychological factors such as control and predictability. Following that, I emphasized the narrow parameters in which they work, and the potential dangers of their simplistic applications. In the subsequent sections on the relevance of social status, temperament, and personality to the stress response, I heavily interpreted findings in those areas in the context of those basic psychological factors. It is important now to interpret those findings further in the context of the narrow parameters in which those factors work. One striking example should make this point.

In the face of a singular stressor, when does a sense of control protect against stress? As discussed, emphasizing or even inflating a sense of control helps when stressors are of only minor severity but is detrimental for catastrophic stressors.

Similarly, when is it beneficial for an individual to have an attributional style in which they *habitually* interpret themselves as being in control? The obvious extension of the dictum just noted is that it works only for the individual whose world is generally benign. When one considers the benign world of comfortably middle-class individuals, that tendency is referred to as an "internal locus of control" and is highly predictive of success, identifying the go-getters, the self-starters, the proverbial captains of their fates with their hands on the rudders. These individuals view their successes as mostly arising from the force and competence of their own efforts.

Yet the same attributional style is so maladaptive in a different setting that it has its own pathologic label. *John Henryism* refers to the folk hero who tried to outrace a steam drill tunneling through a mountain. Hammering with a six-foot-long steel drill, John Henry did the impossible, beating the machine, only to fall dead from the effort. As defined, John Henryism is a predisposition to approach stressful situations with a maximal amount of personal effort. On questionnaires, John Henrys endorse statements such as, "When things don't go the way I want them to, it just makes me work even harder" or "Once I make up my mind to do something, I stay with it until the job is completely done." With enough effort and determination, they feel as though they can regulate all outcomes, the epitome of an inner locus of control.

In a privileged, meritocratic world, these are ideal traits. Yet they define a pathology when occurring in poor people with limited opportunities, where prejudice reigns. In such a setting, an inner locus of control, where one habitually decides that those insurmountable odds could have been surmounted if only you had worked even harder, is maladaptive; John Henryism is highly predictive of hypertension and cardiovascular disease when it appears among working-class African-Americans but not particularly among working-class whites or middle-class African-Americans (James, 1994). Low SES seems to predispose toward some stress-related diseases in a tremendous range of settings. It appears that it particularly does so for the subset of individuals who, while in a low-SES position in part because of some of the more brutal aspects of society, have decided it is all just a matter of insufficient will on their parts.

The links between social status or personality and patterns of physiology or pathophysiology are not monolithic but reflect subtle, context-dependent interactions. Thus, the application of stress-management techniques cannot be monolithic either and can be disastrous if incorrect.

This is a conclusion with moral implications, as well as scientific ones, as emphasized by the late Aaron Antonovsky in his critique of the "well-being" movement (Antonovsky, 1994). Explorations of the mind-body interface as it applies to health—the realm of stress-management techniques, the well-being movement, and holistic medicine—have produced some impressive findings, suggesting that a reframing of the way in which stressors are viewed can be highly salutary. This brings to mind the old parable about the difference between heaven and hell: In heaven, as the story goes, all of eternity is spent in the intensive study of the holy books. In contrast, hell consists of all of eternity spent in the intensive study of the holy books. To some extent, our personalities and the coping techniques that we mobilize alter our perception of the world, determining whether the same events constitute heaven or hell.

However, Antonovsky (1994) noted that it is a moral failure to consider these mind-body relations outside their larger societal context, and much of the ability to finesse hells into heavens concern the minor stressors afflicting the relatively well-off in society. But what if one blithely counsels the same optimistic conclusion to those whose stressors are enormous? What of well-being movement gurus such as the Yale surgeon Bernie Siegel who, writing about terminal disease, opines, "There are no incurable diseases, only incurable people"? (Siegel, 1986, p. 99). What of the clinician who applies the standard middle-class approaches of psychotherapy in working with the homeless? This not only denies the pains of the individual suffering but props up the worst of the status quo. When the individual has the perceptual potential to turn all hells into heavens, there is no imperative to change the world, and one need only rouse oneself from eating peeled grapes while reclining on a sedan chair to point out to victims whose fault it is if they are unhappy. In studying the physiology of how we respond to unhappiness, we have learned many means for modulating the hellishness of numerous types of psychological stressors that may fill many of our everyday lives. But when faced with the truly brutal stressors that life brings so disproportionately to some, it is both bad science and morally unacceptable to preach as an outsider about the techniques for transforming hells into heavens. There is probably little that an outsider can do for people in such cruel circumstances other than to validate the tragedy of their situations and to aid them in their means of denial.

EPILOGUE, 2005

As noted, the chapter above is reproduced from a 1999 book[1] and represents work published up until circa 1997–1998. This epilogue updates the progress on a few key topics in the years since then.

The Basic Conceptualization of the Stress Response and Stress-Related Disease

Since the writing of this chapter, there has been increasing interest in the allostasis concept. Currently, it seems built on three broad ideas: (a) Unlike homeostasis, which is about the body's attempt to reach *the* ideal set point for any of a number of physiological measures, allostasis recognizes that the ideal set point fluctuates in differing circumstances; (b) homeostasis is about reattaining a physiological set point through some local regulation, and allostasis is about set points being reestablished through far-flung physiological modifications, including changes in behavior; (c) homeostasis is about responding to perturbations to set points, and allostasis includes the idea of activating in *anticipation* of perturbations (Schulkin, 2003). The relevance of allostasis to stress physiology is obvious.

The allostasis concept also includes the idea of "allostatic load." This can be thought of as the wear and tear on the body by the cumulative efforts to reestablish set points. Broadly, cumulative load is increased by the frequency of these efforts and their cost (with more far-flung regulatory responses costing more than local ones). In recent years, this appealing but fairly undefined concept has been greatly strengthened by some studies that are data-based, rather than theoretical. The best example asked the question: Even if no single physiological measure in a body is in the abnormal range, is it deleterious to health to have an array of measures that approach the abnormal range? Measuring a variety of somewhat unrelated metabolic, cardiovascular, and stress-related endpoints in a healthy elderly population of humans, the authors showed that the collective degree of skew in these measures (i.e., a surrogate measure of collective allostatic load) was an excellent predictor of risk of an array of diseases and of mortality (Seeman, McEwen, Rowe, & Singer, 2001).

The Physiology and Pathophysiology of the Stress Response

Naturally, this field has progressed with the identification of new hormones, neurotransmitters, and physiological pathways that are sensitive to stress. Some of the most interesting advances concern the immune system and stress. As described in the chapter, stress inhibits immunity, with severe and prolonged stress causing significant immune suppression. As assay techniques have become more sensitive, it has become clear that during the first hour or so of the stress response, the immune system is actually stimulated. This phase occurs before elevated glucocorticoid levels have their effects and is heavily due to the actions of other, faster components of the stress response. This has had three implications: (a) A failure to stimulate the immune system early on in the stress response can be deleterious; (b) the inhibition of immunity by glucocorticoids represents a recovery from the immune stress response (i.e., returning to baseline), and the significant immune suppression that comes with chronic stress represents an overshoot of this recovery phase; and (c) if glucocorticoids fail to have their delayed inhibitory effects during stress, the immune system not only remains activated but may become overly activated; it is now recognized that a variety of autoimmune and inflammatory diseases (i.e., cases of immune overactivation) involve insufficient glucocorticoid secretion during stress (reviewed in Sapolsky, Romero, & Munck, 2000).

Another advance concerns metabolic syndrome. Traditionally, heart disease and metabolic disorders such as diabetes were viewed as very different arenas of medicine, with measures such as cholesterol, blood pressure, and inflammatory markers relevant to the cardiovascular realm and blood glucose and insulin levels relevant to metabolic diseases. Framed within the context of stress, although both areas of disease are stress-related, they are nonetheless very different domains of pathophysiology. Metabolic syndrome is the increasingly common intersection of both classes of risk factors and reflects the fact that damage in one realm increases the risk of damage in the other. The syndrome has received considerable attention in recent years because of the increasing incidence of people suffering from both cardiovascular disease and adult-onset diabetes, the incidence of which is rising at epidemic rates (Zimmel, Alberti, & Shaw, 2001).

Another area is notable because of the *lack* of changes that have occurred in these years; this concerns the links between stress and cancer. First, there remains next to no evidence that stress increases the risk of cancer onset. Second, a number of studies have shown that stress-reducing psychosocial interventions extend cancer survival time; however, there is little reason to believe that this is due to stress directly changing the biology of cancer progression. Instead, the stress reduction probably increases patient compliance with difficult and painful treatment regimes. Finally, there are an equal number of well-done studies showing that psychosocial interventions do not increase cancer survival time (e.g., Goodwin et al., 2001). Despite evidence such as this, it remains a common perception that cancer is a stress-related disease; a recent study of breast cancer patients shows that "stress" is, by a wide margin, the most common attribution that patients make in explaining the causes of their cancer (Stewart et al., 2001).

Finally, there has been considerable and fascinating progress in understanding the links between stress and obesity. One branch concerns insights into who decreases and who increases food intake during stress; the more restrained and self-regulating someone is in his or her everyday eating habits, the more likely he or she is to overeat during periods of stress (Bjorntorp, 1997). A second area of research concerns the anatomy of fat deposition and demonstrates several things: (a) Although chronic stress promotes fat deposition, it preferentially does so in the abdominal area, rather than in the gluteal area of the buttocks, probably due to the fact that abdominal fat cells contain more glucocorticoid receptors than do gluteal fat cells; (b) of the two forms of fat deposition, abdominal fat is more predisposing toward cardiovascular and metabolic disease; and (c) individuals who secrete glucocorticoids in a prolonged manner after the end of stress are atypically prone toward depositing fat in the abdominal area (cf. Epel et al., 2000).

Psychological Elements of Stress

The chapter emphasized the extent to which our everyday stressors are psychological rather than physical in nature and how psychological stress is built around the losses of control, predictability, outlets for frustration, and social support. Yet there have always been two problems with that summary. First, stress is not synonymous with unhappiness, in that there are stressors that we enjoy; we call this *stimulation*. As but one example of this, the classic stress response is activated during sex (Woodson, Macintosh, Fleshner, & Diamond, 2003). The second problem is that often the sorts of mild stressors that we find to be most pleasurably stimulating are ones that involve a certain degree of loss of control and of predictability (e.g., a scary movie or a roller coaster ride). Work in the last few years has helped to clarify this confusion.

Much of the progress has come with an understanding of the role of dopamine in the brain. Dopamine is the primary neurotransmitter in a pathway beginning in a brain region called the *ventral tegmentum*, progressing on to the nucleus accumbens, a projection often referred to as the "pleasure pathway." This appellation arises from two facts. A wide range of species will carry out extraordinarily demanding tasks in order to be stimulated in this pathway, and euphoriant drugs such as cocaine release dopamine in this pathway. Recent work has shown that dopamine is not so much *the* neurotransmitter of pleasure but instead mediates the *anticipation* of pleasure and the motivation derived from that. For example, consider a primate who has learned that a bell signals the start of a session in which pressing a lever 10 times results in access to a desirable food item 10 seconds later. Although dopamine is released by neurons in this pathway in response to the food reward, it is released to a much greater extent in response to the bell (Schultz, Tremblay, & Hollerman, 2000), and that first dopamine rise fuels the performance of the behavior (i.e., the lever pressing) needed to obtain the reward (Phillips, Stuber, Heien, Wightman, & Carelli, 2003). Remarkably, if an element of unpredictability is introduced into this paradigm (i.e., if lever pressing produces a food reward only 50% of the time), there is an even greater release of dopamine, with a strong peak during the interval between the lever pressing and the point where the food is or is not delivered (Fiorillo, Tobler, & Schultz, 2003). This is, in effect, a neurochemical explanation for why intermittent reinforcement is so addictive. When combining studies such as this with the extensive literature on psychological stress, what this teaches is that in a setting in which there is perceived to be a good chance that an outcome is going to be bad, lack of control and predictability is highly aversive and stressful. In contrast, in a situation where there is perceived to be a good chance that an outcome is going to be good, lack of control and predictability adds to the anticipatory pleasure.

Recent work has also revealed the interactions between stress and the dopamine pathway. Strikingly, acute exposure to moderate stress or to moderately elevated levels of glucocorticoids causes release of dopamine in this pathway, and rats will even lever press in order to be infused with the levels of glucocorticoids that maximize dopamine release (Piazza & Le Moal, 1998; Pont-Rouge, Deroche, Le Moal, & Piazza, 1998). This is the essence of what stimulation is, namely, a moderate, transient challenge—it is for this reason that roller coaster rides are for 3 minutes rather than 3 hours. In addition, when stressors or glucocorticoid exposure are more severe and/or more prolonged, there is depletion of dopamine in this pathway and blunting of the responsiveness of neurons to dopamine (Ahmed, Kenny, Koob, & Markou, 2002; Gambarana et al., 1999).

Social Rank, Stress, and Health

The chapter emphasized how there is not a monolithic picture of rank and its physiological correlates. (For example, social subordination is not always associated with higher levels of physical and psychological stressors or of glucocorticoids). Instead, the social meaning of rank (and thus its physiological correlates) varies as a function of the species and population. Two recent papers reviewed this issue, looking across a variety of species (Abbott et al., 2003; Creel 2001). They made two broad points: (a) Subordinate individuals are more prone toward stress-related disease in species/populations in which subordination is a state enforced by those of higher rank and where subordinate animals are subject to high rates of displacement aggression and/or have a paucity of coping outlets; and (b) high-ranking individuals are more prone toward stress-related disease in species/populations where the hierarchy is unstable, dominance must be reestablished frequently, and/or where subordination is a phenomenon of younger siblings biding their time until rising in the hierarchy.

Finally, there have been enormous amounts of work concerning the links among stress, SES, and health. At the time that this chapter was written, it was already clear that issues of medical access and lifestyle risk- and protective-factors did not explain much about the SES/health gradient, implicating stress as a suspect mostly by default. Since then, the case for psychosocial and stress-related factors has become much stronger. This is derived from two areas of the literature: (1) Although SES is a strong predictor of numerous aspects of health, an even better measure in many ways is subjective, perceived SES (Adler, Epel, Castellazzo, & Ickovics, 2000); and (2) in the United States, the more income inequality there is, the steeper is the SES/health gradient. This is independent of absolute income and can be shown at the level of both states and cities (Lynch et al., 1998; Ross et al, 2000). In other words, poor health is not so much predicted by being poor as much as by *feeling* poor and, most basically, being *made to feel* poor by society. This strengthens even more a point emphasized in the original chapter: With the invention of societal stratification, humans have come up with a form of subordination whose impact is unprecedented in the primate world.

NOTES

1. Sapolsky, R. (1999). The physiology and pathophysiology of unhappiness. In D. Kahneman, E. Diener, & N. Schwartz (Eds.), *Well-being: Foundations of hedonic psychology*. New York: Sage. Copyright 1999 Russell Sage Foundation, 112 East 64th Street, New York, NY 10021. Reprinted with permission.

2. *Homeostasis*, as used classically, typically refers to the body's continuous small adjustments needed to keep any given physiological measure in balance. A newer, fancier term, *allostasis*, has been introduced to refer to the integrated balancing of large, interrelated physiological systems in the face of an ever-changing environment [Sterling & Eyer, 1988]. As such, *homeostasis* is a term most relevant to understanding how your body maintains, for example, the same blood pressure over any given 5-minute period. In contrast, *allostasis* is a term more relevant to understanding how all sorts of things in your body have very different set points when you are sleeping deeply in the middle of the night than when you are alert and active at noon. As such, a wildebeest with its innards ripped open and

dragging in the dust after a lion's attack might better be thought of as being allostatically challenged than homeostatically challenged, a distinction that even it would appreciate.

3. The use of the term *psychological* by most stress physiologists—who make livings making precise measurements of how the extent of insults such as blood volume loss, hypothermia, or hypoglycemia trigger the stress response—is most definitely pejorative.

ACKNOWLEDGMENTS

The author and editor thank the Russell Sage Foundation for generously permitting the reprint of material in the midst of this chapter. The material, bracketed in the current form with a prologue and epilogue that update the research, appeared originally as a complete chapter: Sapolsky, R. (1999). The physiology and pathophysiology of unhappiness. In D. Kahneman, E. Diener, & N. Schwartz (Eds.), *Well-being: Foundations of hedonic psychology*. New York: Sage. Copyright 1999 Russell Sage Foundation, 112 East 64th Street, New York, NY 10021. Reprinted with permission.

REFERENCES

Abbott, D., Keverne, E., Bercovith, F., Shively, C., Mendoza, S., Saltzman, W., et al. (2003). Are subordinates always stressed? A comparative analysis of rank differences in cortisol levels among primates. *Hormones and Behavior, 43*, 67–82.

Ader, R., Felten, D., & Cohen, N. (1991). *Psychoneuroimmunology* (2nd ed.). San Diego: Academic Press.

Adler, N., Boyce W. T., Chesney, M. A., Folkman, S., & Syme, S. L. (1993). Socioeconomic inequalities in health: No easy solution. *Journal of the American Medical Association, 269*, 3140–3145.

Adler, N., Epel, E., Castellazzo, G., & Ickovics, J. (2000). Relationship of subjective and objective social status with psychological and physiological function: Preliminary data in healthy white women. *Health Psychology, 19*, 586–592.

Ahmed, S. H., Kenny, P. J., Koob, G. F., & Markou, A. (2002). Brain reward deficit drives compulsive drug use. *Nature Neuroscience, 5*, 625–627.

Alberts, S., Sapolsky, R., & Altmann, J. (1992). Behavioral, endocrine, and immunological correlates of immigration by an aggressive male into a natural primate group. *Hormones and Behavior, 26*, 167–178.

Antonovsky, A. (1968). Social class and the major cardiovascular diseases. *Journal of Chronic Diseases, 21*, 65–106.

Antonovsky, A. (1994). A sociological critique of the "well-being" movement. *ADVANCES: Journal of Mind-Body Health, 10*, 6–44.

APA Task Force on Laboratory Tests in Psychiatry (1987). The dexamethasone suppression test: An overview of its current status in psychiatry. *American Journal of Psychiatry, 144*, 1253–1262.

Berkman, L. (1983). *Health and ways of living: Findings from the Alameda County study*. New York: Oxford University Press.

Bjorntorp, P. (1997). Behavior and metabolic disease. *International Journal of Behavioral Medicine, 3,* 285–302.

Brier, A., Albus, M., Pickar, D., Zahn, T., Wolkowitz, O., & Paul, S. (1987). Controllable and uncontrollable stress in humans: Alterations in mood and neuroendocrine and psychophysiological function. *American Journal of Psychiatry, 144,* 1419–1425.

Brown, L., Tomarken, A., Orth, D., Loosen, P., Kalin, N., & Davidson, R. (1996). Individual differences in repressive-defensiveness predict basal salivary cortisol levels. *Journal of Personality and Social Psychology, 70,* 362–371.

Creel, S. (2001). Social dominance and stress hormones. *Trends in Ecological Evolution, 16,* 491–497.

Diderichsen, F. (1990). Health and social inequities in Sweden. *Social Science and Medicine, 31,* 359–367.

Elias, M. (1981). Cortisol, testosterone, and testosterone-binding globulin responses to competitive fighting in human males. *Aggressive Behavior, 7,* 215–224.

Epel, E., McEwen, B., Seeman, T., Matthews, K., Castellazzo, G., Brownell, K., et al. (2000). Stress and body shape: Stress-induced cortisol secretion is consistently greater among women with central fat. *Psychosomatic Medicine, 62,* 623–632.

Feldman, J., Makuc, D. M., Kleinman, J. C., Cornoni-Huntley, J. (1989). National trends in education differentials in mortality. *American Journal of Epidemiology, 129,* 919–933.

Fiorillo, C., Tobler, P., & Schultz, W. (2003). Discrete coding of reward probability and uncertainty by dopamine neurons. *Science, 299,* 1898–1902.

Gambarana, C., Masi, F., Tagliamonte, A., Scherggi, S., Ghiglieri, O., & De Monti, M. (1999). A chronic stress that impairs reactivity in rats also decreases dopaminergic transmission in the nucleus accumbens: A microdialysis study. *Journal of Neurochemistry, 72,* 2039–2046.

Goldman, L., Coover, G., & Levine, S. (1973). Bidirectional effects of reinforcement shifts on pituitary-adrenal activity. *Physiology and Behavior, 10,* 209–214.

Goodwin, P., Leszcz, M., Ennis, M., Koopmans, J., Vincent, L., Guther, H., et al. (2001). The effect of group psychosocial support on survival in metastatic breast cancer. *New England Journal of Medicine, 345,* 1719–1726.

Green, W., Campbell, M., & David, R. (1984). Psychosocial dwarfism: A critical review of the evidence. *Journal of the American Academy of Child Psychiatry, 23,* 39–48.

Gross, J. J., & Levenson, R. W. (1997). Hiding feelings: The acute effects of inhibiting negative and positive emotion. *Journal of Abnormal Psychology,* 95–103.

Gulley, L., & Nemeroff, C. (1993). The neurobiological basis of mixed depression-anxiety states. *Journal of Clinical Psychiatry, 54,* 16–19.

Gust, D., Gordon, T., Hambright, K., & Wilson, M. (1993). Relationship between social factors and pituitary-adrenocortical activity in female rhesus monkeys (*Macaca mulatta*). *Hormones and Behavior, 27,* 318–331.

House, J., Landis, K., & Umberson, D. (1988). Social relationships and health. *Science, 241,* 540–545.

James, S. (1994). John Henryism and the health of African-Americans. *Culture, Medicine, and Psychiatry, 18,* 163–182.

Kiecolt-Glaser, J., Fisher, L., Ogrocki, P., Stout, J., Speicher, C., & Glaser, R. (1987). Marital quality, marital disruption, and immune function. *Psychosomatic Medicine 49,* 213–229.

Kitagawa, E., & Hauser, P. (1973). *Differential mortality in the United States: A study of socioeconomic epidemiology.* Cambridge, MA: Harvard University Press.

Kunst, A., & Mackenbach, J. (1994). Size of mortality differences associated with educational level in nine industrialized countries. *American Journal of Public Health, 84,* 932–937.

Laudenslager, M., Held, P., Boccia, M., Reite, M., & Cohen, J. (1990) Behavioral and immunological consequences of brief mother-infant separation: A species comparison. *Developmental Psychobiology 23,* 247–264.

Lazarus, R. (1983). The costs and benefits of denial. In S. Breznitz (Ed.), *The denial of stress* (pp. 1–30). New York: International Universities Press.

Leedy, C., & DuBeck, L. (1971). Physiological changes during tournament chess. *Chess Life and Review,* 708–711.

Lenington, S. (1981). Child abuse: The limits of sociobiology. *Ethology and Sociobiology, 2,* 17–29.

Levav, I., Friedlander, Y., Kark, J., & Peritz, E. (1988). An epidemiological study of mortality among bereaved parents. *New England Journal of Medicine, 319,* 457–461.

Levine, S., Coe, C., & Wiener, S. (1989). The psychoneuroendocrinology of stress—A psychobiological perspective. In S. Levine & R. Brush (Eds.), *Psychoendocrinology* (pp. 15–31). New York: Academic Press.

Lundberg, U., & Frankenhaeuser, M. (1980). Pituitary-adrenal and sympathetic-adrenal correlates of distress and effort. *Journal of Psychosomatic Research, 24,* 125–130.

Lynch, J., Kaplan, G., Pamuk, E., Cohen, R., Heck, K., Balfour, J., et al. (1998). Income inequality and mortality in metropolitan areas of the United States. *American Journal of Public Health, 88,* 1074–1080.

Maggioncalda, A. (1995). Testicular hormone and gonadotropin profiles of developing and developmentally arrested adolescent male orangutans. *American Journal of Physiological Anthropology, Supplement 20,* 140.

Marmot, M., Kogevinas, M., & Elston, M. (1987). Social/economic status and disease. *Annual Review of Public Health, 8,* 111–135.

Matthews, K., & Haynes, S. (1986). Type A behavior pattern and coronary disease risk. *American Journal of Epidemiology, 123,* 923–960.

McLeod, P., Moger, W., Ryon, J., Gadbois, S., & Fentress, J. (1996). The relation between urinary cortisol levels and social behaviour in captive timber wolves. *Canadian Journal of Zoology,* 209–216.

Munck, A., Guyre, P., & Holbrook, N. (1984). Physiological actions of glucocorticoids in stress and their relation to pharmacological actions. *Endocrine Reviews, 5,* 25–44.

Natelson, B., Dubois, A., & Sodetz, F. (1977). Effect of multiple stress procedures on monkey gastro-duodenal mucosa, serum gastrin, and hydrogen ion kinetics. *American Journal of Digestive Diseases, 22,* 888–897.

Phillips, P., Stuber, G., Heien, M., Wightman, R., & Carelli, R. (2003). Subsecond dopamine release promotes cocaine seeking. *Nature, 422,* 614–618.

Piazza, P., & Le Moal, M. (1998). The role of stress in drug self-administration. *Trends in Pharmacological Science, 19,* 67–74.

Pincus, T., & Callahan, L. (1995). What explains the association between socioeconomic status and health: Primarily medical access of mind-body variables? *Advances: Journal of Mind-Body Health, 11,* 4–36.

Pincus, T., Callahan, L., & Burkhauser, R. (1987). Most chronic diseases are reported more frequently by individuals with fewer than 12 years of formal education in the age 18–64 United States population. *Journal Chronic Diseases, 40,* 865–874.

Pont-Rouge, F., Deroche, V., Le Moal, M., & Piazza, P. (1998). Individual differences in stress-induced dopamine release in the nucleus accumbens are influenced by corticosterone. *European Journal of Neuroscience, 10,* 3903–3907.

Ray, J., & Sapolsky, R. (1992). Styles of male social behavior and their endocrine correlates among high-ranking baboons. *American Journal of Primatology, 28,* 231–250.

Rose, R., & Fogg, L. (1993). Definition of a responder: Analysis of behavior, cardiovascular, and endocrine response to varied workload in air traffic controllers. *Psychosomatic Medicine, 55,* 325–338.

Ross, N. A., Wolfson, M. C., Dunn, J. R., Berthelot, J. M., Kaplan, G. A., & Lynch, J. W. (2000). Relation between income inequality and mortality in Canada and in the United States: Cross sectional assessment using census data and vital statistics. *British Medical Journal, 320,* 898–902.

Sapolsky, R. (1986). Endocrine and behavioral correlates of drought in the wild baboon. *American Journal of Primatology, 11,* 217–227.

Sapolsky, R. (1991). Testicular function, social rank, and personality among wild baboons. *Psychoneuroendocrinology, 16,* 281–293.

Sapolsky, R. (1992). Cortisol concentrations and the social significance of rank instability among wild baboons. *Psychoneuroendocrinology, 17,* 701–709.

Sapolsky, R. (1993a). Endocrinology alfresco: Psychoendocrine studies of wild baboons. *Recent Progress in Hormone Research, 48,* 437–468.

Sapolsky, R. (1993b). The physiology of dominance in stable versus unstable social hierarchies. In W. Mason & S. Mendoza (Eds.), *Primate social conflict* (pp. 171–204). New York: SUNY Press.

Sapolsky, R. (1994). *Why zebras don't get ulcers: A guide to stress, stress-related diseases, and coping.* New York: W. H. Freeman.

Sapolsky, R. (1997). The physiological and pathophysiological implications of social stress in mammals. In B. McEwen (Ed.), *Handbook of physiology: Endocrinology.* Washington, DC: American Physiological Society.

Sapolsky, R., & Plotsky, P. (1990). Hypercortisolism and its possible neural bases. *Biological Psychiatry, 27,* 937–952.

Sapolsky, R., & Ray, J. (1989). Styles of dominance and their physiological correlates among wild baboons. *American Journal of Primatology, 18,* 1–13.

Sapolsky, R., Romero, M., & Munck, A. (2000). How do glucocorticoids influence the stress-response? Integrating permissive, suppressive, stimulatory, and preparative actions. *Endocrine Reviews, 21,* 55–89.

Schulkin, J. (2003). Allostasis: A neural behavioral perspective. *Hormones and Behavior, 43,* 21–27.

Schultz, W., Tremblay, L., & Hollerman, J. (2000). Reward processing in primate orbitofrontal cortex and basal ganglia. *Cerebral Cortex, 10,* 272–284.

Seeman, T., McEwen, B., Rowe, J., & Singer, B. (2001). Allostatic load as a marker of cumulative biological risk: MacArthur studies of successful aging. *Proceedings of the National Academy of Sciences of the United States of America, 98,* 4770–4775.

Seligman, M. E. P. (1975). *Helplessness: On depression, development, and death.* New York: W. H. Freeman.

Selye, H. (1936). A syndrome produced by diverse nocuous agents. *Nature, 138,* 32.

Selye, H. (1971) *Hormones and resistance.* New York: Springer-Verlag.

Siegel, B. (1986). *Love, medicine, and miracles.* New York: Harper & Row.

Snowdon, D., Ostwald, S., & Kane, R. (1989) Education, survival, and independence in elderly Catholic sisters 1936–1988. *American Journal of Epidemiology, 120,* 999–1012.

Sterling, P., & Eyer, J. (1988). Allostasis: A new paradigm to explain arousal pathology. In S. Fisher & J. Reason (Eds.), *Handbook of life stress, cognition and health* (pp. 629–649). New York: Wiley.

Stewart, D., & Winser, D. (1942). Incidence of perforated peptic ulcer: Effect of heavy air-raids. *Lancet, 28,* 259–261.

Stewart, D. E., Cheung, A. M., Duff, S., Wong, F., McQuestion, M., Cheng, T., et al. (2001). Attributions of cause and recurrence in long-term breast cancer survivors. *Psycho-Oncology, 10,* 179–183.

Suomi, S. (1987). Genetic and maternal contributions to individual differences in rhesus monkey biobehavioral development. In N. Krasnegor, E. Blass, M. Hofer, & W. Smotherman (Eds.), *Perinatal development: A psychobiological perspective* (pp. 397–420). New York: Academic Press.

Surwit, R., Ross, S., & Feingloss, M. (1991). Stress, behavior, and glucose control in diabetes mellitus. In P. McCabe, N. Schneidermann, T. Field, & J. Skyler (Eds.), *Stress, coping and disease* (pp. 97–111). Hillsdale, NJ: Lawrence Erlbaum.

Terman, G., Shavit, Y., Lewis, J., Cannon, J., & Liebeskind, J. (1984). Intrinsic mechanisms of pain inhibition: Activation by stress. *Science, 226,* 1270–1277.

van Schaik, C. P., van Noordwijk, M. A., van Bragt, T., & Blankenstein, M. A. (1991). A pilot study of the social correlates of levels of urinary cortisol, prolactin, and testosterone in wild long-tailed macaques (*Macaca fascicularis*). *Primates, 32,* 345–356.

Weiss, J. (1968). Effects of coping response on stress. *Journal of Comprehensive Physiological Psychology, 65,* 251–260.

Weiss, J. (1972). Psychological factors in stress and disease. *Scientific American, 226,* 104–113.

Williams, R. (1991). A relook at personality types and coronary heart disease. *Progressive Cardiology, 4,* 91–97.

Woodson, J., Macintosh, D., Fleshner, M., & Diamond, D. (2003). Emotion-induced amnesia in rats: Working memory-specific impairment, corticosterone-memory correlation, and fear versus arousal effects on memory. *Learning and Memory, 10,* 326–336.

Worthington, E. L., Jr., & Scherer, M. (2004). Forgiveness is an emotion-focused coping strategy that can reduce health risks and promote health resilience: Theory, review, and hypotheses. *Psychology and Health, 19,* 385–405.

Yabana, T., & Yachi, A. (1988). Stress-induced vascular damage and ulcer. *Digestive Disease Science, 33,* 751–761.

Zimmel, P., Alberti, K., & Shaw, J. (2001). Global and societal implications of the diabetes epidemic. *Nature, 414,* 782–787.

Chapter Eighteen

Unforgiveness, Forgiveness, and Justice: Scientific Findings on Feelings and Physiology

Charlotte vanOyen Witvliet

Interpersonal hurts and offenses affect nearly everyone. Whether committed intentionally or unintentionally, between loved ones or strangers, transgressions can arouse strong and negative emotions connected to guilt and shame in transgressors, and sadness, fear, and anger in victims. These emotions can emerge as an amalgamation of hurt-filled bitterness, or unforgiveness. Transgressors are faced with the decision of whether to apologize and seek forgiveness. Even if never asked, victims are faced with the question of what to do about their unforgiveness. Some may seek to override their pain by stoking the fires of revenge; others may try to reduce their unforgiveness as they accept that bad things happen even to good people, tolerate it, minimize it, ignore it, excuse it, or forbear it. Alternatively, victims can also choose two potentially complementary options to respond to the injustice and reduce their attendant unforgiveness: They can pursue justice, and they can grant forgiveness. In this chapter, I address the peripheral physiological patterns—of facial muscles, skin conductance, and cardiovascular measures—associated with unforgiveness, forgiveness, and justice, organizing the accumulated data patterns within a framework of emotion.

VIEW OF UNFORGIVENESS, FORGIVENESS, AND JUSTICE

Interpersonal offenses often generate perceptions of injustice. Whether these offenses are betrayals, insults, or crimes, victims can experience a discrepancy between the way things are and the way they ought to turn out. Worthington (2003) has termed this an *injustice gap*, noting that it is charged with negative emotions that can coalesce as unforgiveness. Among the means of reducing the injustice gap and its associated unforgiveness are, in theory, justice outcomes that reduce the size of the remaining gap and forgiveness that can bridge the gap by juxtaposing positive emotions against negative emotions incurred by the injustice. Justice is important for holding offenders accountable for their actions and preventing further societal harm. Restorative (cf. retributive) justice approaches further attend to the rights and needs of victims as well as offenders, often through a mediation process that maximizes the potential to arrive at mutually beneficial outcomes (chapter 29 by Hill, Exline, & Cohen and chapter 30 by Armour & Umbreit). Forgiveness carries with it the implication that its target is to blame for having caused harm, involves holding the offender accountable, and may still require justice-oriented interventions for the offender. Against this backdrop—and sensitive to first ensuring the victim's emotional, physical, and spiritual safety—forgiveness involves cultivating positive prosocial responses (e.g., empathy and desiring genuine and ultimate good) toward the offender so that victims eventually edge out the hurt and bitter emotions of unforgiveness.

Because forgiveness involves so many types of shifts—affective, behavioral, cognitive, social, spiritual, and physiological—it is valuable to view forgiveness and related constructs through a lens that can least interact with aspects of these multiple dimensions. My own approach is to situate research on the psychophysiological correlates of unforgiveness, forgiveness, and justice within a broad view of emotion that emphasizes the active response elements of emotion and integrates affective, attentional, and motivational functions. This view is sympathetic to Lang's (1979, 1995) bioinformational theory, which emphasizes that verbal/cognitive, behavioral, and physiological responses are inherent to emotion. It also is consonant with Thayer and Lane's (2000) dynamic systems neurovisceral integration model that further integrates affective, attentional, motivational, and physiological functions.

Furthermore, these theories and empirical investigations of psychophysiology and emotion have emphasized the importance of two dimensions of emotion that organize verbal/cognitive and physiological expressions in response to a broad range of stimuli (Faith & Thayer, 2001). These dimensions are valence (extending from negative to positive) and arousal (ranging from deactivated to highly activated).[1] Within this two-dimensional space, a variety of emotion categories can be situated, recognizing that even within categories, shifts in valence and arousal may occur from time to time. For example, both fear and anger (and unforgiveness) might occupy a negative and activated part of the valence × arousal space, whereas pleasant relaxation and peace (and forgiveness) might be situated in a positive and calmer part of the statespace, although shifts in their precise valence and arousal qualities may vary across particular experiences within each emotion, anticipations of them, and ruminations about them.

REVIEW OF THE LITERATURE

Studies of Victims Using Their Autobiographical Offenses

Unforgiveness Versus Forgiveness: State Effects in Victims.   Based on basic research linking the valence and arousal of *emotional imagery* to patterns of facial EMG, skin conductance, and heart rate (e.g., Witvliet & Vrana, 1995), Witvliet, Ludwig, and Vander

Laan (2001) tested hypotheses about the physiological response patterns that would occur when 71 (36 men and 35 women) college students each adopted two states of unforgiveness (i.e., rumination about the transgression; nursing a grudge toward the offender) versus two states of forgiveness toward a particular real-life offender (cultivating empathy for the offender; forgiving the offender by finding a way to genuinely wish him or her well while releasing hurt and angry emotions). Witvliet et al. (2001) adapted methods used in basic research on emotion and continuous physiology. In a within-subjects design, each participant imagined each of the four types of imagery eight times (32 trials total with continuous physiology), counterbalancing condition orders. For each measure, physiological reactivity during each imagery and recovery trial was calculated by subtracting that measure's values during each trial's 4-s pre-trial baseline from the 16-s imagery trial and 8-s recovery period means.

As predicted, the unforgiving imagery evoked higher arousal and more negative valence ratings, compared with the forgiving imagery. Consistent with the high arousal ratings, unforgiving imagery was associated with higher levels of tonic eye muscle tension (orbicularis oculi [eye] EMG) during imagery and higher heart rate and skin conductance-level scores (indicating sympathetic nervous system activation) during both imagery and recovery periods. Consistent with the negative valence of unforgiving imagery (versus the positive valence of forgiving imagery), participants showed more brow muscle tension (corrugator [brow] EMG) during imagery and recovery periods. Although blood pressure has not been specifically measured in reference to valence and arousal, heightened blood pressure has been linked to state and trait anger, which may be characterized as aroused and negatively valent. Witvliet et al. (2001) found that systolic blood pressure (SBP; during the middle of imagery), diastolic blood pressure (DBP), and mean arterial pressure (MAP) were all significantly higher during unforgiving versus forgiving imagery.

State and Trait Effects. Consistent with these findings, Lawler et al. (2003) found cardiovascular benefits of both trait and state forgiving in 108 (44 men and 64 women) college students. Higher trait forgivingness was associated with lower SBP, DBP, and MAP (when values for each measure were averaged across baseline, three time periods during the parent conflict and peer/partner conflict interviews, and two time periods during recovery from each type of interview). Lower state unforgivingness (i.e., using the Transgression-Related Inventory of Motivations [TRIM]; McCullough et al., 1998) and higher state forgiveness for both parent and peer/partner were associated with lower SBP, DBP, MAP, heart rate, and rate pressure product (SBP × heart rate, an indicator of myocardial oxygen demand and stress). Lawler et al. (2003) also assessed the interaction of trait and state forgiveness variables on physiology during the two types of conflict interviews and the subsequent recovery periods, covarying baseline values. For an interview about a salient memory of conflict with a parent or primary caregiver, high trait forgivers had the least reactivity and best recovery patterns for SBP, DBP, and MAP, rate pressure product, and forehead EMG; low trait forgivers in unforgiving states had the highest levels of cardiovascular reactivity and poorest recovery patterns. When the same participants were interviewed about a conflict with a friend or partner, the only significant effect was that women who were high in state forgiving showed smaller increases in rate pressure products than did the low state-forgiving women. In the subsequent recovery period, high trait forgivingness was associated with lower blood pressure for DBP and MAP. Lawler et al. further found that the physiological measures were unrelated to stress or hostility in their study. Path analyses indicated that trait forgivingness predicted state forgiveness; higher state forgiveness and lower hostility predicted lower stress levels, which in turn predicted lower self-reported illness.

In an interview study, Toussaint and Williams (2003) measured blood pressure in a diverse sample of 100 Midwestern community residents (25 in each cell: 2 SES [high, low] × 2 race [Black, White]; with participant sex almost evenly divided across cells). Across participants, higher levels of total forgiveness (i.e., a composite of forgiveness of others and self, plus feeling forgiven by God) were associated with lower resting DBP. High SES White participants showed lower resting DBP for total forgiveness and, specifically, forgiveness of *self*. By contrast, low SES Blacks showed lower resting DBP with higher forgiveness of *others*, and lower resting cortisol levels with higher levels of total forgiveness, forgiveness of *others*, and perceived *divine* forgiveness. When assessing blood pressure for all participants at baseline, at two points during a 10-minute interview about "a time when you were treated unfairly" and a 5-minute recovery period, Toussaint and Williams found that being forgiving toward others and feeling God's forgiveness were each associated with lower raw blood pressure values during the interview.

Intervention-Induced Forgiveness Effects in Victims.   Waltman (2003) examined how learning to forgive influenced cardiovascular variables over time in 17 middle-aged and elderly men with coronary artery disease. Waltman contrasted those in a 10-week individualized program using an Enright forgiveness intervention to patients in a treatment program addressing the impact of their disease. At pretreatment, post-treatment, and a follow-up another 10 weeks after treatment, patients engaged in anger-recall tasks, focusing on a past real-life hurt, followed by measures of myocardial perfusion, heart rate, and blood pressure. The available abstract for this dissertation reports that comparing pretreatment to 10-week follow-up, patients who completed the forgiveness intervention versus the standard program had significantly better results for anger-induced myocardial perfusion defects. Waltman surmised that it took time for the psychological adjustment involved in forgiving to become evident on this cardiac measure.

Forgiveness Motivation Effects in Victims.   Whereas the other forgiveness and physiology studies used United States samples, Huang and Enright (2000) studied Taiwanese community members. Blood pressure was assessed in 22 matched pairs of men and who tended to forgive, out of either obligation or moral love. When interviewed about a typical day, the groups did not differ in their blood pressure cuff measurements. When interviewed about a past experience with conflict, however, those with obligation-oriented versus unconditional-love forgiveness motives showed differences on 3 of 12 raw blood pressure comparisons. Obligation-oriented forgivers had higher raw SBP at the beginning of the interview and higher raw SBP and DBP 1 minute into the interview, relative to unconditional-love forgiveness motives. The groups did not differ on self-reported anger, but the obligation forgivers cast down their eyes and showed more masking smiles, which the authors interpreted as signs of hidden anger.

Trait Unforgiveness, Forgiveness Toward Others, and Resting Physiology. In an exploratory study, Brenneis (2001) assessed correlations between single raw SBP and DBP blood pressure cuff recordings and their revenge, avoidance, and generally positive statement (i.e., TRIM, McCullough et al., 1998) scores for 175 male clergy recovering from substance dependence or compulsive behavior disorders. Unexpectedly, higher avoidance scores and lower positive statements scores were significantly associated with lower SBP and DBP blood pressures. Perhaps the clergy with more "favorable" scores forgave from obligation rather than genuine moral love (see Huang & Enright, 2000). The results may also be due to other person variables that were not measured (e.g., substance abuse and compulsive behaviors associated with blood pressure), environmental variables (e.g., the context of measurement in the continuing care program), or person X environment variables (e.g., perhaps those who felt obligated to forgive or to present themselves favorably were also more anxious or angry in the continuing care program, thereby increasing their blood pressure). Alternatively, these results may be spurious, reflecting high levels of error variation in the single baseline blood pressure measurements.

In another exploratory investigation, Seybold, Hill, Neumann, and Chi (2001) assessed 68 (12 women, 46 men) Veterans Administration Medical Center and university participants. They correlated Mauger et al.'s (1992) scales of difficulty forgiving oneself, others, and a combined score with a single measure of corrugator EMG and BP obtained at 30 minutes into a period of rest.[2] Given that for each physiological measure, only one data point was obtained (similar to Brenneis' methods), and only at baseline rest, it is not surprising that no statistically significant relationships were found.[3]

Studies of Victims Using Scenario-Based Offenses

The previously discussed research on victims focused on autobiographical offenses, often measuring physiological responses during emotional imagery or interviews about them. Another method is to assess physiology during imagery about offenses described in scripted scenarios. This approach enables us to investigate justice-related outcomes that for procedural and/or ethical reasons we cannot investigate in vivo. The use of standardized scripts of scenarios also improves internal validity by standardizing—to the extent that it is possible—the content of participants' imagery. The benefits of improved internal validity are offset, however, by costs to external validity (e.g., the standard images may not be similar to other real-life offenses or to the experiences of some participants). The following justice-related studies used scenario-based imagery (much like a substantial portion of basic research on emotion and psychophysiology; see Witvliet & Vrana, 1995). The imagery paradigm parallels that used by Witvliet et al. (2001).

Granting Forgiveness in Response to an Apology and Restitution. Examining interpersonal forgiveness, empathy, and unforgiveness as dependent variables, Witvliet, Worthington, and Wade (2002) conducted a within-subjects psychophysiology study of college students ($N = 61$; 29 women, 32 men). They imagined four different outcomes to a scenario in which their residence was burglarized: The offender later apologized, made restitution, both, or neither (2 Apology × 2 Restitution design). Both a strong apology and restitution reliably reduced unforgiveness and increased empathy and forgiveness. Each also had emotional benefits, including reduced arousal, more positively valent emotion, and reduced corrugator EMG reactivity. The apology alone reliably ameliorated orbicularis oculi EMG and heart rate reactivity—consistent with lower emotional arousal reports—and improved rate pressure product reactivity and recovery patterns associated with lower stress.

Granting Forgiveness in Response to No Justice, Punitive Justice, and Restorative Justice Outcomes. Using the same burglary scenario, Witvliet, Root, Sato, and Ludwig (2003) conducted another within-subjects imagery study ($N = 56$; 29 women, 27 men college students) crossing three justice outcomes (no justice, punitive justice, restorative justice) with 2 forgiveness responses (granted, not). Echoing data patterns for an autobiographical offense (Witvliet et al., 2001), imagery of granting (vs. not granting) forgiveness to a fictitious burglar reduced arousal and prompted more positively valent emotion ratings. Consistent with lower arousal levels, orbicularis oculi EMG was lower during forgiveness imagery (as long as the no-justice outcome occurred), and heart rate scores were lower both during imagery and recovery periods. Consistent with its more positive valence, corrugator brow tension levels were lower during forgiveness imagery.

The general pattern of justice effects was that across no justice to punitive justice to restorative justice; unforgiving motivations and anger systematically decreased; and empathy, forgiveness, and positive emotions increased. Furthermore, the reported benefits of the restorative justice condition were similar to those associated with forgiveness imagery. The physiology results indicated two significant justice effects that emerged when forgiveness was not imagined. Skin conductance-level scores were lower—suggesting less sympathetic nervous system activation—during imagery of restorative justice, compared with punitive justice. Rate pressure products were also lower—suggesting lower stress levels—for punitive justice versus no-justice imagery and recovery periods.

Studies of Transgressors Using Their Autobiographical Offenses

As a complement to victim research, Witvliet, Ludwig, and Bauer (2002) conducted a within-subjects psychophysiology imagery study of 40 (20 women, 20 men) college students who reflected on a particular transgression they previously committed. The study compared the effects of ruminating about one's transgression with seeking forgiveness, then compared the effects of three possible responses they could receive from their real-life victims: begrudging, forgiving, or reconciling.

Compared with ruminations about one's transgression or an unforgiving response from the victim, imagery of forgiveness-seeking and merciful responses from victims (forgiveness and reconciliation) prompted improvements in basic emotions (e.g., sadness, anger), moral emotions (e.g., guilt, shame, gratitude, hope), and greater perceived interpersonal forgiveness. Imagery of forgiveness-seeking and of victims' merciful responses prompted less furrowing of the brow muscle (corrugator EMG) associated with negative emotion. Imagery of merciful responses from one's victim also increased smiling activity (zygomatic EMG), consistent with the positive and interpersonal nature of the imagery. Autonomic nervous system measures were largely unaffected by imagery, although skin conductance data suggested greater sympathetic nervous system engagement when victims reconciled with transgressors. When considered in combination with the studies of forgiveness in victims, these data suggest that when it comes to physiological patterns and forgiveness, *it is even better to give than to receive* forgiveness.

SUMMING IT UP: WHAT DOES THE EXTANT EVIDENCE TELL US?

Schwartz et al. (2003) have proposed that lab studies of cardiovascular reactivity often do not generalize well to real life unless they employ tasks that mirror daily life (e.g., recalling, retelling, imagining), aggregate repeated measures across tasks, and measure physiology before, during, and after the conditions of interest. Of the studies reviewed here, those with designs closest to Schwartz et al.'s (2003) ideals show self-report, cardiovascular reactivity, and facial EMG patterns that reliably distinguish unforgiving responses toward others (as a state or trait) as generating more negative and aroused affect and greater reactivity and prolonged activation than do forgiving responses toward others. Nevertheless, it is important to keep in mind that *sustained* elevations in blood pressure predict end-organ damage. The impact of the brief blood pressure peaks measured in the forgiveness studies is unclear (see Schwartz et al., 2003). Hence, the extant data speak primarily to immediate short-term patterns.[4] As we interpret the autonomic and cardiovascular effects, we must keep in mind that they may reflect not only heightened sympathetic nervous system arousal but also impaired parasympathetic response.

NEW RESEARCH DIRECTIONS

Linking Studies of Forgiveness and Physiology with a Theory to Guide Future Investigations: A Dynamic Systems Model of Neurovisceral Integration

Thayer and Lane (2000) have proposed a model of neurovisceral integration that ties together the systems involved in attention, emotion, and motivation—systems that in my view are involved in the multidimensional facets of unforgiveness and forgiveness. In the neurovisceral integration model, a variety of physiological systems underlie and integrate attention, motivation, and emotion, which from a dynamic systems perspective involve feedback and feed-forward circuits that enable self-regulation and efficient functioning. One of the most important features of this model is that it highlights the importance of inhibition. Inhibitory processes are negative feedback circuits that enable one to interrupt behavior and reallocate attention and responses to another task. In our case, inhibition would permit a victim to let go of rumination or grudge-holding to cultivate an empathic and forgiving response.

As Thayer and Lane (2000) detail, when these inhibitory processes fail or when negative feedback mechanisms are ineffective, the resulting *disinhibition* leads to positive feedback loops that perpetuate behaviors in a feed-forward fashion (e.g., when people persist in ruminating about a past injustice or about getting revenge). When emotion is disordered, such as in anxiety disorders (with the most evidence accrued for generalized anxiety disorder), people have a distorted emotional system that prevents them from shifting to process information and generate responses that would be more appropriate or beneficial. This state of being emotionally "stuck" or "inflexible" reflects not only difficulty in shifting to a more appropriate response but also—and more likely—*being unable to inhibit inappropriate responses* (Thayer & Lane, 2000).

This may well correspond to what happens in unforgiveness (see Witvliet et al., 2001; Worthington & Scherer, 2004), because people seem unable to shift their attention to information that could promote empathy or forgiveness. Instead, they seem drawn like magnets to ruminate about past hurts, embellish these narratives with bitter adjectives and adverbs that stir up contempt, exhibit avoidance and revenge motivations, cogitate about the negative features of the offender and offense, and even rehearse a repertoire of grudge and revenge plots. Such processes may both reflect and perpetuate feed-forward circuits subserved by attentional, motivational, physiological, and behavioral subsystems of emotion. Thayer and Lane (2000) further propose that this kind of inefficiency in affective information processing results in affective dysregulation. This can ultimately lead to such problems as a hostile personality, anxiety and depressive disorders, hypertension, and coronary heart disease.

Self-regulation is critical to Thayer and Lane's (2000) model and to an understanding of forgiveness and physiology. A successful shift from unforgiveness to forgiveness requires flexibility in attentional, affective, and motivational processes. Currently, the strongest indicator of self-regulation in attention and affect is cardiac vagal tone (Porges, 1992), often assessed with heart rate variability (HRV). Spectral analysis is a noninvasive method used to transform HRV mathematically in order to determine relative sympathetic and parasympathetic activity (see McCraty, Atkinson, Tiller, Rein, & Watkins, 1995). As a general example, two people may have the same mean heart rate, but one will show less variation around the mean, indicative of lower heart rate variability, lower vagal tone, and poorer self-regulation. Heart rate variability is a quantifiable indicator of self-regulation, reflecting neural feedback mechanisms involved in the integration between the central and autonomic nervous systems (Thayer & Lane, 2000).

FUTURE DIRECTIONS FOR RESEARCH: RESEARCH AND CLINICAL ADVANCES SHOULD BE LINKED TO THEORY

For psychophysiological research and clinical applications of forgiveness and justice to advance, we will need to study additional physiological measures, integrate central and peripheral nervous system measures with each other and with psychological variables, use rigorous designs that are ecologically valid, and evaluate long-term effects—all with a view to advance not only basic research but also clinical applications.

As Thayer and Lane's (2000) neurovisceral integration model suggests, HRV and its related measures (e.g., respiratory sinus arrhythmia) and methods will be important complements to measures of heart rate because they point to the important role of the parasympathetic nervous system, inhibitory processes, and self-regulation. Whereas most research has assessed physiological measures as dependent variables, advances are even more likely to occur if we additionally consider them as *independent* individual difference variables that may exert main effects and also interact with environmental variables. Considering HRV as an individual difference variable, people with predispositions to have poor vagal control will—according to Thayer and Lane's (2000) model—have poorer inhibitory processes and self-regulation.

How might such individual differences in self-regulation interact with values-oriented, spiritual, and religious factors? Might having poor vagal control make it more difficult to grant forgiveness, even for people of faith who value this virtue? Do people with better vagal control find it easier to embody virtues that hinge on self-regulation? Might people devoted to embodying virtue as a way of life ultimately be able to shift their sympathovagal balance in favor of vagal control? Self-regulation appears to be at the heart of a range of virtues and values, including those in Peterson and Seligman's (2004) classification of human strengths and virtues. In addition to forgiveness, for example, courage and temperance seem to hinge on affective, attentional, and motivational modulation as people engage positive responses while steering away from or overriding negative ones. With advances in psychophysiological assessment, more effective applied interventions can be designed, perhaps incorporating relaxation and belief-sensitive meditation approaches in order to improve HRV as an adjunct to various forgiveness intervention models.

We will be most likely to make substantial advances in the field if we employ multimethod designs that integrate genetic, central and peripheral nervous system, neurohormonal, and behavioral measures. In line with Schwartz et al.'s (2003) observations, cardiovascular (and other mental and physical health) responses to stressors ought to be studied in interaction with stress exposures and genetic susceptibilities. For example, chronic or repeated injustices (stressors) are likely to be more strongly associated with the development of cardiovascular disease and mortality. Perhaps the unforgiving personality will show similar patterns because, in effect, such persons tend to interpret even minor slights as major and ruminate about them, thereby generating repeated stressors. This relates to McCullough and Hoyt's (2002) theorizing that neuroticism may involve heightened perceptions of behaviors as offenses and to their data linking neuroticism with unforgiving revenge and avoidance motivations. In emotion and personality research, Yik and Russell (2001) found that neuroticism was strongly associated with negative valence, regardless of arousal level. Agreeableness (inversely related to unforgiving motivations) was associated with positive valence, slightly activated/aroused. Other research links vengeful imagery with negatively valent and aroused emotion reports, and more stressful physiological reactivity and recovery patterns (see Witvliet et al., 2001; Witvliet et al., 2003).

Finally, research is needed to ascertain the relationship between laboratory findings and real-life experiences. Experimental conditions that closely resemble real-life experiences will have the most ecological validity and stronger associations to applied costs and benefits. Perhaps for these reasons, forgiveness and physiology studies have most often used imagery and interview paradigms. Further advances in research may occur with ambulatory monitoring studies that provide a better indication of the role of anticipation, exposure, and remembering/ruminating in the psychophysiological reactivity, and recovery patterns associated with transgressions and contact with transgressors/victims. Additionally, physiological investigations will need to employ longitudinal designs and "hard" health measures.

RELEVANCE FOR CLINICAL AND APPLIED INTERVENTIONS

Unforgiveness and forgiveness involve emotional processes that intersect with a range of clinical issues. Unforgiveness includes a negative emotion complex that overlaps to some extent with rumination and hostility. Psychophysiology research has shown that negative emotion has longer lasting effects on heart rate than does positive emotion (Brosschot & Thayer, 2003). Also, rumination associated with negative emotion may prolong blood pressure activation (Glynn, Christenfeld, & Gerin, 2002). Additionally, states of rumination in normals and persons with generalized anxiety disorder (vs. controls) show impaired parasympathetically mediated HRV; treatments that reduced such worry also improved HRV (see Thayer & Lane, 2000; Thayer, Friedman, & Borkovec, 1996). Both rumination (Kubzansky et al., 1997) and hostility have been associated with coronary heart disease risk (Miller, Smith, Turner, Guijarro, & Hallet,

1996) and lower levels of HRV (Thayer & Lane, 2000), possibly due to inadequate parasympathetic antagonism to sympathetic activity. Further punctuating this view is evidence that sympathetic nervous system activity was more dominant when people recalled life events that continued to arouse anger and/or frustration, whereas beneficial HRV changes occurred when participants focused on feeling sincere appreciation or similarly positive emotions toward someone (McCraty et al., 1995). These data suggest that to the degree that forgiveness can increase such positive emotions, the parasympathetic nervous system may exert better control. In addition, to the extent that forgiveness can reduce or eclipse anger and rumination, sympathetic nervous system activation may be mitigated. These hypotheses warrant testing in light of their promise for interventions.

Clinically, it is also important to consider forgiveness in relation to the various behavioral strategies people use to cope with the stress of unforgiveness. Some coping strategies will likely exacerbate mental and physical health problems, some strategies will mitigate against them, and some will introduce positive effects. People who suppress, binge, smoke, misuse alcohol and other substances, aggress, withdraw, and ruminate to manage unforgiveness will engage in behaviors with known links to adverse health outcomes. Such behaviors may interact with genetic factors, such that some people will increase the likelihood of negative effects on their health (see Schwartz et al., 2003). By contrast, research has demonstrated benefits of several factors that are part of a multidimensional forgiveness response, including reappraising a difficult situation rather than suppressing one's negative emotions (see Gross & John, 2003), engaging social support (see Christenfeld & Gerin, 2000), and cultivating positive emotions (Fredrickson, 1998). For example, McCraty et al. (1995) theorized that the increased parasympathetic mediation associated with positive emotion may assist hypertension treatment and reduce the probability of sudden death in persons with congestive heart failure.

In terms of assessment, psychophysiology may prove useful both to determine individual differences in the capacity for self-regulation and to provide useful outcome measures in clinical trials of forgiveness interventions. Physiological measures can supplement self-reports, other-reports, and behavioral observations. In individual therapy, psychophysiological feedback could be used to inform clients of the physiological changes that accompany their choice to focus on empathy and forgiveness versus transgression rumination or grudge holding. If justice-oriented interventions are developed for clinical use—such as family therapy interventions in which a wayward spouse is directed to seek forgiveness on bended knee (Madanes, 1990)—psychophysiological assessments could also be incorporated for both transgressor and victim.

Of the topics in this chapter, the study of forgiveness in connection to justice is the most nascent, yet it may be among the most significant for victims. When faced with a hurtful offense, the victim generally experiences unforgiveness, which can be reduced in a number of ways—seeking justice and forgiving among them. These two options are not antithetical to one another, although cognitive, emotional, and situational constraints on the victim may necessitate devoting one's energy to pursuing them sequentially rather than concurrently. So far, the available data suggest that justice outcomes can promote forgiveness, with restorative justice enhancing forgiveness more than punitive justice, and punitive more than no-justice outcomes (Witvliet et al., 2003). Questions remain as to whether granting forgiveness affects one's motives to pursue justice, for whom this may hold true, and under what conditions.

PERSONAL THEORETICAL PERSPECTIVES ON THE FIELD

Our current understanding of the psychophysiology of forgiveness and unforgiveness is still in its infancy. The data accrued so far, however, carry more weight than they would in isolation because we can view them through an emotional lens that considers verbal/cognitive, behavioral, and physiological responding as inherent to emotional expression (see Lang's bioinformational theory) and views the systems involved in affect regulation as integrating attentional, motivational, and physiological subsystems (Thayer & Lane's, 2000 neurovisceral integration model). This view highlights connections between findings from the forgiveness literature and the broader literature on emotion and psychophysiology. The data on unforgiveness can also be connected to specific literature on rumination, anger, and hostility, providing further insights that can guide the formation of our hypotheses, methodologies, theoretical interpretations, and applications.

CONCLUSIONS

People have a propensity to offend and be offended. Unforgiveness naturally bubbles up in the wake of hurtful offenses. Both forgiveness and justice may be beneficial in reducing victims' unforgiveness, which is associated with prolonged physiological activation, which in turn is theorized to have more cardiovascular health implications than short-term stress reactivity (Brosschot & Thayer, 2003). Forgiveness research suggests it also promotes positive and prosocial emotions for victims and offenders, calming physiological indicators of negative and aroused emotion. To the degree that forgiveness can calm emotion and make it more positive, the parasympathetic nervous system may exert better control (see McCraty et al., 1995). To the extent that forgiveness may eclipse or reduce anger, sympathetic nervous system activation may be mitigated (McCraty et al., 1995). The net effect may be one that enhances health-promoting effects and buffers against health-eroding effects (see also Witvliet et al., 2001). Justice research suggests that some restorative approaches may be more psychophysiologically beneficial than punitive justice, even promoting forgiveness in victims. Research in this area is in its infancy, and the time is ripe for advances in this area fertile with promise to offer a healing balm.

NOTES

1. Much of the psychophysiology of emotion literature has emphasized valence and arousal. Yik and Russell (2001) assessed the valence and arousal dimensions, as well as a rotation of them: positive activation (extending from high arousal positive to low arousal negative) and negative activation (extending from high arousal negative to low arousal positive). They found that neither set of dimensions was more "basic" than the other.

2. Brenneis (2001) also measured total cholesterol, high-density lipoprotein, low-density lipoprotein, and blood glucose levels, finding no significant relationships with the TRIM inventory by Mc-Cullough, Rachal, Sandage, Worthington, Brown, and Hight (1998).

3. Seybold et al. (2001) also assessed blood and plasma assays. Lower forgiveness of others and total forgiveness (Mauger et al., 1992) were associated with higher hematocrit scores, higher total white blood cell counts, and lower TxPA levels. Lower forgiveness of others and self were correlated with higher T-helper/T-cytotoxic cell ratios.

4. Waltman's (2003) study provides the first long-term evidence of health impact. Waltman's study tested a complex 20-step intervention. Although intervention research is important, the complexity of interventions can possibly obscure the effects of forgiveness by confounding them with demand characteristics of the treatment, differential effects of the components of the intervention, and effects of leaders' and participants' personalities. Furthermore, Waltman used only a 10-week follow-up. Of note, Toussaint and Williams (2001) found that differences in health outcomes with respect to forgiveness emerged only at age 65 and older.

REFERENCES

Brenneis, M. J. (2001). The relationship between forgiveness and physical health indicators in recovering members of the clergy. *Journal of Ministry in Addiction and Recovery, 7,* 43–59.

Brosschot, J. F., & Thayer, J. F. (2003). Heart rate response is longer after negative emotions than after positive emotions. *International Journal of Psychophysiology, 50,* 181–187.

Christenfeld, N., & Gerin, W. (2000). Social support and cardiovascular reactivity. *Biomedicine and Pharmacotherapy, 54,* 251–257.

Faith, M., & Thayer, J. F. (2001). A dynamical systems interpretation of a dimensional model of emotion. *Scandinavian Journal of Psychology, 42,* 121–133.

Fredrickson, B. L. (1998). What good are positive emotions? *Review of General Psychology, 2,* 300–319.

Glynn, L. M., Christenfeld, N., & Gerin, W. (2002). The role of rumination in recovery from reactivity: Cardiovascular consequences of emotional states. *Psychosomatic Medicine, 64,* 714–726.

Gross, J., & John, O. P. (2003). Individual differences in two emotion regulation processes: Implications for affect, relationships, and well-being. *Journal of Personality and Social Psychology, 85,* 348–362.

Huang, S-T. T., & Enright, R. D. (2000). Forgiveness and anger-related emotions in Taiwan: Implications for therapy. *Psychotherapy, 37,* 71–79.

Kubzansky, L. D., Kawachi, I., Spiro, A., Weiss, S. R., Vokonas, P. S., & Sparrow, D. (1997). Is worrying bad for your heart? A prospective study of worry and coronary heart disease in the Normative Aging Study. *Circulation, 95,* 818–824.

Lang, P. J. (1979). A bio-informational theory of emotional imagery. *Psychophysiology, 16,* 495–512.

Lang, P. J. (1995). The emotion probe: Studies of motivation and attention. *American Psychologist, 50,* 372–385.

Lawler, K. A., Younger, J. W., Piferi, R. L., Billington, E., Jobe, R., Edmondson, K., et al. (2003). A change of heart: Cardiovascular correlates of forgiveness in response to interpersonal conflict. *Journal of Behavioral Medicine, 26,* 373–393.

Madanes, C. (1990). *Sex, love, and violence: Strategies for transformation.* New York: W. W. Norton.

Mauger, P. A., Perry, J. E., Freeman, T., Grove, D. C., McBride, A. G., & McKinney, K. (1992). The measurement of forgiveness: Preliminary research. *Journal of Psychology and Christianity, 11,* 170–180.

McCraty, R., Atkinson, M., Tiller, W. A., Rein, G., & Watkins, A. D. (1995). The effects of emotion on short-term power spectrum analysis of heart rate variability. *American Journal of Cardiology, 76,* 1089–1093.

McCullough, M. E., & Hoyt, W. R. (2002). Transgression-related motivational disposition: Personality substrates of forgiveness and their links to the Big Five. *Personality and Social Psychology Bulletin, 28,* 1556–1573.

McCullough, M. E., Rachal, K. C., Sandage, S. J., Worthington, E. L., Brown, S. W., & Hight, T. L. (1998). Interpersonal forgiving in close relationship: II. Theoretical elaboration and measurement. *Journal of Personality and Social Psychology, 75,* 1586–1603.

Miller, T. Q., Smith, T. W., Turner, C. W., Guijarro, M. L., & Hallet, A. J. (1996). Meta-analytic review of research on hostility and physical health. *Psychological Bulletin, 108,* 322–348.

Peterson, C., & Seligman, M. E. P. (2004). *Character strengths and virtues: A handbook and classification.* Washington, DC: American Psychological Association Press and Oxford University Press.

Porges, S. W. (1992). Autonomic regulation and attention. In B. A. Campbell & H. Hayne (Eds.), *Attention and information processing in infants and adults: Perspectives from human and animal research* (pp. 201–223). Hillsdale, NJ: Lawrence Erlbaum.

Seybold, K. S., Hill, P. C., Neumann, J. K., & Chi, D. S. (2001). Physiological and psychological correlates of forgiveness. *Journal of Psychology and Christianity, 20,* 250–259.

Schwartz, A. R., Gerin, W., Davidson, K. W., Pickering, T. G., Brosschot, J. F., Thayer, J. F., et al. (2003). Toward a causal model of cardiovascular responses to stress and the development of cardiovascular disease. *Psychosomatic Medicine, 65,* 22–35.

Thayer, J. F., Friedman, B. H., & Borkovec, T. D. (1996). Autonomic characteristics of generalized anxiety disorder and worry. *Biological Psychiatry, 39,* 255–266.

Thayer, M. F., & Lane, R. D. (2000). A model of neurovisceral integration in emotion regulation and dysregulation. *Journal of Affective Disorders, 61,* 201–216.

Toussaint, L. L., & Williams, D. R. (October, 2003). *Physiological correlates of forgiveness: Findings from a racially and socio-economically diverse sample of community residents.* Paper presented at Scientific Findings About Forgiveness conference, Atlanta, GA.

Waltman, M. A. (2003). The psychological and physiological effects of forgiveness education in male patients with coronary artery disease. *Dissertation Abstracts International: Section B: The Sciences & Engineering, 63,* 3971.

Witvliet, C. V. O., Ludwig, T. E., & Bauer, D. (2002). Please forgive me: Transgressors' emotions and physiology during imagery of seeking forgiveness and victim responses. *Journal of Psychology and Christianity, 21,* 219–233.

Witvliet, C. V. O., Ludwig, T., & Vander Laan, K. (2001). Granting forgiveness or harboring grudges: Implications for emotion, physiology, and health. *Psychological Science, 12,* 117–123.

Witvliet, C. V. O., Root, L., Sato, A., & Ludwig, T. E. (2003). Justice and forgiveness: Psychophysiological effects for victims. *Psychophysiology, Supplement 40,* 87.

Witvliet, C. V. O., & Vrana, S. R. (1995). Psychophysiological responses as indices of affective dimensions. *Psychophysiology, 32,* 436–443.

Witvliet, C. V. O., Worthington, E. L., Jr., & Wade, N. G. (2002). Victims' heart rate and facial EMG responses to receiving an apology and restitution. *Psychophysiology, Supplement 39,* S88.

Worthington, E. L., Jr. (2003). *Forgiving and reconciling: Bridges to wholeness and hope.* Downers Grove, IL: InterVarsity Press.

Worthington, E. L., Jr., & Scherer, M. (2004). Forgiveness is an emotion-focused coping strategy that can reduce health risks and promote health resilience: Theory, review, and hypotheses. *Psychology and Health, 19,* 385–405.

Yik, M. S. M., & Russell, J. A. (2001). Predicting the Big Two of affect from the Big Five of personality. *Journal of Research in Personality, 35,* 247–277.

Chapter Nineteen

Forgiveness, Unforgiveness, Health, and Disease

Alex H. S. Harris
Carl E. Thoresen

Five years ago, we observed that no evidence existed from controlled studies linking forgiveness to physiology, health, or disease (Thoresen, Harris, & Luskin, 2000). Since then, the theory, measurement, and empirical study of forgiveness have developed substantially. Evidence has been produced linking both forgiveness and unforgiveness to short-term physiological variables, such as cortisol reactivity (Berry & Worthington, 2001) as well as blood pressure and skin conductance (Lawler et al., 2003; Witvliet, Ludwig, & Vander Laan, 2001). Coupled with the related literature on stress and health, this evidence makes hypotheses directly linking unforgiveness and forgiveness with health and disease variables more plausible and ripe to be tested. However, direct evidence that forgiveness or unforgiveness are related to health or disease is still virtually nonexistent (cf. Toussaint, Williams, Musick, & Everson, 2001). We write this chapter with hopes of inspiring researchers to address this clinically-relevant gap in our knowledge.

We review hypotheses and theoretical models linking forgiveness and unforgiveness to health and disease, and we present supporting evidence where available. Because evidence supporting these models is generally indirect and/or limited, we focus on specifying the research and evidence that might further our understanding of hypothesized associations between forgiveness and unforgiveness, and health and disease.

PERSONAL ASSUMPTIONS ABOUT FORGIVENESS

Unforgiveness has been defined by Worthington and colleagues (Worthington, Sandage, & Berry, 2000; Worthington & Wade, 1999) as a combination of delayed negative emotions (i.e., resentment, bitterness, hostility, hatred, anger, and fear) toward a transgressor. We view unforgiveness essentially as stress response (see also Worthington & Scherer, 2004) with potential health consequences. Unforgiveness is distinct from the immediate emotional response to a perceived injustice. It can be viewed as getting stuck in negative emotions and a hyperaroused stress response through rumination. Not everyone who experiences an offense experiences unforgiveness. Forgiveness can be seen as one of many ways to reduce or avoid unforgiveness (Worthington, 2001). As such, the hypothesized health benefits of reducing unforgiveness and fostering forgiveness are not necessarily synonymous. We view forgiveness not only as the reduction of unforgiveness through reducing the negative thoughts, emotions, motivations, and behaviors toward the offender but also as the increase of positive emotions and perspectives, such as empathy, hope, or compassion. Although the health benefits of forgiveness should include the health benefits of unforgiveness reduction, there may be additional health benefits associated with the increase of positive states. Furthermore, it may be possible to reduce unforgiveness and reap the hypothesized health benefits without forgiving. We elaborate on these notions below.

REVIEW OF THE THEORETICAL AND EMPIRICAL LITERATURE

We consider three general hypotheses that are relevant to the notion that forgiveness and unforgiveness may be related to physical health and disease: (a) Unforgiveness is associated with health risks; (b) positive states that are characteristic of forgiveness have health benefits beyond those associated with the reduction of unforgiveness; and (c) forgiveness interventions produce changes in health and disease outcomes when evaluated with randomized trials. Here we unpack these broad and multidimensional hypotheses, review relevant evidence, and discuss the nature of future research that might help us understand under what conditions each hypothesis may hold.

Hypothesis 1: Unforgiveness Is Associated With Health Risks

There are physiological, psychological, behavioral, and social paths through which unforgiveness may impact health. Again, unforgiveness does not refer to the immediate transgression-related experience of negative emotions but rather the delayed experience of resentment, blame, bitterness, hostility, hatred, anger, and fear that may be fostered through rumination. No direct evidence exists that either situational or dispositional unforgiveness is related to long-term health or disease. The lack of direct evidence is not surprising, given that the notion of unforgiveness and the means to measure it are fairly recent developments. In fact, no detailed, multidimensional measure of unforgiveness has yet been developed. An exception is the Transgression-Related Interpersonal Motivations Inventory (TRIM; McCullough et al., 1998) that is limited to the state-assessment of avoidance and revenge. Even so, three lines of evidence exist—stated here as propositions—suggesting unforgiveness may be related to health.

Unforgiveness Causes Health Problems in a Manner Similar to Other Chronic Stress Responses. Unforgiveness has been framed as a stress reaction (Worthington & Scherer, 2004). The negative health consequences of chronic stress and the physiological wear and tear of a hyperaroused stress response have been observed in traumatized populations and in people who have endured extreme and/or chronic stressors (e.g., Schnurr & Green, 2004). We hypothesized previously (Thoresen et al., 2000) that the rumination-fueled, chronic experience of stress and negative emotions that constitute unforgiveness may detrimentally impact health through the pathways of chronic sympathetic nervous system hyperarousal and increased allostatic load (McEwen, 1998, 2003). The argument rests on the assumption that transgressions are like other health-endangering stressors and that unforgiveness produces a similar, chronically hyperaroused stress response. Given the substantial evidence that extreme and chronic stressors negatively impact health (see McEwen, 2002) and further, that unforgiveness has been conceptualized as a stress response to a significant stressor, the notion that unforgiveness is linked to health risks is a small leap. Yet the devil may be in the details.

In the short term, unforgiveness has been shown to produce intense negative emotions as well as physiological responses consistent with other stress responses (Witvliet, Ludwig, & Bauer, 2002; Witvliet et al., 2001). Yet outside the lab and over longer periods of time, it is unknown to what extent unforgiveness is like stress responses to extreme stressors for which links to health outcomes have been established. Seybold, Hill, Neumann, and Chi (2001) found some evidence that the blood chemistries of people who are chronically unforgiving are similar to that of people under stress; however, there were many markers for which similarities were not found. We simply do not know whether the physiology, cognition, behavior, and social functioning of the unjustly fired worker or wife of an unfaithful husband, for example, are similar to those of people living in extreme poverty or refugee camps, traumatized combat veterans, or rape survivors. How is interpersonal unforgiveness different from and similar to trauma in terms of physiological, social, and health consequences? The natural history of unforgiveness (i.e., its frequency, intensity, and duration) for specific people in specific contexts is largely unknown.

Knowledge concerning the natural history of unforgiveness is currently a major missing link in the evidentiary chain. For example, it is unknown to what extent the attentional resources of the unforgiving person are devoted to the transgression or at what point rumination becomes problematic. Intuitively, unforgiveness may be characterized by range (i.e., the number of people or situations for which one is unforgiving), frequency (i.e., how often one is actively experiencing a state of unforgiveness), duration (i.e., how long each episode of unforgiveness lasts), and intensity (i.e., the magnitude of the emotional/behavioral stress response). Research that characterizes individuals on these unforgiveness domains and examines the long-term health trajectories of various patterns of unforgiveness would be extremely enlightening. Research such as this would also let us know how much unforgiveness is like other stress responses for which links to health and illness exist. Knowing more about the lived experience of unforgiveness will allow us to understand better its nature and prevalence, and to study its health-related consequences. Long-term studies with frequent assessments, posttransgression physiological monitoring, and disentangling of the health consequences of severe unforgiveness and trauma are important steps to furthering our knowledge in this area.

Unforgiveness Is Defined as the Experience of Emotions Already Linked to Health Risks. The core components of unforgiveness (e.g., anger, hostility, blame, fear) have been associated with health and disease outcomes. It is a short and tempting leap to claim that the health risks associated with the components of unforgiveness apply directly to unforgiveness. Yet again, the devil may be in the details.

The research linking anger and hostility to health, disease, and mortality are extremely nuanced. *Anger* has been defined as an emotional response to a perceived mistreatment that may range in intensity from irritation to rage, and *hostility* as a set of negative attitudes, beliefs, and appraisals concerning others as likely sources of frustration, mistreatment, and provocation (Smith, 1992). The manner in which anger is experienced, responded to, and expressed, how long one stays angry and takes to recover from it, as well as characteristics of the person (e.g., gender) appear to greatly influence the links to health and disease outcomes. As an example of the nuanced and qualified nature of the anger/health association, Hogan and Linden (2004) examined the health consequences of six independent anger-response styles—aggression, assertion, social support seeking, diffusion, avoidance, and rumination—in a sample of 159 hypertensive patients. Although the anger styles were not found to influence resting and ambulatory blood pressure levels, rumination had a detrimental influence on the relation between avoidance and assertion on blood pressure. The moderator effect of rumination also different by gender.

There is also the possibility that some forms of anger may actually improve health (Davidson, MacGregor, Stuhr, Dixon, & MacLean, 2000) and reduce unforgiveness. Davidson and colleagues have distinguished between constructive anger and destructive anger. Constructive anger may involve engaging in instrumental thoughts and actions geared toward rectifying the situation, cognitive restructuring, and interpersonal problem solving. Destructive anger involves rage, revenge, and hostile rumination and imagery. In this framework, anger may be a positive or negative motivating force.

Clearly, it is an oversimplification to follow this form of logic: Anger is a component of unforgiveness; anger is a health risk; therefore, unforgiveness is a health risk. The multidimensional assessment of anger and perhaps of angry rumination should be routinely included in forgiveness and unforgiveness research. Knowing more about the nature and course of anger expression in the context of unforgiveness will further our understanding of the potential health effects of unforgiveness.

Similar issues exist in claiming negative health consequences of unforgiveness based on the link between hostility and disease. For example, Julkunen, Salonen, Kaplan, and Chesney (1994) prospectively studied the link between hostility and anger suppression to the progression of carotid atherosclerosis in a sample of Finnish men ($N = 119$; mean age 54 years). They found a twofold accelerated progression of carotid atherosclerosis in people with high cynical distrust and high anger control, even after controlling for biological and demographic risk factors. Also, there was evidence that the cognitive component of hostility is a more important risk factor for the progression of carotid atherosclerosis than is the affective component. For our purposes, we emphasize here that not all unforgiveness has hostility as a component, nor does all hostility equally endanger health.

It is also important to consider models other than main-effects models that might link unforgiveness to health. Underlying personality characteristics or long-standing psychosocial patterns, such as hostility or suspiciousness, may make one more likely to experience both unforgiveness and negative health consequences (Eysenck, 2000). A mediational model might link personality characteristics to health consequences through the path of unforgiveness.

Less evidence exists that other components of unforgiveness, such as blame and hatred, affect health. Affleck, Tennen, Croog, and Levine (1987) found blaming others for an initial heart attack was predictive of reinfarctions. It is plausible that the physiological arousal associated with chronic experiencing of hatred or blame might endanger health. As with anger, the nature, intensity, frequency, and duration of these experiences in the context of unforgiveness is unknown and would most likely moderate the subsequent impact on health. Again, it would be useful to document the natural history of these components of unforgiveness, especially the ongoing cognitive features, so that we might better understand the associated health risks as well as the impact of reducing unforgiveness and promoting forgiveness. To establish that unforgiveness is a health risk, the construct needs more precise definition and measurement, as well as research specifically dedicated to examining its influence on health.

The Behaviors Associated With Unforgiveness May Cause Health Problems.   Until now, we have implicitly assumed that the mechanisms through which unforgiveness might endanger health primarily involve the intense and chronic experience of its component emotions, resulting in autonomic nervous system hyperarousal and the general wear and tear associated with increased allostatic load. Other mechanisms are plausible. For example, resentment, anger, or hatred could lead to violent revenge or retaliation. Although there may be specific situations when revenge actually makes one safer, we generally assume that engaging in violent retribution leads to poor health, social, and legal outcomes. Furthermore, unforgiveness might be linked to poor health through the consequences of problematic coping styles, such as avoidance coping or substance use.

In addition, the emotional components of unforgiveness may lead directly or indirectly to social isolation, which has been linked to health risks (e.g., Cohen, Gottlieb, & Underwood, 2000). At least two processes might implicate unforgiveness in the erosion of social networks and support. First, the unforgiving person, who may be angry, hostile, ruminating, and attached to his or her victim role, may have friends and acquaintances who tire of attending to the person's misery. Second, the dispositionally unforgiving person, untrusting of people and fearful of revictimization, may avoid social contact or may limit the extent to which he or she allows himself or herself to be vulnerable in relationships. If unforgiveness reduces social contact, support, and integration by these or other mechanisms, the health benefits of these contacts will be lost. It is also important to note that not all social contact is health promoting. In some cases, the anger or fear associated with unforgiveness might motivate healthy changes or reductions in unhealthy social contact.

Currently, no direct evidence exists linking interpersonal transgressions to changes in health-related behavior through the path of unforgiveness. Clearly, this is an important area of future research and is a core aspect of documenting the natural history of unforgiveness.

Conclusions Regarding Hypothesis 1.   One way of proceeding is to show that transgressions are like other extreme or chronic stressors for which links to health have been established. More directly, it would be useful to characterize the physiological, psychological, and social course of unforgiveness across time and to examine possible links of person, course, and context factors to hypothesized health outcomes. We currently have no reliable means to distinguish between the prolonged initial reactions to a transgression from the beginnings of unforgiveness. Nor do we know at what point, in terms of chronicity and intensity, unforgiveness may endanger health. More detailed, multidimensional, and time-structured means of assessing unforgiveness would be helpful.

Hypothesis 2: Forgiveness Has Health Benefits Beyond Those Linked to Reduced Unforgiveness

Toussaint et al. (2001) examined a national probability sample of 1,423 respondents and found relationships between forgiveness of others and self-reports of mental and physical health that varied by age. Specifically, forgiveness of others was more strongly related to self-reported mental and physical health for middle-aged and elderly adults than for young adults. Although intriguing, the cross-sectional nature of these data makes claims regarding underlying mechanisms and causal relationships speculative.

Forgiveness, as noted, is commonly defined as a reduction of unforgiveness plus an increase of positive states, such as empathy, compassion, or hope. At issue here is whether these positive states add health benefits beyond those that may be associated with unforgiveness reduction. First, we discuss the possible mechanisms through which positive affect might be generally linked to better heath. Then we examine the evidence that positive states cause better health. Finally, we discuss evidence that forgiveness involves the affective experiences for which health consequences have been implicated.

Mechanisms Thought Which Positive Affect May Benefit Health.   Salovey, Rothman, Detweiler, and Steward (2000) argue that positive affect may influence health through several different paths: "(a) direct effects of positive affect on physiology, especially the immune system, (b) the information value of emotional experiences, (c) the psychological resources engendered by positive feeling states, (d) the ways in which mood can motivate health-relevant behaviors, and (e) the elicitation of social support" (p. 110). Fredrickson (1998) theorized that positive emotions serve to broaden one's momentary thought-action repertoire, which in turn has the effect of building physical, intellectual, and social resources. The majority of the explanatory models implied by these authors posit mediators, such as increased health-related behaviors or social integration, as critical to the production of health affects. Here we highlight examples of research that bear on these notions.

Evidence That Positive Affect Impacts Health.   Fredrickson and Levenson (1998) found that certain positive emotions speed recovery from the cardiovascular sequelae of negative emotions in the laboratory setting. Many studies have been conducted examining associations between both positive affect and negative affect with blood markers of immune functioning, especially secretory immunoglobulin A. The results have been mixed (e.g., Futterman, Kemeny, Shapiro, & Fahey, 1994) but generally support the idea that positive affect enhances and negative affect compromises immune functioning (e.g., Labott, Ahleman, Wolever, & Martin, 1990). As mentioned previously, evidence has linked forgiveness-related positive emotions to blood pressure and skin conductance (Lawler et al., 2003; Witvliet et al., 2001).

Much less is known about the health (not just transient physiological reactions) and long-term consequences of acute or habitual experiences of positive affect. Some epidemiological evidence exists documenting a prospective association between positive affect and important long-term health outcomes, including mortality (e.g., Moskowitz, 2003). The links between health outcomes and personality characteristics, such as optimism or hostility, may be mediated by the effects of positive and negative emotions. Many gaps exist in our knowledge regarding the associations between positive affect and health, particularly the nature, frequency, duration, and intensity of positive affect required to influence health risks.

Even if we knew that forgiveness-related positive affect was salubrious in certain "doses," we really do not know the emotion-related natural history of forgiveness. We define people as forgiving if they increase in positive states, but it is unknown whether these positive states are of an adequate frequency and intensity to influence health. We suspect that a main-effect model (e.g., forgiveness-related compassion produces positive health outcome) is unlikely to find support. More likely, increases in forgiveness-related positive affect might influence health through more indirect means, such as most of the mechanisms proposed by Salovey et al. (2000) and Fredrickson (1998). Currently, research documenting the experience of forgiveness-related affect is limited by crude instrumentation and infrequent and short-term assessment. Research that tests models linking forgiveness-related affect to health outcomes through mediators such as health behaviors or increased social networks could dramatically advance the field.

Conclusion Regarding Hypothesis 2.   The nature and extent of positive states related to forgiveness remain unclear. More detailed assessment of the natural history of forgiveness-related positive states are needed before we can adequately test claims regarding the health benefits of forgiveness beyond the reduction of unforgiveness. Testing both the main and mediated effects of forgiveness—beyond those associated with unforgiveness reduction—on health and disease will increase our knowledge greatly.

Hypothesis 3: Forgiveness Interventions Have Produced Changes in Health and Disease Outcomes When Evaluated in Randomized Trials

Ideally, forgiveness intervention studies would assess multiple dimensions of forgiveness, unforgiveness, and important health-related variables on frequent occasions for extended periods of time. Furthermore, not only would the main effects of the intervention on these outcomes be explored, but the extent that intervention-related health effects are mediated by unforgiveness reduction and/or increases in forgiveness-related positive affect would be examined. In addition, forgiveness-intervention studies could be conducted with patient samples to observe the effects of forgiveness training on medical course and status. These ideals have not been realized in the published literature, but one dissertation study represents a step in the right direction (Waltman, 2003).

Waltman (2003) examined the psychological and physiological effects of a 10-week forgiveness program with male coronary artery disease patients. Participants were randomized either to an individual forgiveness intervention based on Enright's process model of forgiveness ($n = 13$) or to an individual 10-week support program discussing the impact of heart disease on various aspects of life ($n = 12$). Measures of forgiveness, anger, anxiety, and hope, as well as measures of myocardial perfusion, heart rate, and blood pressure, were taken for 17 participants at pretest, posttest, and 10-week follow-up. Participants also underwent nuclear heart scans at the same measurement points after an anger recall task. Participants in the forgiveness condition significantly improved on measures of forgiveness, state anger, and anger reaction from pretest to posttest but only on forgiveness from pretest to follow-up, in comparison with the support participants. No significant differences on physiological measures were observed between groups from pretest to posttest, but from pretest to follow-up, significant differences in reductions of anger-induced myocardial perfusion defects were found in favor of the forgiveness condition. If this study used a larger sample size, longer term of follow-up, and as a result were able to explore indirect effects, it would represent the kind of research capable of producing evidence directly linking forgiveness and health.

It is unusual but not completely unheard of for forgiveness intervention studies to measure fear, hostility, or anger—hypothesized to be core components of unforgiveness—or hope, compassion, or empathy—hypothesized to be core components of forgiveness. For example, Thoresen et al. (2001) reported significant treatment effects measured at 4 months after intervention for trait anger and perceived stress in an evaluation of a primarily cognitive behavioral forgiveness intervention consisting of six once-weekly, 90-minute sessions conducted in small, same-sex groups. They also found the hypothesized effects on several dimensions of forgiveness (increased positive, reduced negative). Unfortunately, as with virtually all intervention trials to date, no direct or longer term assessments measured important health or disease indicators. Hopefully, future intervention studies will address these issues.

NEW RESEARCH DIRECTIONS NEEDED IN THE AREA

Construct Refinement and Measurement

The advancement of forgiveness research depends on further refining relevant constructs and improving the means of assessing them. For example, different authors have enumerated the components of unforgiveness and forgiveness-related affect differently. Definitions of forgiveness vary, as does the parsing of types of forgiveness. Furthermore, no current assessment instrument or method captures the full complexity of these constructs. Even among the most established and multidimensional instruments, such as the Enright Forgiveness Inventory, assessment of negative and positive affect is kept at the general level. It is possible that several types of unforgiveness exist (e.g., angry, depressed, passive) that may have different effects on health or may operate via different pathways. Worthington and Scherer (2004) have distinguished between decisional and emotional forgiveness, a useful distinction that has yet to be incorporated into other forgiveness research. Because unforgiveness is defined as a delayed pattern of reactions, the time elapsed between the transgression and reaction should be, but has never been, a part of unforgiveness assessment. In other words, better understanding the nature as well as the extent of negative and positive states is important to the future of forgiveness research.

Many authors have lamented the almost exclusive reliance of self-report, questionnaire-based measures in the assessment of forgiveness constructs, typically administered to the offended party on very few occasions spanning short time periods. McCullough, Rachal, and Hoyt (2000) and Thompson and Synder (2003) elaborate further on improvements in forgiveness measurement that are needed. Use of performance-based measures and gathering information from other sources are among the possible advances.

Indirect Models

As Witvliet (2001) noted, there are most likely a host of person factors that influence the nature of offense that is taken from a given interpersonal stimulus, the likelihood of developing unforgiveness, as well as the nature and magnitude of the link between unforgiveness, forgiveness, health, and disease. The exploration of moderator variables, such as ethnicity, educational level, income level, and personality style, within both longitudinal-observational studies and intervention studies will greatly advance our knowledge of the natural history of both unforgiveness and forgiveness. In addition, as noted, mediational models of various forms should be tested (e.g., unforgiveness → substance use → illness, or optimism → forgiveness-related positive affect → health outcome).

Long-Term Longitudinal Studies

Most disease and health processes unfold over time periods that exceed the typical follow-up of forgiveness studies. Long-term longitudinal studies with frequent assessments could help clarify the typical course of harmful physiological states related to unforgiveness. The long-term health risks associated with dispositional unforgiveness need to be documented. The potentially bidirectional, if not multidirectional, nature of the illness–unforgiveness relationship should be explored. The unique health effects of unforgiveness reduction and forgiveness need to be clarified. The long-term health impacts of forgiveness interventions should be tracked. The logistical and financial burdens of such studies are great, but so might be the rewards.

RELEVANCE FOR CLINICAL AND APPLIED INTERVENTIONS

We have stated here that although models exist positing plausible links from unforgiveness reduction and forgivingness-related positive states to health and disease, the current state of evidence is indirect and suggestive at best. Therefore, we make several recommendations and caveats regarding the clinical application of this literature:

1. Clinicians and researchers should not overstate claims about the nature of the forgiveness–health association.
2. Current theory and empirical evidence suggest that many paths exist to unforgiveness reduction besides forgiveness. We know little about the costs and benefits of these paths, and even less about interventions that might facilitate travel along them. Other means of unforgiveness reduction deserve more research attention.
3. Very little attention has been given to potential downsides of forgiveness. When might forgiveness be contraindicated, or what might be potential risks associated with it? Is there such a thing as "premature forgiveness?"
4. All interventions occur within a cultural context. The meaning and perceived value of forgiveness (or grudge holding) is largely culturally determined. What it means to say "I have forgiven" may vary on average by gender, religious affiliation, spiritual perspective, ethnicity, geographical location, or other characteristics. Forgiveness may be valued or denigrated, may be viewed as an important therapeutic goal or seen as making one weak or vulnerable. The multicultural meanings of forgiveness are poorly understood.

5. If unforgiveness reduction, especially through forgiveness, can be shown to reduce the risk of illness, then chronic unforgiveness might be assessed and treated
   in the primary care setting. A patient's tendency to be easily offended and grudge-
   harboring may also have implications for the patient-doctor relationship.

PERSONAL THEORETICAL PERSPECTIVES ON THE FIELD

This chapter focuses on forgiveness and unforgiveness as proximal to health outcomes.
However, given the prevailing proximal and causal perspective of almost all empirical studies, the more distal and indirect relationships linking forgiveness and health
are sorely in need of study. Another important area of future forgiveness research and
application is the recognition and treatment of unforgiveness that results from injury
(including crimes, terrorism, and war) and disease (e.g., HIV/AIDS, hepatitis), as well
as from interactions with the health care system (e.g., medical mistakes). Virtually
ignored are models in which health and disease variables (e.g., pain, HIV, injuries
from violent crimes or medical mistakes) are the kernel around which unforgiveness
grows. For example, U.S. Institute of Medicine (2000) estimates that 44,000–98,000
Americans die each year because of medical errors, and many more are nonfatally injured and disabled. The potential is great for the development of unforgiveness in patients surviving medical mistakes, as well as in their families and friends, and for the
development of self-unforgiveness in health care providers who are responsible for
these events. The stress of unforgiveness in these contexts may exacerbate the already
compromised health in surviving patients, may add additional burdens to family systems already under stress, and may impact the health and professional functioning of
the responsible health care providers.

CONCLUSIONS

The recent work linking unforgiveness and forgiveness to short-term physiological
variables provides a basis from which we can reasonably hypothesize, yet not conclude, that chronic and intense unforgiveness are health risks. Almost no direct evidence has been produced that tests this hypothesis. Distinctions between reducing
unforgiveness and promoting forgiveness and between state and dispositional unforgiveness are important theoretical developments that will allow researchers to posit
and test hypotheses of specific forgiveness and health relationships. We believe the
extensive stress-coping health literature provides a template for research in this area.
More precise construct definition and measurement, more fine-grained and long-term
assessment schedules, methodological pluralism (e.g., randomized trials, longitudinal observational studies, qualitative methods), and studying forgiveness within patient samples will greatly advance our understanding of links between unforgiveness,
forgiveness, health, and disease.

REFERENCES

Affleck, G., Tennen, H., Croog, S., & Levine, S. (1987). Causal attribution, perceived benefits, and morbidity after a heart attack: An 8-year study. *Journal of Consulting and Clinical Psychology, 55*, 29–35.

Berry, J. W., & Worthington, E. L., Jr. (2001). Forgivingness, relationship quality, stress while imagining relationship events, and physical and mental health. *Journal of Counseling Psychology, 48*, 447–455.

Cohen, S., Gottlieb, B. H., & Underwood, L. G. (2000). Social relationships and health. In S. Cohen, L. G. Underwood, & B. H. Gottlieb (Eds.), *Social support measurement and intervention* (pp. 3–28). New York: Oxford University Press.

Davidson, K., MacGregor, M. W., Stuhr, J., Dixon, K., & MacLean, D. (2000). Constructive anger verbal behavior predicts blood pressure in a population-based sample. *Health Psychology, 19*, 55–64.

Eysenck, H. J. (2000). Personality as a risk factor in cancer and coronary heart disease. In D. T. Kenny & J. G. Carlson (Eds.), *Stress and health: Research and clinical applications* (pp. 291–318). Amsterdam, The Netherlands: Harwood Academic.

Fredrickson, B. L. (1998). What good are positive emotions? Special issue: New directions in research on emotion. *Review of General Psychology, 2*, 300–319.

Fredrickson, B. L., & Levenson, R. W. (1998). Positive emotions speed recovery from the cardiovascular sequelae of negative emotions. *Cognition and Emotion, 12*, 191–220.

Futterman, A. D., Kemeny, M. E., Shapiro, D., & Fahey, J. L. (1994). Immunological and physiological changes associated with induced positive and negative mood. *Psychosomatic Medicine, 56*, 499–511.

Hogan, B. E., & Linden, W. (2004). Anger response styles and blood pressure: At least don't ruminate about it! *Annals of Behavioral Medicine, 27*, 38–49.

Julkunen, J., Salonen, R., Kaplan, G. A., & Chesney, M. A. (1994). Hostility and the progression of carotid atherosclerosis. *Psychosomatic Medicine, 56*, 519–525.

Labott, S. M., Ahleman, S., Wolever, M. E., & Martin, R. B. (1990). The physiological and psychological effects of the expression and inhibition of emotion. *Behavioral Medicine, 16*, 182–189.

Lawler, K. A., Younger, J. W., Piferi, R. L., Billington, E., Jobe, R., Edmondson, K., et al. (2003). A change of heart: Cardiovascular correlates of forgiveness in response to interpersonal conflict. *Journal of Behavioral Medicine, 26*, 373–393.

McCullough, M. E., Rachal, K. C., & Hoyt, W. T. (2000). What we know (and need to know) about assessing forgiveness constructs. In M. E. McCullough, K. I. Pargament, & C. E. Thoresen (Eds.), *Forgiveness: Theory, research, and practice* (pp. 65–88). New York: Guilford Press.

McCullough, M. E., Rachal, K. C., Sandage, S. J., Worthington, E. L., Jr., Brown, S. W., & Hight, T. L. (1998). Interpersonal forgiving in close relationships: II. Theoretical elaboration and measurement. *Journal of Personality and Social Psychology, 75*, 1586–1603.

McEwen, B. S. (1998). Protective and damaging effects of stress mediators. *New England Journal of Medicine, 338*, 171–179.

McEwen, B. S. (2002). *The end of stress as we know it.* Washington, DC: Joseph Henry Press.

McEwen, B. S. (2003). Mood disorders and allostatic load. *Biological Psychiatry, 54*, 200–207.

Moskowitz, J. T. (2003). Positive affect predicts lower risk of AIDS mortality. *Psychosomatic Medicine, 65*, 620–626.

Salovey, P., Rothman, A. J., Detweiler, J. B., & Steward, W. T. (2000). Emotional states and physical health. *American Psychologist, 55*, 110–121.

Schnurr, P. P., & Green, B. L. (Eds.). (2004). *Trauma and health: Physical health consequences of exposure to extreme stress*. Washington, DC: American Psychological Association.

Seybold, K. S., Hill, P. C., Neumann, J. K., & Chi, D. S. (2001). Physiological and psychological correlates of forgiveness. *Journal of Psychology and Christianity, 20*, 250–259.

Smith, T. W. (1992). Hostility and health: Current status of a psychosomatic hypothesis. *Health Psychology, 11*, 139–150.

Thompson, L. Y., & Synder, C. R. (2003). Measuring forgiveness. In S. J. Lopez & C. R. Snyder (Eds.), *Positive psychological assessment: A handbook of models and measures* (pp. 301–312). Washington, DC: American Psychological Association.

Thoresen, C. E., Harris, A. H. S., & Luskin, F. (2000). Forgiveness and health: An unanswered question. In M. E. McCullough & K. I. Pargament (Eds.), *Forgiveness: Theory, research, and practice* (pp. 254–280). New York: Guilford Press.

Thoresen, C. E., Luskin, F., Harris, A. H. S., Benisovich, S. V., Standard, S., Bruning, B., et al. (2001, March). *Effects of forgiveness intervention on perceived stress, state and trait anger, and self-reported health*. Paper presented at the annual meeting of the Society of Behavioral Medicine, Seattle, WA.

Toussaint, L. L., Williams, D. R., Musick, M. A., & Everson, S. A. (2001). Forgiveness and health: Age differences in a U.S. probability sample. *Journal of Adult Development. 8*, 249–257.

U.S. Institute of Medicine Committee on Quality of Health Care in America. (Eds.). (2000). *To err is human: Building a safer health system*. Washington, DC: National Academy Press.

Waltman, M. A. (2003). The psychological and physiological effects of forgiveness education in male patients with coronary artery disease. *Dissertation Abstracts International: Section B: The Sciences & Engineering, 63*(8-B), 3971.

Witvliet, C. v. O. (2001). Forgiveness and health: Review and reflections on a matter of faith, feelings, and physiology. *Journal of Psychology and Theology, 29*, 212–224.

Witvliet, C. v. O., Ludwig, T. E., & Bauer, D. J. (2002). Please forgive me: Transgressors' emotions and physiology during imagery of seeking forgiveness and victim responses. *Journal of Psychology and Christianity, 21*, 219–233.

Witvliet, C. v. O., Ludwig, T. E., & Vander Laan, K. L. (2001). Granting forgiveness or harboring grudges: Implications for emotion, physiology, and health. *Psychological Science, 12*, 117–123.

Worthington, E. L., Jr. (2001). Unforgiveness, forgiveness, and reconciliation in societies. In R. G. Helmick, & R. L. Petersen (Eds.), *Forgiveness and reconciliation: Religion, public policy, and conflict transformation* (pp. 161–182). Philadelphia: Templeton Foundation Press.

Worthington, E. L., Jr., Sandage, S. J., & Berry, J. W. (2000). Group interventions to promote forgiveness: What researchers and clinicians ought to know. In M. E. McCullough, K. I. Pargament, & C. E. Thoresen (Eds.), *Forgiveness: Theory, research, and practice* (pp. 228–253). New York: Guilford Press.

Worthington, E. L., Jr., & Scherer, M. (2004). Forgiveness is an emotion-focused coping strategy that can reduce health risks and promote health resilience: Theory, review, and hypotheses. *Psychology and Health, 19*, 385–405.

Worthington, E. L. Jr., & Wade, N. G. (1999). The psychology of unforgiveness and forgiveness and implications for clinical practice. *Journal of Social and Clinical Psychology, 18*, 385–418.

Chapter Twenty

Forgiveness and Health in Persons Living With HIV/AIDS

Lydia R. Temoshok
Rebecca L. Wald

The HIV/AIDS epidemic constitutes an unprecedented phenomenon affecting not only health but all aspects of life for a person living with HIV/AIDS from marriage and intimate relations to child-bearing and parenthood, to work and social functioning, and to psychological and spiritual well-being. There is a large and growing literature on psychosocial and spiritual aspects of cancer, which is probably the disease most akin to HIV/AIDS in its inspiration of fear and its threat to life and well-being. It may be said that perceptions of HIV/AIDS are much like perceptions of cancer 50 years ago: a usually fatal, essentially incurable disease associated with stigma and a sense of hopelessness. Since 1996, advances in treatment options with combination therapies have improved the ability to treat a large proportion of HIV-infected individuals and significantly decrease mortality.

Unlike cancer, however, HIV is an infectious disease, transmissible by two of the most intrinsic human forces—sexuality and procreation. The intense fear and stigma surrounding transmission in these most intimate of human connections have cast the multidimensional concept of forgiveness in a central role for those living with HIV/AIDS and their loved ones. How does a person living with HIV or AIDS come to terms with—and forgive—the person who infected him or her and with God or other spiritual being who seemingly allowed this to happen? How does a person living with HIV or AIDS come to terms with the natural desires for sexual intimacy with one's partner and fears that HIV may be transmitted to a loved one by this most natural of acts? How does someone with HIV deal with the normal human goal to give life and to see life continue through one's children, and with the realistic fear that one's children may be born infected with HIV? How can a person living with HIV or AIDS forgive himself or herself if a partner or child is infected through his or her own actions, even if not intentional? Forgiving the self for becoming infected with HIV in the first place is especially difficult if infection occurred through the doubly socially stigmatized routes of sexual transmission in a same-sex relationship or transmission through injecting illicit drugs. To the extent that language and metaphor often reveal deep mind-body connections, it may not be coincidental that one of the synonyms for forgiveness is *immunity* and that to be forgiven is *to be spared.*

OUR THEORETICAL APPROACH TO FORGIVENESS IN THE CONTEXT OF HIV/AIDS

Our understanding of the role of forgiveness in the lives of persons with HIV/AIDS is located within a biopsychosocial framework (Temoshok, 2004b). The existing body of theory and research on psychoneuroimmunology and HIV suggests that biological, psychological, and behavioral factors interact in a complex manner to affect clinical disease progression (Ader, Felten, & Cohen, 2000; Solomon, Kemeny, & Temoshok, 1991; Solomon & Temoshok, 1987). The main theoretical position of the first author is that more adaptive coping with stress—particularly the appropriate recognition and expression of emotion—is a key factor contributing to immunological processes that affect cancer and HIV outcomes (e.g., Temoshok, 1987, 1990a, 2000a, 2000b, 2002, 2004a; Temoshok & Dreher, 1992).

We hypothesize that the emotional and psychosocial consequences of forgiving and feeling forgiven or the converse—unforgiving/feeling unforgiven—have psychosocial/behavioral and psychoneuroimmunological/biomedical consequences for those infected with HIV, as well as other people they touch in their lives. The mechanisms by which psychosocial and spiritual factors could influence immunological function and disease outcome for a specific disease entity such as HIV remain to be defined. In Figure 20.1, we depict the hypothesized consequences of forgiving and feeling forgiven along two interacting cascades of processes: psychoneuroimmunological and psychosocial/behavioral (cf. Temoshok, 1995).

The hypothesized emotional, behavioral, and biomedical consequences of not forgiving/feeling unforgiven are presented in Table 20.1, which depicts four increasingly wider contexts for considering forgiveness and unforgiveness as multidimensional concepts within the specific situation of individuals infected with HIV/AIDS. Within each context, forgiveness or unforgiveness can be considered as a state or action emanating from the self or from others in relation to the self (i.e., forgiving vs. not forgiving and feeling forgiven vs. unforgiven). For the sake of simplicity, we have presented the contexts and hypothesized consequences for the negative end of the forgiveness/unforgiveness dimension.

Forgiving oneself is hypothesized to be associated with higher self-esteem and self-respect, states associated with more positive health outcomes, in contradistinction to states of guilt, self-hatred, and self-blame (Glaser, Rabin, Chesney, Cohen, & Natelson, 1999; Moulton, Sweet, & Temoshok, 1987). Low self-esteem has been associated with maladaptive ways of dealing with stress, such as substance abuse, which is a contributor to HIV infection and other sexually transmitted diseases, as well as to disease progression because a person using drugs, particularly injecting drugs, is more susceptible to bacterial infections and more likely to have poorer hygiene and nutrition.

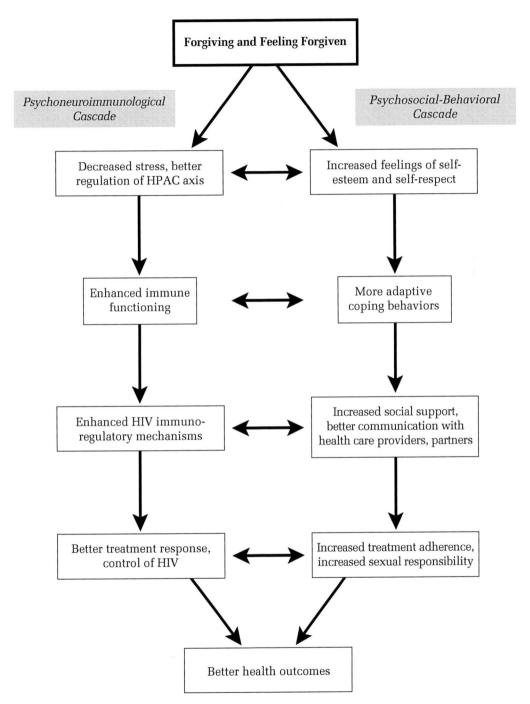

FIGURE 20.1. Hypothesized Consequences of Forgiving and Feeling Forgiven

TABLE 20.1. Contexts of Forgiveness for HIV/AIDS

Contexts of feeling unforgiven/unforgiving	Emotional and psychosocial consequences	Behavioral consequences	Biomedical consequences
Intrapersonal	Low self-esteem, guilt, helplessness, self-blame, depression	Self-destructive behaviors (e.g., drug and alcohol abuse)	Increased stress, immune dysfunction, disease progression
Interpersonal	Anger, resentment, lack of empathy, feeling unloved	Irresponsible sexual behaviors, transmission risk behaviors	Coinfection with other viruses (STDs); HIV "superinfection"; HIV transmission
Health care system and medical providers	Mistrust	Poor patient–provider communication; poor adherence to medical regimens/recommendations	Treatment failure; disease progression
Spiritual	Hopelessness, alienation, despair	Suicidal thoughts/ behaviors, homicidal thoughts/actions, isolation, withdrawal	Multisystem breakdown (mental, biological, and social)

Note: Adapted from Temoshok & Chandra, 2000.

In the interpersonal context, a person who is able to forgive others and let go of unproductive feelings of anger, bitterness, resentment, or disappointment will probably be able to seek and receive social support more easily and effectively from others. Social support has been shown to be a key factor in maintaining good health in general and is particularly relevant for people living with HIV/AIDS, who often feel shunned or rejected by friends, family members, or society at large (Solomon et al., 1991; Zich & Temoshok, 1987).

The trusting and open, mutually forgiving communications that help maintain social relations with friends and family also apply to relations with medical providers. Hope, as a critical ingredient in biopsychosocial processes that result in recovery and healing, is a fragile product of verbal and nonverbal provider-patient communications and can easily turn into hopelessness and despair (e.g., Temoshok, 1996). Mistrust of medical systems and of information about HIV/AIDS promulgated by government agencies is unfortunately prevalent in disadvantaged and alienated groups (Temoshok & Chandra, 2000). This is especially true in some African-American communities whose leaders may remind them of the infamous Tuskegee medical study that observed the course of untreated syphilis in poor, largely African-American research "volunteers" (Temoshok, 1997). We hypothesize that mistrust of medical systems and bitter, unforgiving attitudes toward mainstream medicine for not finding a cure or effective HIV/AIDS treatment will lead to missed appointments and poorer adherence to the HIV medications that must be taken with over 95% accuracy to prevent the development of the drug-resistant virus (e.g., Bartlett & Gallant, 2003). Thus, not forgiving one's medical providers and larger medical systems or feeling unforgiven for having contracted a stigmatized disease can exacerbate a cycle of mistrust, poor patient-provider communication, and withdrawal that can result in treatment failure and disease progression.

In the biomedical realm, being able to "forgive and forget," to let go of angry thoughts and feelings, may have physiological concomitants in being able to return inappropriately hyperaroused physiological systems back to more normal levels of homeostasis (Besedovsky, Herberman, Temoshok, & Sendo, 1996; Temoshok, 1990b, 1991, 2000a, 2002). Forgiveness is hypothesized to be associated with physiological relaxation and autonomic homeostasis, following the paradigm established in a study of physiological patterns associated with long-term survival in men with AIDS (O'Leary et al., 1989; Solomon, Temoshok, O'Leary, & Zich, 1987).

We postulate that being unforgiving or feeling unforgiven keep mental and physiological processes operating in a spiraling feedback loop of hyperarousal in the hypothalamic-pituitary-adrenal-cortical axis. Well-functioning nervous and immune systems are able to respond appropriately to stimuli or antigens—neither over- nor underreacting—and to return to a "resting level" that helps maintain an organism's basic integrity and growth (Temoshok, 2000a, 2002). Additionally, it is hypothesized that a "masked" forgiveness response that covers one's true feelings of unforgiveness will not resolve forgiveness events or dilemmas and will result in autonomic arousal and inappropriate immune activation (Temoshok, 2003a).

This cascade of biopsychosocial events is analogous to the processes theorized to underlie the negative health effects of the Type C pattern, which has been shown to be associated with worse health outcomes in malignant melanoma as well as HIV (Temoshok, 2003b, 2004c; Temoshok & Dreher, 1992). Type C proclivities include not recognizing that anything is wrong internally or externally (and letting stressful or problematic situations continue unaddressed and resolved), presenting a pleasant façade to the world and not expressing needs or feelings—particularly anger.

REVIEW OF THE RELEVANT THEORETICAL AND EMPIRICAL RESEARCH

In studies across a number of diseases, evidence is accumulating to suggest that psychosocial dimensions of quality of life, particularly hope (or its converse, hopelessness), perceived social support (or its converse, isolation and social inhibition), and fighting spirit (or its converse, resignation), can have striking effects on disease susceptibility as well as on recovery and survival time for persons with cancer, AIDS, and heart disease (Denollet et al., 1996; Greer, Morris, Pettingale, & Haybittle, 1990; Miller & Cole, 1998; Temoshok, 1985, 1993). Depression, life stress, and distress have been shown to be associated with poorer health outcomes in HIV (e.g., Balbin, Ironson, & Solomon, 1999; Evans et al., 1997; Ironson et al., 1994; Kemeny & Dean, 1995; Leserman et al., 2000; Lyketsos et al., 1993; Patterson et al., 1995; Vassend, Eskild, & Halvorsen, 1997). The inappropriate and maladaptive nonexpression, suppression, or repression of emotions as the theorized pathogenic core of the Type C coping style (Temoshok, 2003b, 2004c) has been related to exacerbation of HIV and other immunologically mediated diseases (e.g., Cole, Kemeny, Taylor, Visscher, & Fahey, 1996; Mulder, 1994; Mulder, Antoni, Duivenvoorden, Kauffmann, & Goodkin, 1995; Nyklicek, Temoshok, & Vingerhoets, 2004; Solano et al., 1993; Solano et al., 2002; Solomon & Temoshok, 1987; Temoshok, 1985, 1991, 2003).

The effects of spirituality and of forgiveness more specifically on health outcomes have not been well studied, but an important recent study in Australia showed that self-reported or perceived religiousness was an independent and statistically significant protective factor for colorectal cancer in a population-based study of 715 colorectal cancer patients and matched community controls (Kune, Kune, & Watson, 1993). Concealment of homosexual identity may be related to multiple contexts of forgiveness, including concerns about social rejection (interpersonal unforgiveness), condemnation from religious communities (spiritual unforgiveness), and internalized feelings of guilt or shame (intrapersonal unforgiveness). HIV-positive men who conceal their homosexual identity have been found to have quicker disease progression, lower CD4+ counts (which indicate more HIV-related damage to the immune system), more symptoms of depression, and less social support (Ullrich, Lutgendorf, & Stapleton, 2003).

Nondisclosure of HIV status is directly related to fears of judgment and rejection by important social others; in other words, the fear that one's HIV status or circumstances of infection will be viewed as unforgivable in an interpersonal context. Persons with HIV who feel unable to disclose their status to important others have been found to have increased rates of depression (Armistead, Morse, Forehand, Morse, & Clark, 1999) and a poorer quality of life (Chandra, Deepthivarma, Jairam, & Thomas, 2003). HIV-related stigma may be experienced from important social others or may be internalized as shame, or intrapersonal unforgiveness. Internalized stigma has been associated with a greater use of avoidant coping and a decreased use of active coping, both of which in turn are strongly related to depression (Demarco, 1999), and has also been linked directly to depression, hopelessness, and anxiety (Lee, Kochman, & Sikkema, 2003). Lee et al. (2003) found that a high level of internalized HIV stigma is associated with a sense of HIV-related rejection (or unforgiveness) from important others. Perceived stigma from others is associated with chronic depression among HIV-positive persons (Lichtenstein, Laska, & Clair, 2002) and poorer utilization of health care (Chesney & Smith, 1999; Lee et al., 2003; Reece, 2003). Chesney and Smith (1999) reported that perceptions of HIV-related stigma may result in underutilization of HIV testing services by high-risk populations and delayed treatment in infected individuals, with both factors contributing to the spread of the epidemic. Thus, stigma (interpersonal unforgiveness) may have a profound negative impact on public health, in addition to having a negative psychological and physical impact on the stigmatized individual.

There is growing evidence that preventing further spread of HIV in families, partners, and communities is highly correlated with psychological and spiritual dimensions of quality of life (Temoshok & the WHOQOL Group, 1997). For example, anxiety and depression can exacerbate problems of addiction and substance use, which, in turn, increase the risk of HIV transmission (e.g., Nannis, Philipson, & Temoshok, 1993). Fostering a sense of altruism and taking responsibility for protecting loved ones from infection have been discussed as ways to decrease HIV transmission to others and decelerate the rate of epidemic spread (Bayer, 1996; Temoshok & Patterson, 1996).

We conducted a partial test of our theoretical model of forgiveness and health among a sample of 131 adult patients in an inner-city HIV clinic in Baltimore, Maryland. Participants who rated themselves as more similar to forgiving vignettes and less similar to unforgiving vignettes (methods are described in more detail in the next section) reported fewer depressive symptoms as well as fewer current life stressors, and the stressors they reported were rated as being of lower severity (Wald & Temoshok, 2004a). On the World Health Organization's (WHO) Quality of Life (QOL) measure (WHOQOL), both global QOL and health QOL were significantly correlated with global vignette forgiveness scores. Thus, forgiveness was broadly associated with more positive psychological functioning and greater life satisfaction. These results remained significant after controlling for religious involvement, a factor that has also been associated in many health-related studies with lower rates of depression and higher quality of life.

Forgiveness was also found to be significantly related to critical health behaviors. Of the 91 patients who were prescribed antiretroviral medications, feeling unforgiven by important others was associated with significantly more missed doses of medication in the previous week. Because near-perfect adherence is required for successful treatment of HIV, these participants were at a substantially increased risk of treatment failure and hastened disease progression. Better patient-provider communication was the most significant factor predicting better adherence (Wald & Temoshok, 2004b).

In this same study, participants who identified more strongly with those vignette characters who were more forgiving of the people who infected them were significantly less likely to have unprotected sex, indicating that participants who were able to forgive those who infected them were more likely to take steps to protect others from infection (Wald & Temoshok, 2004a). Thus, forgiveness was found in this study to have positive health consequences for both the individual and society at large.

NEW RESEARCH DIRECTIONS AND PERSONAL THEORETICAL PERSPECTIVES

To our knowledge, most measures of forgiveness in the psychological literature have concentrated on the interpersonal context, with only a handful focused on self-forgiveness (see chapter 10 by Tangney, Boone, & Dearing and chapter 11 by Mullet, Neto, and Rivière). We believe that assessing forgiveness in the spiritual, community, or health care contexts, as we have outlined theoretically in Table 20.1 and implemented empirically in our research on HIV/AIDS (Temoshok & Chandra, 2000; Wald & Temoshok,

2004a, 2004b), widens the scope of considering forgiveness and potentially increases the opportunity to reveal relationships with a number of different constructs.

Such a comprehensive approach, however, entails the danger of respondent burden by having multiple measures, as well as the validity of self-report assessment of value-laden constructs. The first author was similarly challenged in the mid-1980s to come up with a more valid method than self-report to assess the Type C coping style (Temoshok & Dreher, 1992), which is highly correlated with social desirability (Kneier & Temoshok, 1984; Temoshok et al., 1985). This was a conundrum because respondents can hardly be expected to report accurately on emotions and thoughts of which they are not conscious or those they are inclined to report positively.

To address this Type C assessment problem, the first author devised the Vignette Similarity Rating method, in which respondents are asked to rate (on scales of 1–5 or 1–10) how similar or dissimilar they are to the person in each vignette, who is described as thinking, feeling, and behaving in ways that depict someone who is avoiding or repressing awareness of problematic emotions or thoughts and focusing instead on what other people may be feeling or needing and how to please these others. Because the vignettes are about other people, being asked to rate similarity to their emotions and behaviors (rather than rating directly one's own emotions and behaviors) appears to circumvent or minimize defensiveness about reporting socially less desirable states and behaviors. Vignettes may be tailored to use language and other details specific to a given culture or population. This vignette method has been shown to be more successful than self-report measures at capturing the complex emotional, cognitive, interpersonal, and behavioral coping proclivities inherent in the Type C construct, is much more accepted and liked by study participants (good face validity), and yields significant predictors (indicating high predictive validity) of health outcomes, such as HIV progression (Solano et al., 1993, Solano et al., 2002; Temoshok, 2003b, 2004c).

For our research on forgiveness in people living with HIV/AIDS, the authors have constructed and validated a series of forgiveness vignettes, using the Vignette Similarity Rating method described above (Wald & Temoshok, 2004a, 2004b). Our instrument presents respondents with 12 scenarios depicting forgiveness and unforgiveness for the different contexts depicted in Table 20.1 (intrapersonal, interpersonal, health care system, and spiritual). It asks them to rate their degree of similarity to each vignette's main character. Vignettes were written in terms of forgiving, unforgiving, feeling forgiven, and feeling unforgiven for each of these contexts. Thus, we have made no theoretical assumptions about bipolarity (i.e., a hypothetical forgiving-unforgiving dimension or a feeling forgiven-feeling unforgiven dimension), allowing for real-life complexity.

We have found excellent respondent acceptance of the vignettes and generally very quick identification or nonidentification with the character in the vignette ("I'm just like that person!" or "That is no way like me!"), as well as more nuanced responses ("I'm like her in some ways but not others; but it's closer to being like her, so I'll rate this "8"). All respondents preferred the vignette method over self-report questionnaires (e.g., of religiousness or forgiveness). From our data analyses, it was apparent that social desirability was still somewhat a problem, in that individuals who were more Type C also tended to report they were more forgiving and felt more forgiven—a hallmark of the Type C style. Our data suggest, however, that this is less of a problem for the vignette method than for the more transparent self-report measures.

Our future research on assessment in this arena will focus on fine-tuning less socially desirable traits and actions of unforgiving characters in vignettes to make it easier for strong Type C copers to recognize and report that they are like these characters. We will also work on validating vignettes to capture "masked forgiveness" (in which the person is more or less conscious about presenting a façade of not truly or genuinely felt forgiveness), as well as "premature forgiveness" (in which the person does not work through the stages and processes of forgiveness but jumps to an unsteady state of incomplete but reported forgiveness).

RELEVANCE FOR CLINICAL AND APPLIED INTERVENTIONS

Clinical Case Example 1

Mr. A was a 38-year-old African American with advanced AIDS, which he had contracted through homosexual behavior. Since early childhood, he was verbally abused and rejected by his father and older brothers over what they perceived to be his effeminacy. He came to regard his homosexuality as a profound moral flaw that had marked him for a lifetime of punishment, in which familial rejection and infection with HIV both played a part. A deeply religious Christian, Mr. A sought comfort from religion but did not feel that it was possible for God to forgive him. He was ambivalent about survival, neglecting to take his HIV medicines and sometimes expressing the belief that it would be better for him to die. With extensive psychotherapy focused on changing Mr. A's perception of himself as unforgiven and unforgivable, Mr. A began to see himself as worthy of life. Although multidrug resistance caused by his years of nonadherence meant that his HIV could not be brought under control, he became diligent about self-care and was adherent to all aspects of his medical regimen. He lived almost a year longer than his doctors predicted, and at the time of his death he felt accepted by himself and by God.

Clinical Case Example 2

Ms. S was a 50-year-old African American who had been infected with HIV by her unfaithful husband. Although Ms. S's physical health remained stable over the 10 years following her infection, lingering anger and resentment directed at her husband, now deceased, caused her substantial psychological distress. She spent much of her time ruminating over the circumstances of how she was betrayed and the unfairness of her situation. Gradually, her resentment toward her husband developed into a more generally hostile attitude toward other people. She had difficulty making emotional connections to other persons with HIV, feeling that her situation differed from theirs because she "didn't do anything wrong" to become infected, and adopted a combative and suspicious attitude toward service providers. She felt that her suffering entitled her to services and benefits, and she became angrily defensive if her need for services was questioned or if she discovered that someone else was given benefits she did not receive. In moments of insight, Ms. S acknowledged that her lingering grudge against her deceased husband impaired her present chances for happiness; however, she was unwilling to consider the possibility of forgiving someone who had wronged her so greatly.

The stories of Mr. A and Ms. S reflect some facets of the powerful role that forgiveness and unforgiveness play in the lives of persons with HIV and AIDS. Individuals often struggle with questions of guilt and self-forgiveness as they come to terms with the role that their own choices and risk behaviors (e.g., intravenous drug use) have played in their illness. They wrestle with concerns about God's forgiveness and with feelings of anger and unforgiveness toward God. Often, as their disease progresses, they find themselves unable to free themselves from lingering feelings of anger and resentment toward the person who infected them, family members who are rejecting or unsupportive, or medical personnel who are unable to cure them. Thus, among persons with HIV/AIDS, forgiveness represents an important concept across multiple intra- and interpersonal contexts, and an individual may simultaneously experience the roles of victim and transgressor in different social relationships. These factors add considerable complexity to the task of conducting forgiveness-related research and clinical interventions with this population.

CONCLUSIONS

In patients with most organic medical disorders, functional health status is strongly influenced by coping skills and social support, yet it has been argued that the mental, emotional, and behavioral dimensions of illness are typically neglected by predominant medical approaches (Sobel, 1995). By helping patients manage not just their disease but also common underlying needs for spiritual meaning, including forgiveness, quality of life as well as health outcomes for the self and loved ones can be markedly improved and at significantly lower costs than when medical interventions alone are used. To the extent that quality of life (well-being across multiple dimensions) and quantity of life (surviving longer) are not only highly correlated but mutually enhancing, it would be important to develop interventions aimed at enhancing quality of life, including the significant dimensions of forgiving and feeling forgiven, and to evaluate the extent to which both quality and quantity of life improve.

REFERENCES

Ader, R., Felten, D. L., & Cohen, N. (2000). *Psychoneuroimmunology,* (3rd ed.). New York: Academic Press.

Armistead, L., Morse, E., Forehand, R., Morse, P., & Clark, L. (1999). African-American women and self-disclosure of HIV infection: Rates, predictors, and relationship to depressive symptomatology. *AIDS & Behavior, 3,* 195–204.

Balbin, E. G., Ironson, G. H., & Solomon, G. F. (1999). Stress and coping: The psychoneuroimmunology of HIV/AIDS. *Ballière's Clinical Endocrinology and Metabolism, 13,* 615–633.

Bartlett, J. G., & Gallant, J. E. (2003). *Medical management of HIV infection, 2003 Edition.* Baltimore: Johns Hopkins University.

Bayer, R. (1996). Sounding board: AIDS prevention—sexual ethics and responsibility. *New England Journal of Medicine, 334,* 1540–1542.

Besedovsky, H. O., Herberman, R. B., Temoshok, L. R., & Sendo, F. (1996). Psychoneuroimmunology and cancer. *Cancer Research, 56,* 4278–4281.

Chandra, P. S., Deepthivarma, S., Jairam, K. R., & Thomas, T. (2003). Relationship of psychological morbidity and quality of life to illness-related disclosure among HIV-infected persons. *Journal of Psychosomatic Research,* 54, 199–203.

Chesney, M., & Smith, A. W. (1999). Critical delays in HIV testing and care: The potential role of stigma. *American Behavioral Scientist, 42,* 1162–1174.

Cole, S., Kemeny, M., Taylor, S., Visscher, B., & Fahey, J. (1996). Accelerated course of HIV infection in gay men who conceal their homosexuality. *Psychosomatic Medicine, 58,* 219–231.

Demarco, F. J. (1999). Coping with the stigma of AIDS: An investigation of the effects of shame, stress, control, and coping on depression in HIV-positive and -negative gay men. *Dissertation Abstracts International, Section B: The Sciences and Engineering, 59,* 5574.

Denollet, J., Sys, S. U., Stroobant, N., Rombouts, H., Gillebert, T. C., & Brutsaert, D. L. (1996). Personality as independent predictor of long-term mortality in patients with coronary heart disease. *Lancet, 347,* 417–421.

Evans, D. L., Leserman, J., Perkins, D. O., Stern, R. A., Murphy, C., Zheng, B., et al. (1997). Severe life stress as a predictor of early disease progression in HIV infection. *American Journal of Psychiatry, 154,* 630–634.

Glaser, R., Rabin, B., Chesney, M., Cohen, S., & Natelson, B. (1999) Stress-induced immunomodulation: Implications for infectious diseases? *Journal of the American Medical Association, 281,* 2268–2270.

Greer, S., Morris, T., Pettingale, K. W., & Haybittle, J. (1990). Psychological response to breast cancer and fifteen-year outcome. *Lancet, 335,* 49–50.

Ironson, G., Friedman, A., Klimas, N., Antoni, M. H., Fletcher, M. A., La Perriere, A., et al. (1994). Distress, denial, and low adherence to behavioral intervention predict faster disease progression in gay men infected with human immunodeficiency virus. *International Journal of Behavioral Medicine, 1,* 90–105.

Kemeny, M. E., & Dean L. (1995). Effects of AIDS-related bereavement on HIV progression among New York City gay men. *AIDS Education and Prevention, 7,* 36–47.

Kneier, A. W., & Temoshok, L. (1984). Repressive coping reactions in patients with malignant melanoma as compared to cardiovascular disease patients. *Journal of Psychosomatic Research, 28,* 145–155.

Kune, G. A., Kune, S., & Watson, L. F. (1993). Perceived religiousness is protective for colorectal cancer: Data from The Melbourne Colorectal Cancer Study. *Journal of the Royal Society of Medicine, 86,* 645–647.

Lee, R. S., Kochman, A., & Sikkema, K. J. (2003). Internalized stigma among people living with HIV-AIDS. *AIDS & Behavior, 6,* 309–319.

Leserman, J., Petitto, J. M., Golden, R. N., Gaynes, B. N., Gu, H., Perkins, D. O., et al. (2000). Impact of stressful life events, depression, social support, coping, and cortisol on progression to AIDS. *American Journal of Psychiatry, 157,* 1221–1228.

Lichtenstein, B., Laska M. K., & Clair, J. M. (2002). Chronic sorrow in the HIV-positive patient: Issues of race, gender, and social support. *AIDS Patient Care, 16,* 27–38.

Lyketsos, C. G., Hoover, D. R., Guccione, M., Senterfitt, W., Dew, M. A., Wesch, J., et al. (1993). Depressive symptoms as predictors of medical outcomes in HIV infection. *Journal of the American Medical Association, 270,* 2563–2567.

Moulton, J. M., Sweet, D. M., & Temoshok, L. (1987). Attributions of blame and responsibility in relation to distress and health behavior change in people with AIDS and AIDS-related complex. *Journal of Applied Social Psychology, 17,* 189–192.

Miller, G. E., & Cole, S. W. (1998). Social relationships and the progression of human immunodeficiency virus infection: A review of evidence and possible underlying mechanisms. *Annals of Behavioral Medicine, 20,* 181–189.

Mulder, C. L. (1994). Psychosocial correlates and the effects of behavioral interventions on the course of human immunodeficiency virus infection in homosexual men. *Patient Education and Counseling, 24,* 237–247.

Mulder, C. L., Antoni, M. H., Duivenvoorden, H. J., Kauffmann, R. H., & Goodkin, K. (1995). Active confrontational coping predicts decreased clinical progression over a one-year period in HIV-infected homosexual men. *Journal of Psychosomatic Research, 39,* 957–965.

Nannis, E. D., Philipson, J., & Temoshok, L. R. (1993). Prevention, education, and counseling efforts in HIV-infected and at-risk populations. *Current Opinion in Infectious Disease, 6,* 205–209.

Nyklicek, I., Temoshok, L. R., & Vingerhoets, A. (Eds.). (2004). *Emotional expression and health: Advances in theory, assessment, and clinical applications.* London: Brunner-Routledge.

O'Leary, A., Temoshok, L., Jenkins, S. R., & Sweet, D. M. (1989). Autonomic reactivity and immune function in men with AIDS. *Psychophysiology, 26,* S47.

Patterson, T. L., Semple, S. J., Temoshok, L. R., Atkinson, J. H., McCutchan, J. A., Straits-Tröster, K. A., et al. (1995). Stress and depressive symptoms prospectively predict immune change among HIV-seropositive men. *Psychiatry, 58,* 299–312.

Reece, M. (2003). HIV-related mental health care: Factors influencing dropout among low-income, HIV-positive individuals. *AIDS Care, 15,* 707–716.

Sobel, D. S. (1995). Rethinking medicine: Improving health outcomes with cost-effective psychosocial interventions. *Psychosomatic Medicine, 57,* 234–244.

Solano, L., Costa, M., Salvati, S., Coda, R., Aiuti, F., Mezzaroma, I., et al. (1993). Psychosocial factors and clinical evolution in HIV-infection: A longitudinal study. *Journal of Psychosomatic Research, 37,* 39–51.

Solano, L., Costa, M., Temoshok, L, Salvati, S., Coda, R., Aiuti, F., et al. (2002). An emotionally inexpressive (Type C) coping style influences HIV disease progression at six- and twelve-month follow-ups. *Psychology and Health, 17,* 641–655.

Solomon, G. F., Kemeny, M. E., & Temoshok, L. (1991). Psychoneuroimmunologic aspects of human immunodeficiency virus infection. In R. Ader, D. L. Felten, & N. Cohen (Eds.), *Psychoneuroimmunology* (2nd ed., pp. 1081–1114). San Diego, CA: Academic Press.

Solomon, G. F., & Temoshok, L. (1987). A psychoneuroimmunologic perspective on AIDS research: Questions, preliminary findings, and suggestions. *Journal of Applied Social Psychology, 17,* 286–308.

Solomon, G. F., Temoshok, L., O'Leary, A., & Zich, J. (1987). An intensive psychoimmunologic study of long-surviving persons with AIDS. *Annals of the New York Academy of Science, 496,* 647–655.

Temoshok, L. R. (1985). Biopsychosocial studies on cutaneous malignant melanoma: Psychosocial factors associated with prognostic indicators, progression, psychophysiology, and tumor-host response. *Social Science and Medicine, 20,* 833–840.

Temoshok, L. R. (1987). Personality, coping style, emotion, and cancer: Toward an integrative model. *Cancer Surveys, 6,* 837–857.

Temoshok, L. R. (1990a). Applying the biopsychosocial model to research on HIV/AIDS. In P. Bennett, J. Weinman, & P. Spurgeon (Eds.), *Current developments in health psychology* (pp. 129–157). Chur, Switzerland: Harwood Academic.

Temoshok, L. R. (1990b). On attempting to articulate the biopsychosocial model: Psychological-psychophysiological homeostasis. In H. Friedman (Ed.), *Personality and disease* (pp. 203–225). New York: Wiley.

Temoshok, L. R. (1991). Malignant melanoma, AIDS, and the complex search for psychosocial mechanisms. *Advances: The Journal of Mind-Body Health, 7,* 20–28.

Temoshok, L. R. (1993). HIV/AIDS, psychoneuroimmunology and beyond: A commentary and review. *Advances in Neuroimmunology, 3,* 141–149.

Temoshok, L. R. (1995). On biobehavioral models of cancer stress and disease course. *American Psychologist, 50,* 1104–1105.

Temoshok, L. R. (1996). On measuring hope and its cultivation. *Advances: The Journal of Mind-Body Health, 13,* 51–53.

Temoshok, L. R. (1997). The risk of HIV exposure in military vs. civilian populations: Implications of the first large-scale military HIV Survey. Geneva: World Health Organization.

Temoshok, L. R. (2000a). Complex coping patterns and their role in adaptation and neuroimmunomodulation: Theory, methodology, and research. *Annals of the New York Academy of Science, 917,* 446–455.

Temoshok, L. R. (2000b). Psychological response and survival in breast cancer. *Lancet, 355,* 404–405.

Temoshok, L. R. (2002). Connecting the dots linking mind, behavior, and disease: The biological concomitants of coping patterns. *Integrative Cancer Therapies, 1,* 387–391.

Temoshok, L. R. (2003a). Congruence matters: A consideration of adaptation and appropriateness. *Advances in Mind-Body Medicine, 19,* 10–12.

Temoshok, L. R. (2003b). Type C coping and cancer progression. In R. Fernandez-Ballesteros (Ed.), *The encyclopedia of psychological assessment* (Vol. 2 pp. 1052–1056). New York: Sage.

Temoshok, L. R. (2004a). Rethinking theory and research on psychosocial interventions in biopsychosocial oncology. *Psycho-Oncology, 13,* 460–467.

Temoshok, L. R. (2004b). Biopsychosocial model. In A. J. Christensen, R. Martin, J. M. Smyth (Eds.), *Encyclopedia of health psychology* (pp. 29–32). New York: Kluwer Academic/Plenum.

Temoshok, L. R. (2004c). Type C coping/behavior pattern. In A. J. Christensen, R. Martin, J. M. Smyth (Eds.), *Encyclopedia of health psychology* (pp. 332–333). New York: Kluwer Academic/Plenum.

Temoshok, L., & Chandra, P. S. (2000). The meaning of forgiveness in a specific situational and cultural context: Persons living with HIV/AIDS in India. In M. E. McCullough, K. I. Pargament, & C. E. Thoresen (Eds.), *Forgiveness: Theory, research, and practice* (pp. 41–64). New York: Guilford Press.

Temoshok, L., & Dreher, H. (1992). *The Type C connection: The behavioral links to cancer and your health.* New York: Random House.

Temoshok, L., Heller, B. W., Sagebiel, R. W., Blois, M. S., Sweet, D. M., DiClemente, R. J., et al. (1985). The relationship of psychosocial factors to prognostic indicators in cutaneous malignant melanoma. *Journal of Psychosomatic Research, 29,* 139–154.

Temoshok, L. R., & Patterson, T. L. (1996). Risk of HIV transmission in infected U.S. military personnel. *Lancet, 347,* 697.

Temoshok L. R., & the WHOQOL Group. (1997). *HIV/AIDS and quality of life: An international perspective.* Geneva: World Health Organization Division of Mental Health.

Ullrich, P. M., Lutgendorf, S. K., & Stapleton, J. T. (2003). Concealment of homosexual identity, social support, and CD4 cell count among HIV-seropositive gay men. *Journal of Psychosomatic Research, 54,* 205–212.

Vassend, P., Eskild, A., & Halvorsen, R. (1997). Negative affectivity, coping, immune status, and disease progression in HIV-infected individuals. *Psychology and Health, 12,* 375–388.

Wald R. L., & Temoshok, L. R. (2004a). Spirituality, forgiveness, and health in a U.S. inner-city HIV clinic. *Proceedings, XV International AIDS Conference, Bangkok, Thailand* (pp. 55–58). Bologna, Italy: Medimond.

Wald, R. L., & Temoshok, L. R. (2004b). Subjective beliefs about health care predict adherence to antiretroviral medications in a U.S. clinic. *Proceedings, XV International AIDS Conference, Bangkok, Thailand* (pp. 257–260). Bologna, Italy: Medimond.

Zich, J., & Temoshok, L. (1987). Perceptions of social support in men with AIDS and ARC: Relationships with distress and hardiness. *Journal of Applied Social Psychology, 17,* 193–215.

Chapter Twenty-One

Theoretical and Empirical Connections Between Forgiveness, Mental Health, and Well-Being

Loren Toussaint
Jon R. Webb

In this chapter, we review theoretical and empirical studies of forgiveness and mental health. Mental health variables are defined, consistent with the DSM-IV (American Psychiatric Association, 1994), and may include symptoms of disorders (e.g., depression) or actual disorders (e.g., major depression). Studies that include relevant mental health variables, such as nonspecific psychological distress and life satisfaction/well-being, are also included.[1] The focus of this chapter is to understand connections between forgiveness and mental health, broadly defined, and critically to examine the state of our knowledge in terms of the potentially salutary effects of forgiveness on mental health and well-being.

Considering mental health correlates and outcomes of forgiveness is important for at least four reasons. First, unforgiveness is often a core component of stress resulting from an *inter*personal offense, and stress is associated with decreased mental health. Second, unforgiveness resulting from *intra*personal transgressions may increase levels of guilt, shame, and regret that in turn negatively impact one's mental health. Forgiveness may be one way of coping with *inter*personal and *intra*personal stress in a fashion that promotes positive adjustment. Third, the cost of mental illness to society is enormous. For instance, in 1996 alone, direct costs exceeded $80 billion (U. S. Department of Health and Human Services, 1999). Fourth, mental health is often linked to physical health, and as such, mental illness may increase costs of physical health care. To the extent that forgiveness can be shown to ameliorate negative mental health consequences of interpersonal and intrapersonal offenses, it will become increasingly recognized as a viable means of treatment and an important protective variable.

PERSONAL ASSUMPTIONS ABOUT FORGIVENESS

A widely accepted definition of forgiveness has been hard to identify. Perhaps this is the result of the many differing contexts in which forgiveness issues arise; hence, most definitions are context specific. Forgiveness may involve oneself (Hall & Fincham, in press), others (Enright, Freedman, & Rique, 1998), God (Exline, Yali, & Lobel, 1999), families (DiBlasio & Proctor, 1993), or entire societies and cultures (Sandage, Hill, & Vang, 2003). Given the broad array of contexts in which forgiveness issues may arise and the multiplicity of factors likely involved, a single, comprehensive definition of forgiveness has remained elusive.

We believe that the key to identifying a more unifying definition of forgiveness lies in building a more comprehensive understanding of the construct. In concurrence with Enright and the Human Development Study Group (1991), we believe that forgiveness should be conceptualized as a multidimensional construct that contains dimensions of affect, behavior, and cognition. We further underscore important distinctions that have been made regarding different *targets* (i.e., oneself, others, God) and *methods* of forgiveness (i.e., offering, feeling, or seeking; Enright & the Human Development Study Group, 1996; Pingleton, 1989; Sandage, Worthington, Hight, & Berry, 2000).

Our definition builds from previous work and is multidimensional and comprehensive. Trait forgiveness involves a *tendency* to offer, feel, or seek changes from negative to positive cognitions, behaviors, and affect pertaining to offenders that include oneself, others, and God. State forgiveness involves a *process* of offering, feeling, or seeking a change from negative to positive cognitions, behaviors, and affect pertaining to *specific* offenses that are perceived to be perpetrated by oneself, others, or God.

Further, we believe that important, distinctive, and core components of the definition of forgiveness that separate it from other forms of adjustment and coping include motivational and volitional factors. As such, we believe that forgiveness is an internal process undertaken by the victim (Worthington, Sandage, & Berry, 2000), which does not require retribution (Rosenak & Harnden, 1992), restitution (Wahking, 1992), reconciliation, or a return to vulnerability by the victim, yet reserves the right to retain accountability from the offender (Enright et al., 1998).

REVIEW OF THE THEORETICAL AND EMPIRICAL LITERATURE

Theoretical Literature

Interest in the psychological and theological understanding of forgiveness has resulted in numerous publications on the topic. We restrict our review to the work we feel has good potential for guiding future empirical work through the development of conceptual models grounded in sound psychological theory and research. A particularly useful conceptual model was proposed by Worthington, Berry, and Parrott (2001). They conceptualize the interplay between forgiveness and health as involving both direct and indirect relationships. Worthington et al. (2001) outline a model of forgiveness and general health, but because of the comprehensive nature of the model, we believe it to be equally applicable to issues of mental health as well. Furthermore, additional insight regarding these relationships is gained through understanding underlying developmental and attributional processes of forgiveness.

Direct Effect. The direct effect of forgiveness on mental health (see Figure 21.1) can be described in terms of unforgiveness, through rumination, and involving the emotions of resentment, bitterness, hatred, hostility, residual anger, and fear (Worthington et al., 2001). Left unaddressed, negative emotions can lead to significant mental health

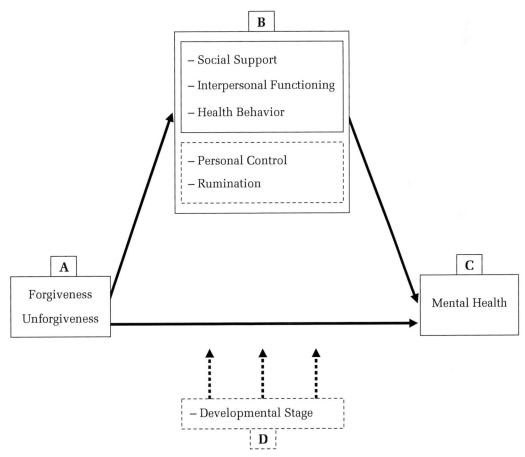

FIGURE 21.1.   Effect of Forgiveness on Mental Health
Note. Adapted from Worthington et al. (2001); dotted lines represent modifications to the model.

problems. There are many ways to address unforgiveness, including retaliation, revenge, justice, denial, and forgiveness (Worthington & Wade, 1999). Forgiveness involves the contamination or prevention of unforgiveness with strong, positive, love-based emotions (Worthington et al., 2001). When describing the emotions of forgiveness and unforgiveness, Worthington et al. (2001) are careful to point out that these are not just subjective feelings, but like all emotions, involve a variety of physiological processes. It is through these physiological changes that forgiveness may likely have its direct effect on mental health and well-being.

Indirect Effect.   Forgiveness is likely to promote mental health indirectly (see Figure 21.1) through variables such as social support, interpersonal functioning, and health behavior (Temoshok & Chandra, 2000; Worthington et al., 2001). These mediating variables are commonly associated with improved mental health (Bausell, 1986; Mohr, Averna, Kenny, & Del Boca, 2001; Saltzman & Holahan, 2002). Worthington et al. (2001) propose that forgiveness is positively related to these mediating variables that in turn are positively related to mental health.

On closer examination, the relationship between forgiveness and mental health may be viewed as indirect in all cases. Although the indirect effect described above is clear, the direct effect described above, in actuality, is thought to operate through rumination and its connection to a variety of negative emotions. However, it may still be helpful to keep the distinction between direct and indirect effects. Because lack of rumination appears to be an underlying determinant of the ability to forgive (see McCullough, 2000), it may go hand in hand with forgiveness and thus may not be a mediating factor. Social support, interpersonal functioning, and health behavior seem less likely to be intertwined with the ability to forgive and thus more likely to be clear mediators.

Developmental Process.   Much work has been completed in describing the developmental process of forgiveness. Enright et al. (1998) provide a summary of 20 steps or units of forgiveness and divide the process into four broad phases: uncovering, decision, work, and deepening. *Uncovering* refers to the awareness of the problem and emotional pain following an offense, including anger and insight. *Decision* includes realizing the need for an alternate resolution. *Work* includes processes such as reframing, empathy, and acceptance of pain. *Deepening* includes finding meaning and universality. It is carefully pointed out that the overall process of forgiveness is not likely to be linear (i.e., an orderly progression between steps).

Depending on one's stage of progression through the developmental process of forgiveness, the relationship between forgiveness and mental health may vary. In the earliest stages of the process (i.e., uncovering and decision), forgiveness may actually be related to poorer mental health. As one works through the later phases (i.e., work and deepening), the effects of forgiveness should become more beneficial. In this way, the developmental stage may act as a moderator of the forgiveness and mental health relationship (see Figure 21.1).

Attributional Process.   The ability to forgive is thought to be positively associated with personal control in one's life (Benson, 1992; Hope, 1987) and the restoration of a sense of personal power (McCullough & Worthington, 1994). Evidence is beginning to emerge in support of this relationship (Witvliet, Ludwig, & Vander Laan, 2001). Internal locus of control, or perceived personal control, refers to an expectation that outcomes are influenced by one's actions (Peterson, Maier, & Seligman, 1993). As such, Coleman (1998) describes a paradoxical relationship between control and forgiveness. One often feels a loss of control when offended and perceives that unforgiveness will enable control to be regained. Over time, unforgiveness actually prevents one from exercising control by continuing to consume (e.g., through rumination) the individual with negative emotions. Given the connection between forgiveness and personal control and the connection between perceptions of control and mental health (Shapiro, Schwartz, & Astin, 1996), it appears that an important indirect pathway from forgiveness to mental health involves perceived personal control (see Figure 21.1).

Empirical Literature

A small number of correlational, experimental, and intervention studies make up the empirical literature on forgiveness and mental health. Although this literature is small in size, the findings from these studies suggest an important role of forgiveness in mental health and psychological well-being. Correlational studies make up the majority of investigations, followed by intervention studies. Finally, only one study was identified that experimentally examined forgiveness and psychological well-being. Correlational studies will be reviewed first. Intervention studies will be reviewed second. The experimental study will be reviewed last.

Correlational Studies.   Thirteen studies that directly examine the relationships between forgiveness and mental health and well-being were identified. Examining these studies (see Table 21.1) reveals interesting characteristics. Seven of the studies rely on undergraduate samples, and six studies utilized other samples from community- and clinic-based settings. College-student samples are convenient and easily accessible, but they come with inherent generalizability issues and other limitations that are particularly important for forgiveness research (i.e., restrictions in age, type of hurt, mental health status). Hence, it is encouraging to find that various populations have been sampled at this early stage of development in the field, and results are consistent across studies using varied samples.

Dimensions of forgiveness that are assessed in relation to mental health have been limited. Although all studies included measures of forgiveness of others, only six included measures of forgiveness of self. Only three studies included measures assessing forgiveness of or by God. Only one study assessed seeking forgiveness. Further, most studies assessed forgiveness at the trait level (10 of 13 studies). Only three studies assessed forgiveness as a state. Trait forgiveness was shown to be associated

TABLE 21.1.   Studies Reporting Correlations Between Forgiveness and Mental Health

Study	Sample (N; number ♀; M_{Age}; population)	Associations
Berry & Worthington (2001)	39; 20; 23; undergrads	Forgiveness positively related to global mental health (r = .52).
Brown (2003)	70; 32; 22.6; undergrads	Forgiveness negatively related to depression (r = −.34).
Exline et al., (1999)	200; 140; 19.7; undergrads	Difficulty forgiving God and self positively related to depression and anxiety (rs .21 to .31). Difficulty forgiving others positively related to anxiety (r = .16).
Kendler et al. (2003)	2,621 twin pairs from Virginia Twin Registry	Forgiveness related to less nicotine dependence and less drug abuse or dependence. Low vengefulness related to less major depression, generalized anxiety, phobia, and bulimia nervosa (ORs = .53 to .90).
Krause & Ellison (2003)	1,316; 763; 74.5; older adults	Forgiveness of others negatively related to depressive affect, depressive somatic symptoms, and death anxiety, and positively to life satisfaction. Forgiveness by God negatively related to depressive affect and positively to life satisfaction ($|\beta s|$ = .07 to .22).
Maltby, Macaskill, & Day (2001)	324; 224; 22; undergrads	Unforgiveness of self and others positively related to depression and anxiety (rs = .16 to .27).
Mauger et al. (1992)	237; outpatient clients in counseling	Unforgiveness of self and others positively related to depression and anxiety (rs = .16 to .56).
McCullough et al. (2001)	91; 55; undergrads	State unforgiveness not related to life satisfaction cross-sectionally or longitudinally.
Rye et al. (2001)	328; 222; 19.2; undergrads	State forgiveness (rs = .21 to .40) but not trait forgiveness positively related to existential well-being.
Seybold, Hill, Neumann, & Chi (2001)	68; 22; 46; community residents	Unforgiveness of self and others positively related to depression, state anxiety, and trait anxiety (rs = .49 to .77).
Subkoviak et al. (1995)	394; 204; 22.1 (50% undergrads)/49.6 (50%; same-gender parent)	State forgiveness negatively related to state anxiety (rs = −.28 to −.60).
Toussaint et al. (2001)	1,423; nationally representative probability sample of U.S. adults	Forgiveness of oneself and others negatively related to psychological distress and positively related to life satisfaction. Seeking forgiveness positively related to distress and negatively related to life satisfaction. Associations vary by age ($|\beta s|$ = .13 to .42).
Witvliet et al. (2004)	213; 0; 50.8; veterans with PTSD	Unforgiveness of oneself positively related to PTSD, depression and anxiety. Unforgiveness of others positively related to PTSD and depression (βs = .16 to .28).

Note: ♀ = female; r = Pearson correlation; β = standardized regression coefficient; OR = odds ratio; $|\beta s|$ = absolute value of standardized regression coefficient; all forgiveness/unforgiveness measures are dispositional unless otherwise indicated.

with mental health in nine of the ten studies. Of the three studies incorporating state forgiveness measures, two showed associations with mental health. More needs to be learned about different types and state-trait considerations of forgiveness in its relation to mental health.

Assessment of mental health outcomes in relation to forgiveness has generally been limited to depression, anxiety, broadly defined mental health, and broadly defined well-being. Nevertheless, findings within this limited range of outcomes appear quite consistent. Nine of thirteen studies examined depression, and all nine showed expected associations with forgiveness. Eight of thirteen examined anxiety, and again all eight showed expected associations with forgiveness. Five of thirteen examined overall mental health and/or well-being, and four of these studies showed expected associations. Other mental health outcomes have received less attention. Only two studies (Kendler et al., 2003; Witvliet, Phipps, Feldman, & Beckham, 2004) exist where variables such as posttraumatic stress disorder (PTSD), phobia, panic, and substance abuse have been considered. Findings from these studies suggest that the connections of forgiveness to mental health reach beyond only depression and anxiety.

The contexts in which forgiveness and mental health have been assessed are limited. For instance, forgiveness and mental health in the context of other health concerns (e.g., traumatic injury, alcoholism, combat-related PTSD) are beginning to receive attention (Hart, 1999; Toussaint & Webb, 2003; Webb, Kalpakjian, & Toussaint, 2003; Webb, Robinson, Brower, & Zucker, 2003; Witvliet et al., 2004), but much more work remains to be done. Many hurts and offenses may be considered traumatic, and the relationship between forgiveness and mental health in the context of traumatic injury or illness should also be examined. Alcohol and substance abuse disorders are often co-morbid with other mental disorders, and these outcomes should also receive further attention. In addition to using assessments of symptoms, it would also be worthwhile to use diagnostic mental health outcome variables that have been verified by a structured clinical interview (e.g., SCID-I; First, Spitzer, Gibbon, & Williams, 1997).

Generally speaking, this small body of literature reveals a relationship between forgiveness and mental health. However, there is a great deal of variability with regard to the magnitude of these associations. Associations have been reported as small as .20 and as large as .70 or greater. An important task is to understand what factors account for such variability. For instance, factors such as age and type of forgiveness have been shown to have an impact, but much remains to be learned here.

Intervention Studies.   Four empirical reports of forgiveness interventions examining mental health variables were identified in the literature (see Part IV for further discussion of forgiveness interventions). A close examination of these four studies (see Table 21.2) reveals that the effect of forgiveness intervention on mental health (i.e., anxiety and depression) is anything but definitive. Three of the four studies show mixed support for the hypothesis that forgiveness has a positive effect on mental health. However, evidence from intervention studies is qualified by a number of factors at present. First, sample sizes are small. Second, intervention protocols differ widely in terms of length and content. Third, anxiety and depression are the only mental health outcomes assessed. Fourth, very specific transgressions (e.g., incest) have been addressed in these studies, so findings likely are not generalizable to other offenses. Apropos, future work should (a) use larger samples, (b) examine the same intervention across different types of offense, (c) examine different interventions within the same type of offense, and (d) broaden the assessment of mental health.

TABLE 21.2. Studies of the Effect of Forgiveness Interventions on Mental Health

Study	Sample	Intervention	Outcomes	General findings
Al-Mabuk, Enright, & Cardis (1995) Studies 1 & 2	$N_1 = 48$ (♀ = 37); $N_2 = 45$ (♀ = 29); $M_{Age} = 20$; love-deprived undergraduates	Study 1: 4 sessions, 2 weeks Study 2: 6 sessions, 6 weeks	Depression and anxiety	Study 2 yielded improvements in trait anxiety but not state anxiety or depression
Coyle & Enright (1997)	$N = 10$ (♀ = 0); $M_{Age} = 28$; hurt by abortion decision of partner	12 sessions, 12 weeks, 90-minute sessions	State anxiety	Intervention yielded improvements in state anxiety
Freedman & Enright (1996)	$N = 12$ (♀ = 12); $M_{Age} = 36$; incest survivors	17 units, average 14.3 months, 60-minute sessions held weekly	State and trait anxiety; depression	Intervention yielded improvements in anxiety and depression
Hebl & Enright (1993)	$N = 24$ (♀ = 24); $M_{Age} = 74.5$	8 sessions, 8 weeks, 60-minute sessions	State and trait anxiety; depression	Improvements in anxiety and depression not attributable to intervention

Note: ♀ = female.

Experimental Study.   Karremans, Van Lange, Ouwerkerk, and Kluwer (2003) have conducted, to our knowledge, the only published experimental investigation of forgiveness and well-being to date. This investigation consisted of a series of four studies focusing on factors explaining when and why forgiveness impacts well-being. A cleverly designed set of instructions allowed the researchers to manipulate forgiveness and observe its effects on psychological well-being. Three major findings are important to review. First, results suggested that forgiveness is associated with well-being, but the association is stronger in relationships of strong rather than weak commitment. Second, results showed that "psychological tension" (i.e., cognitive dissonance) mediated the relationship between forgiveness and well-being. Third, tendencies to forgive one's spouse were more strongly related to well-being than were tendencies to forgive others. In sum, these findings suggest that the mental health benefits of forgiveness are dependent on the relational nature underlying the offense and mediated through reductions in psychological tension. This study provides an excellent starting point from which to build additional experimental support for the link between forgiveness and mental health. Future work would do well to employ nonstudent samples and explore novel ways of manipulating forgiveness levels while controlling for variance in transgressions.

NEW RESEARCH DIRECTIONS NEEDED IN THE AREA

Advancing our understanding of the connections between forgiveness and mental health *requires* at least three things. First, forgiveness measurement issues must be addressed. Currently, there are a handful of good measures of trait and state forgiveness, but these measures focus almost exclusively on forgiveness of others. Dimensions of forgiveness such as forgiveness of self, feeling forgiven, and seeking forgiveness have all but been ignored in terms of developing sound assessment instruments. The field needs appropriate state-trait and multidimensional measures of forgiveness. Second, selecting samples from diverse populations must be a high priority. This will allow an examination of the extent to which ethnicity or socioeconomic status moderates the relationships between forgiveness and mental health. Social psychologists, sociologists, medical sociologists, and psychiatric epidemiologists could serve as excellent colleagues in our pursuit to understand social factors influencing the forgiveness and mental health relationship. Social survey experts can also assist in attaining nationally representative probability samples that will allow for generalization of our findings to broader populations. Third, we must continue to focus on the development and execution of interventions and experiments. This is the only way we will definitively know that forgiveness causes improvements in mental health and not the opposite. Longitudinal, correlational research would also be useful in this regard, but little if any exists showing prospective associations between forgiveness and mental health.

A fourth goal of continuing research efforts should be to understand potential mediators/moderators (e.g., empathy, anger, rumination) of the relationship between forgiveness and mental health. A key variable in this regard is rumination. Rumination is associated with a variety of mental health outcomes, especially depression (e.g., Harrington & Blankenship, 2002). Rumination is also associated with forgiveness (Berry, Worthington, O'Connor, Parrott, & Wade, 2005; Brooks, Toussaint, Worthington, & Berry, 2004; McCullough, Bellah, Kilpatrick, & Johnson, 2001; McCullough et al., 1998; Thompson et al., 2005). Given these associations, two interesting questions arise. First, what is the causal ordering of forgiveness and rumination? Second, what are the unique contributions of each to mental health?

Both of these questions have begun to be addressed. McCullough and Bono (2004) have shown that rumination may play a *causal* role in impeding forgiveness over time, and Brooks (2004) has shown that experimentally manipulating rumination following a transgression lowers subsequent levels of forgiveness. Brooks and Toussaint (2003) have also shown relationships between forgiveness and depression that are fully or partially mediated by rumination. These studies offer a starting point for future work to examine forgiveness and rumination variables in a fashion that allows for clear conclusions about their causal ordering and their unique contributions to mental health. Given the connection of rumination to key mental health outcomes such as depression and anxiety (Harrington & Blankenship, 2002), it is critical that we begin to improve our understanding of the connections it has to forgiveness.

In line with our previous recommendation to understand better the mediators/moderators of the forgiveness-mental health relationship, a fifth suggestion is that interventionists and clinicians studying the therapeutic effects of forgiveness should consider mental health variables as moderators. For instance, improvements in depression, anxiety, life satisfaction, and so forth, that result from a forgiveness intervention may be more pronounced for victims of a traumatic offense who are suffering from PTSD, as compared with others. In this case, mental health status (i.e., presence vs. absence of PTSD) would moderate the effect of forgiveness on depression, anxiety, life satisfaction, and so forth.

Despite the fact that all known studies have treated mental health variables as outcomes, our final recommendation is to use these variables as predictors of forgiveness. Perhaps depressed or anxious individuals will be less motivated to engage in the forgiveness process, or they may not have the necessary energy to invest in such a challenging and taxing venture. In either case, it would be interesting to know the mental health profile of a forgiving versus unforgiving person.

PERSONAL THEORETICAL PERSPECTIVES ON THE FIELD

Our personal approach to the study of forgiveness focuses on understanding the different targets and methods of forgiveness and their relationship to mental health. Our conceptualization can be mapped out in an incomplete three (offer, feel, seek) by three (self, others, God) table that yields seven distinct dimensions of forgiveness that should be investigated. They are: (a) forgiveness of oneself, (b) forgiveness of others, (c) forgiveness of God, (d) feeling others' forgiveness, (e) feeling God's forgiveness, (f) seeking others' forgiveness, and (g) seeking God's forgiveness. We leave feeling and seeking forgiveness from oneself undefined at this point. We hypothesize that these seven dimensions of forgiveness may relate differentially to mental health. Toussaint, Williams, Musick, and Everson (2001) showed that forgiveness of self and others were associated with less distress and greater well-being, but feeling forgiven by God was *not* associated with these outcomes, and seeking forgiveness from others was indeed associated but in the *opposite* direction. We believe that additional gains in understanding the associations between forgiveness and mental health will come as a result of conceptualizing forgiveness as multidimensional and examining the associations between specific dimensions of forgiveness and mental health in carefully planned and executed correlational, experimental, and intervention studies.

CONCLUSIONS

Our review of the literature on forgiveness and mental health suggests that theory and empirical work are at a beginning point. Vast arrays of theoretical and theological positions exist regarding the relationship between forgiveness and mental health. Empirical evidence, although sparse, is growing in support of the notion that forgiveness may have a salutary effect on mental health. With continued attention to issues of conceptualization and measurement, we can expect continued growth in our knowledge of the exciting relationships between forgiveness and mental health.

NOTE

1. The terms *life satisfaction* and *well-being* are used interchangeably to describe one's perceived satisfaction with life.

REFERENCES

Al-Mabuk, R. H., Enright, R. D., & Cardis, P. A. (1995). Forgiveness education with parentally love-deprived late adolescents. *Journal of Moral Education, 24*, 427–444.

American Psychiatric Association. (1994). *Diagnostic and statistical manual of mental disorders* (4th ed.). Washington, DC: Author.

Bausell, R. B. (1986). Health-seeking behavior among the elderly. *The Gerontologist, 26*, 556–559.

Benson, C. K. (1992). Forgiveness and the psychotherapeutic process. *Journal of Psychology and Christianity, 11*, 76–81.

Berry, J. W., & Worthington, E. L., Jr. (2001). Forgiveness, relationship quality, stress while imagining relationship events, and physical and mental health. *Journal of Counseling Psychology, 48*, 447–455.

Berry, J. W., Worthington, E. L., Jr., O'Connor, L. E., Parrott, L., III., & Wade, N. G. (2005). Forgivingness, vengeful rumination, and affective traits. *Journal of Personality, 73*, 1–43.

Brooks, C. W. (2004). *The cognitive processes of unforgiveness: Examining the roles of rumination and counterfactual thinking after a hurtful event.* Pocatello, ID: Idaho State University.

Brooks, C. W., & Toussaint, L. (2003). *The relationship between forgiveness and depression: Rumination as a link.* Poster session presented at the annual meeting of the Association for the Advancement of Behavior Therapy, Boston, MA.

Brooks, C. W., Toussaint, L., Worthington, E. L., Jr., & Berry, J. W. (2004). [Forgiveness, rumination, and depression]. Unpublished raw data.

Brown, R. P. (2003). Measuring individual differences in the tendency to forgive: Construct validity and links with depression. *Personality and Social Psychology Bulletin, 29*, 1–13.

Coleman, P. W. (1998). The process of forgiveness in marriage and the family. In R. D. Enright & J. North (Eds.), *Exploring forgiveness* (pp. 75–94). Madison, WI: University of Wisconsin Press.

Coyle, C. T., & Enright, R. D. (1997). Forgiveness intervention with postabortion men. *Journal of Consulting and Clinical Psychology, 65*, 1042–1046.

DiBlasio, F. A., & Proctor, J. H. (1993). Therapists and the clinical use of forgiveness. *American Journal of Family Therapy, 21*, 175–184.

Enright, R. D., Freedman, S., & Rique, J. (1998). The psychology of interpersonal forgiveness. In R. D. Enright & J. North (Eds.), *Exploring forgiveness* (pp. 46–62). Madison, WI: University of Wisconsin Press.

Enright, R. D., & the Human Development Study Group. (1991). The moral development of forgiveness. In W. Kurtines & J. Gewirtz (Eds.), *Handbook of moral behavior and development* (Vol. 1, pp. 123–152). Hillsdale, NJ: Lawrence Erlbaum.

Enright, R. D., & The Human Development Study Group. (1996). Counseling within the forgiveness triad: On forgiving, receiving forgiveness, and self-forgiveness. *Counseling and Values, 40*, 107–126.

Exline, J. J., Yali, A. M., & Lobel, M. (1999). When God disappoints: Difficulty forgiving God and its role in negative emotion. *Journal of Health Psychology, 4*, 365–379.

First, M. B., Spitzer, R. L., Gibbon, M., & Williams, J. B. W. (1997). *Structured clinical interview for DSM-IV Axis I disorders (SCID-I), clinician version: User's guide.* Washington, DC: American Psychiatric Press.

Freedman, S. R., & Enright, R. D. (1996). Forgiveness as an intervention goal with incest survivors. *Journal of Consulting and Clinical Psychology, 64*, 983–992.

Hall, J. H., & Fincham, F. D. (in press). Self-forgiveness: The stepchild of forgiveness research. *Journal of Social and Clinical Psychology.*

Harrington, J. A., & Blankenship, V. (2002). Ruminative thoughts and their relation to depression and anxiety. *Journal of Applied Social Psychology, 32*, 465–485.

Hart, K. E. (1999). A spiritual interpretation of the 12 steps of Alcoholics Anonymous: From resentment to forgiveness to love. *Journal of Ministry in Addiction and Recovery, 6*, 25–39.

Hebl, J. H., & Enright, R. D. (1993). Forgiveness as a psychotherapeutic goal with elderly females. *Psychotherapy, 30*, 658–667.

Hope, D. (1987). The healing paradox of forgiveness. *Psychotherapy, 24*, 240–244.

Karremans, J. C., Van Lange, P. A. M., Ouwerkerk, J. W., & Kluwer, E. S. (2003). When forgiving enhances psychological well-being: The role of interpersonal commitment. *Journal of Personality and Social Psychology, 84*, 1011–1026.

Kendler, K. S., Liu, X.-Q., Gardner, C. O., McCullough, M. E., Larson, D., & Prescott, C. A. (2003). Dimensions of religiosity and their relationship to lifetime psychiatric and substance use disorders. *American Journal of Psychiatry, 160*, 496–503.

Krause, N., & Ellison, C. G. (2003). Forgiveness by God, forgiveness of others, and psychological well-being in late life. *Journal for the Scientific Study of Religion, 42*, 77–93.

Maltby, J., Macaskill, A., & Day, L. (2001). Failure to forgive self and others: A replication and extension of the relationship between forgiveness, personality, social desirability and general health. *Personality and Individual Differences, 30*, 881–885.

Mauger, P. A., Perry, J. E., Freeman, T., Grove, D. C., McBride, A. G., & McKinney, K. E. (1992). The measurement of forgiveness: Preliminary research. *Journal of Psychology and Christianity, 11*, 170–180.

McCullough, M. E. (2000). Forgiveness as human strength: Theory, measurement, and links to well-being. *Journal of Social and Clinical Psychology, 19*, 43–55.

McCullough, M. E., Bellah, C. G., Kilpatrick, S. D., & Johnson, J. L. (2001). Vengefulness: Relationships with forgiveness, rumination, well-being, and the Big Five. *Personality and Social Psychology Bulletin, 27*, 601–610.

McCullough, M. E., & Bono, G. (2004). *Rumination, affect, and forgiveness: Two longitudinal studies.* Unpublished manuscript submitted for publication, Coral Gables, FL, Miami University.

McCullough, M. E., Rachal, K. C., Sandage, S. J., Worthington, E. L., Jr., Brown, S., & Hight, T. L. (1998). Interpersonal forgiving in close relationships: II. Theoretical elaboration and measurement. *Journal of Personality and Social Psychology, 75*, 1586–1603.

McCullough, M. E., & Worthington, E. L., Jr. (1994). Encouraging clients to forgive people who have hurt them: Review, critique, and research prospectus. *Journal of Psychology and Theology, 22*, 3–20.

Mohr, C. D., Averna, S., Kenny, D. A., & Del Boca, F. K. (2001). "Getting by (or getting high) with a little help from my friends": An examination of adult alcoholics' friendships. *Journal of Studies on Alcohol, 62*, 637–645.

Peterson, C., Maier, S. F., & Seligman, M. E. P. (1993). *Learned helplessness: A theory for the age of personal control*. New York: Oxford University Press.

Pingleton, J. P. (1989). The role and function of forgiveness in the psychotherapeutic process. *Journal of Psychology and Theology, 17*, 27–35.

Rosenak, C. M., & Harnden, G. M. (1992). Forgiveness in the psychotherapeutic process: Clinical applications. *Journal of Psychology and Christianity, 11*, 188–197.

Rye, M. S., Loiacono, D. M., Folck, C. D., Olszewski, B. T., Heinm, T. A., & Madia, B. P. (2001). Evaluation of the psychometric properties of two forgiveness scales. *Current Psychology: Developmental, Learning, Personality, Social, 20*, 260–277.

Saltzman, K. M., & Holahan, C. J. (2002). Social support, self-efficacy, and depressive symptoms: An integrative model. *Journal of Social and Clinical Psychology, 21*, 309–322.

Sandage, S. J., Hill, P. C., & Vang, H. C. (2003). Toward a multicultural positive psychology: Indigenous forgiveness and Hmong culture. *Counseling Psychologist, 31*, 564–592.

Sandage, S. J., Worthington, E. L., Jr., Hight, T. L., & Berry, J. W. (2000). Seeking forgiveness: Theoretical context and an initial empirical study. *Journal of Psychology and Theology, 28*, 21–35.

Seybold, K. S., Hill, P. C., Neumann, J. K., & Chi, D. S. (2001). Physiological and psychological correlates of forgiveness. *Journal of Psychology and Christianity, 20*, 250–259.

Shapiro, D. H., Jr., Schwartz, C. E., & Astin, J. A. (1996). Controlling ourselves, controlling our world: Psychology's role in understanding positive and negative consequences of seeking and gaining control. *American Psychologist, 51*, 1213–1230.

Subkoviak, M. J., Enright, R. D., Wu, C.-R., Gassin, E. A., Freedman, S., Olson, L. M., et al. (1995). Measuring interpersonal forgiveness in late adolescence and middle adulthood. *Journal of Adolescence, 18*, 641–655.

Temoshok, L. R., & Chandra, P. S. (2000). The meaning of forgiveness in a specific situational and cultural context: Persons living with HIV/AIDS in India. In M. E. McCullough, K. I. Pargament, & C. E. Thoresen (Eds.), *Forgiveness: Theory, research, and practice* (pp. 41–64). New York: Guilford Press.

Thompson, L. Y., Snyder, C. R., Hoffman, L., Michael, S. T., Rasmussen, H. N., Billings, L. S., et al. (2005). Dispositional forgiveness of self, others, and situations. *Journal of Personality, 73*, 313–360.

Toussaint, L., & Webb, J. R. (2003). *Forgiveness and health following the September 11th, 2001 terrorist attacks*. Poster presentation at the 111th annual conference of the American Psychological Association, Toronto, Canada.

Toussaint, L. L., Williams, D. R., Musick, M. A., & Everson, S. A. (2001). Forgiveness and health: Age differences in a U. S. probability sample. *Journal of Adult Development, 8*, 249–257.

U.S. Department of Health and Human Services. (1999). *Mental health: A report of the surgeon general*. Rockville, MD: Author.

Wahking, H. (1992). Spiritual growth through grace and forgiveness. *Journal of Psychology and Christianity, 11*, 198–206.

Webb, J. R., Kalpakjian, C. Z., & Toussaint, L. (2003). *Forgiveness, health, and life-satisfaction among people with spinal cord injury.* Paper presentation at the 17th annual conference of the American Association of Spinal Cord Injury Psychologists and Social Workers, Las Vegas, NV.

Webb, J. R., Robinson, E. A. R., Brower, K. J., & Zucker, R. A. (2003). *Forgiveness and alcohol related outcomes among people seeking substance abuse treatment.* Paper presentation at the Scientific Findings About Forgiveness conference, Atlanta, GA.

Witvliet, C. V. O., Ludwig, T. E., & Vander Laan, K. L. (2001). Granting forgiveness or harboring grudges: Implications for emotion, physiology, and health. *Psychological Science, 12*, 117–123.

Witvliet, C. V. O., Phipps, K. A., Feldman, M. E., & Beckham, J. C. (2004). Posttraumatic mental and physical health correlates of forgiveness and religious coping in military veterans. *Journal of Traumatic Stress, 17*, 269–273.

Worthington, E. L., Jr., Berry, J. W., & Parrott, L., III. (2001). Unforgiveness, forgiveness, religion, and health. In T. G. Plante & A. C. Sherman (Eds.), *Faith and health: Psychological perspectives* (pp. 107–138). New York: Guilford Press.

Worthington, E. L., Jr., Sandage, S. J., & Berry, J. W. (2000). Group interventions to promote forgiveness: What researchers and clinicians ought to know. In M. E. McCullough, K. I. Pargament, & C. E. Thoresen (Eds.), *Forgiveness: Theory, research, and practice* (pp. 228–253). New York: Guilford Press.

Worthington, E. L., Jr., & Wade, N. G. (1999). The psychology of unforgiveness and forgiveness and implications for clinical practice. *Journal of Social and Clinical Psychology, 18*, 385–418.

Chapter Twenty-Two

Forgiveness in People Experiencing Trauma

Jennie G. Noll

For centuries, practitioners have linked violent trauma with psychological and physiological dysfunction. A common sequela of a traumatic experience is post-traumatic stress disorder (PTSD), which includes reexperiencing the traumatic event, avoiding traumatic reminders, and chronic hyperarousal (American Psychiatric Association [APA], 1994). There is now considerable support for the usefulness of interventions curtailing the acute and long-term effects of PTSD. Recovery from violent trauma and reducing PTSD symptoms are thought to be enhanced by the survivor's ability to accept that the world can be unsafe and to acquire a less naïve view about justice and safety (Drescher & Foy, 1995). This ability to overcome tragedy is thought to characterize resilience (Richardson, 2002) and has been shown to be related to better physical and mental health, and lower trauma-related distress in PTSD patients (Connor, Davidson, & Lee, 2003). In addition to prolonged exposure therapy (e.g., Foa et al., 1999), cognitive-behavioral treatments designed to help traumatized individuals understand and manage the anxiety and vigilance associated with trauma-related stimuli have proven to be the most effective (Resnick, Kilpatrick, Dansky, Saunders, & Best, 1993). However, the extent to which these therapies involve intensive focus on overcoming negative feelings specifically associated with the transgressor (or perpetrator) of a trauma is not well understood. How do maintaining stagnating resentment, harboring hatred, retaining anger, plotting revenge, avoiding contact, and harboring general ill-will toward an offender affect the recovery process? Would interventions designed to target ill-will toward a perpetrator be more effective than therapies focusing solely on the generalized anxiety or vigilant reactions to the trauma? The application of forgiveness to the aid and treatment of trauma victims has been generally overlooked in empirical study. This chapter provides some guidelines for the study and treatment of transgressor-specific violent traumas and the use of forgiveness-based intervention; how forgiving a perpetrator might differ from other types of forgiving; the extent to which forgiving a perpetrator is a multifaceted and dynamic process; and the potential costs and benefits of forgiving a perpetrator of violent trauma.

Violent trauma comes in many forms. The death of a loved one, physical and emotional alienation or abandonment, witnessing domestic or community violence, serious accidents or natural disasters, and trauma associated with war or combat are situations likely to produce a PTSD reaction for many victims. Theories about recovery from trauma rarely include aspects of forgiveness. Perhaps this dearth of focus on forgiveness is in part due to the lack of an identifiable or blameworthy transgressor for many traumatic experiences. For example, it is not always easy to identify a specific, tangible transgressor in the aftermath of a natural disaster. Culpability in an accident may not always be clear. War veterans may hold an entire country responsible for the deaths of fellow soldiers. However, with such violent trauma as sexual abuse and assault, where the perpetrator can be clearly identified, the appropriateness of transgressor-specific forgiving might be more readily integrated into theories of recovery. Because violent trauma includes such a wide range of experiences and because the process of forgiving a specific transgressor likely differs from the forgiveness of global, nonspecific, or intangible transgressors, this chapter will be devoted to the discussion of forgiveness of violent trauma that can be attributed to a specific transgressor. Childhood sexual abuse is universally accepted as among the most heinous forms of victimization and usually involves a discernable offender. After briefly providing a general account of how forgiveness has been studied in the treatment of PTSD, I will primarily focus on the violent trauma of childhood sexual abuse as an example of how models of transgressor-specific forgiving might be upheld as viable treatment options to enhance recovery.

PERSONAL ASSUMPTIONS ABOUT FORGIVENESS

Although there is currently no gold-standard definition of forgiveness, several distinct operational definitions of forgiveness have been offered. For purposes of this chapter, forgiving a transgressor-specific trauma will include the following broad definitional components as borrowed from several prominent theorists and researchers: (a) the cessation of negative affect (Enright, Gassin, & Wu, 1992), (b) the cancellation of perpetrator debt (Exline & Baumeister, 2000), (c) decreased motivation for retaliation and estrangement from the perpetrator (McCullough et al., 1998), and (d) prosocial change toward a blameworthy transgressor (McCullough, Pargament, & Thoresen, 2000). In addition, it is also assumed that forgiveness is a dynamic process that may ebb and flow with the passage of time and the development of accommodating cognitive strategies. Further, as outlined by McCullough, Fincham, and Tsang (2003) and discussed in chapter 7 by McCullough and Root, the notion that forgiveness includes several distinct phases is adopted here. These phases include an initial forbearance (relatively low initial ill-will), trend forgiveness (overall reductions in ill will), and temporary forgiveness (transient reductions in ill-will). Finally, it is assumed that forgiveness is a multifaceted construct and should be studied as such. Simply collapsing the various aspects of forgiving into a single total-score may result in the masking of potential costs as well as benefits of forgiving and may preclude the examination of individual differences in distinct forgiveness profiles.

REVIEW OF THE THEORETICAL AND EMPIRICAL LITERATURE REGARDING FORGIVENESS AND TRAUMA

Forgiveness and PTSD

As noted earlier, there has been little empirical research examining a specific link between forgiveness and the recovery from trauma. Moreover, the theoretical interplay between PTSD and unforgiveness has yet to be adequately articulated. There is some limited work with PTSD patients which, when taken in aggregate, might provide an initial theoretical foundation for future research. A recent study of 213 treatment-seeking veterans diagnosed with PTSD reported that a dispositional approach to forgiving others was related to lower depression and decreased PTSD symptom severity (Witvliet, Phipps, Feldman, & Beckham, 2004). This study also demonstrated the particular importance of war veterans' forgiveness of self; prolonged guilt and self-blame associated with a lack of dispositional intrapersonal forgiveness predicted depression, anxiety, and persisting PTSD. Other studies have demonstrated that harboring anger and revenge (both indicative of unforgiveness) were correlated with heightened short- and long-term PTSD symptoms in combat veterans and assault victims (Feeny, Zoellner, & Foa, 2000; Van der Kolk, 1985). Similarly, rumination about the trauma (arguably an additional aspect of unforgiveness) was shown to be among the strongest predictors of subsequent PTSD in a study of accident survivors (Murray, Ehlers, & Mayou, 2002). Rumination regarding the loss of a loved-one, however, has been shown to be associated with greater social support and subsequently greater long-term psychological health (Nolen-Hoeksema & Davis, 1999).

These results suggest that forgiving in the context of trauma may need to encompass both *interpersonal* and, in the presence of guilt and self-blame, *intrapersonal* forgiving. Rumination about the trauma may have both *positive* and *negative* consequences, depending on the specific nature of the trauma. Although there seems to be some correlational connection between the two, extant evidence does not suggest a single mechanistic model that would explain how PTSD and forgiving are functionally related. It remains unclear, for example, whether PTSD symptoms might complicate forgiving and/or whether forgiving might interfere with the treatment of PTSD. It is also possible that PTSD and unforgiveness are different expressions of the same syndrome and that focus on one will enhance the treatment of the other. If hatred that fuels the fires of anger and revenge is quenched, will nightmares and hypervigilance associated with PTSD be simultaneously reduced? What is clear, however, is that forgiveness intervention should not commence without an adequate assessment of the nature and severity of coexisting PTSD symptoms.

Forgiveness and Childhood Sexual Abuse

It has been estimated that: (a) About 33% of women in the general population of the United States will experience some form of sexual abuse or assault in their lifetime

(Resnick et al., 1993); (b) 94% of victims will have moderate to severe PTSD symptoms immediately following the trauma; and (c) roughly 50% will experience persistent PTSD symptoms. Acute responses to childhood sexual abuse (defined here as unwanted or forced sexual contact with a minor by a caregiver or another older individual where a clear power differential exists) have been shown to include behavioral problems, depression, dissociative tendencies, sexual acting out, poor self-esteem, and less family cohesion (see reviews by Beitchman et al., 1992; Kendall-Tackett, Williams, & Finkelhor, 1993; Trickett, Noll, Reiffman, & Putnam, 2001). Long-term sequelae uniquely attributable to childhood sexual abuse include persisting PTSD and pathological dissociation (Putnam, 1997, 2003); depression (Bifulco, Brown, & Adler, 1991; Fergusson, Horwood, & Lynskey, 1996); psychiatric and substance abuse disorders (Kendler et al., 2000); sexual distortion (Loeb et al., 2002; Miller, Monson, & Norton, 1995; Noll, Trickett, & Putnam, 2003); early coital initiation and teen pregnancy (Fiscella, Kitzman, Cole, Sidora, & Olds, 1998; Stock, Bell, Boyer, & Connell, 1997); increased obesity and poor physiological health (Sickel, Noll, Moore, Putnam, & Trickett., 2002); higher rates of subsequent victimization, including physical and sexual assaults and self-inflicted harm (Briere, 1992; Gidycz, Hanson, & Layman, 1995; Messman-Moore, & Long, 2003; Noll, Horowitz, Bonanno, Trickett, & Putnam, 2003; Van der Kolk, 1989); and hormone dysregulation (Breier, 1989; Chrousos & Gold, 1992; Heim, Jeffrey, Bonsall, Miller, & Nemeroff, 2001). Given this wide range of sequelae, there has been surprisingly little intervention outcome research, and models for the effective treatment of childhood sexual abuse have yet to be tested or even adequately articulated.

Forgiveness in the context of childhood sexual abuse likely differs from forgiving other transgressions, due to a number of factors. First, perpetrators of childhood sexual abuse are often responsible for the safety and welfare of the child and are extremely emotionally intimate with their victims. The betrayal of trust coupled with the violation of safety involved in sexual abuse is profound and may be especially difficult to forgive. Second, forgiving childhood sexual abuse is likely a complex and dynamic process, being difficult to initiate and requiring a significant passage of time. This dynamic process is likely revisited throughout development as issues related to the abuse arise and become developmentally salient, and as victims become increasingly capable of accommodating more sophisticated aspects of forgiving (i.e., Enright, Santos, & Al-Mabuk, 1989). Finally, prosocial motivational change toward an offender may be impractical and/or not encouraged. As is often the case in many sexually abusing families, court-mandated jail or removal from the home results in the physical absence of the perpetrator, making reconciliation difficult or even impossible. Further, reconciliation with a perpetrator may put victims at risk for re-abuse. Thus, the potential costs associated with forgiving a sexual abuse perpetrator should be considered.

Several researchers and theorists have cautioned against forgiveness when the perpetrator has not shown remorse, when the violation is too severe, or when the wounds from the offense are too fresh (McCullough & Worthington, 1999; Worthington, Sandage,

& Berry, 2000). Forgiveness of violent offenses has been criticized for being both physically and psychologically dangerous for victims (Bass & Davis, 1988; Engel, 1989). Forgiveness is very often equated with reconciliation, and encouraging a victim to repair a relationship with a violent offender may result in substantial risk for revictimization. Because forgiveness also connotes pardoning, offenders may interpret forgiveness as a condonation and may revert to abusive tendencies, causing additional damage and perpetuating abuse (Katz, Street, & Arias, 1997; Olio, 1992). However, it has been suggested that forgiveness can occur without reconciling and that one can achieve emotional, cognitive, and behavioral transformation toward a perpetrator without any physical proximity. One can give up the qualities of revenge, anger, resentment, and hatred without entering into a relationship with a perpetrator (Enright, Eastin, Golden, Sarinopoulos, & Freedman, 1992; Freedman & Enright, 1996; Spring, 2004).

There has been very little empirical work focusing on forgiving sexual abuse. One study tested the effectiveness of a forgiveness intervention on 12 incest survivors and reported that the intervention resulted in decreased anxiety and depression, and increased forgiveness and hope (Freedman & Enright, 1996). These authors insist that forgiveness interventions have been too quickly dismissed by critics and that therapies focused on forgiving an incest perpetrator can be psychologically beneficial for survivors. It should be noted that the forgiveness intervention tested in this study did not require victims to be reconciled with perpetrators. Prosocial change toward perpetrators was simply the result of regarding the perpetrator with greater empathy and compassion, and enabling victims to see the imperfect nature of all human beings, including their perpetrators.

A slightly different approach was taken by Noll and colleagues (Noll, 2003; Noll & McCullough, 2004) to test the connection between forgiveness and the psychological well-being of sexual abuse survivors. In this prospective, longitudinal study, 55 sexually abused and 65 nonabused comparison women indicated their subjective levels of both forbearance and forgiveness on four independent aspects of forgiveness (letting go of anger, the cessation of revenge, conciliation, and moving on in life despite the offense) 10 years after the disclosure of abuse.[1] Results showed that sexually abused women were significantly less likely to report initial forbearance (i.e., they reported higher initial anger and revenge, and lower initial conciliation and moving on). However, the abused and comparison subjects reported very similar levels of actual forgiveness (i.e., prosocial change toward less anger and revenge, and greater conciliation and moving on). Results also indicated that most aspects of forgiveness (moving on and letting go of anger and revenge) were generally associated with higher self-esteem and lower anxiety, depression, and PTSD. On the other hand, high scores on conciliation were associated with more *negative* outcomes, such as higher anxiety and more disturbed relationships with maternal caregivers for abused participants.[2] Results also indicated that incest abuse by a biological father (i.e., as opposed to other relatives, including grandfathers, uncles, siblings) was especially difficult to forgive. Religious involvement correlated positively with several aspects of both forbearance and forgiveness but only for nonabused women. The association between religious involvement and all aspects of forgiveness was found to be near zero for sexually abused women.

These limited empirical results suggest that a forgiveness intervention may be effective for some sexual abuse victims and that many aspects of forgiving (letting go of anger, cessation of revenge, moving on with life) would likely benefit the recovery process. However, opening oneself to reconciling and moving back into a relationship with the perpetrator or merely adopting a conciliatory stance toward the perpetrator should be encouraged only with the utmost sensitivity and care. Results also suggest that religious involvement does not adequately explain the motivation for forgiving a sexual abuse perpetrator.

NEW RESEARCH DIRECTIONS NEEDED IN THE AREA

Transgressor-specific forgiveness is a potentially valuable tool for trauma victims, particularly those suffering from PTSD. The causal directionality and mechanistic nature of the relationship between forgiveness and PTSD is not well understood and is an area ripe for creative and ambitious future research designs. We are beginning to understand forgiveness as a complex, multifaceted process that should be studied as such. Not every aspect of forgiving operates exactly the same way in all individuals. Reconciliation, for example, should be studied either in isolation from other aspects of forgiving or as a distinct, independent construct, thus enabling a more comprehensive understanding of the potential costs and benefits of forgiving a violent perpetrator. Further, additional research needs to be conducted before an unequivocal endorsement of all aspects of forgiving can be adopted for victims of sexual trauma.

The intrinsic motivations for engaging in forgiving a sexual abuse perpetrator are increasingly unclear. Why do victims forgive? It has been demonstrated that religiosity is but a minor motivating factor in forgiving transgression-specific offenses (Subkoviak, Enright, Wu, & Gassin, 1995) and that religiousness has very little to do with forgiving a sexual abuse perpetrator (Noll, 2003). Future research endeavors aimed at exploring possible motivational substrates for forgiving could provide information about the types and characteristics of individuals for whom forgiveness intervention would prove most effective. It has also been shown that forgiving incest by a biological father is especially difficult (Noll, 2003). Sexual abuse by a biological father is often accompanied by large degrees of guilt, shame, and self-blame because this type of abuse is frequently perpetrated under the auspices of a "loving" relationship, and the victim often sees herself as a willing participant (Herman, Russel, & Trocki, 1986). Incest victims may need to forgive the self as well as forgive the perpetrator to achieve full forgiveness. Research on intrapersonal forgiving of sexual trauma may provide further insight into why certain types of sexual trauma are very difficult to overcome.

As our knowledge of sexual trauma sequelae grows, it is increasingly apparent that acute and long-term effects of trauma differ and that each new developmental stage may bring with it novel associations with the original trauma. For example, the development of secondary sex characteristics, initiation into sexual activity, choosing a romantic partner, and becoming a parent are milestones that can trigger delayed reactions to the trauma of childhood sexual abuse. With these delayed reactions may come a renewed interest in or heightened urgency for forgiveness intervention. Comprehensive assessments of forgiving (as well as treatment) should go beyond a single point in time or any single stage of development. Future research should acknowledge that any isolated forgiveness assessment may occur at a time when victims are inordinately upset by recent reminders of a trauma or, conversely, at a time when victims exhibit atypical adjustment or health. To curtail attenuated or artificially inflated forgiveness levels, multiple assessments of forgiveness at distinct periods throughout development are warranted.

RELEVANCE FOR CLINICAL INTERVENTIONS

The transgression of childhood sexual abuse may be among the most "unforgivable." Such an injury disrupts or assaults core belief systems and shatters the internal and external world of the self. Janoff-Bulman (1992) outlines how victims' basic set of assumptions about the self and the world are violated in the aftermath of sexual trauma. Upon realizing the extent of the violation, victims may begin to question their self-worth, the meaning of life, and their own presumptions of goodness, protection, and justice. As Flanigan (1992, 1998) asserts, the more damage to one's "assumptive set," the more difficult is forgiveness. Further, Flanigan asserts that the degree to which one can offer forgiveness depends on the degree to which one can rebuild these shattered life assumptions. A thorough understanding of the extent of damage to victims' assumptive set will give practitioners insight into the potential complexity of the forgiveness process. For example, incestual abuse by a biological parent likely damages many, if not most, core assumptive beliefs. Such a profound violation of trust by the individual who is upheld as one's supreme protector may be especially difficult to forgive, or forgiveness may never be obtained in any complete form (Hargrave, 2001). Victimization or exploitation by others outside the family (coaches, teachers, and pastors or priests) may result in a shattering of life assumptions, but this damage may manifest in slightly different ways and/or to a lesser degree than with incest. Thus, depending on the depth of the injury, forgiveness in cases of abuse outside the family may take an entirely different course or may be more fully and swiftly attainable than forgiving incestual abuse.

The issue of failing to protect children is in itself a blameworthy transgression. Forgiveness of a nonabusing caretaker who enabled the abuse or allowed it to persist may be an additional issue for childhood sexual abuse victims. Indeed, a substantial portion of sexual abuse victims attribute much of their suffering to the lack of protection of a nonabusing caretaker—usually the mother (Noll, 2003; Spring, 2004). The nonabusing parent should be counseled to expect a time when he or she becomes the target of rage and blame on behalf of the child victim. It is possible for nonabusing parents to be instruments of healing and forgiveness. Spring (2004) outlines nicely how these parents can facilitate their child's forgiveness process by (a) admitting mistakes and bearing witness to their child's pain, (b) apologizing genuinely and nondefensively, (c) understanding and revealing their own contribution to the injury, (d) working to earn back trust, and (e) engaging in self-forgiveness for injuring their child. By owning their part in the abuse and allowing forgiveness to unfold within their own relationship with the child, nonabusing parents model healthy forgiving. Such modeling can ultimately enable the victim to engage in the healthy forgiving of the offender.

PERSONAL THEORETICAL PERSPECTIVES ON THE FIELD

The limited empirical evidence (Freedman & Enright, 1996; Noll, 2003), coupled with the extensive anecdotal experience of several clinicians (Flanigan, 1998; Hargrave, 2001; Spring, 2004), suggests that forgiveness as an intervention in the treatment of sexual abuse and assault should generally be encouraged. However, there may be aspects of forgiving that are more easily attainable than others for some victims. It is clear that survivors should be encouraged to let go of anger directed toward the offender and should refrain from perseverating on ways to retaliate. Victims should also be encouraged to move ahead with adaptive life goals and not to stagnate in the paralyzing fear that all humans are capable of violation and exploitation. Perhaps to a greater degree than other aspects of forgiving, less emphasis should be placed on reconciling a relationship with a violent offender.

Several theorists have offered *acceptance* of the perpetrator as an alternative to reconciliation. Acceptance involves understanding the depth of a perpetrator's woundedness, giving up the need for revenge, learning from (as opposed to forgetting) past traumatic experiences, recognizing the enemy, and anticipating and avoiding harm (Hargrave, 2001; Spring, 2004). Acceptance is an internal process and does not necessarily involve the participation of the offender. This is not to say that individuals should actively avoid all contact with anyone who has offended them, but instead it should be recognized that reconciliation is a highly subjective and complex process requiring considerable passage of time, intensive therapy, sophisticated cognitive resources, adequate social supports, and the self-protective strategies necessary to avoid, curtail, or escape re-abuse.

The life-changing nature of experiencing a violent trauma should not be underestimated. Thus, levels of dispositional forgiveness might be dictated or transformed as a result of enduring such trauma. For some victims, violence will shatter the self irreparably. They may devolve from a person with a forgiving disposition to a person who is wholly damaged and unable or unwilling to forgive. For others, recovery from trauma may involve making sense of the event and finding benefit and spiritual growth. Janoff-Bulman and Frantz (1997) describe a process of making sense of a trauma by understanding how the trauma fits with one's view of the world and reorganizing beliefs about justice, fairness, and the predictability life. Learning about one's strength in the face of adversity, gaining insight into the meaning of life, and developing deeper, more satisfying relationships are examples of the potential benefits that may help to mitigate the negative effects of a traumatic experience (Nolen-Hoeksema & Davis, 2002). Such life-changing transformations have also been associated with spiritual conversion. As individuals begin to overcome the desecration of those things previously held as sacred (e.g., innocence, trust, safety, parental love), they can begin to experience a phenomenological transformation that may radically alter their understanding of themselves, the world, their relationships, and their ultimate place within the universe (Mahoney & Pargament, 2004). Thus, individuals who where unlikely to possess a forgiving disposition before a traumatic event may likely adopt a forgiving disposition through discerning benefits from trauma and/or engaging in profound spiritual transformation as a result of the trauma.

CONCLUSION

Trauma changes lives. The deleterious effects of trauma can to some degree be curtailed by engaging in the work of forgiveness, but we possess an inadequate understanding of exactly how and why forgiveness might facilitate recovery. Overall, forgiveness of offenders should be encouraged, but most researchers and theorists would agree that forgiveness is a complex, multifaceted process and includes several distinct psychological mechanisms. This is important because there is some evidence that reconciliation (one important aspect of forgiving) is potentially harmful for victims of sexual abuse. Hence, reconciliation should be encouraged only with the utmost sensitivity and care. Those engaging in forgiveness efforts with sexual abuse victims should consider alternatives to reconciliation that do not necessarily require the victim to repair the relationship with the offender but that simply culminate in some level of empathy or acceptance of the offender's flaws and failures. The degree to which one can forgive depends on the degree of damage to basic life assumptions. The violation of basic trust and protection of incestual abuse may be particularly difficult to forgive. Further, incest victims may need to engage in aspects of *intrapersonal* forgiving of the self (see chapter 10 by Tangney, Boone, & Dearing) if, as is often the case with incest, there is any guilt or self-blame associated with being abused. Making sense of a trauma and finding benefit in the experience are among the most effective ways to cope with victimization. Learning to forgive or acquiring a forgiving disposition may be perceived as potential benefits of having gone through a life-changing traumatic experience.

NOTES

1. Another main objective of this study was to validate empirically a new measure of forgiveness, the Process of Forgiving (POF) scale. The POF measures participants' retrospective levels of initial forbearance and their current levels of forgiveness while taking into account initial forbearance. Participants

respond to a set of items regarding how they feel about a perpetrator currently, then respond to that same set of items regarding how they (retrospectively) felt about the same perpetrator at a time when they felt the worst about him or her. Four factors of forgiving were confirmed and shown to be invariant in a pilot sample of college students and across retrospective and present time points: (a) lack of revenge, (b) cessation of anger, (c) desire for conciliation, and (d) a desire to move on in life despite the offense. *Forbearance* scores are simply participants' scores on the initial retrospective factors. *Forgiveness* scores, on the other hand, are participants' scores on the present forgiving factors with initial forbearance scores statistically residualized. Thus, forgiveness represents current levels of forgiving with initial forbearance taken into account. This residualizing procedure was preferred, relative to a difference-score approach, because it allows the process of forgiving to be captured by taking into account initial levels, thus eliminating the possibility of equating the forgiveness of two individuals whose change scores may be equivalent but for whom initial forbearance was quite disparate. Ideally, this would be accomplished by multiple assessments at several time points, but this design is not always attainable. The POF provides a viable option to either single-administration devices or unrealistic, multiple-assessment strategies.

2. It should be noted that until this study, no measure of transgression-specific forgiveness had been designed to assess reconciliation as a stand-alone, independent construct. Instead, items assessing reconciliation had been included in other subscales, making it difficult to ascertain the unique contribution of reconciliation to the forgiveness process and the extent to which there are costs and benefits associated with this aspect of forgiving. Given the controversy surrounding reconciliation, Noll and colleagues were careful to characterize reconciliation (a) to include instances where the perpetrator is absent or unwilling to admit the transgression, (b) to be devoid of perpetrator pardoning, and (c) as a willingness to take a conciliatory stance, achieving emotional proximity to the perpetrator (e.g., "If he wanted to say 'sorry,' I would listen") rather than requiring reconciliation. Hence, the term *conciliation* (as opposed to *reconciliation*) was used to define this unique construct. High scores on this construct do not necessarily reflect a reconciled relationship with the perpetrator but rather the adopting of a "conciliatory stance" toward the perpetrator and an acceptance of the perpetrator's flaws and failures.

REFERENCES

American Psychiatric Association (1994). *Diagnostic and statistical manual of mental disorders* (4th ed.). Washington, DC: Author.

Bass, E., & Davis, L. (1988). *The courage to heal: A guide for women survivors of child sexual abuse.* New York: Harper & Row.

Beitchman, J. H., Zucker, K. J., Hood, J. E., DaCosta, G. A., Akman, D., & Cassavia, E. (1992). A review of the long-term effects of child sexual abuse. *Child Abuse and Neglect, 16,* 101–118.

Bifulco, A., Brown, G. W., & Adler, Z. (1991). Early sexual abuse and clinical depression in adult life. *British Journal of Psychiatry, 159,* 115–122.

Breier, A. (1989). Experimental approaches to human stress research: Assessment of neurobiological mechanisms of stress in volunteers and psychiatric patients. *Biological Psychiatry, 26,* 438–462.

Briere, J. N. (1992). *Child abuse trauma: Theory and treatment of the lasting effects.* Newbury Park, CA: Sage.

Chrousos, G. P., & Gold, P. W. (1992). A concept of stress and stress system disorder: Overview of physical and behavioral homeostasis. *Journal of the American Medical Association, 267,* 1244–1255.

Connor, K. M., Davidson, J., & Lee, L. C. (2003). Spirituality, resilience, and anger in survivors of violent trauma: A community survey. *Journal of Traumatic Stress, 16,* 487–494.

Drescher, K. D., & Foy, D. W. (1995). Spirituality and trauma treatment: Suggestions for including spirituality as a coping resource. *National Center for PTSD Clinical Quarterly, 5*, 4–5.

Engel, B. (1989). *The right to innocence: Healing the trauma of childhood sexual abuse.* Los Angeles: Jeremy P. Tarcher.

Enright, R. D., Eastin, D. L., Golden, S., Sarinopoulos, I., & Freedman, S. R. (1992). Interpersonal forgiveness within the helping professions: An attempt to resolve differences of opinion. *Counseling and Values, 36*, 84–103.

Enright, R. D., Gassin, E. A., & Wu, C. (1992). Forgiveness: A developmental view. *Journal of Moral Education, 21*, 95–110.

Enright, R. D., Santos, M. J. D., & Al-Mabuk, R. (1989). The adolescent as forgiver. *Journal of Adolescence, 12*, 95–110.

Exline, J. J., & Baumeister, R. F. (2000). Expressing forgiveness and repentance: Benefits and barriers. In M. E. McCullough, K. I. Pargament, & C. E. Thoresen (Eds.), *Forgiveness: Theory, research, and practice* (pp. 133–155). New York: Guilford Press.

Feeny, N. C., Zoellner, L. A., & Foa, E .B. (2000). Anger, dissociation, and posttraumatic stress disorder among female assault victims. *Journal of Traumatic Stress, 13*, 89–100.

Fergusson, D. M., Horwood, L. J., & Lynskey, M. T. (1996). Childhood sexual abuse and psychiatric disorder in young adulthood: II. Psychiatric outcomes of childhood sexual abuse. *Journal of the American Academy of Child and Adolescent Psychiatry, 34*, 1365–1374.

Fiscella, K., Kitzman, H. J., Cole, R. E., Sidora, K. J., & Olds, D. (1998). Does child abuse predict adolescent pregnancy? *Pediatrics, 101*(4 Pt 1), 620–624.

Flanigan, B. (1992). *Forgiving the unforgivable: Overcoming the bitter legacy of intimate wounds.* New York: Macmillan.

Flanigan, B. (1998). Forgiver and the unforgivable. In R. D. Enright & J. North (Eds.), *Exploring forgiveness* (pp. 95–105). Madison, WI: University of Wisconsin Press.

Foa, E. B., Dancu, C. V., Hembree, E. A., Jaycox, L. H., Meadows, E. A., & Street, G. P. (1999). A comparison of exposure therapy, stress inoculation training, and their combination for reducing posttraumatic stress disorder in female assault victims. *Journal of Consulting and Clinical Psychology, 67*, 194–200.

Freedman, S. R., & Enright, R. D. (1996). Forgiveness as an intervention goal with incest survivors. *Journal of Consulting and Clinical Psychology, 64*, 983–992.

Gidycz, C. A., Hanson, K., & Layman, M. J. (1995). A prospective analysis of the relationships among sexual assault experiences: An extension of previous findings. *Psychology of Women Quarterly, 19*, 5–29.

Hargrave, T. (2001). *Forgiving the devil: Coming to terms with damaged relationships.* Phoenix, AZ: Zeig, Tucker, & Theisen.

Heim, C., Jeffrey, N. D., Bonsall, R., Miller, A. H., & Nemeroff, C. B. (2001). Altered pituitary-adrenal axis responses to provocative challenge tests in adult survivors of childhood abuse. *American Journal of Psychiatry, 158*, 575–581.

Herman, J., Russel, D., & Trocki, K. (1986). Long-term effects of incestuous abuse in childhood. *American Journal of Psychiatry, 143*, 1293–1296.

Janoff-Bulman, R. (1992). *Shattered assumptions: Towards a new psychology of trauma.* New York: Free Press.

Janoff-Bulman, R., & Frantz, C. M. (1997). The impact of trauma on meaning: From meaningless world to meaningful life. In M. Power & C. R. Brewin (Eds.), *The transformation of meaning in psychological therapies* (pp. 91–106). New York: Wiley.

Katz, J., Street, A., & Arias, I. (1997). Individual differences in self-appraisals and responses to dating violence scenarios. *Violence and Victims, 12*, 265–276.

Kendall-Tackett, K. A., Williams, L. M., & Finkelhor, D. (1993). Impact of sexual abuse on children: A review and synthesis of recent empirical studies. *Psychological Bulletin, 113*, 164–180.

Kendler, K., Bulik, C., Silberg, J., Hettema, J., Myers, J., & Prescott, C. (2000). Childhood sexual abuse and adult psychiatric and substance abuse disorders in women. *Archives of General Psychiatry, 57*, 953–959.

Loeb, T. B., Williams, J. K., Carmona, J. V., Rivkin, I., Wyatt, G. E., Chin, D., et al. (2002). Child sexual abuse: Associations with the sexual functioning of adolescents and adults. *Annual Review of Sex Research, 13*, 307–345.

Mahoney, A., & Pargament, K. I. (2004). Sacred changes: Spiritual conversion and transformation. *Journal of Clinical Psychology, 60*, 481–492.

McCullough, M. E., Fincham, F. D., & Tsang, J. (2003). Forgiveness, forbearance, and time: The temporal unfolding of transgression-related interpersonal motivations. *Journal of Personality and Social Psychology, 84*, 540–557.

McCullough, M. E., Pargament, K. I., & Thoresen, C. E. (2000). The psychology of forgiveness: History, conceptual issues, and overview. In M. E. McCullough, K. I. Pargament, & C. E. Thoresen (Eds.), *Forgiveness: Theory, research, and practice* (pp. 1–16). New York: Guilford Press.

McCullough, M. E., Sandage, S. J., Brown, S. W., Rachal, K. C., Worthington, E. L., Jr., & Hight, T. L. (1998). Interpersonal forgiving in close relationships: II. Theoretical elaboration and measurement. *Journal of Personality and Social Psychology, 75*, 1586–1603.

McCullough, M. E., & Worthington, E. L., Jr. (1999). Religion and the forgiving personality. *Journal of Personality, 67*, 1141–1164.

Messman-Moore, T. L., & Long, P. J. (2003). The role of childhood sexual abuse sequelae in the sexual revictimization of women: An empirical review and theoretical reformulation. *Clinical Psychology Review, 23*, 537–571.

Miller, B. C., Monson, B. H., & Norton, M. C. (1995). The effects of forced sexual intercourse on white female adolescents. *Child Abuse and Neglect, 19*, 1289–1301.

Murray, J., Ehlers, A., & Mayou, R. A. (2002). Dissociation and post-traumatic stress disorder: Two prospective studies of road traffic accident survivors. *British Journal of Psychiatry, 180*, 363–368.

Nolen-Hoeksema, S., & Davis, C. G. (1999). "Thanks for sharing that": Ruminators and their social support networks. *Journal of Personality and Social Psychology, 77*, 801–814.

Nolen-Hoeksema, S., & Davis, C. G. (2002). Positive responses to loss: Perceiving benefits and growth. In C. R. Snyder & S. J. Lopez (Eds.), *Handbook of positive psychology* (pp. 598–607). New York: Oxford University Press.

Noll, J. G. (2003, October). *The process of forgiving childhood sexual abuse.* Paper presented at the conference on Scientific Findings About Forgiveness, Atlanta, GA.

Noll, J. G., Horowitz, L. A., Bonanno, G. A., Trickett, P. K., & Putnam, F. W. (2003). Revictimization and self-harm in females who experienced childhood sexual abuse: Results from a prospective study. *Journal of Interpersonal Violence, 18*, 1452–1471.

Noll, J. G., & McCullough, M. E. (2004). *The process of forgiving childhood sexual abuse: The costs and benefits of forbearance and forgiveness.* Unpublished manuscript submitted for publication, Cincinnati.

Noll, J. G., Trickett, P. K., & Putnam, F. W. (2003). A prospective investigation of the impact of childhood sexual abuse on the development of sexuality. *Journal of Consulting and Clinical Psychology, 71*, 575–586.

Olio, K. (1992). Recovery from sexual abuse: Is forgiveness mandatory? *Voices, 28*, 73–74.

Putnam, F. W. (1997). *Dissociation in children and adolescents: A developmental perspective.* New York: Guilford Press.

Putnam, F. W. (2003). Ten-year research update review: Child sexual abuse. *Journal of the American Academy of Child and Adolescent Psychiatry, 42*, 269–278.

Resnick, H. S., Kilpatrick, D. G., Dansky, B. S., Saunders, B. E., & Best, C. L. (1993). Prevalence of civilian trauma and posttraumatic stress disorder in a representative national sample of women. *Journal of Consulting and Clinical Psychology, 61*, 984–991.

Richardson, G. E. (2002). The meta-theory of resilience and resiliency. *Journal of Clinical Psychology, 58*, 307–321.

Sickel, A. E., Noll, J. G., Moore, P. J., Putnam, F. W., & Trickett, P. K. (2002). The long-term physical health and healthcare utilization of women who were sexually abused as children. *Journal of Health Psychology, 7*, 583–598.

Spring, J. A. (2004). *How can I forgive you? The courage to forgive, the freedom not to.* New York: HarperCollins.

Stock, J. L., Bell, M. A., Boyer, D. K., & Connell, F. A. (1997). Adolescent pregnancy and sexual risk-taking among sexually abused girls. *Family Planning Perspectives, 29*, 200–227.

Subkoviak, M. J., Enright, R. D., Wu, C., & Gassin, E. A., (1995). Measuring interpersonal forgiveness in late adolescence and middle adulthood. *Journal of Adolescence, 18*, 641–655.

Trickett, P. K., Noll, J. G., Reiffman, A., & Putnam, F. W. (2001). Variants of intrafamilial sexual abuse experience: Implications for short- and long-term development. *Development and Psychopathology, 13*, 1001–1019.

Van der Kolk, B. A. (1985). Adolescent vulnerability to posttraumatic stress disorder. *Psychiatry: Journal for the Study of Interpersonal Processes, 48*, 365–370.

Van der Kolk, B. A. (1989). The compulsion to repeat the trauma: Reenactment, revictimization, and masochism. *Psychiatric Clinics of North America, 12*, 341–389.

Witvliet, C. V. O., Phipps, K. A., Feldman, M. E., & Beckham, J. C. (2004). Posttraumatic mental and physical health correlates of forgiveness and religious coping in military veterans. *Journal of Traumatic Stress, 17*, 269–273.

Worthington, E. L., Jr., Sandage, S. J., & Berry, J. W. (2000). Group interventions to promote forgiveness: What researchers and clinicians ought to know. In M. E. McCullough, K. I. Pargament, & C. E. Thoresen (Eds.), *Forgiveness: Theory, research, and practice* (pp. 228–253). New York: Guilford Press.

Part Six

INTERVENING TO PROMOTE FORGIVENESS

Chapter Twenty-Three

Facilitating Forgiveness in Individual Therapy as an Approach to Resolving Interpersonal Injuries

Wanda Malcolm
Serine Warwar
Leslie Greenberg

In their 1997 review, McCullough, Worthington, and Rachal pointed out that most of the forgiveness literature has focused on *interpersonal* forgiveness, the form of forgiveness that has as one of its goals the possibility of restoring relationships, provided that it is wise and safe to do so. In this chapter, we depart from this tradition by reviewing the theoretical and empirical literature germane to *unilateral* forgiveness, the form of forgiveness that may be facilitated in individual psychotherapy as an approach to resolving interpersonal emotional injuries when restoring the relationship is not a goal of therapy, either because it is not possible to restore the relationship (as is the case when the injurer is dead or unwilling to reconcile) or because doing so is likely to expose the client to the risk of reinjury.

PERSONAL ASSUMPTIONS ABOUT UNILATERAL FORGIVENESS AS A PSYCHOTHERAPEUTIC TASK

It is not uncommon to find discussions of the value of forgiveness as a response to interpersonal injury in the clinical literature (e.g., Akhtar, 2002; Berecz, 2001; Davenport, 1991; Enright & Fitzgibbons, 2000; Fitzgibbons, 1986; Karen, 2001), and in our own research we have found the resolution of such injuries to be a psychotherapeutic task that may include forgiveness in significant ways (Greenberg & Foerster, 1996; Malcolm, 1999). It is noteworthy then that along with other clinicians (Ferch; 1998; McCullough & Worthington, 1994), we have noted (Malcolm & Greenberg, 2000) that it has been difficult to gain specific knowledge of how best to facilitate the process of forgiveness in individual therapy. Similarly, in a survey of family and marriage therapists, DiBlasio (1992; DiBlasio & Proctor, 1993) found that most therapists (especially those of middle age or older) held a positive view of the value of forgiveness but reported a lack of skills specific to facilitating forgiveness as a therapeutic task.

REVIEW OF EMPIRICAL AND THEORETICAL LITERATURE

Review of Empirical Literature

Excluding group interventions, there are only three reports of psychotherapy outcome studies associated with unilateral forgiveness interventions. The results of these three studies provide initial support for the hypothesis that unilateral forgiveness has both short- and long-term psychological benefits. Freedman and Enright (1996) investigated the effectiveness of an intervention program for incest survivors in which forgiveness was the end goal of treatment. The intervention used a yoked, randomized experimental and control group design where six pairs of women were matched on variables related to demographics, the abuse, and the abuser. One woman in each matched pair was randomly selected to receive therapy, and the other woman served as a member of the comparison group. Those who were wait-listed received therapy after the first group completed treatment, thereby serving as their own comparison group. Duration of therapy averaged 14 months of weekly sessions conducted in accordance with an intervention manual. Based on significant change from pre- to posttreatment, the study demonstrated that unilateral forgiveness could be successfully promoted and that the intervention was associated with increases in self-esteem and hope, as well as decreases in depression and anxiety.

Coyle and Enright (1997) replicated the Freedman and Enright (1996) study by investigating the psychological benefits of promoting forgiveness among a set of 10 men who identified themselves as having been hurt by a partner's choice to terminate a pregnancy. Half of the men were seen for 12 weekly individual sessions of approximately 90 minutes, and the other five men served as a wait-list comparison group. The men in the comparison group subsequently received treatment as well. Analysis of a set of outcome measures demonstrated significant positive change from pre- to posttreatment associated with therapy alone in terms of increased forgiveness and decreased anxiety, anger, and grief.

The York Forgiveness Project (Greenberg, Warwar, & Malcolm, 2003) examined the differential treatment effects of resolving emotional injuries in individual Emotion-Focused Therapy (EFT; Greenberg, 2002), compared with a psychoeducational group intervention. Treatment focused on facilitating the resolution of a specific interpersonal emotional injury that had occurred at least 2 years prior to the start of therapy and continued to be distressing to the client. In this study, 23 clients were assigned to individual therapy and 23 to group psychoeducation. Both interventions involved 12 hours of treatment spread over approximately 12 weeks. Clients presented issues of betrayal, criticism, neglect, abandonment, and physical and sexual abuse as foci for resolution. Most of these clients were dealing with injuries caused by one or both parents.

Clients in the individual EFT treatment showed significantly more improvement than those in the psychoeducation group on the global severity index of the SCL-90-R (Derogatis, 1983), on positive change in key target complaints (Battle et al., 1968), on the Enright Forgiveness Inventory (Enright, Rique, & Coyle, 2000), and on measures assessing the degree to which clients had let go of distressing feelings and unmet needs in relation to the injurer. In addition, significantly more EFT clients than psychoeducation group members reported that they forgave the injurer. Taken as a whole, this study provides support for the differential effectiveness of an emotion-focused approach for resolving emotional injuries over a psychoeducation group intervention of the same duration.

It is interesting that all who reported that they forgave the injurer, regardless of group, also indicated that they had let go of the distressing feelings and unmet needs previously associated with the injury. In contrast, there were some individuals who indicated that they had let go of the distressing feelings and unmet needs associated with the injury but had not forgiven the injurer. This suggests that letting go of persisting unresolved feelings such as anger, grief, sadness and/or hurt is necessary to achieve forgiveness but that this aspect of the process is not the equivalent of forgiveness.

REVIEW OF THEORETICAL PERSPECTIVES

Numerous clinicians and researchers underscore the importance of the emotion work involved in forgiveness (Davenport, 1991; Enright & Fitzgibbons, 2000; Fitzgibbons, 1986; Hope, 1987; Karen, 2001), and McCullough and his colleagues have carried out an impressive body of research that has shown the mediating role of empathy in successful forgiveness (e.g., McCullough et al., 1998; McCullough, Worthington, et al., 1997). Because of the emphasis in the forgiveness literature on the emotion work and development of empathy, these two aspects of the resolution process need further elaboration.

Emotion Work Involved in Unilateral Forgiveness Interventions. Our assumption (further outlined in Greenberg, 2002; Greenberg & Elliott, 2002) is that emotion is a biologically based meaning system that is fundamentally adaptive, gives people feedback about what is important and meaningful for them on a moment-by-moment basis, and organizes them for adaptive action (Frijda, 1986). Working within the client's emotion system is therefore seen as having a key place in the therapeutic process.

Sadness over loss, anger in the face of violation, or fear in response to threat are examples of initial adaptive and automatic emotional responses people have in response to interpersonal injuries. They produce biologically based relational action tendencies, which constitute a readiness to act in a particular way so as to establish, maintain, or alter the relationship with one's environment. The therapist's role is to guide clients toward these primary adaptive emotions and to facilitate their evocation for the purpose of accessing their adaptive information and action tendency. They are core and irreducible responses, and their symbolization and expression is of value in and of itself.

Emotion schemes (syntheses of emotion, cognition, motivation, memories, and action tendencies) are formed as the product of learning and experience. Once formed, they produce complex, bodily felt responses that are not the result of purely innate responses to specific cues. Because emotion schemes emerge from one's lived experience, they may be either adaptive or maladaptive.

Forgiveness and unforgiveness are both complex, bodily felt responses. In the feeling of unforgiveness, the cognitive component involves a sense of being unfairly wronged and rightfully deserving of revenge or restitution. There is also an affective component of corrosive anger, a smouldering type of resentment, coupled with feelings of sadness and possibly shame and pain. In contrast, forgiveness reciprocally involves soft affects such as compassion and lovingkindness, and the ability to see and understand the unfolding of events surrounding the injury from the other's perspective. It involves acceptance of what happened instead of continuing to fight against the unfairness of it and a letting go of the desire to retaliate. Forgiveness involves a giving out of something, sending out positive feelings of compassion, and a feeling with and possibly even for the other person rather than feeling against the other.

One of the premises of the EFT approach is that the suppression or blocking of primary biologically adaptive emotions subverts healthy boundary setting, self-respectful anger, and necessary grieving. Numerous clinicians (for example, Akhtar, 2002; Baures, 1996; Enright & Eastin, 1992) emphasize the importance of facilitating expressions of adaptive anger and suggest that facilitating forgiveness requires an acknowledgment of the legitimacy of emotions such as resentment and hatred toward the offender. Baures (1996), Boss (1997), and Fincham (2000) consider resentment and desires for revenge to be closely linked with self-respect, and Greenberg and Paivio (1997) suggest that there may be times when it is therapeutic to encourage clients to talk about their revenge fantasies. The desire to retaliate is normalized as a sign of how damaged the injured person feels. Such expressions of anger also teach clients to accept and tolerate their anger, and to work with it rather than against it. Encouraging such expressions is not the same thing as promoting outer-directed blaming or hurling of insults. In encouraging speaking from one's inner experience, the therapist is promoting ownership of a client's emotional experience and is empowering clients to assign responsibility appropriately for harm done. It also helps clients focus on their own concerns rather than get stuck in blaming the other or feeling victimized. Owning one's intense feelings of anger and desire to make the other suffer as one has suffered generates a sense of self as a person of worth who has been treated unfairly and deserves to be treated differently. The danger in short-circuiting expressions of anger is that the client may end up condoning or excusing the injurer's hurtful behavior, or inappropriately taking too much responsibility for the unfolding of events surrounding the injury. Furthermore, it is difficult to let go of self-protective anger if one feels weak and vulnerable.

Therapists also need to attend to the process of grieving the loss of or damage to a significant relationship, as well as the shattering of the client's view of self and the world that may have been caused by the injury. Akhtar (2002) addresses the relationship between mourning and forgiveness, and Greenberg and Paivio (1997) emphasize that work with betrayal and abandonment can be a process of facilitating normal grieving in which anger and sadness play central roles. Facilitating an imaginary dialogue with the injurer can help the client grieve and say goodbye to what has been lost or irreparably damaged as a consequence of the injury.

Which Emotions Need Changing?   A key element of therapist skill resides in his or her ability to assess the nature of the emotion expressed in therapy and to intervene in appropriate ways, because different kinds of emotional reactions require different therapist interventions. This in turn requires that the therapist be empathically attuned to the client and the nature of the emotion schemes that are evoked when processing the impact of an unresolved emotional injury. The difficult, lingering emotions a client struggles with are primarily seen as the path to accessing and transforming underlying maladaptive emotional schemes.

When clients indicate that they are stuck in bad feelings, the expressed emotions are often secondary reactive experiences that obscure underlying and possibly unacceptable primary emotional responses (Greenberg, 2002). People also have feelings about their primary emotional responses and can, for example, be afraid of their anger or ashamed of their fear, or they may have learned that their sadness is unacceptable. In terms of forgiveness interventions, McCullough et al. (1998) point to the connection between rumination and maintenance of thoughts of seeking revenge that serve to sustain a disinclination to forgive. In our experience, this is likely to happen when clients are stuck in secondary anger. In that event, the therapist needs to facilitate the client's tolerance for distressing but primary adaptive feelings. When clients are helped to attend to and symbolize their adaptive emotions, they are able to create new meaning and act effectively to solve problems. For example, if a client is helped to recognize how he has learned to cover an underlying fear of being reinjured with aggressive anger, he can begin to work toward meeting his needs for comfort and connection in adaptive ways.

Expressions of instrumental emotion are maladaptive responses that are used to influence or manipulate others. Holding a grudge because of the interpersonal advantage it offers is an example of instrumental anger and resentment. These expressions do not provide useful information about the significance of events and have no underlying primary emotion that would be useful to access for adaptive information. Instead, the therapist's goal would be either to bypass such expressions or gently to confront the function served by them.

Principles of Therapeutic Work with Emotion.   Empirical evidence is mounting in support of the importance of changing one emotion with another (Greenberg 2002, 2004) and suggests that a maladaptive emotion state is transformed best by replacing it with another, more adaptive emotion. Applying the concept of changing one emotion with another is not new to the forgiveness field (e.g., Worthington's 1998 and 2001 discussions of emotion replacement), but we would emphasize that the process may entail work that is not directly related to the forgiveness effort per se, because there may be work to be done that involves changing emotions in response to self-representations, and the self-work may take precedence over work that involves changing feelings about the injurer. For example, it appears that the likelihood of forgiving the injurer is related to the degree to which the injured person is able to overcome the negative feelings caused by the injurer and gain or renew a positive sense of self-worth and -esteem.

The key to transforming maladaptive emotions is to access alternate healthy adaptive emotions to act as resources in the self (Greenberg & Paivio, 1997). In the view proposed here, the maladaptive feeling does not simply attenuate by virtue of the person feeling and getting used to it. Instead, a different feeling is used to transform or undo the maladaptive one. In essence, withdrawal emotions from one side of the brain are transformed by approach emotions from another part of the brain, or vice versa (Davidson, 2000). Once the alternate emotion has been accessed, it transforms, undoes, or replaces the original state. The newly accessed, alternate feelings are resources in the personality that help change the maladaptive state.

The transformation process is not one of counter-conditioning or reciprocal inhibition, as suggested in desensitization, but rather a dialectical synthesis of a new response from the prior ones by a process of integration of elements. Change is seen as occurring when opposing emotions are co-activated, and new, higher level schemes are formed that incorporate both emotions by synthesizing compatible elements from the co-activated schemes. Just as schemes for standing and falling in a toddler can be dynamically synthesized by a dialectical process into a higher level scheme for walking, so too can schemes of different emotional states be synthesized to form new integrative structures that become primary and adaptive complex feelings (Pascual-Leone, 1991; Greenberg & Pascual-Leone, 1995). This type of activation of emotions and reflection on them is much more likely to be facilitated in the safety of therapy. Clients are helped to attend to the felt sense of these complex feelings in order to access and explore the implicit meaning that is carried with them. Being able to attend to these adaptive responses also helps clients notice bodily felt shifts or changes that accompany the emergence of newly constructed meaning.

Role of Empathy in Forgiving.   Our study of the therapeutic resolution of past emotional injuries leads us to propose that empathy is an essential component of successful forgiveness. This proposition is consistent with the clinical observation, theory, and empirical evidence of others working in the forgiveness field (Macaskill, Maltby, & Day, 2002; McCullough, Worthington, & Rachal, 1997; McCullough, Rachal, Sandage, & Worthington, 1997; Worthington & Wade, 1999). When accessed, empathy is a primary and adaptive complex feeling that facilitates forgiveness in the face of an interpersonal injury. The ability to feel empathy for the injurer appears in our sample to be preceded by the process of helping clients access and face their own pain, which in turn enables them to imagine that the injurer could see and understand it too. Only when a client experiences himself or herself as someone who is strong enough to own and express painful and distressing emotions can he or she envision another who is similarly strong enough to hear and take responsibility for harm done. Engaging in imaginary dialogues with the injurer in an empathic therapeutic environment seems to facilitate these processes.

As Rowe et al. (1989) have pointed out, empathy toward the injurer involves being able to see the other person as acting in a quintessentially human manner, which may flow out of the context of his or her own self-focused needs and perceptions. It includes (but does not require) the possibility of recognizing that what the injurer did was similar to something one has done or could do under the same circumstances. In addition to assisting in the revision of how one sees the injurer, cognitive perspective taking sometimes allows the injury itself to be recast within a broader understanding of the context of the unfolding of events. Cognitive perspective taking of this nature does not have to involve warm, benevolent feelings. In fact, understanding the other's perspective may be part of what informs the injured person that resuming a relationship would be ill advised (Berecz, 2001).

Considerations of cognitive perspective taking highlight the role of acceptance of the other as part of empathy, but acceptance alone will not necessarily bring one all the way to forgiveness, because it is possible to accept another's behavior by condoning or excusing rather than forgiving. Something more is required, and that appears to be compassion for the other, or affective empathy.

Affective empathy is best understood as a means of imaginative entry into the world of the other, which generates a bodily felt sense of understanding what the other person may have been feeling without actually sharing the same experience (Greenberg & Rosenberg, 2002). Berecz (2001) suggests that rather than the client focusing inward and using his or her own feelings as the point of reference for understanding the injurer's perspective (which is difficult to do in the face of an egregiously hurtful interaction), the task is for the injured person to transpose himself or herself imaginatively into the other person's place in an attempt to understand the unfolding of events from the injurer's perspective.

In the York Forgiveness Study, we also found it helpful to have the client imagine what the injurer might feel if he or she were capable of comprehending the consequences and impact of his or her actions on the client. The empty-chair technique employed in EFT is a particularly effective tool in this regard. In imaginatively bringing the injurer and injury alive, the client moves from a cognitive discussion with the therapist to an imaginal confrontation and dialogue with the injurer. In so doing, the client is helped to move reified inner representations of self and other into a transitional space in conscious awareness where the representations can be reexamined, reworked, and resolved.

Role of Self-Other Representations in the Empathy-Forgiveness Equation.   Part of what is needed to achieve the primary, adaptive, and complex feeling of forgiveness is a shift from viewing self as wholly injured and other as wholly bad to a view of self as "not all good" and other as "not all bad" (Akhtar, 2002). There is a connection between such shifts, the emotion work, and emerging feelings of empathy and compassion. When people permit themselves to feel their resentment and acknowledge their desire to retaliate or to access their intense feelings of loss, shame, or fear, the groundwork is laid for the necessary shift in view of self and other.

This shift in how the other is represented and viewed is crucial to forgiveness. Greenberg and Paivio (1997) highlight how important it is that an injured person in therapy come to believe that if the injurer were present in the room, he or she would be able to hear and empathize with the client's emotional pain and distress, take responsibility for harm done, and seek to make amends if he or she could. It is only then that the client can soften and begin to empathize with the others' limitations.

BRIEF CLINICAL APPLICATION

Part of the function of dialectic imagination in empty-chair work is to facilitate the client in imaginatively projecting himself or herself into an enactment of the other as empathic. Doing so fosters an empathic response within the client, thereby opening up the possibility of revising his or her representations of the other from inhuman monster to "not all bad" and therefore forgivable.

An example of this is reported by Malcolm and Greenberg (2000). Early in therapy, a client often slipped into reactive anger and other-focused blame and complaint. It was not until after the therapist assisted her past the reactive anger to the core and adaptive expression of intense sadness and grief in the face of her mother's suicide that the client was able to enact her mother as saying, "I wish there were something that I could do to change what I did. You're making me understand the devastation I caused and the aftermath. It wasn't just about me; it was about a lot of other people. I really wish that you could forgive me." The mother was also enacted at a later point in the therapy process, saying, "My suicide wasn't about you kids at all. You're the reason I stayed as long as I did. . . . It was about a life I just thought was hopeless. . . . You have every right to feel ashamed of what I did. And I don't want you to feel guilty. You didn't cause it. . . . It's about me being out of control. I take responsibility for what I did."

NEW RESEARCH DIRECTIONS NEEDED IN THE AREA

This chapter has concerned itself with the process of facilitating unilateral forgiveness in individual psychotherapy. In order to understand and evaluate the benefits of such interventions adequately, we draw on the work of colleagues who are doing research in other areas of the forgiveness field. For example, to assess the success of our interventions, we turn to the work of those who have developed self-report forgiveness measures (Enright, Rique, & Coyle, 2000; Hargrave & Sells, 1997; Mauger et al., 1992; McCullough et al., 1998; Wade, 1989) and methods of assessing change when individuals report that they have forgiven another person (e.g., McCullough, Fincham, & Tsang, 2003). The development of such tools is a significant challenge, given that such instruments are typically based on an understanding of forgiveness that is defined in ideal terms, terms that may not be shared by those who come for therapy and are asked to report the degree to which they have forgiven (see, for example, DeCourville & Belicki [2004] for a discussion of this problem). As advances are made in the testing and refining of measurement tools, the assessment of forgiveness-specific outcomes will improve, and our collective efforts within the forgiveness field will gain credibility.

As we move beyond the initial stages of research in this area, we also need to be cognizant of the impact of issues such as possible gender differences in propensity to forgive or manner of working through forgiveness issues, the relevance of the timing of interventions after a hurtful interpersonal experience, and factors that could argue against the wisdom of working toward forgiveness. For example, Paivio and colleagues (Paivio & Nieuwenhuis, 2001; Paivio, Hall, Holowaty, Jellis, & Tran, 2001) suggest that facilitating self-validation, self-assertion, and holding the other accountable has priority when working with clients who have been victims of traumatic abuse. Similarly, feminist writers, such as Boss (1997), are outspoken critics of unqualified promotions of the value of forgiveness on the part of those working with abuse victims. This underscores the fact that forgiveness is only one way of reducing unforgiveness (Wade & Worthington, 2003; Worthington & Wade, 1999) and reminds us that some traumatic experiences are unforgivable to the sufferer of the injury (Akhtar, 2002) and ought to be respected as such.

PERSONAL THEORETICAL PERSPECTIVES ON THE FIELD

The empirical and clinical study of unilateral forgiveness is an important area within the larger field of forgiveness studies that can be further pursued in fruitful ways. As a start, although all three existing studies of unilateral forgiveness interventions (Freedman & Enright, 1996; Coyle & Enright, 1997; Greenberg et al., 2003) have demonstrated significant benefits when individual therapy interventions are compared with a wait-list control or psychoeducational group, none have yet examined the differential benefits of successful forgiveness outcomes when compared with successful outcomes of some other form. Consistent with previous studies (Malcolm, 1999; Paivio & Greenberg, 1995), for example, there were clients in the York Forgiveness Project who experienced significant improvements without forgiving, and comparing the differential benefits of these different forms of successful outcomes is important in deepening our understanding of the value of forgiveness interventions.

In addition, qualitative studies of successful interpersonal forgiveness processes have been carried out (Holeman, 2003), but there have been no qualitative studies of unilateral forgiveness. Nor are there any that have compared improved versus nonimproved clients' psychotherapy sessions to elucidate the crucial differences in process that might account for different outcomes. Qualitative studies and differential benefit studies are of value across all types of theoretical approaches in deepening our understanding of the therapeutic task of unilateral forgiveness. Within a given approach, task analyses of the theorized process would also be useful in the effort to integrate theory and clinical practice.

CONCLUSION

In this chapter, we reviewed the theoretical and empirical literature germane to *unilateral* forgiveness. This is the form of forgiveness that may be facilitated in individual psychotherapy as an approach to resolving interpersonal emotional injuries when restoring the relationship is not a goal of therapy, either because it is not possible to restore the relationship (as is the case when the injurer is dead or unwilling to reconcile) or because doing so is likely to expose the client to the risk of reinjury.

The importance of emotion work in forgiveness is emphasized in the clinical and research literature, and what emerges is an emphasis on reexperiencing, reprocessing, and transforming emotions related to the injury. Affective empathy is also a key aspect that plays a fundamental role in the forgiveness process. It is facilitated first by helping clients face and process the pain of their injuries, then by imagining that the injurer could feel empathy for the client's suffering if he or she were to understand and take responsibility for the pain caused by the injury. Therapeutic interventions have been built using theoretical models in conjunction with assessment tools developed to measure both process and outcome variables related to forgiveness. The refinement of these tools will allow us more successfully to evaluate the impact of our interventions and more clearly specify the process of forgiveness, which in turn will help us more effectively facilitate this process with our clients. Furthermore, a consideration of individual difference variables and the differential nature of client injuries will allow therapists to tailor their interventions to different client populations and specific types of injuries.

REFERENCES

Akhtar, S. (2002). Forgiveness: Origins, dynamics, psychopathology, and technical relevance. *Psychoanalytic Quarterly, 71*, 175–212.

Battle, C., Imber, S., Hoehn-Saric, R., Stone, A., Nash, C., & Frank, J. (1968). Target complaints as criteria of improvements. *American Journal of Psychotherapy, 20*, 184–192.

Baures, M. M. (1996). Letting go of bitterness and hate. *Journal of Humanistic Psychology, 36*(1), 75–90.

Berecz, J. M. (2001). All that glitters is not gold: Bad forgiveness in counseling and preaching. *Pastoral Psychology, 49*, 253–275.

Boss, J. (1997). Throwing pearls to the swine: Women, forgiveness, and the unrepentant abuser. In L. D. Kaplan & L. F. Bove (Eds.) *Philosophical perspectives on power and domination: Theories and practices* (pp. 235–247). Amsterdam-Atlanta, GA: Rodopi.

Coyle, C. T., & Enright, R. D. (1997). Forgiveness intervention with postabortion men. *Journal of Consulting and Clinical Psychology, 65,* 1042–1046.

Derogatis, L. R. (1983). *SCL-90-R administration, scoring, and procedures manual for the revised version.* Towson, MD: Clinical Psychiatric Research.

Davenport, D. S. (1991). The functions of anger and forgiveness: Guidelines for psychotherapy with victims. *Psychotherapy, 28,* 140–144.

Davidson, R. (2000). Affective style, mood, and anxiety disorders: An affective neuroscience approach. In R. Davidson (Ed.), *Anxiety, depression, and emotion* (pp. 88–108). London: Oxford University Press.

DeCourville, N., & Belicki, K. (2004, June). *Subjective experiences of forgiveness in a community sample.* Paper presented at the Canadian Psychological Association Convention, St. John's, Newfoundland.

DiBlasio, F. A. (1992). Forgiveness in psychotherapy: Comparison of older and younger therapists. *Journal of Psychology and Christianity, 11,* 181–187.

DiBlasio, F. A., & Proctor, J. H. (1993). Therapists and the clinical use of forgiveness. *American Journal of Family Therapy, 21,* 175–184.

Enright, R. D., & Eastin, D. L. (1992). Interpersonal forgiveness within the helping professions: An attempt to resolve differences of opinion. *Counseling and Values, 36,* 84–103.

Enright, R. D., & Fitzgibbons, R. P. (2000). *Helping clients forgive: An empirical guide for resolving anger and restoring hope.* Washington, DC: American Psychological Association.

Enright, R. D., Rique, J., & Coyle, C. T. (2000). *The Enright Forgiveness Inventory (EFI) user's manual.* Madison, WI: International Forgiveness Institute.

Ferch, S. R. (1998). Intentional forgiving as a counseling intervention. *Journal of Counseling and Development, 76,* 261–270.

Fincham, F. D. (2000). The kiss of the porcupines: From attributing responsibility to forgiving. *Personal Relationships, 7,* 1–23.

Fitzgibbons, R. P. (1986). The cognitive and emotive uses of forgiveness in the treatment of anger. *Psychotherapy, 23,* 629–633.

Freedman, S. R., & Enright, R. D. (1996). Forgiveness as an intervention goal with incest survivors. *Journal of Consulting and Clinical Psychology, 64,* 983–992.

Frijda, N. H. (1986). *The emotions.* Cambridge, England: Cambridge University Press.

Greenberg, L. (2004). Emotion-focused therapy. *Clinical Psychology and Psychotherapy* (special issue), 11, 3–16.

Greenberg, L. S. (2002). *Emotion-focused therapy: Coaching clients to work through feelings.* Washington, DC: American Psychological Association.

Greenberg, L. S., & Elliott R. (2002). Emotion focused therapy: A process experiential approach. In J. Lebow & F. Kaslow (Eds.), *Comprehensive handbook of psychotherapy* (pp. 213–241). New York: Wiley.

Greenberg, L. S., & Foerster, F. (1996). Resolving unfinished business: The process of change. *Journal of Consulting and Clinical Psychology, 64,* 439–446.

Greenberg, L. S., & Paivio, S. C. (1997). *Working with emotions in psychotherapy.* New York: Guilford Press.

Greenberg, L. S., & Pascual-Leone, J. (1995). A dialectical constructivist approach to experiential change. In R. Neimeyer & M. Mahoney (Eds.), *Constructivism in psychotherapy* (pp. 169–191). Washington, DC: American Psychological Association.

Greenberg L. S., & Rosenberg R. (2002). Therapist experience of empathy. In J. C. Watson, R. N. Goldman, & M. Warner (Eds.), *Client-centered and experiential psychotherapy in the 21st century: Advances in theory, research, and practice*. Ross-on Wye, Herefordshire, UK: PCCS Books.

Greenberg, L. S., Warwar, S., & Malcolm, W. (2003, June). *Differential effects of emotion focused therapy and psychoeducation for resolving emotional injuries*. Paper presented at the International Society for Psychotherapy Research, Weimar, Germany.

Hargrave, T. D., & Sells, J. N. (1997). The development of a forgiveness scale. *Journal of Marital and Family Therapy, 23*, 41–62.

Holeman, V. (2003). *Marital reconciliation: A qualitative study.* Paper presented at Scientific Findings About Forgiveness conference, Atlanta, GA.

Hope, D. (1987). The healing paradox of forgiveness. *Psychotherapy, 24*, 240–244.

Karen, R. (2001). *The forgiving self: The road from resentment to connection.* New York: Doubleday.

Macaskill, A., Maltby, J., & Day, L. (2002). Forgiveness of self and others and emotional empathy. *Journal of Social Psychology, 142*, 663–665.

Malcolm, W. M. (1999). *Relating process to outcome in the process-experiential resolution of unfinished business.* Unpublished doctoral dissertation. Toronto, ON: York University.

Malcolm, W. M., & Greenberg, L. (2000). Forgiveness as a process of change in individual psychotherapy. In M. E. McCullough, K. I. Pargament, & C. E. Thoresen (Eds.) *Forgiveness: Theory, practice, and research* (pp. 179–202). New York: Guilford Press.

Mauger, P. A., Freedman, T., McBride, A. G., Perry, J. E., Grove, D. C., & McKinney, K. E. (1992). The measurement of forgiveness: Preliminary research. *Journal of Psychology and Christianity, 11*, 170–180.

McCullough, M. E., Fincham, F. D., & Tsang, J. (2003). Forgiveness, forbearance, and time: The temporal unfolding of transgression-related interpersonal motivations. *Journal of Personality and Social Psychology, 84*, 540–557.

McCullough, M. E., Rachal, K. C., Sandage, S. J., & Worthington, E. L. Jr. (1997, August). *A sustainable future for the psychology of forgiveness.* Paper presented at the meeting of the American Psychological Association, Chicago, IL.

McCullough, M. E., Rachal, K. C., Sandage, S. J., Worthington Jr., E. L., Brown, S. W., & Hight, T. L. (1998). Interpersonal forgiving in close relationships: II. Theoretical elaboration and measurement. *Journal of Personality and Social Psychology, 75*, 1586–1603.

McCullough, M. E., & Worthington, E. L., Jr. (1994). Encouraging clients to forgive people who have hurt them: Review, critique, and research prospectus. *Journal of Psychology and Theology, 22*, 3–20.

McCullough, M. E., Worthington, E. L., Jr., & Rachal, K. C. (1997). Interpersonal forgiving in close relationships. *Journal of Personality and Social Psychology, 73*, 321–336.

Paivio, S. C., & Greenberg, L. S. (1995). Resolving "unfinished business." Efficacy of experiential therapy using empty-chair dialogue. *Journal of Consulting and Clinical Psychology, 63*, 419–425.

Paivio, S. C., & Nieuwenhuis, J. A. (2001). Efficacy of emotion focused therapy for adult survivors of childhood abuse: A preliminary study. *Journal of Traumatic Stress, 14*, 115–134.

Paivio, S. C., Hall, I., Holowaty, K., Jellis, J. & Tran, N. (2001). Imaginal confrontation for resolving child abuse issues. *Psychotherapy Research, 11*, 433–453.

Pascual-Leone, J. (1991). Emotions, development, and psychotherapy: A dialectical constructivist perspective. In J. Safran & L. Greenberg (Eds.), *Emotion, psychotherapy and change* (pp. 302–335). New York: Guilford Press.

Rowe, J. O., Halling, S., Davies, E., Leifer, M., Powers, D., & Van Bronkhorst, J. (1989). The psychology of forgiving another: A dialogal research approach. In R. S. Valle & S. Halling (Eds.), *Existential-phenomenological perspective in psychology: Exploring the breadth of human experience* (pp. 233–244). New York: Plenum Press.

Wade, S. J. (1989). *The development of a scale to measure forgiveness.* Unpublished dissertation, Fuller Theological Seminary, Pasadena, CA.

Wade, N. G., & Worthington, E. L., Jr. (2003). Overcoming interpersonal offenses: Is forgiveness the only way to deal with unforgiveness? *Journal of Counseling and Development, 81*, 343–353.

Worthington, E. L., Jr. (1998). The pyramid model of forgiveness: Some interdisciplinary speculations about unforgiveness and the promotion of forgiveness. In Everett L. Worthington, Jr. (Ed.), *Dimensions of forgiveness: Psychological research and theological perspectives* (pp. 107–138). Philadelphia: Templeton Foundation Press.

Worthington, E. L., Jr. (2001). *Five steps to forgiveness: The art and science of forgiving.* New York: Crown Publishers.

Worthington, E. L., Jr., & Wade, N. G. (1999). The psychology of unforgiveness and forgiveness and implications for clinical practice. *Journal of Social and Clinical Psychology, 18*, 385–418.

Chapter Twenty-Four

A Progress Report on the Process Model of Forgiveness

Suzanne Freedman
Robert D. Enright
Jeanette Knutson

The past 19 years have seen a birth of interest in forgiveness by psychologists, counselors, psychiatrists, researchers, religious leaders, and the general public. For example, Konstam, Marx, Schurer, Emerson Lombardo, and Harrington (2002), in their research with mental health counselors, found that "90% of respondents indicated that forgiving is an important clinical issue and would be interested in pursuing professional training focusing on forgiveness related issues in clinical practice" (p. 69).

The purpose of this chapter is to present a summary of the progress on the process model of forgiveness developed by Enright and the Human Development Study Group (1991). We begin with a definition of forgiveness. The process model will be defined, followed by a discussion of pioneering studies using this model. Recent work using the process model follows, with a brief review of a meta-analysis conducted on empirical studies. A response to critics follows.

What Forgiveness Is and Is Not

After studying this topic since 1985, we define *forgiving* as the following.

> People, upon rationally determining that they have been unfairly treated, forgive when they willfully abandon resentment and related responses (to which they have a right) and endeavor to respond to the wrongdoer based on the moral principle of beneficence, which may include compassion, unconditional worth, generosity, and moral love (to which the wrongdoer, by nature of the hurtful act or acts, has no right). (Enright & Fitzgibbons, 2000, p. 29)

Abandonment of anger is not something that happens overnight, as the definition seems to imply. In practical terms, our definition includes decreases in negative affect, cognition, and behavior. Over time, possible increases in positive affect, cognition, and behavior toward the offender may occur.

In addition to defining what forgiveness is, Enright, Freedman, and Rique (1998) discuss how forgiveness is more than accepting what happened, ceasing to be angry, and making oneself feel good. Forgiveness is not the same as forgetting, condoning, excusing, legally pardoning, or automatic reconciliation, which is defined as getting back together in a relationship (see Enright, 2001 for a more expanded discussion of what forgiveness is and is not).

We find that the most frequently occurring misunderstanding is the equating of forgiveness with reconciliation. It is possible to forgive and not reconcile (Freedman, 1998). An injured individual can work on the process of forgiveness knowing that reconciliation is not possible if, for example, the offender remains entrenched in a hurtful pattern of behavior toward the offended person.

Contexts Surrounding Forgiveness

Forgiveness occurs in a moral context of the offender's injustice and the offended person's mercy. Often forgiveness is viewed as something one does for oneself without taking the offender into account. Forgiveness takes the other into consideration and is not solely a self-help strategy. When one completes the forgiveness process, he or she is doing good for the offender, for the self, and perhaps for others with whom he or she is in close interaction.

Because forgiveness takes place in a context of injustice, the solution to that injustice need not be only forgiveness or only a quest for fairness. Forgiveness and justice can and should coexist.

Forgiveness is an individual decision and should not be forced on anyone (Baskin & Enright, 2004). One can be educated about forgiveness but then must make his or her own decision regarding whether to forgive. It is one's choice. If one is forced into forgiving, pseudo-forgiveness rather than genuine forgiveness may result (Enright, Freedman, & Rique, 1998).

THE PROCESS MODEL OF FORGIVENESS DEVELOPED FROM THE DEFINITION

After clarifying what forgiveness is and what it is not, the group began constructing psychological models of forgiveness. Hepp-Dax (1996) writes, "One of the advantages of the construct of forgiveness as presented by Enright et al. (1991), is that it is viewed as a multidimensional construct that combines cognitive, affective, and behavioral factors, since all are involved in forgiveness" (p. 35).

Enright et al. (Enright & the Human Development Study Group, 1991) asserted that the process of forgiveness can occur in 20 units. Unlike the definition of forgiveness, which we have come to realize has a core meaning that is unchanging, the pathways to forgiving are many. After a thorough review of the literature in the areas of psychology, psychiatry, philosophy, and theology, and after numerous discussions with people who have forgiven, Enright et al. (1991) developed this model as their best estimate of the process people go through when trying to forgive.

The model is not to be viewed as a "rigid, step-like sequence, but a flexible set of processes with feedback and feed-forward loops" (Enright et al., 1998, p. 12). The authors explain how some people may skip units and others may go back and rework units previously experienced, because there is great individual variation in how people forgive. This process model of forgiveness may not be an exhaustive description of how each person forgives, but it illustrates how complex the journey of forgiveness is and that it is not a process that occurs overnight. Each person approaches forgiveness differently, based on his or her previous experiences and role models. In fact, the interventions described below to assess this model have incorporated slight variations of the model over the years (Baskin & Enright, 2004). The 20-unit model is divided into four different phases, which are briefly described here.

Units 1–8 represent the *uncovering phase* as the person gets in touch with the pain and explores the injustice he or she experienced. Working through these eight units allows the injured to experience both the pain and the reality of the injury and how it has affected him or her. Feeling pain from the injury motivates some people to see a need for change, and gradually they realize that previous ways of coping may not have been effective or are no longer serving their purpose.

Units 9–11 represent the *decision phase,* which we view as a critical part of the forgiveness process. The Decision Phase illustrates that one explores the idea of forgiveness and what is involved in the process of forgiveness before committing to actually forgiving. As Freedman and Enright (1996) point out, one may make the cognitive decision to forgive, even though he or she does not feel forgiving at the time.

The *work phase* of the model encompasses four units beginning with Unit 12, which involves seeing the offender with new eyes or reframing who he or she is by viewing the wrongdoer in context. The individual who is hurt tries to understand the context of the offender to understand better how the injury could have occurred. Reframing often leads to feelings of empathy (Unit 13) and compassion (Unit 14). Unit 15 deals with acceptance and absorption of the pain and is seen as the heart of forgiveness (Enright et al., 1998). The injured accepts and absorbs his or her own pain as well as the pain of the offender instead of passing it on to others or back to the offender.

The *outcome phase* represents the last four units in the model. The injured realizes that as he or she gives the gift of forgiveness to the offender, healing is experienced. The entire process of forgiveness may lead to improved psychological health. See Enright (2001) and Enright et al. (1998) for a more thorough description of the 20-unit process model.

Early Studies Using the Process Model of Forgiveness

Hebl and Enright (1993) conducted the first empirical intervention using forgiveness as the goal. Before their study, all published works of forgiveness were anecdotal and case study reports (Hebl & Enright, 1993). The purpose of the Hebl and Enright (1993) study was empirically to examine an 8-week group therapy program with elderly women who had miscellaneous hurts. The participants' goal was to forgive one person who had hurt them deeply. Participants were randomly assigned to either a forgiveness or a control group. The forgiveness group followed the process model developed by Enright et al. (Enright & the Human Development Study Group, 1991). The control group met for the same amount of time—60 minutes weekly—and discussed general topics suggested by the group during the first session. Forgiveness was not discussed in the control group. Posttests showed that the experimental group had a significantly higher forgiveness profile, compared with the control group. Both groups had a significant decrease in anxiety and depression from pretest to posttest. As the first empirically based experimental study using forgiveness as a goal, Hebl and Enright's (1993) study is noteworthy.

Freedman and Enright (1996) conducted a forgiveness intervention with 12 women who were incest survivors. The goal was for the incest survivors to forgive their abusers. The women ranged in age from 24 to 54 years old, were Caucasian, and lived in a Midwestern city. Using a yoked, randomized, experimental and control group design, the participants were randomly assigned to an experimental group (receiving forgiveness education immediately) or a wait-list control group (receiving the intervention after the experimental group). See Freedman and Enright (1996) for a detailed description of the intervention procedure.

After the intervention, the experimental group gained significantly more than the control group in forgiveness and hope, and decreased significantly more than the control group in anxiety and depression. After members of the control group completed the forgiveness intervention, they showed similar gains in forgiveness and hope, as well as in self-esteem, and greater decreases in anxiety and depression. Members of the experimental group were also posttested again 1 year from the date they completed the intervention. The change patterns were maintained (Freedman & Enright, 1996). This study illustrated the effectiveness of a forgiveness intervention for incest survivors. A more forgiving attitude toward one's abuser and greater psychological well-being resulted after participation in the forgiveness intervention (Freedman & Enright, 1996). Verbal reports from the incest survivors illustrate psychological benefits from forgiving as well. One survivor stated that after forgiving her father, she was able to use the forgiveness model with her mother for not protecting her. Other early work can be found in Al-Mabuk, Enright, and Cardis (1995), Coyle and Enright (1997), and Lin (1998).

Recent Work

Meta-analysis of Intervention Studies. Baskin and Enright (2004) conducted a meta-analysis to investigate whether forgiveness interventions are effective in increasing forgiveness and psychological well-being. Nine published studies with empirical results were used in the meta-analysis. Although the field is still early in its development, the analysis could be useful for those designing future studies on forgiveness (Baskin & Enright, 2004).

The authors described three basic models of forgiveness gleaned from the literature. The first model is the Enright et al. (Enright & the Human Development Study Group, 1991) process model described earlier in this chapter.

The second model identified by Baskin and Enright (2004) was developed by Mc-Cullough, Worthington, and Rachal (1997) and is described as fostering "both cognitive and affective empathy" (Baskin & Enright, 2004, p. 9). It includes nine different components, with the first component similar to the first eight units in the Enright et al. (Enright & the Human Development Study Group, 1991) model. The other eight steps are also similar to various units in Enright and colleagues' 20-unit model, such as developing empathy, practicing cognitive reframing, thinking about when one has needed forgiveness from others, and considering the offender's needs (see Baskin & Enright, 2004, for a thorough description).

The third model was developed by McCullough and Worthington (1995) and was designed to introduce people to the idea of forgiveness and to consider the decision to forgive in a 1-hour session. In all three models, participants focus on one person who hurt them deeply and work on forgiving that person. The first two models are process based, and the third model is decision based. Process-based models include the decision to forgive as well as other cognitive and affective units. Decision-based models emphasize making the decision to forgive and can be placed solely in the cognitive domain. According to Fitzgibbons (1986) and as previously mentioned, people first approach forgiveness cognitively, then emotionally.

Baskin and Enright's (2004) meta-analysis appears to be one of only a few assessments of all existing published forgiveness interventions. Other criteria for a study's inclusion were the use of a control group, publication in a refereed journal, and the use of quantitative measurement. The nine studies included in the analysis were categorized into three groupings: (a) decision-based studies, (b) process-based studies with a group format, and (c) process-based studies with an individual format.

Results illustrate the effectiveness of forgiveness interventions for adults and older adolescents. Baskin and Enright (2004) make a number of conclusions based on the data. First, effect size scores were low for the decision-based forgiveness interventions, compared with both the individual and group process-based interventions. Specifically, there was no significant difference in forgiveness between those receiving a decision-based intervention and those receiving no intervention. Second, *individual*-based process interventions had a higher effect size, compared with the *group* process-based interventions (1.66 vs. 0.82). Baskin and Enright (2004) emphasize how this finding highlights the time and energy required by both participants/clients and educators/counselors to forgive a person for a deep injustice completely and successfully. Forgiveness interventions seem to be particularly well suited for incest survivors, adolescents hurt by emotionally distant parents, and men hurt by their partner's decision to have an abortion.

The difference in findings between the process-based models and decision-based models of forgiveness support the use of a process-based model of forgiveness in educational interventions or counseling. The 0.82 effect size on process-based group forgiveness interventions can be viewed in terms of the average person in the intervention doing as well or better than 75% of the control group (Baskin & Enright, 2004). For the results of the process-based individual intervention, the effect size was 1.66, meaning that the average person in the intervention group did as well or better than 95% of the people in the control group (Baskin & Enright, 2004). Effect sizes for the mental health variables also illustrate the effectiveness of forgiveness. The effect size of 0.59 for the process-based group interventions means that the average person in the forgiveness group did better than 65% of the control group (Baskin & Enright, 2004). Even more striking is the effect size for the mental health variables for the process-based individual interventions, which was 1.42. These results clearly support a link between forgiveness and mental health. These results are almost three times the minimum level for a large effect size (Lipsey, 1990).

Studies Recently Completed. Lin, Mack, Enright, Krahn, and Baskin (2004) investigated the use of forgiveness therapy with 14 patients with substance abuse dependence from a local residential treatment facility. Participants were randomly assigned to and completed approximately 12 twice-weekly sessions of individual forgiveness therapy or approximately 12 twice-weekly sessions of an alternative individual treatment based on routine drug and alcohol therapy topics. The latter treatment is the typical therapy implemented at the residential facility. Participants who had completed forgiveness therapy had significantly greater increases in self-esteem and significantly greater decreases in depression, anger, anxiety, and vulnerability to drug use than did those who went through the alternative form of therapy. Most benefits of the forgiveness therapy remained superior to the alternative at a 4-month follow-up. Participants were initially quite low in forgiveness—lower than the average for a nonclinical adult population sample (Lin et al., 2004). At posttest, the forgiveness therapy participants averaged higher than the published norm for the adult sample, and this gain was maintained at follow-up.

Forgiveness therapy goes beyond treating only symptoms to treating the underlying causes of substance abuse. Past research has illustrated that substance abuse is often a symptom of underlying resentments and related emotional issues. Forgiveness therapy can be a successful addition to traditional therapies for substance abusers.

The results of Lin et al.'s (2004) study provide support for forgiveness therapy to be used as an effective new treatment for substance abuse clients.

Hansen (2002) showed that implementing a forgiveness intervention with terminal cancer patients led to significantly greater increases in forgiveness of the offender, hope, and quality of life; it also led to significantly less anger than did a control intervention. Forgiveness, as illustrated in both Hebl and Enright's (1993) study and Hansen's (2002) work, has the potential to be helpful for those facing end-of-life issues.

Gambaro's (2002) dissertation also illustrated the impact forgiveness education can have on young adolescents. Gambaro (2002) implemented a forgiveness intervention with adolescents (ages 12–14) who had higher than average levels of anger. In a group setting, half of the students received the forgiveness education, and the other half (control condition) received a Rogerian-based support-group experience. At posttest, participants in the experimental group demonstrated greater decreases in "anger as a trait," "having an angry temperament," and "predilection to react in an angry manner" than did control subjects. The experimental group showed significantly greater improvements in their attitudes toward school and family and in the quality of their relationships with friends and family. These differences were maintained at follow-up 9 months after the intervention had ended. Gambaro (2002) also looked at school grades, detentions, and in-school suspensions and found that the experimental group was significantly higher in academic achievement and significantly lower in detentions and suspensions than the control group. Other recent work is described in Knutson (2003), Freedman and Knupp (2003), and Park (2003).

Response to Critics

Although the forgiveness research has been favorably acknowledged by many, it has also been subject to criticism. We interpret such criticism as a positive sign that researchers and those in the helping professions are beginning to take seriously the ideas presented (Enright & Coyle, 1998). Lamb and Murphy (2002), in particular, have put forth a number of objections to the forgiveness research in their edited book, *Before Forgiving: Cautionary Views of Forgiveness in Psychotherapy*. We include here eight of Lamb's (2002) concerns regarding the forgiveness research, followed by our response.

1. Lamb (2002) argues that there is no consensus regarding the definition of forgiveness and its set of necessary conditions. She is accurate in her statement of definitional confusion, as McCullough, Pargament, and Thoresen (2000) have pointed out. Enright and colleagues (1998) anticipated the development of myriad definitions and cautioned researchers to take care as they answered the question: What is forgiveness? Although the caution was not always heeded, research from a variety of laboratories has maintained a fair level of stability and integrity, despite varied definitions of the concept. We believe that the core definition of forgiveness remains constant, regardless of whether researchers agree.

2. Another concern is that there is little justification for the theories developed for the forgiveness process, and the ones that do exist were developed using clinical observation. As Enright (2001) explains, we regard the four phases of the process model and the 20 units within the phases as guideposts that most people experience. We do not consider these phases and units to be carved in stone or rigidly fixed. Numerous studies have indicated that when participants are led through the units of this model, they have learned to forgive and have experienced emotional healing. In addition, when we tested the model with these different populations, we had to change some of the guideposts or units to fit the participants' actual experiences better.

3. The topic of unilateral forgiveness, in which nothing is expected from the perpetrator of the wrongdoing because of its unconditional nature, raises additional concerns for Lamb. According to Andrews (2000), "The forgiver and forgiven need each other for justice to be enacted and to require remorse from a perpetrator is not to confuse justice and forgiveness, but to show their interdependence" (cited in Lamb, 2002, p. 8). Negotiated forgiveness seems to imply some type of ongoing relationship between the injured and injurer; however, it is not always possible or feasible for such a relationship to occur. We believe forgiveness is best offered freely and in one's own time, regardless of the offender's actions. Lamb (2002) appears to be arguing that an injustice may be committed through the process of unconditional forgiveness. As stated previously, Enright et al. (1998) discuss specific expectations that exist for reconciliation (getting back together in a relationship) but are not necessary for forgiveness. Although an admittance of wrongdoing, an apology, and acts of remorse by the offender may certainly make forgiving easier, forgiveness can occur in their absence.

4. Murphy (2002, 2003) suggests that releasing negative and vindictive feelings may be equivalent to "letting go of self-respect, self-defense, and allegiance to moral order" (Lamb, 2002, p. 8). Forgiveness researchers have not properly addressed this criticism. In response to this point, we defer to Holmgren's (2002) eloquent discussion of the necessary steps leading to forgiveness. The first step is that the client who has been injured needs to recover his or her self-respect and recognize that the injury he or she received was wrong. This involves recognizing that he or she (the injured) is a valuable person who deserves to be treated well and that the offensive behavior was not his or her fault. In this context, the act of forgiveness is a sign of self-respect and an allegiance to moral order. It is the offering of mercy toward the offender in the face of wrongdoing.

5. Lamb (2002) and Richards (2002) ask whether other counseling or treatment approaches may be more effective than forgiveness. We do not think that those who study forgiveness are claiming that forgiveness is the only way to heal after being deeply injured but that forgiveness is *one way* to heal and effectively decrease anger and resentment. Before illustrating that forgiveness is better or as effective, compared with another approach, the Enright et al. (Enright & the Human Development Study Group, 1991) group wanted to show that forgiveness is effective in

its own right. Recent research has shown that forgiveness education and therapy is as effective and even more effective than alternative therapies (see Chapman et al., 2001; Gambaro, 2002; Hansen, 2002; Lin et al., 2004; Park, 2003). If a medical researcher found a drug to cure cancer, should she exclaim, "Wait! Let's not use the drug. There may be a drug that is as effective or perhaps even more effective"?

6. Lamb claims that a lot of what is discussed in the Enright et al.'s (Enright & the Human Development Study Group, 1991) model of forgiveness is covered in traditional therapy, such as feelings of guilt and shame, confrontation of anger, how one has been changed as a result of being hurt, and reframing who the wrongdoer is. Yet here is the large difference between traditional therapies and forgiveness therapy: No therapy before forgiveness therapy has deliberately taken the spotlight off of the client and pointed it straight at the offender. The client in forgiveness therapy must step outside of a primary self-focus toward a moral focus on the offender. As paradoxical as this seems for therapy, it works. So yes, the ingredients of the Enright model have similarities with traditional therapy, but they are used in different ways, creating a new and innovative therapy for clients.

7. Lamb (2002) is troubled by the lack of attention to the moral question: Why forgive? She says, to answer that question, forgiveness researchers need to answer why, morally, people may not and should not forgive. Enright and Fitzgibbons (2000) examine in considerable depth whether forgiveness qualifies as a moral virtue. The reader is encouraged to read their exposition of forgiveness as a virtue to determine whether they were successful.

8. Finally, she concludes her introductory criticisms of forgiveness with a discussion of how forgiveness theorists ignore the context of forgiveness. We hope that this chapter has illustrated our emphasis on context. We include the following points to make this clear. Lamb (2002) and Murphy (2002, 2003) both imply that the forgiveness advocated by forgiveness educators and counselors is a Christian-based perspective. Although it is hard not to think of religion when one hears the word *forgiveness*, the Enright group has studied forgiveness from a psychological perspective without adhering to any one religion. This decision was made early in the development of the forgiveness program so that the therapy and education that flowed from the model would be open to all people. Throughout the years, we have worked successfully in forgiveness therapy and education with people from all of the monotheistic faiths, Buddhism, Hinduism, atheism, and religious indifference. They are given the freedom to apply the process model to their particular worldview.

To say that all of forgiveness centers only on Christianity is to neglect the fact that many who study and practice forgiveness come from other perspectives. The first author of this chapter is Jewish, and the process model does not contradict Jewish teachings. As another example, a graduate student from our group was interviewing for a college teaching job at a school on one of the coasts. The student is Muslim. A professor attending the student's colloquium, clearly annoyed by the presentation of forgiveness, used his higher status and power to ask, "Will you be giving your report to the Pope tomorrow?" as he stormed out. The professor did not take the time to find out that this student is a faithful Muslim. The comment was an insult. (But the student forgave the grumpy professor!)

We now turn to four of Murphy's (2002, 2003) criticisms of our process model and the research surrounding it.

1. Murphy questions why we would count greater tendencies to forgive as a gain after a group has been taught to forgive. Increases in forgiveness illustrate that the intervention is effective in helping people forgive. For example, just because one takes a math class, it should not be assumed that he or she is going to learn the math. There could be a variety of reasons why the student completes the math class without learning much at all. One reason is because the math class was not taught well. We count increases in forgiveness as a gain because it shows us that the process model is working.

2. Murphy questions the benefits that research has demonstrated regarding forgiveness. He asks what an increase in self-esteem means and questions the contexts surrounding decreases in depression and anxiety. He implies that the increases in psychological well-being are synonymous with leaving the victim powerless and in his or her status of a victim. Our first response is this: In general, "across all of the studies, there was not one instance in which a group experiencing forgiveness education showed a decline in psychological health. In fact, statistically significant improvements in variables such as hope and self-esteem, and significant decreases in anxiety and depression were more the rule than the exception" (Enright & Coyle, 1998, p. 154). Our second response is that in addition to statistical increases in well-being, verbal and behavioral reports from participants illustrate that after forgiving an offender, participants in Freedman and Enright's (1996) study were more at peace, more productive at work, better able to handle relationships, better able to make decisions regarding career and relationship issues, and also able to use the forgiveness model with other people in their lives. In Lin et al. (2004), those haunted by the specter of drug use reported no psychological depression and greater control over substance use. The control group was not as fortunate. Is any of this *powerlessness* by those *forgiving*?

3. When he talks about the dangers of premature forgiveness, we agree with him. We always have warned against hasty forgiving (see Enright & the Human Development Study Group, 1991). We do not see the beef here. We are in agreement with Murphy that premature forgiveness is false forgiveness.

4. Murphy (2002, 2003) argues that it is morally permissible to hold onto resentment and rejection without forgiveness. He tells the story of a former student, Ralph, who was seeking advice for a personal problem. The student's father, who had repeatedly sexually abused him as a child, wanted his son back in his life after

many years of separation. The father showed no repentance and "still seemed to be his same old arrogant self" (p. 48). Ralph did not want to begin a relationship with his father now, but his friends from church and minister were telling him that it was his duty to forgive and to welcome his father back into his family life, at least on limited terms. Ralph wanted to maintain his strategy of resentment and rejection but wanted to be validated for doing so (Murphy, 2002). After speaking with Murphy, Ralph decided to maintain his attitude of resentment, which had seemed to work for him in the past. As an aside, we do not know enough about Ralph's life to know whether this is true or not. For example, Ralph may experience psychological benefits as a result of forgiving that he did not know were possible because he has held on to resentment for so long.

First, let us say, "Poor Ralph." No one seems to be giving him accurate advice regarding forgiveness and reconciliation; no wonder he is confused. Murphy asks what Enright would say about a case like this and assumes that Enright would say these cases do not occur. These cases do occur (common sense alone would tell us that). We believe that Ralph is being put in an unfair situation because he is being asked not only to forgive but also to reconcile with an unrepentant abuser. Ralph's religious leader is confusing forgiveness with reconciliation, and Murphy (2002) does not recognize the difference when he gives advice to Ralph. Regarding the religious leader's belief that it is Ralph's duty to forgive, we say that forgiveness is not a duty when Ralph is confused about the meaning of forgiveness. What, exactly, is poor Ralph doing when he "forgives," especially when he has such confusion?

Forgiveness from a psychological perspective comes from a choice when one is aware of what forgiveness is and is not, of what is involved in the process of forgiveness, and that forgiveness takes time. Forgiveness should not be rushed or forced on anyone because it can lead to false forgiveness. Forgiveness should not be brushed aside because of fear of exploitation (because the quest for forgiveness and justice can occur concomitantly and because forgiveness and reconciliation can occur separately). Ralph can forgive if he decides to do so. Ralph can work on forgiveness at his own pace and initially for his own well-being, but he may choose not to enter into a relationship with his father until his father apologizes, admits his wrongdoings, and illustrates that he has changed. As a result of forgiving, Ralph may hope that his father recognizes his past offenses, makes reparations, and changes his hurtful behavior. What we would like to ask Murphy is this: How would true forgiveness, as described by Enright (2001; Enright & Fitzgibbons, 2000) and Holmgren (2002), affect Ralph? Would forgiveness bring Ralph more peace and psychological well-being than his present strategy of resentment and rejection? Based on what we have been finding in our scientific studies as described in this chapter, what would common sense say to Ralph if he tried to forgive with the process model?

NEW RESEARCH DIRECTIONS NEEDED

The intervention studies reviewed raise some significant issues for forgiveness research. What should be the duration of interventions to make it possible for subjects actually to forgive? Is it possible to come up with an actual time line that would capture the progression of the average person's experience with the forgiveness model? How does forgiveness change over time for individuals? Because forgiveness is individual for each person, is forgiveness education that occurs in a group setting as effective as forgiveness education that is individually focused? Are there certain benefits to group education? How often should the education occur? Once a week, twice a week? Does the whole model need to be experienced for forgiveness to occur and are there certain steps that are more critical than others in promoting forgiveness? There may be a number of different ways to educate effectively for forgiveness. One format may be best suited to people with particular kinds of hurts. More research on forgiveness needs to be conducted with different populations. If we can aid professionals to find the maximum psychological benefits to participants in the least amount of time necessary to achieve such benefits, those professionals may be able to serve more clients.

CONCLUSION

The state of forgiveness intervention work using Enright's process model is sound. Randomized, experimental and control group trials have produced initially interesting results, especially as seen in the meta-analysis described here. Experimental designs have begun to mature by including active control groups. Diverse educators and therapists who lead such research show, when all are taken together, that positive results are not the result of only a few very talented leaders. We need a continued effort with larger samples and an emphasis on the benefits for the one forgiven. Our emphasis on the forgiver's outcomes is a clinical choice based on therapeutic efficacy and should not be taken as a sign that forgiveness is a self-serving enterprise.

The response-to-critics section is by no means an attempt to address all critics' remarks about forgiveness. We value the criticisms because they aid us in the clarification of our own ideas. All clarification, whether borne out of independent inquiry or in response to critics, is a service to clients because it points more strongly to the truth. Just as we take risks by presenting our ideas and science to the scholarly community, so too do the critics open themselves to the risk of challenge. We have tried to illustrate that many of the criticisms aimed at forgiveness seem to result from incomplete formulations of definitions or misunderstanding of the contexts surrounding forgiveness.

Those who do forgiveness research and counseling do so because of an interest in the question: Can forgiveness help people to heal? What is clear is that both victims of injustice and their counselors are in need of more education regarding forgiveness and how to forgive. As Lamb and Murphy remind us, we need to do more research on when a person's level of anger begins to be maladaptive. Not all anger is counter-productive. We need to know when a person is ready to forgive so that we do not simply presume that all who seek help will embrace forgiveness (and an accurate concept of it). Yet the field to date is healthy precisely because the important work of clarifying definitions and examining effective pathways to forgiveness has been done. The science, although still in its initial stages, is surprisingly strong. Come, critics, let us at least temporarily join in acknowledging the truth that forgiveness, properly understood and practiced, is good, and the examination of it to date is helpful to the hurting.

REFERENCES

Al-Mabuk, R. H., Enright, R. D., & Cardis, P. A. (1995). Forgiveness education with parentally love-deprived late adolescents. *Journal of Moral Education, 24*, 427–444.

Andrews, M. (2000). Forgiveness in context. *Journal of Moral Education, 29*, 75–86.

Baskin, T. W., & Enright, R. D. (2004). Intervention studies of forgiveness: A meta-analysis. *Journal of Counseling and Development, 82*, 79–90.

Chapman, R. F., Maier, G., Owen, A., Nousse, V., Park, J. H., & Enright, R. D. (2001, July). *Healing forgiveness: Group cognitive therapy for abused male forensic patients*. Paper presented at the World Congress of Behavioral and Cognitive Therapies, Vancouver, Canada.

Coyle, C. T., & Enright, R. D. (1997). Forgiveness intervention with postabortion men. *Journal of Consulting and Clinical Psychology, 65*, 1042–1046.

Enright, R. D. (2001). *Forgiveness is a choice: A step-by-step process for resolving anger and restoring hope*. Washington, DC: APA Life Tools.

Enright, R. D., & Coyle, C. T. (1998). Researching the process model of forgiveness within psychological interventions. In E. L. Worthington, Jr., (Ed.), *Dimensions of forgiveness: Psychological research and theological perspectives* (pp. 139–162). Philadelphia: Templeton Foundation Press.

Enright, R. D., & Fitzgibbons, R. P. (2000). *Helping clients forgive: An empirical guide for resolving anger and restoring hope*. Washington, DC: American Psychological Association.

Enright, R. D., Freedman, S. R., & Rique, J. (1998). The psychology of interpersonal forgiveness. In R. D. Enright & J. North (Eds.), *Exploring forgiveness*. Madison, WI: University of Wisconsin Press.

Enright, R. D., & the Human Development Study Group (1991). The moral development of forgiveness. In W. Kurtines & J. Gewirtz (Eds.), *Handbook of moral behavior and development* (Vol. 1, pp. 123–152). Hillsdale, NJ: Lawrence Erlbaum.

Fitzgibbons, R. P. (1986). The cognitive and emotional uses of forgiveness in the treatment of anger. *Psychotherapy, 23*, 629–633.

Freedman, S. (1998). Forgiveness and reconciliation: The importance of understanding how they differ. *Counseling and Values, 42*, 200–216.

Freedman, S. R., & Enright, R. D. (1996). Forgiveness as an intervention goal with incest survivors. *Journal of Consulting and Clinical Psychology, 64*, 983–992.

Freedman, S. R., & Knupp, A. (2003). The impact of forgiveness on adolescent adjustment to parental divorce. *Journal of Divorce and Remarriage, 39*, 135–165.

Gambaro, M. E. (2002). *School-based forgiveness education in the management of trait anger in early adolescents*. Unpublished doctoral dissertation, University of Wisconsin, Madison.

Hansen, M. J. (2002). *Forgiveness as an educational intervention goal for persons at the end of life.* Unpublished doctoral dissertation, University of Wisconsin, Madison.

Hebl, J. H., & Enright, R. D. (1993). Forgiveness as a psychotherapeutic goal with elderly females. *Psychotherapy, 30,* 658–667.

Hepp-Dax, S. H. (1996). *Forgiveness as an educational goal with fifth-grade inner-city children.* Unpublished doctoral dissertation. Fordham University, New York.

Holmgren, M. R. (2002). Forgiveness and self-forgiveness in psychotherapy. In S. Lamb & J. G. Murphy (Eds.), *Before forgiving: Cautionary views of forgiveness in psychotherapy* (pp. 112–135). New York: Oxford University Press.

Konstam, V., Marx, F., Schurer, J., Emerson Lombardo, N., & Harrington, A. K. (2002). Forgiveness in practice: What mental health counselors are telling us. In S. Lamb & J. G. Murphy (Eds.), *Before forgiving: Cautionary views of forgiveness in psychotherapy* (pp. 54–71). New York: Oxford University Press.

Knutson, J. A. (2003). *Strengthening marriages through the practice of forgiveness.* Unpublished doctoral dissertation, University of Wisconsin, Madison.

Lamb, S. (2002). Women, abuse, and forgiveness: A special case. In S. Lamb & J. Murphy (Eds.), *Before forgiving: Cautionary views of forgiveness in psychotherapy* (pp. 155–171). New York: Oxford University Press.

Lamb, S., & Murphy, J. G. (Eds.). (2002). *Before forgiving: Cautionary views of forgiveness in psychotherapy.* New York: Oxford University Press.

Lin, W. N. (1998). *Forgiveness as an intervention goal with late adolescents with insecure attachment in Taiwan.* Unpublished masters thesis, University of Wisconsin, Madison.

Lin, W., Mack, D., Enright, R., Krahn, D., & Baskin, T. (2004). Effects of forgiveness therapy on anger, mood, and vulnerability to substance use among inpatient substance-dependent clients. *Journal of Consulting and Clinical Psychology, 72* 1114–1121.

Lipsey, M. W. (1990). *Design sensitivity: Statistical power for experimental research.* Newbury Park, CA: Sage.

McCullough, M. E., Pargament, K. I., & Thoresen, C. E. (2000). The psychology of forgiveness: History, conceptual issues, and overview. In M. E. McCullough, K. I. Pargament, & C. E. Thoresen (Eds.), *Forgiveness: Theory, research, and practice* (pp. 1–14). New York: Guilford Press.

McCullough, M. E., & Worthington, E. L., Jr. (1995). Promoting forgiveness: The comparison of two brief psychoeducational interventions with a waiting-list control. *Counseling and Values, 40,* 55–68.

McCullough, M. E., Worthington, E. L., Jr., & Rachal, K. C. (1997). Interpersonal forgiving in close relationships. *Journal of Personality and Social Psychology, 73,* 321–336.

Murphy, J. G. (2002). Forgiveness in counseling: A philosophical perspective. In S. Lamb & J. G. Murphy (Eds.), *Before forgiving: Cautionary views of forgiveness in psychotherapy* (pp. 19–41). New York: Oxford University Press.

Murphy, J. G. (2003). *Getting even: Forgiveness and its limits.* New York: Oxford University Press.

Park, J. H. (2003). *Validating a forgiveness education program for adolescent female aggressive victims in Korea.* Unpublished doctoral dissertation, University of Wisconsin, Madison.

Richards, N. (2002). Forgiveness as therapy. In S. Lamb & J. Murphy (Eds.), *Before forgiving: Cautionary views of forgiveness in psychotherapy* (pp. 72–87). New York: Oxford University Press.

Chapter Twenty-Five

Forgiveness in Couples: Divorce, Infidelity, and Couples Therapy

Kristina Coop Gordon
Donald H. Baucom
Douglas K. Snyder

Most clinicians would agree that betrayals and forgiveness are significant issues for many couples. However, despite the prevalence of the need for forgiveness, until recently most couples therapists have been reluctant to use therapeutic strategies that relate explicitly to forgiveness (DiBlasio & Proctor, 1993). Fortunately, in the last few years, forgiveness has been increasingly incorporated into couples treatment, and its use has begun to receive empirical support. In this chapter, we present our integrative, trauma-based model of forgiveness; then we review recent applications of forgiveness to couples therapy that have received initial empirical support. We conclude by outlining directions for future research and intervention.

THEORETICAL ASSUMPTIONS ABOUT FORGIVENESS

We define *forgiveness* as a process whereby partners pursue increased understanding of themselves, each other, and their relationship in order to free themselves from being dominated by negative thoughts, feelings, and behaviors after experiencing a major interpersonal betrayal. This process is distinguished from a view of forgiveness as excusing or forgetting that a relationship injury or betrayal has occurred, or as requiring a decision to reconcile the couple's relationship. An important aspect of our conceptualization of forgiveness is that it does *not* stipulate that partners must reconcile in order for forgiveness to occur. Partners can decide to terminate the relationship and still fulfill the conditions of forgiveness.

Instead, our model asserts that forgiveness consists of three components: (a) a realistic, nondistorted, balanced view of the relationship, (b) a release from being controlled by negative affect toward the participating partner, and (c) a lessened desire to punish the participating partner. For a more thorough explication of this approach to understanding forgiveness and its place in the forgiveness literature, see Gordon and Baucom (1998). The forgiveness process also allows for the possible development of warmer and more positive feelings toward the participating partner. However, healthy forgiveness requires a realistic appraisal of the partner, not an assessment that ignores real and dangerous aspects of the partner or the relationship. Forgiveness means that negative affect no longer dominates individuals' lives or controls their actions toward their partners and that this event has been resolved to such an extent that the injured partner no longer carries its negative effects into other relationships. Furthermore, another key issue in our definition of forgiveness is the stipulation that forgiveness is a process, not an event. Most theorists agree that forgiveness of a serious transgression takes a great deal of time and emotional work (e.g., Worthington et al., 2000).

Finally, our model of forgiveness also proposes that forgiveness in relationships often closely parallels recovery from a traumatic event. Research reported in the trauma literature has suggested that posttraumatic stress reactions evolve from "violated assumptions" (e.g., Janoff-Bulman, 1989). The "betrayal" that requires forgiveness may be seen as an interpersonal trauma that upsets the person's previous assumptions and expectations of his or her partner and relationships in general. These violated assumptions often can leave the "victim" feeling out of control and no longer able to predict future behaviors on the part of his or her partner. Therefore, the forgiveness process results in part from attempts to reconstruct these former cognitions and regain a sense of interpersonal control, predictability, and safety in the relationship.

Thus, we believe that there are three major stages in the forgiveness process, each of which parallels the general stages that are believed to occur in recovery from a psychological trauma: (a) impact, (b) a search for meaning, and (c) recovery, or moving on. The primarily cognitive emphasis is not to suggest that the experience of forgiveness is wholly an intellectual one. This process is likely to be suffused with overwhelmingly intense negative affect to such a degree that the process seems to be primarily emotional in tone. However, the current theory suggests that accomplishing these cognitive goals is a key factor in moving through these stages. Thus, within each stage there are important cognitive tasks that must be accomplished before moving on to the next stage. However, within each of these stages there are also distinct emotional and behavioral components in addition to cognitive ones.

In the first stage, called the *impact stage*, people recollect details related to the betrayal in an attempt to comprehend what has happened. However, because this betrayal often has major implications for the injured person's well-being, this cognitive process is accompanied by an overwhelming array of emotions, such as fear, hurt, or anger. These emotions often alternate with a sense of numbness or disbelief. Additionally, people may find themselves acting toward their partners in ways that are punitive, erratic, or unlike their usual selves. These are natural reactions to an unexpected, painfully traumatic event and are similar to the approach-avoidance strategies used by victims of traumatic stress (e.g., Horowitz, 1985).

The goal in the second stage, the *meaning* stage, is to discover why the event happened and to give it meaning. Research on the reactions of trauma victims suggests that a major strategy in their recovery is a search for some meaning behind the trauma (e.g., Horowitz, 1985; Janoff-Bulman, 1989). This meaning may come from two sources—identifying causes of the trauma (e.g., "I didn't lock my door" or "I made a bad choice in dating partners") or some positive impact the event had on their lives (e.g., greater spiritual growth, better understanding of life). Similarly, the injured person in the relationship also begins to look for the meaning behind the event, such as a deeper understanding of the partner's motives and the relationship as a whole. This meaning helps the victims regain some sense of control over their lives. If they know "why" the transgression happened, it gives them the ability to try to prevent it from happening again, and it may give them the sense of safety needed to approach a decision to forgive, which happens in the next stage, *moving on.*

Again, similar to trauma victims, in this recovery or moving on stage, the injured person must move beyond the event and stop allowing it to control his or her life. In the current conceptualization, forgiveness involves moving on by giving up the control that negative affect can have over the injured person's thoughts and behaviors and by giving up the right to punish the partner. In this theory, the injured person must also reevaluate the relationship and reach a decision regarding whether he or she wishes to continue with the relationship. Forgiveness does not require reconciliation. Furthermore, forgiveness does not require that anger disappear completely. More likely, the emotions and thoughts associated with the event will recur; however, these thoughts and feelings are no longer as severe or as disruptive as they once were.

REVIEW OF THE THEORETICAL AND EMPIRICAL LITERATURE ON FORGIVENESS AND COUPLES TREATMENT

As yet, treatment-outcome studies on the use of forgiveness in couples therapy are still scarce, although the concept of forgiveness is quite prominent in the clinical and theoretical literature. In general, forgiveness has been empirically evaluated as a therapeutic option for couples therapy in at least three instances: infidelity and betrayal, marital enrichment, and increasing the quality of co-parenting following a divorce. In this section, we will review the existing literature, the theories underlying the treatments, and the research findings in each of these areas.

Infidelity and Major Betrayals

Integrative Forgiveness-Based Treatment for Infidelity. Based on the forgiveness model we described earlier in this chapter and elsewhere (Gordon & Baucom, 1998; Gordon, Baucom, & Snyder, 2004), we have developed and evaluated a treatment based on this model and on empirical evidence from our basic research (Gordon et al., 2004;

Snyder, Gordon, & Baucom, 2004). The first stage of the treatment aids the couple in developing skills to contain and regulate their negative emotions and to discuss more effectively with each other the impact that infidelity has had on themselves and their relationship. Thus, the first several sessions use well-established cognitive-behavioral strategies (Epstein & Baucom, 2002) to deal primarily with helping the couple to (a) set appropriate boundaries around themselves individually and as a couple, (b) manage their emotions, and (c) express and identify their reactions to the impact of the infidelity. In the second stage, the therapy integrates more insight-oriented as well as cognitive techniques (Snyder, 1999) as the partners attempt to understand why the affair happened and examine both current and developmental issues within themselves and in their relationship that may have contributed to the affair. The developmental aspect of this treatment often is critical. The injured and participating partners often already know or have access to information about their relationship that may have influenced the participating partner's decision to have an affair; however, they are often unaware of deeper or unacknowledged needs or motives from their partner's past history that may be impacting their current behaviors. Gaining this new understanding often results in an increase in compassion for the partner and tolerance of his or her flaws. Thus, our treatment is designed to help the couple to (a) explore these factors in a neutral, supportive, and structured environment; (b) develop empathy and understanding for each other to the extent possible; and (c) attempt to alter any negative or problematic issues that they pinpoint as contributing influences to the person's decision to have an affair.

Finally, in the third stage, the treatment again becomes more present- and future-focused, which in turn calls for more cognitive-behavioral strategies. As the couple begins to understand why the affair happened, they need to evaluate the viability of their relationship, its potential for change, and their commitment to work toward change. In addition, the process of forgiveness becomes a focus of intervention. The therapist explains to the couple how they have been progressing through the forgiveness process as they have gone through this treatment. Their misconceptions of and resistance to forgiveness are examined, and any blocks to this process are addressed. This treatment then helps them to evaluate important aspects of their relationship in order to reach a well-considered decision about whether they wish to continue their marriage. Depending on this decision, the couple either continues to work on rebuilding their relationship or receives the therapist's support and guidance as they work through the necessary issues of terminating the marriage. The latter course retains efforts toward increased understanding and forgiveness of traumatic events in the marriage in order to move on in their individual lives.

We have conducted a replicated case study that allowed us to explore in depth the efficacy of our integrative treatment designed to help couples recover from an affair (Gordon et al., 2004; Snyder et al., 2004). Six couples entered and completed treatment. By the end of treatment, the majority of these couples were less emotionally distressed (e.g., less posttraumatic stress symptomatology or less depression, as measured by the Beck Distress Inventory) and less maritally distressed, and the injured partners reported greater forgiveness regarding the affair. Five of the six couples showed clinically significant changes on measures of forgiveness, demonstrating that this treatment was able to shift the injured partners' levels of forgiveness of the affairs significantly in the intended direction. The treatment effect sizes for the group were comparable to those of other empirically supported marital treatments and were significantly greater than the average effect sizes for wait-list controls across marital treatment-outcome studies (Baucom, Hahlweg, & Kuschel, 2003). However, a third of the couples did not respond as favorably to treatment, and group-mean data showed some deterioration in marital satisfaction and depression scores from posttest to 6-month follow-up. Couples showing less favorable response were those in which one or both partners exhibited enduring individual, emotional, or behavioral difficulties independent of the affair (e.g., features of a borderline or antisocial personality disorder).

Decision-Based Forgiveness Treatment for Infidelity.   DiBlasio (2000) has developed a unique decision-based forgiveness intervention for couples based on the premise that forgiveness, or at least the decision to forgive, can take place in a single session. He suggests that this cognitive decision to forgive leads to shifts in emotional reactions to the betrayal and quickly to more emotional peace, whereas forgiveness driven primarily by emotions leaves a client powerless and at the mercy of time. Although DiBlasio also acknowledges that forgiveness often does take time, he defines decision-based forgiveness as:

> The cognitive letting go of resentment, bitterness, and need for vengeance. By this definition, emotional readiness is not a factor in the decision process. There is a separation of reason from feelings in making the forgiveness decision, followed by an act of will. (DiBlasio, 2000, p. 150)

There are 13 steps involved in DiBlasio's decision-based forgiveness for infidelity (DiBlasio, 1998, 2000). The first three steps involve defining decision-based forgiveness, discussing its benefits, and preparing the ground for the decision. Then each partner is given the opportunity to seek forgiveness for his or her own wrongful actions, the intent of which is to create an atmosphere of personal accountability. During this step, DiBlasio suggests that therapists must attend to their clients' expectations concerning how their partners should respond and help each person avoid coercive attempts to make his or her partner admit behaviors that the individual sees as wrong.

The couple then takes turns going through steps 4–12. During these steps, the offense is stated, the offender provides an explanation for his or her behavior, and the reasons for this behavior are further explored, as are the offended person's reactions. Following these steps, offenders are encouraged to be empathic about the effects of their behaviors on their partners and to develop a plan to stop or prevent the behaviors. Then the offended partners are asked to recognize the offenders' emotions—such as guilt, shame, or fear—about the offense or the effects of the offense, which can be facilitated by either tracing patterns back to offenders' childhoods or by the offended partners identifying their own failures in their relationships. The next two steps involve recognizing the "choice and commitment involved in letting go" (DiBlasio, 2000, p. 155) and a formal ritual of seeking and granting forgiveness between partners. Finally, the last step consists of a ceremonial ritual or act that symbolizes the couple's commitment to forgiveness and decision to let go of the pain of the betrayal.

These steps are accomplished within a lengthy (2- to 3-hour) single treatment session. Although DiBlasio acknowledges that many therapists would find this framework too compressed to address an issue as complex as an extramarital affair adequately, he also argues that the forgiveness session may be an early step that would then facilitate more traditional therapy to heal the relationship completely. Similarly, he responds to criticisms that forgiveness is more a process than a decision by suggesting that his decision-based treatment also is a process, albeit a process that unfolds in a very short period of time.

Recently, DiBlasio (2003) presented preliminary findings on a treatment outcome project examining the efficacy of this treatment. Couples were randomly assigned to three groups: a secular, forgiveness-based group; an alternative treatment group; and a no-treatment control group. Couples were also allowed to choose the option of entering an explicitly Christian forgiveness group. Results showed no difference between the secular forgiveness and alternative treatment group and trends toward greater improvement in forgiveness and contentment when comparing the secular forgiveness group and the no-treatment control. Statistically significant differences in forgiveness, marital satisfaction, and individual contentment outcomes were found comparing the Christian forgiveness-based group with the no-treatment control. However, because this group was not randomly assigned to this treatment, it is unclear whether these differences were due to the treatment or to a systematic selection bias in the type of couple who would choose this treatment.

A Contextual Model of Families and Forgiveness.   Hargrave has developed a theoretical framework of forgiveness for use in family and couples therapy that has received some empirical support. Hargrave's (1994) model suggests that forgiveness involves a response to a violation of an innate sense of justice or a disruption between the implicit balance of give (obligations) and take (entitlements) inherent in healthy family functioning. He further suggests that the betraying member—the one who disrupts this balance and violates the justice standard—has likely experienced a violation of trust in a prior relationship and consequently feels justified in enacting hurtful behaviors within the current relationship. As a result, the betrayed partner faces the realization that the betraying family member may not be reliable or trustworthy, which can engender a number of emotional reactions, such as rage and shame. If this injustice is not satisfactorily resolved, betrayed individuals are likely to carry the results forward into new relationships and thus play out their own roles of destructive entitlement in their own family relationships. Forgiveness is theorized to be an effective method to end the cycle of intergenerational transmission of discord and betrayal.

Thus, Hargrave posits that the work of forgiveness in families is made up of both *exonerating* and *forgiving* in an attempt to right injustice and rebalance the ratio of obligations and entitlements in the family system. *Exonerating* includes gaining insight into and understanding of the motive behind the betrayal. The increased insight gained in this "station" of forgiveness allows the individual to become aware of how familial patterns are repeated and to understand or "identify with the victimizer's position, limitations, development, efforts, and intent" (Hargrave & Sells, 1997, p.44). On the other hand, *forgiving* involves the injured person engaging in an overt act of forgiving, which involves direct discussion between the victimizer and victim about developing a new, trustworthy relationship in the future. In addition, forgiving also might involve giving the offender the opportunity for compensation, such as allowing the victimizer to engage in a series of behaviors designed to show increased signs of trustworthiness. Thus, *exoneration* appears to be cognitive in nature, whereas *forgiving* is more behavioral. Hargrave emphasizes that these components are not stages that people progress through in succession; instead, he hypothesizes that people vary between these strategies as they forgive.

Some empirical evidence exists for the use of this model in group therapy with couples. Sells, Giordano, and King (2002) developed a protocol for group couples therapy based on Hargrave's theoretical framework, in which couples received modules in empathic listening, conflict resolution and anger management, and forgiveness. The treatment lasted for 8 sessions over 8 weeks. The forgiveness modules involved three components: (a) expression of relational injury, (b) setting goals surrounding regaining trust and achieving insight, and (c) focusing on the group's spontaneous reactions to the materials given for homework. Participants were five couples recruited from a large private-practice agency; it was unclear whether these couples were specifically recruited for the occurrence of a betrayal. Results indicated that couples were successful in acquiring and, to some extent, retaining forgiveness skills at 3-month follow-up, and forgiveness was correlated with marital satisfaction and psychological symptoms. However, these correlations were small, and the researchers noted that there was an increase in state anger at follow-up, as well as a decline in the forgiveness skills (although these were still higher than pretreatment levels), marital satisfaction, and psychological health, which they interpret as an atrophy effect. The general conclusions were that forgiveness may be achieved through these group interventions but that couples require a longer period of "reinforcement and support to form an internal reorientation and sustain the development of new habit[s]" (Sells et al., 2002, p. 164).

Forgiveness and Marital Enrichment and Prevention Programs

A Pyramid Model of Forgiveness and Reconciliation in Couples Therapy.   Worthington and colleagues have developed a pyramid model of forgiveness that hypothesizes three central components to forgiveness: empathy, humility, and commitment (e.g., Worthington, 1998; Worthington & Drinkard, 2000). Empathy between partners regarding each other's situation is believed to be critical in facilitating a softened atmosphere between partners, enabling them to risk forgiving each other. Humility on the part of each partner also furthers this process by requiring that the hurt partner acknowledge that she or he is not perfect by recalling times when she or he hurt the offending partner. Worthington (1998) theorizes that this recognition of human fallibility and of one's own imperfections brings with it the realization that forgiveness, which releases the offender from one's own hate, anger, or retribution, is the just or fair thing to do; therefore, forgiveness is seen as "the natural response to empathy and humility" (Worthington, 1998, p. 64). Finally, although an individual might internally experience forgiveness, Worthington suggests that forgiveness lacks a degree of reality until the individual formally commits to forgiving through overt behaviors.

Based on this model of forgiveness, Worthington has developed a forgiveness intervention described by the acronym REACH. First, the injured individual must *recall* the hurt by acknowledging the offense and examining the nature of the injury. The focus of the intervention then centers on promoting *empathy* in each partner for the experience of the other partner. Interventions may include writing a letter from the other person's point of view or describing the hurtful events in a session from the other's perspective. Third, the partners are invited to give an *altruistic gift of forgiveness*, in which participants explore times when they have needed and been granted forgiveness and the impact on them when forgiveness was received. This experience may achieve the quality of humility by accessing the realization that one is not perfect. It promotes awareness of one's partner's suffering as well as a desire to alleviate that suffering by granting forgiveness. The fourth step in the model is for the partners to *commit* verbally to forgive, once the therapist believes that the partners have experienced enough empathy and developed enough humility to take this step. Finally, the partners are encouraged to find ways in which they can *hold on to forgiveness*, because it is inevitable that past hurts will be remembered. In a sense, the couple is inoculated against these unavoidable recapitulations by the therapist encouraging them to make the distinction between simply remembering past pain and continuing to reexperience bitterness and hatred.

Worthington's pyramid model of forgiveness has been tested in two studies involving interventions (Burchard et al., 2003; Ripley & Worthington, 2002). In both of these studies, the forgiveness intervention was used either as a preventive measure or as a means to enrich currently stable marriages; in neither study were couples recruited for existing betrayals and an expressed need for forgiveness. Ripley and Worthington (2002) provided an initial test of the pyramid model of forgiveness by comparing two marital enrichment groups, a HOPE (Handling Our Problems Effectively) communication-based group and a REACH forgiveness-based group, with a no-treatment control, using a wider range of married couples. These components together comprised what Worthington et al. (1997) termed *hope-focused marital enrichment*. In Ripley and Worthington (2002), neither treatment significantly affected self-report measures of marital quality, communication, or forgiveness. The only difference between the groups was that the HOPE treatment created significant improvements in observational measures of couples' communication.

In the follow-up study (Burchard et al., 2003), 20 newlywed couples were recruited from the community to participate in an intervention involving couples who met as a pair with a marriage consultant. The aims were to prevent the development of marital distress and to enhance their marital functioning. These couples were randomly assigned to one of two marital enrichment programs, HOPE or Forgiveness and Reconciliation through Experiencing Empathy (FREE), or to an assessment-only control. FREE was based on teaching couples the pyramid model of forgiveness and reasons why forgiveness is important, and on teaching reconciliation skills. Couples practiced the skills under the attention of a consultant. Both of these interventions consisted of four sessions of about 2–2.5 hours each (9 total hours of consultation) over 3–5 weeks. Results indicated that both interventions improved the participants' quality of life posttreatment, whereas the general quality of life for the control group decreased; however, the hypothesis that the forgiveness-based intervention would create significantly better quality of life than the more traditional communication-based intervention was not supported.

Both of the above studies were sequential pilot studies to refine the method used in a larger research effort involving 156 newly married couples. Worthington et al. (2003) reported preliminary results at a conference. Using the method of Burchard et al. (2003) but using a 9-month follow up, Worthington et al. reported that both HOPE and FREE were superior in forgiveness measures and marital satisfaction to assessment-only controls at 1 month posttreatment. On some measures, HOPE reflected more improvement than did FREE. However, at 9 months posttreatment, FREE was superior to HOPE, and both were superior to the assessment-only controls on most measures. In these preliminary results, only self-report measures were analyzed. Behavioral and salivary cortisol data were still being analyzed at that time. Worthington et al. (2003) showed that the FREE intervention had preventive benefits that showed up at a longer follow-up after treatment. When couples were followed up within a month of treatment (i.e., Burchard et al., 2003; Ripley & Worthington, 2002; Worthington et al., 2003, posttest), however, few positive preventive effects of the forgiveness intervention were found.

In summary, neither of these treatment studies indicated that forgiveness interventions provide a greater general enhancement to marital and individual well-being over and above a more traditional conflict-resolution approach. However, it should be noted that these groups were not targeted for specific betrayals. A forgiveness-based intervention might be more useful for individuals who are currently experiencing a pressing need to forgive a major betrayal, rather than as a preventive measure. Furthermore, the follow-up periods for two of the treatments were quite short; because major hurts or betrayals may not have occurred in this time period, the studies' designs may not give an adequate sampling of the behaviors of interest or an opportunity for the intervention to demonstrate its effects.

Forgiveness and Divorce

Rye and colleagues (Rye et al., 2004) have developed an intervention targeting individuals' experience of anger and bitterness after divorce that is designed to increase their levels of forgiveness toward ex-spouses. Loosely based on Worthington's REACH model and conducted in a group therapy modality, this treatment contained five steps: (a) discussion of feelings of betrayal; (b) coping with anger; (c) forgiveness education, obstacles to forgiveness, and strategies for achieving forgiveness; (d) self-care and self-forgiveness; and (e) relapse prevention and closure. A sample of 149 divorced individuals was randomly assigned to a secular forgiveness group, a religiously integrated forgiveness group (similar to the secular group except that participants were also encouraged to draw on their spiritual beliefs while working toward forgiveness), or a wait-list control group that was also similar to a treatment-as-usual group because it allowed individuals to seek out available community resources. Results indicated that there were significant intervention effects for levels of forgiveness and depression posttreatment, such that individuals in the two intervention groups had more self-reported forgiveness and less depression at the end of treatment. Notably, unlike DiBlasio's (2003) findings, there were no differences between the secular and the religious groups on these variables. Rye et al. (2004) also had friends and family members reporting on the individuals' levels of forgiveness. There were no significant intervention effects for these observer ratings. Furthermore, the participants also completed a measure regarding their forgiveness in parenting, which essentially assessed how well the participants interacted with their ex-spouses around parenting issues; again, no significant differences in treatment outcomes for the groups were found on this measure.

Although the findings regarding forgiveness were mixed and were not significant for parenting, these results still provide partial support, indicating that individuals' levels of forgiveness toward their ex-spouses can be increased by a relatively brief intervention. Given the emotional impact that parental conflict after divorce can have on children (Amato, 1996), any intervention that may reduce the level of that conflict ultimately might have beneficial effects beyond the individual who is participating. Consequently, this is an area of forgiveness intervention that deserves more study and innovation.

Summary

All of these interventions to some degree promote a better understanding of each partner and suggest that this better understanding should consequently lead to increased emotional empathy. This improved insight and heightened emotional empathy are considered to be central to the forgiveness process. Furthermore, these interventions all promote forgiveness as beneficial to the relationship, and some even suggest that forgiveness may go beyond ameliorative effects on a relationship to have preventive effects on marital deterioration.

At the same time, there are several distinctions to be made among these treatments; each model promotes its own "twist" on the forgiveness process. The integrative forgiveness model put forth by Gordon et al. (2004) emphasizes forgiveness as a necessary reconstructive process after a relational trauma. Thus, their model highlights individuals' need to rebuild safety before forgiving by reconstructing disrupted assumptions and achieving cognitive insight into themselves and the relationship. Consequently, their model places less emphasis on compassion between the partners as a condition of forgiveness, although such compassion may be a frequent consequence of the forgiveness process. Although DiBlasio (2003) lays out a similar process of forgiveness to the other clinical models, his decision-based model compresses this process into a shorter time frame and emphasizes mutual seeking of forgiveness in the beginning phase. Worthington's (1998) pyramid model places more weight on empathy and, like DiBlasio's model, emphasizes mutual fallibility and need for forgiveness. Finally, Hargrave and Sells (1997) adopt a family systems approach to forgiveness that acknowledges the intergenerational context of betrayal. The implications of their model for understanding why betrayals occur might be clinically very useful through its explication of how interpersonal hurts and styles of relating may be handed down across generations. However, a problem with this treatment might arise in the language used to describe the stations of forgiveness; in particular, the word *exoneration* could be problematic for some persons because its connotations may play into preexisting negative stereotypes of forgiveness as excusing or condoning negative behaviors.

At this time, the data remain inconclusive regarding the impact of couples-based forgiveness interventions. There is some evidence that forgiveness treatments affect forgiveness (Gordon et al., 2004; Rye et al., 2004; Sells et al., 2002; and possibly DiBlasio, 2003). However, there is only mixed evidence that treatments go beyond forgiveness to affect individual and dyadic functioning; evidence favoring generalized effects include findings from Gordon et al. (2004), Ripley and Worthington (2002), Rye et al. (2004), and possibly DiBlasio (2003), whereas evidence against generalized effects include findings from Sells et al. (2002) and Burchard et al. (2003). It is possible that difference in treatment effectiveness might arise when forgiveness is taught in a primary prevention context as opposed to a secondary or tertiary intervention. It seems that the strongest effects occur when forgiveness is addressed in the context of existing interpersonal hurt; otherwise, the strategies might not have the resonance necessary for them to be encoded in the couples' repertoire of responses. At the same time, it is possible that we could teach individuals to be more forgiving but also possible that new interventions might be needed or longer follow-ups required to capture these interventions, effects as suggested by Worthington et al.'s (2003) long-term follow-up findings.

NEW RESEARCH DIRECTIONS

More, More, More

Research in this area is still in its infancy. Although the studies reviewed here are a promising start, more and higher quality trials are needed. All of the existing studies are plagued by methodological flaws that make it difficult to assess their efficacy adequately, let alone the effectiveness of these interventions. For example, studies often have a low sample size or no control groups, or the participants are not randomly assigned to treatments. Although the study on forgiveness after divorce by Rye et al. (2004) was exemplary in many ways, the authors did not specify their means of recruiting couples. Whether individuals were recruited specifically for forgiveness interventions might have introduced a selection bias with the unintended artifact that these programs are working only because people want them to work—that is, participants are already predisposed to forgive by choosing an intervention that is advertising forgiveness. If this is true, what about individuals who are adamantly opposed to forgiveness? Can or should we help them to forgive as well?

Divorce

As noted earlier, a particularly promising line of research is the study of forgiveness to decrease the bitterness and conflict that occurs between parents after divorce. Although Rye and colleagues (2004) were unable to show changes in parenting behaviors posttreatment, more targeted interventions that explicitly discuss how lack of forgiveness may affect parenting and, consequently, the family as a whole or that involve both spouses participating in the same intervention might yield more powerful results. Because conflict after divorce is a particularly damaging phenomenon, efforts targeting this problem are worthy of greater attention. Forgiveness interventions may have considerable potential in this area.

What Works for Whom?

We do not yet know which forgiveness interventions work best with which individuals or couples. DiBlasio's (2003) data suggest that religiously based forgiveness interventions may be quite efficacious for individuals who choose that modality. However, what type of intervention works best for a bitter, angry partner who is not spiritually oriented and bristles at the mere mention of forgiveness? Our own intervention with couples struggling with infidelity was less successful with emotionally dysregulated individuals. Such couples might benefit from more emotion-focused treatments or a combination of individual treatment focusing on emotion regulation as well as conjoint therapy. Finally, forgiveness interventions may not be effective as preventive strategies but instead may be more applicable to individuals who are in the throes of interpersonal trauma or betrayals.

CONCEPTUAL CONFOUNDS

Forgiving one's partner for failing to pick up the dry cleaning is not the same as forgiving one's partner for infidelity or even a major betrayal of a personal confidence to a friend. All of these instances of forgiveness are likely to be important in the healthy functioning of a relationship, yet the forgiveness process is likely to be different for each one. A great deal more emotional work is required to respond to a major interpersonal betrayal, whereas a simple attributional shift (from "my partner doesn't care about my needs" to "my partner was busy and forgot about the errand but still cares") may be required to deal with the dry-cleaning incident. Thus, it may be that talking to premarital couples about how to deal with the daily hurts and irritations may be efficacious, but it is not effective to teach them in advance how to deal with major betrayals and hurts because the kind of major effort involved in helping partners overcome these severe difficulties does not lend itself well to brief preventive group interventions.

Moreover, when conducting forgiveness interventions in couples therapy, what is an optimal forgiveness outcome? As Ripley and Worthington (2002) note, measures that assess only "unforgivingness," such as revenge and anger, may not adequately capture the entire range of forgiveness. Is forgiveness simply the absence of negatives, or does it necessarily contain positive elements such as reconciliation, compassion, or wishing one's partner well? It is likely that the answers to such questions are complex and that the definition of optimal forgiveness might vary depending on the situation. Forgiveness may be more adequately conceptualized as multidimensional or as involving diverse types or modalities. For example, one type of forgiveness may be high on positive affect (reconciliation, compassion for partner, wishing him or her well) and low on negative affect (revenge, anger, rumination); by comparison, in other situations, such as when a partner is likely to reengage in the hurtful behavior, an optimal forgiveness outcome might be moderate positive affect (compassion for the partner and wishing him or her well but without reconciliation) and low negative affect (no wish for revenge or rumination and moderate anger). Finally, in the case of a continuing abusive situation, low positive affect (no compassion, little wishing him or her well, no reconciliation) but also low negative affect (no revenge or rumination, moderate anger) might be the most realistic goal. Indeed, recent research indicates that women residing in a domestic violence shelter who are highly forgiving of their partners are more likely to intend to return to them (Gordon, Burton, & Porter, 2004). Encouraging reconciliation or even compassion for the partner may not always be an appropriate intervention.

CONCLUSIONS

If allowed only one word to describe the state of research on forgiveness interventions in couples therapy, that word would be *beginning*. If allowed two words to describe this state of affairs, the words would be *reasonable beginning*. Finally, if allowed three words to capture our progress, they would be *reasonable beginning only*. Incorporating forgiveness in couples interventions and interventions after divorce shows a great deal of promise; however, as a field, we still have far to go before that potential is fully realized.

REFERENCES

Amato, P. R. (1996). Explaining the intergenerational transmission of divorce. *Journal of Marriage and the Family, 58,* 628–640.

Baucom, D. H., Hahlweg, K., & Kuschel, A. (2003). Are waiting list control groups needed in future marital therapy outcome research? *Behavior Therapy, 34,* 179–188.

Burchard, G. A., Yarhouse, M. A., Kilian, M. K., Worthington, E. L., Jr., Berry, J. W., & Canter, D. E. (2003). A study of two marital enrichment programs and couples' quality of life. *Journal of Psychology and Theology, 31,* 240–252.

DiBlasio, F. A. (1998). The use of a decision-based forgiveness intervention within intergenerational family therapy. *Journal of Family Therapy, 20,* 77–94.

DiBlasio, F. A. (2000). Decision-based forgiveness treatment in cases of marital infidelity. *Psychotherapy, 37,* 149–158.

DiBlasio, F. A. (2003). *Preliminary experimental findings of forgiveness therapy.* Paper presented at the conference on Scientific Findings About Forgiveness, Atlanta, GA.

DiBlasio, F. A., & Proctor, J. H. (1993). Therapists and the clinical use of forgiveness. *Journal of Family Therapy, 21,* 175–184.

Epstein, N., & Baucom, D. H. (2002). *Enhanced cognitive-behavioral therapy for couples: A contextual approach.* Washington, DC: American Psychological Association.

Gordon, K. C., & Baucom, D. H. (1998). Understanding betrayals in marriage: A synthesized model of forgiveness. *Family Process, 37,* 425–450.

Gordon, K. C., Baucom, D. H., & Snyder, D. K. (2004). An integrative intervention for promoting recovery from extramarital affairs. *Journal of Marital and Family Therapy, 30,* 213–231.

Gordon, K. C., Burton, S., & Porter, L. (2004). The role of forgiveness: Predicting women in domestic violence shelters intentions to return to their partners. *Journal of Family Psychology, 18,* 331–338.

Hargrave, T. D. (1994). *Families and forgiveness: Healing wounds in the intergenerational family.* Philadelphia: Brunner/Mazel.

Hargrave, T. D., & Sells, J. N., (1997). The development of a forgiveness scale. *Journal of Marital and Family Therapy, 23,* 41–62.

Horowitz, M. J. (1985). Disasters and psychological responses to stress. *Psychiatric Annals, 15,* 161–167.

Janoff-Bulman, R. (1989). Assumptive worlds and the stress of traumatic events: Applications of the schema construct. *Social Cognition, 7,* 113–136.

Ripley, J. S., & Worthington, E. L., Jr. (2002). Hope-focused and forgiveness-based group interventions to promote marital enrichment. *Journal of Counseling and Development, 80,* 452–472.

Rye, M. S., Pargament, K. I., Pan, W., Yingling, D. W., Shogren, K. A., & Ito, M. (2004). *Forgiveness and divorce: Can group interventions facilitate forgiveness of a former spouse?* Manuscript submitted for publication, University of Dayton, OH.

Sells, J. N., Giordano, F. G., & King, L., (2002). A pilot study in marital group therapy: Process and outcome. *The Family Journal: Counseling and Therapy for Couples and Families, 10,* 156–166.

Snyder, D. K. (1999). Affective reconstruction in the context of a pluralistic approach to couples therapy. *Clinical Psychology: Science and Practice, 6,* 348–365.

Snyder, D. K., Gordon, K. C., & Baucom, D. H. (2004). Treating affair couples: Extending the written disclosure paradigm to relationship trauma. *Clinical Psychology: Science and Practice, 11,* 155–160.

Worthington, E. L., Jr. (1998). An empathy-humility-commitment model of forgiveness applied within family dyads. *Journal of Family Therapy, 20,* 59–71.

Worthington, E. L., Jr., & Drinkard, D. T. (2000). Promoting reconciliation through psychoeducational and therapeutic interventions. *Journal of Marital and Family Therapy, 26,* 93–101.

Worthington, E. L., Jr., Berry, J. W., Canter, D. E., Sharp, C., Yarhouse, M., & Scherer, M. (2003, October). *Forgiveness and communication in marital enrichment with parents.* Paper presented at the conference on Scientific Findings About Forgiveness, Atlanta, GA.

Worthington, E. L., Jr., Hight, T. L., Ripley, J. S., Perrone, K. M., Kurusu, T. A., & Jones, D. R. (1997). Strategic hope-focused relationship-enrichment counseling with individual couples. *Journal of Counseling Psychology, 44,* 381–389.

Worthington, E. L., Jr., Kurusu, T. A., Collins, W., Berry, J. W., Ripley, J. S., & Baier, S. N. (2000). Forgiving usually takes time: A lesson learned by studying interventions to promote forgiveness. *Journal of Psychology and Theology, 28,* 3–20.

Chapter Twenty-Six

But Do They Work?
A Meta-Analysis of Group
Interventions to Promote
Forgiveness

Nathaniel G. Wade
Everett L. Worthington, Jr.
Julia E. Meyer

W hen people are seriously hurt by others, they often seek help from professional or friendship helpers to resolve the problems these hurts create. Several models of explicit forgiveness-promoting interventions from a variety of
perspectives have been explored experimentally (see Table 26.1). Are such interventions effective at promoting forgiveness? If so, what are the active ingredients of these
interventions?

PERSONAL ASSUMPTIONS ABOUT FORGIVENESS

First, forgiveness can be understood by what it is not. Many in this volume agree that
forgiveness is not condoning, forgetting, accepting, justifying, excusing, or overlook-
ing the event. Nor is it reconciling (Worthington & Drinkard, 2000). Furthermore,
forgiveness is not merely reducing *unforgiveness*. We have defined *unforgiveness* as a
combination of delayed emotions, including resentment, bitterness, hatred, hostility,
anger, and fear, that develops after ruminating about a transgression and can motivate desires for retaliation against or avoidance of the offender (Worthington & Wade,
1999). We have shown experimentally that people can lower unforgiveness without
reporting they have forgiven (Wade & Worthington, 2003). Instead, we define two
types of forgiveness (Exline, Worthington, Jr., Hill, & McCullough, 2003; Worthington, 2003). *Decisional forgiveness* is a behavioral intention statement to forswear one's
revenge and avoidance (unless it is unsafe to interact with the offender) and to release

the offender from the social debt incurred by the wrongdoing. *Emotional forgiveness* is the replacement of negative emotions with positive, other-oriented emotions. Thus, emotional forgiveness leads to a reduction in the uncomfortable or negative emotions and motivations associated with unforgiveness and might yield an increase in positive regard toward the offender (although that is usually limited to ongoing close relationships). This definition differs from the practice of some interventionists, who focus solely on reducing unforgiveness. Even when researchers endorse a definition of forgiveness involving both *a reduction in unforgiveness* and an increase in positive, other-oriented emotions, they often measure only reduced unforgiveness and assume that people forgave. Although this assumption is theoretically dubious, when an explicit effort has been made to promote forgiveness, the assumption is more tenable. As a result, because we are reviewing interventions, we consider reductions in unforgiveness and promotion of forgiveness synonymous for this review.

REVIEW AND META-ANALYSIS OF THE EMPIRICAL LITERATURE

The large majority of studies have investigated the efficacy of interventions provided in group formats. A few studies of forgiveness interventions with individuals exist. We limit our analysis to forgiveness interventions provided in group formats. We focus on the (a) efficacy of interventions to promote forgiveness, (b) shared techniques used by the interventions, and (c) efficacy as a function of the time spent on various shared techniques, or components.

Method

Procedure. Intervention studies seeking to promote forgiveness in a group setting were identified by searching PsycINFO (www.apa.org/psycinfo), using keywords such as *forgive* and *forgiveness interventions*. Interventions were also identified from psychology conferences and from Web pages of known forgiveness researchers. Interventions were included if they describe a group program to help people forgive and report analyses of outcome data intended to measure the degree of reduced unforgiveness or increased forgiveness the participants held for the offenders. We included journal articles, conference presentations, unpublished manuscripts, and doctoral dissertations. In several situations, a study investigated two or more types of groups to promote forgiveness. Each unique group was included separately. Two dissertations were omitted because they reported only subscales of the outcome variable (Enright Forgiveness Inventory [EFI]; Subkoviak et al., 1995), not the overall scores. Enright, Rique, and Coyle (2000) urged researchers not to use the subscales as stand-alone measures because the subscales alone can distort the assessment of forgiveness. As of July 2004, 39 forgiveness interventions, 10 alternate treatments, and 16 no-treatment control groups from 27 studies fit the criteria (see Table 26.1).

TABLE 26.1. Means and Standard Deviations With Effect Sizes and Time for Each Intervention Condition

Study	n Post	Forgiveness measure				Group Type I	Group Type II	Total time
		Mean (SD) pre	Mean (SD) post	ES I	ES II			
Al-Mabuk, Enright, & Cardis (1995) S1 treatment	24	—	90.7 (13.1)	—[a]	-.30	FT	P	240
Al-Mabuk, Enright, & Cardis (1995) S2 treatment	24	81.0 (18.1)	101.5 (14.4)	1.21	1.17	FT	F	480
Al-Mabuk, Enright, & Cardis (1995) S2 control	21	82.2 (11.8)	86.6 (9.8)	.39	—	AT	P	480
Freedman & Knupp (2003) treatment	5	121.6 (65.5)	221.6 (44.1)	1.79	.38	FT	F	480
Freedman & Knupp (2003) control	5	167.4 (36.5)	204.2 (47.7)	.87	—	NT	N	0
Hart & Shapiro (2002) secular intervention	31	3.32 (0.7)	2.76 (0.8)	.73	—	FT	F	1200
Hart & Shapiro (2002) spiritual intervention	30	3.75 (.7)	2.67 (.8)	1.4	—	FC	F	1200
Hebl & Enright (1993) treatment	13	—	113.85 (19.1)	—[a]	.70	FT	F	480
Humphrey (1999) treatment	9	166.3 (86.6)	213.7 (73.2)	.53	.40	FT	F	1155
Humphrey (1999) control	11	169.0 (87.0)	177.9 (93.0)	.09	—	NT	N	0
Jackson (1998) treatment	14	39.5 (12.8)	68.5 (18.4)	1.84	.91	FT	F	720
Jackson (1998) control	13	36.4 (13.2)	48.5 (25.2)	.60	—	NT	N	0
Lin (1998) treatment	15	224.8 (39.2)	254.2 (37.5)	1.03	.20	FT	F	1800
Lin (1998) perspective taking	12	237.5 (49.7)	243.5 (69.7)	.10	—	AT	P	780
Lin (2001) treatment	7	174.7 (58.7)	280.1 (33.8)	2.20	2.43	FT	F	720
Lin (2001) support	7	185.5 (18.2)	182.7 (45.6)	-.08	—	AT	F	720
Luskin & Thoresen (1998) treatment	23	24.29 (7.8)	19.65 (7.0)	.60	.12	FT	F	360
Luskin & Thoresen (1998) control	23	24 (7.4)	20.52 (7.8)	.44	—	NT	N	0
Luskin, Thoresen et al. (2001) treatment	101	47.2 (9.6)	57.9 (11.5)	1.00	.61	FT	F	540
Luskin, Thoresen et al. (2001) control	86	46.1 (11.4)	50.6 (12.3)	.38	—	NT	N	0
Luskin & Bland (2000) HOPE 1	5	36.8 (19.2)	52.8 (15.0)	.68	—	FT	F	900

TABLE 26.1. Means and Standard Deviations With Effect Sizes and Time for Each Intervention Condition (continued)

Study	n Post	Forgiveness measure		ES I	ES II	Group Type I	Group Type II	Total time
		Mean (SD) pre	Mean (SD) post					
Luskin & Bland (2001) HOPE 2	17	47.4 (10.9)	49.6 (12.5)	.18	—	FT	F	900
McCullough & Worthington (1995) interpersonal	30	23.1 (9.4)	22 (8.1)	.12	.12	FT	P	60
McCullough & Worthington (1995) self-enhancement	35	23.2 (7.7)	20 (7.1)	.42	.38	FC	P	60
McCullough & Worthington (1995) control	21	20.2 (9.8)	23 (8.7)	-.29	—	NT	N	0
McCullough, Worthington, & Rachal (1997) empathy	13	13.4 (4.7)	18.25 (5.5)	.88	.53	FT	F	480
McCullough, Worthington, & Rachal (1997) self-enhancement	17	13.8 (6.7)	12.3 (8.0)	-.19	-.45	FC	P	480
McCullough, Worthington, & Rachal (1997) control	40	15.3 (5.4)	15.2 (5.6)	-.02	—	NT	N	0
Osterndorf (2000) treatment	6	203.2 (36.1)	241.5 (30.4)	1.15	-.08	FT	F	1080
Osterndorf (2000) conflict resolution	6	208.7 (52.7)	246.7 (84.7)	.54	—	AT	F	1080
Park (2003) treatment	8	58.4 (15.0)	74.9 (18.2)	.99	1.10	FT	F	720
Park (2003) skillstream	8	68.8 (13.2)	57.7 (13.5)	-.83	.13	AT	F	720
Park (2003) control	8	68.3 (14.6)	55.8 (16.6)	-.64	—	NT	N	0
Ripley & Worthington (2002) FREE	28	14.5 (4.2)	12.9 (4.8)	.34	-.20	FT	F	360
Ripley & Worthington (2002) HOPE	30	17.5 (6.9)	14.7 (7.2)	.39	-.39	AT	F	360
Ripley & Worthington (2002) control	28	15.2 (8.1)	11.3 (9.8)	.42	—	NT	N	0
Rye & Pargament (2002) secular	20	47.4 (8.2)	62.0 (7.9)	1.74	1.18	FT	F	540
Rye & Pargament (2002) religious	19	50.2 (7.9)	64.8 (7.8)	1.78	1.47	FC	F	540
Rye & Pargament (2002) control	19	48.6 (11.6)	50.8 (10.6)	.19	—	NT	N	0
Rye et al. (2004) secular	49	41.5 (3.7)	47.4 (3.1)	1.69	1.09	FT	F	720
Rye et al. (2004) religious	50	41.6 (4.6)	47.1 (4.0)	1.26	.87	FC	F	720
Rye et al. (2004) control	50	44.9 (3.6)	43.9 (3.3)	-.27	—	NT	N	0

Sandage (1997) empathy	30	159.6 (60.1)	192.2 (65.1)	.51	.24	FT	F	360
Sandage (1997) self-enhancement	30	168.4 (68.4)	203.7 (74.9)	.48	.39	FC	P	360
Sandage (1997) control	36	187.6 (61.3)	177.1 (63.0)	-.17	—	NT	N	0
Van Loon (1997) treatment	17	268.3 (36.7)	291.3 (37.6)	.62	.81	FT	F	360
Van Loon (1997) human relations	15	229.2 (62.3)	243.9 (75.2)	.21	—	AT	P	360
Wade (2002) REACH	25	36.6 (9.6)	32.2 (10.0)	.43	-.22	FT	F	360
Wade (2002) REAXX	25	33.5 (12.2)	28.9 (10.4)	.59	.06	FT	P	360
Wade (2002) RXXCH	26	37.4 (12.4)	30.3 (11.0)	.39	-.06	FT	P	360
Wade (2002) RXXXX	24	33.0 (12.6)	30.2 (10.2)	.24	-.05	FT	P	360
Wade (2002) stress reduction	41	31.7 (13.8)	26.8 (13.4)	.37	.22	AT	P	360
Wade (2002) control	26	32.3 (13.4)	29.6 (13.4)	.20	—	NT	N	0
Waltman (2003) treatment	13	187.3 (60.2)	253.5 (70.7)	1.01	.94	FT	F	650
Waltman (2003) support	12	164.1 (55.4)	183.5 (79.0)	.28	—	AT	P	650
Worthington et al. (2000) S1, treatment	80	227.7 (19.5)	233.7 (22.0)	.29	-.12	FT	P	60
Worthington et al. (2000) S1, control	10	235.8 (16.9)	236.4 (14.9)	.03	—	NT	N	0
Worthington et al. (2000) S2, workshop + specific	23	28.8 (11.1)	28.4 (9.8)	.14	.13	FC	P	130
Worthington et al. (2000) S2, workshop + general	19	34.3 (12.3)	32.2 (11.3)	.17	-.22	FC	P	130
Worthington et al. (2000) S2, workshop	13	36.8 (13.2)	31.2 (10.9)	.43	-.14	FT	P	120
Worthington et al. (2000) S2, control	9	31.4 (11.3)	29.7 (10.1)	.14	—	NT	N	0
Worthington et al. (2000) S3, forgiveness	27	34.6 (10.4)	30.4 (10.2)	.40	-.20	FT	P	120
Worthington et al. (2000) S3, public commitment	29	28.8 (10.8)	28.4 (10.9)	.14	-.06	AT	P	120
Worthington et al. (2000) S3, both	23	30.2 (11.4)	28.3 (9.4)	.18	.00	FC	P	120
Worthington et al. (2000) S3, control	26	30.3 (9.6)	28.9 (9.5)	.04	—	NT	N	0

Note: ES I (effect size) was measured as a standardized mean gain (Lipsey & Wilson, 2001, p.44), using pre and post scores for each intervention group (including control groups). *ES* II (effect size) was measured with standardized mean difference scores (Lipsey & Wilson, 2001, p. 48), comparing treatments with their control groups at posttest. Group Type I was coded as FT = forgiveness treatment, FC = forgiveness-focused comparison, AT = alternate treatment, and NT = no treatment. Group Type II was coded such that F = full intervention (whether forgiveness or not), P = partial intervention, and N = no treatment. Total time is the duration of the intervention (in minutes). [a]No data were collected at pretest with which to compute *ES* as with others in this column.

Means, standard deviations, and sample sizes for each treatment group were collected from results sections or from the primary authors to calculate effect sizes. The method sections of these articles and the treatment manuals were used to determine what types of materials, exercises, and techniques were used to promote forgiveness. We adopted a theoretical frame to summarize the content of the interventions. The two obvious candidates were Enright's (2001) and Worthington's (2001) models because each was involved in multiple studies. However, neither model incorporated all the observed contents, so we added two categories (i.e., defining forgiveness and overcoming unforgiveness) to Worthington's (2001) five components. This resulted in a seven-component taxonomy plus a generic "other topics" category for analyzing the contents of the interventions (see Table 26.2). This taxonomy was used to categorize all the techniques that were reported in the interventions.

TABLE 26.2. Summary of Amount of Time Spent on Each Component and Correlations With Overall Effect Sizes for Forgiveness

	D	R	E	A	C	H	OU	Total
Mean time[a]	26.2	41.0	39.5	21.0	30.6	12.7	19.1	396.4
(SD)	(32.0)	(53.6)	(52.7)	(29.0)	(41.7)	(25.3)	(38.8)	(391.9)
r[b]	.56*	.60*	.64*	.52*	.62*	.44*	.53*	.52*
N	63	63	63	63	63	63	63	63
Mean time[c]	43.8	73.5	68.2	37.3	50.8	21.7	277	542.3
(SD)	(31.1)	(56.7)	(54.9)	(32.9)	(46.0)	(30.0)	(42.3)	(388.2)
r[b]	.37	.43	.51*	.32	.52*	.29	.44*	.43
n	37	37	37	37	37	37	37	37

Note: D = defining forgiveness, R = recalling the hurt, E = empathizing with the offender, A = acknowledging one's own offenses, C = committing to forgive, H = holding on to forgiveness, OU = overcoming unforgiveness.
[a]Includes all intervention groups, treatment and no-treatment control (analyzed using zero as the time spent). Time is provided in minutes.
[b]Correlation represents the relationship between the before and after effect size of a given study (see Table 26.2) and the amount of time that study spent on a given component.
[c]Includes only treatment and comparison groups that specifically attempted to promote forgiveness (FT and FC groups; see Table 26.1).
*$p < .006$, Bonferroni-corrected alpha level for each set of correlation analyses (.05/8).

Once components were identified, the amount of time spent on each was estimated from the available written material. In some cases, time estimates of individual components were not provided by the researchers. In these situations, we estimated the time spent on individual components by dividing the total time of the session by the number of components covered in that session. Because manuals and method sections were not always fully explicit, measurement error for the time dimension creates some uncertainty about our results. However, we believe that these estimates, if correctly understood, can provide a guideline for understanding the relationship between the time spent intervening with individual components and efficacy.

Measures.   There was variation of measures used across the different studies. The most popular measures of forgiveness were the EFI (Subkoviak et al., 1995) and the Transgression-Related Interpersonal Motivations Inventory (TRIM; McCullough et al., 1998). The EFI is a 60-item self-report questionnaire. Items are rated on 6-point Likert scales. Scores range from 60 to 360. Higher scores indicate more forgiveness. The TRIM is a 12-item self-report questionnaire. Items are rated on 5-point Likert scales. Scores range from 12 to 60. Higher scores indicate more *un*forgiving motivations (i.e., less forgiveness).

Another measure used was the Rye Forgiveness Scale (RFS; Rye et al., 2001). The RFS is a 15-item, 5-point, Likert-scale self-report questionnaire. Scores range from 15 to 75. Higher scores indicate more forgiveness. The Wade Forgiveness Scale (WFS; Wade, 1989) is an 83-item, 5-point, Likert-scale self-report measure. The WFS has nine subscales with total scores ranging from 83 to 415; higher scores indicate more forgiveness. The last measure of forgiveness was a proxy measure taken from the Estrangement subscale of the Interpersonal Distance Scale (IDS; Luskin & Thoresen, 1998). Although not originally intended to measure forgiveness, the IDS was hypothesized to measure forgiveness that would be associated with interpersonal outcomes such as reconnecting with offenders. Lower scores of estrangement indicate more forgiveness.

Results and Discussion

Analyses.   We used meta-analytic techniques to explore the efficacy of the identified interventions and to compare the interventions across the different measures of the outcome variable. Two forms of effect sizes were calculated for each intervention group (if the data were available), using methods outlined by Lipsey and Wilson (2001). The first effect size, which is reported in Table 26.1 but not discussed in the text, compared the differences in the means of the outcome measure at postintervention between the treatment group and its associated control group (a between-group effect size). This effect size represented the difference between the treatment and control groups following the intervention and was calculated by making an adjustment to Cohen's *d* that controls for the bias of sample size. We did not discuss these findings in the text for two reasons. First, the types of control groups differed across studies; some were comparison groups, and others were untreated test-retest controls. This makes the comparisons of effect sizes based on these differences problematic. Second, we wished to avoid the difficulties inherent in postmeasurement-only designs. Without a control for pretest scores, it is impossible to know whether the groups were truly comparable prior to the intervention. This is particularly problematic in designs using non- or partially random selection or assignment with smaller samples, which was often the case in the studies reviewed.

The second form of effect size (standardized mean gain score) compared the pre-intervention score with the postintervention score for each of the groups, treatment and control (a within-groups effect size). This measure of effect was corrected for the correlation between measurement times, which can unrealistically inflate the effect size. The correlation of the measurement times was calculated from raw data (where available) and estimated from published test-retest reliabilities of the outcome measures. The directions (positive or negative) of the effect sizes have all been modified so that positive effect sizes represent positive changes in forgiveness (increasing forgiveness or decreasing unforgiveness).

Enright's Group. Enright and the Human Development Study Group (1991) developed a 17-step model of forgiveness that has been the basis for interventions in 10 separate studies. However, two of these studies did not include measurement of the outcome variable prior to the intervention, due to concerns that a questionnaire about forgiveness might be confounded with the intervention (Al-Mabuk, Enright, & Cardis, 1995; Study 1; Hebl & Enright, 1993). The 17-step model has been used with elderly women (Hebl & Enright, 1993) and with college students who felt that their parents were emotionally neglectful (Al-Mabuk et al., 1995). In Study 1, Al-Mabuk et al. (1995) used only a portion of the full intervention model. They did not find significant differences between the treatment and control groups. However, the interventions that used the full 17-step model reported that the treatment group showed more forgiveness than the control group.

The 17-step model was eventually expanded to a 21-step model and has been applied in a wide variety of adult populations. Van Loon (1997) investigated the Enright et al. (1991) model with clergy struggling with interpersonal issues. Osterndorf (2000) used the model as the basis for an intervention with adult children of alcoholics. Lin (2001) studied the model's effectiveness with individuals in a drug rehabilitation center. Waltman (2003) explored the effects on male veterans with heart problems. These studies found that participants receiving the forgiveness interventions reported more forgiveness than support-based comparison groups. However, in a comparison of an adapted Enright model and a "spiritual" intervention based on the 12-step model of Alcoholics Anonymous for people in recovery from chemical dependency, Hart and Shapiro (2002) reported that the spiritually based intervention resulted in more forgiveness than the adapted Enright intervention. It is not surprising that these participants responded better to an intervention that was connected to something they knew well, a 12-step program.

Enright's forgiveness intervention model has also been used with adolescent populations, with varied degrees of success (Freedman & Knupp 2003; Lin 1998; Park 2003). In applications with older adolescents in Taiwan (Lin, 1998) and adolescent girls in Korea who were victims of aggression (Park, 2003), participants reported more forgiveness following the intervention than the comparison conditions. Freedman and Knupp (2003), however, did not find differences between treatment and control groups in a sample of Midwestern junior high students. These discrepancies could be due to the length of treatment (longer in the former studies) and limited sample sizes (smaller in the latter study). However, enough evidence has amassed to suggest that this model of intervening has considerable promise in multiple settings.

Worthington's Group.   A second set of interventions derives from a model developed by McCullough and Worthington (1995; McCullough, Worthington, & Rachal, 1997). The Pyramid Model to REACH Forgiveness delineates five steps toward forgiving a specific harm or offense (for a review of the contents of this model and the others described in this chapter, see Wade & Worthington, 2004). Eight studies have applied this model to help participants forgive a variety of interpersonal offenses. Similar to Al-Mabuk et al. (1995), Worthington's colleagues have investigated their model, attempting to determine which components are most effective.

Four studies have investigated the full REACH model (Jackson, 1998; McCullough et al., 1997; Ripley & Worthington, 2002; Wade, 2002). Each of these four treatments resulted in moderate to strong effects for helping participants overcome their unforgiveness across time and were more effective than no-treatment controls. Still, in several studies, the full model was compared to other conditions. It is unclear whether the full model is *more* effective than the comparison conditions. In McCullough et al. (1997), REACH was more effective than deciding to forgive. But in Ripley and Worthington (2002) and in Wade (2002), REACH did not differ from a communication-based intervention and combination of components, respectively.

Five studies representing nine treatment groups and five control conditions used an early version of the REACH model that focused on only three (REA) of the five steps (McCullough & Worthington, 1995; Sandage, 1997; Worthington et al., 2000). Four versions of the REA psychoeducational groups illustrated that small gains in forgiveness are possible in brief interventions of 1–2 hours. In tests of the full REACH model, effect sizes for pre- to postchange range from .35 to .95. This suggests that 6- to 8-hour psychoeducational interventions produce modest gains in forgiveness that may be more clinically significant than shorter interventions (or than partial treatments), which produce gains between .12 and .40. However, from this research it is still not clear whether the specific forgiveness interventions are more effective than comparison treatments.

Rye's Group.   Rye and Pargament (2002) examined the differences in efficacy of a secular versus a religiously integrated forgiveness intervention (using religious concepts and terminology to describe forgiveness). The two treatment groups promoted more forgiveness over time than did a wait-list control group. Rye and his colleagues (2004) extended their initial intervention from 9 hours to 12 hours and investigated its efficacy with divorced individuals. Participants in the treatment groups reported greater degrees of forgiveness for their ex-spouses than did participants in the control group. Rye's model shows great promise. The four intervention groups have effect sizes from before to after that range from 1.28 to 1.86. The distinctive elements of Rye's approach include (a) investigating religiously tailored groups, (b) focusing on failed relationships, and (c) working toward self-forgiveness. Rye's approach also incorporated relaxation and was longer on average than the other intervention programs.

Luskin's Group. Luskin and his colleagues have conducted four separate forgiveness intervention studies, although none of them are yet published. In two of the intervention studies, they compared forgiveness interventions that included instruction and practice in relaxation, meditation, and guided imagery, and drew heavily from cognitive behavioral and rational emotive therapy techniques with no-treatment control groups (Luskin & Thoresen, 1998; Luskin et al., 2001). In the first study, Luskin and Thoresen (1998) found no differences between the treatment and control conditions. However, in an investigation of a much larger sample, Luskin et al. (2001) demonstrated that their forgiveness intervention produced more forgiveness than did a no-treatment control group. Besides investigations, Luskin and Bland (2000, 2001) used a similar intervention for participants from Northern Ireland who had lost someone close to them due to murder. The intervention lasted for 15 hours over a 1-week period and took place in California. In the first study, participants reported increases in forgiveness from before to after. On average, participants in the second study did not become more forgiving.

Similar to Luskin's group, Humphrey (1999) incorporated the use of meditation and relaxation to help people deal with interpersonal injuries. Nine people participated in a forgiveness intervention implemented through audiotapes (approximately 18 hours within 8 weeks) that participants listened to at home. Although Humphrey's study did not use a pure group format, participants met together on three occasions for 1 hour each and completed the same intervention protocol. Compared with a wait-list group, participants in the forgiveness group were not significantly more forgiving over time, although the effect size was larger. This may have been a result of low statistical power due to the small sample size.

Meta-Analyses

Effect Sizes. Effect sizes for each intervention, calculated as described above, are listed in Table 26.1. First, we coded the interventions into separate groups for comparison. Interventions were coded as either forgiveness treatment (FT, if the intervention was based on a forgiveness model and explicitly attempted to promote forgiveness); forgiveness comparison treatment (FC, if it used an alternate method to promote forgiveness, such as Hart & Shapiro's [2002] 12-step groups); alternate comparison treatment (AT, if a treatment did not intend to specifically promote forgiveness, such as Ripley & Worthington's (2002) communication-based marriage enrichment group); and no-treatment groups (NT, if the participants were assessed but did not attend an intervention, including wait-list controls). We then calculated mean effect sizes weighted by the inverse of the variance, as described in Lipsey and Wilson (2001). Forgiveness-oriented treatments, both theoretically-grounded (FT, $ES = .57$, 95% confidence interval [CI] = .51 to .63) and those used for comparison purposes, (FC, $ES = .43$, CI = .33 to .53), had the highest effect sizes and were not significantly different. Alternate comparison treatments (AT) were significantly less effective than FT at producing forgiveness but not less effective than FC ($ES = .26$, CI = .16 to .36). Treatments of any kind (FT, FC, and AT) were more effective than no treatment ($ES = .10$, CI = .04 to .16).

Next, we compared full interventions (forgiveness or not) and groups that were partial treatments or used no treatments (see Table 26.1). Interventions were coded as partial if they were a comparison group in a component analyses study, were early (partial) versions of a forgiveness treatment, were alternate comparison groups intended as placebo groups (such as general discussion or support groups), or were one-component interventions. The mean weighted effect size for full interventions was .77 (CI = .70 to .84); for partial interventions, .28 (CI = .22 to .34); and for no treatment, .10 (CI = .04 to .16). All intervention types had a mean $ES > 0$. The full interventions had larger effect sizes than did the partial. Both had larger effect sizes than did no treatment.

In both of the above analyses, theoretically grounded, comparison, and full interventions were the most effective. It is important to note that these analyses did not control for the potential confound of time with the forgiveness or full interventions. (These interventions were often longer in duration than were the comparison groups.) Therefore, we conducted two hierarchical weighted (by the inverse variance) regression analyses on the effect sizes to determine whether there was a difference beyond the effects of time (a) between forgiveness, two types of comparison (FC and AT), and no treatment groups; and (b) between full, partial, and no interventions. Because we conducted two analyses, we set the alpha at .025 (.05/2). For each regression, total time spent on the intervention was entered in step 1, and the comparisons were entered in step 2. To determine overall model fit, we used the Q_R statistic, which is the regression sum-of-squares with degrees of freedom equaling the number of predictors and significance determined from the chi-square table (Lipsey & Wilson, 2001). To determine significance of the change in R^2 from step 1 to step 2, we tested the difference between Q_R at steps 1 and 2 (ΔQ_R), using the number of predictors at step 2 as the degrees of freedom. Following Lipsey and Wilson (2001), individual predictors were analyzed for significance by correcting the standard errors of the nonstandardized regression coefficients (B), using the mean square residual as a divisor. The corrected standard error was then used to divide B to create a z-test.

In the first regression, time was entered at step 1 and was a significant predictor of effect size, $R^2 = .33$, $Q_R (1) = 151.92$, $p < .001$. As expected, the z-test of the corresponding B was significant ($z = 17.54$, $p < .001$). In step 2, type of treatment was dummy coded, with FT used as the reference category. The overall model was significant at step 2, as was the change in R^2, $\Delta R^2 = .06$, $\Delta Q_R (4) = 29.38$, $p < .01$, indicating that the four group categories (FT, FC, placebo, and no treatment) predicted treatment effectiveness beyond time spent on the intervention. Analyses of the nonstandardized regression weights supported the results above: Explicit FT promoted more forgiveness than did AT (z = 3.57, $p < .01$) or NT (z = 4.48, $p < .01$); FT was no more effective than FC.

In the second regression, time was entered at step 1. At step 2, the intervention type (full, partial, or none) was dummy coded and entered with full interventions as the reference group. The addition of step 2 again was significant, $\Delta R^2 = .13$, $\Delta Q_R (3) = 57.037$, $p < .001$. Analyses of the regression coefficients indicated that partial interventions (z = −5.26, $p < .01$) and no-treatment groups (z = −5.74, $p < .01$) had significantly lower effect sizes than did full interventions, even after controlling for the effect of the duration of the intervention.

These regression analyses indicate that even when controlling for the amount of time spent on treatment, explicit forgiveness versus general treatments and full versus partial interventions are more helpful for promoting forgiveness. This might suggest that the contents plus the coherence—fully integrated versus components—make interventions more successful. One note of caution regarding the above regression equations must be cited. Statisticians have argued that in meta-analyses models should be specified (i.e., residual variance of the model should be no more than would be expected from sampling error), and conclusions on unspecified models should be tentative (Lipsey & Wilson, 2001). Each of the regression models above was unspecified, meaning there was more variance in the residuals than was expected by sampling error. Thus, the results should be taken with caution until substantiated by future research.

Correlations Between Effect Size and Time Spent. Time spent on the individual component techniques was calculated as described earlier. Many researchers used the same components to promote forgiveness. For example, most interventions defined forgiveness (87%), encouraged recalling the hurt (95%), and helped participants empathize with the offender (89%). Two of the components were used much less frequently—promoting maintenance of (or holding on to) forgiveness (53%) and overcoming unforgiveness (37%). To determine whether the time spent on particular components was related to forgiveness outcomes, bivariate correlations were computed between the amount of time an intervention spent on a given component and effect size (see Table 26.2). Time spent on each component was significantly correlated with effect size.

These results could possibly be an artifact of the inclusion of groups that did not use any of the components and so were coded with zero as the time spent. Such groups had smaller effect sizes, as seen in the previous analyses. Therefore, we computed the same correlations using only those groups that explicitly attempted to promote forgiveness (FT and FC from Table 26.1) to see whether particular components were more strongly related to forgiveness outcomes in explicit forgiveness intervention models. In these analyses, the pattern of results changed substantially. The only components significantly related to effect size were empathizing with the offender, committing to forgive, and overcoming unforgiveness by using strategies such as relaxation or anger management (see Table 26.2). Not even overall time was significantly related to outcome. However, excluding studies in this way reduced our power. Thus, although some relationships were not statistically significant, they may be clinically significant.

DIRECTIONS FOR FUTURE RESEARCH

Are Forgiveness Interventions Stronger Than Placebo or Alternate Treatments?   What seems clear from the research is that the simple passage of time, although mildly effective, is not as effective as an explicit intervention. In each analysis, forgiveness interventions and alternate treatments outperformed no-treatment controls. Although forgiveness interventions may be more powerful than the passage of time, are specific forgiveness-promoting interventions more effective than other, alternate treatments? What roles do common curative factors (e.g., empathic listening, social support, catharsis) play in promoting forgiveness? Is it important to intervene in specific "forgiveness-promoting" ways to help people overcome their hurts? This meta-analysis provides some support for the specific effectiveness of explicit forgiveness interventions for promoting forgiveness. However, many of the studies we reviewed did not use *strong* control groups. Rather, they provided alternate treatments that were more "attention control" than bona fide treatment. Those that did use strong controls did not find a difference (e.g., Hart & Shapiro, 2002; Ripley & Worthington, 2002; Wade, 2002, stress reduction). In addition, this meta-analysis explored only the effects on self-reported forgiveness and not psychological symptoms. It is important that future research compare forgiveness treatments with strong alternatives—not mere placebos—and examine the effects on psychological symptoms in addition to achievement of forgiveness.

Does Any Particular "Forgiveness-Promoting" Intervention Really Matter?   If using explicit forgiveness interventions is more effective than general treatments, the next logical question would be *which* explicit interventions are the most effective. A few studies reviewed in this chapter compared different methods of promoting forgiveness (e.g., Hart & Shapiro, 2002) and found no differences. Additionally, in the few component analyses that have been conducted, no specific method of intervening appears to be better than another. However, our analyses indicated that perhaps empathizing with offenders, committing to forgiveness, and overcoming feelings of unforgiveness are more effective components (with recalling the offense considered potentially important as well). These conflicting results could be clarified with further studies that examine the effective elements of explicit forgiveness interventions.

RELEVANCE FOR CLINICAL AND APPLIED INTERVENTIONS

Along with the amount of time spent intervening, specified programs or techniques of forgiving also have a valuable role. First, explicit forgiveness interventions appear to promote forgiveness more than general treatments. This implies that for therapists to help clients as fully as possible, it may be necessary to introduce forgiveness explicitly. However, clinical caution must be exercised. All the clients in these interventions gave their consent to receive forgiveness interventions *prior to the start of the intervention*. It is uncertain whether these findings will apply to clients already in psychotherapy, some of whom might not value forgiving. Some initial evidence suggests that explicit forgiveness interventions with actual clients may help promote forgiveness and reduce psychological symptoms (Wade, Bailey, & Shaffer, 2004). However, the nuances of how, when, and with whom to intervene to promote forgiveness are still uncertain.

Second, full interventions were more predictive of larger effects than were either partial or no treatments, even when controlling for time. This suggests that providing a coherent treatment, rather than a smattering of disjointed interventions, may lead to better outcomes.

Third, several of the components appeared to be related to larger effects. Clinicians might assist clients the most by promoting an active commitment to forgive. Commitment to forgiveness took on two primary functions in the interventions (see Wade & Worthington, 2004). They attempted to help clients commit to *trying* to forgive (commit to the process of forgiveness) and commit to the forgiveness that they achieved during the intervention. Helping clients to empathize with their offenders also appears to be an effective component, which is supported by previous research on empathy (McCullough et al., 1997). Again, however, caution and sound clinical judgment are needed to determine how and when one seeks to promote empathy for an offender such that the client is not victimized further by a perception of being judged or a misunderstanding that the client should reconcile with the offender.

CONCLUSION

The data appear to speak clearly: Forgiveness interventions are effective. However, beyond that conclusion, ambiguity and uncertainty exist. Data suggest that specific forgiveness interventions are helpful beyond time spent intervening and beyond common curative factors. However, it is unclear whether forgiveness interventions are helpful in real-life clinical settings, such as adjuncts to traditional therapy, or whether forgiveness interventions can lead to better mental and emotional health over time. The research is promising, but thus far clinical science has not established forgiveness interventions as clearly helpful beyond other modes of bona fide therapy. Other issues—such as cost-effectiveness, effects on relationships, effects on health, and match to type of clientele—still need to be addressed.

REFERENCES

*Al-Mabuk, R. H., Enright, R. D., & Cardis, P. A. (1995). Forgiveness education with love-deprived late adolescents. *Journal of Moral Education, 24,* 427–444.

Enright R. D. (2001). *Forgiveness is a choice: A step-by-step process for resolving anger and restoring hope.* Washington, DC: American Psychological Association.

Enright R. D., & the Human Development Study Group. (1991). The moral development of forgiveness. In W. Kurtines & J. Gerwirtz (Eds.), *Handbook of moral behavior and development* (Vol. I, pp. 123–152). Hillsdale, NJ: Lawrence Erlbaum.

Enright, R. D., Rique, J., & Coyle, C. T. (2000). *The Enright Forgiveness Inventory user's manual.* Madison, WI: International Forgiveness Institute.

Exline, J. J., Worthington, E. L., Jr., Hill, P. C., & McCullough, M. E. (2003). Forgiveness and justice: A research agenda for social and personality psychology. *Personality and Social Psychology Review 7,* 337–348.

*Freedman, S., & Knupp, A. (2003). The impact of forgiveness on adolescent adjustment to parental divorce. *Journal of Divorce and Remarriage, 39,* 135–165.

*Hart, K. E., & Shapiro, D. A. (2002, August). *Secular and spiritual forgiveness interventions for recovering alcoholics harboring grudges.* Paper presented at the annual convention of the American Psychological Association, Chicago, IL.

*Hebl, J. H., & Enright, R. D. (1993). Forgiveness as a psychotherapeutic goal with elderly females. *Psychotherapy, 30,* 658–667.

*Humphrey, C. W. (1999). *A stress management intervention with forgiveness as the goal.* Unpublished doctoral dissertation, Union Institute, Cincinnati, OH.

*Jackson, R. E. (1998). *Reducing shame through forgiveness and empathy: A group therapy approach to promoting prosocial behavior.* Unpublished doctoral dissertation, Fuller Theological Seminary, Pasadena, CA.

*Lin, W. (2001). *Forgiveness as an educational intervention goal within a drug rehabilitation center.* Unpublished doctoral dissertation, University of Wisconsin-Madison.

*Lin, W. N. (1998). *Forgiveness as an intervention for late adolescents with insecure attachment in Taiwan.* Unpublished doctoral dissertation, University of Wisconsin-Madison.

Lipsey, M. W., & Wilson, D. B. (2001). *Practical meta-analysis.* London: Thousand Oaks.

*Luskin, F., & Bland, B. (2000). *Stanford-Northern Ireland HOPE-1 project.* Unpublished manuscript, Stanford University, Palo Alto, CA.

*Luskin, F., & Bland, B. (2001). *Stanford-Northern Ireland HOPE-2 project.* Unpublished manuscript, Stanford University, Palo Alto, CA.

*Luskin, F., & Thoresen, C. (1998). *Effectiveness of forgiveness training on psychosocial factors in college-aged adults.* Unpublished manuscript, Stanford University, Palo Alto, CA.

*Luskin, F., Thoresen, C, Harris, A., Benisovich, S., Standard, S., Bruning, J., et al. (2001). *Effects of group forgiveness interventions on perceived stress, state and trait anger, symptoms of stress, self-reported health and forgiveness.* Unpublished manuscript, Stanford University, Palo Alto, CA.

McCullough, M. E., Rachal, K. C., Sandage, S. J., Worthington, E. L. Jr., Brown, S. W., & Hight, T. L. (1998). Interpersonal forgiveness in close relationships: Theoretical elaboration and measurement. *Journal of Personality and Social Psychology, 75,* 1586–1603.

*McCullough, M. E., & Worthington, E. L. Jr. (1995). Promoting forgiveness: A comparison of two brief psycho-educational interventions with a waiting list control. *Counseling and Values, 40,* 55–68.

*McCullough, M. E., Worthington, E. L., Jr., & Rachal, K. C. (1997). Interpersonal forgiving in close relationships. *Journal of Personality and Social Psychology, 73,* 321–336.

*Osterndorf, C. L. (2000). *Effects of a forgiveness education intervention with adult children of alcoholics.* Unpublished doctoral dissertation, University of Wisconsin-Madison.

*Park, J. (2003). *Validating the effectiveness of a forgiveness intervention program for adolescent female aggressive victims in Korea.* Unpublished doctoral dissertation, University of Wisconsin-Madison.

*Ripley, J. S., & Worthington, E. L., Jr., (2002). Comparison of hope-focused communication and empathy-based forgiveness group interventions to promote marital enrichment. *Journal of Counseling and Development, 80,* 452–463.

Rye, M. S., Loicono, D. M., Folck, C. D., Olszewski, B. T., Heim, T. A., & Madia, B. P. (2001). Evaluation of the psychometric properties of two forgiveness scales. *Current Psychology, 20,* 260–277.

*Rye, M. S., & Pargament, K. I. (2002). Forgiveness and romantic relationships in college: Can it heal the wounded heart? *Journal of Clinical Psychology, 54,* 419–441.

*Rye, M. S., Pargament, K. I., Pan, W., Yingling, D. W., Shogren, K. A., & Ito, M. (2004). *Forgiveness and divorce: Evaluation of an intervention to break the cycle of pain.* Manuscript submitted for publication, University of Dayton, OH.

*Sandage, S. J. (1997). *An ego-humility model of forgiveness.* Unpublished doctoral dissertation, Virginia Commonwealth University, Richmond.

Subkoviak, M. J., Enright, R. D., Wu, C. R., Gassin, E. A., Freedman, S., Olson, L. M., et al. (1995). Measuring interpersonal forgiveness in late adolescence and middle adulthood. *Journal of Adolescence, 18,* 641–655.

*Van Loon, P. C. (1997). *A cognitive development intervention for clergy: Forgiveness education.* Unpublished doctoral dissertation, Northern Illinois University, Dekalb.

*Wade, N. G. (2002). *Understanding REACH: A component analysis of a group intervention to promote forgiveness.* Unpublished doctoral dissertation, Virginia Commonwealth University, Richmond.

Wade, N. G., Bailey, D., & Shaffer, P. (2004, August). *Forgiveness in therapy: Prevalence and outcome data.* Paper presented at the annual convention for the American Psychological Association, Honolulu, HI.

Wade, N. G., & Worthington, E. L. Jr. (2003). Overcoming interpersonal offenses: Is forgiveness the only way to deal with unforgiveness? *Journal of Counseling and Development, 81,* 343–353.

Wade, N. G., & Worthington, E. L., Jr. (2004). *In search of a common core: A content analysis of interventions to promote forgiveness.* Manuscript submitted for publication, Iowa State University, Ames.

Wade, S. H. (1989). *The development of a scale to measure forgiveness.* Unpublished doctoral dissertation. Fuller Graduate School of Theology, Pasadena, CA.

*Waltman, M. A. (2003). *The psychological and physiological effects of forgiveness education in male patients with coronary artery disease.* Unpublished doctoral dissertation, University of Wisconsin-Madison.

Worthington, E. L., Jr. (2001). *Five steps to forgiveness: The art and science of forgiving.* New York: Crown Publishers.

Worthington, E. L., Jr. (2003). Hope-focused marriage. Recommendations for researchers and church workers. *Journal of Psychology and Theology, 31,* 231–239.

Worthington, E. L., Jr., & Drinkard, D. T. (2000). Promoting reconciliation through psychoeducational and therapeutic interventions. *Journal of Marital and Family Therapy, 26,* 93–101.

*Worthington, E. L., Jr., Kurusu, T. A., Collins, W., Berry, J. W., Ripley, J. S., & Baier, S. B. (2000). Forgiving usually takes time: A lesson learned by studying interventions to promote forgiveness. *Journal of Psychology and Theology, 28,* 3–20.

Worthington, E. L., Jr., & Wade, N.G. (1999). The social psychology of unforgiveness and forgiveness and implications for clinical practice. *Journal of Social and Clinical Psychology, 18,* 358–415.

*Indicates a study used in the meta-analyses.

Part Seven

SOCIETAL ISSUES
INVOLVING FORGIVENESS

Chapter Twenty-Seven

Constructive Rather Than Harmful Forgiveness, Reconciliation, and Ways to Promote Them After Genocide and Mass Killing

Ervin Staub

INTRODUCTION TO FORGIVENESS, RECONCILIATION, AND PERSONAL ASSUMPTIONS

There is little empirical research or theory on forgiveness after intense violence between groups or between individuals who have harmed each other acting as members of their groups (but see Byrne, 2003a, 2003b; Hewstone et al., in press; Quinn, 2003; Staub, 2004; Staub & Pearlman, 2001, 2004; Staub, Pearlman, Gubin, & Hagengimana, in press; Worthington, 2001). In considering forgiveness after genocide or mass killing, I will draw on our work in Rwanda. That work involved both formal research and observations in the course of a series of interventions between 1998 and 2004 that aimed to promote healing, reconciliation, and forgiveness in the aftermath of the 1994 genocide (Staub, 2000, 2004; Staub & Pearlman, 2001, 2004; Staub, Pearlman, & Miller, 2003; Staub et al., in press). In that genocide, the majority Hutus killed about 700,000 Tutsis and about 50,000 Hutus because they saw them as opposing the genocide, as political enemies, or for other reasons. The killings were done by part of the army, by paramilitary groups composed of young men, and by neighbors. In some mixed families, even relatives participated (Des Forges, 1999; Mamdani, 2002; Prunier, 1995). Obviously, forgiveness after such violence is intensely difficult. What kind of forgiveness is "constructive" versus potentially harmful after a genocide? What avenues or practices promote it?

Research findings show that after more severe experiences with violence, people are less ready to forgive (Subkoviak et. al., 1995). In Northern Ireland, people who themselves, their relatives, or the neighborhoods they lived in experienced more violence were less willing to forgive (Hewstone et al., in press). While it is the experience of violence that is likely to matter most, the actual amount of violence is incomparably greater in a genocide than it was in Northern Ireland, where about 3,000 people were killed in a 40-year period (Cairns & Derby, 1998). In genocides, usually hundreds of thousands if not millions of people are killed.

Definitions of Forgiveness and Its Relationship to Reconciliation

When groups continue to live together after intense violence between them, reconciliation is crucial for the prevention of new violence. Without it, violence is likely to resume (de la Rey, 2001; de Silva & Samarasinghe, 1993; Staub, 2004). One reason for the importance of forgiveness is to help improve the lives of victims; another is its supposed relationship to reconciliation (Arthur, 1999; Hayner, 1999; Lederach, 1998; Shriver, 1995; Staub, 2004; Staub & Bar-Tal, 2003; Staub & Pearlman, 2001).

A strong relationship between the two concepts/processes is suggested by their definitions. McCullough, Fincham, and Tsang (2003) see central elements of forgiveness as change from negative emotions and thoughts about the offender, such as anger, resentment, and the desire for revenge, to more positive, benevolent ones. This definition overlaps with the definition of reconciliation my associates and I have offered (see Staub, 2000, 2004; Staub & Bar-Tal, 2003; Staub & Pearlman, 2001, 2004). One version of this is the following:

> Reconciliation may be defined as mutual acceptance by groups of each other. The essence of reconciliation is a changed psychological orientation toward the other. Reconciliation means that victims and perpetrators, or members of hostile groups, do not see the past as defining the future . . . [that they] . . . come to see the humanity of one another, accept each other, and see the possibility of a constructive relationship (Staub & Pearlman, 2001; Staub & Bar-Tal, 2003). This definition is consistent with other definitions that focus on restoring a damaged relationship and on both the processes involved and the outcomes (de la Rey, 2001; Kriesberg, 1998a, b; Lederach, 1997). (Staub, 2004, p. 8)

A change from a negative to a more positive, benevolent orientation to the other seems a core component of all definitions of forgiveness (see also Worthington, 2001).

Although the literature clearly suggests that the other party has a role in forgiveness, for example, by apologizing or asking for forgiveness, still forgiveness can be one-sided—a change in the harmed party. In contrast, the essence of reconciliation is mutuality—a change in both parties. However, I see beneficial, constructive forgiveness, especially after genocide and when people who were harmed continue to live next to or have contact or a relationship with perpetrators, as requiring acknowledgment of harmdoing by perpetrators, empathy for the victims, and expressions of regret. Without this, forgiveness can be harmful rather than beneficial. Such feelings and actions require significant change in the perpetrators and, in the case of mass violence, in other members (supporters, passive bystanders) of the perpetrator group.

Forgiveness and reconciliation can both vary in degree. The two processes seem intertwined. Some degree of forgiveness, of letting go of fear and anger, may be required for reconciliation to begin. In continuing relationships, it is likely that reconciliation has to proceed before deep forgiveness can occur. Deep forgiveness is the end of a process and of a continuum ranging from anger, hostility, even hatred and the desire for revenge, to understanding the other's actions, acceptance of the other, and an ultimate form of acceptance. The influences I will describe as promoting constructive forgiveness also promote reconciliation. Given the overlapping definitions and my argument about the essential role of mutuality after genocide, it may be that reconciliation, which is inherently mutual, should be the primary process to focus on after genocide, with forgiveness as an aspect of it.

Some Views of Forgiveness in Rwanda: Religion, Authority, Culture, and Genocide

I conducted informal interviews in Rwanda, asking people what forgiveness is, whether it is possible after the genocide, and what may be required for it to occur.

What is the cultural/societal background to forgiveness in Rwanda? Rwandans are a religious people, mostly Christian and predominantly Catholic, a religion in which forgiveness is a deeply held value (Auerbach, 2004). Religiousness has been assumed to promote forgiveness. However, Hewstone et al. (in press), did not find this in Northern Ireland. There religion was the basis of conflict, and religious authorities often supported the violence. This is the case in many instances of group violence. According to Quinn (2003), not to forgive those who belong to other religions is explicit in the Koran because religions draw a line between those who follow the true faith and those who do not. Religiousness may not contribute to and may even inhibit forgiveness when perpetrators are members of another religious group.

In Rwanda, many people who work in the community to promote reconciliation, many of them Tutsis, have strong religious beliefs. In addition, the government actively promotes reconciliation. The government also promotes the notion that the division between Hutu and Tutsi was imposed on the people by Belgian colonialists, that no differences exist, and that all the people in the country are Rwandans. Talking about Hutus and Tutsis is discouraged. Implicit in this is the need to forgive.

At the same time and in contrast, there are trials of perpetrators of the genocide in the international court set up for Rwanda, in regular Rwandan courts, and in special courts—the *gacaca*, where perpetrators are tried by groups of elected judges in front of and with the participation of local communities (Honeyman et al., 2004; Staub, 2004). Moreover, taking revenge is deeply embedded in Rwandan culture. Revenge is a family duty. Proverbs advocate and express the obligation for revenge.

Adding to this complex picture in Rwanda, when a person is asked to forgive, he or she is supposed to forgive. We have seen and heard of instances in Rwanda when, presumably due to the cultural norm, perpetrators asked for but did not receive immediate expressions of forgiveness, they responded with anger (see Formative Research Report, 2004).

In response to the question, "What is forgiveness?" an army Colonel said (paraphrased from my informal interviews in Rwanda), "Forgiveness is necessary. We cannot live by revenge. We can't live in the past. We must look to a positive future. To bring about forgiveness requires that we discuss the issues between us." Two boys, 13 and 14 years old, whose Tutsi family, refugees from Rwanda, returned after the genocide, agreed that to forgive means to give people a second chance. They also said (paraphrased from my informal interviews in Rwanda), "You cannot forgive people who have killed. They would kill again. If the killers have been punished, you can forgive them but only if they have changed. And one can only judge that from their actions. Hutus who did not kill one can forgive. But maybe one does not even have to. They did not do anything."

The most complex information about forgiveness came from several writers of radio programs. One informant said, "Perpetrators have to ask forgiveness. They must say 'I recognize what I have done and I am sorry.' Then the victim is responsible to give forgiveness. Only those who have been saved by God can forgive without being asked." It is relatively rare that those who forgive will give up anger and feel benevolent toward the perpetrator. It seems that this writer sees forgiveness as usually more form than substance.

Another writer said that when people cannot do anything against the perpetrator, in order to forget what happened they say, "I forgive." Real forgiveness, the writer continued, comes after answering several questions. Did a person who killed have enough time to think before acting? Did the person really plan the actions? Was the person sent by others? How was this person affected by his or her actions? In apparent reference to the powerful role of authorities and obedience to them in Rwanda, this respondent said, "Finding that the person was sent by people he is not in agreement with would contribute to forgiveness." This respondent's son was killed by a neighbor. She told him, "I forgive you, because I realize you did not do it in your own behalf." (Interestingly, immediately after this, the neighbor moved away.) Forgiving gave her relief. This consideration of the context of perpetration as important in forgiveness is consistent with our findings about the importance of understanding the roots of violence, as discussed later in this chapter.

Constructive Versus Harmful Forgiveness: Mutuality and Evolution

Forgiveness as a unilateral rather than mutual process can have harmful effects (Perlman, 2002). Victimization creates wounds, as well as an imbalance in the relationship between victim and perpetrator (Berscheid, Boye, & Walster, 1968). It diminishes the status of the former in relation to the latter in the eyes of harmdoers and of people in general. After one-sided perpetration, as in a genocide—in contrast to mutual and relatively equal group violence, as in some intractable conflicts—when the two groups continue to live together, as in Rwanda, forgiveness without mutuality can be destructive. It supports impunity, offers acceptance without effort and change by perpetrators, and may make violence by them more likely. The more perpetrators acknowledge their actions and the harm they have created, assume responsibility, express regret and apologize, show empathy and concern for the pain and suffering of the victims, and offer money or compensatory action as reparation, the more they help survivors feel safe, affirm their worth, and balance the relationship. After genocide, it is probably necessary to punish the planners and the perpetrators of the most heinous acts as individuals, and for the group as a whole to be forgiven.

Regret and apology are important but may be transitory. For forgiveness to be "deserved," for it to affirm the survivors and create balance, and for it to be part of a genuine change in relations that make violence by former perpetrators less likely, compensatory actions are also important. Genocide usually evolves progressively. Important changes occur along the way in perpetrators as individuals and as a group. However, beneficial changes are also gradual. To an important extent, people learn by doing. People change as a result of their own actions and others' responses to them (Staub, 1989, 2003). Initial positive actions by former perpetrators can result in a positive cycle of interactions and lead to more genuine regret and deeper forgiveness.

Unilateral forgiveness enhances the imbalance. It accepts impunity. Descriptions of their acts by perpetrators without indications of regret appear to harm survivors (see also Byrne, 2003a, 2003b; and Gibson, 2002, on the role of perceptions of justice). Members of the perpetrator group who did not participate in perpetration may greatly contribute to forgiveness and reconciliation by acknowledging the harm done by their group and apologizing for its actions.

Genuine and Superficial Forgiveness

Some of my informants in Rwanda indicated that people may say they forgive because they believe they are expected to by religion, authorities, or cultural custom. Genuine rather than superficial forgiveness requires significant psychological change. Religion and authorities may but do not necessarily promote the processes that bring these about.

Limited procedures that guide people to make a decision to forgive do not work (see McCullough & Worthington, 1995). The more that procedures engage people in processes theoretically considered important, the more successful they have been (Enright & Coyle, 1998; McCullough, Worthington, & Rachal, 1997; see chapter 26 by Wade, Worthington, and Meyer). Apparently, people have to engage in an extended, deep process—even if harm is limited, as in much of the forgiveness research, and certainly when harm is as extreme as in a genocide. The influence of authority or the authority of religion is ongoing and continuous. However, if people simply obey authorities rather than engage with processes that create change, they may develop two separate systems—one a way of talking and expressing forgiveness when expected, the other a way of thinking and feeling. Genocide and mass killing create a permanent imprint, like a fault line or cleavage in the earth. This can probably heal over but is not erased. In the face of new conflict and threat driven by extreme ideas—destructive ideologies (Staub, 1989)—that activate memories of past experiences and deep feelings, the cleavage opens up. Neighbors come to kill neighbors again. Deep change in attitude toward the other person makes this less likely.

Who Is to Be Forgiven?

When members of one's family have been killed, the perpetrators are potential recipients of forgiveness. Other potential recipients include perpetrators as a group, passive bystanders, and the whole group of which the perpetrators are members. Although it was evident to us in Rwanda that Tutsis hold both individual perpetrators and the Hutus as a group responsible, most Tutsis find forgiving members of the group who were not actual perpetrators to be the easiest. Given that they are usually the great majority, this is essential for reconciliation.

Forgiving people who harmed oneself or one's family is partly an individual or family process. The other kinds of forgiveness can be either individual or group processes. But what does it mean to forgive as a group? Is it a matter of how many individuals in the group forgive? Is it a matter of forgiveness by leaders? Can leaders forgive in the name of the group? Leaders and group actions expressing forgiveness are likely to promote forgiveness by group members. But unless individuals experience genuine forgiveness with a change in leadership and circumstance, negative attitudes, anger, and persisting desire for revenge are likely to come to the fore.

Identification with a group (Hewstone et al., in press), increased by shared suffering, may interfere with forgiveness. One of my students, a mother of three young children, came to my office one day and broke down crying. In applying course material to her life in her papers, she began to understand her parents and to forgive them for the abuse she has suffered as a child. But she felt that she thereby betrayed her similarly abused, hurt, and angry siblings. Leaders forgiving in the name of a group may lessen such feelings of betrayal by individuals who forgive.

Benefits of Forgiveness After Mass Violence

Research indicates that forgiveness helps relieve the pain and distress of those who have been harmed, injured, or victimized by other individuals. The beneficial changes include enhanced self-respect; more positive mental states not dominated by negative thoughts and resentment; improved emotional states with less anger, anxiety, depression and guilt; and the ability to pursue constructive goals in place of revenge (see chapter 21 by Toussaint & Webb). These benefits are similar to what one would expect in people who are healing from emotional traumas (Herman, 1992; McCann & Pearlman, 1990; see chapter 22 by Noll). Healing from the trauma created by victimization is an important avenue to forgiveness. Forgiveness, in turn, may promote healing.

A significant potential benefit of forgiveness is its contribution to reconciliation. Forgiveness means acceptance, which can lessen the perpetrators' defensiveness. It can make it less likely that they engage in violence motivated by fear of revenge and more likely that they acknowledge the harm they have done. Small changes in survivors may initiate changes in perpetrators, leading to a positive cycle. Forgiveness can also make contact in working for shared goals possible. Anger, hostility, and unforgiveness (Worthington, 2001) interfere with the possibility of such contact. Forgiveness can also contribute to the creation of a shared history, which is essential to avoid future violence (discussed later in this chapter).

REVIEW OF THE THEORETICAL AND EMPIRICAL LITERATURE

Apology, Acknowledgment of Harm, Regret, Sorrow, and Empathy

As reviews of research on forgiveness by individuals indicate, apology or a show of remorse facilitates forgiveness (Weiner, Graham, Peter, & Zmuidinas, 1991). Is this also the case after intense violence between groups?

In one study (Byrne, 2003a), Black survivors in South Africa who testified before the Truth and Reconciliation Commission (TRC) were exposed to different "accounts" of their actions given by perpetrators. These survivors suffered brutal violence either to themselves or to close relatives—torture, murder, acts as extreme as children or adults burned to death. Survivors were exposed to justifications, excuses, or apologies, offered not by the perpetrators who harmed them but by other perpetrators testifying in front of the Commission. Their anger was reduced more by excuses (e.g., "I had to follow orders given") and apologies (e.g., "I am sorry") than by justifications (e.g., "We were at war"). Apologies had numerically slightly greater effects.

In all three conditions, more survivors said they would not forgive than said they would forgive. Among those who said they would forgive, excuses and apologies were more likely to lead to forgiveness, consistent with past research (Hewstone, et al., in press; Subkoviak, et al., 1995). People gave the severity of the acts and lack of remorse as reasons for not forgiving. In addition, the apology in the study consisted only of perpetrators saying they were sorry and was not directed at participants. Apology may be regarded as a summary term for acknowledgment of harm done, assumption of responsibility for it, expression of seemingly genuine regret, sorrow for the harm one has caused, and empathy for the victims—each important in its own right.

These emotions and actions are, however, extremely rarely shown by perpetrators of group violence. Perpetrators defend themselves from shame, guilt (Staub, 2004), and the feeling that their actions placed them outside the moral order (Nadler, 2003).

They surround themselves with a psychological shield, maintaining that their actions were justified by the need to defend themselves against their victims or by "higher ideals" of ideologies that perpetrators usually adopt (Staub, 1989, 2004; Staub & Pearlman, 2001; Staub et al., 2003). In the healing and reconciliation section that I moderated at a *New York Times* Internet conference in 1995, members of each ethnic group in the former Yugoslavia blamed the other groups for the conflict. Hewstone et al. (in press) found that members of both Protestant and Catholic paramilitary groups in Northern Ireland saw their actions as justified at the time and were less likely than other members of their group to ask for or give forgiveness.

Very few perpetrators in front of the TRC did more than describe their actions, which was a requirement to be considered for amnesty. But confessing to extremely violent deeds without apparent regret causes renewed pain for survivors (Byrne, 2003a, 2003b). In Rwanda as well, when some perpetrators who were brought back to their communities described their actions and even asked for forgiveness without apparent regret or empathy, this created distress in survivors.

Asking for forgiveness is a type of apology, although indirect. However, such requests can be difficult to refuse, especially in cultures like Rwanda's, where people are expected to respond to them positively. When people say they forgive without actually forgiving, rather than benefiting them, this may create added stress and psychological damage.

Healing As an Avenue to Forgiveness

Survivors of mass violence are deeply wounded. They experience great loss, grief, and pain. They feel diminished and see the world as dangerous, a combination that makes them feel vulnerable. Their suffering also creates anger and hostility toward the perpetrators and toward a hostile world. New conflict or threat may give rise to an intense need for self-defense. This can lead to violence to protect the group and its members, even when this is unnecessary (Staub, 1998, 1999, 2004; Staub & Pearlman, 2001, 2004).

Healing may reduce pain and vulnerability, enable survivors to lead better lives, and reduce the likelihood of violence by them. Especially in combination with other influences, healing can make survivors more open to and empathic with perpetrators. One avenue to healing is engagement with painful experience. Following group trauma, this is especially useful when it happens in groups. The presence of people with the same experience can provide support. The presence of empathic others can provide acknowledgment of suffering and the opportunity to reconnect with people (Herman, 1992; Staub & Pearlman, 2004; Staub et al., 2003). Acknowledgment of the group's suffering by perpetrators as well as any parties outside the victim group is another avenue to healing.

Testimonials, ceremonies, and memorialization can help larger numbers of people engage with their victimization. The nature of such group ceremonies matters, however. They can focus on the cruelty and violence in the world and on the harm done to the group, making the wounds persist, or they can help people grieve but also point to the possibilities of a better future. As an increasing amount of literature indicates, perpetrators of extreme violence are also wounded (Laufer, Brett, & Gallops, 1985; McNair, 2002; Parson, 1984; Rhodes, 1999; Rhodes, Allen, Nowicki, & Cillesen, 2002). To do their terrible acts, they must distance themselves from victims, devalue them, justify their suffering, and exclude them from the moral universe (Fein, 1979; Staub, 1989, 2004). In the end, devaluation and a destructive ideology combine to create a reversal of morality in which killing the victims becomes the moral thing to do. All of this is wounding, especially killing large numbers of people in cruel and inhumane ways. When the genocide is stopped, perpetrators face loss of power and status, shame, and potential guilt, all of which activate powerful psychological defenses.

Healing may enable perpetrators to feel empathy with themselves and in turn with people they have harmed, to acknowledge their actions, and to apologize. Empathy for the perpetrators and passive bystanders (Gobodo-Madikezela, 2003), although it can be difficult to offer, may be important for healing by them. Understanding the influences that led to their actions may promote healing and empathy while also helping perpetrators avoid using these influences as justification or exposing themselves to the stories of survivors, both part of our procedure in Rwanda in the study described in the next section (Staub et al., in press).

Acknowledging people in the perpetrator group who were not passive bystanders—who either opposed the genocide or rescued or attempted to rescue victims—may be important to help members of the group feel reincluded in the moral community. A combination of our advocacy of this in seminars with national leaders in Rwanda (see Staub & Pearlman, 2002) and other influences, such as a book on rescuers (Africa Rights, 2002), might have led to rescuers being acknowledged in the 2003 commemoration of the genocide.

Promoting Healing, Reconciliation, and Forgiveness in Rwanda

In an intervention, we trained 35 people, Tutsis (about two-thirds of the group) and Hutus who worked for local organizations involved with groups in the community (Staub et al., in press). The participants then used our approach, integrated with their prior approach, with groups in the community. This integration was an aspect of the training.

There were brief lectures and extensive discussions. We explored the impact of traumatizing events, such as genocide. The purpose of this was to help people understand changes in themselves and others around them, and to help them see these changes as a natural, normal consequence of extreme and abnormal events. We examined avenues to healing. A third topic was understanding the origins of genocide, with the group applying this understanding to Rwanda.

A fourth topic was basic human needs. I see the frustration of these needs giving rise to the psychological and societal processes leading to genocide (Staub, 1989). Victimization and violence, in turn, profoundly frustrate these needs (McCann & Pearlman, 1990; Staub, 2003; Staub & Pearlman, 2001). The needs for security, a positive identity, positive connection to other people, a feeling of effectiveness and control, and an understanding of the world and of one's place in it (Staub, 1989, 1996, 2003) require some degree of fulfillment for healing to occur.

Participants also shared their experiences during the genocide. People were asked to think about and then talk about them in small groups. There was a great deal of open and highly emotional sharing of painful experiences (Staub et al., 2003; Staub et al., in press). Although it was Tutsis, the survivors of the genocide, who talked about their experiences, they did this in a mixed group, with Hutus present as empathic witnesses. This was likely to contribute to another important element of healing—reconnecting with other people. Reconnecting with members of the other group may contribute to healing by members of both groups.

The effects of the training were evaluated, not on the people who participated in the training but on people in community groups with which they subsequently worked (Staub et al., in press). New groups were created, led by some of the people we trained. They integrated their traditional approach with the content of the training they received (*integrated* groups). Other newly created groups were led by facilitators who did not receive the training (*traditional* groups). These groups met for 4 weeks, twice a week for 2 hours. In *control* groups, community members did not receive treatment but were evaluated using questionnaires, the same way and about the same time as participants in the treatment groups: before the treatment, immediately afterward, and 2 months later.

The participants in the integrated group showed a reduction in trauma symptoms from before the treatment to 2 months afterward, both over time and in relation to the two other groups, which showed some deterioration. They also showed a more positive orientation toward members of the other group, both over time and in relation to the traditional and control groups, which did not change on this dimension. This positive orientation consisted of an awareness of the complexity of the roots of violence; a willingness to work together for a better future; some positive views of Hutus (that some endangered their lives to help); and "conditional forgiveness," which is greater openness to forgiving members of the other group under certain conditions ("I can forgive those who acknowledge the harm they have done . . . who requested forgiveness of my group . . . who make amends for what their group did").

We used elements of this approach in our work in Rwanda with community and national leaders, journalists, and the staff of Non-Governmental Organizations. We also trained trainers in this approach. Starting in May 2004, a twice-weekly radio drama series that incorporates the elements of this approach began to broadcast in Rwanda. There will also be a second informational radio program. In most of this work, we provided information about the traumatic impact of victimization, about avenues to healing, and about the origins of genocide and violence by groups against other groups.

Understanding the Origins of Violence As an Avenue to Forgiveness

Understanding is a way-station to forgiveness. Inherent in understanding is taking the other's role (Staub, 1979). One of the resilient survivors of childhood abuse in O'Connell Higgins's book (1994), as he comes to understand the reasons for his father's great rage and violent behavior, says that he accepts his father but cannot forgive him. Most likely, his acceptance represents a limited degree of forgiveness.

We could not independently evaluate in our study the impact of understanding the origin of genocide. But in the course of the training and in work with other groups in Rwanda, such information seemed to have powerful effects. In discussions after presenting how genocide originates and giving examples from other societies, survivors seemed to feel humanized. They no longer felt they were the objects of incomprehensibly evil acts or uniquely selected by God for such suffering. Understanding seemed to help survivors heal, fulfill their need for a comprehension of reality, and develop a meaningful story about their painful experiences (Staub, 2004; Staub et al., in press), which is important in healing (Herman, 1992; McCann, & Pearlman, 1990; Pearlman & Saakvitne, 1995).

Understanding the origins of violence also offers hope. It points to avenues to prevention. In describing social conditions (e.g., economic problems, political disorganization, group conflict), their psychological effects (e.g., the frustration of fundamental psychological needs), and the resulting destructive social processes (e.g., scapegoating, the creation of destructive ideologies, the evolution of violence), such understanding also suggests alternative ways to respond to such conditions. By indicating what characteristics of culture make mass violence more likely, such as devaluation of some group, overly strong respect for authority, and past victimization and woundedness, it points to societal changes that people can strive to attain (Staub, 1989, 2004). Understanding how their actions came about also humanizes perpetrators and passive bystanders. It creates some openness to them and increases the potential for forgiveness. We found that discussing the origins of genocide had powerful appeal to every group we worked with in Rwanda.

Although the extent to which we focused on understanding the roots of violence is probably unique, one element of change procedures that has been found effective in promoting forgiveness (see Enright & Coyle, 1998; McCullough et al., 1997) is a focus on the offender's psychological state and general situation in life on their effect on the context in which the offender acted. Successful procedures also helped victims explore the impact of the harm done to them, similar to the information we provide about the traumatic impact of victimization. Thus, our procedures are consistent with past research but focus more on healing and understanding.

Truth, Justice, Creation of a Shared History, and Contact As Avenues to Forgiveness

All of these topics are important for reconciliation (*Proceedings*, 2002; Staub, 2004), and all have a role in forgiveness. Survivors of mass violence desperately want justice. Justice affirms their innocence. It affirms the moral order, thereby increasing feelings of safety. It negates impunity and creates some balance in the relationship between victims and perpetrators. Forms of justice can include retributive, restorative or compensatory, and procedural justice. But to promote forgiveness, victims must *experience* justice. Truth is a prerequisite for justice. It is important, however, to establish the truth in all its complexity. Even in a genocide, the perpetrators may have suffered at an earlier time at the hands of their current victims. For example, in Rwanda, Tutsis ruled over and oppressed Hutus before 1959 under Belgian colonial rule, and Hutu civilians were killed in the course of fighting before, during, and after the genocide (des Forges, 1999; Mamdani, 2002). Acknowledgment of the prior suffering of perpetrators should make it easier for members of a perpetrator group to acknowledge and take responsibility for their actions during the genocide. However, because survivors' suffering is usually so much greater and because it is difficult for groups to acknowledge harm they have done, survivor groups find it extremely difficult to acknowledge their own harmful actions.

The creation of a shared history is essential to avoid renewed violence between groups. Usually, groups hold conflicting views of what happened between them and, even more important, of the causes of events. Each tends to blame the other, unable to consider the experience of the other. Some level of forgiveness may be required for working on the creation of a shared history. As such a history emerges, it contributes in turn to further forgiveness.

We have experimented in Rwanda with using information about the origins of violence as a tool in building a shared history. We discussed the Hutu revolt in 1959 against severe Tutsi oppression, which some in Rwanda called genocide, as an example of a response to severe and persistent injustice. We suggested that Hutus were psychologically wounded by their oppression. However, the persecution of the Tutsis by Hutus after 1959, rather than helping Hutus heal, further wounded them, increased fear of revenge, and made the subsequent genocide more likely. We also applied understanding of genocide at the societal level to describing the evolution of a particular perpetrator, a member of the militias composed of young men (Staub, 2004).

Both theory and research show that significant contact (Pettigrew & Tropp, 2000), working together for shared goals, whether children in a classroom (Aronson, Stephan, Sikes, Blaney, & Snapp, 1978) or adults in a community (Wessells & Montiero, 2001), can help overcome devaluation, prejudice, and hostility. Although some degree of prior forgiveness may be required for such contact, in turn it can promote further, deeper forgiveness.

RELEVANCE FOR CLINICAL AND APPLIED INTERVENTIONS

Elements of our approach can be used in applied clinical interventions. They include (a) basic psychological needs and their role in violence and trauma (Pearlman & Saakvitne, 1995; Staub, 1989, 2003); (b) the traumatic impact of violence (as well as of acting violently) in terms of symptoms, psychological changes in the self in attitudes toward people and the world; (c) avenues to healing—given the huge number of people affected in a genocide, we emphasized person-to-person healing, how people in the community can help each other, especially by empathic listening and support; (d) understanding the origins of violence between groups and the implications of this for preventing violence and for reconciliation; and (e) people sharing their experiences during the genocide, which we did only in long seminars and workshops because it requires prior building of trust and enough time for debriefing.

NEW RESEARCH DIRECTIONS NEEDED IN THE AREA

Forgiveness after genocide is an unexplored domain. A major proposition in this chapter requiring study is that when there is ongoing relationship, forgiveness without mutuality can make future violence more likely and worsen rather than improve the psychological well-being of the victim. Continued power imbalance can add to the problem.

Research is needed on what leads perpetrators to heal, on the extent to which healing by them leads to acknowledgment and regret, and on the extent to which this facilitates forgiveness by survivors after genocide and other intense group violence. More generally, further research is needed on all of the influences I identified as contributing to forgiveness: how can we help large numbers of people—whole groups—heal after mass violence; whether such healing contributes to forgiveness; the contribution of understanding the origins of violence to helping survivors (and perpetrators) heal, forgive, and reconcile; and the contributions of contact and the creation of shared history to forgiveness and reconciliation. The proposition that some avenues to forgiveness require some prior forgiveness and can in turn promote higher levels of forgiveness also needs to be empirically explored.

PERSONAL THEORETICAL PERSPECTIVES ON THE FIELD

I see reconciliation, which is inherently mutual, as essential for preventing new violence and promoting a peaceful future after genocide and mass killing. The beginning of healing by survivors may lead to less fear and anger by them. Public manifestation of this can lead to responses by perpetrators and a cycle or evolution of increasing forgiveness and reconciliation.

Forgiveness and reconciliation are the "tasks" of the people who have been involved in conflict and violence. But third parties can have an important role. They can be active bystanders who offer their services to the extent the parties involved are open to them and who provide information and initiate and facilitate interaction, acting with sensitivity and respect.

CONCLUSION

Reconciliation after mass violence is a difficult task that is essential to prevent new violence and create a peaceful future. Forgiveness is an important component of reconciliation. Without mutuality, forgiveness can be harmful. Understanding the origins of violence and healing by both parties is an essential tool or aspect of forgiveness and reconciliation.

REFERENCES

Africa Rights (2002). *Tribute to courage*. Kigali, Rwanda and London: Author.

Aronson, E., Stephan, C., Sikes, J., Blaney, N., & Snapp, M. (1978). *The jigsaw classroom*. Beverly Hills, CA: Sage.

Arthur, P. (1999). The Anglo-Irish peace process: Obstacles to reconciliation. In R. L. Rothstein (Ed.), *After the peace: Resistance and reconciliation* (pp. 85–109). Boulder, CO: Lynne Rienner.

Auerbach, Y. (2004, July). *Forgiveness and reconciliation: The religious dimension*. Presented at the meeting of International Society for Political Psychology, Lund, Sweden.

Berscheid, E., Boye, D., & Walster, E. (1968). Retaliation as a means of restoring equity. *Journal of Personality and Social Psychology, 10*, 370–376.

Byrne, C. (2003a). Responses of victims to perpetrators' justifications, excuses, and apologies: Accounts in the context of the South African Truth and Reconciliation Commission. *Dissertation Abstracts International*, DAI-B 63/10, 4963, April, 2003.

Byrne, C. (2003b). *Benefit or burden: Victims' reflections on TRC participation*. Manuscript submitted for publication. Solomon Asch Center for Study of Ethnopolitical Conflict. University of Pennsylvania, Philadelphia.

Cairns, E., & Darby, J. (1998). The conflict in Northern Ireland. *American Psychologist, 53*, 754–776.

de la Rey, C. (2001). Reconciliation in divided societies. In D. J. Christie, R. V. Wagner, & D. D. Winter (Eds.), *Peace, conflict, and violence* (pp. 251–262). Upper Saddle River, NJ: Prentice Hall.

Des Forges, A. (1999). *Leave none to tell the story: Genocide in Rwanda*. New York: Human Rights Watch.

de Silva, K. M., & Samarasinghe, S. W. R. de A. (Eds.). (1993). *Peace accords and ethnic conflicts*. London: Pointer.

Enright, R., & Coyle, C., (1998). Researching the process model of forgiveness within psychological interventions. In E. L. Worthington, Jr. (Ed.), *Dimensions of forgiveness: Psychological science and theological perspectives* (pp. 139–162). Philadelphia: Templeton Foundation Press.

Fein, H. (1979). *Accounting for genocide: Victims and survivors of the holocaust.* New York: Free Press.

Formative Research Report (2004). Labenevolencija Radio Project. Rwanda.

Gibson, J. L. (2002). Truth, justice, and reconciliation: Judging the fairness of amnesty in South Africa. *American Journal of Political Science, 46,* 540–556.

Gobodo-Madikezela, P. (2003). *A human being died that night: A South African story of forgiveness.* Boston: Houghton-Mifflin.

Hayner, P. B. (1999). In pursuit of justice and reconciliation: Contributions of truth telling. In C. J. Arnson (Ed.), *Comparative peace processes in Latin America* (pp. 363–383). Stanford, CA: Stanford University Press.

Herman, J. (1992). *Trauma and recovery.* New York: Basic Books.

Hewstone, M., Cairns, E., Voci, A., McLernon, F., Niens, U., & Noor, M. (in press). Intergroup forgiveness and guilt in Northern Ireland: Social psychological dimensions of "The Troubles." In N. Branscombe & B. Doosje (Eds), *Collective guilt: International perspectives.* New York: Cambridge University Press.

Honeyman, C., Hudami, S., Tiruneh, A., Hierta, J., Chirayath., L., Iliff, A., et al. (2004). Establishing collective norms: Potentials for participatory justice in Rwanda. *Peace and Conflict: Journal of Peace Psychology, 10,* 1–24.

Kriesberg, L. (1998a). Intractable conflicts. In E. Weiner (Ed.), *The handbook of interethnic coexistence* (pp. 332–342). New York: Continuum.

Kriesberg, L. (1998b). Coexistence and the reconciliation of communal conflicts. In E. Weiner (Ed.), *The handbook of interethnic coexistence* (pp.182–198). New York: Continuum.

Laufer, R. S., Brett, E., & Gallops, M. S. (1985). Symptom patterns associated with posttraumatic stress disorder among Vietnam veterans exposed to war trauma. *American Journal of Psychiatry, 142,* 1304–1311.

Lederach, J. P. (1997). *Building peace: Sustainable reconciliation in divided societies.* Washington, DC: United States Institute of Peace Press.

Lederach, J. P. (1998). Beyond violence: Building sustainable peace. In E. Weiner (Ed.), *The handbook of interethnic coexistence* (pp. 236–245). New York: Continuum.

Mamdani, M. (2002). *When victims become killers.* Princeton: Princeton University Press.

McCann, I. L., & Pearlman, L. A. (1990). *Psychological trauma and the adult survivor: Theory, therapy, and transformation.* New York: Brunner/Mazel.

McCullough, M. E., & Worthington, E. L., Jr. (1995). Promoting forgiveness: A comparison of two brief psychoeducational group interventions with a waiting-list control. *Counseling and Values, 40,* 55–69.

McCullough, M. E., Fincham, F. D., & Tsang, J., (2003). Forgiveness, forbearance, and time: The temporal unfolding of transgression-related interpersonal motivations. *Journal of Personality and Social Psychology, 84,* 540–557.

McCullough, M. E., Worthington, E. L., Jr., & Rachal, K. C. (1997) Interpersonal forgiving in close relationships. *Journal of Personality and Social Psychology, 73,* 321–336.

McNair, R. M., (2002). *Perpetration-induced traumatic stress.* London: Praeger.

Nadler, A. (2003, October). *Opening comments on the social psychology of reconciliation.* Presentation at the conference on Social Psychology of Reconciliation: Moving from Violent Confrontation to Peaceful Coexistence, University of Connecticut, Storrs.

O'Connell Higgins, G. (1994). *Resilient adults overcoming a cruel past.* San Francisco: Jossey-Bass.

Parson, E. O. (1984). The reparation of the self: Clinical and theoretical dimensions in the treatment of Vietnam combat veterans. *Journal of Contemporary Psychotherapy, 4,* 4–56.

Pearlman, L. A., & Saakvitne, K. W. (1995). *Trauma and the therapist: Countertransference and vicarious traumatization in psychotherapy with incest survivors.* New York: W. W. Norton.

Perlman, D. (2002). *Reparalogy: Toward a scientific evolutionary model of healing after protracted collective trauma.* Unpublished manuscript.

Pettigrew, T. F., & Tropp, L. R. (2000). Does intergroup contact reduce prejudice? Recent meta-analytic findings. In S. Oskamp (Eds.), *Reducing prejudice and discrimination* (pp. 93–114). London: Lawrence Erlbaum.

Proceedings of the Stockholm International Forum on Truth, Justice, and Reconciliation. (2002, April). Stockholm: Sweden.

Prunier, G. (1995). *The Rwanda crisis: History of a genocide.* New York: Columbia University Press.

Quinn, J. (2003). *The politics of acknowledgement: Truth commissions in Uganda and Haiti.* Unpublished dissertation, McMaster University, Hamilton, Ontario,.

Rhodes, R (1999). *Why they kill.* New York: Knopf.

Rhodes, G., Allen, G. J., Nowincki, J., & Cillesen, A. (2002). The violent socialization scale: Development and initial validation. In J. Ulmer & L. Athens (Eds.), *Violent acts and violentization: Assessing, applying, and developing Lonnie Athens' theories* (Vol. 4, pp. 125–144). New York: Elsevier Science.

Shriver, D. W., Jr., (1995). *An ethic for enemies: Forgiveness in politics.* New York: Oxford University Press.

Staub, E. (1979). *Positive social behavior and morality: Socialization and development* (Vol. 2). New York: Academic Press.

Staub, E. (1989). *The roots of evil: The origins of genocide and other group violence.* New York: Cambridge University Press.

Staub, E. (1996). Cultural-societal roots of violence: The examples of genocidal violence and of contemporary youth violence in the United States. *American Psychologist, 51,* 17–132.

Staub, E. (1998). Breaking the cycle of genocidal violence: Healing and reconciliation. In Harvey, J. (Ed.), *Perspectives on loss: A sourcebook* (pp. 231–241). Washington DC: Taylor and Francis.

Staub, E. (1999). The roots of evil: Personality, social conditions, culture and basic human needs. *Personality and Social Psychology Review, 3,* 179–192.

Staub, E. (2000). Genocide and mass killing: Origins, prevention, healing, and reconciliation. *Political Psychology, 21,* 367–382.

Staub, E. (2003). *The psychology of good and evil: Why children, adults, and groups help and harm others.* New York: Cambridge University Press.

Staub, E. (2004). *Reconciliation after genocide, mass killing or intractable conflict: Healing, understanding the roots of violence and the prevention of new violence.* Unpublished manuscript, University of Massachusetts at Amherst.

Staub, E. (in press). The roots of goodness: The fulfillment of basic human needs and the development of caring, helping, and nonaggression, inclusive caring, moral courage, active bystandership, and altruism born of suffering. In G. Carlo & C. Edwards (Eds.), *Moral motivation.* Nebraska Symposium on Motivation. Lincoln: Nebraska University Press.

Staub, E., & Bar-Tal, D. (2003). Genocide, mass killing and intractable conflict: Roots, evolution, prevention and reconciliation. In D. Sears, L. Huddy, & R. Jervis (Eds.), *Handbook of political psychology* (pp. 710–754). New York: Oxford University Press.

Staub, E., & Pearlman, L. A. (2001). Healing, reconciliation, and forgiving after genocide and other collective violence. In R. G. Helmick & R. L. Petersen (Eds.), *Forgiveness and recon-*

ciliation: Religion, public policy, and conflict transformation, (pp. 195–217). Philadelphia: Templeton Foundation Press.

Staub, E., & Pearlman, L. A. (2002). Facilitators' summary of observations and recommendations from leaders seminar. Retrieved from *www.heal-reconcile-rwanda.org.*

Staub, E., & Pearlman, L. A., (2004). *Advancing healing and reconciliation in Rwanda—and elsewhere.* Unpublished manuscript, University of Massachusetts at Amherst.

Staub, E., Pearlman, L. A., & Miller, V. (2003). Healing the roots of genocide in Rwanda. *Peace Review, 15,* 287–294.

Staub, E., Pearlman, L.A., Gubin, A., & Hagengimana, A. (in press). Healing, reconciliation, and the prevention of violence after genocide or mass killing: An intervention and its experimental evaluation in Rwanda. *Journal of Social and Clinical Psychology.*

Subkoviak, M. J., Enright, R. D., Wu, C., Gassin, E. A., Freedman, S., Olson, L. M., et al. (1995). Measuring interpersonal forgiveness in late adolescence and middle adulthood. *Journal of Adolescence, 18,* 641–655.

Weiner, B., Graham, S., Peter, O., & Zmuidinas, M. (1991). Public confession and forgiveness. *Journal of Personality, 59,* 281–321.

Wessells, M., & Monteiro, C. (2001). Psychosocial Interventions and post-war reconstruction in Angola: Interweaving Western and traditional approaches. In D. J. Christie, R. V. Wagner, & D. D. Winter (Eds.), *Peace, conflict, and violence* (pp. 262–277). Upper Saddle River, NJ: Prentice Hall.

Worthington, E. L., Jr. (2001). Unforgiveness, forgiveness, and reconciliation and their implications for societal interventions. In R. J. Helmick & R. L. Petersen, (Eds.), *Forgiveness and reconciliation: Religion, public policy, and conflict transformation* (pp. 171–193). Philadelphia: Templeton Foundation Press.

Chapter Twenty-Eight

Intergroup Forgiveness and Intergroup Conflict: Northern Ireland, A Case Study

Ed Cairns
Tania Tam
Miles Hewstone
Ulrike Niens

I get down on my knees and do what must be done
And kiss Achilles' hand, the killer of my son.

—*Ceasefire*, Michael Longley, 1994[1]

With the end of the Cold War, the world has had to come to grips with new or at least hitherto hidden types of conflict. In these conflicts, the combatants inhabit the same battlefield. This means that even when the actual fighting fades, the lives of the opposing groups remain interlocked. Subjective elements of conflict often persist long after its "objective" elements disappear. They can become independent of the initiating, more objective causes of the conflict and contribute to an escalation and continuation of violence even after the initial causes have become irrelevant (Deutsch, 1973; Tajfel & Turner, 1979). Thus, the formal resolution of a conflict is often merely the first step toward peaceful coexistence. To promote peace and reconciliation, a psychological process is required to change people's often deeply-entrenched beliefs and feelings about the outgroup, their ingroup, and the relationship between the two (Bar-Tal, 2000). Group loyalty and the maintenance of group boundaries are dominant features of such conflicts, as are communal memories of victimization. Together they create psychological processes that, if not countered, will lead to further cycles of violence.

In this chapter, we examine the contributions that a fuller understanding of intergroup forgiveness can make in an attempt to resolve or at least contain these identity-based conflicts. To do this, we will begin by sketching out some of the more important psychological processes involved in protracted ethnic conflicts, in particular, their intergroup (as opposed to interpersonal) nature and the role of the past. We will then draw on our research in Northern Ireland to illustrate the process of intergroup forgiveness.

PERSONAL ASSUMPTIONS ABOUT INTERGROUP CONFLICT AND INTERGROUP FORGIVENESS

Intergroup Conflict

One of these psychological factors is undoubtedly the intergroup nature of the conflict. Tajfel (1978) proposed that *intergroup* behavior could be distinguished from *interpersonal* behavior when it involved two clearly identifiable social categories and when there was little variability of behavior or attitude within each group. Also, members of one group should show little variability in their perception or treatment of members of the other group (i.e., "they" are "all alike"). There is now extensive evidence that people's behavior is indeed qualitatively different in intergroup and interpersonal settings (see Brown & Turner, 1981; Cairns & Hewstone, 2002; Hewstone, Rubin, & Willis, 2002).

In a similar vein, Brewer (1997) has proposed three principles likely to operate in any social situation in which a particular ingroup/outgroup categorization is made salient. The "intergroup accentuation principle" suggests that all members of the ingroup are seen as more similar to the self than are members of the outgroup. The "ingroup favoritism principle" refers to the selective generalization of positive affect (trust, liking) to fellow ingroup, but not outgroup, members. The "social competition principle" suggests that intergroup social comparison is typically perceived in terms of competition, rather than comparison, with the outgroup. Indeed, intergroup conflict is often perceived as a zero-sum game by the parties involved (Esses, Jackson, & Armstrong, 1998).

The Past in the Present.   The "social competition principle," we believe, is key to understanding the role of the past in the present. Groups involved in intergroup conflict are often encouraged to "move on" or to try to "face up to" the past. The problem about the past where ethnic conflict is concerned, however, is that it is intimately part of the present. Instead the past forms part of the ongoing intergroup competition central to any intergroup conflict, with people in Northern Ireland apparently clinging tenaciously to battles fought long ago. As a result, certain dates appear to be fixed like beacons in the folklore and mythology of people in Northern Ireland so that they "trip off the tongue during ordinary conversations like the latest football scores in other environments" (Darby, 1983, p. 13).

Of course, rituals, symbols, commemoration, and reparations can play an important role in any process of healing, bereavement, and addressing personal trauma. They can help grieving by allowing individuals to focus exclusively on their grief and to share their feelings with others (Cairns & Roe, 2003). However, we would argue that only the promotion of intergroup forgiveness will lead to long-term intergroup reconciliation.

Intergroup Forgiveness

Because intergroup bias is such a pervasive phenomenon and is present at public and private, explicit and implicit levels (see Hewstone et al., 2002), we should not be surprised if we find evidence that "we" are reluctant to forgive "them." Indeed, intergroup forgiveness may be thwarted not only by blatant feelings of hatred but also through very subtle processes, such as the tendency for more differentiated, secondary emotions to be attributed to ingroup than outgroup members (see Leyens et al., 2000). In the context of an ongoing ethnic conflict, promoting intergroup forgiveness is a difficult issue to broach and not just to those who have suffered directly. As Duncan Morrow, Director of Northern Ireland's Community Relations Council, put it, "What makes forgiveness so burning in Northern Ireland is not that many victims are left with their injury, but that so many of the injuries are understood as the grief not only of individuals but of whole communities."

Notwithstanding our expectation that intergroup forgiveness will prove different from interpersonal forgiveness, we are convinced that it is a hugely important topic (especially for a society such as Northern Ireland), although one that has so far generated remarkably little research (for an exception, see Roe, Pegg, Hodges, & Trimm, 1999; see also a study investigating religious groups, Azar, Mullet, & Vinsonneau, 1999).

Intergroup forgiveness has, however, begun to take its place on the world stage (Montiel, 2002), either in the form of apologies, as a means to promote reconciliation, or in truth commissions, aimed at supporting a process of reconciliation after political violence and human rights abuses (Borris & Diehl, 1998).

Apologies.   The 1990s have seen a dramatic increase in apologies offered by political, social, and religious leaders (Dodds, 2003). For example, in 1994, German President Roman Herzog asked the Polish people for forgiveness for the suffering they had to experience during World War II. In 1998, U.S. President Bill Clinton apologized for a failure to act during the Rwandan genocide. In 2000, Pope John Paul II asked God's forgiveness for the wrongs committed by Roman Catholics in the past, including offenses against specific minority groups. In Northern Ireland in 2002, the IRA published an apology addressed to the families of "noncombatants" who had been killed or injured by the IRA. All of these apologies were positively received by some people but criticized by others for not being explicit enough or falling short of an acceptance of guilt.

Truth Commissions.   Over the past 30 years, truth commissions, public enquiries, and tribunals have been set up across the world in countries and societies that had experienced political violence. The commissions sought to deal with the past, construct collective memory and history, and move forward a process of reconciliation. The majority of truth commissions focused either on giving a voice to the victims of political violence or on issues of social justice. For example, in Rwanda, a reduced penalty was granted only to those perpetrators who admitted their offenses and expressed their remorse. The Truth and Reconciliation Commission (TRC) in South Africa has probably been the most widely discussed of these, partly because it was the first to attempt to give a voice to victims of injustice as well as to provide amnesty to perpetrators under the condition that they reported full details of past crimes. In a keynote speech at the "Peacebuilding After Peace Accords" conference organized by the Joan B. Kroc Institute for International Peace Studies, Archbishop Tutu recalled a victim of apartheid who said, "We would like to forgive. We would just like to know who to forgive" (Stowe, 2003, p. 20). However, although the TRC provided a forum for victims to hear who to forgive and for all people to debate reconciliation and a shared memory of the past (Hamber & Wilson, 2002; Kulle & Hamber, 2000), it has also been criticized for providing insufficient support to victims and perpetrators (Hamber, 1998).

REVIEW OF RELEVANT EMPIRICAL AND THEORETICAL LITERATURE

Empirical Research

Although forgiveness and reconciliation at an interpersonal level are now being extensively researched (as evidenced throughout this book), there is little systematic research on intergroup forgiveness. Azar et al. (1999) conducted a survey in Lebanon using scenarios. The scenarios described politically motivated shootings and experimentally varied four factors to test for their effect on propensity to forgive. These factors were: proximity to the offender (own community/other community), intent to harm (deliberate/accidental shooting), long-term consequences (negative/positive), and apologies from the offender (apologized/did not apologize). The sample included people from the three main Lebanese Christian communities: Catholics, Maronites, and Orthodox. Results indicated overall relatively high levels of forgiveness in all three communities with lack of intent to harm, cancellation of consequences and, in particular, apologies, significantly increasing respondents' propensity to forgive.

Using attribution theory, Gibson and Gouws (1999) investigated assumptions underlying the work of the TRC in South Africa and factors affecting the willingness to forgive perpetrators of political violence in South Africa. The representative panel survey sample included respondents identified as Asian, Black, Colored, and White. Again, short vignettes describing acts of political murders were employed in order to vary four factors: actor roles (African National Congress or South African Police), obedience (leader or follower), consequences (harming innocent people or people directly involved in violence), and motive (hatred or ideology). These factors were hypothesized as affecting attributions of blame and the propensity to forgive. In contrast to the findings of Azar et al. (1999), results indicated a significant main effect for actor roles, with respondents expressing lower levels of blame if the perpetrator was identified as a member of an organization associated with the respondent's community (Gibson & Gouws, 1999). A slightly weaker main effect was revealed for obedience, with respondents blaming leaders more than followers. No significant effects were found in relation to motive and consequences or motive. Forgiveness, in turn, was positively related to attitudes toward amnesty and negatively related toward the belief that it was right to sue the perpetrator. More generally, Hamber, reporting on the effectiveness of the TRC in South Africa, points out that the truth-telling process led to psychological benefits for individuals and society but that knowledge and "truth alone will not lead to reconciliation" (1998, p. 26).

Staub (2000; chapter 27) summarizes the experiences of an intervention project aimed at promoting forgiveness and reconciliation in Rwanda after the 1994 genocide. Although he affirms the importance of knowledge about the origins and possibilities of solving conflict, the necessity for forgiveness as a precondition for reconciliation is emphasized. In different sociopolitical contexts, a lack of cancellation of wider consequences, especially through persisting inequalities between communities, is thought to impede the process of reconciliation (Hamber, 1998; Staub, 2000).

Empirical research on intergroup forgiveness in societies emerging from ethnopolitical conflict is particularly difficult for ethical, political, and psychometric reasons. For example, the very mention of the term *forgiveness* as part of a qualitative or quantitative survey may cause individual trauma or revive intergroup anxiety and distrust (McLernon, Cairns, & Hewstone, 2002; Staub & Pearlman, 2000). Hence, researchers need to take care when designing the research in order to minimize the possibility of a negative impact on participants. The measurement of intergroup forgiveness must also go beyond personalized trauma to ensure that forgiveness is explored at a community or societal level rather than at an individual level. Scenarios or other measures priming the participant to the intergroup context or group research, such as focus groups, help to facilitate responses at the level of intergroup forgiveness.

Intergroup Forgiveness in Northern Ireland: A Case Study

Surprisingly, for a society that is struggling to overcome the effect of prolonged political violence, intergroup forgiveness is not high on the agenda. For example, although Northern Ireland is a particularly "churched" part of the world, and although the main churches have all officially condemned violence, one has to look to exceptional individual church leaders to find attempts to encourage the recognition and acknowledgment of past wrongs and injustices by both sides. For example, one church leader (Stevens, 1986) had suggested that in Northern Ireland, "without forgiveness there cannot be reconciliation" (p. 63), and another (Dunlop) has suggested that some acknowledgment of collective guilt could help to promote forgiveness in Northern Ireland (Giffin, McDonagh, Dunlop, McMaster, & Smyth, 1996).

Politicians in Northern Ireland appear to be even more reticent to speak about forgiveness. One has to look not to *local* politicians but to politicians from other nations to find references to the need for forgiveness in Northern Ireland. In an address during the 1995 visit by U.S. President Bill Clinton to Belfast, he likened the conflict in Northern Ireland to the American Civil War when he said:

> We have all done wrong. No one can say his heart is altogether clean, and his hands altogether pure. Thus as we wish to be forgiven, let us forgive those who have sinned against us and ours. That was the beginning of America's reconciliation, and it must be the beginning of Northern Ireland's reconciliation.

Exceptions exist, however, and private individuals from both sides of the religious divide in Northern Ireland have called for forgiveness even in the face of personal hurt. The best known of examples of public demonstrations of intergroup forgiveness have come from two bereaved fathers—Michael McGoldrick and Gordon Wilson (McKittrick, Kelters, Feeney, & Thornton, 1999). Michael McGoldrick's 31-year-old son was shot by Protestant paramilitaries in July 1996, yet he felt able to say, "Bury your hate with my boy. Love one another. I can love the man that murdered my son" (p. 1996). Similarly, Gordon Wilson, whose daughter, Marie, was killed in an IRA bomb attack in 1987, said: "I bear no ill will. I bear no grudge. That will not bring her back" (p. 1098). For most survivors in Northern Ireland, however, the journey to forgiveness appears to be a bridge too far.

Intergroup Forgiveness in Northern Ireland: Empirical Research

Despite this lack of interest in the topic of intergroup forgiveness in Northern Ireland, we have over the last 5 years begun a program of research to investigate this topic. In this section, we will briefly describe our ongoing research in which we have used a range of qualitative and quantitative methodologies to investigate intergroup forgiveness and its correlates in Northern Ireland (see Hewstone, Cairns, Voci, McLernon, Niens, & Noor, 2004). We focus here on our studies developing and using a new measure of intergroup forgiveness in this context, but we have also undertaken research using the Enright Forgiveness Inventory (see McLernon, Cairns, Hewstone, & Smith, 2004), which we believe is less able to capture the specifically intergroup aspects of forgiveness in Northern Ireland. In our research program, we first conducted a series of focus groups to examine what people in Northern Ireland thought of forgiving the other community. Second, surveys elucidated psychological processes involved in intergroup forgiveness. Finally, an experimental study systematically examined factors that lead people to forgive the other side.

The Conflict in Northern Ireland.   Before discussing our work on intergroup forgiveness in Northern Ireland, it is necessary to consider the background to the "Troubles," as they are commonly known. In common with many if not most of current ethnic conflicts, the conflict in Northern Ireland has a long history. It is possible to trace the Irish conflict with the English to at least the 16th century. Northern Ireland really came to the world's attention, however, only because of the violence that has dominated the last 30 years, leading to some 3,000 deaths and tens of thousands of injuries due to increasing community divisions. Today, despite the recent peace process, the conflict in Northern Ireland remains largely a struggle between those who wish to see Northern Ireland remain part of the United Kingdom (the Protestant/Unionists) and those who wish to see the reunification of the island of Ireland (the Catholic/Nationalists). Complicating this picture, however, is the fact that the conflict is underpinned by a mix of historical, religious, political, economic, and psychological elements (Cairns & Darby, 1998).

Focus Groups.   People from lay and church-based organizations devoted to the reduction of conflict, ex-paramilitaries, and victims themselves participated in a series of focus groups conducted between June 1999 and February 2000 (see McLernon et al., 2002). All saw forgiveness as based on ideas of compassion, mercy, humanity, or empathy, which parallels previous research on *interpersonal* forgiveness (e.g., Enright & the Human Development Study Group, 1991). However, most agreed that it was easier to forgive an individual than a group, because it was easier to trust an individual than each member of the other community.

There were, however, disagreements about intergroup forgiveness; victims, particularly from the Catholic/Republican side, were hostile to the idea of forgiveness and thought that in forgiving, they were justifying the wrongs that were done to them. Members of the ex-paramilitary groups also felt that their acts were fully justified at the time and that they did not feel the need to ask for or to offer forgiveness.

The focus groups also showed that many participants felt that forgiveness becomes easier if others acknowledge and validate the pain of a hurtful act; in Northern Ireland, they felt, intense bitterness develops without this acknowledgment. Indeed, a show of remorse from the perpetrator promotes forgiveness. Finally, it was stressed by all groups that preaching forgiveness or trying to force it was likely to be counterproductive, but an act of remembrance such as a monument might give others the opportunity to share the loss and make forgiving easier.

Survey 1. University student sample—Collective guilt, outgroup attitudes, and ingroup identification as predictors of forgiveness. Hewstone et al. (2004) developed a forgiveness scale from the focus-group sessions to examine the relation between forgiveness and variables such as religiosity, contact with members of the other community, and personal experience of victimhood during the Troubles. Using a sample of Catholic and Protestant university students in Northern Ireland, they found that the strongest predictors of forgiveness were collective guilt and outgroup attitudes, whereas identification with one's own religious community was a negative predictor. This model explained a large proportion of the variance in forgiveness (31% for Catholics and 52% for Protestants). Interestingly, personal self-reports of religiosity did not relate to intergroup forgiveness at all. On examining victimization experience of the Troubles, Hewstone et al. (in press) found that those who had experienced high levels of victimization reported significantly lower collective guilt and forgiveness than those who experienced little victimization.

Survey 2. Representative sample—Trust, perspective taking, and ingroup identification as predictors of forgiveness. Hewstone et al. (2004) then surveyed a representative sample of the Northern Irish population, adding measures of perspective taking, trust of the other community, and an objective index of participants' exposure to violence (based on how much sectarian violence had taken place in their area of residence). Forgiveness was positively associated with more contact with outgroup friends, more positive outgroup attitudes, greater ability to take the perspective of the other community, and greater outgroup trust. The strongest predictor of forgiveness for Catholics was trust, which alone explained 23% of the variance in forgiveness, whereas for Protestants, there were two strong positive predictors (trust and perspective taking) and one strong negative predictor (identification with one's own group); these three predictors together explained 41% of the variance in forgiveness for Protestants. As in Survey 1, respondents who experienced more violence reported significantly less forgiveness than those who experience less violence.

Surveys 3 and 4. Infrahumanization as mediator of the effect of contact on forgiveness. Tam et al. (2004) focused on the link between intergroup contact and forgiveness. They replicated the finding that higher levels of contact between Catholics and Protestants predict intergroup forgiveness. They also examined how this occurs. According to the psychological essentialism perspective on intergroup bias (Haslam, Rothschild, & Ernst, 2000; Hirschfeld, 1996), people tend to infuse an essence (biological, cultural, religious, etc.) into social groups to explain their differences. An ingroup perceived as superior may be endowed with the human essence (Schwartz & Struch, 1989), whereas outgroups are seen as "infra-humans." This form of bias has been suggested to lead to "delegitimization" (Bar-Tal, 1989, p.358) and "moral exclusion" (Opotow, 1990, p.1; Staub, 1989) in extreme cases; for example, Nazi Germans regarded Jews as being subhuman.

Researchers (e.g., Demoulin et al., 2004) have observed that people perceive what emotion researchers (e.g., Ekman, 1992) call *secondary emotions* (e.g., nostalgia, guilt) as more unique to humans than are primary emotions (e.g., anger, pleasure). Evidence suggests further that individuals attribute more specifically human secondary emotions to the ingroup than to the outgroup—infrahumanizing the outgroup (Leyens et al., 2000). Tam et al. (2004) selected primary and secondary emotions from a pretested list (see Demoulin et al., 2004): positive primary emotions (surprise, calmness, attraction, enjoyment, caring, excitement, pleasure), positive secondary emotions (optimism, love, passion, elation, nostalgia, admiration, hope), negative primary emotions (pain, fear, anger, fury, panic, fright, suffering), and positive secondary emotions (humiliation, shame, guilt, disgust, melancholy, disconsolate, disenchantment). They found that both Catholics and Protestants indeed attributed more secondary emotions to their ingroup than to the outgroup, thus infrahumanizing members of the other community.

Tam et al. (2004) further examined this process of infrahumanization as a mediator of the effect of contact on forgiveness. They found that higher levels of contact with members of the other community in Northern Ireland predicted lower levels of infrahumanization. Furthermore, lessening the tendency to attribute secondary emotions to the ingroup than to the outgroup (i.e., seeing the outgroup as *more* human) mediated the effect of contact on willingness to forgive the outgroup for past wrongdoings over and above other variables, such as the attribution of primary emotions, as well as feelings of empathy, respect, and lessened anxiety. This model explained 11% of the variance in forgiveness.

Tam et al. (2004) replicated this result in a second study, which adopted a more refined scale measure of secondary and primary emotions. The attribution of secondary emotions to members of the other community again mediated the effect of contact on forgiveness, over and above the attribution of primary emotions and feelings of empathy, positive and negative emotions toward the outgroup. This model explained even more of the variance in outgroup forgiveness: 16%. Catholic-Protestant contact is thus a possible means of humanizing the other community in Northern Ireland, thereby promoting the vital act of forgiving.

Experimental (Scenario) Study.   Finally, in an experimental study, Hewstone et al. (2004) presented participants with one of several versions of a scenario describing an act of paramilitary violence (based on Gibson and Gouws' [1999] methodology). The conditions in the scenario were manipulated in a four-factor between-subjects design: 2 (religious group membership of participant: Catholic vs. Protestant) × 2 (religious group membership of perpetrator: Catholic vs. Protestant) × 2 (intention to kill the victim: intentional vs. unintentional) × 2 (motivation: retaliation vs. no apparent motivation). Participants were asked to attribute blame and forgiveness in these situations and whether they would make a recommendation for the perpetrator to be granted early release. Under the terms of the Good Friday or Belfast Agreement, signed April 10, 1998, prisoners convicted of terrorist offenses could be released immediately or be required to serve a minimum of 2 more years. Participants also completed measures of the importance of religion, intergroup contact, outgroup perspective taking, outgroup attitudes, intergroup forgiveness, and ingroup identification.

Both Catholics and Protestants were biased in favor of their own groups. Catholics were more forgiving of a Catholic than a Protestant perpetrator. Protestants were more forgiving of a Protestant than a Catholic perpetrator. Blame attributions and recommendations for early release followed a similar pattern. Interestingly, however, forgiveness was moderated by participants' identification with their own religious groups; those who were "low" in identification with their religious groups (i.e., as Catholic or Protestant) were not more forgiving of the ingroup perpetrators than the outgroup perpetrators, but those who highly identified with their religious groups showed an even stronger pattern of bias toward forgiving *ingroup* members than in the overall analysis. This reinforces the survey results, highlighting the importance of ingroup identification in forgiveness, because ingroup identification was clearly driving the intergroup forgiveness bias in this experiment and was much more important than manipulations of the perpetrator's intention or motivation.

CONCLUSIONS FROM OUR ONGOING CASE STUDY

In the context of the conflict in Northern Ireland, forgiveness may be best thought of as an intergroup, rather than as an interpersonal, construct—as sociopolitical rather than religious. Whereas religiosity was a weak predictor of forgiveness, identification with one's religious group and attitudes toward the other community were especially strong predictors. An experiment reinforced the relative importance of ingroup identification over sectarian perpetrators' intention or motivation. Intergroup forgiveness was also closely related to collective guilt, outgroup perspective taking, and outgroup trust.

We also showed subtle processes involved in inhibiting intergroup forgiveness, such as the tendency to attribute more secondary emotions to the ingroup than to the outgroup. Contact with the other community was an important predictor of forgiveness, and this process was mediated by infrahumanization. In other words, attenuating the tendency to infrahumanize was a mechanism by which this works. When people in Northern Ireland have higher levels of contact with members of the other community, they humanize the other community more, thereby becoming more forgiving of the outgroup. In a society as starkly segregated as Northern Ireland (see Hewstone et al., 2004), we believe that cross-community contact is an essential part of any solution to the Troubles, ultimately helping the two communities progress toward cross-community forgiveness and reconciliation.

DIRECTIONS FOR FUTURE RESEARCH

More research that focuses specifically on intergroup forgiveness is needed. To begin with, research should explore the similarities and differences between intergroup and interpersonal forgiveness. As this volume shows, a great deal of information is being accumulated about interpersonal forgiveness. Too often, however, authors assume that this literature can be applied directly to intergroup forgiveness. As we noted previously, interpersonal and intergroup *conflict* are distinct phenomena, and it is therefore likely that interpersonal and intergroup *forgiveness* are distinct phenomena. However, this is an empirical question that as yet remains to be answered.

We believe our research has blazed an important trail in this area. Other important issues are still to be resolved. In particular, even if we accept that intergroup contact plays an important role in promoting intergroup forgiveness in the context of the conflict in Northern Ireland, what we need to know is whether this is generalizable to other conflicts in other, for example, non-Christian cultures. Also, it would be essential to learn at what stage of any conflict attempts to foster intergroup forgiveness can be made. Our research in Northern Ireland has been carried out in a postconflict phase. Would it have worked as well at an earlier stage of the conflict? Indeed, would it work better if we had waited until the peace process in Northern Ireland had made even more progress?

Future research should, therefore, at the very least, attempt to replicate our Northern Irish research in the context of other conflicts and, we hope, at other periods in the life cycle of a conflict. In addition, research that addresses the relationship between intergroup forgiveness and three key concepts in any intergroup conflict—forgetting, revenge, and reconciliation—is needed. The current literature does include some mention of these relationships (Hewstone et al., 2004) but mostly in the context of interpersonal forgiveness (Enright, Freedman, & Rique, 1998).

PERSONAL THEORETICAL PERSPECTIVES

Forgiving and forgetting are regarded as closely linked, sometimes synonymous concepts. Therefore, often the admonition is to "forgive and forget." Despite this, it can be argued that there can be no forgiving if forgetting has already occurred. This is because some form of remembering is necessary if forgiveness is to take place. For these reasons, forgiveness must not be confused with forgetting (see Enright & Coyle, 1994).

Current theoretical accounts of the process of forgiveness indicate that the concepts of revenge and forgiveness are, implicitly or explicitly, placed at the opposite poles of a single dimension (see Enright et al., 1998: McCullough, Worthington, & Rachal, 1997). In contrast, acceptance of reparation or forgiveness of perpetrators may be perceived by relatives of the dead and injured as a disrespectful act that betrays the memory of their loss. Finally, there is disagreement in the literature on the relationship between forgiveness and reconciliation. What is perhaps most often debated is whether there can be reconciliation without forgiveness and/or forgiveness without reconciliation.

Enright, Gassin, Longinovic, and Loudon (1994) argue that it is possible to forgive without reconciliation and maintains that the process of forgiveness does not involve any predictable gains on the victim's part (such as restored relationship/reconciliation). This implies that forgiveness should not be thought about or calculated in terms of equity or reciprocity. Rather, an unconditional process of forgiveness frees the victim from the control of the transgressor. A less positive implication of this notion of unconditional forgiveness is that the burden or responsibility of forgiveness may be placed solely on the victim, who may already be carrying a heavy load due to the infliction of a severe transgression. Power (1994), in contrast, regards any acts of forgiveness that do not point in the direction of reconciliation as incomplete. Including the concept of reconciliation in the process of forgiveness implies a shared responsibility of forgiveness between the wronged party and the offender.

Although, as this volume testifies, work is proceeding at pace on interpersonal forgiveness, intergroup forgiveness remains a "quandary" (Smedes, 1984) still to be understood. Unfortunately, as Pargament et al. (2000, p. 308) note:

There is no shortage of deep-seated social and political conflict. Mistrust and hatred represent powerful naturalistic laboratories for the study of forgiveness.

APPLICATION FOR PRACTICE: POLICY IMPLICATIONS

A problem for many societies torn apart by civil war or racial conflict, according to Ignatieff (1966), is that "what is mythic—and hence what is poisonous—about the past . . . is that it is not past at all." This, he cautions, makes the process of coming to terms with the past much more complicated than "simply sifting fact from fiction, lies from truth" (p. 121). With the apparent success of the South African TRC has come the belief in some societies that truth commissions are the *open sesame* to lasting peace in deeply divided societies.

Work on intergroup forgiveness may have implications for the conduct of future truth commissions. It could certainly be argued that if the poisonous past is to be dealt with, some form of intergroup forgiveness is likely to play an important role. For this reason, non-governmental organizations, governments, and others involved in peacemaking and peacekeeping (in its broadest sense) should pay close attention to work in this area. Similarly, those involved in peace education in its broadest sense would do well to learn from this literature. One of the clearest challenges to peacemakers is to prevent the recurrence or reemergence of long-standing conflict. Again, an acknowledgment of the potential role of intergroup forgiveness in this area could lead to important progress.

This is not the only area in which we believe intergroup forgiveness can play a role in promoting reconciliation in situations of ethnic conflict. As Worthington (2001) has suggested, what is required is for policy makers to adopt a "multilayered war . . . against the centrifugal forces that threaten to disintegrate society" (p. 181). In this war, we believe that policy makers should take note of the research outlined above that points to a key role for intergroup contact in helping to promote forgiveness.

CONCLUSIONS

Although we have tried to approach our work with a certain amount of dispassion, we are mindful of the hurt and suffering that the words *the Troubles* contain. One insight into the human side of the Troubles can be seen in the book *Lost Lives* (McKittrick et al., 1999), which chronicles the deaths of Northern Ireland's 3,600 victims in some detail. Of course, the political conflict in Northern Ireland is a mere blip on the graph of world deaths in similar conflicts. It is our belief, however, that if the world is to stem this tide of suffering in Northern Ireland and in many other societies, what is needed is not just sympathy but hard-nosed theoretically based research. Given the suffering that has gone on, an essential part of this research we believe will, of necessity, have to focus on intergroup forgiveness. As the recent joint declaration of the British and Irish governments notes, although it is not "possible to complete the transition to . . .

peace and stability by dwelling forever on . . . the past, neither is it possible to create a new beginning without taking account of, and addressing, its legacies (April, 2003).

NOTE

1. This poem, a reworking of a section of Homer's *Iliad* about the reconciliation of Achilles and Priam, was first published in the *Irish Times* in 1994. A few days later, the IRA announced its own ceasefire.

REFERENCES

Azar, F., Mullet, E., & Vinsonneau, G. (1999). The propensity to forgive: Findings from Lebanon. *Journal of Peace Research*, 36, 161–181.

Bar-Tal, D. (2000). From intractable conflict through conflict resolution to reconciliation: Psychological analysis. *International Journal of Political Society, 21*, 362–365.

Borris, E., & Diehl, P. F. (1998). Forgiveness, reconciliation, and the contribution of international peacekeeping. In H. L. Langholtz (Ed.), *The psychology of peacekeeping* (pp. 207–222). Westport: Praeger.

Brewer, M. B. (1997). The social psychology of intergroup relations: Can research inform practice? *Journal of Social Issues, 53*, 197–211.

Brown, R. J., & Turner, J. C. (1981). Interpersonal and intergroup behavior. In J. C. Turner & H. Giles (Eds.), *Intergroup behavior* (pp. 33–64). Chicago: University of Chicago Press.

Cairns, E., & Darby, J. (1998). The conflict in Northern Ireland—Causes, consequences, and controls. *American Psychologist, 53*, 754–760.

Cairns E., & Hewstone, M. (2002). Northern Ireland: The impact of peacemaking in Northern Ireland on intergroup behavior. In G. Salomon & B. Neov (Eds.), *Peace education: The concept, principles and practices around the world* (pp. 217–228). Hillsdale, NJ: Lawrence Erlbaum.

Cairns, E., & Roe, M. (Eds.). (2003). *The role of memory in ethnic conflict.* London: Palgrave Macmillan.

Darby, J. (1983). *Northern Ireland: The background to the conflict.* Belfast: Appletree Press.

Demoulin, S., Leyens, J., Paladino, P. M., Rodriguez, A. P., Rodriguez, R. T., & Dovidio, J. (2004). Dimensions of "uniquely" and "non uniquely" human emotions. *Cognition and Emotion, 18,* 71–96.

Deutsch, M. (1973). *The resolution of conflict.* New Haven, CT: Yale University Press.

Dodds, G. M. (2003). *Political apologies: Chronological list.* Penn National Commission on Society, Culture, and Community. Retrieved August 19, 2004, from http://www.upenn.edu/pnc/politicalapologies.html.

Enright, R. D., & Coyle, C. (1994). Researching the process model of forgiveness within psychological interventions. In E. L. Worthington, Jr. (Ed.), *Dimensions of forgiveness: Psychological research and theological perspectives* (pp. 139–161). Philadelphia: Templeton Foundation Press.

Enright, R. D., Freedman, S., & Rique, J. (1998). The psychology of interpersonal forgiveness. In R. D. Enright & J. North (Eds.), *Exploring forgiveness* (pp. 46–63). Madison: University of Wisconsin Press.

Enright, R. D., Gassin, E. A., Longinovic, T., & Loudon, D. (1994, December). *Forgiveness as a solution to social crisis.* Paper presented at the Morality and Social Crisis conference, Institute for Educational Research, Beograd, Serbia.

Enright, R. D., & the Human Development Study Group. (1991). The moral development of forgiveness. In W. Kurtines & J. Gewirtz (Eds.), *Handbook of moral behavior and development* (pp. 123–152). Hillsdale, NJ: Lawrence Erlbaum.

Ekman, P. (1992). An argument for basic emotions. *Cognition and Emotion, 6,* 169–200.

Esses, V. M., Jackson, L. M., & Armstrong, T. L. (1998). Intergroup competition and attitudes toward immigrants and immigration: An instrumental model. *Journal of Social Issues, 54,* 699–724

Gibson, J. L., & Gouws, A. (1999). Truth and reconciliation in South Africa: Attributions to blame and the struggle over apartheid. *American Political Science Review, 93,* 501–517.

Giffin, V. E., McDonagh, J., Dunlop, J., McMaster, J., & Smyth, G. (1996). *Brokenness, forgiveness, healing, and peace.* Unpublished lectures delivered in St. Anne's Cathedral, Belfast.

Hamber, B. (1998). The burdens of truth: An evaluation of the psychological support services and initiatives undertaken by the South African Truth and Reconciliation Commission. *American Imago, 55,* 9–28.

Hamber, B., & Wilson, R. (2002). Symbolic closure through memory, reparation, and revenge in post-conflict societies. *Journal of Human Rights, 1,* 35–53.

Haslam, N., Rothschild, L., & Ernst, D. (2000). Essentialist beliefs about social categories. *British Journal of Social Psychology, 39,* 127–139.

Hewstone, M., Cairns, E., Voci, A., McLernon, F., Niens, U., & Noor, M. (2004). Intergroup forgiveness and guilt in Northern Ireland: Social psychological dimensions of "The Troubles." In N. R. Branscombe & B. Doosje (Eds.), *Collective guilt: International perspectives* (pp. 193–215). New York: Cambridge University Press.

Hewstone, M., Rubin, M., & Willis, H. (2002). Intergroup bias. *Annual Review of Psychology, 53,* 575–604.

Hirschfeld, L. A. (1996). *Race in the making: Cognition, culture, and the child's construction of human kinds.* Cambridge, MA: MIT Press.

Ignatieff, M. (1996). There's no place like home: The politics of belonging. In S. Dunant & R. Porter (Eds.), *The age of anxiety.* London: Virago.

Kulle, D., & Hamber, B. (2000). Introduction. In *Future policies for the past. Democratic dialogue, Report No. 13.* Retrieved May 3, 2004 from http://cain.ulst.ac.uk/dd/report13/report13a.htm.

Leyens, J. P., Paladino, P. M., Rodriguez, R. T., Vaes, J., Demoulin, S., Rodriguez, A. P., et al. (2000). The emotional side of prejudice: The role of secondary emotions. *Personality and Social Psychology Review, 4,* 186–197.

McCullough, M. E., Worthington, E. L., Jr., & Rachal, K. C. (1997). Interpersonal forgiving in close relationships. *Journal of Personality and Social Psychology, 73,* 321–336.

McKittrick, D., Kelters, S., Feeney, B., & Thornton, C., (1999). *Lost lives: The stories of the men, women, and children who died as a result of the Northern Ireland Troubles.* London: Mainstream.

McLernon, F., Cairns, E., & Hewstone, M. (2002). Views on forgiveness in Northern Ireland. *Peace Review, 14,* 285–290.

McLernon, F., Cairns, E., Hewstone, M., & Smith, R. (2004). The development of intergroup forgiveness in Northern Ireland. *Journal of Social Issues, 60,* 587–601.

Montiel, C. J. (2002). Sociopolitical forgiveness. *Peace Review, 14,* 271–277.

Morrow, D. Forgiveness and reconciliation. In *Future policies for the past. Democratic dialogue, Report No. 13*. Retrieved from http://cain.ulst.ac.uk/dd/report13/report13a.htm.

Opotow, S. (1990). Moral exclusion and injustice: An introduction. *Journal of Social Issues, 46*, 1–20.

Pargament, K. I., McCullough, M. E., & Thoresen, C. E. (2000). The frontier of forgiveness: Seven directions for psychological study and practice. In M. E. McCullough, K. I. Pargament, & C. E. Thoresen (Eds.), *Forgiveness: theory, research, and practice* (pp. 299–319). New York: Guilford Press.

Power, F. C. (1994). Commentary. *Human Development, 37*, 81–85.

Roe, M. D., Pegg, W., Hodges, K, & Trimm, R. A. (1999). Forgiving the other side: Social identity and ethnic memories in Northern Ireland. In J. P. Harrington & E. Mitchell (Eds.), *Politics and performance in contemporary Northern Ireland* (pp. 122–156). Amherst: University of Massachusetts Press.

Schwartz, S. H., & Struch, N. (1989). Values, stereotypes, and intergroup antagonism. In D. Bar-Tal, C. F. Graunman, A. W. Kruglanski, & W. Stroebe (Eds.), *Stereotyping and prejudice: Changing conceptions* (pp. 151–167). New York: Springer-Verlag.

Smedes, L. B. (1984). *Forgive and forget: Healing the hurts we don't deserve*. New York: Harper & Row.

Staub, E. (1989). *The roots of evil: The origins of genocide and other group violence*. New York: Cambridge University Press.

Staub, E. (2000). Genocide and mass killings: Origin, prevention, healing, and reconciliation. *Political Psychology, 21*, 367–382.

Staub, E., & Pearlman, L. A. (2000). *Healing, forgiveness, and reconciliation in Rwanda: Project summary and outcome*. Rwanda: Advanced Healing and Reconciliation. Retrieved March 5, 2004, from http://www.heal-reconcile-rwanda.org/Tempfinal.htm.

Stevens, D. (1986). Forgiveness and reconciliation in political perspective. *Doctrine and Life, 35*, 60–72.

Stowe, J. (2003). Tutu promotes South Africa's example of restorative justice. Nation: Desmond Tutu. *National Catholic Reporter*. Retrieved August 19, 2004 from http://www.findarticles.com/p/articles/mi_m1141/is_42_39/ai_108838266.

Tajfel, H. (1978). *Differentiation between social groups: Studies in the social psychology of intergroup relations*. London: Academic Press.

Tajfel, H., & Turner, J. C. (1979). An integrative theory of intergroup conflict. In W. G. Austin & S. Worchel (Eds.), *The social psychology of intergroup relations* (pp. 33–47). Monterey, CA: Brooks-Cole.

Tam, T., Hewstone, M., Kenworthy, J., Cairns, E., Voci, A., & Marinetti, C. (2004). *Intergroup contact and infra-humanization*. Manuscript in preparation, University of Oxford, Oxford, England.

Worthington, E. L., Jr. (2001). Unforgiveness, forgiveness, and reconciliation and their implications for societal interventions. In R. G. Helmick & R. L. Petersen (Eds.), *Forgiveness and reconciliation: Religion, public policy, and conflict transformation* (pp. 161–181). Philadelphia: Templeton Foundation Press.

Chapter Twenty-Nine

The Social Psychology of Justice and Forgiveness in Civil and Organizational Settings

Peter C. Hill
Julie Juola Exline
Adam B. Cohen

This chapter will focus on the role of justice in civil and organizational relationships, with a particular focus on when that sense of justice has been violated. To do so, we must consider how people think of justice, how they perceive injustice, and how they react to a sense of injustice, whether they are the aggrieved party or not.

Consider the following true story. Three 12-year-old girls in Garden Grove, California recently faced trial for sending an innocent man to jail for 8 months ("Three preteens get up to...", 2004). The girls, one of whom feared her parents' reaction to being 20 minutes late coming home from school, lacerated themselves and concocted a tale about a homeless drifter attacking them. Collectively, they identified a man from a police photo lineup as the guilty party. At the man's trial 8 months later, one of the girls confessed, and the man was freed. At their own trial, the girls expressed remorse ("Girls express remorse...", 2004), with one penning a letter addressed to the court saying that if the man who was wronged were present, "I would kneel down in front of him and ask for his forgiveness" (p. 5). Though the girls were eventually sentenced to 45 days in prison (with the possibility of early release for good behavior), the District Attorney originally asked that the girls be incarcerated for 253 days—1 day more than the wronged man had served. The homeless man himself was willing to forgive the girls, claiming that "Kids are kids. Kids do bonehead things. If the police had done their job right, this wouldn't have happened" ("Three preteens get up to...", 2004, p. 1).

Though the age of the girls is undoubtedly a mitigating factor, this story involves many of the key principles that will be discussed in this chapter: injustice (sending an innocent man to jail), the scope of distributive justice (a homeless drifter perhaps perceived as an easy target), remorse and guilt (from the girls over the accusations), retributive justice (the DA wanting the girls incarcerated for 1 day beyond the period of incarceration for the innocent man), perceived procedural injustice (perceived by the homeless man at the hands of the police; the harsh punishment perceived by the girls for being late), confession (by one of the girls at the innocent man's trial), and forgiveness (of the homeless drifter toward the girls), among others. We'll return to this story as we discuss some of these principles.

PERSONAL ASSUMPTIONS ABOUT FORGIVENESS

The guiding premise of this chapter, as it applies both to the workplace and in civilian relationships in general, is simple: People maintain some sense of what is right or just in human relationships, and when that sense has been violated (whether against one's self or others), there is a tendency to recapture that sense of justice through a myriad of possible reactions. Forgiveness is but one of those many ways to react (Worthington, 2001). However, other reactions (e.g., retaliation, seeking retribution) may appear to be better tactics if the goal is to reestablish justice. (For a detailed review of issues related to justice and forgiveness, see Exline, Worthington, Hill, & McCullough, 2003.) Some tactics are likely to result in a lingering unforgiveness where the individual remains mired in negative emotion. Other reactions to reassert justice may actually have similar effects of reducing the negative emotions of unforgiveness. However, as Worthington argues, it is only as those negative emotions are replaced by such positive emotions as empathy and compassion that the individual will experience forgiveness. Therefore, this paper will focus on research, particularly within an organizational and civilian context, that centers primarily around the following issues: (a) how people conceive of justice as a prescriptive norm for social relationships, (b) some factors that influence the perception that the justice norm has been violated, and (c) ways in which people can respond to justice violation. We will conclude our review of the literature with a special focus on implications for forgiveness.

REVIEW OF THEORETICAL AND EMPIRICAL RESEARCH

Given the interdependent nature of the workplace, one might expect that the recent surge of research interest in forgiveness would extend to organizational psychology. In fact, only recently have organizational researchers begun theoretically (Aquino, Grover, Goldman, & Folger, 2003) or empirically (Aquino, Tripp, & Bies, 2001; Bradfield & Aquino, 1999) to study forgiveness and reconciliation. Instead, organizational researchers on interpersonal relationships (e.g., Bies & Tripp, 1996, 1998) have focused far more on revenge and related problem behaviors such as violence (Folger & Baron, 1996), aggression (Folger & Starlicki, 1998), and employee theft (Greenberg, 1990) in response to perceived wrongdoing.

JUSTICE AS A PRESCRIPTIVE NORM

Justice norms that help regulate behavior are developed as guidelines for fair interactions that are mutually beneficial. Our sense of justice makes us aware of boundaries of acceptable behavior, provides a sense of predictability in human relationships, and instills confidence that future outcomes will be adequately distributed (Folger & Cropanzano, 1998). Research suggests that actions are viewed as just when the allocations or outcomes that individuals receive are believed to be equitable (*distributive justice*) and when the procedures for allocating resources, often influenced by how decisions are made, are perceived to be fair (*procedural justice*). To the extent that distributive and procedural justice criteria are met, negative emotions associated with a sense of injustice (e.g., hurt, anger) may not occur; thus, forgiveness may not be an issue (Volf, 2001). When either of these justice principles is violated, however, individuals may find that they are engulfed by unforgiving emotions (Worthington, 2001, 2003; Worthington & Wade, 1999).

Though people desire to maximize both long-term and short-term self-interests, equity theory (Adams, 1965) proposes that they also recognize the importance of equitable distribution of benefits relative to the effort put into the relationship. That is, people are happier when both parties receive appropriate benefits based on their respective contributions. The ill will of those who do not receive a fair appropriation is paralleled, in equity theory terms, by the guilt of those who are overcompensated. As a result, both parties are motivated to restore balance or equity in the relationship. Though perhaps counterintuitive and fascinating, the utility of the distributive justice construct is limited because judgments of distributive justice are subject to bias (Thompson & Lowenstein, 1992). Thus, two interactive parties using different standards in determining the degree of favorable outcomes they deserve will have differing opinions on whether distributive justice has been achieved.

It also appears that concerns about the allocation of resources are perhaps even *less* important than the procedures for distributing those limited resources (Alexander & Ruderman, 1987). For example, if procedures used in making decisions are perceived as fair, people are sometimes willing to accept decisions by authority figures that negatively affect them (see Tyler & Smith, 1998). Research on organizational justice (Folger, 1977; Greenberg & Folger, 1983) has documented the importance to a sense of procedural justice of *voice* (Thibaut & Walker, 1975)—the opportunity to be heard and the perception that one's say is given due consideration by decision makers, even if it has little or no desired influence on the outcome (Lind, Kanfer, & Earley, 1990).

Furthermore, research suggests that what often appears to be key in perceptions of procedural fairness and justice is the quality of interpersonal treatment, or *interactional* justice (Bies, 1987; Bies & Moag, 1986). Though concerns of allocation and procedures remain important in one's perception of justice, what is also important is *how* the distribution outcome and procedures are communicated. Therefore, the degree to which an authority figure displays interpersonal sensitivity, which may (or may not) communicate a sense of respect and dignity, will often play an important role in perceptions of justice (Greenberg, 1993).

Violations of Justice

When basic principles of distributive, procedural, and interactive justice are violated, an *injustice gap* (Worthington, 2003) is established. The size and personal importance of the injustice gap is predicted by many factors, including the intentionality behind the offensive behavior, the severity of the offense, and the extent to which the victim was deserving of the offense. When these factors are heightened, it may be especially difficult for a victim to respond with forgiveness (see Exline et al., 2003, for a review.)

Intentional Offenses.   Offender motives are important. To the extent that a person purposely violates a justice principle, the perceived injustice should be greater, and it may be more difficult to forgive. Relative to unintentional offenses, intentional offenses lead to greater assessments of responsibility and blame (Shaver, 1985), more anger (Folger & Cropanzano, 1998), harsher punishments (Darley & Huff, 1990), and less forgiveness (Boon & Sulsky, 1997).

Offense Severity.   More severe offenses are seen as more unjust, and thereby may be more difficult to forgive. People judge even accidental offenses harshly if the offenses violate one's sense of distributive justice due to severe negative consequences (Walster, 1966), especially if they involve a betrayal of trust (Gordon, Baucom, & Snyder, 2000). Offenses prompt harsher judgments and more retaliation when they violate procedural justice norms through insults or symbolic harm (Gabriel, 1998), particularly when committed against collectives as opposed to individuals (Tyler, Boeckmann, Smith, & Huo, 1997).

Undeserving Victim.   Distributive, procedural, and interactive justice are all potentially violated when the offended party, including oneself, did nothing to deserve harm (Feather 1999). Justice, however, is maintained and less sympathy given to people who, as offended parties, are seen as somehow responsible for their negative outcomes (Lerner, 1980; Weiner, 1993).

The true story presented at the beginning of this chapter highlights all three forms of (in)justice which, when taken together, may make the expressed forgiveness by the homeless victim toward the girls whose story placed him in prison for 8 months somewhat remarkable. The girls' offense was clearly intentional and deliberate. The story they concocted and the extreme measures they went to, simply so that one of the girls might avoid being punished for coming home 20 minutes late, clearly could add (despite their age) to an assessment of greater responsibility, to more blame, to harsher punishments (the DA's suggestion that they serve 1 day longer in jail than the innocent victim), and to less forgiveness. The severity of the offense drew considerable attention to their actions (daily newspaper accounts in a county of almost 3 million people), especially when they jointly pointed to one helpless individual who perhaps, as a homeless individual, became for the girls a depersonalized model without identity and, therefore, beyond the "scope" of justice (Clayton & Opotow, 2003). Indeed, as Clayton and Opotow point out, both personal and group identities evoke assessments of value, status, and power, which in turn influence justice judgments and when, why, and how justice matters. The procedural injustice by law enforcement authorities that the victim suffered by (a) allowing the girls collectively rather than independently to identify him as the supposed perpetrator and (b) not seeking verifying information (e.g., other witness accounts) could very well have been different had the individual been a respected leader or even a common tax-paying homeowner in the community. Indeed, the newspaper accounts made little or no mention of these procedural injustices beyond the victim's sole comment that, from his view, the police were to blame for not having done their job right ("Three preteens get up to...", 2004). Yet the victim was willing to forgive the girls.

Responding to Perceived Injustice: Retribution and Restoration

If one experiences an injustice, how can that sense of justice be restored? The criminal judicial system has established formal means that focus either on punishing the wrongdoer (retributive justice) or on compensation to the victim and/or restoration of the offender to a status of productive member of the community (restorative justice; see chapter 30 by Armour & Umbreit). We will consider some social psychological dynamics that underlie these two orientations, again particularly as they apply to civil and organizational relationships.

Motives for Retribution.   The desire for punishment, or what Darley and Pittman (2003) call the "impulse to punish" (p. 326), is a core part of retributive justice reasoning (Darley & Pittman, 2003; Miller, 2000). The *deterrence* view, the predominant contemporary retribution perspective, justifies the use of punishment presumably because it deters people from breaking the law, thereby maximizing the general social good (see LaFave, 2000). Thus, suitable punishment "in proportion to the moral gravity of the offense committed" (Darley & Pittman, 2003, p. 326) has become standard fare in justice reasoning and is perhaps one reason why retaliation that allows one to get even in the amount of punishment received, as pointed out earlier, is often morally justified (Tripp & Bies, 1997) and even aesthetically pleasing (Tripp, Bies, & Aquino, 2002). Such retributive desires can reflect (a) self-interested or *material* aims, as when offended parties retaliate to regain power (perhaps based on a sense of violated distributive justice), (b) *relational* aims, such as feeling protective anger when loved ones are harmed (Exline, 2002), (c) *esteem-related* aims in which people who feel demeaned seek to bolster their self-esteem (Miller, 2000; Worthington, 2001), or (d) *deontic* aims (Folger, 2001; Turillo, Folger, Lavelle, Umphress, & Gee, 2002) that emphasize a moral commitment to ethical standards of fairness. Whether the motive for retribution is driven by self-interest, as in the first three aims, or, as in the last aim, driven by a principle beyond self-interest (even to the point of self-sacrifice, see Turillo et al., 2002), people often see punishment as an effective way to maintain social order, safety, and equity in the wake of an offense.

Thus, the idea that an individual "should get what he or she deserves" is not necessarily bad, provided that it is grounded in some morality-based principle, such as the correction of harmful behavior on the part of the wrongdoer or the restoration of the victim's status (Tripp & Bies, 1997; Tripp et al., 2002). Under such circumstances, however, retributive reasoning gives way to a second means of reestablishing a sense of justice: restorative justice. A revenge orientation, in and of itself, may find that its only benefit is some sense that the injustice gap has been reduced.

Motives for Restoration.   Whereas retributive justice focuses on reestablishing justice through punishment for the offender, restorative justice focuses on preserving the rights and dignity of both victims and offenders, a philosophy that has had considerable reforming influence on the justice system, both in the United States and elsewhere (see chapter 30 by Armour & Umbreit; Bazemore, 1998; Umbreit, 2001). Proponents of restorative justice argue that it is a process offering hope to three co-participants: the victim, the offender, and the community. Bazemore (1998) points out that restorative justice processes (e.g., providing opportunities for offenders and victims to meet together in carefully supervised settings; providing opportunities for correspondence via letter writing, video, or phone conversation; providing opportunities for the offender to provide services to the victim or others) offers (a) victims greater opportunity to be heard and greater hope for restitution, (b) offenders the opportunity to express remorse and other expressions of accountability directly to victims and communities (e.g., restitution through community service), and (c) the community more accessible justice processes and potentially greater crime prevention and control but also greater accountability and obligation for involvement. Defenders of the restorative justice view (e.g., Brunk, 2001) argue that restoration is a sufficient deterrent to potential offenders because the long-term effects of integrating offenders back into a constructive relationship with the community are far greater and more positive than are the psychological and moral debilitation resulting from the penal system.

Motivations to restore fairness after a perceived injustice can be viewed as part of procedural and interactive justice, described earlier. For the victim, justice may be restored simply through "voice," or the opportunity to be heard (Folger, 1977). Restoring justice may also create a greater sense of distributive justice, especially if the restoration process involves some form of restitution to the victim or community. The extent to which the interaction (either direct or indirect) between perpetrator and victim is done with respect and dignity may help establish a greater sense of interactional justice.

Implications for Forgiveness

Of the many conceptual models of forgiveness, we find Worthington's (2001, 2003; Worthington & Wade, 1999) model, because of its strong focus on *unforgiveness*, particularly relevant to considerations of the violation of justice in the workplace and society. Worthington proposes that forgiveness is best conceptualized as an emotional replacement of negative unforgiving emotions (e.g., anger, bitterness) with positive pro-relational emotions, such as empathy and compassion. However, this does not imply that unforgiving emotions necessarily impede the development of forgiveness; in fact, to the extent that unforgiving emotions help reduce or close the injustice gap, an individual may find it easier under some circumstances to replace such emotions with empathy and compassion that may lead to forgiveness.

On the other hand, purely from a justice perspective, one could argue that forgiveness becomes irrelevant if justice needs are adequately met by other means. If one's only motive is to reduce the injustice gap by "getting even," for example, then retaliation is all that is necessary. Still, however, the desire to reestablish justice, whether through retributive or restorative means, has important implications for forgiveness. In fact, a psychophysiological study by Witvliet and her colleagues (Witvliet, Root, Sato, & Ludwig, 2003) found that unforgiving emotions and motivations decreased, whereas positive emotions, empathy, and forgiveness increased when going from no justice to punitive justice to restorative justice conditions (also see chapter 18 by Witvliet).

Listed below are some factors that might influence the forgiveness decision.

Retributive Motives. A key factor in forgiveness is the extent to which retributive motives in the victim reflect cold emotions of revenge or retaliation driven by self-interest, or reflect a genuine societal concern for the welfare of others and/or commitment to an ethical standard of fairness (Worthington, 2001, 2003). To be sure, it is far too simplistic and inaccurate to equate the desire for retribution with unforgiveness, because a retribution motive can not only potentially lower the injustice gap and therefore reduce negative emotions (Worthington, 2003) but also reflect concerns beyond the self.

Punishment motives affect how both a victim and offender react to an offense. For the victim, the motive will frequently lead to a desire for punishment for the sake of fairness, whereas for the offender, the motive will often involve avoiding punishment. In both cases, there may be a justice motive at work because victims and offenders frequently see and remember the offense in different terms (Stillwell & Baumeister, 1997). For the victim, unforgiveness driven by a desire for retribution may be influenced by such factors as the offender's blameworthiness (Bradfield & Aquino, 1999) and the offender's level of unrepentance (Schwartz, Kane, Joseph, & Tedeschi, 1978). For the offender, the unwillingness to seek forgiveness may be influenced by whether the offense was perceived as justified in the first place.

Restorative Motives.   A poignant example of the power of a restorative motive to forgiveness is provided by Gobodo-Madikizela (2002), a former member of the Truth and
Reconciliation Commission in South Africa. She reports a face-to-face meeting between two women, Pearl and Doreen, with Eugene de Kock, the head of the apartheid
government's covert operations and commander of an army of death squads. de Kock
begged for forgiveness, and the following quotation was an explanation provided by
one of the women, Pearl, on why she forgave de Kock.

> I was profoundly touched by him, especially when he said he wished he could bring
> our husbands back.... I felt the genuineness in his apology. I couldn't control my
> tears.... I was just nodding, as a way of saying yes, I forgive you. I hope that when he
> sees our tears, he knows that they are not only tears for our husbands, but tears for
> him as well.... I would like to hold him by the hand, and show him that there is a
> future, and that he can still change. (p. 17)

Many factors are at work where both justice may be restored and forgiveness facilitated. For example, forms of procedural justice, such as the simple opportunity
(under proper circumstances) to interact with the offender, may be enough to satisfy
the victim's yearning for justice. As Bazemore (1998) points out, having a say in what
will happen to the offender, having the choice to express forgiveness, or even having
the knowledge that just seeing the victim and perhaps the victim's suffering might
create a greater sense of remorse in the offender may help reestablish a sense of equity.
Likewise, for the offender, the opportunity to express remorse, either verbally or behaviorally (e.g., engaging in community service) may create a greater sense of justice.

Perhaps nothing is more central to a sense of restorative justice than a direct and
forthright apology. Suggesting that empathy may be "the central facilitative condition
that leads to forgiving" (p. 322), McCullough, Worthington, and Rachal (1997) found
that when an offending party apologizes for offensive behavior, the apology results in
increased empathy in the offended party, which may in turn facilitate a willingness to
forgive. Interaction between the offender and the victim may promote greater empathy
in both parties, thereby perhaps reducing motivation for retribution and increasing motivation for restoration, as communicated in the earlier quotation by Pearl's forgiveness
of Eugene de Kock. Also, greater empathy may evoke a greater sense of genuine remorse
in the offender, once the damage to the victim is further realized. Expressions of apology that clearly communicate a sincere remorse, though perhaps difficult to discern, are
more likely to lead to forgiveness (McCullough et al., 1997, 1998).

In the case presented at the beginning of this chapter of the young girls who
wrongly implicated a homeless man for a crime he did not do, restorative justice procedures along the lines described here were not employed. In fact, one girl desired the
opportunity to express her remorse directly to the victim. It is very possible that the
experiences of forgiving and being forgiven would have been even further enhanced
with more opportunity for the perpetrators and victim to interact.

NEW RESEARCH DIRECTIONS

Our brief analysis suggests many crucial avenues for future research linking concerns for justice to forgiveness. One such avenue is to explore further on what basis people think that justice or injustice has been served. That is, despite repeated demonstrations of the importance of fairness in human relationships, little research has examined what comprises fairness judgments—taking into account that people are subject to bias with regard to considerations of justice, such as differential notions of what constitutes justice and differential perceptions of the offense (e.g., the recent Kobe Bryant case) that may have important implications for what constitutes a just resolution (Baumeister, 1997). We encourage further research such as that reported by Blader and Tyler (2003) that begin to analyze a combination of specific criteria used by people to evaluate, in their research, judgments of procedural fairness: two aspects of group formal procedures (those that relate to decision making and those that relate to quality of treatment) and two aspects of group authorities (quality of decision making by such authorities and the quality of treatment from those authorities). Further understanding of such criteria may help us disentangle the conditions under which the fulfillment of justice concerns promote (or fail to promote) forgiveness.

Similarly, victims often feel entitled to a sincere apology, and people are more likely to forgive when they judge apologies to be genuine (McCullough et al., 1997, 1998). Are people good at judging the authenticity of an apology? Though research has examined offender accounts, it remains unclear on what basis (and how accurate) are judgments of the genuineness of an apology. We further note that it may be hard for people to evaluate, even within themselves, the extent to which concerns for justice as a morality-based principle are involved in strongly felt negative emotions that may motivate revenge; yet little research to date has been conducted on how people make such judgments.

Another important avenue to consider for future research is a differential understanding of justice as influenced by cultural processes (also see chapter 4 by Sandage & Williamson). For example, perceptions of justice and its violation in a collectivist society may involve considerations beyond the self, even when it appears that an offense has been committed against one person alone (Sandage, Hill, & Vang, 2003).

Differences may also exist between religious groups. For example, in Christianity, forgiveness is a supreme value, even to the point of discounting considerations of justice (Marty, 1998), whereas in Judaism, forgiveness is predicated more on concerns of justice (Cohen, Hall, Koenig, & Meador, 2005; Dorff, 1998). Thus, for example, the Christian may think it right to forgive whether the offender has apologized; the Jew may (and perhaps should) withhold forgiveness until the offender has engaged in a process of repentance, or *tshuvah*.

RELEVANCE FOR CLINICAL AND APPLIED INTERVENTIONS

When considering the utility of forgiveness in justice-oriented settings, it is crucial to remember that people vary widely in their ideas about what forgiveness means and how it relates to justice (Exline et al., 2003). Some believe that forgiveness, by its very nature, opposes justice or negates the need to restore justice. Although forgiveness researchers are unlikely to share these views, the views are nonetheless common within the broader public. As such, we urge the use of caution and clarity when addressing forgiveness-related issues in justice contexts. For example, it may be unwise to use the term *forgiveness* unless there is ample opportunity to define the term—that is, to clarify that forgiveness does not imply condoning, excusing, forgetting, trusting, or reconciling. Despite this difficulty with terminology, it may still be useful to discuss anger-related issues with offended parties. In what ways is their anger helping and/or hurting them? What strategies might be helpful in reducing their anger?

We also propose that, where possible, apologies should be encouraged when perpetrators seem to be experiencing genuine (which, again, is often difficult to discern) remorse. Apologies are robust predictors of forgiveness, as reviewed earlier. Apologies also serve the important moral function of acknowledging the social norm that has been broken (Tavuchis, 1991), which is a key factor in restoring a perpetrator to the community. Granted, there are cases in which an apology can in no way repay the debt, and it may even be helpful to acknowledge this shortcoming as part of an apology. Despite its limitations, we contend that the careful and compassionate use of apology can be a key factor in restoring a sense of justice.

PERSONAL THEORETICAL PERSPECTIVES ON THE FIELD

For decades, researchers who study relationships in the workplace and in civilian life have focused extensively on justice and have conceptualized many different types of justice concerns. We agree with the underlying assumption that the establishment of justice is, in many circumstances, a healthy and moral response; that is, not only are concerns about justice often a noble reaction to an offense but efforts to reduce injustice can provide potential benefits to all parties involved and, to the extent that a healthy concern for justice becomes normative, to society as a whole. Justice researchers, however, have been slow in extending their research to forgiveness (Aquino et al., 2003, Aquino et al., 2001), perhaps implying that rectifying injustice should itself be the ultimate goal in restoring damaged relationships. Thus, for example, though forgiveness is an implicit concept in much of the restorative justice process (Zehr, 1990), the focus has been primarily on restoring justice rather than promoting forgiveness (Worthington, 2000). In fact, *forgiveness* has become an unpopular term among many writers in the crime victims' movement because it might be seen by some victims or communities as exculpating offenders, forgetting or trivializing the offense, or victims might feel coerced to forgive implicitly (if not explicitly), suggesting that the ability to forgive is somehow related to greater worthiness for social concern (for a review, see chapter 30 by Armour & Umbreit). In this sense, it is argued, the victims are further victimized, thereby increasing the injustice gap.

Although certainly these concerns are legitimate, it may also be true that the potential benefits of a restored justice include not just the reestablished sense of equity. Rather, restored justice may also be the means by which other healthy interpersonal and intrapersonal responses are facilitated. We have argued that one such response—through the victims' ability to overcome negative feelings associated with injustice—is forgiveness. Thus, by replacing negative feelings of unforgiveness in some form other than one of external coercion, the victim is not further victimized but rather may be empowered to place the victimization experience behind him or her and thereby move on in life with a greater sense of hope, meaning, and perhaps restored dignity. In this sense, fulfilling a justice concern may facilitate forgiveness.

CONCLUSION

Justice is, within the individual, both perceived and multifaceted. When a sense of justice is violated, whether in the workplace, in civil relationships, or in other types of relationships, forgiveness is but one of an interdependent myriad of possible responses. Further investigating the combination of individual, interactional, and contextual variables in considerations of justice that may facilitate forgiveness is a potentially fruitful research endeavor.

REFERENCES

Adams, J. S. (1965). Inequity in social exchange. In L. Berkowitz (Ed.), *Advances in experimental social psychology* (Vol. 2, pp. 267–299). New York: Academic Press.

Alexander, S., & Ruderman, A. (1987). The role of procedural and distributive justice in organizational behavior. *Social Justice Research, 1,* 177–198.

Aquino, K., Grover, S. L., Goldman, B., & Folger, R. (2003). When push doesn't come to shove: Interpersonal forgiveness in workplace relationships. *Journal of Management Inquiry, 12,* 209–216.

Aquino, K., Tripp, T. M., & Bies, R. J. (2001). How employees respond to personal offense: The effects of blame attribution, victim status, and offender status on revenge and reconciliation in the workplace. *Journal of Applied Psychology, 86,* 52–59.

Bazemore, G. (1998). Restorative justice and earned redemption: Communities, victims, and offender reintegration. *American Behavioral Scientist, 41,* 768–813.

Baumeister, R. F. (1997). *Evil: Inside human violence and cruelty.* New York: Freeman.

Bies, R. J. (1987). The predicament of injustice: The management of moral outrage. In L. L. Cummings & B. M. Staw (Eds.), *Research in organizational behavior* (Vol. 9, pp. 289–319). Greenwich, CT: JAI Press.

Bies, R. J., & Moag, J. S. (1986). Interactional justice: Communication criteria of fairness. In R. J. Lewicki, B. H. Sheppard, & M. H. Bazerman (Eds.), *Research in negotiation in organizations* (Vol. 1, pp. 43–55). Greenwich, CT: JAI Press.

Bies, R. J., & Tripp, T. M. (1996). Beyond distrust: "Getting even" and the need for revenge. In R. M. Kramer & T. R. Tyler (Eds.), *Trust in organizations* (pp. 246–260). Newbury Park, CA: Sage.

Bies, R. J., & Tripp, T. M. (1998). The many faces of revenge: The good, the bad, and the ugly. In R. W. Griffin, A. O'Leary-Kelly, & J. Collins (Eds.), *Dysfunctional behavior in organizations: Vol. 1. Part B. Violent behaviors in organizations* (pp. 49–67). Greenwich, CT: JAI Press.

Blader, S. L., & Tyler, T. R. (2003). A four-component model of procedural justice: Defining the meaning of a "fair" process. *Personality and Social Psychology Bulletin, 29*, 747–758.

Boon, S. D., & Sulsky, L. M. (1997). Attributions of blame and forgiveness in romantic relationships: A policy-capturing study. *Journal of Social Behavior and Personality, 12*, 19–44.

Bradfield, M. O., & Aquino, K. (1999). The effects of blame attributions and offender likableness on revenge and forgiveness in the workplace. *Journal of Management, 25*, 607–631.

Brunk, C. G. (2001). Restorative justice and the philosophical theories of criminal punishment. In M. L. Hadley (Ed.), *The spiritual roots of restorative justice* (pp. 31–56). Albany, NY: SUNY Press.

Clayton, S., & Opotow, S. (2003). Justice and identity: Changing perspectives on what is fair. *Personality and Social Psychology Review, 7*, 298–310.

Cohen, A. B., Hall, D. E., Koenig, H. G., & Meador, K. (2005). Social versus individual motivation: Implications for normative definitions of religious orientation. *Personality and Social Psychology Review, 9*, 48–61.

Darley, J. M., & Huff, C. W. (1990). Heightened damage assessment as a result of the intentionality of the damage-causing act. *British Journal of Social Psychology, 29*, 181–188.

Darley, J. M., & Pittman, T. S. (2003). The psychology of compensatory and retributive justice. *Personality and Social Psychology Review, 7*, 324–336.

Dorff, E. N. (1998). The elements of forgiveness: A Jewish approach. In E. L. Worthington, Jr. (Ed.), *Dimensions of forgiveness: Psychological research and theological perspectives* (pp. 29–55). Philadelphia: Templeton Foundation Press.

Exline, J. J. (2002). *When loved ones suffer harm: Protectiveness, loyalty, and other's forgiveness as predictors of one's own anger.* Poster session presented at a meeting of the Society for Personality and Social Psychology, Savannah, GA.

Exline, J. J., Worthington, E. L., Jr., Hill, P. C., & McCullough, M. E. (2003). Forgiveness and justice: A research agenda for social and personality psychology. *Personality and Social Psychology Review, 7*, 337–348.

Feather, N. T. (1999). Judgments of deservingness: Studies in the psychology of justice and achievement. *Personality and Social Psychology Review, 3*, 86–107.

Folger, R. (1977). Distributive and procedural justice: Combined impact of "voice" and improvement on experienced inequity. *Journal of Personality and Social Psychology, 35*, 108–119.

Folger, R. (2001). Fairness as deonance. In M. Schminke (Ed.), *Managerial ethics: Morally managing people and processes* (pp. 13–34). Mahwah, NJ: Lawrence Erlbaum.

Folger, R., & Baron, R. A. (1996). Violence and hostility at work: A model of reactions to perceived injustice. In G. R. Vandenbos & E. Q. Bulato (Eds.), *Workplace violence* (pp. 51–85). Washington, DC: American Psychological Association.

Folger, R., & Cropanzano, R. (1998). *Organization justice and human resource management.* Thousand Oaks, CA: Sage.

Folger, R., & Starlicki, D. P. (1998). A popcorn metaphor for employee aggression. In R. W. Griffin, A. O'Leary-Kelly, & J. Collins (Eds.), *Dysfunctional behavior in organizations: Vol. 1. Violent behaviors in organizations* (pp. 43–81). Greenwich, CT: JAI Press.

Gabriel, Y. (1998). An introduction to the social psychology of insults in organizations. *Human Relations, 51,* 1329–1354.

Girls express remorse over accusations (2004). *The Orange County Register*, March 5, p. 5.

Gobodo-Madikizela, P. (2002). Remorse, forgiveness, and rehumanization: Stories from South Africa. *Journal of Humanistic Psychology, 42,* 7–32.

Gordon, K. C., Baucom, D. H., & Snyder, D. K. (2000). The use of forgiveness in marital therapy. In M. E. McCullough, K. I. Pargament, & C. E. Thoresen (Eds.), *Forgiveness: Theory, research, and practice* (pp. 203–227). New York: Guilford Press.

Greenberg, J. (1990). Employee theft as a reaction to underpayment inequity: The hidden cost of pay cuts. *Journal of Applied Psychology, 75,* 561–568.

Greenberg, J. (1993). The social side of fairness: Interpersonal and informational classes of organizational justice. In R. Cropanzano (Ed.), *Justice in the workplace: Approaching fairness in human resource management* (pp. 79–103). Hillsdale, NJ: Lawrence Erlbaum.

Greenberg, J., & Folger, R. (1983). Procedural justice, participation, and the fair process effect in groups and organizations. In P. B. Paulus (Ed.), *Basic group processes* (pp. 235–256). New York: Springer-Verlag.

LaFave, W. (2000). *Criminal law* (3rd. ed.). St Paul, MN: West Publishers.

Lerner, M. J. (1980). *The belief in a just world.* New York: Plenum.

Lind, E. A., Kanfer, R., & Earley, P. C. (1990). Voice, control, and procedural justice: Instrumental and noninstrumental concerns in fairness judgments. *Journal of Personality and Social Psychology, 59,* 952–959.

Marty, M. E. (1998). The ethos of Christian forgiveness. In E. L. Worthington, Jr. (Ed.), *Dimensions of forgiveness: Psychological research and theological perspectives* (pp. 9–28). Philadelphia: Templeton Foundation Press.

McCullough, M. E., Rachal, K. C., Sandage, S. J., Worthington, E. L., Jr., Brown, S. W., & Hight, T. L. (1998). Interpersonal forgiving in close relationships. II: Theoretical elaboration and measurement. *Journal of Personality and Social Psychology, 75,* 1586–1603.

McCullough, M. E., Worthington, E. L., Jr., & Rachal, K. C. (1997). Interpersonal forgiving in close relationships. *Journal of Personality and Social Psychology, 73,* 321–336.

Miller, D. T. (2000). Disrespect and the experience of injustice. *Annual Review of Psychology, 52,* 527–553.

Sandage, S. J., Hill, P. C., & Vang, H. C. (2003). Toward a multicultural positive psychology: Indigenous forgiveness and Hmong culture. *Counseling Psychologist, 31,* 564–592.

Schwartz, G. S., Kane, T. R., Joseph, J. M., & Tedeschi, J. T. (1978). The effects of post-transgression remorse on perceived aggression, attributions of intent, and level of punishment. *British Journal of Social and Clinical Psychology, 17,* 293–297.

Shaver, K. G. (1985). *The attribution of blame.* New York: Springer-Verlag.

Stillwell, A. M., & Baumeister, R. F. (1997). The construction of victim and perpetrator memories: Accuracy and distortion in role-based accounts. *Personality and Social Psychology Bulletin, 23,* 1157–1172.

Tavuchis, N. (1991). *Mea culpa: A sociology of apology and reconciliation.* Stanford, CA: Stanford University Press.

Thibaut, J., & Walker, L. (1975). *Procedural justice: A psychological analysis.* Hillsdale, NJ: Lawrence Erlbaum.

Thompson, L., & Lowenstein, G. (1992). Egocentric interpretations of fairness and interpersonal conflict. *Organizational Behavior and Human Decision Processes, 51,* 176–197.

Three preteens get up to 45 days (2004). *The Orange County Register,* March 5, p. 1.

Tripp, T. M., & Bies, R. J. (1997). What's good about revenge: The avenger's perspective. In R. J. Lewicki, R. J. Bies, & B. H. Sheppard (Eds.), *Research on negotiation in organizations* (Vol. 6, pp. 145–160). Greenwich, CT: JAI Press.

Tripp, T. M., Bies, R. J., & Aquino, K. (2002). Poetic justice or petty jealousy? The aesthetics of revenge. *Organizational Behavior and Human Decision Processes, 89,* 966–984.

Turillo, C. J., Folger, R., Lavelle, J. J., Umphress, E., & Gee, J. (2002). Is virtue its own reward? Self-sacrificial decisions for the sake of fairness. *Organizational Behavior and Human Decision Processes, 89,* 839–865.

Tyler, T. R., Boeckmann, R. J., Smith, H. J., & Huo, Y. J. (1997). *Social justice in a diverse society.* Boulder, CO: Westview.

Tyler, T. R., & Smith, H. J. (1998). Social justice and social movements. In D. T. Gilbert & S. T. Fiske (Eds.), *The handbook of social psychology,* (Vol. 2, 4th ed., pp. 595–629). Oxford: Oxford University Press.

Umbreit, M. S. (2001). *The handbook of victim offender mediation.* San Francisco: Jossey-Bass.

Volf, M. (2001). Forgiveness, reconciliation, and justice: A Christian contribution to a more peaceful social environment. In R. G. Helmick & R. L. Petersen (Eds.), *Forgiveness and reconciliation: Religion, public policy, and conflict transformation* (pp. 27–49). Philadelphia: Templeton Foundation Press.

Walster, E. (1966). Assignment of responsibility for an accident. *Journal of Personality and Social Psychology, 3,* 73–79.

Weiner, B. (1993). On sin versus sickness: A theory of perceived responsibility and social motivation. *American Psychologist, 48,* 957–965.

Witvliet, C. V. O., Root, L., Sato, A., & Ludwig, T. E. (2003). Justice and forgiveness: Psychophysiological effects for victims. *Psychophysiology, Supplement 40,* 87.

Worthington, E. L., Jr. (2000). Is there a place for forgiveness in the justice system? *Fordham Urban Law Journal, 27,* 1721–1734.

Worthington, E. L., Jr. (2001). Unforgiveness, forgiveness, and reconciliation in societies. In R. G. Helmick & R. L. Petersen (Eds.), *Forgiveness and reconciliation: Religion, public policy, and conflict transformation* (pp. 161–182). Philadelphia: Templeton Foundation Press.

Worthington, E. L., Jr. (2003). *Forgiving and reconciling: Bridges to wholeness and hope.* Downers Grove, IL: InterVarsity Press.

Worthington, E. L., Jr., & Wade, N. G. (1999). The social psychology of unforgiveness and forgiveness and implications for clinical practice. *Journal of Social and Clinical Psychology, 18,* 385–418.

Zehr, H. (1990). *Changing lenses: A new focus for crime and justice.* Scottsdale, PA: Herald Press.

Chapter Thirty

The Paradox of Forgiveness in Restorative Justice

Marilyn Peterson Armour
Mark S. Umbreit

estorative justice has emerged internationally as a viable response to the harm caused by crime. As an alternative to systems that focus nearly exclusively on retributive justice, it seeks to elevate the role of crime victims and community members, hold offenders directly accountable to the people they have violated, and restore the emotional and material losses of victims. It provides a range of opportunities for dialogue, negotiation, and problem solving that can lead to a greater sense of community safety, conflict resolution, and healing for all involved (Umbreit, 2001). Most restorative justice practitioners use a humanistic approach to mediation that is dialogue- rather than settlement-driven.

PERSONAL ASSUMPTIONS ABOUT FORGIVENESS AND RESTORATIVE JUSTICE

The growing clinical and scholarly interest in the healing potential of forgiveness (e.g., Enright & North, 1998; Witvliet, Ludwig, & Vander Laan, 2001; Worthington & Wade, 1999) has pulled restorative justice into the limelight because of its ability to achieve emotional repair for the victim through processes that reduce vengefulness or increase empathy, factors that influence a forgiveness response (Strang & Sherman, 2003). In light of the parallels, it would be tempting to align restorative justice with forgiveness and draw the erroneous conclusion that restorative justice explicitly promotes forgiveness. It is time for restorative justice proponents to clarify the question of forgiveness and provide guidance to prevent the reductionism that might otherwise simplify and distort the use of forgiveness. The purpose of this chapter, therefore, is to delineate the dimensions of forgiveness in restorative justice dialogue, review empirical and theoretical data that address forgiveness or forgiveness-related constructs in restorative justice programs, and offer suggestions for clinical applications and future research.

Description of Prevalent Restorative Justice Dialogue Programs

Three empirically grounded programs use restorative justice dialogue as a mechanism to address harm and foster accountability in more than 2000 communities throughout the United States and abroad. The programs are distinguished on the basis of who participates, the nature of the crime, and when the mediated dialogue occurs.

Victim Offender Mediation (VOM) programs, sometimes referred to as Victim Offender Reconciliation Programs (VORP), are the most widely used and empirically substantiated form of restorative justice dialogue. More than 1,400 programs operate in 17 countries (Umbreit, 2001). VOM programs focus primarily on dialogue that is limited to the victim, juvenile or adult offender, and his or her immediate family members. Family Group Conferencing (FGC) involves the victim and the offender and the family, friends, and key supporters of both in deciding the resolution of a criminal or delinquent act. Most VOM and FGC programs work with property crimes and minor assaults. Victim Offender Mediated Dialogue (VOMD) in severely violent cases is an emerging, post-sentence, victim-driven initiative that occurs between the offender and victim. These dialogues work with the victim and offender, and often include support people, in cases of murder, rape, and aggravated assault. It requires more intense case development, preparation, and extensive mediator training before bringing people together to address the horrific violence and suffering that accompany these crimes.

Role of Forgiveness in Restorative Justice Dialogue

Restorative justice dialogue fosters the possibility for forgiveness—but only if the victim voluntarily chooses that path (Gehm, 1992; Peachey, 1992). In this regard, forgiveness can release the victim from the negative power of the crime (Zehr, 1995), raise the offender back to the status of a human being (Van Biema, 1999), facilitate the offender's reintegration into the community (Cragg, 1992), restore the victim's peace of mind (Van Strokkom, 2002), and potentially contribute to the victim's mental (e.g., Coyle & Enright, 1997; Freedman & Enright, 1996) and physical health (e.g. Witvliet et al., 2001). Forgiveness has remained resolutely embedded in the restorative justice process while out of sight of examination. We believe that explicating the current and implicit dimensions of forgiveness may increase understanding of its unique role in restorative justice dialogue and hopefully corral how outsiders view it. Because restorative justice is systemic in its focus, the concept of forgiveness can have one or more of the following dimensions:

1. From the victim's perspective, forgiveness refers to a conscious decision to free himself or herself of the negative power that the offense and the offender have over a person while not condoning or excusing the actor (Zehr, 1995). Letting go of the negative power usually refers to disconnecting from the trauma or releasing bitterness and vengeance. This reduction in negative motivations neither precludes nor includes positive feelings toward the offender.

2. From the offender's perspective, the experience of being forgiven is associated with feeling accepted by representatives of the community (e.g. victim, mediator, neighborhood residents) who participate in a restorative justice conference. The feeling of having been reinstated in the community as a moral citizen (Van Biema, 1999) occurs as the outgrowth of offender engagement in a process of accountability, remorse, and reparation.

3. From the victim's perspective, forgiveness involves a transformed sense of meaning about a transgression or crime (Armour, 2003). Restorative justice dialogue has no absolute standard for assessing whether forgiveness has occurred or is even feasible. Rather, the crucial dimension of forgiving is that a participant experiences a shift in understanding of and relationship to the other person, oneself, and the world.

4. Mediators maintain neutrality about forgiveness as an outcome. The potential for victim exploitation in restorative justice dialogues exists. Forgiveness must, thus, be approached from a position of mediator disinterest in order to protect the integrity of the dialogue and the victim's safety. The institutional practice of promoting offender apologies as a way to reduce recidivism does not recognize, for example, its potential to place victims in an obligatory position to grant forgiveness. Likewise, crime victims are sometimes severely revictimized by religious prescriptions for unconditional forgiveness. The internalization of these prescriptions may compromise the ability of victims to exercise free choice in their decision making. Umbreit and colleagues (Umbriet, Vos, Coates, & Brown, 2003) maintain that restorative justice dialogue must be anchored in creating a safe place that maximizes the opportunity of the involved parties to enter into a direct dialogue about the impact of the crime on their lives and their community. Mediators, therefore, need to guard the victim's emotional safety and the opportunity for authentic dialogue by remaining personally de-invested in the outcome, other than to support a process of healing that may include a change in attitude toward the offender, as is inherent in the concept of forgiveness.

5. Forgiveness is implicit. Some critics have argued that for many individual victims, terms such as *forgiveness* and *reconciliation* are interpreted as devaluing their criminal victimization or as judging their legitimate anger and rage as inappropriate (Murphy, 2000). Therein lies the paradox. On one hand, forgiveness and reconciliation represent a powerful potential outcome of the process of mediator-assisted dialogue and mutual aid between crime victims and offenders. On the other hand, the more one talks about these concepts, the more likely they will be heard as behavioral prescriptions, and the less likely victims will participate and have the opportunity to experience elements of forgiveness and reconciliation (Umbreit, 1995). Because the word *forgiveness* is a lightning rod for many crime victims and their advocates, the power of forgiveness in restorative justice may be tied to keeping it an implicit part of the process, rather than making it explicit (Hill, 2001). Indeed, forgiveness may occur as a by-product that is communicated nonverbally through a shift in attitude (e.g., letting go of anger) or behavior (e.g., no longer fighting against the offender's parole).

6. Forgiveness within restorative justice may involve a bilateral process. Restorative-justice dialogue is based on the premise that victim and offender are together, in part, because each has the power by virtue of his or her physical presence and behavior potentially to help heal the other. For many victims and offenders, forgiving and feeling forgiven in the context of restorative justice dialogue may be inseparable from the dyadic relationship. In unilateral forgiveness, victims work independently of those who have offended them. In the bilateral process surrounding forgiveness, victims work through the stages with the offender, dealing with issues of acknowledgment of wrongdoing, acceptance of responsibility, apology, offers of restoration, requests for forgiveness, and (perhaps) the granting of forgiveness (Dickey, 1998; Kittle, 1999). In this regard, bilateral processes surrounding forgiveness involve numerous elements and steps, rather than a one-time, all-or-nothing event.

Forgiveness in restorative justice is multifaceted and conditioned by a protective reactivity against the imposition of religious doctrine or social expectation. For the offender, forgiveness generally refers to offender reinstatement in the community. For the victim, forgiveness refers to transformed meaning that reduces unforgiveness in the victim. Forgiveness, in the context of restorative justice, is often a derivative of a bilateral process that requires victim and offender to be emotionally available to each other. The emergence of authentic forgiveness is protected by the mediator's de-investment in a particular outcome and awareness that forgiveness is an implicit rather than explicit part of the process. Notwithstanding the forgoing comments, restorative justice advocates also recognize and accept that many victims choose to forgive because granting forgiveness is congruent with their personal or religious beliefs.

THEORETICAL AND EMPIRICAL LITERATURE ON FORGIVENESS

Applied studies of forgiveness in restorative justice dialogues are thin. Outcome studies have focused on participant satisfaction (Umbreit, Coates, & Vos, 2002) or offender recidivism (e.g., Nugent, Umbreit, Wiinamaki, & Paddock, 2001) rather than forgiveness as indicators of change. Little is empirically known, therefore, about whether restorative justice dialogue realizes its full potential (Strang, 2002). Theoretical formulations as well as findings from clinical and experimental studies, however, have repeatedly shown relationships between forgiveness-related constructs (i.e., apology and offender remorse, and empathy and victim forgiveness; McCullough, Worthington, & Rachal, 1997; McCullough et al., 1998) and forgiveness and justice (Exline & Baumeister, 2000).

Forgiveness in Minor and Major Crimes

Outcome studies that specifically address forgiveness and changes in victim attitudes toward offenders have been conducted on family group conferencing in Australia

(Strang, 2002) and VOMD in Ohio and Texas (Umbreit et al., 2003). Reviews of victim satisfaction in VOM programs in North America and Europe also provide some data on forgiveness-related constructs (Umbreit, 2001; Umbreit, Coates, & Vos, 2002).

Family Group Conferencing. A study known as the Reintegrative Shaming Experiments (RISE) project in Canberra, Australia (Strang, 2002) analyzed victim effects after random assignment of 275 offenders to court or diversionary restorative justice conference for violent crimes ($n = 100$) and property crimes ($n = 175$). Victim-based response rate was 89% (88% for property crimes and 91% for violent crimes). Victims who attended a restorative justice conference later said that they forgave their offenders in 39% of the cases. A forgiving attitude may be indicated by the fact that 36% of all conference victims reported that wanting to help the offender was an important reason for their participation. Statistically significant differences between conference and court victims were found for anger reduction (63% vs. 29%), sympathy for the offender (48% vs. 19%), incidence of apology (72% vs. 19%), sincerity of apology (77% vs. 41%), and effect of the intervention on closure (60% vs. 20%). Conference victims also felt that meeting with the offender repaired the harm (54%), helped reduce shame and embarrassment (28%), and assisted them in feeling more settled (41%). Fewer victims reported fear after the conference (14%) than before meeting with the offender (38%).

The RISE experiment also analyzed the differential impact of crime (property vs. violent offenses) on conference victim's pre- and postconference responses. Increase in sympathy for offenders was greater for victims of property crime (22% to 58%) than for violent crime (14% to 34%). Reduction in anger was greater for victims of property crime (58% to 24%) than violent crime (67% to 36%). Reduction in anxiety was greater for victims of violent crime (58% to 42%) than for property crime (40% to 31%). Reduction in shame was greater for victims of violent crime (57% to 38%) than for property crime (28% to 17%).

Victim Offender Mediation (VOM). Reviews of victim satisfaction in over 50 studies of VOM programs in North America and Europe also provide some data on forgiveness-related constructs (Umbreit, 2001; Umbreit et al., 2002). Two multisite assessments (Coates, Burns, & Umbreit, 2002; Umbreit, Coates, & Vos, 2001), for example, showed that the top-ranking victim reason for choosing to participate was to help the offender. Moreover, offenders participate to take direct responsibility for their own actions, pay back the victim, and apologize for the harm (Umbreit, 2001). Reasons for participation suggest that both parties feel a pull to "reach" the other in some meaningful way.

In addition, victims indicate that financial or material reparations are less important to them than the opportunity to talk to the offender about the crime (Coates & Gehm, 1989; Strang, 2002; Umbreit, 1995; Umbreit & Coates, 1993). Victims who participated in VOM were 2.6 times more likely to forgive the offender (Poulson, 2000) and feel less fear (11%) than were victims in court (31%; Umbreit, 1995). They also reported more satisfaction (79%) than did victims in court (57%; Umbreit, 1994; Umbreit & Coates, 1993). Secondary analysis of satisfaction data from a U.S. study and a Canadian study found that 40% of the variance was associated with three variables: (1) The victim felt good about the mediator; (2) the victim perceived the resulting restitution agreement as fair; and (3) the victim, for whatever reason, had a strong initial desire to meet the offender (Bradshaw & Umbreit, 1998; Umbreit & Bradshaw, 1999).

A review of four studies found that offenders were 6.9 times more likely to apologize to the victim in VOM and family group conferences than in court (Poulson, 2000). That is, nearly three of four (74%) offenders in restorative justice apologized, whereas almost three of four (71%) offenders in court did not apologize. Umbreit and Coates (1992) found also that 9 of 10 offenders listed "apologizing to the victim" as one of the four most important issues in the mediation process.

Although these studies did not measure forgiveness, reviews of VOM studies show that offenders have opportunities to hear the victims' perspective, apologize, explain their actions, and offer restitution, all of which can facilitate forgiveness by victims (Gehm, 1992; Peachey, 1992).

Victim Offender Mediated Dialogue.   There is speculation that the greatest benefit from restorative justice may be found in the most serious crimes because the higher level of emotional engagement by victims and offenders is the mechanism leading to the emotions of empathy and remorse (Strang & Sherman, 2003). Although information on the results of VOMD is limited to case studies, in a program evaluation in Canada (Roberts, 1995) and in a multisite, qualitative study of pioneering efforts in two states (Umbreit et al., 2003), participant self-reports indicate exceptionally high levels of client satisfaction with the process.

Umbreit and colleagues (2003) conducted extensive post-VOMD interviews with the first 79 participants (victims and offenders) in Texas and Ohio. Among other reasons, victims participated to share forgiveness (23%) and out of concern for the offender (18%). Offenders participated to apologize (38%) and to benefit victims (95%), including helping victims heal (38%) and release anger (13%). Over half the sample spoke spontaneously of forgiveness issues during the interviews. Forgiveness was mentioned by 64% of offenders. Although forgiveness is not a stated goal of VOMD, this study suggests that forgiveness is an important consideration in the minds of victims and offenders. Self-reports indicate less victim anger and offender remorse. Some interest in greater "reconciliation" is shown by the fact that 18% of participants either wanted or were already engaged in additional contact with each other.

Conditions That Facilitate Victim Forgiveness

Restorative justice dialogue implicitly relies on the importance of emotional processes. Although forgiveness has not been widely examined, there is a wealth of theoretical and empirical knowledge about emotional dispositions that increase the possibility of forgiveness and have application to restorative-justice dialogues, namely, apology, remorse, and empathy.

Apology.   There is clear evidence that crime victims want apologies (Strang, 2002) and that apologies influence whether forgiveness occurs (Witvliet, Worthington, Wade, & Berry, 2002). Apology stimulates emotional dissonance and humility, which allows victims to recognize their own transgressions and respond on the basis of commonalities rather than differences (Kelln & Ellard, 1999; Levenson & Ruef, 1991; Takaku, 2001).

The giving and receiving of apology, however, have sparked debate about issues of power and control between victim and offender. For example, the emphasis on victim need to receive an apology allows the offender to maintain control (Kittle, 1999), and waiting for the apology as a precondition for forgiveness gives the offender too much power (Regehr & Gutheil, 2002). Umbreit (1994) also argues that victims may feel bound by social protocol to give young offenders the opportunity to make amends. In contrast, Petrucci (2002) maintains that the offender's taking of responsibility empowers the victim and contributes to the offender's positive self-attributions.

Apology making has also raised concerns about the authenticity of the offender's response. Bazemore (1999) states that the practice of having juvenile offenders write apology letters to their victims is gaining increasing acceptance. Coerced apologies that are perceived as lacking authenticity raise concerns about revictimization (Lavery & Achilles, 1999). It can also turn a potentially healing process into something mechanical and offensive. Because even weak or indirect apologies influence the willingness to forgive (Bennett & Dewberry, 1994; Girard, Mullet, & Callahan, 2002), it is important to recognize strong social norms that encourage victims to accept an apology, regardless of its strength (Petrucci, 2002).

Offender Remorse.   Although the emotional dynamics of confrontations have yet to be investigated (Van Strokkom, 2002), victim-perceived offender remorse has shown the largest overall multivariate effect on measures of victim forgiveness (Gold & Weiner, 2000). Remorse also increases the likelihood of getting more positive judgments from victims (Daly, 2001). Although speculative, victim-perceived remorse likely impacts victims' future expectations of offenders. Specifically, expression of remorse can affect perceived internalizations of a person's moral code and be experienced as proof of sincerity. Moreover, victims report reduced revenge and avoidance, less anger, less fear, and more forgiveness only after a "strong" apology (Witvliet et al., 2002). It is hypothesized that victim empathy is evoked because the remorseful offender appears as a wounded person in pain, and pain cannot be evil. (Gobodo-Madikizela, 2002; Shabad, 1988; Tavuchis, 1991). Apology also removes the victim's shame. In its place, victims may compare themselves to the offender and feel hypocritical (Exline, Worthington, Hill, & McCullough, 2003; Takaku, 2001) because they know that they too have done wrong. The cognitive dissonance is reduced by the victim's acknowledgment of shame associated with past deeds, which creates a bond between victim and offender (Scheff, 1998).

Empathy.   Empathy is the only psychological variable shown to facilitate forgiveness when induced experimentally (McCullough, 2001). Indeed, empathy completely mediates the apology-forgiveness connection (McCullough et al., 1997; McCullough et al., 1998), which suggests that the linear sequence is from apology to empathy to forgiving, rather than from apology to forgiving. Moreover, empathy-based forgiveness results in more forgiveness than does non–empathy-based forgiveness (McCullough et al., 1997). Empathy reduces the injustice gap by helping victims to see themselves as less innocent and their offenders as less evil (Exline et al, 2003; Worthington, 2003).

Conditions that affect forgiveness include offender apology, offender attributions, victim empathy, and relationship closeness (McCullough, 2001). Victim perception of offender intentionality (Zechmeister & Romero, 2002) and severity of the transgression (e.g., Bonach, 2001) also influence the willingness to forgive. Many of these relationships have been established in experimental or clinical settings but now need to be shown in applied settings, such as restorative justice dialogues. Victim participation in restorative-justice dialogues consistently shows a generalized reduction in fear and anxiety, both fear of being revictimized by the particular offender as well as more free-floating anxiety (Umbreit, 1994, 1995). Specific studies (e.g., Strang, 2002) have shown less anger, shame, and reduced suffering from the harm. The decrease in unforgiveness may result from the affective interplay between victim and offender that reduces the sense of injustice through apology making, remorse, and empathy.

NEW RESEARCH DIRECTIONS NEEDED IN THE AREA

Restorative justice populations offer a unique, real-world opportunity to examine formulations about forgiveness and forgiveness-related constructs. Moreover, because restorative justice can examine these constructs in the context of specific crimes, it can reduce possible measurement error due to variation in perceived severity, salience, and recency of the transgression. Restorative justice populations also allow a focus on the dyad, which broadens the perspective to include more than just the person doing the forgiving. In this regard, we need more research on bilateral processes surrounding forgiveness, including attention to how variables interact concurrently, not just how they predict or relate in a unidirectional manner (Moore, 1997).

We hope that researchers will also examine the following issues. Little is known about who does and does not elect to participate in restorative justice, what their attitudes are toward forgiveness, and the impact of the mediator on the process. Specifically, what are the postmediation outcomes for victims who forgive, who, prior to the dialogue, have already forgiven, intend to forgive, are open to forgiving, or do not intend to forgive? What events occur during the dialogue to generate or impede victim forgiveness?

Studies are also needed on motives for victim forgiveness for those victims who elect to forgive. Do victims forgive to reduce discomfort, to behave in accordance with principles and beliefs, to express acceptance of the offender after receiving an apology, or possibly to reduce offender's fear of the victim and gain the offender's co-operation in dealing with unanswered questions about the crime? Moreover, how do motives affect the interaction and outcome?

Although crime type influences victim response, are certain crimes more un-forgivable than others? Some restorative justice advocates (e.g., Umbreit et al., 2003) argue that restorative justice may be applied most meaningfully to crimes of severe violence. Although forgiveness is not an inherent part of this consideration, empirical studies are needed to ascertain the impact of crime type on victim response, includ-ing receptivity to forgiveness, and to examine possible change in victim perception of criminal intent in restorative justice dialogue.

Longitudinal studies might also provide information about the significance of preparation on both victims and offenders. A growth curve analysis might offer infor-mation about the role of time and the cumulative effect of premeeting preparation on victim forgiveness. Examination of the mediator's influence on victims and offenders might also provide data about effective interventions on victim rumination or anger and offender denial, proclivities that negatively influence victims' forgiveness.

Research is needed on the impact of forgiveness on offenders. Does this induce-ment of prosocial behavior suggest that receiving victim forgiveness positively influ-ences offender behavior generally? Studies are also needed on offender behavior after forgiveness is granted.

We have argued against making forgiveness an explicit part of the process in re-storative justice dialogues. This position, however, makes forgiveness more difficult to research because it is not the primary focus and participants' forgiveness-related be-haviors may not be overt. Greater attention, therefore, must be given to participants' perceptions of having given or received forgiveness and their verbal and non-verbal communication with each other. Phenomenological studies on participants' experience of themselves and each other or analysis of videotaped mediations might begin to delin-eate the dimensions of implicit forgiveness. The study of implicit forgiveness presents new and exciting challenges. For example, if forgiveness remains covert, how do we know if forgiveness or an apology has occurred? Does the transformation of bitterness and resentment into compassion mean that forgiveness has occurred? Does assuming responsibility and expressing genuine sorrow and regret constitute an apology? Might the answers to these questions vary based on differences in the perceptions of victim and offender? Are there other behaviors that each party may perceive as equivalent to forgiving or apologizing?"

PERSONAL THEORETICAL PERSPECTIVES ON THE FIELD

Our current research applies both theory and findings from experimental and clinical studies to a real-world population of victim and offender participant dyads in a VOMD program for crimes of severe violence. It uses a combination of surveys, standardized measures, and inmate behavior and recidivism reports to gather information at four points on whether change occurs in victim and offender attitudes (e.g., revenge, rumination, forgiveness, empathy, gratitude) and spirituality, victim physical and psychological symptoms, and offender behavior. As the first empirical study to date of the VOMD intervention, it offers a unique opportunity with an unusual sample of victims and offenders involved in severely violent crime to test relationships between forgiveness-related constructs and the cumulative or dosage effects of an intense intervention in an applied and dyadic context.

RELEVANCE FOR CLINICAL AND APPLIED INTERVENTIONS

Whereas restorative justice is an applied intervention, the things we have learned can apply to other clinical situations as well—family and couple therapy, conflict negotiation, and multiple forms of mediation. That is, they can help us understand that forgiveness is multifaceted and conditioned by a protective reactivity against the imposition of religious doctrine or social expectation; the bilateral nature of authentic forgiveness; and, notwithstanding the victim's desire *to forgive*, the practitioner's de-investment in a particular outcome.

CONCLUSION

Proponents of restorative justice face a significant dilemma. Forgiveness has been demonstrated to occur in the most horrendous of crimes (Umbreit et al., 2003). The extrapolation of forgiveness for study, however, gives it preeminence over the other components of healing and raises valid concerns among victim advocates and victim-services staff about the possible imposition of external agendas on victims. Because victims have historically been given no voice or were valued only as witnesses by the criminal justice system, it is imperative to protect their safety and the integrity of the restorative justice process by paying close attention to the emergence of scholarly interest in the health-promoting effects of forgiveness related to criminal offenses.

Our belief is that the significance of both forgiveness and restorative justice is their potential to facilitate victim healing. If victim healing is paramount, then constructs such as reduced anger and increased empathy may be as important as forgiveness. Moreover, victim healing in restorative justice requires, and is intricately wrapped up in, restoring victim safety and security. Victim safety and protection from prescribed forgiveness have been ensured, so far, by making forgiveness "irrelevant" (unless victims specifically request help with forgiving), which allows it to play naturally in the background. The goal in restorative justice, therefore, needs to remain on creating conditions that further healing, including conditions such as offender apology and remorse that may facilitate victim-desired forgiveness.

Forgiveness in the context of restorative justice remains a paradox. If the concept of forgiveness is used as an explicit intervention, many victims and victim advocates will, at best, feel unsafe or even preached at. Some may feel quite offended. On the other hand, the more forgiveness remains in the background with the focus on creating a safe place for dialogue, the more likely it is that many if not most victims will feel safe enough to travel the path of authentic forgiveness, if that is what they truly desire.

REFERENCES

Armour, M. P. (2003). Meaning making in the aftermath of homicide. *Death Studies, 27,* 519–540.

Bazemore, G. (1999). Crime victims, restorative justice, and the juvenile court: Exploring victim needs and involvement in the response to youth crime. *International Review of Victimology, 6,* 295–320.

Bennett, M., & Dewberry, C. (1994). "I've said I'm sorry, haven't I?" A study of the identity implications and constraints that apologies create for their recipients. *Current Psychology: Developmental, Learning, and Personality, Social, 13,* 457–464.

Bonach, K. (2001). The mediating role of forgiveness in the relationship between post-divorce cognitive processes and coparenting quality: A context, process, outcome model. *Dissertation Abstracts International Section A: Humanities & Social Sciences, 62(5-A),* 1942.

Bradshaw, W., & Umbreit, M. S. (1998). Crime victims meet juvenile offenders: Contributing factors to victim satisfaction with mediated dialogue. *Juvenile and Family Court Journal, 49,* 17–25.

Coates, R., Burns, H., & Umbreit, M. (2002). *Victim participation in victim offender conferencing: Washington County, Minnesota Community Justice Program.* St. Paul, MN: Center for Restorative Justice & Peacemaking.

Coates, R. B. & Gehm, J. (1989) An empirical assessment. In M. Wright & B. Galaway (Eds.), *Mediation and criminal justice* (pp. 251–263). London: Sage Publications

Coyle, C. T., & Enright, R. D. (1997). Forgiveness intervention with postabortion men. *Journal of Consulting and Clinical Psychology, 65,* 1042–1046.

Cragg, W. (1992). *The practice of punishment.* London: Routledge.

Daly, K., (2001). Conferencing in Australia and New Zealand: Variations, research findings, and prospects. In A. Morris & G. Maxwell (Eds.), *Restorative justice for juveniles: Conferencing, mediation, and circles* (pp. 59–89). Oxford, England: Hart.

Dickey, W. J. (1998). Forgiveness and crime: The possibilities of restorative justice. R. D. Enright & J. North (Eds.), *Exploring forgiveness* (pp. 106–120). Madison: University of Wisconsin Press.

Enright, R. D., & North, J. (Eds.). (1998). *Exploring forgiveness.* Madison: University of Wisconsin Press.

Exline, J. J., & Baumeister, R. F. (2000). Expressing forgiveness and repentance. In M. E. McCullough, K. I. Pargament, & C. E. Thoresen (Eds.), *Forgiveness: Theory, research, and practice* (pp. 133–155). New York: Guilford Press.

Exline, J. J., Worthington, E. L., Jr., Hill, P. C., & McCullough, M. E. (2003). Forgiveness and justice: A research agenda for social and personality psychology. *Personality and Social Psychology Review, 7,* 337–348.

Freedman, S. R., & Enright, R. D. (1996). Forgiveness as an intervention goal with incest survivors. *Journal of Consulting and Clinical Psychology, 64,* 983–992.

Gehm, J. R. (1992). The function of forgiveness in the criminal justice system. In J. Messmer & H-U. Otto (Eds.), *Restorative justice on trial: Pitfalls and potentials of victim-offender mediation—International research perspectives* (pp. 541–550). Boston: Kluwer Academic.

Girard, M., Mullet, E., & Callahan, S. (2002). Mathematics of forgiveness. *American Journal of Psychology, 115*, 351–375.

Gobodo-Madikizela, P. (2002). Remorse, forgiveness, and rehumanization: Stories from South Africa. *Journal of Humanistic Psychology, 42*, 7–32.

Gold, G. J., & Weiner, B. (2000). Remorse, confession, group identity, and expectancies about repeating a transgression. *Basic and Applied Social Psychology, 22,* 291–300.

Hill, W. E. (2001). Understanding forgiveness as discovery: Implications for marital and family therapy. *Contemporary Family Therapy, 23*, 369–384.

Kelln, B. R. C., & Ellard, J. H. (1999). An equity theory analysis of the impact of forgiveness and retribution on transgressor compliance. *Personality and Social Psychology Bulletin, 25*, 864–872.

Kittle, B. (1999). Forgiveness in the criminal justice system: Necessary element or impossible dream. *World of Forgiveness, 2*, 3–11.

Lavery, C., & Achilles, M. (1999). Apologies: Balancing the needs of victims and offenders. *VOMA Connections, 3*, 6.

Levenson, R. W., & Ruef, A. M. (1991). Empathy: A physiological substrate. *Journal of Personality and Social Psychology, 63*, 234–246.

McCullough, M. E. (2001). Forgiveness: Who does it and how do they do it. *Current Directions in Psychological Science, 10,* 194–197.

McCullough, M. E., Sandage, S. J., Brown, S. W., Rachal, K. C., Worthington, E. L., Jr., & Hight, T. L. (1998). Interpersonal forgiving in close relationships: II. Theoretical elaboration and measurement. *Journal of Personality and Social Psychology, 75*, 1586–1603.

McCullough, M. E., Worthington, E. L., Jr., & Rachal, K. C. (1997). Interpersonal forgiving in close relationships. *Journal of Personality and Social Psychology, 73*, 321–336.

Moore, D. (1997). Pride, shame, and empathy among peers: Community conferencing as transformative justice in education. In K. Rigby & P. T. Slee (Eds.), *Children's peer relations* (pp. 254–271), London: Routledge.

Murphy, J. G. (2000). Forgiveness, reconciliation, and responding to evil: A philosophical overview. *Fordham Urban Law Journal 27*, 1353–1366.

Nugent, W. R., Umbreit, M., Wiinamaki, L., & Paddock, J. (2001). Participation in victim-offender mediation and severity of subsequent delinquent behavior: Successful replications? *Journal of Research in Social Work Practice, 11*, 5–23.

Peachey, D. E. (1992). Restitution, reconciliation, retribution: Identifying the forms of justice people desire. In H. Messmer & H-U. Otto (Eds.), *Restorative justice on trial* (pp. 551–557). Dordrecht: Kluwer.

Petrucci, C. J. (2002). Apology in the criminal justice setting: Evidence for including apology as an additional component in the legal system. *Behavioral Sciences and the Law, 20*, 337–362.

Poulson, B. (2000). A third voice: A review of empirical research on the psychological outcomes of restorative justice. *Utah Law Review, 167*, 1–17.

Regehr, C., & Gutheil, T. (2002). Apology, justice, and trauma recovery. *Journal of the American Academy of Psychiatry and Law, 30*, 425–30.

Roberts, T. (1995). *Evaluation of the victim offender mediation project. Langley, BC: Final Report.* Victoria, BC, Canada: Focus Consultants.

Scheff, T. J. (1998). Therapeutic jurisprudence forum: Community conferences: Shame and anger in therapeutic jurisprudence. *Revista Juridica Universidad de Puerto Rico, 67*, 97–119.

Shabad, P. (1988). Remorse: The echo of inner truth. *Psychotherapy Patient, 5*, 113–133.

Strang, H. (2002). *Repair or revenge: Victims and restorative justice.* Oxford, England: Clarendon Press.

Strang, H., & Sherman, L. W. (2003). Repairing the harm: Victims and restorative justice. *Utah Law Review, 15*, 15–42.

Takaku, S. (2001). The effects of apology and perspective taking on interpersonal forgiveness: A dissonance-attribution model of interpersonal forgiveness. *Journal of Social Psychology, 141*, 494–508.

Tavuchis, N. (1991). *Mea culpa: A sociology of apology and reconciliation.* Stanford, CA: Stanford University Press.

Umbreit, M. S. (1994). *Victim meets offender: The impact of restorative justice and mediation.* Monsey, NY: Criminal Justice Press.

Umbreit, M. S. (1995). *Mediation of criminal conflict: An assessment of programs in four Canadian provinces.* St. Paul: University of Minnesota, Center for Restorative Justice and Peacemaking.

Umbreit, M. S. (2001). *Handbook of victim offender mediation.* San Francisco: Jossey-Bass.

Umbreit, M. S., & Bradshaw, W. (1999). Factors that contribute to victim satisfaction and mediated offender dialogue in Winnipeg: An emerging area of social work practice. *Journal of Law and Social Work, 9*, 35–51.

Umbreit, M. S., & Coates, R. B. (1992). The impact of mediating victim offender conflict: An analysis of programs in three states. *Juvenile and Family Court Journal, 43*, 21–28.

Umbreit, M. S., & Coates, R. B. (1993). Cross-site analysis of victim-offender mediation in four states. *Crime and Delinquency 39*, 565–585.

Umbreit, M. S., Coates, R. B., & Vos, B. (2001). *Juvenile victim offender mediation in six Oregon counties.* Salem, OR: Oregon Dispute Resolution Commission.

Umbreit, M. S., Coates, R. B., & Vos, B. (2002). The impact of restorative justice conferencing: A multi-national perspective. *British Journal of Community Justice, 1*, 21–48.

Umbreit, M. S., Vos, B., Coates, R. B., & Brown, K. A. (2003). *Facing violence: The path of restorative justice and dialogue.* Monsey, NY: Criminal Justice Press.

Van Biema, D. (1999). Should all be forgiven? *Time*, March 22.

Van Strokkom, B. (2002). Moral emotions in restorative justice conferences: Managing shame, designing empathy. *Theoretical Criminology, 6*, 339–360.

Witvliet, C., Ludwig, T. E., & Vander Laan, K. (2001). Granting forgiveness or harbouring grudges: Implications for emotion, physiology, and health. *Psychological Science, 12*, 117–123.

Witvliet, C. V. O., Worthington, E. L., Jr., Wade, N. G., & Berry, J. W. (2002, April). *Physiological reactivity to apology and restitution.* Paper presented at the meeting of the Society of Behavioral Medicine, Washington, DC.

Worthington, E. L., Jr. (2003). *Forgiving and reconciling: Bridges to wholeness and hope..* Downers Grove, IL: InterVarsity Press.

Worthington, E. L., Jr., & Wade, N. G. (1999). The social psychology of unforgiveness and forgiveness and implications for clinical practice. *Journal of Social and Clinical Psychology, 18*, 385–418.

Zechmeister, J. S., & Romero, C. (2002). Victim and offender accounts of interpersonal conflict: Autobiographical narratives of forgiveness and unforgiveness. *Journal of Personality and Social Psychology, 82*, 675–686.

Zehr, H. (1995). *Changing lenses: A new focus on crime and justice.* Scottsdale, PA: Herald Press.

Part Eight

PRESENT AND FUTURE OF FORGIVENESS

Chapter Thirty-One

Forgiveness Bibliography

Michael Scherer
Kathryn L. Cooke
Everett L. Worthington, Jr.

This bibliography represents our ambitious attempt to accumulate an up-to-date bibliography of forgiveness and forgiveness-related scientific literature and to organize it into a directory (by topic), which can facilitate research. This includes, but is not limited to, scientific journal articles, book chapters, dissertations, and books in the field. In consideration of space, we chose to omit dissertations when it appeared that the dissertation study had been published in a refereed journal. We understand that, despite our efforts to be comprehensive, many important journal articles, books, dissertations, and book chapters may have been inadvertently overlooked. As such, we offer our most sincere apologies to all researchers and authors that were excluded from this endeavor. Please, forgive us.

ACKNOWLEDGMENTS

We acknowledge support from *A Campaign for Forgiveness Research* and the John Fetzer Institute for the funding of the preparation of this bibliography.

IN PRESS (AS OF LAST QUARTER OF 2004) FORGIVENESS REFERENCES

Baucom, D. H., Gordon, K. C., & Snyder, D. K. (in press). Marital infidelity. In J. Lebow (Ed.), *Handbook of clinical family therapy.* New York: Brunner-Mazel.

Berry, J. W., Worthington, E. L., Jr., Wade, N. G., Witvliet, C. V. O., & Kiefer, R. (in press). Forgiveness, moral identity, and perceived justice in crime victims and their supporters. *Humboldt Journal of Social Issues.*

Bono, G., & McCullough, M. E. (in press). Positive responses to benefit and harm: Bringing forgiveness and gratitude into cognitive psychotherapy. *Journal of Cognitive Psychotherapy.*

Bono, G., Root, L. M., & McCullough, M. E. (in press). Religion and forgiveness. In R. Paloutzian & C. Park (Eds.), *Handbook of the psychology of religion and spirituality.* New York: Guilford Press.

Brown, R. P. (in press). Vengeance is mine: Narcissism, vengeance, and the tendency to forgive. *Journal of Research in Personality.*

Brown, R. P., & Phillips, A. (in press). Letting bygones be bygones: Further evidence for the validity of the tendency to forgive scale. *Personality and Individual Differences.*

Cairns, E., Hewstone, M., Hamberger, J., Niens, U., & Voci, A. (in press). The contact hypothesis, forgiveness, and peace psychology in identity-based conflicts: Northern Ireland. *Journal of Social Issues.*

Exline, J. J., Baumeister, R. F., Bushman, B. J., Campbell, W. K., & Finkel, E. J. (in press). Too proud to let go: Narcissistic entitlement as a barrier to forgiveness. *Journal of Personality and Social Psychology.*

Fincham F. D., & Kashdan, T. B. (in press). Facilitating forgiveness: Developing group and community interventions. In P. A. Linley & S. Joseph (Eds.), *International handbook of positive psychology in practice: From research to application.* Hoboken, NJ: Wiley.

Fincham, F. D., Jackson, H., & Beach, S. R. H. (in press). Transgression severity and forgiveness: Different moderators for objective and subjective severity. *Journal of Social and Clinical Psychology.*

Freedman, S., & Knupp, A. (in press). Impact of forgiveness education on adolescent adjustment to parental divorce. *Journal of Divorce and Remarriage.*

Gauché, M., & Mullet, E. (in press). Do we forgive physical aggression in the same way that we forgive psychological aggression? *Aggressive Behavior.*

Gauché, M., Mullet, E., & Chasseigne, G. (in press). Forgiveness: The self and the norm. *Advances in Psychological Research.*

Gordon, K. C., Baucom, D. H., & Snyder, D. K. (in press). An integrative intervention for promoting recovery from extramarital affairs. *Journal of Marital and Family Therapy.*

Gordon, K. C., Burton, S., & Porter, L. (in press). The role of forgiveness: Predicting women in domestic violence shelters intentions to return to their partners. *Journal of Family Psychology.*

Hall, J. H., & Fincham, F. D. (in press). Self-forgiveness: The stepchild of forgiveness research. *Journal of Social and Clinical Psychology.*

Kachadourian, L. K., Fincham, F. D., & Davila, J. (in press). The tendency to forgive in dating and married couples: The role of attachment and relationship satisfaction. *Personal Relationships.*

Kadiangandu, J. K., & Mullet, E. (in press). "Can whole nations repent?": An African perspective. *Peace and Conflict: A Peace Psychology Journal.*

Karremans, J. C., & Van Lange, P. A. M. (in press). Does activating justice help or hurt in promoting forgiveness? *Journal of Experimental Social Psychology.*

Lawler, K. A., Younger, J. W., Piferi, R. L., Jobe, R. L., Edmondson, K., & Jones, W. H. (in press). The unique effects of forgiveness on health: An exploration of pathways. *Journal of Behavioral Medicine.*

Luskin, F. M., Ginzburg, K, & Thoresen, C. E. (in press). The effect of forgiveness training on psychosocial factors in college age adults. *Humboldt Journal of Social Relations.*

Luskin, F. M. (in press). Optimal healing environments: Transformative practices for integrating mind, body, and spirit. *Journal of Complementary and Alternative Medicine, Supplement 10.*

McCullough, M. E. (in press). Religion, gratitude, forgiveness, and positive psychology. In R. Paloutzian & C. Park (Eds.), *Handbook of the psychology of religion and spirituality*. New York: Guilford Press.

Muñoz Sastre, M. T., Vinsonneau, G., Chabrol, H., & Mullet, E. (in press). Forgivingness and the paranoid personality style. *Personality and Individual Differences.*

Ristovski, A., & Wertheim, E. H. (in press). The effects of source of compensation and trait empathy on forgiveness and satisfaction with outcome in the criminal context. *Australian Psychologist.*

Rye, M. S., Folck, C. D., Heim, T. A., Olszewski, B. T., & Traina, E. (in press). Forgiveness of an ex-spouse: How does it relate to mental health following a divorce? *Journal of Divorce and Remarriage.*

Sutton, G. W., & Thomas, E. K. (in press). Can derailed pastors be restored? Effects of offense and age on restoration. *Pastoral Psychology.*

Tsang, J-A., McCullough, M. E., & Hoyt, W. T. (in press). Psychometric and rationalization accounts for the religion-forgiveness discrepancy. *Journal of Social Issues.*

Wade, N. G., & Worthington, E. L., Jr. (in press). In search of a common core: A content analysis of interventions to promote forgiveness. *Psychotherapy.*

Wertheim, E. H., Love, A., Peck, C., & Littlefield, L. (in press). *"Building relationships" in skills for resolving conflict: A co-operative problem solving approach* (2nd ed.). Melbourne: Eruditions.

Wohl, M. J. A., & Branscombe, N. R. (in press). Forgiveness and collective guilt assignment to historical perpetrator groups depend on level of social category inclusiveness. *Journal of Personality and Social Psychology.*

Wohl, M. J. A., & Branscombe, N. R. (in press). Importance of social categorization for forgiveness and collective guilt assignment for the Holocaust. In N. R. Branscombe & B. Dooje (Eds.), *Collective guilt: International perspectives*. New York: Cambridge University Press.

Wohl, M. J. A., & Reeder, G. D. (in press). When bad deeds are forgiven: Judgments of morality and forgiveness for intergroup aggression. In F. Columbus (Ed.), *Psychology of aggression*. New York: Nova Science.

Worthington, E.L., Jr. (in press). The development of forgiveness. In E.M. Dowling & W.G. Scarlette (Eds.), *Encyclopedia of religious and spiritual development in childhood and adolescence*. Thousand Oaks, CA: Sage.

Worthington, E. L., Jr. (in press). Promoting forgiveness and reconciliation. In T. Clinton & G. Ohlschlager (Eds.), *Caring for people God's way: Volume 1A: Personal, emotional, grief, loss, and trauma issues*. Sisters, OR: Multnomah Publishers.

Worthington, E. L., Jr., Scherer, M., & Cooke, K. L. (in press). Forgiveness in alcohol dependence, abuse, and their treatment. *Alcohol Treatment Quarterly.*

Worthington, E. L., Jr., Witvliet, C. V. O., Lerner, A. J., & Scherer, M. (in press). Forgiveness in health research and medical practice. *EXPLORE: The Journal of Science and Healing.*

Younger, J. W., Piferi, R. L., Jobe, R., & Lawler, K. A. (in press). Dimensions of forgiveness: The views of laypersons. *Journal of Social and Personal Relationships.*

FORGIVENESS PUBLICATIONS

Adams, J. M., & Jones, W. H (Eds.). (1999). *Handbook of interpersonal commitment and relationship stability*. New York: Kluwer Academic/Plenum.

Affinito, M. G. (2001). When to forgive. *Family Therapy, 28,* 113.

Affinito, M. G. (2002). Forgiveness in counseling: Caution, definition, and application. In S. Lamb & J. Murphy (Eds.), *Before forgiving: Cautionary views of forgiveness in psychotherapy* (pp. 88–111). New York: Oxford University Press.

Ahn, T. (1999). Healing shame in a Korean context: The contributions of Heinz Kohut and Donald Eric Capps. *Dissertation Abstracts International, 1A, 60,* 0167.

Akhtar, S. (2002). Forgiveness: Origins, dynamics, psychopathology, and technical relevance. *Psychoanalytic Quarterly, 71,* 175–212.

Al-Mabuk, R. H. (1990). The commitment to forgive in parentally love-deprived college students. (Doctoral dissertation, University of Wisconsin-Madison, 1990). *Dissertation Abstracts International, A51,* 3361.

Al-Mabuk, R. H., Dedrick, C. V. L., & Vanderah, K. M. (1998). Attribution retraining in forgiveness therapy. *Journal of Family Psychotherapy, 9,* 11–30.

Al-Mabuk, R. H., & Downs, W. R. (1996). Forgiveness therapy with parents of adolescent suicide victims. *Journal of Family Psychotherapy, 7,* 21–39.

Al-Mabuk, R. H., Enright, R. D., & Cardis, P. A. (1995). Forgiveness education with parentally love-deprived late adolescents. *Journal of Moral Education, 24,* 427–444.

Alvaro, J. A. (2001). An interpersonal forgiveness and reconciliation intervention: The effect on marital intimacy. *Dissertation Abstracts International, 3B, 62,* 1608.

Andres, B. S. (2002). A qualitative phenomenological analysis of the critical incidents in the native Hawaiian peacemaking process of "ho`oponopono." *Dissertation Abstracts International: Section B: Sciences & Engineering, 63,* 2048.

Andrews, M. (2000). Forgiveness in context. *Journal of Moral Education, 29,* 75–86.

Aoki, W. T., & Turk, A. A. (1997). Adolescent suicide: A review of risk factors and implications for practice. *Journal of Psychology and Christianity, 16,* 273–279.

Aponte, H. J. (1998). Love, the spiritual wellspring of forgiveness: An example of spirituality in therapy. *Journal of Family Therapy, 20,* 37–58.

Applegate, B. K., Cullen, F. T., Fisher, B. S., & Vander Ven, T. (2000). Forgiveness and fundamentalism: Reconsidering the relationship between correctional attitudes and religion. *Criminology, 38,* 719–750.

Aquino, K., Glover, S. L., Goldman, B., & Folger, R. (2003). When push doesn't come to shove: Interpersonal forgiveness in workplace relationships. *Journal of Management Inquiry, 12,* 209–216.

Armour, M. P. (2003). Meaning making in the aftermath of homicide. *Death Studies, 27,* 519–540.

Arthur, P. (1999). The Anglo-Irish peace process: Obstacles to reconciliation. In R. L. Rothstein (Ed.), *After the peace: Resistance and reconciliation* (pp. 85–109). Boulder: Lynne Rienner.

Ashton, M. C., Paunonen, S. V., Helmes, E., & Jackson, D. N. (1998). Kin altruism, reciprocal altruism, and the Big Five personality factors. *Evolution and Human Behavior, 19,* 243–255.

Atkinson, D. (1982a). The importance of forgiveness. *Third Way, 5,* 4–7.

Atkinson, D. (1982b). Forgiveness and personality development. *Third Way, 5,* 18–21.

Augsburger, D. (1992). *Conflict mediation across cultures: Pathways and patterns.* Louisville, KY: Westminster John Knox.

Augsburger, D. W. (1996). *Helping people forgive.* Westminster, KY: Westminster John Knox Press.

Aune, M. B. (1984). A Lutheran understanding and experience of repentance and forgiveness. *New Catholic World, 227,* 33–36.

Aureli, F., Das, M., & Veenema, H. C. (1997). Differential kinship effect on reconciliation in three species of macaques (*Macaca fascicularis, M. fuscata,* and *M. sylvanus*). *Journal of Comparative Psychology, 111,* 91–99.

Ayoub, M. (1997). Repentance in the Islamic tradition. In A. Etzioni & D. E. Carney (Eds.), *Repentance: A comparative perspective* (pp. 96–121). New York: Rowaman & Littlefield.

Azar, F., & Mullet, E. (2001). Interpersonal forgiveness among Lebanese: A six-community study. *International Journal of Group Tensions, 30,* 161–181.

Azar, F., & Mullet, E. (2002). "Forgiveness": Overall level and factor structure in a sample of Muslim and Christian-Lebanese. *Peace and Conflict: A Peace Psychology Journal, 8,* 17–30.

Azar, F., & Mullet, E. (2002). Muslim and Christian in Lebanon: Common views regarding political issues. *Journal of Peace Research, 39,* 735–746.

Azar, F., & Mullet, E. (2002). Willingness to forgive: A study of Muslim and Christian Lebanese. *Peace and Conflict: Journal of Peace Psychology, 8,* 17–30.

Azar, F., Mullet, E., & Vinsonneau, G. (1999). The propensity to forgive: Findings from Lebanon. *Journal of Peace Research, 36,* 169–181.

Baker, D. (2002). Beyond forgiveness: The healing touch of church discipline. *Leadership, 5,* 96–97.

Barros, J. H. (2002). Forgiveness: Concept and evaluation: Presentation of a new scale. [Portuguese]. *Psicologia Educaca Cultura, 6,* 303–320.

Barros, J. H. (2003). Forgiveness and happiness: A cross-cultural approach. [Portuguese]. *Psicologia Educaca Cultura. 7,* 283–312.

Bar-Tal, D. (2000). From intractable conflict through conflict resolution to reconciliation: Psychological analysis. *Political Psychology, 21,* 351–362.

Bartoli, A. (1998). Forgiveness and reconciliation in the Mozambique peace process. In R. G. Helmick & R. L. Petersen (Eds.), *Forgiveness and reconciliation: Religion, public policy, and conflict transformation* (pp. 351–371). Philadelphia: Templeton Foundation Press.

Baskin, T. W., & Enright, R. D. (2004). Intervention studies on forgiveness: A meta-analysis. *Journal of Counseling and Development, 82,* 79–90.

Bauer, L., Duffy, J., Fountain, E, Halling, S., Holzer, M., Jones, E., et al. (1992). Exploring self-forgiveness. *Journal of Religion and Health, 21,* 149–160.

Baumeister, R. F. (1998). Empathy, shame, guilt, and narratives of interpersonal conflicts: Guilt-prone people are better at perspective taking. *Journal of Personality, 66,* 1–37.

Baumeister, R. F., & Exline, J. J. (2000). Self-control, mortality, and human strength. *Journal of Social and Clinical Psychology, 19,* 29–42.

Baumeister, R. F., Exline, J. J., & Sommer, K. L. (1998). The victim role, grudge theory, and two dimensions of forgiveness. In E. L. Worthington, Jr. (Ed.), *Dimensions of forgiveness: Psychological research and theological perspectives* (pp. 79–106). Philadelphia: Templeton Foundation Press.

Baumeister, R. F., & Newman, L. S. (1994). How stories make sense of personal experiences: Motives that shape autobiographical narratives. *Personality and Social Psychology Bulletin, 20,* 676–690.

Baumeister, R. F., Stillwell, A. M., & Heatherton, T. F. (1994). Guilt: An interpersonal approach. *Psychological Bulletin, 115,* 243–247.

Baumeister, R. F., Stillwell, A. M., & Wotman, S. R. (1990). Victim and perpetrator accounts of interpersonal conflict: Autobiographical narratives about anger. *Journal of Personality and Social Psychology, 59,* 994–1005.

Baures, M. M. (1996). Letting go of bitterness and hate. *Journal of Humanistic Psychology, 36,* 75–91.

Bazemore, G. (1999). Crime victims, restorative justice, and the juvenile court: Exploring victim needs and involvement in the response to youth crime. *International Review of Victimology, 6,* 295–320.

Beck, J. R. (1995). When to forgive. *Journal of Psychology and Christianity, 14,* 269–273.

Benn, P. (1996). Forgiveness and loyalty. *Philosophy, 71,* 369–385.

Bennett, M. L. (1998). A study of the relationship of prayer between family caregiver and cancer patient in easing caregiver burden. *Dissertation Abstracts International, 1B,* 59, 169.

Bennett, M., & Dewberry, C. (1994). "I've said I'm sorry, haven't I?" A study of the identity implications and constraints that apologies create for their recipients. *Current Psychology: Developmental, Learning, Personality, and Social, 13,* 457–464.

Benson, C. K. (1992). Forgiveness and the psychotherapeutic process. *Journal of Psychology and Christianity, 11,* 76–81.

Berecz, J. M. (2001). All that glitters is not gold: Bad forgiveness in counseling and preaching. *Pastoral Psychology, 49,* 253–275.

Bergin, A. E. (1988). Three contributions of a spiritual perspective to counseling, psychotherapy, and behavior change. *Counseling and Values, 33,* 21–31.

Berry, J. W., & Worthington, E. L., Jr., (2001). Forgivingness, relationship quality, stress while imagining relationship events, and physical and mental health. *Journal of Counseling Psychology, 48,* 447–455.

Berry, J. W., Worthington, E. L., Jr., O'Connor, L., Parrott, L., III, & Wade, N. G. (2005). Forgiveness, vengeful rumination, and affective traits. *Journal of Personality, 73,* 1–43.

Berry, J. W., Worthington, E. L., Jr., Parrott, L., III, O'Connor, L., & Wade, N. G. (2001). Dispositional forgivingness: Development and construct validity of the Transgression Narrative Test of Forgivingness (TNTF). *Personality and Social Psychology Bulletin, 27,* 1277–1290.

Bonach, K. (2001). The mediating role of forgiveness in the relationship between post-divorce cognitive processes and coparenting quality: A context, process, outcome model. *Dissertation Abstracts International Section A: Humanities and Social Sciences, 62(5-A),* 1942.

Bonach, K., & Sales, E. (2002). Forgiveness as a mediator between post-divorce cognitive processes and coparenting quality. *Journal of Divorce and Remarriage, 38,* 17–38.

Bonar, C. (1989). Personality theories and asking forgiveness. *Journal of Psychology and Christianity, 8,* 45–51.

Bono, G., & McCullough, M. E. (2004). Forgiveness, religion, and adjustment in older adulthood. In K. W. Schaie, N. Krause, & A. Booth (Eds.), *Religious influences on health and well-being in the elderly* (pp. 163–186). New York: Springer.

Boobyer, G. H. (1954). Mark II, 10a and the interpretation of the healing of the paralytic. *Harvard Theological Review, 47,* 115–120.

Boon, S. C., & Sulsky, L. M. (1997). Attributions of blame and forgiveness in romantic relationships: A policy-capturing study. *Journal of Social Behavior and Personality, 12,* 19–44.

Borris, E., & Diehl, P. F. (1998). Forgiveness, reconciliation, and the contribution of international peacekeeping. In H. L. Langholtz (Ed.), *The psychology of peacekeeping* (pp. 207–222). Westport: Praeger.

Boss, J. (1997). Throwing pearls to the swine: Women, forgiveness, and the unrepentant abuser. In L. D. Kaplan & L. F. Bove (Eds.), *Philosophical perspectives on power and domination: Theories and practices.* Amsterdam-Atlanta, GA: Rodopi.

Bowman, E. S. (2000). The assets and liabilities of conservative religious faith for persons with severe dissociative disorders. *Journal of Psychology and Christianity, 19,* 122–138.

Bradfield, M., & Aquino, K. (1999). The effects of blame attributes and offender likableness on forgiveness and revenge in the workplace. *Journal of Management, 25,* 607–631.

Brandsma, J. M. (1982). Forgiveness: A dynamic, theological, and therapeutic analysis. *Pastoral Psychology, 31,* 40–50.

Branscomb, H. (1934). "Son thy sins are forgiven." *Journal of Biblical Literature, 53,* 53–60.

Braun, K. L., & Zir, A. (2001). Roles for the church in improving end-of-life care: Perceptions of Christian clergy and laity. *Death Studies, 25,* 685–704.

Brenneis, M. J. (2000). Personality and demographic factors predicting conflicted attitudes toward authority in clergy who have completed residential psychiatric treatment. *Dissertation Abstracts International, 61,* 2-A.

Brenneis, M. J. (2001). The relationship between forgiveness and physical health indicators in recovering members of the clergy. *Journal of Ministry in Addiction and Recovery, 7,* 43–59.

Brink, T. L. (1985). The role of religion in later life: A case of consolation and forgiveness. *Journal of Psychology and Christianity, 4,* 22–25.

Brown, E. M. (2000). Working with marital affairs: Learning from the Clinton triangles. In L. Vandecreek & T. L. Jackson (Eds.), *Innovations in clinical practice: A source book,* (Vol. 18, pp. 471–478). Sarasota, FL: Professional Resource Press.

Brown, E. M. (2001). *Patterns of infidelity and their treatment* (2nd ed.). New York: Brunner-Routledge.

Brown, H. O. (1997). Godly sorrow, sorrow of the world: Some Christian thoughts on repentance. In A. Etzioni (Ed.), *Repentance: A comparative perspective* (pp. 31–42). Lanham, MD: Rowman & Littlefield.

Brown, K. D. (2001). A theory of forgiveness in marriage and family therapy: A critical review of the literature. *Dissertation Abstracts International, 1B, 62* (538).

Brown, R. P. (2003). Measuring individual differences in the tendency to forgive: Construct validity and links with depression. *Personality and Social Psychology Bulletin, 29,* 759–771.

Brown, S. W., Gorsuch, R., Rosik, C. H., & Ridley, C. R. (2001). The development of a scale to measure forgiveness. *Journal of Psychology and Christianity, 20,* 40–52.

Bryant, D. (1987). Forgiveness: Learning forgiveness as a way of life. *World Christian, 6,* 172–196.

Bryant, W. J. (1999). The application of cognitive dissonance theory in a forgiveness workshop: Inducing hypocrisy to create a commitment to give. *Dissertation Abstracts International: Section B: Sciences & Engineering, 59,* 5164.

Bucello, G. L. (1991). Family of origin and personality characteristics as predictive of a high capacity for forgiveness in ongoing relationships. *Dissertation Abstracts International, B52,* 4968.

Burchard, G. A., Yarhouse, M. A., Worthington, E. L., Jr., Berry, J. W., Killian, M., & Canter, D. E. (2003). A study of two marital enrichment programs and couples' life. *Journal of Psychology and Theology, 31,* 230–245.

Burkle, H. (1989). Guilt and its resolution outside of the Christian tradition. *Communio, 6,* 172–196.

Butler, D. S. (1998). The effects of personality and general health on choosing interpersonal forgiveness in the workplace. *Dissertation Abstracts International: Section B: Sciences & Engineering, 58,* 4498.

Butler, D. S., & Mullis, F. (2001). Forgiveness: A conflict resolution strategy in the workplace. *Journal of Individual Psychology, 57,* 259–272.

Butler, M. H., Dahlin, S. K., & Fife, S. T. (2002). "Languaging" factors affecting clients' acceptance of forgiveness intervention in marital therapy. *Journal of Marital and Family Therapy, 28,* 285–298.

Call, J., Aureli, F., & de Waal, F. B. M. (1999). Reconciliation patterns among stumptail macaques: A multivariate approach. *Animal Behaviour, 58,* 165–172.

Cameron, K. S., & Caza, A. (2002). Organizational and leadership virtues and the role of forgiveness. *Journal of Leadership and Organizational Studies, 9,* 33–48.

Cameron, K. S., & Caza, A. (2004). Exploring the relationships between organizational virtuousness and performance. *American Behavioral Scientist, 47,* 766–690.

Canale, J. R. (1990). Altruism and forgiveness as therapeutic agents in psychotherapy. *Journal of Religion and Health, 29,* 297–301.

Caplan, B. (1992). Forgiving the loss of parent in childhood: Three case studies. (Doctoral dissertation, Harvard University, 1992). *Dissertation Abstracts International B53,* 4993.

Caprara, G. V. (1986). Indicators of aggression: The Dissipation-Rumination scale. *Personality and Individual Differences, 7,* 763–769.

Caprara, G. V., Cinanni, V., D'Imperio, G., Passerini, S., Renzi, P., & Travaglia, G. (1985). Indicators of impulsive aggression: Present status of research on irritability and emotional susceptibility scales. *Personality and Individual Differences, 6,* 665–674.

Caprara, G. V., Cinanni, V., & Mazzotti, E. (1989). Measuring attitudes toward violence. *Personality and Individual Differences, 10,* 479–481.

Caprara, G. V., Coluzzi, M., Mazzotti, E., Renzi, P., & Zelli, A. (1985). Effect of insult and dissipation-rumination on delayed aggression and hostility. *Archivio di Psicologia Neurologia e Psichiatra, 46,* 130–139.

Caprara, G. V., Manzi, J., & Perugini, M. (1992). Investigating guilt in relation to emotionality and aggression. *Personality and Individual Differences, 13,* 519–532.

Care, N. S. (2002). Forgiveness and effective agency. In S. Lamb & J. Murphy (Eds.), *Before forgiving: Cautionary views of forgiveness in psychotherapy* (pp. 215–231). New York: Oxford University Press.

Carlsmith, J. M., & Gross, A. E. (1969). Some effects of guilt on compliance. *Journal of Personality and Social Psychology, 11,* 232–239.

Carone, D. A., Jr., & Barone, D. F. (2001). A social cognitive perspective on religious beliefs: Their functions and impact on coping and psychotherapy. *Clinical Psychology Review, 21,* 989–1003.

Carver, C. S., Scheier, M. F., & Weintraub, J. K. (1989). Assessing coping strategies: A theoretically based approach. *Journal of Personality and Social Psychology, 56,* 267–283.

Casarjian, R. (1992). *Forgiveness: A bold choice for a peaceful heart.* New York: Bantam Books.

Case, B. T. (1998). Further validation of the Forgiveness of Self (FOS) and Forgiveness of Others (FOO) scales and development of the Potential Barriers to Forgiveness scale. *Dissertation Abstracts International, 58,* 12-A.

Casey, K. L. (1998). Surviving abuse: Shame, anger, forgiveness. *Pastoral Psychology, 46,* 223–231.

Cassiday-Shaw, A. K. (2002). *Family abuse and the Bible: The scriptural perspective.* New York: Haworth Press.

Cavell, M. (2003) Freedom and forgiveness. *International Journal of Psycho-Analysis, 84,* 515–531.

Chambliss, B. B. (2002). Contemporary women peacemakers: The hidden side of peacemaking. *Dissertation Abstracts International, 63,* 2025.

Chapman, A. R. (1998). Truth commissions as instruments of forgiveness and reconciliation. In R. G. Helmick & R. L. Petersen (Eds.), *Forgiveness and reconciliation: Religion, public policy, and conflict transformation* (pp. 247–267). Philadelphia: Templeton Foundation Press.

Chapman, A. R. (1999). Coming to terms with the past: Truth, justice, and/or reconciliation. *Annals of the Society of Christian Ethics, 19,* 237–260.

Chapman, A. R., & Spong B. (Eds.). (2003). *Religion and reconciliation in South Africa*. Philadelphia: Templeton Foundation Press.

Childs, B. H. (1981). Forgiveness in community in light of Pauline literature and the experience among pre-school children. *Dissertation Abstracts International, 42*, 1683.

Clark, D. K. (1985). Philosophical reflections on self-worth and self-love. *Journal of Psychology and Theology, 13*, 3–11.

Cloke, K. (1993). Revenge, forgiveness, and the magic of mediation. Special issue: Beyond technique: The soul of family mediation. *Mediation Quarterly, 11*, 67–78.

Close, H. T. (1970). Forgiveness and responsibility: A case study. *Pastoral Psychology, 21*, 19–25.

Coates, D. (1997). The correlations of forgiveness of self, forgiveness of others, and hostility, depression, anxiety, self-esteem, life adaptation, and religiosity among female victims of domestic violence. *Dissertation Abstracts International 5B, 58*.

Coleman, P. W. (1998). The process of forgiveness in marriage and the family. In R. D. Enright & J. North (Eds.), *Exploring forgiveness* (pp. 75–94). Madison, WI: University of Wisconsin Press.

Compaan, A. (1985). Anger, denial, and the healing of memories. *Journal of Psychology and Christianity, 4*, 83–85.

Connery, T. J. (2002). Forgiveness: A correlational study between the spirit of forgiveness and physical health in senior citizens. *Dissertation Abstracts International, 6A, 63*.

Connor, K. M., Davidson, J. R. T., & Lee, L. (2003). Spirituality, resilience, and anger in survivors of violent trauma: A community survey. *Journal of Traumatic Stress, 16*, 487–494.

Conran, M. (1993). Some considerations of shame, guilt, and forgiveness derived principally from King Lear. *Revista de Psicoanalsis, 50*, 839–857.

Consoli, A. J. (1995). Psychotherapists' personal and mental health values according to their theoretical/professional orientation. *Dissertation Abstracts International: Section B: Sciences & Engineering, 56*, 1695.

Cords, M. (1992). Post-conflict reunions and reconciliation in long-tailed macaques. *Animal Behaviour, 44*, 57–61.

Cornock, B. L. (2002). Forgiveness in everyday life: An examination of gender similarities and differences. *Dissertation Abstracts International, 41*, 4.

Couch, L. L., Jones, W. H., & Moore, D. S. (1999). Buffering the effects of betrayal: The role of apology, forgiveness, and commitment. In J. Adams & W. H. Jones (Eds.), *Handbook of interpersonal commitment and relationship stability* (pp. 451–469). New York: Kluwer Academic/Plenum.

Countryman, L. W. (1998). *Forgiven and forgiving*. Milwaukee, MN: Morehouse.

Coyle, C. T., & Enright, R. D. (1997). Forgiveness intervention with postabortion men. *Journal of Consulting and Clinical Psychology, 65*, 1042–1046.

Crohn, J., Markman, H. J., Blumberg, S. L., & Levine, J. R. (2000). *Fighting for your Jewish marriage: Preserving a lasting promise*. San Francisco: Jossey-Bass.

Cunningham, B. B. (1985). The will to forgive: A pastoral theological view of forgiving. *Journal of Pastoral Care, 39*, 141–149.

Curtis, N. C. (1989). The structure and dynamics of forgiving another. *Dissertation Abstracts International B50*, 1152.

Darby, B. W., & Schlenker, B. R. (1982). Children's reactions to apologies. *Journal of Personality and Social Psychology, 43*, 742–753.

Davenport, D. S. (1991). The functions of anger and forgiveness: Guidelines for psychotherapy with victims. *Psychotherapy, 28*, 140–144.

Davidson, D. L. (1993). Forgiveness and narcissism: Consistency in experience across real and hypothetical hurt situations. *Dissertation Abstracts International, 54,* 2746.

Davidson, L. L. (2001). Forgiveness and attachment in college students. *Dissertation Abstracts International: Section B: The Sciences and Engineering, 61,* 6129.

Davies, W. W. (1920). The law of forgiveness. *Methodist Review, 103,* 807–813.

De Cantanzaro, C. J. (1962). Forgiveness in the Old Testament. *American Church Quarterly, 2,* 26–39.

De Jong, P. (1951). Divine and human forgiveness: An investigation into the biblical data about God's and man's forgiveness and the relations between them, followed by a comparison of the biblical data and some of the systematic and ethical approaches to the problem. (Doctoral dissertation, Union Theological Seminary, 1951). *Dissertation Abstracts International A49,* 103.

de Waal, F. B. M. (1993). Reconciliation among primates: A review of empirical evidence and unresolved issues. In W. A. Mason & S. P. Mendoza (Eds.), *Primate social conflict* (pp. 111–144). Albany: State University of New York Press.

Denton, R. T., & Martin, M. W. (1998). Defining forgiveness: An empirical exploration of process and role. *American Journal of Family Therapy, 26,* 281–292.

Deshea, L. (2000). Development and validation of a scale measuring willingness to forgive. *Dissertation Abstracts International, 8B,* 60.

Deshea, L. (2003). A scenario-based scale of willingness to forgive. *Individual Differences Research, 1,* 201–217.

DiBlasio, F. A. (1992). Forgiveness in psychotherapy: Comparison of older and younger therapists. *Journal of Psychology and Christianity, 11,* 181–187.

DiBlasio, F. A. (1993). The role of social workers' religious beliefs in helping family members forgive. *Families in Society, 74,* 163–170.

DiBlasio, F. A. (1998). The use of decision-based forgiveness intervention within intergenerational family therapy. *Journal of Family Therapy, 20,* 77–94.

DiBlasio, F. A. (2000). Decision-based forgiveness treatment in cases of marital infidelity. *Psychotherapy, 37,* 149–158.

DiBlasio, F. A., & Benda, B. B. (1991). Practitioners, religion, and the use of forgiveness in the clinical setting. *Journal of Psychology and Christianity, 10,* 166–172.

DiBlasio, F. A., & Benda, B. B. (2001). Effects of religiosity and forgiveness on violence among adolescents. *Marriage and Family: A Christian Journal, 4,* 393–404.

DiBlasio, F. A., & Benda B. B. (2002). The effect of forgiveness treatment on self-esteem of spouses: Initial experimental results. *Marriage and Family: A Christian Journal, 5,* 511–523.

DiBlasio, F. A., & Proctor, J. H. (1993). Therapists and the clinical use of forgiveness. *American Journal of Family Therapy, 21,* 175–184.

Dickey, W. J. (1998). Forgiveness and crime: The possibilities of restorative justice. In R. D. Enright & J. North (Eds.), *Exploring forgiveness* (pp. 106–120). Madison, WI: University of Wisconsin Press.

Dillon, R. S. (2001). Self-forgiveness and self-respect. *Ethics, 112,* 53–83.

Dimitroff, M., & Hoekstra, S. (1998). The spiritually or religiously disordered couple. In J. Carlson & L. Sperry (Eds.), *The disordered couple* (pp. 121–138). New York: Brunner/Mazel.

Domeris, W. R. (1986). Biblical perspectives on forgiveness. *Journal of Theology for Southern Africa, 54,* 48–50.

Donnelly, D. (1984). Forgiveness and recidivism. *Pastoral Psychology, 33,* 15–24.

Donnelly, D. (1984). The human side of forgiveness and what it tells us about how God forgives. *New Catholic World, 227,* 28–30.

Dorff, E. N. (1992). Individual and communal forgiveness. In D. H. Frank (Ed.), *Autonomy and Judaism* (pp. 193–218). Albany, NY: State University of New York Press.

Dorff, E. N. (1998). The elements of forgiveness: A Jewish approach. In E. L. Worthington, Jr. (Ed.), *Dimensions of forgiveness: Psychological research and theological perspectives* (pp. 29–55). Philadelphia: Templeton Foundation Press.

Dorn, T. J. (1998). Relationships amongst guilt-proneness, shame-proneness, and the forgiveness of others. *Dissertation Abstracts International, 37* (1052), 3.

Doyle, G. (1999). Forgiveness as an intrapsychic process. *Psychotherapy, 36,* 190–198.

Dreelin, E. D. (1994). Religious functioning and forgiveness. (Doctoral dissertation, Fuller Theological Seminary, 1994). *Dissertation Abstracts International, 55,* 2397A.

Drinnon, J. E. R. (2001). Assessing forgiveness: Development and validation of the Act of Forgiveness Scale. *Dissertation Abstracts International, 61* (6185), 11-B.

Droll, D. M. (1985). Forgiveness: Theory and research (Doctoral dissertation, University of Nevada, 1985). *Dissertation Abstracts International, 45,* 2732B.

Duggar, C. D. (1995). An investigation of selected elements of religious ideation as related to particular categories of psychopathology. *Dissertation Abstracts International: Section B: Sciences & Engineering, 56,* 2321.

Educational Psychology Study Group. (1990). Must a Christian require repentance before forgiving? *Journal of Psychology and Christianity, 9,* 16–19.

Edwards, L. M., Lapp-Rincker, R. H., Magyar-Moe, J. L., Rehfeldt, J. D., Ryder, J. A., Brown, J. C., et al. (2002). A positive relationship between religious faith and forgiveness: Faith in the absence of data? *Pastoral Psychology, 50,* 147–152.

Egleston, P. N., Lee, K. H., Brown, W. H., Green, R. D. J., Farrow, T. F. D., Hunter, M. D., et al. (2004). Treatment induced brain changes during forgiveness tasks in patients with schizophrenia. *Schizophrenia Research, 67,* 193.

Elder, J. W. (1998). Expanding our options: The challenge of forgiveness. In R. D. Enright & J. North (Eds.), *Exploring forgiveness* (pp. 150–161). Madison, WI: University of Wisconsin Press.

Elshatain, J. B. (1999). Politics and forgiveness: The Clinton case. In C. Fackne (Ed.), *Judgment day at the White House* (pp. 11–17). Grand Rapids, MI: Eerdmans.

Emerson, J. G. (1964). *The dynamics of forgiveness.* Philadelphia: Westminster Press.

Emmons, R. A. (2000). Personality and forgiveness. In M. E. McCullough, K. I. Pargament, & C. E. Thoresen (Eds.), *Forgiveness: Theory, research, and practice* (pp. 156–175). New York: Guilford Press.

Enright, R. D. (1998). Comprehensive bibliography on interpersonal forgiveness. In R. D. Enright & J. North (Eds.), *Exploring forgiveness* (pp. 165–186). Madison, WI: University of Wisconsin Press.

Enright, R. D. (1999). "Interpersonal forgiving in close relationships": Correction to McCullough et al. (1997). *Journal of Personality and Social Psychology, 77,* 218.

Enright, R. D. (2001). *Forgiveness is a choice: A step-by-step process for resolving anger and restoring hope.* Washington, DC: American Psychological Association.

Enright, R. D., & Coyle, C. T. (1998). Researching the process model of forgiveness within psychological interventions. In E. L. Worthington Jr. (Ed.), *Dimensions of forgiveness: Psychological research and theological perspectives* (pp. 139–161). Philadelphia: Templeton Foundation Press.

Enright, R. D., & Eastin, D. L. (1992). Interpersonal forgiveness within the helping professions: An attempt to resolve differences of opinion. *Counseling and Values, 36,* 84–103.

Enright, R. D., Eastin, D. L., Golden, S., Sarinopoulos, I., & Freedman, S. (1992). Interpersonal forgiveness within the helping professions: An attempt to resolve differences of opinion. *Counseling and Values, 36,* 84–103.

Enright, R. D., & Fitzgibbons, R. P. (2000). *Helping clients forgive: An empirical guide for resolving anger and restoring hope.* Washington, DC: American Psychological Association.

Enright, R. D., Freedman, S., & Rique, J. (1998). The psychology of interpersonal forgiveness. In R. D. Enright & J. North (Eds.), *Exploring forgiveness* (pp. 46–62). Madison, WI: University of Wisconsin Press.

Enright, R. D., Gassin, E. A., & Wu, C. (1992). Forgiveness: A developmental view. *Journal of Moral Education, 21,* 99–114.

Enright, R. D., Mullet, E., & Fitzgibbons, R. P. (2001). Le pardon comme mode de regulation emotionnelle. *Journal de Therapie Comportementale et Cognitive, 11,* 123–135.

Enright, R. D., & North, J. (Eds). (1998). *Exploring forgiveness.* Madison, WI: University of Wisconsin Press.

Enright, R. D., Santos, M. J., & Al-Mabuk, R. (1989). The adolescent as forgiver. *Journal of Adolescence, 12,* 99–110.

Enright, R. D., & the Human Development Study Group (1991). The moral development of forgiveness. In W. Kurtines & J. Gerwitz (Eds.), *Handbook of moral behavior and development* (Vol. 1; pp. 123–152). Hillsdale, NJ: Lawrence Erlbaum.

Enright, R. D., & the Human Development Study Group (1994). Piaget on the moral development of forgiveness: Identity or reciprocity? *Human Development, 37,* 63–80.

Enright, R. D., & the Human Development Study Group (1996). Counseling within the forgiveness triad: On forgiving, receiving forgiveness, and self-forgiveness. *Counseling and Values, 40,* 107–126.

Enright, R. D., & Zell, R. (1989). Problems encountered when we forgive one another. *Journal of Psychology and Christianity, 8,* 52–60.

Exline, J. J., & Baumeister, R. F. (2000). Expressing forgiveness and repentance: Benefits and barriers. In M. E. McCullough, K. I. Pargament, & C. E. Thoresen (Eds.), *Forgiveness: Theory, research, and practice* (pp. 133–155). New York: Guilford Press.

Exline, J. J., & Smith, C. (2004). The value of forgiveness in pastoral care. In D. Herl & M. L. Berman (Eds.), *Building bridges over troubled waters: Enhancing pastoral care and guidance* (pp. 259–275). Lima, OH: Wyndham Hall.

Exline, J. J., Worthington, E. L., Jr., Hill, P. C., & McCullough, M. E. (2003). Forgiveness and justice: A research agenda for social and personality psychology. *Personality and Social Psychology Review, 7,* 337–348.

Exline, J. J., Yali, A. M., & Lobel, M. (1999). When God disappoints: Difficulty forgiving God and its role in negative emotion. *Journal of Health Psychology, 4,* 365–379.

Fagenson, E. A., & Cooper, J. (1987). When push comes to power: A test of power restoration theory's explanation for aggressive conflict escalation. *Basic and Applied Social Psychology, 8,* 273–293.

Falconi, A., & Mullet, E. (2003). Cognitive algebra of love through the adult life. *International Journal of Aging and Human Development, 57,* 277–292.

Farrow, T. F. D., Zheng, Y., Wilkinson, I. D., Spence, S. A., Deakin, J. F. W., Tarrier, N., et al. (2001). Investigating the functional anatomy of empathy and forgiveness. *NeuroReport, 12,* 2433–2438.

Fennel, D. L. (1993). Characteristics of long-term first marriages. *Journal of Mental Health Counseling, 15,* 446–460.

Ferch, S. R. (1998). Intentional forgiving as a counseling intervention. *Journal of Counseling and Development, 76,* 261–270.

Ferch, S. R. (1999). Marital forgiveness: A case study of forgiveness and multiple extramarital affairs. *Marriage and Family: A Christian Journal, 2,* 159–170.

Ferch, S. R. (2000). Meanings of touch and forgiveness: A hermeneutic phenomenological inquiry. *Counseling and Values, 44,* 155–173.

Ferch, S. R., & Ramsey, M. I. (2003). Sacred conversation: A spiritual response to unavoidable suffering. *Canadian Journal of Counseling, 37,* 16–27.

Fincham, F. D. (2000). The kiss of the porcupines: From attributing responsibility to forgiving. *Personal Relationships, 7,* 1–23.

Fincham, F. D. (2003). Marital conflict: Correlates, structure, and context. *Current Directions in Psychological Science, 12,* 23–27.

Fincham, F. D., & Beach, S. R. H. (2001). Forgiveness: Toward a public health approach to intervention. In J. H. Harvey & A. Wenzel (Eds.), *A clinician's guide to maintaining and enhancing close relationships* (pp. 277–300). Mahwah, NJ: Lawrence Erlbaum.

Fincham, F. D., & Beach, S. R. H. (2002). Forgiveness in marriage: Implications for psychological aggression and constructive communication. *Personal Relationships, 9,* 239–251.

Fincham, F. D., & Beach, S. R. H. (2002). Forgiving in close relationships. In F. Columbus (Ed.), *Advances in psychology research* (Vol. 7, pp. 163–197). Huntington, NY: Nova Science.

Fincham, F. D., Beach, S. R. H., & Davila, J. (2004). Forgiveness and conflict resolution in marriage. *Journal of Family Psychology, 18,* 72–81.

Fincham, F. D., Paleari, F. G., & Regalia, C. (2002). Forgiveness in marriage: The role of relationship quality, attributions, and empathy. *Personal Relationships, 9,* 27–37.

Fincham, F. D., Paleari, F. G., & Regalia C. (2003) Adolescents' willingness to forgive their parents: An empirical model. *Parenting, 3,* 155–174.

Finkel, E. J., Rusbult, C. E., Kumashiro, M., & Hannon, P.A. (2002). Dealing with betrayal in close relationships: Does commitment promote forgiveness? *Journal of Personality and Social Psychology, 82,* 956–974.

Fittipaldi, S. E. (1982). Zen-mind, Christian-mind, and empathy-mind. *Journal of Ecumenical Studies, 19,* 69–84.

Fitzgibbons, R. P. (1986). The cognitive and emotive use of forgiveness in the treatment of anger. *Psychotherapy, 23,* 629–633.

Flanigan, B. J. (1987). Shame and forgiving in alcoholism. *Alcoholism Treatment Quarterly, 4,* 181–195.

Flanigan, B. J. (1994). *Forgiving the unforgivable: Overcoming the bitter legacy of intimate wounds.* Foster City, CA: IDG Books Worldwide.

Flegel, H. (1990). The individual and the psychotherapeutic community: Based on Levinas' "Totalite et Infini." *International Journal of Therapeutic Communities, 11,* 33–41.

Floristan, C., & Duquoc, C. (Eds.). (1986). *Forgiveness.* Edinburgh: Concilium.

Fow, N. R. (1988). An empirical-phenomenological investigation of the experience of forgiving another. (Doctoral dissertation, University of Pittsburgh, 1989). *Dissertation Abstracts International B50,* 1097.

Fow, N. R. (1996). The phenomenology of forgiveness and reconciliation. *Journal of Phenomenological Psychology, 27,* 219–233.

Frankel, E. (1998). Repentance, psychotherapy, and healing through a Jewish lens. *American Behavioral Scientist, 41,* 814–833.

Freedman, S. R. (1998). Forgiveness and reconciliation: The importance of understanding how they differ. *Counseling and Values, 42,* 200–216.

Freedman, S. R. (1999). A voice of forgiveness: One incest survivor's experience forgiving her father. *Journal of Family Psychotherapy, 10,* 37–60.

Freedman, S. R. (2000). Creating an expanded view: How therapists can help their clients forgive. *Journal of Family Psychotherapy, 23,* 629–633.

Freedman, S. R., & Enright, R. D. (1996). Forgiveness as an intervention goal with incest survivors. *Journal of Consulting and Clinical Psychology, 64,* 983–992.

Freedman, S. R., & Knupp, A. (2003). The impact of forgiveness on adolescent adjustment to parental divorce. *Journal of Divorce and Remarriage, 39,* 135–165.

Freemesser, G. F. (1985). Clinical role of religion: New vistas or perceptions. In R. E. Kogan & J. T. Salvendy (Eds.), *Outpatient psychiatry: Progress, treatment, prevention. POCA perspectives, No. 9* (pp. 38–51). Tuscaloosa: University of Alabama Press.

Fukuno, M., & Ohbuchi, K. (1998). How effective are different accounts of harm-doing in softening victims' reactions? A scenario investigation of the effects of severity, relationship, and culture. *Asian Journal of Social Psychology, 1,* 167–178.

Galindo, J. (2002). Understanding the construct of forgiveness: An empirical study. *Dissertation Abstracts International: Section B: Sciences & Engineering, 63,* 2582.

Gartner, J. (1988). The capacity to forgive: An object relations perspective. In M. Finn & J. Gartner (Eds.), *Object relations theory and religion* (pp. 21–33). Westport, CT: Praeger.

Gartner, J. (1996). Religious commitment, mental health, and prosocial behavior: A review of the empirical literature. In E. P. Shafranske (Ed.), *Religion and the clinical practice of psychology* (pp. 187–214). Washington, DC: American Psychological Association.

Garzon, F., Richards, J., Witherspoon, M., Garver, S., Wu, Z., Burkett, L., et al. (2002). Forgiveness in community cultural contexts: Applications in therapy and opportunities for expanded professional roles. *Journal of Psychology and Christianity, 21,* 349–356.

Gassin, E. A. (1995). Social cognition and forgiveness in adolescent romance: An intervention study. *Dissertation Abstracts International, 56,* 1290.

Gassin, E. A. (1998). Receiving forgiveness as moral education: A theoretical analysis and initial empirical investigation. *Journal of Moral Education, 27,* 71–87.

Gassin, E. A. (2000). Are Christians NOT obligated to forgive? A response to Martin (1997). *Journal of Psychology and Theology, 28,* 36–42.

Gassin, E. A. (2001). Interpersonal forgiveness from an Eastern Orthodox perspective. *Journal of Psychology and Theology, 29,* 187–200.

Gassin, E. A., & Enright, R. D. (1995). The will to meaning in the process of forgiveness. *Journal of Psychology and Christianity, 14,* 38–49.

Gehm, J. R. (1991). The function of forgiveness in the criminal justice system. In J. Messmer & H-U. Otto (Eds.), *Restorative justice on trial: Pitfalls and potentials of victim-offender mediation—International research perspectives* (pp. 541–550). Boston: Kluwer Academic.

Gentilone, F., & Regidor, J. R. (1986, April). The political dimension of reconciliation: A recent Italian experience. In C. Florstein & A. Duquoc (Eds.). *Forgiving* (Special Issue). Concilium, Edinburgh: T & T Clark.

Geoghegan, E. B. (2000). Abortion and loss: A psychological and theological study of religious coping, forgiveness, and grief. *Dissertation Abstracts International: Section B: Sciences and Engineering, 61,* 1080.

Gerber, L. A. (1987). Experiences of forgiveness in physicians whose medical treatment was not successful. *Psychological Reports, 61,* 236.

Gerber, L. A. (1990). Transformations in self-understanding in surgeons whose treatments efforts were not successful. *American Journal of Psychotherapy, 44,* 75–84.

Gibson, J. L., & Gouws, A. (1999). Truth and reconciliation in South Africa: Attributions to blame and the struggle over apartheid. *American Political Science Review, 93,* 501–517.

Girard, M., & Mullet, E. (1997). Forgiveness in adolescents, young, middle-aged, and older adults. *Journal of Adult Development, 4,* 209–220.

Girard, M., & Mullet, E. (1997). Forgiveness: An exploratory factor analysis and its relationship to religious variables. *Review of Religious Research, 34,* 333–347.

Girard, M., Mullet, E., & Calahan, S. (2002). Mathematics of forgiveness. *American Journal of Psychology, 115,* 351–375.

Gisi, T. M. (1999). Evaluating the relationship between traumatic brain injury, anger, and forgiveness. *Dissertation Abstracts International, 59* (4463), 8-B.

Gisi, T. M., & D'Amato, R.C. (2000). What factors should be considered in rehabilitation: Are anger, social desirability, and forgiveness related in adults with traumatic brain injuries? *International Journal of Neuroscience, 105,* 121–133.

Gladson, J. A. (1992). Higher than the heavens: Forgiveness in the Old Testament. *Journal of Psychology and Christianity, 11,* 125–135.

Gobodo-Madikizela, P. (2002). Remorse, forgiveness, and rehumanization: Stories from South Africa. *Journal of Humanistic Psychology, 42,* 7–32.

Goins, S. L. (1987). The concept of forgiveness as reflected in the writings of Albert Ellis and Jay Adams. (Master's thesis, University of West Florida, 1988). *Masters Abstracts International, 26,* 291.

Gold, G. J., & Weiner, B. (2000). Remorse, confession, group identity, and expectancies about repeating a transgression. *Basic and Applied Social Psychology, 22,* 291–300.

Golding, M. (1984–1985). Forgiveness and regret. *Philosophical Forum, 16,* 121–137.

Gonzales, M. H., Haugen, J. A., & Manning, D. J. (1994). Victims as "narrative critics": Factors influencing rejoinders and evaluative responses to offenders' accounts. *Personality and Social Psychology Bulletin, 20,* 691–704.

Gonzales, M. H., Manning, D. J., & Haugen, J. A. (1992). Explaining our sins: Factors influencing offender accounts and anticipated victim responses. *Journal of Personality and Social Psychology, 62,* 958–971.

Gordon, K. C., & Baucom, D. H. (1998). Understanding betrayals in marriage: A synthesized model of forgiveness. *Family Process, 37,* 425–449.

Gordon, K. C., & Baucom, D. H. (1999). A multi-theoretical intervention for promoting recovery from extramarital affairs. *Clinical Psychology—Science and Practice, 6,* 382–399.

Gordon, K. C., & Baucom, D. H. (2003). Forgiveness and marriage: Preliminary support for a synthesized model of recovery from a marital betrayal. *American Journal of Family Therapy, 31,* 179–199.

Gordon, K. C., Baucom, D. H., & Snyder, D. K. (2000). The use of forgiveness in marital therapy. In M. E. McCullough, K. I. Pargament, & C. E. Thoresen (Eds.), *Forgiveness: Theory, research, and practice* (pp. 203–227). New York: Guilford Press.

Gordon, K. C., Baucom, D. H., & Snyder, D. K. (2004). An integrative intervention for promoting recovery from extramarital affairs. *Journal of Marital and Family Therapy, 30,* 213–232.

Gordon, K. C., Burton, S., & Porter, L. (2004). The role of forgiveness: Predicting women in domestic violence shelters intentions to return to their partners. *Journal of Family Psychology, 18,* 331–338.

Gorsuch, R. L., & Hao, J. Y. (1993). Forgiveness: An exploratory factor analysis and its relationships to religious variables. *Review of Religious Research, 34,* 333–347.

Graham, K. H. (1994). Forgiveness: A personal and pastoral imperative. (Doctoral dissertation, Fuller Theological Seminary, 1994.) *Dissertation Abstracts International A, 55,* 991.

Graham-Pole, J., Wass, H., Eyeberg, S. M., & Chu, L. (1989). Communicating with dying children and their siblings: A retrospective analysis. *Death Studies, 13,* 465–483.

Gregory, W. H. (2002). Resiliency in the Black family. *Dissertation Abstracts International, 62* (4786), 10-B.

Grosskopf, B. (1999). *Forgive your parents, heal yourself: How understanding your painful family legacy can transform your life.* New York: Free Press.

Haaken, J. (2002). The good, the bad, and the ugly: Psychoanalytic and cultural perspectives on forgiveness. In S. Lamb & J. G. Murphy (Eds.), *Before forgiving: Cautionary views of forgiveness in psychotherapy* (pp. 172–191). London: Oxford University Press.

Haley, W. E., & Strickland, B. R. (1986). Interpersonal betrayal and cooperation: Effects on self-evaluation in depression. *Journal of Personality and Social Psychology, 50,* 386–391.

Halling, S. (1994). Shame and forgiveness. *Humanistic Psychologist, 22,* 74–87.

Halling, S. (1995). Embracing human fallibility: On forgiving oneself and forgiving others. *Journal of Religion and Health, 33,* 107–113.

Halpain, M. C., Harris, M. J., McClure, F. S., & Jeste, D. V. (1999). Training in geriatric mental health: Needs and strategies. *Psychiatric Services, 50,* 1205–1208.

Hannon, M. A. (2001). Perpetrator behavior and forgiveness in close relationships. *Dissertation Abstracts International, 62* (1642), 3-B.

Hansen, M. J. (2002). Forgiveness as an educational intervention goal for persons at the end of life. *Dissertation Abstracts International, 63,* 1224.

Hanson-Richardson, R. J. (1999). Forgiveness: Its nature and facilitation. *Dissertation Abstracts International: Section B: Sciences and Engineering, 60,* 0410.

Harakas, S. S. (1998). Forgiveness and reconciliation: An Orthodox perspective. In R. G. Helmick & R. L. Petersen (Eds.), *Forgiveness and reconciliation: Religion, public policy, and conflict transformation* (pp. 51–77). Philadelphia: Templeton Foundation Press.

Hargrave, T. D. (1994). Families and forgiveness: A theoretical and therapeutic framework. *The Family Journal: Counseling and Therapy for Couples and Families, 2,* 339–348.

Hargrave, T. D. (1994). *Families and forgiveness: Healing wounds in the intergenerational family.* New York: Brunner/Mazel.

Hargrave, T. D. (2001). *Forgiving the devil: Coming to terms with damaged relationships.* Phoenix, AZ: Zeig, Tucker, & Theisen.

Hargrave, T. D., & Sells, J. N. (1997). The development of a forgiveness scale. *Journal of Marital and Family Therapy, 23,* 41–64.

Harris, A. H. S., & Thoresen, C. E. (2003). Strength-based health psychology: Counseling for total human health. In W. B. Walsh (Ed.), *Counseling psychology and optimal human functioning. Contemporary topics in vocational psychology* (pp. 199–227). Mahwah, NJ: Lawrence Erlbaum.

Harris, A. H. S., Thoresen, C. E., McCullough, M. E., & Larson, D. B. (1999). Spiritually and religiously oriented health interventions. *Journal of Health Psychology, 4,* 413–433.

Harris, J. W. (1986). Lawyers and forgiveness: Until seventy times seven? *Modern Christianity, 28,* 32–41.

Harris, M. L. (1999). Personological predictors of forgiveness: An investigation of a process model. *Dissertation Abstracts International, 59,* 4464.

Harris, R. (2002). *Christ-centered therapy: Empowering the self.* New York: Haworth Press.

Hart, K. E. (1999). A spiritual interpretation of the 12-steps of Alcoholics Anonymous: From resentment to forgiveness to love. *Journal of Ministry in Addiction and Recovery, 6,* 25–39.

Harvey, J. (1993). Forgiving as an obligation of the moral life. *International Journal of Moral and Social Studies, 8,* 211–222.

Harvey, J. H., & Wenzel, A. (Eds.). (2002). *A clinician's guide to maintaining and enhancing close relationships.* Mahwah, NJ: Lawrence Erlbaum.

Harvey, R. W., & Brenner, D. G. (1997). *Choosing the gift of forgiveness: How to overcome hurts and brokenness.* Grand Rapids, MI: Baker Book House.

Hauerwas, S. (1983). Constancy and forgiveness: The novel as a school for virtue. *Notre Dame English Journal, 15,* 23–54.

Hebl, J. H., & Enright, R. D. (1993). Forgiveness as a psychotherapeutic goal with elderly females. *Psychotherapy, 30,* 658–667.

Heller, S. (1998). Emerging field of forgiveness studies explores how we let go of grudges. *Chronicle of Higher Education, 17,* A18–A20.

Helmick, R. G. (2001). Does religion fuel or heal in conflicts? In R. G. Helmick & R. L. Petersen (Eds.), *Forgiveness and reconciliation: Religion, public policy, and conflict transformation* (pp. 81–95). Philadelphia: Templeton Foundation Press.

Helmick, R. G., & Petersen, R. L. (Eds.). (2001). *Forgiveness and reconciliation: Religion, public policy, and conflict transformation.* Philadelphia: Templeton Foundation Press.

Herford, R. T. (1964). Repentance and forgiveness in the Talmud: With some reference to the teaching of the gospels. *Hibbert Journal, 40,* 55–64.

Hestevold, H. S. (1985). Justice to mercy. *Philosophy and Phenomenological Research, 46,* 281–291.

Hewstone, M., Cairns, E., Voci, A., McLernon, F., Niens, U., & Noor, M. (2004). Intergroup forgiveness and guilt in Northern Ireland: Social psychological dimensions of "The Troubles." In N. R. Branscombe & B. Doosje (Eds.), *Collective guilt: International perspectives* (pp. 193–215). New York: Cambridge University Press.

Hill, W. E. (2001). Understanding forgiveness as discovery: Implications for marital and family therapy. *Contemporary Family Therapy, 23,* 369–384.

Hodgins, H. S., Liebeskind, E., & Schwartz, W. (1996). Getting out of hot water: Facework in social predicaments. *Journal of Personality and Social Psychology, 71,* 300–314.

Holbrook, M. I., White, M. H., & Hutt, M. J. (1995). The Vengeance Scale: Comparison of groups and an assessment of external validity. *Psychological Reports, 77,* 224–226.

Holeman, V. T. (1995). The relationship between forgiveness of a perpetrator and current marital adjustment for female survivors of childhood sexual abuse. *Dissertation Abstracts International: Section B: Sciences & Engineering, 55,* 4592.

Holeman, V. T. (1997). Couples forgiveness exercise. *Family Journal: Counseling and Therapy for Couples and Families, 5,* 263–266.

Holeman, V. T. (1999). Mutual forgiveness: A catalyst for relationship in the moral crucible of marriage. *Marriage and Family: A Christian Journal, 2,* 147–157.

Holeman, V. T. (2003). Marital reconciliation: A long and winding road. *Journal of Psychology and Christianity, 22,* 30–42.

Holeman, V. T. (2004). *Reconcilable differences: Hope and healing for troubled marriages.* Downers Grove, IL: InterVarsity Press.

Holeman, V. T., & Myers, R. (1998). Effects of forgiveness of perpetrators on marital adjustment for survivors of sexual abuse. *Family Journal: Counseling and Therapy for Couples and Families, 6,* 182–188.

Holmgren, M. R. (1993). Forgiveness and the intrinsic value of persons. *American Philosophical Quarterly, 30,* 341–352.

Holmgren, M. R. (1998). Self-forgiveness and responsible moral agency. *Journal of Value Inquiry, 32,* 75–91.

Holmgren, M. R. (2002). Forgiveness and self-forgiveness in psychotherapy. In S. Lamb & J. G. Murphy (Eds.), *Before forgiving: Cautionary views of forgiveness in psychotherapy* (pp. 112–135). London: Oxford University Press.

Hope, D. (1987). The healing paradox of forgiveness. *Psychotherapy, 24,* 240–244.

Howard, N. C., McMinn, M. R., Bissell, L. D., Faries, S. R., & VanMeter, J. B. (2000). Spiritual directors and clinical psychologists: A comparison of mental health and spiritual values. *Journal of Psychology and Theology, 28,* 308–320.

Huang, S. T, & Enright, R. D. (2000). Forgiveness and anger-related emotions in Taiwan: Implications for therapy. *Psychotherapy, 37,* 71–79.

Huang, S. T. (1990). Cross-cultural and real-life validations of the theory of forgiveness in Taiwan, the Republic of China. *Dissertation Abstracts International, 51,* 2644.

Hughes, P. M. (1993). What is involved in forgiving? *Journal of Value Inquiry, 27,* 331–340.

Human Development Study Group (1991). Five points on the construct of forgiveness within psychotherapy. *Psychotherapy, 28,* 493–496.

Humphrey, C. W. (1999). A stress management intervention with forgiveness as the goal (meditation, mind-body medicine). *Dissertation Abstracts International: Section B: Sciences & Engineering, 60,* 1855.

Hunter, R. C. A. (1987). Forgiveness, retaliation, and paranoid reactions. *Canadian Psychiatric Association Journal, 23,* 167–173.

Hyer, L. A., & Sohnle, S. J. (2001). *Trauma among older people: Issues and treatment.* Philadelphia: Brunner-Routledge.

Hylen, S. E. (2000). Forgiveness and life in community. *Interpretation: A Journal of Bible and Theology, 54,* 146–157.

Ingersoll, R. E. (1995). Construction and initial validation of the Spiritual Wellness Inventory. (Doctoral dissertation, Kent State University, 1995). *Dissertation Abstracts International,l B56,* 5827.

Introini, M., & Paleari, F. G. (2002). The quality of the marital relationship as a bidimensional construct. *Bollettino di Psicologia Applicata, 236,* 61–70.

Jackson, R. E. (1999). Reducing shame through forgiveness and empathy: A group therapy approach to promoting prosocial behavior. *Dissertation Abstracts International, 60,* 1856.

Jackson, S. M. (1998). The influence of forgiveness on intimacy and trust in marital and committed relationships. *Dissertation Abstracts International, 58* (4452) 8-B.

Jacobson, S. T. (1959). The interpersonalism of guilt and forgiveness as seen in the writings of Harry Stack Sullivan and Emil Brunner. (Doctoral dissertation, Princeton Theological Seminary). *Dissertation Abstracts International.* 1959.

Jeffress, R. (2000). *When forgiving doesn't make sense.* Colorado Springs, CO: WaterBrook.

Johnson, S. (1984). Reconciliation counselling: A Christian's approach to mental health. *Mental Health in Australia, 1,* 35–36.

Jones, J. I., & King, A. L. (2001). Violence and the offender: Interrupting the cycle of violence. In D. S. Sandhu, (Ed.), *Faces of violence: Psychological correlates, concepts, and intervention strategies* (pp. 103–125). Huntington, NY: Nova Science.

Jones, L. G. (1995). *Embodying forgiveness: A theological analysis.* Grand Rapids, MI: Eerdmans.

Jones, L. G. (2000). Crafting communities of forgiveness. *Interpretation: A Journal of Bible and Theology, 54,* 121–134.

Jones-Haldeman, M. (1992). Implications from selected literary devices for a New Testament theology of grace and forgiveness. *Journal of Psychology and Christianity, 11,* 136–146.

Jorgensen, D. (1984). Pain and the healthy individual: A religious perspective. *Counseling and Values, 28,* 134–140.

Kachadourian, L. K., Fincham, F. D., & Davila, J. (2005). Attitudinal ambivalence, rumination and forgiveness of partner transgressions in marriage. *Personality and Social Psychology Bulletin, 31,* 334–342.

Kachadourian, L. K., Fincham, F. D., & Davila, J. (2004). The tendency to forgive in dating and married couples: Association with attachment and relationship satisfaction. *Personal Relationships, 11,* 373–393.

Kadiangandu, J. K., Mullet, E., & Vinsonneau, G. (2001). Forgivingness: A Congo-France comparison. *Journal of Cross-Cultural Psychology, 32,* 504–511.

Kaminer, D., Stein, D. J., Mbanga, I., & Zungu-Dirwayi, N. (2001). The Truth and Reconciliation Commission in South Africa: Relation to psychiatric status and forgiveness among survivors of human rights abuses. *British Journal of Psychiatry, 178,* 373–377.

Kanz, J. E. (2000). How do people conceptualize and use forgiveness? The Forgiveness Attitudes Questionnaire. *Counseling and Values, 44,* 174–188.

Kaplan, B. H. (1992). Social health and the forgiving heart: The Type B story. *Journal of Behavioral Medicine, 15,* 3–14.

Kaplan, B. H. (1993). Two topics not covered by Aldridge: Spirituality in children and forgiveness and health. *Advances, 9,* 30–33.

Kaplan, B. H., Munroe-Blum, H., & Blazer, D. G. (1993). Religion, health, and forgiveness: Traditions and challenges. In J. S. Levin (Ed.), *Religion in aging and health: Theoretical foundations and methodological frontiers* (pp. 52–77). Thousand Oaks, CA: Sage.

Karen, R. (2001). *The forgiving self: The road from resentment to connection.* New York: Doubleday.

Karremans, J. C., & Van Lange, P. A. M. (2004). Back to caring after being hurt: The role of forgiveness. *European Journal of Social Psychology, 34,* 207–227.

Karremans, J. C., Van Lange, P. A. M., Ouwerkerk, J. W., & Kluwer, E. S. (2003). When forgiving enhances psychological well-being: The role of interpersonal commitment. *Journal of Personality and Social Psychology, 84,* 1011–1026.

Kasper, W. (1989). The church as a place of forgiveness. *Communio: International Catholic Review, 16,* 160–171.

Kaufman, M. E. (1984). The courage to forgive. *Israel Journal of Psychiatry and Related Sciences, 21,* 177–187.

Kearns, J. N., & Fincham, F. D. (2005). Victim and perpetrator accounts of interpersonal transgressions: Self-serving or relationship-serving biases. *Personality and Social Psychology Bulletin, 31,* 321–333.

Kearns, J. N., & Fincham, F. D. (2004). A prototype analysis of forgiveness. *Personality and Social Psychology Bulletin, 30,* 838–855.

Kelley, D. L. (1998). The communication of forgiveness. *Communication Studies, 49,* 1–17.

Kelln, B. R. C., & Ellard, J. H. (1999). An equity theory analysis of the impact of forgiveness and retribution on transgressor compliance. *Personality and Social Psychology Bulletin, 25,* 864–872.

Kendler, K. S., Liu, X., Gardner, C. O., McCullough, M. E., Larson, D., & Prescott, C. A. (2003). Dimensions of religiosity and their relationship to lifetime psychiatric and substance use disorders. *American Journal of Psychiatry, 160,* 496–503.

Kennington, P. A. (1994). Encouraging friendship relationships between women who volunteer and women who live in shelters: An educational action research study focusing on social justice, interpersonal forgiveness, and womanist identity. (Doctoral dissertation, North Carolina State University, 1994). *Dissertation Abstracts International, A55,* 868.

Keyes, C. L. M., & Lopez, S. J. (2002). Toward a science of mental health: Positive directions in diagnosis and interventions. In C. R. Snyder & S. J. Lopez (Eds.), *Handbook of positive psychology* (pp. 45–59). London: Oxford University Press.

Kidder, J. (1975). Requital and criminal justice. *International Philosophical Quarterly, 15,* 255–278.

Kirkpatrick, C. K. (1995). The interpersonal construct of human forgiveness: Comparing perceptions of clinical psychologists and pastoral counselors. (Doctoral dissertation, United States International University, 1995). *Dissertation Abstracts International, A56,* 463.

Kirkup, P. A. (1993). Some religious perspectives on forgiveness and settling differences. Beyond techniques: The soul of family mediation. *Mediation Quarterly, 11,* 79–94.

Kittle, B. (1999). Forgiveness in the criminal justice system: Necessary element or impossible dream. *The World of Forgiveness, 2,* 3–11.

Klassen, W. (1966). *The forgiving community.* Philadelphia: Westminister Press.

Koenig, H. G. (1999). *The healing power of faith: Science explores medicine's last great frontier.* New York: Simon and Schuster.

Konstam, V., Chernoff, M., & Deveney, S. (2001). Toward forgiveness: The role of shame, guilt, anger, and empathy. *Counseling and Values, 46,* 26–39.

Konstam, V., Marx, F., Schurer, J., Harrington, A., Lombardo, N. E., & Deveney, S. (2000). Forgiving: What mental health counselors are telling us. *Journal of Mental Health Counseling, 22,* 253–267.

Konstam, V., Marx, F., Schurer, J., Emerson Lombardo, N., & Harrington, A. K. (2002). Forgiveness in practice: What mental health counselors are telling us. In S. Lamb & J. G. Murphy (Eds.), *Before forgiving: Cautionary views of forgiveness in psychotherapy* (pp. 54–71). New York: Oxford University Press.

Kraus, P. A. (1999). The journey from role identity to self identity: A study of cognitive development and personal spiritual growth among middle-aged Catholic women. *Dissertation Abstracts International: Section B: Sciences and Engineering, 60,* 1887.

Krause, N., & Ellison, C. G. (2003). Forgiveness by God, forgiveness of others, and psychological well-being in late life. *Journal for the Scientific Study of Religion, 42,* 77–93.

Krause, N., & Ingersoll-Dayton, B. (2001). Religion and the process of forgiveness in late life. *Review of Religious Research, 42,* 252–276.

Krejci, M. J. (2004). Forgiveness in marital therapy. In P. S. Richards & A. E. Bergin (Eds.), *Casebook for a spiritual strategy in counseling and psychotherapy* (pp. 87–102). Washington, DC: American Psychological Association.

Kremer, J. F., & Stephens, L. (1983). Attributions and arousal as mediators of mitigation's effect on retaliation. *Journal of Personality and Social Psychology, 45,* 335–343.

Kuert, W. P. (2003). A study of the redemptive change process from a biblical and psychological perspective. *Dissertation Abstracts International, 63* (3490), 7-B.

Kurusu, T. A. (2000). The effectiveness of pretreatment intervention on participants of a forgiveness-promoting psychoeducational group in various stages of change. *Dissertation Abstracts International, 60,* 3270.

Kus, R. (1992). Spirituality in everyday life: Experiences of gay men of Alcoholics Anonymous. *Journal of Chemical Dependency Treatment,* 5, 49–66.

Lamb, S. (2002). Women, abuse, and forgiveness: A special case. In S. Lamb & J. G. Murphy (Eds.), *Before forgiving: Cautionary views of forgiveness in psychotherapy* (pp. 155–171). New York: Oxford University Press.

Lamb, S., & Murphy, J. G. (Eds.). (2002). *Before forgiving: Cautionary views of forgiveness in psychotherapy.* New York: Oxford University Press.

Landman, J. (2002). Earning forgiveness: The story of a perpetrator, Katherine Ann Power. In S. Lamb & J. G. Murphy (Eds.), *Before forgiving: Cautionary views of forgiveness in psychotherapy* (pp. 232–264). New York: Oxford University Press.

Lang, B. (1994). Forgiveness. *American Philosophical Quarterly, 31,* 105–117.

Larson, E. (1992). *From anger to forgiveness.* New York: Ballantine Books.

Lauritzen, P. (1987). Forgiveness: Moral prerogative or religious duty? *Journal of Religious Ethics, 15,* 141–150.

Lavery, C., & Achilles, M. (1999). Apologies: Balancing the needs of victims and offenders. *VOMA Connections, 3,* 6.

Lawler, K. A., Younger, J. W., Piferi, R. L., Billington, E., Jobe, R., Edmondson, K., et al. (2003). A change of heart: Cardiovascular correlates of forgiveness in response to interpersonal conflict. *Journal of Behavioral Medicine, 26,* 373–393.

Leach, M. M., & Lark, R. (2003). Does spirituality add to personality in the study of trait forgiveness? *Personality and Individual Differences, 30,* 881–885.

Lena, M. (1984). Education in the sense of forgiveness. (J. Lyon, Trans.). *International Catholic Review, 11,* 308–321.

Lester, A. D., & Lester, J. L. (1998). *It takes two: The joy of intimate marriage.* Louisville, KY: Westminster/John Knox Press.

Lim, B. K. (2001). Conflict resolution styles, somatization, and marital satisfaction in Chinese couples: The moderating effect of forgiveness and willingness to seek professional help. *Dissertation Abstracts International: Section B: Sciences & Engineering, 61,* 3902.

Lim, B. R., & Tan, S. (2001). Regret and forgiveness: Principles for intervening in counterfactual thinking. *Journal of Psychology and Christianity, 20,* 85–90.

Lin, W. N. (1998). Forgiveness as an intervention for late adolescents with insecure attachment in Taiwan. *Dissertation Abstracts International: Section B: Sciences & Engineering, 59,* 2456.

Lin, W. N. (2002). Forgiveness as an educational intervention goal within a drug rehabilitation center. *Dissertation Abstracts International, 62,* 2342.

Linn, M., & Linn, D. (1978). *Healing life's hurts.* New York: Paulist Press.

Loewen, J. A. (1970). Four kinds of forgiveness. *Practical Anthropology, 11,* 153–168.

Long, W. J., & Brecke, P. (2003). *War and reconciliation: Reason and emotion in conflict resolution.* Cambridge, MA: MIT Press.

Lopez, S. J., & Snyder, C. R. (Eds.). (2003). *Positive psychological assessment: A handbook of models and measures.* Washington, DC: American Psychological Association.

Lourenco, O., & Fonseca, E. (2003). The force of emotion: Transgressions, emotions, and forgivingness in 5–6 and 7–8 year-olds. *Psicologia Educaca Cultura, 7,* 177–201.

Luebbert, M. C. (1999). The survival value of forgiveness. In D. H. Rosen & M. C. Luebbert (Eds.), *Evolution of the psyche: Human evolution, behavior, and intelligence* (pp. 169–187). Westport, CT: Greenwood.

Luebbert, M. C. (2000). Attachment, psychosocial development, shame, guilt, and forgiveness. *Dissertation Abstracts International: Section B: Sciences and Engineering, 60(8-B),* 4234.

Lukasik, V. J. (2001). Predictors of the willingness to use forgiveness as a coping strategy in adolescent friendships. *Dissertation Abstracts International, 61* (3908), 10-A.

Luskin, F. M. (1999) The art and science of forgiveness. *Stanford Medicine, 3,* 32–40.

Luskin, F. M. (1999). The effect of forgiveness training on psychosocial factors in college-age adults. *Dissertation Abstracts International, 60* (1026), 4-A.

Luskin, F. M. (2001) The art of forgiveness. In E. Rosenbaum & I. Rosenbaum (Eds.), *Cancer supportive care: A comprehensive guide for patients and their families* (pp. 181–183). Toronto: Somerville.

Luskin, F. M. (2001). *Forgive for good: A proven prescription for health and happiness.* San Francisco: Harper.

Luskin, F. M. (2004). The effect of forgiveness training on physical and emotional well-being. In M. Schlitz, T. Amorak, & M. Micozzi (Eds.), *Consciousness and healing: Integral approaches to mind body medicine.* New York: CV Mosby.

Luskin, F. M., & Curtis, D. (2000). The power of forgiveness. *California Lawyer, 4,* 25–27.

Luskin, F. M., Thoresen, C., Harris, A., Standard, S., Benisovich, S., Bruning J., et al. (2001). Effects of group forgiveness intervention on perceived stress, state and trait anger, self reported health, symptoms of stress and forgiveness. *Alternative Therapies in Health and Medicine, 7,* 106.

Lynch, L. W. (1983). Fear, freedom, and forgiveness: A goal toward wholeness and healing for single parents with custody. (Doctoral dissertation, Claremont School of Theology, 1983). *Dissertation Abstracts International A44,* 789.

Macaskill, A., Maltby, J., & Day, L. (2002). Forgiveness of self and others and emotional empathy. *Journal of Social Psychology, 142,* 663–665.

Mackintosh, H. R. (1927). *The Christian experience of forgiveness.* London: Nisbet & Company.

Malcolm, W. M. (1999). Relating process to outcome in the resolution of unfinished business in process experiential psychotherapy. *Dissertation Abstracts International: Section B: Sciences & Engineering, 60,* 4235.

Malcolm, W. M., & Greenberg, L. S. (2000). Forgiveness as a process of change in individual psychotherapy. In M. E. McCullough, K. I. Pargament, & C. E. Thoresen (Eds.), *Forgiveness: Theory, research, and practice* (pp. 179–202). New York: Guilford Press.

Maltby, J., Macaskill, A., & Day, L. (2001). Failure to forgive self and others: A replication and extension of the relationship between forgiveness, personality, social desirability and general health. *Personality and Individual Differences, 30,* 881–885.

Mamalakis, P. M. (2001). Painting a bigger picture: Forgiveness therapy with pre-marital infidelity: A case study. *Journal of Family Psychotherapy, 12,* 39–54.

Mamula, K. M. (1997). The effects of guided spiritual exploration on sexually abused women's understanding of God. *Dissertation Abstracts International, 57,* 4792.

Marks, M. (1988). Remorse, revenge, and forgiveness. *Psychotherapy Patient, 5,* 317–330.

Maroda, K. J. (1991). Saint or sadist: Who is the self-righteous patient? *Psychotherapy Patient, 7,* 125–135.

Marty, M. E. (1998). The ethos of Christian forgiveness. In E. L. Worthington, Jr. (Ed.), *Dimensions of forgiveness: Psychological research and theological perspectives* (pp. 9–28). Philadelphia: Templeton Foundation Press.

Mauger, P. A., Freedman, T., McBride, A. G., Perry, J. E., Grove, D. C., & McKinney, K. E. (1992). The measurement of forgiveness: Preliminary research. *Journal of Psychology and Christianity, 11,* 170–180.

Mauldin, F. L. (1983). Singularity and a pattern of sin, punishment, and forgiveness. *Perspectives in Religious Studies, 10,* 41–50.

Mauldin, G. R. (2003). "Forgive and forget": A case example of contextual marital therapy. *Family Journal: Counseling and Therapy for Couples and Families, 11,* 180–184.

Mauldin, G. R., & Anderson, W. T. (1998). Forgiveness as an intervention in contextual family therapy: Two case examples. *TCA Journal, 26,* 123–132.

Mazor, A., Batiste-Harel, P., & Gampel, Y. (1998). Divorcing spouses' coping patterns, attachment bonding, and forgiveness processes in the post-divorce experience. *Journal of Divorce and Remarriage, 29,* 65–81.

McAllister, E. W. C. (1983). Christian counseling and human needs. *Journal of Psychology and Christianity, 2,* 50–60.

McCullough, M. E. (1997). Marital forgiveness. *Marriage and Family: A Christian Journal, 1,* 77–93.

McCullough, M. E. (1999). Review of Enright Forgiveness Inventory—United States version. In P. C. Hill & R. W. Hood (Eds.), *Measures of religiosity* (pp. 457–460). Birmingham, AL: Religious Education Press.

McCullough, M. E. (1999). Review of Wade's Forgiveness Scale. In P. C. Hill & R. W. Hood (Eds.), *Measures of religiosity* (pp. 460–464). Birmingham, AL: Religious Education Press.

McCullough, M. E. (2000). Forgiveness as human strength: Theory, measurement, and links to well-being. *Journal of Social and Clinical Psychology, 19,* 43–55.

McCullough, M. E. (2001). Forgiveness: Who does it and how do they do it? *Current Directions in Psychological Science, 10,* 194–197.

McCullough, M. E. (2001). Forgiving. In C. R. Snyder (Ed.), *Coping with stress: Effective people and processes* (pp. 93–113). New York: Oxford University Press.

McCullough, M. E. (2004). Forgiveness. In C. Peterson & M. E. P. Seligman (Eds.), *Character strengths and virtues: A handbook and classification* (pp. 445–459). New York: Oxford/American Psychological Association.

McCullough, M. E., Bellah, G. C., Kilpatrick, S. D., & Johnson, J. L. (2001). Vengefulness: Relationships with forgiveness, rumination, well-being, and the Big Five. *Personality and Social Psychology Bulletin, 27,* 601–610.

McCullough, M. E., Exline, J. J., & Baumeister, R. F. (1998). An annotated bibliography of research on forgiveness and related topics. In E. L. Worthington, Jr. (Ed.), *Dimensions of forgiveness: Psychological research and theological perspectives* (pp. 193–317). Philadelphia: The Templeton Foundation Press.

McCullough, M. E., Fincham, F. D., & Tsang, J. (2003). Forgiveness, forbearance, and time: The temporal unfolding of transgression-related interpersonal motivations. *Journal of Personality and Social Psychology, 84,* 540–557.

McCullough, M. E., & Hoyt, W. T. (2002). Transgression-related motivational dispositions: Personality substrates of forgiveness and their links to the Big Five. *Personality and Social Psychology Bulletin, 28,* 1556–1573.

McCullough, M. E., Hoyt, W. T., & Rachal, K. C. (2000). What we know (and need to know) about assessing forgiveness constructs. In M. E. McCullough, K. I. Pargament, & C. E. Thoresen (Eds.), *Forgiveness: Theory, research, and practice* (pp. 65–88). New York: Guilford Press.

McCullough, M. E., Pargament, K. I., & Thoresen, C. E. (Eds.). (1999). *Forgiveness: Theory, research, and practice.* New York: Guilford Press.

McCullough, M. E., Pargament, K. I., & Thoresen, C. E. (2000). The psychology of forgiveness: History, conceptual issues, and overview. In M. E. McCullough, K. I. Pargament, & C. E. Thoresen (Eds.), *Forgiveness: Theory, research, and practice* (pp. 1–14). New York: Guilford Press.

McCullough, M. E., Rachal, K. C., Sandage, S. J., Worthington, E. L., Jr., Brown, S. W., & Hight, T. L. (1998). Interpersonal forgiving in close relationships. II. Theoretical elaboration and measurement. *Journal of Personality and Social Psychology, 73,* 321–336.

McCullough, M. E., Sandage, S. J., & Worthington, E. L., Jr. (1995). Charles Williams on interpersonal forgiveness: Theology and therapy. *Journal of Psychology and Christianity, 14,* 355–364.

McCullough, M. E., Sandage, S. J., & Worthington, E. L., Jr. (1997). *To forgive is human: How to put your past in the past.* Downers Grove, IL: InterVarsity Press.

McCullough, M. E., & Witvliet, C. V. O. (2002). The psychology of forgiveness. In C. R. Snyder & S. J. Lopez (Eds.), *Handbook of positive psychology* (pp. 446–458). New York: Oxford University Press.

McCullough, M. E., & Worthington, E. L., Jr. (1994). Encouraging clients to forgive people who have hurt them: Review, critique, and research prospectus. *Journal of Psychology and Theology, 22,* 3–20.

McCullough, M. E., & Worthington, E. L., Jr. (1994). Models of interpersonal forgiveness and their applications to counseling. Review and critique. *Counseling and Values, 39,* 2–14.

McCullough, M. E., & Worthington, E. L., Jr. (1995). Promoting forgiveness: Psychoeducational group interventions with a wait-list control. *Counseling and Values, 4,* 55–68.

McCullough, M. E., & Worthington, E. L., Jr. (1999). Religion and the forgiving personality. *Journal of Personality, 67,* 1141–1164.

McCullough, M. E., Worthington, E. L., Jr., & Rachal, K. C. (1997). Interpersonal forgiving in close relationships. *Journal of Personality and Social Psychology, 73,* 321–336.

McDaniel, S. H., Hepworth, J., & Doherty, W. J. (1999). The shared emotional themes of illness. *Journal of Family Psychotherapy, 10,* 1–8.

McLernon, F., Cairns, E., & Hewstone, M. (2002). Views on forgiveness in Northern Ireland. *Peace Review, 14,* 285–290.

McLernon, F., Cairns, E., Hewstone, M., & Smith, R. (2004). The development of intergroup forgiveness in Northern Ireland. *Journal of Social Issues, 60,* 587–601.

McLernon, F., Cairns, E., Lewis, C. A., & Hewstone, M. (2003). Memories of recent conflict and forgiveness in Northern Ireland. In E. Cairns & M. Roe (Eds.), *The role of memory in ethnic conflict* (pp. 125–143). London: Palgrave Macmillan.

McNally, R. E. (1977). The Counter-Reformation's view of sin and penance. *Thought, 52,* 151–166.

McNeill, D. P. (1971). The dynamics of forgiveness in community: A study of the theological meaning and pastoral implications of processes of forgiveness in experiences other than the celebration of the sacrament of penance. (Doctoral dissertation, Princeton Theological Seminary, 1971). *Dissertation Abstracts International A32,* 563.

Meek, K. R., & McMinn, M. R. (1997). Forgiveness: More than a therapeutic technique. *Journal of Psychology and Christianity, 16,* 51–61.

Meek, K. R., Albright, J. S., & McMinn, M. R. (1995). Religious orientation, guilt, confession, and forgiveness. *Journal of Psychology and Theology, 23,* 190–197.

Meninger, W. (1996). *The process of forgiveness.* New York: Continuum.

Messenger, J. C. (1959). The Christian concept of forgiveness and Anang morality. *Practical Anthropology, 6,* 97–103.

Meyer, L. R. (2000). Forgiveness and public trust. *Fordham Urban Law Journal, 27,* 1515–1540.

Middleton, H. K. (1997). How do adolescents understand and define forgiveness? *Dissertation Abstracts International, 57,* 5352.

Miller, D. H. (1996). A matter of consequence: Abortion rhetoric and media messages. R. L. Parrott & C. M. Condit (Eds.), *Evaluating women's health messages: A resource book* (pp. 33–48). Thousand Oaks, CA: Sage.

Miller, T. Q., Smith, T. W., Turner, C. W., Guijarro, M. L., & Hallet, A. J. (1996). Meta-analytic review of research on hostility and physical health. *Psychological Bulletin, 119,* 322–348.

Minow, M. (1998). *Between vengeance and forgiveness: Facing history after genocide and mass violence.* Boston, MA: Beacon Press.

Mitchell, C. E. (1995). A model for forgiveness in family relationships. *Family Therapy, 22,* 25–30.

Molander, P. (1985). The optimal level of generosity in a selfish, uncertain environment. *Journal of Conflict Resolution, 29,* 611–618.

Molina, C. L. (2000). Experiencing the phenomenon of reconciliation: A heuristic study. *Dissertation Abstracts International, 61,* 2-A.

Mongeau, P. A., Hale, J. L., & Alles, M. (1994). An experimental investigation of accounts and attributions following sexual infidelity. *Communication Monographs, 61,* 326–344.

Montiel, C. J. (2002). Sociopolitical forgiveness. *Peace Review, 14,* 271–277.

Montville, J. V. (1989). Psychoanalytic enlightenment and the greening of diplomacy. *Journal of the American Psychoanalytic Association, 37,* 297–318.

Moon, G. W. (1999). "Forgiving" God: A matter of heart over head. *Marriage and Family: A Christian Journal, 2,* 177–185.

Moore, D. B. (1993). Shame, forgiveness, and juvenile justice. *Criminal Justice Ethics, 12,* 3–25.

Morgan, D. D. (1982). Needs assessment in churches: A Christian community's need for professional counseling services. *Journal of Psychology and Theology, 10,* 242–250.

Morris, H. (1988). Murphy on forgiveness. *Criminal Justice Ethics, 7,* 15–19.

Moss, D. B. (1986). Revenge and forgiveness. *American Imago, 43,* 191–210.

Mullet, E., Azar, F., Vinsonneau, G., & Girard, M. (1998). What is known about forgiveness. *Psicologia Educaca Cultura, 2,* 281–294.

Mullet, E., Barros, J., Frongia, L., Usaï, V., Neto, F., & Shafighi, S.R. (2003). Religious involvement and the forgiving personality. *Journal of Personality, 71,* 1–19.

Mullet, E., & Girard, M. (1999). Developmental and cognitive points of view on forgiveness. In M. E. McCullough, K. I. Pargament, & C. E. Thorensen (Eds.). *Forgiveness: Theory, research, and practice* (pp. 111–132). New York: Guilford Press.

Mullet, E., Girard, M., & Bakhshi, P. (2004). Conceptualizations of forgiveness. *European Psychologist, 9,* 78–86.

Mullet, E., Houdbine, A., Laumonnier, S., & Girard, M. (1998). Forgivingness: Factorial structure in a sample of young, middle-aged, and elderly adults. *European Psychologist, 3,* 289–297.

Muñoz Sastre, M. T., Vinsonneau, G., Neto, F., Girard, M., & Mullet, E. (2003). Forgivingness and satisfaction with life. *Journal of Happiness Studies, 4,* 323–335.

Murphy, J. G. (1982). Forgiveness and resentment. *Midwest Studies on Philosophy, 7,* 503–516.

Murphy, J. G. (1988). Forgiveness, mercy, and the retributive emotions. *Criminal Justice Ethics,* *7,* 3–15.

Murphy, J. G. (1997). Repentance, punishment, and mercy. In A. Etzioni (Ed.), *Repentance: A comparative perspective* (pp. 143–170). Lanham, MD: Rowman & Littlefield.

Murphy, J. G. (2002). Forgiveness in counseling: A philosophical perspective. In S. Lamb & J. G. Murphy (Eds.), *Before forgiving: Cautionary views of forgiveness in psychotherapy* (pp. 19–41). New York: Oxford University Press.

Murphy, J. G. (2003). *Getting even: Forgiveness and its limits.* New York: Oxford University Press.

Murphy, J. G., & Hampton, J. (1988). *Forgiveness and mercy.* Cambridge: Cambridge University Press.

Murray, M. (1975). Spirituality and forgiveness. (Master's thesis, Duquesne University, 1995). *Masters Abstracts International, 13,* 455.

Murray, R. J. (2002). Forgiveness as a therapeutic option. *Family Journal: Counseling and Therapy for Couples and Families, 10,* 315–321.

Murray, R. J. (2002). The therapeutic use of forgiveness in healing intergenerational pain. *Counseling and Values, 46,* 188–198.

Nelson, M. K. (1992). A new theory of forgiveness. (Doctoral dissertation, Purdue University, 1992). *Dissertation Abstracts International B53,* 4381.

Neto, F., Mullet, E., Deschamps, J. C., Barros, J., Benvindo, R., Camino, L., et al. (2000). Cross-cultural variations in attitudes toward love. *Journal of Cross-Cultural Psychology, 31,* 626–635.

Neto, F., & Mullet, E. (2004). Personality, self-esteem, and self-construal as correlates of forgivingness. *European Journal of Personality, 18,* 15–30.

Neu, J. (2002). To understand all is to forgive all—or is it? In S. Lamb & J. G. Murphy (Eds.), *Before forgiving: Cautionary views of forgiveness in psychotherapy* (pp. 1–17). New York: Oxford University Press.

Neumann, J. K., & Chi, D.S. (1999). Relationship of church giving to immunological and TxPA stress response. *Journal of Psychology and Theology, 27,* 43–51.

Neusner, J. (1997). Repentance in Judaism. In A. Etzioni & D. E. Carney (Eds.), *Repentance: A comparative perspective* (pp. 60–75). New York: Rowman and Littlefield.

Newberg, A. B., d'Aquili, E. G., Newberg, S. K., & deMarici, V. (2000). The neuropsychological correlates of forgiveness. In M. E. McCullough, K. I. Pargament, & C. E. Thoresen (Eds.), *Forgiveness: Theory, research, and practice* (pp. 91–110). New York: Guilford Press.

Newberry, P. A. (1995). Forgiveness and emotion. (Doctoral dissertation, Claremont Graduate School, 1995). *Dissertation Abstracts International A56,* 2269.

Newberry, P. A. (2001). Joseph Butler on forgiveness: A presupposed theory of emotion. *Journal of the History of Ideas, 62,* 233–244.

Newman, L. E. (1987). The quality of mercy: On the duty to forgive in the Judaic tradition. *Journal of Religious Ethics, 15,* 141–150.

Norris, D. A. (1983). Forgiving from the heart: A biblical and psychotherapeutic exploration. (Doctoral dissertation, Union Theological Seminary, 1984.) *Dissertation Abstracts International A44,* 3091.

North, J. (1997). Wrongdoing and forgiveness. *Philosophy, 61,* 499–508.

North, J. (1998). The 'ideal' of forgiveness: A philosopher's exploration. In R. D. Enright & J. North (Eds.), *Exploring forgiveness* (pp. 15–34). Madison: University of Wisconsin Press.

Nqweni, Z. C. (2002). A phenomenological approach to victimization of families subjected to political violence. *Journal of Psychology in Africa, South of the Sahara, the Caribbean and Afro-Latin America, 12,* 180–195.

Nqweni, Z. C. (2002). A phenomenological approach to victimization of families subjected to political violence. *Dissertation Abstracts International: Section B: Sciences & Engineering, 62,* 4797.

O'Malley, M. N., & Greenberg, J. (1983). Sex differences in restoring justice: The down payment effect. *Journal of Research in Personality, 17,* 174–185.

O'Shaughnessy, R. J. (1967). Forgiveness. *Philosophy, 42,* 336–352.

Oberholzer, F. (1984). The transformation of evil into sin and into sorrow and forgiveness: Lessons from analytic psychology and theology. (Doctoral dissertation, Graduate Theological Union, 1984). *Dissertation Abstracts International, A45,* 1444.

O'Driscoll, L. H. (1983). The quality of mercy. *Southern Journal of Philosophy, 21,* 229–258.

Ohbuchi, K., Kameda, M., & Agarie, N. (1989). Apology as aggression control: Its role in mediating appraisal of and response to harm. *Journal of Personality and Social Psychology, 56,* 219–227.

Ohbuchi, K., & Takada, N. (2001). Escalation of conflict and forgiveness: A social psychological model of forgiveness. *Tohoku Psychologica Folia, 60,* 61–71.

Olson, M. M., Russell, C. S., Higgins-Kessler, M., & Miller, R. B. (2002). Emotional processes following disclosure of an extramarital affair. *Journal of Marital and Family Therapy, 28,* 423–434.

Omuro-Yamamoto, L. K. (2001). Ho`oponopono: A phenomenological investigation of a native Hawaiian harmony restoration process for families. *Dissertation Abstracts International, 62* (2114), 4-B.

Osterndorf, C. L. (2000). Effects of a forgiveness education intervention with adult children of alcoholics. *Dissertation Abstracts International, 61,* 1-A.

Painter, R. M. (1998). Attending to evil: Fiction, apperception, and the growth of consciousness. *Dissertation Abstracts International, 59,* 5-A.

Palamattathil, G. V. (2001). The impact of an integrated forgiveness intervention in enhancing the psychological well-being among recently divorced adults. *Dissertation Abstracts International: Section B: Sciences & Engineering, 62,* 4799.

Paleari, F. G., Regalia, C., & Fincham, F. D. (2005). Marital quality, forgiveness, empathy, and rumination: A longitudinal analysis. *Personality and Social Psychology Bulletin, 31,* 368–378.

Paleari, F. G., Regalia, C., & Fincham, F. D. (2003). Adolescents' willingness to forgive their parents: An empirical model. *Parenting: Science and Practice, 3,* 155–174.

Pargament, K. I., Koenig, H. G., & Perez, L. M. (2000). The many methods of religious coping: Development and initial validation of the RCOPE. *Journal of Clinical Psychology, 56,* 519–543.

Pargament, K. I., McCullough, M. E., & Thoresen, C. E. (2000). The frontier of forgiveness: Seven directions for psychological study and practice. In M. E. McCullough, K. I. Pargament, & C. E. Thoresen (Eds.), *Forgiveness: Theory, research, and practice* (pp. 299–319). New York: Guilford Press.

Pargament, K. I., & Rye, M. S. (1998). Forgiveness as a method of religious coping. In E. L. Worthington, Jr. (Ed.), *Dimensions of forgiveness: Psychological research and theological perspectives* (pp. 59–78). Philadelphia: Templeton Foundation Press.

Pargament, K. I., Smith, B. W., Koenig, H. G., & Perez, L. (1998). Patterns of positive and negative religious coping with major life stressors. *Journal for the Scientific Study of Religion, 37,* 710–724.

Park, S. R., & Enright, R. D. (2000). Forgiveness across cultures. In F. Aureli & F. B. M. de Waal (Eds.), *Natural conflict resolution* (pp. 359–361). Berkeley: University of California Press.

Park, Y. O., & Enright, R. D. (1997). The development of forgiveness in the context of adolescent friendship conflict in Korea. *Journal of Adolescence, 20,* 393–402.

Parsons, R. D. (1988). Forgiving-not-forgetting. *Psychotherapy Patient, 5,* 259–273.

Pastor, M. (1986). The nature of forgiveness in the Christian tradition, modern Western psychology and a course in miracles. (Doctoral dissertation, California Institute of Integral Studies, 1986). *Dissertation Abstracts International, A47,* 940.

Pattison, E. M. (1965). On the failure to forgive or to be forgiven. *American Journal of Psychotherapy, 19,* 106–115.

Patton, J. (2000). Forgiveness in pastoral care and counseling. In M. E. McCullough, K. I. Pargament, & C. E. Thoresen (Eds.), *Forgiveness: Theory, research, and practice* (pp. 281–293). New York: Guilford Press.

Peddle, N. A. (2001). Forgiveness in recovery/resiliency from the trauma of war among a selected group of adolescents and adult refugees. *Dissertation Abstracts International, 62* (2252), 5-B.

Pedersen, J. E. (1974). Some thoughts on biblical view of anger. *Journal of Psychology and Theology, 2,* 210–215.

Petersen, R. L. (2001). A theology of forgiveness: Terminology, rhetoric, and the dialect of interfaith relationships. In R. G. Helmick & R. L. Petersen (Eds.), *Forgiveness and reconciliation: Religion, public policy, and conflict transformation* (pp. 3–25). Philadelphia: Templeton Foundation Press.

Peterson, J. O. (2001). A psychological theistic model of forgiveness for Latter-Day Saint clients. *Dissertation Abstracts International: Section B: Sciences and Engineering, 62,* 2073.

Phillips, A. (1986). Forgiveness reconsidered. *Christian Jewish Relations, 19,* 14–21.

Phillips, C. E. (1994). Forgiveness in the healing process. (Doctoral dissertation, Northern Arizona University, 1994). *Dissertation Abstracts International A55,* 871.

Phillips, L. J., & Osborne, J. W. (1989). Cancer patients' experiences of forgiveness therapy. *Canadian Journal of Counseling, 23,* 236–251.

Phillips, R. E., Lakin, R., & Pargament, K. I. (2002). Development and implementation of a spiritual issues psychoeducational group for those with serious mental illness. *Community Mental Health Journal, 38,* 487–495.

Pingleton, J. P. (1989). The role and function of forgiveness in the psychotherapeutic process. *Journal of Psychology and Theology, 17,* 27–35.

Pingleton, J. P. (1997). Why we don't forgive: A biblical and object relations theoretical model for understanding failures in the forgiveness process. *Journal of Psychology and Theology, 25,* 403–413.

Plante, T. G., & Sherman, A. C. (Eds.). (2001). *Faith and health: Psychological perspectives.* New York: Guilford Press.

Plantinga, C. (1996). Embodying forgiveness: A theological analysis. *Christianity Today, 40,* 31–33.

Pollard, M. W. (1995). The construction of a family forgiveness scale. (Doctoral dissertation, Texas Woman's University, 1995). *Dissertation Abstracts International A56,* 829.

Pollard, M. W., Anderson, R. A., Anderson, W. T., & Jennings, G. (1998). The development of a family forgiveness scale. *Journal of Family Therapy, 20,* 95–109.

Poloma, M. M., & Gallup, G. H. (1991). Unless you forgive others: Prayer and forgiveness. *Varieties of prayer* (pp. 85–106). Philadelphia: Trinity Press.

Power, C. (1994). Commentary. *Human Development, 37,* 81–83.

Puka, B. (2002). Forgoing forgiveness. In S. Lamb & J. G. Murphy (Eds.), *Before forgiving: Cautionary views of forgiveness in psychotherapy* (pp. 136–152). London: Oxford University Press.

Putnam, J. W. (2001). Revenge and forgiveness: Mutually exclusive or coexisting constructs? *Dissertation Abstracts International, 61* (4424), 8-B.

Rabinowitz, A. (2004). Judaic therapeutic spiritual counseling: Guiding principles and case histories. In P. S. Richards & A. E. Bergin (Eds.), *Casebook for a spiritual strategy in counseling and psychotherapy* (pp. 119–140). Washington, DC: American Psychological Association.

Rackley, J. V. (1993). The relationship of marital satisfaction, forgiveness, and religiosity. (Doctoral dissertation, Virginia Polytechnic Institute and State University, 1993). *Dissertation Abstracts International A54,* 1556.

Rayburn, C. A. (2000). Psychotherapy with Seventh-Day Adventists. In S. P. Richards & A. E. Bergin (Eds.), *Handbook of psychotherapy and religious diversity* (pp. 211–234). Washington, DC: American Psychological Association.

Reed, H. L. (2002). Claiming the future: The efficacy of a group therapy protocol for sexually abused women within the criminal justice system. *Dissertation Abstracts International: Section B: Sciences & Engineering, 63,* 2600.

Reed, H., Burkett, L., & Garzon, F. (2001). Exploring forgiveness as an intervention in psychotherapy. *Journal of Psychotherapy in Independent Practice, 2,* 1–16.

Renouf, R. W. (1981). Freedom and alcoholism. *Dissertation Abstracts International, 42,* 1688.

Rhode, M. G. (1990). Forgiveness, power, and empathy. (Doctoral dissertation, Fuller Theological Seminary, 1990). *Dissertation Abstracts International B51,* 2606.

Richards, N. (1988). Forgiveness. *Ethics, 99,* 77–97.

Richards, N. (2002). Forgiveness as therapy. In S. Lamb & J. G. Murphy (Eds.), *Before forgiving: Cautionary views of forgiveness in psychotherapy* (pp. 72–87). New York: Oxford University Press.

Richards, P. S., & Bergin, A. E. (Eds.). (2004). *Casebook for a spiritual strategy in counseling and psychotherapy.* Washington, DC: American Psychological Association.

Richards, P. S., & Potts, R. W. (1995). Using spiritual interventions in psychotherapy: Practices, successes, failures, and ethical concerns of Mormon psychotherapists. *Professional Psychology: Research and Practice, 26,* 163–170.

Ripley, J. S., & Worthington, E. L., Jr. (2002). Hope-focused and forgiveness-based group interventions to promote marital enrichment. *Journal of Counseling and Development, 80,* 452–463.

Rique, J. N. (2000). A cross-cultural study on the Enright Forgiveness Inventory: A measure for interpersonal forgiveness. Samples from Brazil and the United States. *Dissertation Abstracts International, 61* (512), 2-A.

Ritzman, T. A. (1987). Forgiveness: Its role in therapy. *Journal of the American Academy of Medical Hypnoanalysts, 2,* 4–13.

Roberts, J. E., Gilboa, E., & Gotlib, I. H. (1998). Ruminative response style and vulnerability to episodes of dysphoria: Gender, neuroticism, and episode duration. *Cognitive Therapy and Research, 22,* 401–423.

Roberts, R. C. (1991). Mental health and the virtues of community: Christian reflections on contextual therapy. *Journal of Psychology and Theology, 19,* 319–333.

Roberts, R. C. (1993). *Taking the word to heart: Self and others in an age of therapies.* Grand Rapids, MI: Eerdmans.

Roberts, R. C. (1995). Forgivingness. *American Philosophical Quarterly, 32,* 289–306.

Robinson, L. J. (1988). The role of forgiving in emotional healing: A theological and psychological analysis. (Doctoral dissertation, Fuller Theological Seminary, 1989). *Dissertation Abstracts International, B49,* 2872.

Roby, D. C. (1997). Forgiveness, parental nurturance, and self-esteem (adolescents, high school students). *Dissertation Abstracts International, 58,* (3024), 8A.

Roe, M. D., Pegg, W., Hodges, K., & Trimm, R. A. (1999). Forgiving the other side: Social identity and ethnic memories in Northern Ireland. In J. P. Harrington & E. Mitchell (Eds.), *Politics and performance in contemporary Northern Ireland* (pp. 122–156). Amherst: University of Massachusetts Press.

Romig, C. A., & Veenstra, G. (1998). Forgiveness and psychosocial development: Implications for clinical practice. *Counseling and Values, 42,* 185–199.

Rooney, A. J. (1989). Finding forgiveness through psychotherapy: An empirical phenomenological investigation. (Doctoral dissertation, Georgia State University, 1989). *Dissertation Abstracts International B51,* 1001.

Roscoe, B., Cavanaugh, L. E., & Kennedy, D. R. (1988). Dating infidelity: Behaviors, reasons, and consequences. *Adolescence, 23,* 35–43.

Rosenak, C. M., & Harnden, G. M. (1992). Forgiveness in the psychotherapeutic process: Clinical applications. *Journal of Psychology and Christianity, 11,* 188–192.

Rosenzwig-Smith, J. (1988). Factors associated with successful reunions of adult adoptees and biological parents. *Child Welfare, 67,* 411–422.

Rotter, J. C. (2001). Letting go: Forgiveness in counseling. *Family Journal: Counseling and Therapy for Couples and Families, 9,* 174–177.

Rowe, J. O., Halling, S., Davies, E., Leifer, M., Powers, D., & Van Bronkhorst, J. (1989). The psychology of forgiving another: A dialogal research approach. In R. S. Valle & S. Halling (Eds.), *Existential-phenomenological perspective in psychology: Exploring the breadth of human experience* (pp. 233–244). New York: Plenum Press.

Rusbult, C. E., Kumashiro, M., Finkel E. J., & Wildschut, T. (2002). The war of the roses: An interdependence analysis of betrayal and forgiveness. In P. Noller & J. A. Feeney (Eds.), *Understanding marriage: Developments in the study of couple interaction* (pp. 251–281). New York: Cambridge University Press.

Rutledge, T. (1997). *The self-forgiveness handbook: A practical and empowering guide.* Oakland, CA: New Harbinger.

Rye, M. S. (1999). Evaluation of a secular and religiously integrated forgiveness group therapy program for college students who have been wronged by a romantic partner. *Dissertation Abstracts International: Section B: Sciences & Engineering, 59,* 6495.

Rye, M. S., Loiacono, D. M., Folck, C. D., Olszewski, B. T., Heim, T. A., & Madia, B. P. (2001). Evaluation of the psychometric properties of two forgiveness scales. *Current Psychology, 20,* 260–277.

Rye, M. S., & Pargament, K. I. (2002). Forgiveness and romantic relationships in college: Can it heal the wounded heart? *Journal of Clinical Psychology, 58,* 419–441.

Rye, M. S., Pargament, K. I., Ali, A., Beck, G. L., Dorff, E. N., Hallisey, C., et al. (2000). Religious perspectives on forgiveness. In M. E. McCullough, K. I. Pargament, & C. E. Thoresen (Eds.), *Forgiveness: Theory, research, and practice* (pp. 17–40). New York: Guilford Press.

Safer, J. (1999). *Forgiving and not forgiving: A new approach to resolve intimate betrayal.* New York: Avon Books.

Sandage, S. J. (1999). An ego-humility model of forgiveness: A theory-driven empirical test of group interventions. *Dissertation Abstracts International, 59* (3712), 7-B.

Sandage, S. J. (1999). An ego-humility model of forgiveness: Theoretical foundations. *Marriage and Family: A Christian Journal, 11,* 188–197.

Sandage, S. J., Hill, P. C., & Vang, H. C. (2003). Toward a multicultural positive psychology: Indigenous forgiveness and Hmong culture. *Counseling Psychologist, 31,* 564–592.

Sandage, S. J., & Wiens, T. W. (2001). Contextualizing models of humility and forgiveness: A reply to Gassin. *Journal of Psychology and Theology, 29,* 201–211.

Sandage, S. J., Worthington, E. L., Jr., Hight, T. L., & Berry, J. W. (2000). Seeking forgiveness: Theoretical context and initial empirical study. *Journal of Psychology and Theology, 28,* 21–35.

Sandberg, J. G. (1999). "It just isn't fair": Helping older families balance their ledgers before the note comes due. *Family Relations: Journal of Applied Family and Child Studies 48,* 177–179.

Sarinopoulos, I. (2000). Forgiveness and physical health. *Dissertation Abstracts International: Section B: Sciences & Engineering, 60,* 4908.

Schelert, R. (1999). Relational reconciliation as a theological and practical framework for Christian ministry. *Dissertation Abstracts International, 60,* 2098.

Schimmel, S. (1988). Joseph and his brothers: A paradigm for repentance. *Judaism: A Quarterly Journal of Jewish Life and Thought, 37,* 60–65.

Schimmel, S. (2002). *Wounds not healed by time: The power of repentance and forgiveness.* New York: Oxford.

Schmidt, M. I. (1986). Forgiveness as the focus theme in group counseling. (Doctoral dissertation, North Texas State University, 1986). *Dissertation Abstracts International A47,* 3985.

Scobie, E. D., & Scobie, G. E. W. (1998). Damaging events: The perceived need for forgiveness. *Journal for the Theory of Social Behavior, 28,* 373–401.

Scobie, G. E. W., & Scobie, E. D. (2000). A comparison of forgiveness and pro-social development. *Early Child Development and Care, 160,* 33–45.

Scobie, G. E. W., & Scobie, E. D. (2003). Measuring children's understanding of the construct of forgiveness. In P. H. Roelofsma, J. M. T. Coreleyn, & J. W. van Saane (Eds.), *One hundred years of psychology and religion* (pp 105–121). Amsterdam: VU University Press.

Scobie, G. E. W., Scobie, E. D., & Kakavoulis, A. K. (2002). A cross-cultural study of the construct of forgiveness: Britain, Greece, and Cyprus. *Psychology: Journal of the Hellenic Psychological Society, 9,* 22–36.

Scott, J. A. (1976). Self-forgiveness. *Journal of the American Institute of Hypnosis, 17,* 131–132.

Scott, J. W. (1991). Idealism and the conception of forgiveness. *International Journal of Ethics, 21,* 189–198.

Seibold, M. (2001). When the wounding runs deep: Encouragement for those on the road to forgiveness. In M. McMinn & T. Phillips (Eds.), *Care for the soul: Exploring the intersection of psychology and theology* (pp. 294–308). Downers Grove, IL: InterVarsity Press.

Sells, J. N., Giordano, F. G., & King, L. (2002). A pilot study in marital group therapy: Process and outcome. *Family Journal: Counseling and Therapy for Couples and Families, 10,* 156–166.

Sells, J. N., & Hargrave, T. D. (1998). Forgiveness: A review of the theoretical and empirical literature. *Journal of Family Therapy, 20,* 21–36.

Server, R. C. (1986). The freedom of forgiveness. *Discipleship Journal, 6,* 44–46.

Sexton, R. O., & Maddock, R. C. (1978). The Adam and Eve syndrome. *Journal of Religion and Health, 17,* 163–168.

Seybold, K. S., Hill, P. C., Neumann, J. K., & Chi, D. S. (2001). Physiological and psychological correlates of forgiveness. *Journal of Psychology and Christianity, 20,* 250–259.

Shackelford, T. K., Buss, D. M., & Bennett, K. (2002). Forgiveness or breakup: Sex differences in responses to a partner's infidelity. *Cognition and Emotion, 16,* 299–307.

Sharma, A., & Cheatham, H. E. (1986). A women's center support group for sexual assault victims. *Journal of Counseling and Development, 64,* 525–527.

Shoemaker, A., & Bolt, M. (1977). The Rokeach Value Survey and perceived Christian values. *Journal of Psychology and Theology, 5,* 139–142.

Shontz, F. C., & Rosenak, C. (1988). Psychological theories and the need for forgiveness: Assessment and critique. *Journal of Psychology and Christianity, 7,* 23–31.

Shriver, D. W., Jr. (1980). The pain and promise of pluralism. *Christian Century, 97,* 345–350.

Shriver, D. W., Jr. (1995). *An ethic for enemies: Forgiving in politics.* New York: Oxford University Press.

Shriver, D. W., Jr. (1998). Is there forgiveness in politics? Germany, Vietnam, and America. In R. D. Enright & J. North (Eds.), *Exploring forgiveness* (pp. 131–149). Madison, WI: University of Wisconsin Press.

Shriver, D. W., Jr. (1998). What is forgiveness in a secular political form? In R. G. Helmick & R. L. Petersen (Eds.), *Forgiveness and reconciliation: Religion, public policy, and conflict transformation* (pp. 151–157). Philadelphia: Templeton Foundation Press.

Shults, F. L., & Sandage, S. J. (2003). *The faces of forgiveness: Searching for wholeness and salvation.* Grand Rapids, MI: Baker Academic.

Shuman, D. W., & Smith, A. M. (Eds.). (2000). *Justice and the prosecution of old crimes: Balancing legal, psychological, and moral concerns. The law and public policy.* Washington, DC: American Psychological Association.

Sigmund, E. W. (1999). Ho'oponopono: A traditional Hawaiian practice for setting relationships right. *Transactional Analysis Journal, 29,* 73–76.

Sims, M. J. (2002). Incest and child sexual abuse in the African American community: African American ministers' attitudes and beliefs. *Dissertation Abstracts International: Section B: Sciences & Engineering, 63,* 2605.

Smadi, A., & Haddad, A. (1999). Investigating modifying the Counseling Relationship Scale. *Dirasat: Educational Sciences, 26,* 483–494.

Smedes, L. B. (1984). *Forgive and forget: Healing the hurts we don't deserve.* New York: Harper & Row.

Smedes, L. B. (1996). *Art of forgiving: When you need to forgive and don't know how.* New York: Ballantine Books.

Smedes, L. B. (1998). Stations on the journey from forgiveness to hope. In E. L. Worthington, Jr. (Ed.), *Dimensions of forgiveness: Psychological research and theological perspectives* (pp. 341–354). Philadelphia: Templeton Foundation Press.

Smith, M. C. (1989). Penitential bread: The Eucharist as locus of forgiveness. *Saint Luke's Journal of Theology, 32,* 99–106.

Smith, M. C., & Pourchot, T. (Eds.). (1998). *Adult learning and development: Perspectives from educational psychology.* Mahwah, NJ: Lawrence Erlbaum.

Smyth, G. O. P., (1998). Brokenness, forgiveness, healing, and peace in Ireland. In R. G. Helmick & R. L. Petersen (Eds.), *Forgiveness and reconciliation: Religion, public policy, and conflict transformation* (pp. 319–349). Philadelphia: Templeton Foundation Press.

Snow, N. E. (1993). Self-forgiveness. *Journal of Value Inquiry, 27,* 75–80.

Snyder, C. R. (Ed.). (2001). *Coping with stress: Effective people and processes.* New York: Oxford University Press.

Snyder, C. R., & Lopez, S. J. (Eds.). (2002). *Handbook of positive psychology.* London: Oxford University Press.

Snyder, C. R., & McCullough, M. E. (2000). A positive psychology field of dreams: "If you build it, they will come…" *Journal of Social and Clinical Psychology, 19,* 151–160.

Snyder, C. R., & Thompson, L. Y. (2003). Measuring forgiveness. In S. J. Lopez & C. R. Snyder (Eds.), *Positive psychological assessment: A handbook of models and measures* (pp. 301–312). Washington, DC: American Psychological Association.

Snyder, C. R., & Yamhure, L. (1999). Forgiveness and getting on with our lives: The President Clinton "affair" and other transgressions. *Clio's Psyche, 5,* 94–96

Snyder, D. K., Gordon, K. C., & Baucom, D. H. (2004). Treating affair couples: Extending the written disclosure paradigm to relationship trauma. *Clinical Psychology: Science and Practice, 11,* 155–159.

Solomon, N. (1986). The forgiveness debate. *Christian Jewish Relations, 19,* 3–24.

Spidell, S., & Liberman, D. (1981). Moral development and the forgiveness of sin. *Journal of Psychology and Theology, 9,* 159–163.

Spring, J. A. (1999). After the affair: Rebuilding trust and personal intimacy. *Issues in Psychoanalytic Psychology, 21,* 53–62.

Spring, J. A. (2004). *How can I forgive you? The courage to forgive, the freedom not to.* New York: HarperCollins.

Stanley, S. M., & Trathen, D. W. (1994). Christian PREP: An empirically based model for marital and premarital intervention. *Journal of Psychology and Christianity, 13,* 158–165.

Staub, E., & Pearlman, L. A. (2001). Healing, reconciliation, and forgiving after genocide and other collective violence. In R. G. Helmick & R. L. Petersen (Eds.). *Forgiveness and reconciliation: Religion, public policy, and conflict resolution* (pp. 195–215). Philadelphia: Templeton Foundation Press.

Stein, V. (2001). The importance of forgiveness in marital therapy. *Dissertation Abstracts International, 61* (4430), 8-B.

Stevens, D. (1986). Forgiveness and reconciliation in political perspective. *Doctrine and Life, 35,* 60–72.

Stillwell, A. M., & Baumeister, R. F. (1997). The construction of victim and perpetrator memories: Accuracy and distortion in role-based accounts. *Personality and Social Psychology Bulletin, 23,* 1157–1172.

Stipe, A. M. (1996). Forgiveness and psychotherapy. (Doctoral dissertation, University of Maryland at Baltimore, 1996). *Dissertation Abstracts International A56,* 3312.

Stoop, D. (2001). *Real solutions for forgiving the unforgivable.* Ann Arbor, MI: Servant Publications.

Stoop, D., & Masteller, J. (1996). *Forgiving our parents, forgiving ourselves: Healing adult children of dysfunctional families.* Ann Arbor, MI: Servant Publications.

Strasser, J. A. (1984). The relation of general forgiveness and forgiveness type to reported health in the elderly. (Doctoral dissertation, Catholic University of America, 1984). *Dissertation Abstracts International B45,* 1733.

Strong, S. R. (1977). Christian counseling. *Counseling and Values, 20,* 151–160.

Stuckless, N., & Goranson, R. (1992). The Vengeance Scale: Development of a measure of attitudes toward revenge. *Journal of Social Behavior and Personality, 7,* 25–42.

Subkoviak, M. J., Enright, R. D., Wu, C., Gassin, E. A., Freedman, S., Olson, L. M., et al. (1995). Measuring interpersonal forgiveness in late adolescence and middle adulthood. *Journal of Adolescence, 18,* 641–655.

Sugimoto, N. (1997). A Japan-U.S. comparison of apology styles. *Communication Research, 24,* 349–369.

Symington, S. H., Walker, D. F., & Gorsuch, R. L. (2002). The relationship of forgiveness and reconciliation to five and sixteen factors of personality. *Journal of Psychology and Christianity, 21,* 141–150.

Takaku, S. (2000). Testing a dissonance-attribution model of interpersonal forgiveness. *Dissertation Abstracts International: Section B: Sciences & Engineering, 61,* 2277.

Takaku, S. (2001). The effects of apology and perspective taking on interpersonal forgiveness: A dissonance-attribution model of interpersonal forgiveness. *Journal of Social Psychology, 141,* 494–508.

Takaku, S., Weiner, B., & Ohbuchi, K. (2001). A cross-cultural examination of the effects of apology and perspective taking on forgiveness. *Journal of Language and Social Psychology, 20,* 144–166.

Tangney, J., Wagner, P. E, Hill-Barlow, D., Marschall, D. E., & Gramzow, R. (1996). Relation of shame and guilt to constructive versus destructive responses to anger across the lifespan. *Journal of Personality and Social Psychology, 70,* 797–809.

Tavuchis, N. (1991). *Mea culpa: A sociology of apology and reconciliation.* Palo Alto, CA: Stanford University Press.

Teahan, J. E. (1987). Alcohol expectancies, values, and drinking of Irish and U.S. collegians. *International Journal of the Addictions, 22,* 621–638.

Tefler, W. (1959). *The forgiveness of sins: An essay in the history of Christian doctrine and practice.* London: SCM.

Temoshok, L. R., & Chandra, P. S. (2000). The meaning of forgiveness in a specific situational and cultural context: Persons living with HIV/AIDS in India. In M. E. McCullough, K. I. Pargament, & C. E. Thoresen (Eds.), *Forgiveness: Theory, research, and practice* (pp. 41–64). New York: Guilford Press.

Thackeray, A. M. (2001). Children's relational perceptions of God. *Dissertation Abstracts International, 61* (4189), 10-A.

Thomas, J. M., & Garrod, A. (2002). Forgiveness after genocide? Perspectives from Bosnian youth. In S. Lamb & J. G. Murphy (Eds.), *Before forgiving: Cautionary views of forgiveness in psychotherapy* (pp. 192–211). London: Oxford University Press.

Thompson, L. Y., & Synder, C. R. (2003). Measuring forgiveness. In S. J. Lopez & C. R. Snyder (Eds.), *Positive psychological assessment: A handbook of models and measures* (pp. 301–312). Washington, DC: American Psychological Association.

Thompson, L. Y., Snyder, C. R., Hoffman, L., Michael, S. T., Rasmussen, H. N., Billings, L. S., et al. (2005). Dispositional forgiveness of self, others, and situations. *Journal of Personality, 73,* 313–359.

Thompson, R. D. (1983). The Wesleyan and the struggle to forgive. *Wesleyan Theological Journal, 18,* 81–92.

Thoresen, C. E., Harris, A. H. S., & Luskin, F. (2000). Forgiveness and health: An unanswered question. In M. E. McCullough, K. I. Pargament, & C. E. Thoresen (Eds.), *Forgiveness: Theory, research, and practice* (pp. 254–280). New York: Guilford Press.

Thoresen, C. E., Luskin, F., & Harris, A. H. S. (1998). Science and forgiveness interventions: Reflections and recommendations. In E. L. Worthington, Jr. (Ed.), *Dimensions of forgiveness: Psychological research and theological perspectives* (pp. 163–192). Philadelphia: Templeton Foundation Press.

Tobin, E. (1993). *How to forgive yourself and others: Steps to reconciliation.* Liguori, MO: Liguori Press.

Todd, E. (1993). The value of confession and forgiveness according to Jung. *Journal of Religion and Health, 24,* 39–48.

Torrance, A. (1986). Forgiveness: The essential socio-political structure of personal being. *Journal of Theology for Southern Africa, 56,* 47–59.

Toussaint, L. L., Williams, D. R., Musick, M. A., & Everson, S. A. (2001). Forgiveness and health: Age differences in a U.S. probability sample. *Journal of Adult Development, 8,* 249–257.

Townsend-Simmons, R. (1985). All roads lead home: Nourishment, transformation, and grace. *Hakomi Forum, 3,* 46–47.

Tracy, S. (1999). Sexual abuse and forgiveness. *Journal of Psychology and Theology, 27,* 219–229.

Trainer, M. F. (1984). Forgiveness: Intrinsic, role-expected, expedient, in the context of divorce. (Doctoral dissertation, Boston University, 1984). *Dissertation Abstracts International, B45,* 1325.

Triandis, H. C. (1995). *Individualism and collectivism.* Boulder, CO: Westview Press.

Trzyna, T. N. (1987). Forgiveness and truth: Literary reflections of Christian ethics. *Seattle Pacific University Review, 5,* 7–36.

Trzyna, T. N. (1992). Forgiveness and time. *Christian Scholar's Review, 22,* 7–21.

Turell, S. C., & Thomas, C. R. (2001). Where was God? Utilizing spirituality with Christian survivors of sexual abuse. *Women and Therapy, 24,* 133–147.

Twambley, P. (1976). Mercy and forgiveness. *Analysis, 36,* 84–90.

Valcour, F. (1990). The treatment of child sex abusers in the church. In S. J. Rossetti (Ed.), *Slayer of the soul: Child sexual abuse and the Catholic Church* (pp. 45–66). New York: Twenty-Third.

Van Loon, P. C. (1998). A cognitive development intervention for clergy: Forgiveness education. *Dissertation Abstracts International, 58* (4604), 12-A.

Vangelisti, A. L., & Maguire, K. (2002). Hurtful messages in family relationships: When the pain lingers. In J. H. Harvey & A. Wenzel, (Eds.), *A clinician's guide to maintaining and enhancing close relationships* (pp. 43–62). Mahwah, NJ: Lawrence Erlbaum.

Vas, S. N. (2002). Expressive writing about interpersonal offenses: Effects on forgiveness and health. *Dissertation Abstracts International, 63* (3028), 6-B.

Vaughan, L. A. (2001). The relationship between marital satisfaction levels associated with participation in the free (forgiveness and reconciliation through experiencing empathy) and hope-focused marital enrichment program. *Dissertation Abstracts International 62*(1124), 2-B.

Veenstra, G., Jr., (1993). Forgiveness: A critique of adult child approaches. *Journal of Psychology and Christianity, 12,* 58–68.

Vinsonneau, G., & Mullet, E. (2001). Willingness to forgive among young adolescents: An European-Maghrebi comparison. *International Journal of Group Tensions, 30,* 267–278.

Vitz, P. C., & Mango, P. (1997). Kernbergian psychodynamics and religious aspects of the forgiveness process. *Journal of Psychology and Theology, 25,* 72–80.

Vitz, P. C., & Mango, P. (1997). Kleinian psychodynamics and religious aspects of hatred and a defense mechanism. *Journal of Psychology and Theology, 25,* 64–71.

Volf, M. (1996). *Exclusion and embrace: A theological exploration of identity, otherness, and reconciliation.* Nashville, TN: Abingdon.

Volf, M. (1999). Original crime, primal care. In L. B. Lampman & M. D. Shattuck (Eds.), *God and the victim: Theological reflections on evil, victimization, justice, and forgiveness* (pp. 17–35). Grand Rapid, MI: Eerdmans.

Volf, M. (2000). The social meaning of reconciliation. *Interpretation: A Journal of Bible and Theology, 54,* 158–171.

Volf, M. (2001). Forgiveness, reconciliation, and justice: A Christian contribution to a more peaceful social environment. In R. G. Helmick & R. L. Petersen (Eds.), *Forgiveness and reconciliation: Religion, public policy, and conflict transformation* (pp. 27–49). Philadelphia: Templeton Foundation Press.

Wade, N. G. (2002). Understanding REACH: A component analysis of a group intervention to promote forgiveness. *Dissertation Abstracts International: Section B: Sciences & Engineering, 63,* 2611.

Wade, N. G., & Worthington, E. L., Jr. (2002). Overcoming interpersonal offenses: Is forgiveness the only way to deal with unforgiveness? *Journal of Counseling and Development, 81,* 343–353.

Wade, S. H. (1989). The development of a scale to measure forgiveness. (Doctoral dissertation, Fuller Theological Seminary, 1990). *Dissertation Abstracts International, B50,* 5338.

Wahking, H. (1992). Spiritual growth through grace and forgiveness. *Journal of Psychology and Christianity, 11,* 198–206.

Wahkinney, R. L. (2002). Self-forgiveness Scale: A validation study. *Dissertation Abstracts International, 62,* 3296.

Walker, D. F., & Gorsuch, R. L. (2002). Forgiveness within the Big Five personality model. *Personality and Individual Differences, 32,* 1127–1137.

Walker, D. F., & Doverspike, D. (2001). The relationship between forgiveness experiences and the masculine gender role among Christian men. *Journal of Psychology and Christianity, 20,* 29–39.

Walker, P. J. (1993). The relationship between forgiveness and marital adjustment. (Master's thesis, University of Alberta, 1993). *Masters Abstracts International, 33,* 26.

Walrond-Skinner, S. (1998). The function and role of forgiveness in working with couples and families: Clearing the ground. *Journal of Family Therapy, 20,* 3–19.

Walters, R. P. (1984). Forgiving: An essential element in effective living. *Studies in Formative Spirituality, 5,* 365–374.

Waltman, M. A. (2003). The psychological and physiological effects of forgiveness education in male patients with coronary artery disease. *Dissertation Abstracts International, 63,* 3971.

Wapnick, K. (1985). Forgiveness: A spiritual psychotherapy. *Psychotherapy Patient, 1,* 47–53.

Watson, P. J., Hood, R. W., Jr., & Morris, R. J. (1985). Religiosity, sin, and self-esteem. *Journal of Psychology and Theology, 13,* 116–128.

Watts, F., & Gulliford, L. (Eds.). (2004). *Forgiveness in context: Psychology and theology in creative dialog.* Dulles, VA: T. & T. Clark.

Watts, R. E. (1992). Biblical agape as a model of social interest. *Individual Psychology, 48,* 35–40.

Wauters, J. W., Jr., & Moser, R. S. (2000). Religious and spiritual factors in youth violence. In R. S. Moser & C. E. Frantz (Eds.), *Shocking violence: Youth perpetrators and victims—A multidisciplinary perspective* (pp. 113–124). Springfield, IL: Charles C. Thomas.

Weinberg, N. (1994). Self-blame, other-blame, and desire for revenge: Factors in recovery from bereavement. *Death Studies, 18,* 583–593.

Weiner, B. A. (1994). The sins of the parents. (Doctoral dissertation, University of California, 1995). *Dissertation Abstracts International A55,* 2978.

Weiner, B. A. (1995). *Judgments of responsibility.* New York: Guilford Press.

Weiner, B. A., Graham, S., Peter, O., & Zmuidinas, M. (1991). Public confession and forgiveness. *Journal of Personality, 59,* 281–312.

West, W. (2001). Issues relating to the use of forgiveness in counselling and psychotherapy. *British Journal of Guidance and Counselling, 29,* 415–423.

Whipple, V. (1988). Counseling battered women from fundamentalist Christian backgrounds. *Counseling and Values, 32,* 140–143.

Wiesenthal, S. (1998). *The sunflower: On the possibilities and limits of forgiveness.* New York: Schocken Books.

Williams, C. (1942/1984). *The forgiveness of sins.* Grand Rapids, MI: Eerdmans.

Williams, R., & Williams, V. (1993). *Anger kills.* New York: Random House.

Wilson, W. P. (1974). Utilization of Christian beliefs in psychotherapy. *Journal of Psychology and Theology, 2,* 125–131.

Witvliet, C. V. O. (2001). Forgiveness and health: Review and reflections on a matter of faith, feelings, and physiology. *Journal of Psychology and Theology, 29,* 212–224.

Witvliet, C. V. O., Ludwig, T. E., & Bauer, D. J. (2002). Please forgive me: Transgressors' emotions and physiology during imagery of seeking forgiveness and victim responses. *Journal of Psychology and Christianity, 21,* 219–233.

Witvliet, C. V. O., Ludwig, T. E., & Vander Laan, K. L. (2001). Granting forgiveness or harboring grudges: Implications for emotion, physiology, and health. *Psychological Science, 121,* 117–123.

Witvliet, C. V. O., Phipps, K. A., Feldman, M. E., & Beckham, J. C. (2004). Posttraumatic mental and physical health correlates of forgiveness and religious coping in military veterans. *Journal of Traumatic Stress, 17,* 269–273.

Witvliet, C. V. O., & Vrana, S. R. (1995). Psychophysiological responses as indices of affective dimensions. *Psychophysiology, 32,* 436–443.

Witvliet, C. V. O., & Vrana, S. R. (2000). Emotional imagery, the visual startle, and covariation bias: An affective matching account. *Biological Psychology, 52,* 187–204.

Woodman, T. (1992). The role of forgiveness in marital adjustment. *Dissertation Abstracts International, 53(4).* (UMI 9225999).

Worthington, E. L., Jr. (1998). An empathy-humility-commitment model of forgiveness applied within family dyads. *Journal of Family Therapy, 20,* 59–76.

Worthington, E. L., Jr. (Ed.). (1998). *Dimensions of forgiveness: Psychological research and theological perspectives.* Philadelphia: Templeton Foundation Press.

Worthington, E. L., Jr. (1998). Empirical research in forgiveness: Looking backward, looking forward. In E. L. Worthington, Jr. (Ed.), *Dimensions of forgiveness: Psychological research and theological perspectives* (pp. 321–339). Philadelphia: Templeton Foundation Press.

Worthington, E. L., Jr. (1998). The pyramid model of forgiveness: Some interdisciplinary speculations about unforgiveness and the promotion of forgiveness. In E. L. Worthington Jr. (Ed.), *Dimensions of forgiveness: Psychological research and theological perspectives* (pp. 107–137). Philadelphia: Templeton Foundation Press.

Worthington, E. L., Jr. (2000). Is there a place for forgiveness in the justice system? *Fordham Urban Law Journal, 27,* 1721–1734.

Worthington, E. L., Jr. (2001). *Five steps to forgiveness: The art and science of forgiving.* New York: Crown Publishers.

Worthington, E. L., Jr. (2001). Unforgiveness, forgiveness and reconciliation and their implications for societal interventions. In R. G. Helmick & R. L. Petersen (Eds.), *Forgiveness and reconciliation: Religion, public policy, and conflict transformation* (pp. 161–182). Philadelphia: Templeton Foundation Press.

Worthington, E. L., Jr. (2003). *Forgiving and reconciling: Bridges to wholeness and hope.* Downers Grove, IL: InterVarsity Press.

Worthington, E. L., Jr. (2005). The new science of forgiveness. *Greater Good, 1,* 6–9

Worthington, E. L., Jr., Berry, J. W., & Parrott, L. III (2001). Unforgiveness, forgiveness, religion, and health. In T. G. Plante & A. C. Sherman (Eds.), *Faith and health: Psychological perspectives* (pp. 107–138). New York: Guilford Press.

Worthington, E. L., Jr., Berry, J. W., Shivy, V. A., & Brownstein, E. (2005). Forgiveness and positive psychology in business ethics and corporate responsibility. In R.A. Giacalone, C. Dunn, & C.L. Jurkiewicz (Eds.), Positive psychology in business ethics and corporate social responsibility (pp. 265-284). Greenwich, CT: Information Age Publishing.

Worthington, E. L., Jr., & DiBlasio, F. A. (1990). Promoting mutual forgiveness within the fractured relationship. *Psychotherapy, 27,* 219–223.

Worthington, E. L., Jr., & Drinkard, D. T. (2000). Promoting reconciliation through psychoeducational and therapeutic interventions. *Journal of Marital and Family Therapy, 26,* 93–101.

Worthington, E. L., Jr., Kurusu, T. A., Collins, W., Berry, J. W., Ripley, J. S., & Baier, S. N. (2000). Forgiving usually takes time: A lesson learned by studying interventions to promote forgiveness. *Journal of Psychology and Theology, 28,* 3–20.

Worthington, E. L., Jr., Mazzeo, S. E., & Canter, D. E. (2005). Forgiveness-promoting approach: Helping clients REACH forgiveness through using a longer model that teaches reconciliation. In Len Sperry and Edward P. Shafranske (Eds.), *Spiritually-oriented psychotherapy* (pp. 235-257). Washington, D.C.: American Psychological Association.

Worthington, E. L., Jr., Mazzeo, S. E., & Kliewer, W. L. (2002). Addictive and eating disorders, unforgiveness, and forgiveness. *Journal of Psychology and Christianity, 21,* 257–261.

Worthington, E. L., Jr., O'Connor, L. E., Berry, J. W., Sharp, C. B., Murray, R., & Yi, E. (2005). Compassion and forgiveness: Implications for psychotherapy. In P. Gilbert (Ed.), *Compassion: Nature and use in psychotherapy* (pp. 168-192). East Sussex, England: Psychology Press.

Worthington, E. L., Jr., Sandage, S. J., & Berry, J. W. (2000). Group interventions to promote forgiveness: What researchers and clinicians ought to know. In M. E. McCullough, K. I. Pargament, & C. E. Thoresen (Eds.), *Forgiveness: Theory, research, and practice* (pp. 228–251). New York: Guilford Press.

Worthington, E. L., Jr., & Scherer, M. (2004). Forgiveness is an emotion-focused coping strategy that can reduce health risks and promote health resilience: Theory, review, and hypotheses. *Psychology and Health, 19,* 385–405.

Worthington, E. L., Jr., & Wade, N. G. (1999). The psychology of unforgiveness and forgiveness and implications for clinical practice. *Journal of Social and Clinical Psychology 18,* 385–418.

Wuthnow, R. (2000). How religious groups promote forgiving: A national study. *Journal for the Scientific Study of Religion, 39,* 125–139.

Yamhure-Thompson, L., & Shahen, P. E. (2002). Forgiveness in the workplace. In R. A. Giacalone & C. L. Jurkiewicz (Eds.), *The handbook of workplace spirituality and organizational performance* (pp. 405–420). Armonk, NY: M. E. Sharpe.

Yancey, P. (1988). *Disappointment with God: Three questions no one asks aloud.* New York: HarperCollins.

Zechmeister, J. S., & Romero, C. (2002). Victim and offender accounts of interpersonal conflict: Autobiographical narratives of forgiveness and unforgiveness. *Journal of Personality and Social Psychology, 82,* 675–686.

Zeiders, C. L. (1999). A Christian depth psychology of forgiveness leading to the resurrection effect. *Journal of Christian Healing, 21,* 3–23.

Zillman, D., & Cantor, J. R. (1976). Effect of timing of information about mitigating circumstances on emotional responses to provocation and retaliatory behavior. *Journal of Experimental Social Psychology, 12,* 38–55.

FORGIVENESS DIRECTORY: AID TO RESEARCH

Methodological Issues

Methods

Baskin & Enright (2004)
Fow (1996)
Girard et al. (2002)
Hughes (1993)
Kanz (2000)
Lopez & Snyder (2003)
McCullough & Worthington (1994)
McCullough, Exline, et al. (1998)
McCullough, Rachal et al. (2000)
McCullough et al. (1997)
Meninger (1996)
Pargament, McCullough et al. (2000)
Witvliet & Vrana (2000)
Worthington (1998)
Worthington (2001)

Creation of Tests and Measurements

Barros (2002)
Berry et al. (2001)
Brown et al. (2001)
Caprara (1986)
Caprara et al. (1985)
Case (1998)
Deshea (2000)
Deshea (2003)
Drinnon (2001)
Hargrave & Sells (1997)
Holbrook et al. (1995)
Ingersoll (1995)
Ingersoll (1996)
McCullough (1999)
McCullough, Rachal et al. (1998)
Pargament, Koenig et al. (2000)
Pollard (1995)
Pollard et al. (1998)
Rique (2000)
Rye et al. (2001)
Sandage (1999)
Scobie & Scobie (2003)
Shoemaker & Bolt (1977)
Smadi & Haddad (1999)
Snyder & Thompson (2003)
Stanley & Trathen (1994)
Stuckless & Goranson (1992)
Subkoviak et al. (1995)
Takaku (2000)
Thompson & Synder (2003)
Wahkinney (2002)

Definitions

Affinito (2002)
Akhtar (2002)
Denton & Martin (1998)
Doyle (1999)
Droll (1985)
Emerson (1964)
Galindo (2002)
Goins (1987)
Hanson-Richardson (1999)
Hauerwas (1983)
Hope (1987)
McCullough & Worthington (1994)
Mullet et al. (2004)
Mullet et al. (1998)

Nelson (1992)
North (1998)
Sandage & Wiens (2001)
Worthington (2003)
Worthington (1998)
Sandage et al. (2000)
Scobie et al. (2002)
Scott (1991)
Sells & Hargrave (1998)
Shontz & Rosenak (1988)
Snyder & Lopez (Eds.) (2002)
Snyder & Yamhure (1999)
Takaku (2001)
Worthington (2005)

Forgiveness and Health

Biological/Physiological Mechanisms

Akhtar (2002)
Aureli et al. (1997)
Egleston et al. (2004)
Farrow (2001)

Neumann & Chi (1999)
Newberg et al. (2000)
Seybold et al. (2001)
Witvliet et al. (2002)

Physical Health

Bennett (1998)
Berry & Worthington (2001)
Butler (1998)
Gisi & D'Amato (2000)
Gisi (1999)
Hart (1999)
Kendler et al. (2003)
Lawler et al. (2003)
Luskin (2004)
McDaniel et al. (1999)
Miller et al. (1996)
Phillips & Osborne (1989)
Sarinopolous (2000)
Sexton & Maddock (1978)

Seybold et al. (2001)
Strasser (1984)
Temoshok & Chandra (2000)
Thoresen et al. (2000)
Toussaint et al. (2001)
Vas (2002)
Waltman (2003)
Witvliet & Vrana (1995)
Witvliet (2001)
Witvliet et al. (2001)
Witvliet et al. (2004)
Worthington et al. (2001)
Worthington et al. (2002)

Mental Health

Berry & Worthington (2001)
Consoli (1995)
Fincham & Beach (2001)
Gartner (1996)
Halpain et al. (1999)
Harris & Thoresen (2003)
Howard et al. (2000)
Johnson (1984)
Jorgensen (1984)

Kaplan et al. (1993)
Keyes & Lopez (2002)
Luskin (2001)
Luskin (2004)
Roberts (1991)
Shelton et al. (1995)
Snyder (2001)
Worthington & Scherer (2004)

Social Psychology

Religious/Spiritual Forgiveness

Aoki & Turk (1997)
Aponte (1998)
Applegate et al. (2000)
Aune (1984)
Baker (2002)
Beck (1995)
Bennett (1998)
Berecz (2001)
Bergin (1988)
Bono & McCullough (2004)
Boobyer (1954)
Brown (1997)
Bryant (1987)
Burkle (1989)
Carone & Barone (2001)
Cassiday-Shaw (2002)
Childs (1981)
Close (1970)
Coates (1997)
Compaan (1985)
Connor, Davidson, & Lee (2003)
Crohn, Markman, Blumberg, & Levine (2000)
Cunningham (1985)
Davies (1920)
De Cantanzaro (1962)
De Jong (1951)
DiBlasio & Benda (1991)
DiBlasio (1993)
Dimitroff & Hoekstra (1998)
Domeris (1986)

Donnelly (1984)
Dorff (1992)
Dorff (1998)
Dreelin (1994)
Duggar (1995)
Educational Psychology Study Group (1990)
Edwards et al. (2002)
Exline & Smith (2004)
Ferch & Ramsey (2003)
Fittipaldi (1982)
Frankel (1998)
Freemesser (1985)
Gartner (1988)
Gartner (1996)
Gassin & Enright (1995)
Gassin (2000)
Gassin (2001)
Geoghegan (2000)
Girard & Mullet (1997)
Gladson (1992)
Gorsuch & Hao (1993)
Graham (1994)
Halling (1995)
Harakas (1998)
Harris (1986)
Harris (2002)
Harris et al. (1999)
Hart (1999)
Helmick & Petersen (2001)
Helmick (2001)
Herford (1964)

Howard et al. (2000)
Hylen (2000)
Johnson (1984)
Jones-Haldeman (1992)
Jorgensen (1984)
Kaplan (1993)
Kaplan et al. (1993)
Kasper (1989)
Kendler et al. (2003)
Kirkup (1993)
Koenig (1999)
Kraus (1999)
Kuert (2003)
Kus (1992)
Lauritzen (1987)
Leach & Lark (2003)
Mackintosh (1927)
Marty (1998)
Mauger et al. (1992)
Mauldin (1983)
McAllister (1983)
McCullough & Worthington (1999)
McNally (1977)
Meek et al. (1995)
Messenger (1959)
Morgan (1982)
Mullet et al. (2003)
Murray (1975)
Neumann & Chi (1999)
Neusner (1997)
Newman (1987)
Norris (1983)
Oberholzer (1984)
Pargament & Rye (1998)
Pargament et al. (1998)
Pastor (1986)
Patton (2000)
Pedersen (1974)
Petersen (2001)
Phillips (1986)
Pingleton (1997)
Plante & Sherman (2001)
Plantinga (1996)
Poloma & Gallup (1991)
Rabinowitz (2004)
Rackley (1993)
Rayburn (2000)

Richards & Potts (1995)
Roberts (1991)
Robinson (1988)
Rosenak & Hamden (1992)
Rye (1999)
Rye & Pargament (2002)
Rye, Pargament, Ali, Beck, Dorff, Hallisey, et al. (2000)
Rye et al. (2000)
Sandage et al. (1995)
Sandage et al. (2000)
Schelert (1999)
Schimmel (1988)
Schimmel (2002)
Seibold (2001)
Server (1986)
Sexton & Maddock (1978)
Seybold et al. (2001)
Shoemaker & Bolt (1977)
Shontz & Rosenak (1988)
Shriver (1980)
Shults & Sandage (2003)
Sims (2002)
Smith (1989)
Solomon (1986)
Spidell & Liberman (1981)
Stanley & Trathen (1994)
Strong (1977)
Tefler (1959)
Thompson (1983)
Todd (1993)
Townsend-Simmons (1985)
Tracy (1999)
Trzyna (1987)
Trzyna (1992)
Turell & Thomas (2001)
Twambley (1976)
Valcour (1990)
Van Loon (1998)
Veenstra (1993)
Vitz & Mango (1997)
Volf (1996)
Volf (1999)
Volf (2000)
Volf (2001)
Wahking (1992)
Walker & Doverspike (2001)

Walters (1984)
Wapnick (1985)
Watson et al. (1985)
Watts (1992)
Wauters & Moser (2000)
Weiner (1994)
Whipple (1988)
Williams (1942/1984)

Wilson (1974)
Witvliet (2001)
Worthington (1998)
Worthington et al. (2001)
Wuthnow (2000)
Young (1984)
Zeiders (1999)

Forgiveness and the Divine

Bennett (1998)
Brown (1997)
De Jong (1951)
Donnelly (1984)
Exline et al. (1999)

Krause & Ellison (2003)
Mamula (1997)
Moon (1999)
Thackeray (2001)
Yancey (1988)

Other Social Psychology

Andres (2002)
Armour (2003)
Ayoub (1997)
Barros (2003)
Baumeister & Newman (1994)
Bowman (2000)
Brandsma (1982)
Branscomb (1934)
Braun & Zir (2001)
Brenneis (2000)
Brink (1985)
Caprara, Cinanni, & Mazzotti (1989)
Carone & Barone (2001)
Darby & Schlenker (1982)
Dorn (1998)
Exline & Baumeister (2000)
Exline, Worthington, Hill, & McCullough
    (2003)
Fagenson & Cooper (1987)
Fukuno & Ohbuchi (1998)
Gassin (1995)
Gerber (1987)
Gold & Weiner (2000)
Gregory (2002)
Haaken (2002)
Harvey (1993)
Hestevold (1985)

Hodgins, et al. (1996)
Hylen (2000)
Jeffress (2000)
Jones (1995)
Jones (2000)
Kaplan (1992)
Karremans & Van Lange (2004)
Klassen (1966)
Lavery & Achilles (1999)
Luskin (1999)
McCullough & Witvliet (2001)
McCullough (1995)
McNeill (1971)
Messenger (1959)
Ohbuchi & Takada (2001)
Rique (2000)
Roe, Pegg, Hodges, & Trimm (1999)
Sandage, Hill, & Vang (2003)
Scobie & Scobie (1998)
Scobie & Scobie (2000)
Scobie et al. (2002)
Shontz & Rosenak (1988)
Shriver (1998)
Shuman & Smith (2000)
Sigmund (1999)
Sims (2002)
Smedes (1984)

Snyder & Lopez (2002)
Snyder & McCullough (2000)
Snyder & Yamhure (1999)
Staub & Pearlman (2001)
Stillwell & Baumeister (1997)
Sugimoto (1997)
Takaku, Weiner, & Ohbuchi (2001)
Tangney et al. (1996)
Tavuchis (1991)
Teahan (1987)
Temoshok & Chandra (2000)
Thomas & Garrod (2002)

Torrance (1986)
Twambley (1976)
Volf (2000)
Walker & Doverspike (2001)
Weiner (1995)
Wiesenthal (1998)
Williams & Williams (1993)
Worthington (1998)
Worthington (2000)
Worthington (2001)
Zillman & Cantor (1976)

Personality

Andrews (2000)
Aron & Aron (1997)
Ashton et al. (1998)
Atkinson (1982)
Baumeister & Exline (2000)
Baumeister (1998)
Baumeister et al. (1990)
Baures (1996)
Benn (1996)
Berry et al. (2005)
Bonar (1989)
Brenneis (2000)
Brown (2003)
Bucello (1991)
Butler (1998)
Cameron & Caza (2002)
Caprara et al. (1985)
Caprara et al. (1992)
Carver et al. (1989)
Casey (1998)
Compaan (1985)
Connor et al. (2003)
Conran (1993)
Cornock (2002)
Davenport (1991)
Davidson (1993)
Dorn (1998)
Emmons (2000)
Enright (2001)
Exline et al. (2003)
Gonzales et al. (1994)

Gonzales et al. (1992)
Haley & Strickland (1986)
Harris (1999)
Holmgren (1993)
Hunter (1987)
Kaplan (1992)
Kaufman (1984)
Kearns & Fincham (2004)
Kendler et al. (2003)
Konstam et al. (2001)
Larson (1992)
Leach & Lark (2003)
Lourenco & Fonseca (2003)
Marks (1988)
Maroda (1991)
McCullough & Worthington (1999)
McCullough (2000)
McCullough (2001)
McCullough (2004)
McCullough, Bellah et al. (2001)
Moss (1986)
Mullet et al. (2003)
Muñoz Sastre et al. (2003)
Murphy (1982)
Murphy (1988)
Murphy (1997)
Neto & Mullet (2004)
Newberry (1995)
O'Malley & Greenberg (1983)
O'Driscoll (1983)
Ohbuchi et al. (1989)

Putnam (2001)
Roberts (1995)
Roberts et al. (1991)
Symington et al. (2002)
Tangney et al. (1996)

Triandis (1995)
Walker & Gorsuch (2002)
Weiner et al. (1991)
Zechmeister & Romero (2002)

Interpersonal Forgiveness

Professional Relationships

Aquino et al. (2003)
Bradfield & Aquino (1999)
Butler (1998)
Butler & Mullis (2001)
Cameron & Caza (2004)

Enright & Eastin (1992)
Enright et al. (1992)
Yamhure-Thompson & Shahen (2002)
Worthington et al. (2005)

Personal Relationships (Friends, Families, Marriage)

Affinito (2001)
Al-Mabuk (1990)
Al-Mabuk et al. (1998)
Alvaro (2001)
Baucom & Epstein (1990)
Berry & Worthington (2001)
Boon & Sulsky (1997)
Boss (1997)
Brown (2000)
Brown (2001)
Bucello (1991)
Burchard et al. (2003)
Coleman (1998)
Couch et al. (1999)
DiBlasio & Benda (2002)
DiBlasio (1993)
Enright (1999)
Fenel (1993)
Ferch (1999)
Fincham & Beach (2001)
Fincham & Beach (2002)
Fincham (2000)
Fincham (2003)
Fincham et al. (2004)
Fincham et al. (2002)
Gordon & Baucom (1998)
Gordon & Baucom (1999)
Gordon & Baucom (2003)
Gordon et al. (2000)

Gordon et al. (2004)
Graham-Pole et al. (1989)
Grosskopf (1999)
Hannon (2001)
Hargrave (1994)
Hill (2001)
Holeman & Myers (1998)
Holeman (1995)
Holeman (1999)
Holeman (2003)
Holeman (2004)
Introini & Paleari (2002)
Kachadourian et al. (2005)
Karremans et al. (2003)
Krejci (2004)
Mauldin & Anderson (1998)
Mauldin (2003)
Mazor et al. (1998)
McCullough (1997)
Noller & Feeney (2002)
Olson et al. (2002)
Paleari et al. (2005)
Paleari et al. (2003)
Rackley (1993)
Roby (1997)
Rosenzwig-Smith (1988)
Rusbult et al. (2002)
Safer (1999)
Sandberg (1999)

Schimmel (2002)
Stoop & Masteller (1996)
Tracy (1999)

Trainer (1984)
Vangelisti & Maguire (2002)
Worthington (2003)

Romantic Relationships

Adams & Jones (1999)
Alvaro (2001)
Finkel et al. (2002)
Flanigan (1994)
Gassin (1995)
Gordon et al. (1959)
Kachadourian et al. (2004)
Lester & Lester (1998)
Mongeau et al. (1994)
Roscoe et al. (1988)

Rusbult et al. (2002)
Rye & Pargament (2002)
Rye (1999)
Safer (1999)
Shackelford et al. (2002)
Spring (1999)
Trainer (1984)
Woodman (1992)
Worthington & DiBlasio (1990)
Wu (2001)

Other Interpersonal

Adams, & Jones (1999)
Azar, & Mullet (2001)
Baumeister (1998)
Baumeister et al. (1998)
Baumeister et al. (1994)
Bennett & Dewberry (1994)
Berry et al. (2001)
Cords (1992)
Curtis (1989)
Enright & Zell (1989)
Enright (1998)
Enright (1999)
Enright et al. (1998)
Fow (1988)
Gassin (2001)
Halling (1994)
Halling (1995)
Hargrave (2001)
Harvey & Wenzel (2002)
Jones & King (2001)
Kearns & Fincham (2005)
Kelley (1998)
Kelln & Ellard (1999)
Kennington (1994)
Kirkpatrick (1995)
Landman (2002)
Linn & Linn (1978)
Loewen (1970)

McCullough & Hoyt (2002)
McCullough et al. (2003)
McCullough et al. (1995)
McCullough, Worthington et al. (1997)
Murphy & Hampton (1988)
Pattison (1965)
Rhode (1990)
Roberts (1993)
Rowe et al. (1989)
Sandage et al. (2000)
Schelert (1999)
Seibold (2001)
Sharma & Cheatham (1986)
Sims (2002)
Smedes (1984)
Smedes (1996)
Smedes (1998)
Snyder & Lopez (2002)
Snyder & Yamhure (1999)
Stillwell & Baumeister (1997)
Stoop (2001)
Subkoviak et al. (1995)
Takaku (2000)
Takaku (2001)
Triandis (1995)
Wade & Worthington (2002)
Weinberg (1994)
Zechmeister & Romero (2002)

Forgiveness of Self

Bauer et al. (1992)
Baumeister (1998)
Baumeister et al. (1994)
Burkle (1989)
Caprara et al. (1992)
Carlsmith & Gross (1969)
Clark (1985)
Coates (1997)
Dillon (2001)
Dorn (1998)
Enright & the Human Development Study
     Group (1996)
Gerber (1990)
Halling (1995)
Holmgren (1998)
Holmgren (2002)
Karen (2001)
Macaskill et al. (2002)
Maltby et al. (2001)
Roberts (1993)
Rutledge (1997)
Scott (1976)
Snow (1993)
Tobin (1993)

Development

Attachment Styles

Al-Mabuk (1990)
Coates (1997)
Davidson (2001)
Holeman (1995)
Kachadourian et al. (2004)
Lin (1998)
Luebbert (2000)
Roby (1997)

Development of Forgiveness Reasoning

Al-Mabuk (1990)
Aoki & Turk (1997)
Baumeister & Newman (1994)
Brink (1985)
Call et al. (1999)
Caplan (1992)
Connery (2002)
DiBlasio (1998)
Enright & the Human Development Study
     Group (1994)
Enright et al. (1989)
Falconi & Mullet (2003)
Fincham et al. (2003)
Freedman & Knupp (2003)
Girard & Mullet (1997)
Kaplan (1993)
Krause & Ingersoll-Dayton (2001)
Lin (1998)
Lourenco & Fonseca (2003)
Lukasik (2001)
Middleton (1997)
Mullet et al. (1998)
Roby (1997)
Scobie & Scobie (2000)
Scobie & Scobie (2003)
Scott (1991)
Spidell & Liberman (1981)
Strasser (1984)
Subkoviak et al. (1995)

Other Development

Aureli, Das, & Veenema (1997)
Coyle & Enright (1997)
de Waal (1993)
Enright & the Human Development Study
    Group (1991)
Enright, Gassin, & Wu (1992)
Luebbert (1999)
Mullet & Girard (1999)
Murray (2002)

Roby (1997)
Romig & Veenstra (1998)
Scobie & Scobie (2000)
Scobie & Scobie (2003)
Smith & Pourchot (1998)
Tangney, Wagner, Hill-Barlow, Marschall, &
    Gramzow (1996)
Vinsonneau & Mullet (2001)

Forgiveness Applications

Therapy/Counseling

Affinito (2002)
Al-Mabuk et al. (1998)
Aponte (1998)
Augsburger (1996)
Benson (1992)
Berecz (2001)
Bergin (1988)
Canale (1990)
Cavell (2003)
Cloke (1993)
Davenport (1991)
DiBlasio & Benda (1991)
DiBlasio & Proctor (1993)
DiBlasio (1992)
DiBlasio (1998)
Enright & Coyle (1998)
Enright & Fitzgibbons (2000)
Enright & the Human Development Study
    Group (1996)
Ferch (1998)
Ferch (2000)
Fitzgibbons (1986)
Flanigan (1987)
Frankel (1998)
Freedman & Enright (1996)
Freedman (2000)
Garzon et al. (2002)
Gordon & Baucom (1999)
Hart (1999)
Harvey & Brenner (1997)
Hebl & Enright (1993)

Heller (1998)
Holmgren (2002)
Human Development Study Group (1991)
Humphrey (1999)
Hyer & Sohnle (2001)
Kremer & Stephens (1983)
Kurusu (2000)
Lamb & Murphy (2002)
Lamb (2002)
Lim & Tan (2001)
Luskin et al. (2001)
Malcolm & Greenberg (2000)
Malcolm (1999)
McCullough et al. (1999)
Meek & McMinn (1997)
Murphy (2002)
Murphy (2003)
Murray (2002)
Nielsen et al. (2000)
Parsons (1988)
Phillips & Osborne (1989)
Pingleton (1989)
Puka (2002)
Reed et al. (2001)
Richards & Bergin (2004)
Richards & Potts (1995)
Richards (2002)
Ritzman (1987)
Roberts (1991)
Roberts (1993)
Roberts, Gilboa, & Gotlib (1998)

Romig & Veenstra (1998)
Rooney (1989)
Rosenak & Hamden (1992)
Rotter (2001)
Sandage et al. (1995)
Smadi & Haddad (1999)
Snyder (2001)
Stipe (1996)
Strong (1977)
Thoresen et al. (1998)

Wade & Worthington (2002)
Walrond-Skinner (1998)
Wapnick (1985)
West (2001)
Whipple (1988)
Wilson (1974)
Worthington & Wade (1999)
Worthington, Kurusu et al. (2000)
Worthington et al. (2005)
Young (1984)

Couple/Family

Al-Mabuk & Downs (1996)
Bonach & Sales (2002)
Bonach (2001)
Butler et al. (2002)
DiBlasio (2000)
Freedman & Knupp (2003)
Freedman (1999)
Holeman (1997)
Jackson (1998)
Konstam et al. (2000)
Konstam et al. (2002)
Lynch (1983)
Mamalakis (2001)
Mauldin & Anderson (1998)
Mitchell (1995)
Palamattathil (2001)
Ripley & Worthington (2002)
Rosenzwig-Smith (1988)
Rotter (2001)

Rotter (2001)
Rusbult et al. (2002)
Sandberg (1999)
Sells & Hargrave (1998)
Sells et al. (2002)
Snyder et al. (2004)
Spring (1999)
Stanley & Trathen (1994)
Stein (2001)
Stoop & Masteller (1996)
Trainer (1984)
Vangelisti & Maguire (2002)
Vaughan (2001)
Veenstra (1993)
Walker (1993)
Walrond-Skinner (1998)
Worthington & DiBlasio (1990)
Worthington (1998)

Group Therapy or Psycho-educational

Al-Mabuk et al. (1995)
Bryant (1999)
Care (2002)
Enright et al. (2001)
Flegel (1990)
Freedman (1998)
Gassin (1998)
Hansen (2002)
Jackson (1999)
Lena (1984)
Lin (2002)
McCullough & Worthington (1995)
Peddle (2001)

Phillips et al. (2002)
Sandage (1999)
Schmidt (1986)
Sells et al. (2002)
Sharma & Cheatham (1986)
Wade (2002)
Worthington & Drinkard (2000)
Worthington (2003)
Worthington (2001)
Worthington, Sandage et al. (2000)
Wu (2001)
Wuthnow (2000)

Political and Legal Applications

Ahn (1999)
Arthur (1999)
Augsburger (1992)
Azar & Mullet (2001)
Azar & Mullet (2002)
Azar et al. (2000)
Bartoli (1998)
Bazemore (1999)
Borris & Diehl (1998)
Chambliss (2002)
Chapman & Spong (2003)
Chapman (1998)
Chapman (1999)
Dickey (1998)
Elshatain (1999)
Gehm (1991)
Gentilone & Regidor (1986)
Gibson & Gouws (1999)
Gobodo-Madikizela (2002)
Harris (1986)
Huang & Enright (2000)
Huang (1990)
Kadiangandu et al. (2001)
Kaminer et al. (2001)
Kidder (1975)
Kittle (1999)
Lim (2001)
Long & Brecke (2003)
Luskin & Curtis (2000)
McLernon et al. (2002)
McLernon et al. (2004)

McLernon et al. (2003)
Meyer (2000)
Minow (1998)
Montiel (2002)
Montville (1989)
Moore (1993)
Morris (1988)
Neto et al. (2000)
Nqweni (2002)
Omuro-Yamamoto (2001)
Park & Enright (1997)
Park & Enright (2000)
Reed (2002)
Roe et al. (1999)
Sandage et al. (2003)
Sandage et al. (1995)
Scobie et al. (2002)
Shriver (1995)
Shriver (1998)
Shuman & Smith (2000)
Sigmund (1999)
Smyth (1998)
Snyder & Yamhure (1999)
Staub & Pearlman (2001)
Stevens (1986)
Sugimoto (1997)
Takaku et al. (1987)
Temoshok & Chandra (2000)
Thomas & Garrod (2002)
Worthington (2002)

Chapter Thirty-Two

More Questions About Forgiveness: Research Agenda for 2005–2015

Everett L. Worthington, Jr.

A fter completing our odyssey through the reviews of forgiveness, we are poised to reflect on the current status of the field. In chapter 1, I posed eight questions which I thought (at the start of work on this book in 2002) were fundamental. Of course, that was not the first time that stock had been taken in the field. In 1998, I assayed the field (see column 1, Table 32.1). In 2000, McCullough, Pargament, and Thoresen similarly reflected on the field (see column 2, Table 32.1). Comparing those books, it was clear how much had been learned in a few short years of intensive research into forgiveness. I also summarized my 2002 questions (see column 3, Table 32.1). From Table 32.1, you can see that the questions posed in 1997 have not changed. The answers have.

STATUS OF FORGIVENESS STUDIES AND IMPLICATIONS FOR THE FUTURE

Question 1: What Is Forgiveness?

In the *Handbook of Forgiveness*, each reviewer defined forgiveness. Routinely, the reviewers said there was no consensus understanding of forgiveness. After reading the chapters, I disagree. There seems to be a near consensus. Most investigators said forgiveness is not to be confused with excusing, exonerating, justifying, condoning, pardoning, or reconciling. Virtually all investigators agree on what forgiveness *is not*. What forgiveness *is* also achieves consensus if we accept that forgiveness has not one but several definitions. That is not simply because investigators can't agree. It is because there are several types of forgiveness (see Table 32.2). Two definitions predominate. Some investigators limit forgiveness to *an individual's experience of forgiveness*. Other investigators see forgiveness as a complex *interpersonal process of forgiveness*.

TABLE 32.1.   Three Sets of Questions to Evaluate Progress in the Scientific Study of Forgiveness

Worthington (1998)	McCullough, Pargament, and Thoresen (2000)	Worthington (this volume)
Are there consensus definitions of major constructs?	2. From one to many meanings: Exploring the variety of meanings of forgiveness	1. What is forgiveness?
Are there a diversity of validated methods and measures of unforgiveness, forgiveness, and concepts that are related to theory?	4. From single to multiple levels of analysis: Drawing on multiple perspectives of forgiveness	2. How is forgiveness best measured?
Has forgiveness of and by God been investigated?		3. What is the role of religion (if any) in forgiveness?
Has forgiveness been investigated at the following levels? • For discrete acts of harm • Of self • Of and by God • Within relationships • Of a partner (for numerous acts) • As a trait or personal characteristic	3. From isolation to integration: Weaving forgiveness into psychological theory 6. From conceptualization to research: Expanding the empirical study of forgiveness	4. What are the forgiveness processes at individual, dyadic, and societal levels?
Are there heuristic theories or models of unforgiveness, naturally occurring forgiveness, and the promotion of forgiveness? What is the adequacy of evidence for each?		
Have precursors, covariates, consequences, and sequelae of both unforgiveness and forgiveness been identified?		5. What are the benefits (and under what conditions) of forgiveness?

5. From the expected to the unexpected: Openness to the downside of forgiveness

Have conditions that indicate when forgiveness is not warranted and not likely to be effective been identified?

1. From distant to close-up: Conducting proximal studies of forgiveness

To what extent have highly relevant target populations been studied and interventions tailored to promote forgiveness within those populations?

7. From intuition to information: Building an empirically informed approach to forgiveness in clinical practice

To what extent have nomothetic investigations revealed information about unforgiveness and forgiveness in general?

To what extent have idiographic investigations revealed information specific to different populations?

How high is the quality of publication outlets?

How many of the objectives for placement of publications have been achieved?

• Have major publications been published in medical and psychological journals?
• Have critical reviews been published?
• Have important scholarly books been published?
• Has a federally funded RFP been initiated?
• Has broad dissemination occurred?

6. What are the costs, limits, and iatrogenic effects of forgiveness?

7. Are there particularly effective ways to promote forgiveness with individuals, dyads, and social or societal units?

8. Is there a future for forgiveness studies?

Note: Numbers refer to the explicit ordering of questions in the works cited.

Forgiveness as an Individual's Experience.   Two types of definitions are used to describe an individual's experience. To some investigators, forgiveness is giving up a grudge (i.e., resentment and bitterness) and not holding an offender's injustice against him or her. To other investigators, forgiveness is not only giving up negative thoughts, feelings, motivations, and behaviors, but also involves replacing those with positive thoughts, feelings, motivations, and behaviors. In some cases, this replacement is seen as a mechanism for affecting an experience of forgiveness (Worthington & Scherer, 2004). In other cases, this replacement is the end result of forgiving (Fincham, Beach, & Davila, 2004). Whereas these two definitions seem to be at odds with each other, the resolution is in the type of relationship in which the transgression occurred (see chapter 12 by Rusbult, Hannon, Stocker, & Finkel).

Forgiveness Is Different in Noncontinuing Versus Continuing Close Relationships. Most investigators who define forgiveness as reducing negative feelings, thoughts, motivations, and behaviors study relationships between strangers, acquaintances, or people who do not expect their relationship to continue. For example, if a person robs a victim or a physician makes a medical error, forgiveness is legitimately defined as giving up negative feelings, thoughts, motivations, and behaviors toward the offender. On the other hand, when a betrayal or major disappointment occurs between romantic partners, family members, or close friends, forgiveness is defined as reducing of negative experiences coupled with replacing them with positive experiences. Fincham and his colleagues (2004) argued forcefully that both experiences must be part of forgiveness in marriage, parenting, and other family relationships.

Some situations are ambiguous. For example, in a workplace, if a co-worker or a supervisor offends a worker, the nature of the relationship affects how the worker will define forgiveness. If the worker does not believe that an ongoing relationship is important, the worker will likely define full forgiveness as reducing or eliminating negative experiences. On the other hand, if workers must work closely together, the worker will likely not feel content simply to reduce negative experiences. He or she will want to rebuild positive experiences into that relationship.

Forgiveness as a Decision to Control One's Behavior.   Some investigators emphasize the importance of a victim's decision about controlling his or her behavior toward the offender. DiBlasio's (1998) decision-based forgiveness is based on making willful decisions. Enright has long included a decision to try to forgive as part of his process model (see Enright & Fitzgibbons, 2000, for a summary). McCullough and Worthington (1995) tested decision-based interventions as early as 1995. Baskin and Enright (2004) have shown in a meta-analysis that such decision-based models of intervention are less effective in promoting experiences of forgiveness than are empathy-based models. The mental health, physical health, and relational and spiritual effects of making a decision to forgive are virtually untested. Worthington (Exline, Worthington, Hill, & McCullough, 2003; Worthington & Scherer, 2004) has differentiated decisional from emotional forgiveness. In decisional forgiveness, people make a behavioral intention statement to eliminate their negative behavior in noncontinuing relationships and also to restore positive behavior in continuing close relationships. The person might (or might not) later *experience* forgiveness and might (or might not) *express* his or her decision to the transgressor.

Experience of Forgiveness.   Victims experience forgiveness internally. Virtually all investigators would agree that an experience of forgiveness involves a prosocial transformation of cognition, emotion, motivation, and behavior. Investigators, however, tend to disagree about which aspect of this experience to use as the sine qua non that marks forgiveness. Some focus on cognition (Flanigan, 1996; Luskin, 2001; Thompson et al., 2005; see chapter 12 by Rusbult et al.); some, motivation (i.e., McCullough and early Worthington); others, emotion (i.e., Worthington & Scherer, 2004; see chapter 23 by Malcolm, Warwar, & Greenberg et al.); and still others, a confluence of changes (i.e., Enright & Fitzgibbons, 2000).

Expression of Forgiveness (Within a Complicated Interpersonal Process Within a Dyad).   Some people see forgiveness as incorporating interactions around a transgression (see chapter 12 by Rusbult et al.). This process includes the experiences of an individual (see above). However, they argue, other processes would be necessary to understand the entire interpersonal surround of the "forgiveness process." Investigators who define forgiveness interpersonally tend to be social psychologists who study interpersonal interactions or social scientists who study forgiveness processes within societal applications (see chapter 27 by Staub; chapter 28 by Cairns, Tam, Hewstone, & Niens; chapter 29 by Hill, Exline, & Cohen; chapter 30 by Armour & Umbreit).

The interpersonal processes involved in forgiveness might begin with a transgression or a perceived transgression. The person might exert restraint (see chapter 12 by Rusbult et al.), forbearance (McCullough, Fincham, & Tsang, 2003), and silently grant decisional forgiveness (Worthington & Scherer, 2004). Many ways of dealing with the transgression exist, including getting even, exacting vengeance, seeking justice, excusing, exonerating, justifying the offense, and attempting to reconcile after the offense. These events are part of the process surrounding forgiving but are not the same as the individual experience of forgiving.

An important part of this interpersonal forgiveness process has to do with the immediate accommodations by both parties involved. Accommodations can include immediate exits from interaction or discussion of the transgression. Later, discussion involves reproaches by the injured party (i.e., requests for the perpetrator to explain why he or she offended) and accounts (i.e., the explanations) by the perpetrator (see chapter 12 by Rusbult et al. and chapter 13 by Fincham, Hall, & Beach). Reproaches and accounts depend on and lead to attributions of causality by both parties. The wrongdoer might experience guilt or shame, let himself or herself off the hook (see chapter 10 by Tangney et al.), or repent (i.e., apologize, confess, and seek to be forgiven for the wrongdoing). Offender accounts might be denials, refusals to acknowledge wrongdoing, or justifications for wrongdoing. To mitigate wrongdoing, offenders might either make excuses (i.e., describe the mitigating circumstances) or concessions of wrongdoing, which might involve apologies, offering restitution, and seeking forgiveness.

If the victim decides to forgive and begins to experience forgiveness (or sometimes even if such experiences are not genuine; Baumeister, Exline, & Sommer, 1998), then forgiveness may be *expressed*, verbally or nonverbally, by the victim. The wrongdoer might then accept forgiveness from the victim and either forgive the self or stew in his or her guilt and (perhaps) shame.

Forgiveness Within Societal and Intergroup Contexts. In society, interpersonal interactions occur within a context of a history between or among groups. Often, such interactions have an audience. Friends and community members observe dyadic interactions around transactions. Ethnic groups attend to and interpret the interactions in light of intergroup history and intragroup assumptions. Group interactions are complicated because not everyone holds the same view of history or assumptions about what should and should not occur. Also, some wrongdoing violates either social norms or explicit laws (see Gobodo-Madikizela, 2002). Prominent examples are crime and terrorism. Legal penalties are prescribed for crime. Victim impact-statements, which describe the suffering victims have undergone, as well as victim forgiveness might be taken into consideration in sentencing. However, courts are not obligated to do so. Through such testimonies, there is, therefore, a formal mechanism by which forgiveness or lack of forgiveness can be considered and perhaps communicated in ways that affect the outcome of a trial.

Justice and forgiveness are not more closely tied together in society for several reasons. First, criminals and terrorists are brought to justice infrequently. Second, many societal transgressions are violations of social norms or senses of common decency but are not violations of law. Insensitive ethnic insults—even delivered unaware—can wound. Deliberate slights and insults that are short of discrimination or hate speech do not fall under legal jurisdiction but nevertheless keep ethnic conflict on the front burner.

I have devoted substantial discussion to definitional issues not because disagreement across theoreticians is still characteristic of the field of forgiveness, as it has been up to now, but because I believe that definitional issues are mostly settled, or soon will be. They are settled because both theory and measurement have become more precise. However, definitional clarity is now more advanced than is measurement.

Question 2: How Is Forgiveness Best Measured?

One's definition of forgiveness in a particular research study or with a particular client should determine the measurement of forgiveness. As definitions have become more precise, so have measures. Yet the development of measures currently lags definitional clarity.

If a person's individual experience of forgiveness is being measured, investigators must make finer distinctions than have previously been made about what forgiveness is. For example, both positive and negative aspects of forgiveness need to be measured and reported. The Enright Forgiveness Inventory (Subkoviak et al., 1995) has subscales for positive and negative affect, behavior, and cognition. Likewise, laboratories directed by Rye (Rye et al., 2001), McCullough (McCullough et al., 2003), and Worthington (Berry, Worthington, Jr., O'Connor, Parrott, III, & Wade, 2005) have the capabilities to report both reductions in unforgiving emotions and motivations and increases in forgiveness. Reporting both—even if, for example, there is no change in forgiveness—and reporting separate effects on affect, behavior, cognition, motivation, and physiology can enrich our understanding of forgiveness and its alternatives as they occur in different types of relationships. Measures other than straightforward self-report questionnaires are needed. Investigators have developed such measures (see chapter 20 by Temoshok & Wald and chapter 22 by Noll). Physiological measures have been developed using brain imagery (see chapter 16 by Farrow & Woodruff), peripheral physiology (see chapter 18 by Witvliet), and cortisol (Berry & Worthington, 2001). Other non-questionnaire measures are needed.

Let us look at measurement in a different way. Instead of focusing on questionnaires or other types of measures, let's ask about research design and statistical treatment. McCullough and Root (see chapter 7) have argued that research design must become increasingly sophisticated. Indeed, it is doing so (see chapter 13 by Fincham et al.). Studies of couples must consider (a) both partners and their reciprocal effects on each other, (b) the context (i.e., sentiment override) and its effect on measures, and (c) couple behaviors, physical reactions, and self-reports of thoughts, attributions, beliefs, perceptions, and attitudes. Hoyt and McCullough (see chapter 8) have also made a strong case for measurement rooted in the most recent psychometric theory and involving multiple modalities. Have these recommendations been heeded thus far? Clearly, the reviewers represented in this book would answer in unison, "Far too infrequently."

Perhaps a more cogent question is this: Will the recommendations be heeded in the future? At the present, it appears the answer is again, "Far too infrequently." Complicated designs require big samples and sophisticated statistical competence. Big samples require money. Most forgiveness research is unfunded. In thesis and dissertation research, participants often are undergraduate students. Dissertation research is not often federally funded. Even if it is, it is not funded long enough to collect the huge samples needed for the statistics discussed in the chapters by McCullough and Root, Fincham et al., and Hoyt and McCullough. In addition, even though many doctoral programs require students to learn sophisticated statistics, most students cannot absorb enough in a few semesters to carry out the analyses at the level suggested by our reviewers.

Does this mean that the field is doomed to second-class status because of terminal methodological inadequacy? No. All fields face the same challenge. That challenge is met in several ways. First, senior researchers need to seek funding. Not only would funded investigators bring resources to bear on research, but also spin-off master's thesis and dissertation research would increase. Second, researchers can string together two or three dissertations plus a faculty-initiated study into a multiple-study publication. Third, researchers can collaborate across laboratories, which allows faculty members, each with graduate (and perhaps undergraduate) assistants, to focus on a single problem. Fourth, collaboration in intervention research between large clinical practices and academic researchers is also becoming more common. In summary, measurement is becoming more sophisticated. However, it lags definitional clarity, and it requires larger-scale research for sophistication in measurement to advance to the highest level.

Question 3: How and for Whom Is Interpersonal Forgiveness Related to Religion?

For many years, forgiveness was considered to be practically owned by religion. That was particularly true in the United States when the nation held a majority of people who professed Christianity. Christianity is characterized by forgiveness (Marty, 1998). Early research on the relationship between forgiveness and religion focused on establishing a relationship between religious beliefs and values, and a forgiving disposition. People who are more religious, especially Christians, reported being more dispositionally forgiving. As McCullough and Worthington (1999) observed, however, high dispositional forgiveness in religious people did not strongly predict the level of forgiveness in particular transgressions, and they suggest reasons why. Tsang, McCullough, and Hoyt (in press) investigated those suggestions. For example, if responses to transgressions are aggregated, a stronger relationship can be detected between forgiving specific transgressions and reports of dispositional forgivingness.

Recently, researchers have moved beyond investigating this state-trait correlation to finer-grained studies. Let me mention four examples. First, Exline and Martin (see chapter 6) have studied people's anger and disappointment with God. They observe that people usually resolve their anger satisfactorily. Some people, however, resolve it by rejecting their faith. Second, Mahoney, Rye, and Pargament (see chapter 5) have observed that people treat overtly religious acts and symbols (e.g., the cross, baptism, or the sacraments) as being sacred. People often treat secular objects such as marriage, family, or country as sacred. When sacred objects are deemed to have been desecrated, people are reluctant to forgive those transgressions (see chapter 5 by Mahoney et al.). Third, Wuthnow (2000) has studied forgiveness in religious groups. Such groups, even if they do not focus on forgiveness per se, were found to promote forgiving attitudes. Fourth, Krause and his colleagues (e.g., Krause & Ellison, 2003) studied Christians using qualitative interviews. They found doctrinal errors in beliefs about forgiveness that could affect people's forgiveness.

A similar increase in sophistication has occurred in the study of clinical and societal interventions. Rye et al. (2004) have studied a religiously tailored forgiveness intervention (see chapter 26 by Wade, Worthington, & Meyer). That intervention promoted more forgiveness with religious students and women who had undergone divorce than did a similar secular intervention. Cairns et al. (see chapter 28 by Cairns, et al.) described the conflict in Northern Ireland between Irish Protestants and Roman Catholics (see also chapter 27 on Rwanda by Staub). Religion empowered each group to hold on to its beliefs and made conflict difficult to resolve. Perhaps the reason might be found in Mahoney et al.'s (see chapter 5) view that desecrated sacred objects are invested with emotion.

Many important questions about religion and forgiveness have not been addressed. For example, no investigations have sought to determine whether forgiveness can induce spiritual transformations or whether spiritual transformations can promote forgiveness. No one has thoroughly documented empirically the negative effects of forgiveness. For example, many Christians believe that their divine forgiveness is dependent on their interpersonal forgiveness. Might this religious pressure to grant forgiveness lead to people saying they forgive but holding emotional unforgiveness, to the detriment of their physical and mental health (see Baumeister et al.'s, 1998, hollow forgiveness). Might they squelch legitimate resentment (see chapter 3 by Murphy)? Might they forgive quickly and thus not hold perpetrators accountable? Might perpetrators assume that forgiveness from their victim implies that the perpetrators need not be accountable and thus take advantage of victims repeatedly? Might guilt-ridden religious people be reluctant to forgive themselves (see chapter 10 by Tangney et al.)? Might self-absorbed and narcissistic religious people let themselves off the hook through glib forgiveness that short-circuits apology, restitution, and making amends? Researchers have also not investigated how people forgive when religious differences are strongly embedded in historical conflict between religions.

In summary, as the scientific study of forgiveness began, investigators generally held religious issues at arm's length. They seemed to want to establish that forgiveness could be studied apart from its religious roots. That has been established. Now we must ask the hard questions about the intersection of religion and forgiveness.

Question 4: How Does Forgiveness Affect the Participants in the Forgiveness Process?

What is the status of our understanding of the processes surrounding forgiving? Let's use Table 32.2 to guide our evaluation. For transgressions perpetrated by strangers, little research has been done on decisional forgiveness. We don't know whether making a decision to forgive affects the internal experience of forgiveness—emotionally, cognitively, motivationally, and behaviorally. We also don't know whether granting decisional forgiveness affects expressing that forgiveness to a person with whom one does not anticipate having a close ongoing relationship. For instance, in restorative justice, what effects will either granting or not granting forgiveness have on the victim, offender, and perhaps involved observers (see chapter 29 by Hill et al. and chapter 30 by Armour & Umbreit)? Decisional forgiveness of a stranger has not been examined from the offender's point of view. The offender might (a) experience guilt, (b) be self-condemning, or (c) finding out that a victim has granted forgiveness, grant self-forgiveness more readily than when knowing nothing about the victim or knowing that the victim still bears a grudge. Those three outcomes are starkly different, and we currently know nothing about any of the three.

TABLE 32.2.   **Emerging Consensus Definitions of Forgiveness**

Type of forgiveness	Definitions if transgressor is a stranger or if continuing relationship is not desired	Definitions if transgressor is in a close relationship and continued relationship is desired
Decisional forgiveness	A private behavioral intention statement to eschew getting even, seeking revenge, or acting to bring harm or disadvantage to the offender.	A private behavioral intention statement (1) to eschew getting even, seeking revenge, avoiding, or acting to bring harm or disadvantage to the offender and (2) to attempt to heal relational damage and, if possible, strengthen the relationship.
Experience of forgiveness	To give up a grudge so that one eliminates negative cognition, emotions, motivations, and behaviors toward the offender.	(1) To give up a grudge toward the offender and (2) to reach net positive cognition, emotions, motivations, and behaviors toward the offender.
Process of interpersonal forgiveness	Forgiveness is either internal or is achieved through discussion with a third party (e.g., counselor, friend). Decisional or experienced forgiveness are not usually expressed to the transgressor but possibly could be expressed to the third party. Thus, accounts might (or might not) have occurred, but interactions are not ongoing.	Interpersonal forgiveness includes interpersonal interactions surrounding a transgression, which include (a) the transgression, (b) accommodation processes by either party, (c) attributions (e.g., of blame by the victims or of justification by the offender), (d) reproaches, (e) accounts by the offender, (f) seeking forgiveness or rejecting the need for forgiveness by the offender, (g) a victim's decisions about of forgiveness, (h) a victim's expressions of emotional forgiveness, (i) acceptance of forgiveness by the offender, and perhaps (j) self-forgiveness by the offender. In society, such dyadic interactions surrounding transgressions occur within historical, in-group/out-group, and social normative (or legal) contexts that affect interpretation of events.

Many questions are also ripe for investigation in close interpersonal interactions. Does making a private decision to forgive a partner affect the victims' thoughts, feelings, motivations, or behaviors? Furthermore, can the offender detect the changes if a decision is made but not communicated explicitly? If the victim experiences forgiveness, what further effects might this have on the victim? Will it affect physical (see chapter 19 by Harris & Thoresen) or mental health (see chapter 21 by Toussaint & Webb)? Behavior in the future? Furthermore, if the victim experiences thorough forgiveness but does not communicate that to the offender and if the offender detects that the victim has forgiven but is reluctant to express that, then does that perceived incongruity affect the offender's behavior or judgments toward the victim? Little has been done in studying the expression of forgiveness between victim and offender and the consequences of different communications. Complex interactions were described in chapter 1, yet few of those had been studied empirically.

In summary, despite all the research that has been done on forgiveness, the bulk of the research has concentrated on the victim's experience. The complexity of the process—especially the interactions around transgressions—remains largely unexplored.

Question 5: What Are Benefits of Forgiveness?

Perhaps as much progress has been made on documenting potential benefits of forgiveness as any topic on forgiveness. Yet despite accumulated research on physical health benefits (see Worthington & Scherer, 2004), little has been established *definitively* (see chapter 19 by Harris & Thoresen). Investigations in the young science of forgiveness have not employed longitudinal designs necessary to document that forgiveness has a causal relationship to physical health or ill health. Researchers have not disentangled the effects of reducing unforgiveness and forgiving. Although mental health benefits of spontaneously forgiving and intervention-induced forgiveness have been found (see chapter 21 by Toussaint & Webb), criticisms similar to the ones that Harris and Thoresen levied against the study of forgiveness and physical health could be levied against forgiveness and mental health. Research has not been longitudinal and has not disaggregated the effects of reducing unforgiveness from those granting or experiencing forgiveness. Substantial research has been done on forgiveness's benefits to relationships. Fincham and his colleagues (see chapter 13) and others have shown that behaviors by one partner in a couple affects behaviors by the other partner. Forgiveness benefits relationships, even if ratings of overall relationship satisfaction are used as covariates.

For the most part, researchers have assumed that forgiveness is genuinely beneficial. Two significant deficits thus characterize the literature.

1. Costs have been less well documented.
2. The difficult and detailed scientific work of establishing causal relationships as opposed to correlational relationships has yet to be done.

Thus, the exciting investigation of causality must now be undertaken.

Question 6: What are the Costs, Limits, and Iatrogenic Effects of Forgiveness?

Early in forgiveness studies, researchers were often enthusiastic about studying forgiveness and did not specify or study the costs, limits, and iatrogenic effects of forgiveness. Popular books bordered on boosterism (see chapter 3 by Murphy). Clinical reports and scientific studies emphasized the benefits of forgiveness. No experience is universally beneficial. In the last 7 years, reports have begun to document the limits of forgiveness. Of course, many people criticized forgiveness for years (i.e., Wiesenthal, 1998). Philosophers objected to uncritical forgiveness (Lamb & Murphy, 2002). Criticism-lite flirtation with forgiveness crashed to the ground on September 11, 2001. With the attack on the United States, motives for getting even, justice, revenge, and retribution were set ablaze. The United States struck back. Reactions to invasions of Afghanistan and Iraq were galvanized within and outside of the United States. Retaliation mentality and anti-U.S. reactions divided rather than promoted reconciliation. As a consequence, a social backlash against forgiveness has recently coincided with dissatisfaction at an often-uncritical approach to forgiveness by clinicians and scientists. Thus, scientific approaches have become more critical since 2001. Researchers are now more often combining their study of forgiveness with identifying the benefits of vengeance, revenge, resentment, and payback (see Chapman & Spong, 2003; Horowitz, 2004; Lamb & Murphy, 2002; see chapter 3 by Murphy and chapter 27 by Staub.

Question 7: Are There Particularly Effective Ways to Promote Forgiveness With Individuals, Families, and Larger Social or Societal Units?

Many forgiveness interventions have been proposed and tested. Enright's process model of forgiveness is the gold standard (see chapter 24 by Freedman, Enright, & Knutson), but Rye's model (Rye et al., 2004) shows excellent outcomes in relational context. The meta-analysis by Wade et al. (see chapter 26) identifies common factors in interventions to promote forgiveness. Most interventions have helped people change their internal experiences of forgiveness. Few investigators have examined forgiveness within contexts of reconciliation or devised interventions to promote reconciliation (cf. see chapter 25 by Gordon, Baucom, & Snyder).

Research has suggested that interventions, especially in groups, that are targeted toward a particular problem, such as Rye et al.'s (2004) attempt to help divorced people forgive or most of Enright's studies, are generally more effective than are nontargeted forgiveness interventions. Both targeted and non-targeted interventions have their places. On one hand, therapeutic efficiency is possible with groups aimed generally at forgiving. Most practices of clinical psychology do not have enough clients to constitute a group of people focused on adults who desire to forgive a significant hurt from (a) the parents of origin, (b) divorce, or (c) marital problems. However, a clinical practice might have many people who are dealing with significant interpersonal hurts for which a non-targeted forgiveness intervention is appropriate. Thus, it is important to study the efficacy of non-targeted group interventions. If settings can sustain targeted interventions, current research suggests that those will produce the most forgiveness. For example, if a trauma center ran groups dealing with trauma (even if different types), a marriage clinic ran groups for marital or parenting issues, or a rehabilitation center ran groups for issues related to substance abuse, those groups would likely be more effective than would groups that combined people with a variety of problems.

The common expectation that evidence-based interventions are de rigueur leaves open the issue of which forgiveness interventions are evidence based. Although numerous interventions have some empirical support for their efficacy (see chapter 14 by Battle & Miller, chapter 23 by Malcolm et al., chapter 24 by Freedman et al., chapter 25 by Gordon et al., and chapter 26 by Wade et al.), none has reached the level of an officially designated "empirically supported" intervention. To reach that status, at least two independent controlled clinical trials conducted in different laboratories must support the efficacy of treatment. The field is too young and funding too meager to date to meet such criteria.

Question 8: Is There a Future for Forgiveness Studies?

Have the Low-Hanging Scientific Fruits Been Plucked?   Fields of scientific study often follow a predictable path. At the beginning, the questions are bold, broad, and breathtakingly exciting. New research tends to answer the big questions. The next generation of questions is more nuanced. Answers have less widespread appeal. Later, questions are increasingly specialized until the field collapses upon itself: Knowledge is precise but no one gives a rip about the jots and tittles. Where is the field of forgiveness studies? Have the big questions been answered? Are the answers now prefaced with so many qualifications, hems, and haws that experts sound to the public like eggheads? My answer: Big questions are plentiful.

Basic Research Questions.   Empirical questions about the fundamental processes involved in forgiveness abound. Measurement is becoming increasingly sophisticated, as are the questions that are being asked (see chapter 7 by McCullough & Root and chapter 8 by Hoyt & McCullough). Yet huge questions remain unaddressed.

Personality.   Mullet, Neto, and Riviére (see chapter 11) suggest that people with vengeful personalities act differently than do people who hold grudges (Exline & Baumeister, 2000), maintain resentment (see chapter 3 by Murphy), or experience unforgiveness (Worthington & Wade, 1999). Researchers need to identify different patterns of behavior and different interventions for each of these types of people.

Understudied Topics.   Some important areas that were reviewed in the present volume are thoroughly underresearched. For example, trauma (see chapter 22 by Noll), family (see chapter 14 by Battle), children (see chapter 9 by Denham, Neal, Wilson, Pickering, & Boyatzis), restorative justice (see chapter 29 by Hill et al. and chapter 30 by Armour & Umbreit), and forgiveness of self (see chapter 10 by Tangney et al.) are all understudied.

Domination by a Few Active Researchers.   Many of the topics reviewed in this book are well researched; however, the field is dominated by only a few active researchers. They provide an in-depth view of the area, but the view depends largely on one research lab with one methodology and often one or two theoretical foci. For example, understanding forgiveness in marriage is dominated by Fincham's work. Interventions are more broadly represented (see chapter 26 by Wade et al.) but the Enright, Worthington, and Rye labs dominate what is known about interventions. In the areas of personality (see the four tables in chapter 11 by Mullet et al.) and social psychology, the findings are more balanced across investigators.

Are there funds for research in forgiveness?   From 1998 through 2005, fourteen funding partners from private sources fueled forgiveness research, contributing to *A Campaign for Forgiveness Research*. At present, though, funding is scarce, despite much talk about how important forgiveness is. Federal funding agencies have not been forthcoming with RFAs. Nor have major grants been awarded to study forgiveness by any major federal agency. Is there a future for forgiveness studies?

CATCH MY PASSION

I hope this book will persuade you to invest your resources in forgiveness. If you are a researcher, you can invest your future in this field. The questions are exciting. They touch the heart and are useful. You can help better people's lives through research. In the practical matters of research success, you can be assured that there are both high-level outlets for your research and eager graduate students who want to study forgiveness.

If you are a practitioner, you can use powerful interventions to help families, adults, children, those who have been victimized, and those who have been traumatized. You can invest your time and effort in running forgiveness groups or using forgiveness in counseling, family life education, and community prevention. Basic research has fed practice (broadly defined), and practice has fed ideas back into the laboratory.

If you are a religious leader, you can use or adapt the many findings to benefit those under your care. Invest your effort and time in learning and teaching people how to forgive and what they can expect (and should not expect) when they try to forgive.

If you are a philanthropist, I hope you have seen that *research can help people*. If you are a federal funding agency, I hope you can see that *this field will help contribute to solving individual and societal problems*. Excellent researchers have developed workable paradigms, accumulated promising pilot data, and developed scientific tools to help solve significant social problems.

If you are a public policy specialist, I hope you see that forgiveness studies are relevant for government support. The common welfare involves helping heal individual hurts, holding marriages together, giving children their best chance to thrive and grow into social contributors, reforming the criminal justice system (through more restorative justice), helping civil disputes be settled out of court more often, preventing lawsuits in the area of medical malpractice, and contributing to foreign and domestic relations. Public policy applications are plentiful.

But whether you are a researcher, graduate student, practitioner, religious leader, philanthropist, government funder, or public policy specialist, the proof is in your own life. Have transgressions touched you or those you love? Do you wish we knew more to ease that pain, smooth out social bumps, and soothe psychological bruises? We *can* know more as we invest in the scientific study of forgiveness.

REFERENCES

Baskin, T. W., & Enright, R. D. (2004). Intervention studies on forgiveness: A meta-analysis. *Journal of Counseling and Development, 82,* 79–90.

Baumeister, R. F., Exline, J. J., & Sommer, K. L. (1998). The victim role, grudge theory, and two dimensions of forgiveness. In E. L. Worthington, Jr. (Ed.), *Dimensions of forgiveness: Psychological research and theological perspectives* (pp. 79–104). Philadelphia: Templeton Foundation Press.

Berry, J. W., & Worthington, E. L., Jr., (2001). Forgiveness, relationship quality, stress while imagining relationship events, and physical and mental health. *Journal of Counseling Psychology, 48,* 447–455.

Berry, J. W., Worthington, E. L., Jr., O'Connor, L., Parrott, L. III, & Wade, N. G. (2005). Forgiveness, vengeful rumination, and affective traits. *Journal of Personality, 73,* 1–43.

Chapman, A. R., & Spong, B. (Eds.). (2003). *Religion and reconciliation in South Africa.* Philadelphia: Templeton Foundation Press.

DiBlasio, F. A. (1998). The use of decision-based forgiveness intervention within intergenerational family therapy. *Journal of Family Therapy, 20,* 77–94.

Enright, R. D., & Fitzgibbons, R. P. (2000). *Helping clients forgive: An empirical guide for resolving anger and restoring hope.* Washington, DC: American Psychological Association.

Exline, J. J., & Baumeister, R. F. (2000). Expressing forgiveness and repentance: Benefits and barriers. In M. E. McCullough, K. I. Pargament, & C. E. Thoresen (Eds.), *Forgiveness: Theory, research, and practice* (pp. 133–155). New York: Guilford Press.

Exline, J. J., Worthington, E. L., Jr., Hill, P., & McCullough, M. E. (2003). Forgiveness and justice: A research agenda for social and personality psychology. *Personality and Social Psychology Review 7,* 337–348.

Fincham, F. D., Beach, S. R., & Davila, J. (2004). Forgiveness and conflict resolution in marriage. *Journal of Family Psychology, 18,* 72–81.

Flanigan, B. (1996). *Forgiving yourself.* New York: Macmillan.

Gobodo-Madikizela, P. (2002). Remorse, forgiveness, and rehumanization: Stories from South Africa. *Journal of Humanistic Psychology, 42,* 7–32.

Horowitz, J. (2004, June 16). Vatican City: The inquisition wasn't that bad. *New York Times*, 8.

Krause, N., & Ellison, C. G. (2003). Forgiveness by God, forgiveness of others, and psychological well-being in late life. *Journal for the Scientific Study of Religion, 42*, 77–93.

Lamb, S., & Murphy, J. G. (2002). *Before forgiving: Cautionary views of forgiveness in psychotherapy.* London: Oxford University Press.

Luskin, F. (2001). *Forgive for good: A proven prescription for health and happiness.* San Francisco: Harper.

Marty, M. E. (1998). The ethos of Christian forgiveness. In E. L. Worthington, Jr. (Ed.), *Dimensions of forgiveness: Psychological research and theological perspectives* (pp. 9–28). Philadelphia: Templeton Foundation Press.

McCullough, M. E., Fincham, F. D., & Tsang, J-A. (2003). Forgiveness, forbearance, and time: The temporal unfolding of transgression-related interpersonal motivations. *Journal of Personality and Social Psychology, 84*, 540–557.

McCullough, M. E., Pargament, K. I., & Thoresen, C. E. (2000). The psychology of forgiveness: History, conceptual issues, and overview. In M. E. McCullough, K. I. Pargament, & C. E. Thoresen (Eds.), *Forgiveness: Theory, research, and practice* (p. 1–16). New York: Guilford Press.

McCullough, M. E., & Worthington, E. L., Jr. (1995). Promoting forgiveness: A comparison of two psychoeducational group interventions with a waiting-list control. *Counseling and Values, 40*, 55–68.

McCullough, M. E., & Worthington, E. L., Jr. (1999). Religion and the forgiving personality. *Journal of Personality, 67*, 1141–1164.

Rye, M. S., Loiacono, D. M., Folck, C. D., Olszewski, B. T., Heim, T. A., & Madia, B. P. (2001). Evaluation of the psychometric properties of two forgiveness scales. *Current Psychology, 20*, 260–277.

Rye, M. S., Pargament, K. I., Ali, A., Beck, G. L., Dorff, E. N., Hallisey, C., et al. (2000). Religious perspectives on forgiveness. In M. E. McCullough, K. I. Pargament, & C. E. Thoresen (Eds.). *Forgiveness: Theory, research, and practice* (pp. 17–40). New York: Guilford Press.

Rye, M. S., Pargament, K. I., Pan, W., Yingling, D. W., Shogren, K. A., & Ito, M. (2004). *Forgiveness and divorce: Evaluation of an intervention to break the cycle of pain.* Manuscript submitted for publication. OH: University of Dayton.

Subkoviak, M. J., Enright, R. D., Wu, C. R., Gassin, E. A., Freedman, S., Olson, L. M., et al. (1995). Measuring interpersonal forgiveness in late adolescence and middle adulthood. *Journal of Adolescence, 18*, 641–655.

Thompson, L. Y., Snyder, C. R., Hoffman, L., Michael, S. T., Rasmussen, H. N., Billings, L. S., et al. (2005). Dispositional forgiveness of self, others, and situations. *Journal of Personality, 73*, 313–359.

Tsang, J., McCullough, M. E., & Hoyt, W. T. (in press). Psychometric and rationalization accounts for the religion-forgiveness discrepancy. *Journal of Social Issues.*

Wiesenthal, S. (1998). *The sunflower: On the possibilities and limits of forgiveness* (Revised and expanded edition). New York: Schocken.

Worthington, E. L., Jr. (Ed.). (1998). *Dimensions of forgiveness: Psychological research and theological perspectives.* Philadelphia: Templeton Foundation Press.

Worthington, E. L., Jr., & Scherer, M. (2004). Forgiveness is an emotion-focused coping strategy that can reduce health risks and promote health resilience: Theory, review, and hypotheses. *Psychology and Health, 19*, 385–405.

Worthington, E. L., Jr., & Wade, N. G. (1999). The social psychology of unforgiveness and forgiveness and implications for clinical practice. *Journal of Social and Clinical Psychology, 18*, 385–418.

Wuthnow, R. (2000). How religious groups promote forgiving: A national study. *Journal for the Scientific Study of Religion, 39,* 125–139.

Author Index

Epstein, N., 200, 229, 410
Erdley, C. A., 135
Ernst, D., 468
Eskild, A., 339
Eslinger, P. J., 264, 268
Esses, V. M., 462
Evans, D. L., 339
Evans, K., 189, 193, 194, 195
Everson, S. A., 7, 321, 358
Exline, J. J., 4, 8, 64, 66, 67, 68, 73, 74, 75, 76, 77, 78, 79, 80, 82, 83, 84, 93, 144, 186, 217, 350, 354, 423, 478, 480, 481, 486, 494, 497, 498, 560, 562, 565, 569
Eyer, J., 298
Eysenck, H. J., 247, 325

Faber, J., 66, 67
Fahey, J., 327, 340
Faragher, B., 261
Farrow, T. F. D., 260, 261, 263, 264, 265, 266, 267
Faulhaber, H-D., 249
Fawbert, D., 261, 264, 266, 267
Feather, N. T., 480
Fee, R., 128, 129, 133, 146
Feeney, B., 466, 472
Feeny, N. C., 365
Fein, H., 451
Feingloss, M., 278
Feldman, J., 289
Feldman, M. E., 354, 355
Feldman, S. S., 189, 193, 194
Felten, D., 279, 336
Fenell, D., 207
Fennel, D. L., 237
Fentress, J., 288
Ferch,, 379
Fergusson, D. M., 366
Festinger, L., 65
Fife, S. T., 228
Fincham, F. D., 4, 41, 44, 76, 80, 98, 99, 136, 137, 144, 146, 152, 154, 190, 191, 192, 193, 194, 195, 196, 198, 199, 207, 208, 209, 210, 211, 212, 213, 214, 215, 216, 217, 219, 220, 222, 231, 232, 350, 364, 382, 387, 560, 561, 563
Finkel, E. J., 4, 75, 76, 187, 189, 190, 191, 193, 195, 196, 198
Finkelhor, D., 366
Fiorillo, C., 297
FirstM. B., 355
Fiscella, K., 366
Fisher, L., 284
Fisher, M., 79
Fiske, A. P., 42, 49
Fiske, D. W., 111, 113, 116
Fitchett, G., 74, 78
Fitzgibbons, R. P., 4, 28, 41, 48, 62, 159, 379, 381, 393, 397, 401, 403, 560, 561
Flanigan, B. J., 4, 60, 369, 561
Fleshner, M., 297
Fletcher, M. A., 339
Fletcher, P., 268
Flett, G. L., 148
Foa, E. B., 363, 365
Foerster, F., 379
Fogg, L., 288
Folck, C. D., 161, 163, 164, 169, 170, 171, 354, 563
Folger, R., 478, 479, 480, 481, 482, 486
Folkman, S., 248, 289, 290
Forehand, R., 340
Formative Research Report, 446
Foy, D. W., 373
Frackowiak, R. S. J., 268
Frank, J., 381
Frankenhaeuser, M., 291
Frantz, C. M., 370
Fredrickson, B. L., 327
Freedman, S. R., 9, 62, 129, 132, 164, 197, 207, 232, 233, 264, 350, 352, 354, 356, 367, 370, 380, 386, 387, 394, 395, 396, 399, 400, 402, 425, 430, 431, 443, 449, 471, 492, 563
Freeman, T., 145, 151, 160, 161, 166, 171, 172, 173, 354
Freier, K., 249
Friedlander, Y., 283
Friedman, A., 339
Frijda, N. H., 381
Frith, C. D., 266, 268,
Frith, U., 268
Frongia, L., 160, 161
Fu, H., 175, 176
Fulker, D. W., 247
Fultz, J., 74, 79
Futterman, A. D., 327

Gabriel, Y., 480
Gadbois, S., 288
Gallagher, H. L., 268
Gallant, J. E., 338
Gallops, M. S., 451
Gallup, G., 57
Gallup, G. G., Jr., 27
Gambarana, C., 297
Gambaro, M. E., 399, 401
Gano-Phillips, S., 222